# Entrepreneurship and Global Capitalism
Volume II

# The International Library of Entrepreneurship

*Series Editor*: David B. Audretsch
*Max Planck Institute of Economics, Jena, Germany and Ameritech Chair of Economic Development Indiana University, USA*

1. Corporate Entrepreneurship and Growth
*Shaker A. Zahra*
2. Women and Entrepreneurship: Contemporary Classics
*Candida G. Brush, Nancy M. Carter, Elizabeth J. Gatewood, Patricia G. Greene and Myra M. Hart*
3. The Economics of Entrepreneurship
*Simon C. Parker*
4. Entrepreneurship and Technology Policy
*Albert N. Link*
5. Technological Entrepreneurship
*Donald S. Siegel*
6. Entrepreneurship and Economic Growth
*Martin Carree and A. Roy Thurik*
7. New Firm Startups
*Per Davidsson*
8. International Entrepreneurship
*Benjamin M. Oviatt and Patricia Phillips McDougall*
9. Entrepreneurship Education
*Patricia G. Greene and Mark P. Rice*
10. Entrepreneurship and Global Capitalism (Volumes I and II)
*Geoffrey G. Jones and R. Daniel Wadhwani*

Future titles will include:

Financing Entrepreneurship
*Philip Auerswald and Ant Bozkaya*

The Political Economy of Entrepreneurship
*Magnus Henrekson and Robin Douhan*

Wherever possible, the articles in these volumes have been reproduced as originally published using facsimile reproduction, inclusive of footnotes and pagination to facilitate ease of reference.

# Entrepreneurship and Global Capitalism Volume II


*Edited by*

Geoffrey Jones

*Isidor Straus Professor of Business History*
*Harvard Business School, USA*

*and*

R. Daniel Wadhwani

*Assistant Professor of Management*
*and Fletcher Jones Professor of Entrepreneurship*
*University of the Pacific, USA*



THE INTERNATIONAL LIBRARY OF ENTREPRENEURSHIP

**An Elgar Reference Collection**
Cheltenham, UK • Northampton, MA, USA

Published by
Edward Elgar Publishing Limited
Glensanda House
Montpellier Parade
Cheltenham
Glos GL50 1UA
UK

Edward Elgar Publishing, Inc.
William Pratt House
9 Dewey Court
Northampton
Massachusetts 01060
USA

A catalogue record for this book is available from the British Library

Library of Congress Control No. 2007927982

ISBN: 978 1 84542 407 7 (2-volume set)

Printed and bound in Great Britain by MPG Books Ltd, Bodmin, Cornwall

# Contents

# Acknowledgements

The editors and publishers wish to thank the authors and the following publishers who have kindly given permission for the use of copyright material.

Blackwell Publishing Ltd for article: Mira Wilkins (1988), 'The Free-Standing Company, 1870–1914: An Important Type of British Foreign Direct Investment', *Economic History Review*, **XLI** (2), 259–82.

Business History Conference for article: Mark Casson (1997), 'Entrepreneurial Networks in International Business', *Business and Economic History*, **26** (2), Winter, 811–23.

Cambridge University Press for articles: Mira Wilkins (1974), 'The Role of Private Business in the International Diffusion of Technology', *Journal of Economic History*, **XXXIV** (1), March, 166–88; Shannon R. Brown (1981), 'Cakes and Oil: Technology Transfer and Chinese Soybean Processing, 1860–1895', *Comparative Studies in Society and History*, **23** (3), July, 449–63; A.G. Hopkins (1987), 'Big Business in African Studies', *Journal of African History*, **28** (1), 119–40; William W. Culver and Cornel J. Reinhart (1989), 'Capitalist Dreams: Chile's Response to Nineteenth-Century World Copper Competition', *Comparative Studies in Society and History*, **31** (4), October, 722–44; Susanne Freidberg (1997), 'Contacts, Contracts, and Green Bean Schemes: Liberalisation and Agro-Entrepreneurship in Burkina Faso', *Journal of Modern African Studies*, **35** (1), 101–28.

Harvard Business School for articles: Kwang-Ching Liu (1954), 'Financing a Steam-Navigation Company in China, 1861–62', *Business History Review*, **XXVIII** (2), June, 154–81; John A. DeNovo (1959), 'A Railroad for Turkey: The Chester Project, 1908–1913', *Business History Review*, **XXXIII** (3), Autumn, 300–29; Vincent Ponko, Jr. (1969), 'The Colonial Office and British Business Before World War I: A Case Study', *Business History Review,* **XLIII** (1), Spring, 39–58; John P. McKay (1974), 'Foreign Enterprise in Russian and Soviet Industry: A Long Term Perspective', *Business History Review*, **XLVIII** (3), Autumn, 336–56; Geoffrey Jones and Judith Wale (1998), 'Merchants as Business Groups: British Trading Companies in Asia Before 1945', *Business History Review*, **72**, Autumn, 367–408.

*Itinerario* for article: Gijsbert Oonk (2004), '"After Shaking His Hand, Start Counting Your Fingers": Trust and Images in Indian Business Networks, East Africa 1900–2000', *Itinerario*, **XXVIII** (3), 70–88.

*Journal of European Economic History* for article: Ioanna Pepelasis Minoglou and Helen Louri (1997), 'Diaspora Entrepreneurial Networks in the Black Sea and Greece, 1870–1917', *Journal of European Economic History*, **26** (1), Spring, 69–104.

New York University Press for excerpt: Marcelo Bucheli (2005), 'The United Fruit Company in Latin America: Business Strategies in a Changing Environment', in *Bananas and Business: The United Fruit Company in Columbia, 1899–2000*, Chapter 3, 44–85, 194–200.

Oxford University Press for excerpts: Mark Casson (1990), 'Multinational Enterprises in Less Developed Countries: Cultural and Economic Interactions', in *Enterprise and Competitiveness: A Systems View of International Business*, Chapter 6, 125–52, references; Mira Wilkins (1998), 'The Free-Standing Company Revisited', in Mira Wilkins and Harm Schröter (eds), *The Free-Standing Company in the World Economy 1830–1996*, Chapter 1, 3–64.

Société Française d'Histoire d'Outre-Mer (www.sfhom.com) for excerpt: William Gervase Clarence-Smith (2001), 'Indian and Arab Entrepreneurs in Eastern Africa (1800–1914)', in Hubert Bonin and Michel Cahen (eds), *Négoce blanc en Afrique noire: L'évolution du commerce à longue distance en Afrique noire du 18è au 20è siècles*, 335–49.

Every effort has been made to trace all the copyright holders but if any have been inadvertently overlooked the publishers will be pleased to make the necessary arrangement at the first opportunity.

In addition the publishers wish to thank the Marshall Library of Economics, University of Cambridge, UK, the Library at the University of Warwick, UK, and the Library of Indiana University at Bloomington, USA, for their assistance in obtaining these articles.

# Part I
# Global Start-ups and International Venture Capitalists

# [1]

*Economic History Review*, 2nd ser., XLI, 2(1988), pp. 259–282

# *The free-standing company, 1870-1914: an important type of British foreign direct investment*[1]

By MIRA WILKINS

The 'free-standing company' is a novel phrase that redefines a particular type of British foreign direct investment, which although familiar to all students of British capital exports in the period 1870-1914, is none the less inadequately analysed in the extensive literature on British overseas investment.[2] This article seeks to fill this gap in the literature, by employing a new typology that focuses on the individual firm as an operating entity.

A recent estimate shows the proportion of overseas assets in British national wealth was 30 per cent just before World War I.[3] Some of this overseas investment was strictly financial in character (in the form of loans to foreign governments and capital for private firms abroad), but some of it was foreign 'direct investment', defined here (following the U.S. Department of Commerce) as investments abroad made for business purposes with the investors intending to control or having the potential to control the foreign operations.

Foreign direct investments differed from bank loans or other 'portfolio' investments where the relationship between the investor and the recipient was at arm's length. In the latter case, the foreign lender (investor) evaluated the borrower and made the loan or provided the equity capital; thereafter, the money was at the disposal of the recipient. By contrast, what characterized the foreign direct investor was the power retained to control and run the business abroad.

While the existence of British direct investments overseas in this

[1] I have discussed my ideas on free-standing companies with Alfred D. Chandler, John McKay, Geoffrey Jones, Tony Corley, Les Hannah, Ra Lundström, Phil Cottrell, Christopher Platt, Jean-François Hennart, Rondo Cameron, John Dunning, Stanley Chapman, and Lou Wells, all of whom have contributed significantly in clarifying my views. Likewise, the work of Oliver Williamson, Kenneth Arrow, and Mark Casson has been important in my thinking, as has that of R.C. Michie and P.L. Payne. This paper was presented at two seminars—one at Florida International University and the other at the Wharton School, University of Pennsylvania. In both cases, I want to thank the participants for their stimulating comments.

[2] The literature on British overseas investment 1870-1914 is enormous. The notes to Pollard, 'Capital exports', provide a good start in bibliography. See also Edelstein's superb *Overseas investment*. In this paper, I use the words 'foreign' and 'overseas' as synonymous, that is, to cover British investments outside England, Wales, Scotland, and Ireland.

[3] Edelstein, *Overseas investment*, p. 25.

period has long been acknowledged,[4] its quantitative significance has been understated and is still not clear. In 1970 Dunning concluded that only 10 per cent of British overseas investments on the eve of World War I were direct investments. By 1983 substantial new research led Dunning to suggest that 35 per cent was probably a more reliable estimate.[5]

Research on the history of British foreign direct investment has taken two distinct directions, both identifying the sizeable extent of such stakes. On the one hand, there have been the students of multinational enterprise, who knew how American companies behaved and assumed British ones followed the American model. These authors studied businesses with headquarters and operations in the United Kingdom which made direct investments abroad to sell or to manufacture in foreign lands, or alternatively to obtain sources of supply overseas. On the other hand, some researchers on British foreign investment knew nothing of or ignored the American model. They found that there were many British-managed companies overseas and described them as foreign direct investments.

The research revealed many British multinationals operating in the same pattern as their American counterparts. But there were also enterprises domiciled abroad, managed by British migrants who had been born and brought up in Britain but who resided overseas; such enterprises might not have a British head office or a British parent company. The individual Briton who settled abroad did *not* create a foreign direct investment, since there remained no obligation to anyone in Britain, whereas the expatriate who went abroad for years, who considered himself British and who then returned home, retaining an interest in his overseas business, became thereby on his return a foreign investor. In those instances where the expatriate tapped British capital markets, establishing a company or companies in England or Scotland, the British *company* became the foreign direct investor.[6]

[4] Paish wrote of 'private capital employed abroad' that could not be documented. Paish, 'Great Britain's capital', p. 187, and *idem*, 'Export of capital'. Sometimes this has been called 'direct investment', i.e. investment bypassing British money markets. On the variations in definition see Wilkins, 'Modern European economic history', p. 585. Platt, *Britain's investment overseas*, pp. 54, 60, 115, 137, and 139, wants to increase the amount of foreign direct investment in the British overseas investment estimates. On direct investments, see also Remer, *Foreign investments*; Brayer, 'Influence of British capital'; Clements, 'British-controlled enterprise'; Spence, *British investments*; and Rippy, *British investment*.

[5] Dunning, *Studies*, p. 2, used the 90 per cent portfolio (10 per cent direct) investment figure, which has frequently and mistakenly been repeated as gospel. His newer tentative estimates are in *idem*, 'Changes', p. 87. Platt's 16 per cent estimate is equally impressionistic (Platt, *Britain's investment overseas*, p. 60). Dunning and Platt defined 'direct' investments differently, with the former using a more encompassing definition. The new research includes Dahl, thesis; Coram, thesis; Jackson, *Enterprising Scot*; McFarlane, 'British investment'; Stopford, 'Origins'; Wilson, 'Multinational'; Paterson, 'British direct investment'; Kerr, *Scottish capital*; Stone, 'British direct and portfolio investment'; Svedberg, 'Portfolio-direct composition'; Nicholas, 'British multinational investment'; Jones, 'State and business practice'; Jones, ed., *British multinationals*.

[6] Remer, *Foreign investments*, dealt with both resident and non-resident British direct investment, as did Coram, thesis. Methodologically, this is wrong. Here again, it is useful to accept the U.S.Department of Commerce definition that a 'foreign investment' must be by a *nonresident*; otherwise, there is no on-going 'foreign' obligation. Since America was a country of immigrants, not emigrants, students of the history of U.S. business abroad rarely had to deal with the expatriate investor, although some cases bore a resemblance to British expatriates' behaviour. It is true that emigrants (and expatriates) transferred capital (especially human capital), but the absence of any continuing obligation to *owners* in Britain meant the lack of an ongoing foreign direct investment. If the British expatriate raised money in Britain without forming a British company, such *investments* would be portfolio ones by definition.

Of key importance, such research showed that there were thousands of companies registered in England or Scotland to conduct business overseas, most of which, unlike the American model, did *not* grow out of the domestic operations of existing enterprises that had headquarters in Britain. Some of these thousands of companies had their origins in expatriates' behaviour. Most were what I have called free-standing companies.[7] Typically, they were included in studies of British portfolio investment, because usually their formation involved capital markets.[8] Yet they were direct investments, since they were designed to conduct business operations abroad, to manage and to direct the specific business.[9]

Students of multinational enterprise have paid little attention to them, since they failed to conform to the expected model. Likewise, in the literature on British portfolio investments, capital exports, and overseas finance, authors have frequently ignored the foreign investment carried out by these 'firms', referring to the *owners of the securities* of the British enterprise as the overseas investors. Thus, the real foreign investors (the companies) often became invisible. Accordingly, their role in overseas investment has been inadequately understood. The free-standing company was, however, probably the most typical mode of British direct investment abroad. The purpose of this article is to analyse and to explain the institutional dimensions and performance of these companies, considering the free-standing company as a governance structure.[10]

## I

In London, and to a far lesser extent in other British cities, notably Edinburgh, Glasgow, and possibly Dundee, between 1870 and 1914 thousands of free-standing companies were organized to engage in business overseas,[11] though their precise number is unknown. Such companies represented a

[7] See Wilkins, 'Defining a firm', pp. 84-91. Many free-standing companies were neither 'expatriate' investments as defined by Stopford ('Origins', pp. 305-8), nor did they fit the U.S. model of foreign direct investment.

[8] Paish in Wilkins, ed., *British overseas investments*; Hall, *London capital market*; Simon, 'The pattern'; Davis and Huttenback, 'Export of British finance' and *idem*, *Mammon*.

[9] Both Svedberg, 'Portfolio-direct composition', and Paterson, *British direct investment*, recognized this.

[10] The phrase 'governance structure' is from Williamson, *Economic institutions*, p. 13.

[11] The basic files on these companies are in the Companies Registration Office, England and the Companies Registration Office, Scotland. The files of defunct English companies are at the Public Record Office. They are often cited with registration number and the designation, BT 31. See also the *Stock Exchange year book*, *Burdett's official intelligence* and its successor, *Stock Exchange official intelligence*; Ashmead, *Twenty-five years*, is helpful on the overseas mining companies. Guildhall, London, has Stock Exchange records and added data on these firms. Ostrye, *Foreign investment*, pp. 96, 129-67 lists roughly 1,800 free-standing companies set up to operate in the North American west, 1870-1914. The U.S. Federal Trade Commission, *Report on cooperation*, II, pp. 537-74, contains a 'partial' list of more than 2000 'British-organized or controlled companies whose properties were located outside of the United Kingdom, United States, and Canada'. Most of these companies were organized and registered in Britain. Michie, *Money, mania*, p. 154, noted that 'The most prominent feature of Scottish joint-stock company promotion in the second half of the [nineteenth] century was the growing number of concerns, in an increasing variety of fields, that were formed to operate outside of Scotland', that is, overseas. His book contains useful data on such firms.

sizeable proportion of the proliferation of British joint-stock companies.[12] Each of the companies set up to conduct business abroad was registered in England or Scotland as a joint-stock, limited liability company.[13] Each had a board of directors and stockholders who might or might not be British; a memorandum of association and articles of association defined corporate objectives and functions; and their capital was denominated in sterling. Usually the enterprises operated (or were intended to operate) directly abroad, although they might be holding companies, owning securities of a subsidiary or subsidiaries that operated overseas, a distinction which for the purpose of this article made no difference.[14]

The companies were to operate in numerous countries at various stages of development, inside and outside the Empire, worldwide, although usually, initially at least, on a bi-national basis, that is, with a headquarters in the United Kingdom and operations in only one foreign country (for example, Anglo-Brazilian, Anglo-Australian, or Anglo-Russian). While each typically operated in only a single economic sector, the companies were to be found in such widely differing activities as agriculture, timber, cattle raising, mining, oil production, manufacturing, transportation, public utilities, banking, land-mortgages, and land development.[15] Sometimes a company acquired an existing business overseas, and sometimes it commenced afresh.

Legally, the companies were separate units, corporate persons. At times, an existing British firm might establish a legally distinct corporation for overseas activities.[16] If an existing British business did so as an extension of its home operations, while juridically free-standing the new corporation would not be free-standing by the definition employed here. A free-standing company, at origin, was administratively as well as legally independent—that is, its management strategy was not subordinated to, nor coordinated with, that of a British parent company operating at home in the same industry. Similarly, specifically excluded from the free-standing category are subsidiaries or affiliates of a multinational enterprise whose headquarters was overseas.[17] In short, the thousands of free-standing companies considered here were legally separate units which were neither controlled by an operating

[12] As of 1914, Hall found that of the 5,337 companies registered in England and Scotland *and* listed in the *Stock Exchange official intelligence*, 1,976 (or 37 per cent) were operating mainly or wholly overseas. Hall, *London capital market*, p. 201. This number is in no way a proxy for the far larger number of companies registered in England and Scotland, 1870-1914, to do business abroad, since many had come and gone, and many were never listed in the *Stock Exchange official intelligence*.

[13] The free-standing *companies* considered herein were *legally domiciled* in Britain.

[14] The description is based mainly on material cited in notes 4, 5, 8 and 11 above. If they were holding companies, they typically had 'double boards' of directors: a board in London and one (or more) abroad. Many companies when set up never did any business; they were stillborn (in these cases, the formulation should be 'were intended to operate').

[15] Very few operated in more than one host country initially. Figures given in Paish, 'Export of capital', pp. v-vi, on 'countries to which Great Britain has supplied capital' and 'purposes for which capital has been subscribed' provide a rough breakdown by country and economic sector.

[16] Liability questions (foreign operations had higher risk and were more prone to bankruptcy), tax considerations, U.S. antitrust law (if the business operated in America), raising outside capital, joint-venture arrangements, and continuity were among the various reasons why an existing British firm might start up an affiliated *British* limited company for business abroad.

[17] To conduct business in Britain and perhaps elsewhere, foreign-based multinationals often formed companies registered in the U.K. Jones, 'Foreign multinationals'; Wilkins, *Emergence*.

enterprise in Britain nor functioned as an operating extension of a foreign multinational enterprise.[18]

Typically, the purpose of a free-standing company was to obtain capital by bringing together profitable or potentially profitable operations overseas with British investors seeking financial opportunities superior to those at home—though frauds were not infrequent. By presenting a new corporation in Britain, the founders sought to attract British savings. The costs of the promotion, legal fees, and other payments have been estimated at from 17 to 33 per cent of the amount raised,[19] which leads to the question why so many companies of this type were floated. It seems to have been assumed that no sensible Briton would invest in the totally unknown, and that foreigners should not be trusted to manage British investments.[20] The free-standing companies would provide an institutional framework that minimized such risks, managed the savings of British investors, and could attract foreign as well as British investment.[21] William Lazonick has suggested that they gave the 'borrower' privileged access to capital.[22] Most were not, however, simply financial intermediaries. They differed from contemporary investment companies in that the latter in many cases operated solely within Britain as institutional portfolio investors,[23] whereas the free-standing company's administration was committed to managing a specific business overseas. Since these companies were expensive to establish, often their capital structure was inflated to cover formation and other costs.[24]

In raising capital the British limited liability company enjoyed two major advantages over a company in the recipient country. The first was that the investor in the British firm enjoyed liquidity; he could sell his sterling-denominated shares (or bonds) with ease if he was unhappy with the overseas

[18] If a U.S. (or other foreign) multinational formed a British-registered company *to acquire the American* (the original) business, if the legal *headquarters* moved to Britain, this new British company *would* qualify as free-standing, since it did not arise out of the *operations* of any existing company possessing headquarters in Britain nor did it develop out of the *operating requirements* of a foreign multinational.

[19] Wilkins, *History of foreign investment*. Some companies were not floated, and thus incurred no such large expense. These typically served to manage the monies of a small group of individuals.

[20] Payne, *Early Scottish limited companies*, p. 49, makes the point (citing Michie) that investors are not ready to release their funds 'to an anonymous foreigner'. My argument is that the British free-standing company was an alternative to such arm's-length release.

[21] Spence, *British investments*, p. 219, found that 'probably a majority of Anglo-American companies registered in London or Edinburgh had at least some foreign shareholders on their roster'. Many had American owners, i.e. holdings of 'vendors'. But others were cosmopolitan. Still others, he found, were controlled by continental European investors. On this matter, see also U.S. Federal Trade Commission, *Report on cooperation*, II, p. 537. Apparently, two very large companies involved in public utilities (electric power and tramways) in Argentina were organized and registered in Great Britain, but attracted German ownership. See ibid., I, p. 282, and II, pp. 543-4.

[22] Comments made at the Business History Conference, Wilmington, Dela., 13 March 1987.

[23] Often investment companies had no 'operations' abroad. Their 'foreign' portfolio investments were made *in Britain*. Sometimes, however, they did operate abroad, appointing agents in a foreign country and actually managing a network of lenders. Kerr, *Scottish capital*, quite properly considers such companies as direct investors. Financial intermediaries can be direct investors; in their operations, they are 'producing' a service for their customers. See Michie, 'Crisis and opportunity', pp. 125-47, showing how the investment company—the British Assets Trust—'managed' money, international investments; all this firm's investments were portfolio ones; it had 'agents' in America.

[24] Commentators on these companies have noted that the assets acquired were frequently overvalued. In the American case, promoters offered U.S. owners what seemed like preposterous sums. The inflated 'cost' of the assets was then reflected in the nominal capital.

project—assuming that the whole affair was not a sham. The existence of a British company, traded on British markets, with the securities denominated in sterling, thus encouraged the investments of British individuals and financial intermediaries.

The second, and probably more important, advantage of the free-standing British company as a conduit of British capital was that the British company was designed to provide the institutional apparatus for the management of the specific business investment.[25] The investment instrument was subject to British law. The directors of the free-standing company—the representatives of the shareholders—were mandated to monitor the overseas operations, to be sure that the investors' money was not misused. Those at the British headquarters were expected to select the managers of the business abroad, to receive reports, and to ensure prudent and efficient management of operations. As the managing director of one free-standing company wrote in a private letter: 'We [the London board members] are the men who stand to be shot at in the event of anything going wrong'.[26] The board of directors were charged with providing responsible management of the capital entrusted to their care.

While the free-standing companies were set up to manage the business investments abroad, their British head offices normally comprised a corporate secretary and the board of directors (whose members participated in other activities in Britain), and little else. This was why many of these companies could, in fact, be referred to as 'little more than a brass nameplate some place in the City',[27] representing an enterprise that could disappear as suddenly as it had emerged.

The limited size of the typical head office was ultimately the crucial feature that distinguished these companies from contemporary U.S. multinationals. American businessmen of this era learned at home about multi-regional operations over the vastness of the United States; American companies became large multi-functional, multi-regional enterprises that developed management talents. Domestic business was a training ground for multinational enterprise, whereas the compact, geographically small domestic market in Britain provided an unsuitable basis for developing skills in business administration comparable with those learned by American managers.[28] The free-standing company, therefore, served as an alternative in many instances to the extension of the British home-based operating enterprises abroad, though the need to manage the business overseas was still there and provided a formidable challenge, and one that the free-standing companies often failed to meet.

[25] Powell wrote that the São Paulo Railroad was an English company, of English registration, under London management, owning and working a railroad in Brazil. This was a preferable investment to the Armavir-Touapse Railway, where the 'locus' was wholly Russian, since both that railway and its management were within the dominion of the czar, and bondholders were 'merely creditors'. Powell, *Mechanism*, pp. 144-5.

[26] Frank Spencer, managing director, Pillsbury-Washburn Flour Mills Company, Ltd., London, to William de la Barre, 7 May 1907. De la Barre Papers, Minnesota Historical Society, St Paul, Minnesota.

[27] Nicholas, 'British multinational investment', p. 606.

[28] Wilkins, *Emergence*; Chandler, *Visible hand*; Wilkins, 'History of European multinationals'.

## II

Although the companies were free-standing, they were not always entirely independent of one another. They were in clusters (based on varied rationales and interest groups), consisting of numerous overlapping circles of individuals and enterprises. While the resulting governance structure sometimes approximated to a multinational enterprise, in most cases the connections within the clusters were too partial and too weak to be so designated.[29] The loose clusters were united by founders, directors, and suppliers, many of whom were also shareholders; as a result there were conflicts of interest.[30] Despite difficulties of definition and the insuperable difficulty of quantification, it is possible to list ten interrelated cluster sets. Identical patterns prevailed in the Empire and the rest of the world. Common to all clusters, because of the free-standing companies' limited head office facilities and absence of internal 'know how', was the provision of services. The clusters may be categorized as follows:

*Promoters*: free-standing companies were designed to link British capital to overseas opportunities. Promoters identified these opportunities; the promoter might serve as an intermediary setting up the company, and never owning its securities. More often, he was the equivalent of an underwriter, obtaining securities for resale,[31] or he might be a principal in the transaction, expecting to continue to hold the new company's securities. The promoter of a British free-standing company might be English or Scottish, or a national of the host or a third country.[32] Early in the period he would often contract for a property, and only purchase and sell it to the new company if the flotation was successful. By the late nineteenth century promoters more frequently purchased mines, acquired concessions, bought factories, and offered them in Britain through the free-standing company. Since typically the promoter was the purchaser of the property, the words vendor (to the new company) and promoter were in these cases synonymous, as the vendor would sell the property to the new British company.[33] The promoter might be a finance company (especially in relation to mining), an investment trust company, or an agency house.[34] Irrespective of whether the promoter was an individual or individuals, a finance company, an investment trust or

[29] At one point Vernon described the multinational enterprise as a cluster of firms, but his cluster had a common administrative organization, a defined headquarters; it was one that arose out of the operations of a single firm. Wilkins, 'Defining a firm', p. 81. The clusters described herein are entirely different. On clusters, see McKay, 'House of Rothschild (Paris)'; Chapman, 'British-based investments'; Payne, *Early Scottish limited companies*, p. 49; Scott and Hughes, *Anatomy*; Hall, *London capital market*, pp. 111ff; Porter, *Victorian shipping*, esp. pp. 152-60; Jones, 'Who invested'.

[30] Hennart noted this in conversation; apparently, none of the British participants saw anything inappropriate in these arrangements.

[31] When Davis and Huttenback, *Mammon*, studied these firms' owners, they considered companies that were at least several years old to eliminate the 'investments' of the mere promoter.

[32] O'Hagan, *Leaves*; Hall, *London capital market*, p. 98; Sprague, *Money mountain*, pp. 212-5.

[33] The original owners, the first-stage vendors, would very likely be paid for the property by funds raised in the flotation and sometimes in securities of the new company; thus, it was not atypical for the original owners to have a continuing role, as shareholders, bondholders, and sometimes as local management—or even, on occasion, sometimes as members of the London board. Hall, *London capital market*, pp. 27-8.

[34] Firms such as Bewick, Moreing & Co. handled mine finance. On this company, see Nash, *Herbert Hoover*. On agency houses as promoters, Stillson, 'Financing', p. 592.

agency house, each exercised the entrepreneurial function of connecting the overseas project to potential investors; the skill acquired in doing this for one venture enabled the promoter to repeat it many times, creating the cluster of companies.[35]

*British investment trust companies:* these financial intermediaries were formed to obtain higher returns for middle-class investors than those available in the home economy. Some investment trusts which had operations abroad could qualify as free-standing companies.[36] Some viewed the shares in free-standing companies as excellent investments. Sometimes the investment trust company actually acted as a promoter (and underwriter); at other times, it was simply involved as a shareholder, frequently with a coterie of other investment trust companies. Groups of investment trust companies that invested in free-standing companies in tandem often possessed interlocking directorates, and also directors that interlocked with the free-standing companies as well. The pattern of investment is partly explained by a desire to spread risks and partly by a wish to let 'friends' share in a profitable opportunity. By providing capital in this way the investment trust company became a portfolio investor in the free-standing company.[37]

*Solicitors:* law firms were instrumental in establishing free-standing companies, with the clients of partnerships, such as Ashurst's, Linklater's, and Freshfield's, probably forming another set of clusters.

*Accountants:* firms of accountants called on to verify the accounts of free-standing companies also generated a distinctive cluster set, which was frequently linked, or overlapped, with those joined by promoters, investment trusts, and law firms.[38]

*Members of Parliament or other 'ornamental' directors*: prestige for a flotation and lustre for a prospectus could be secured by placing a titled aristocrat or prominent Member of Parliament on the board of directors.[39] Certain promoters called on the same men to enhance the image of different companies.

*Geographical locations:* British businessmen participating in trade or investments in a country or region tended to make unrelated (or only remotely related) investments in the same geographical area. Their involvements through directorships and shareholdings in free-standing companies formed yet another cluster set, the common element being the availability of information.[40]

*Mining engineers:* mining finance houses provided engineers for evaluation

[35] For one such cluster, see the list of the 1888-91 issues of the Trustees', Executors' and Securities' Insurance Company in *Investors' Review*, 1 (1892), p. 34-5.

[36] See note 23.

[37] Data in the Stillman Papers, Columbia University, New York. See also *Investors' Review, passim.*

[38] Wilkins, *History of foreign investment.*

[39] For example, in 1894 Sir H.S. King, M.P., was on the board of the American Freehold Land Co., the Canadian Agricultural Coal and Colonization Co., the Queensland Investment and Land Mortgage Co., and the Indian and General Trust Co. *Investors' Review*, 3 (1894), pp. 200-1. See Jefferys, *Business organisation*, p. 423, on 'ornamental' directors, who were 'decoys on the front page of the prospectus'.

[40] The Coats family, for instance, had investments in thread in America—multinational enterprise type investments—but members of the family were also directors and shareholders in free-standing companies in other industries (timber and mining) in the United States. Jackson, *Enterprising Scot*, pp. 221, 229.

and management purposes, which is how such leading firms as Bewick, Moreing, & Co. and John Taylor & Sons became associated with sets of mining enterprises in many parts of the world.

*Non-mining industry networks:* typically, the board of directors of a free-standing company contained a man (or men) active in the same or in a closely associated economic sector. The board membership (and often stockholdings) was based on familiarity with the industry and capability in assessing opportunities, an eagerness to determine what competitors were doing, and the potential for complementarity (i.e. the free-standing companies could become alternatives to vertical integration by British firms). The first of these three rationales can be perceived from the standpoint both of the promoter and of the director (*qua* stockholder). For example, the appointment of a prominent British brewer to the board of a South African brewery at its promotion would appear to the potential, less well-informed, investor to be a well-informed endorsement, increasing the attraction of shareholding.[41] Extending this example, from the directors' and shareholders' standpoints, experienced brewers were in a position to assess the profitability of a brewery investment (for *themselves* as well as for others). Thus, they wanted to be involved. So, too, a stock raiser in Scotland could judge for himself the financial viability of raising cattle in the United States. Hennart found that individual Cornish tin producers were directors of, and investors in, free-standing companies mining tin in Malaya, their participation being related in large part, it seems, to their knowledge of the industry, which enabled them to recognize profitable opportunities;[42] analysed in terms of transaction costs, information reduced costs substantially.

The second basic reason for the industry clusters is connected with possible competition; board membership made it feasible, for example, for the stock raiser in Scotland to obtain superior intelligence about potential competition from America.[43] In a number of instances, the development of new businesses abroad might offer rivalry to existing British industries or to British investments in third countries. Men in the same sector sought to be involved not only to profit from the potential competitive activity, but also to remain informed and *possibly* to influence the course of events by controlling, stabilizing, and neutralizing the competition.

The third reason is associated with complementarity. Pillsbury-Washburn Flour Mills Ltd., a typical free-standing company, was promoted in London. On its board was Sydney T. Klein, whose trading company handled part of the British flour trade for this American miller. Unlike the typical multinational enterprise, Klein's *trading house* was not integrating backwards into U.S. production. Klein was at the same time the principal figure in his trading house and a director and substantial stockholder in the large Pillsbury

[41] On the British-owned *American* breweries, Wiman (in 'British capital', p. 228) wrote that the British parent companies were 'officered by men of prominence and position, whose presence in a board of directors is a guarantee to capitalists that thorough investigation has taken place, and that the business will be honestly and efficiently administered'.

[42] Hennart, 'Internalization', pp. 131-43, esp. p. 141. He never uses the phrase 'free-standing companies'.

[43] Scottish stock raisers invested in American cattle companies at the time when U.S. meat exports to the United Kingdom were rising rapidly.

company, though he had no exclusive rights. Through his position on the Pillsbury board Klein presumably had an insider's advantage.[44]

Many free-standing companies were producers abroad, selling their output in Britain. When this was the case, they were often in industries that provided *inputs* for businesses in Britain. The British customer wanted knowledge, which with the free-standing company could be acquired without vertical integration of the British enterprise. Casson has suggested that when economies of scale are dissimilar at different stages of the production, and by implication the distribution, process, vertical integration is often undesirable.[45] This insight and others on asymmetrical production units would seem relevant in explaining why, for example, individuals served on boards of free-standing companies while their own companies did not integrate backward. Also, in some cases, British capital goods producers appear to have wished to *sell* to the free-standing firms. In his study of British free-standing companies in the Queensland gold-mining industry in the late 1880s, Lougheed found 'that some English engineering firms bought into several of the companies in order to sell them mining equipment'.[46] Presumably shareholders received preferential treatment over independent suppliers.

The business interests of members of the boards and shareholders of the free-standing companies (interests directly linked with their own British firms) were different from relationships characterizing multinational enterprise, since there was no clear, overall, administrative direction provided by the businessman's company, although it might be involved in marketing contracts, construction contracts, banking arrangements, and other specific functional interlocking associations.[47]

*Trading companies:* like the ties produced by mining engineers, the linkage associated with the trading company is to some extent a subset of the industry connection. Trading houses were often allied with what Chapman has called 'investment groups'.[48] Firms such as Balfour, Williamson & Co. of Liverpool[49] and Matheson & Co. of London[50] were intimately linked with British-incorporated free-standing companies. Cottrell notes that in the decade before 1914 many London 'mercantile firms' entered the new issue market: 'Eastern agency houses established [rubber] plantation companies and provided their protégés with local management and financial services.'[51] The merchants, Harrison & Crosfield, for example, promoted new issues in London for tea estates and tobacco companies in Java and India, as well as for Borneo timber, Japanese silk concerns, and Malayan rubber enterprises.[52] For the tea, tobacco, and rubber properties, the trading companies served

[44] Wilkins, *History of foreign investment.*
[45] Casson, *Multinationals*, p. 56.
[46] Lougheed, 'British company formation', p. 78.
[47] See Jefferys, *Business organisation*, p. 423.
[48] Chapman, 'British-based investment groups'.
[49] See Hunt, *Heirs.*
[50] Chapman, 'British-based investment groups', p. 235.
[51] Cottrell, *British overseas investment*, p. 33.
[52] Stillson, 'Financing', p. 592; Chapman, *Rise of merchant banking*, p. 144; on Scottish trading companies and tea plantation companies, see Michie, *Money, mania*, p. 158.

as suppliers of management services. Very often, in the course of their existing commercial business, trading companies saw opportunities abroad and assisted in the formation of British-registered free-standing companies. Stillson found that in Malaya the same agency houses that floated the companies' new issues and provided management of the rubber estates also 'serviced the financing'.[53] In short, free-standing companies were often grouped around the activities of a particular mercantile house.

*Merchant banks:* Chapman noted that 'There was no clear line demarcating investment groups with financial functions from merchant banks active in the promotion of . . . overseas shares.'[54] Merchant banks acted as promoters and as trading houses. Likewise, merchant bankers, such as the Rothschilds, engaged in the metals trades, were at centre stage *vis-à-vis* clusters of free-standing mining companies.[55] There appear to have been two tiers of British merchant banks: the large ones that only handled the best-quality issues and the smaller ones that might be less prudent. The various roles of merchant banks in relation to free-standing companies need much more study.[56]

For the most part, each of the ten cluster sets described above seems to have had a functional relationship to the free-standing units—emphasizing a particular function (or functions), rather than, as in the prototype U.S. multinational enterprise, offering an entire package, including product, process, marketing ability, technological know how, capital, *and* management. What seems evident is that the basic reason for the clusters lay in the severe limits to home office decision-making and governance of the free-standing company. For example, in the case of a typical American multinational enterprise the decision to invest abroad involved not only a consideration of financial requirements, but also the provision of operating and administrative needs. Growing out of conditions that arose in domestic business operations, the decision to invest was made by experienced senior managers in the home office, whose knowledge of the same industry in the large and diverse U.S. domestic market could be transferred abroad *within* the firm.

Lacking a comparable home office and in-house expertise, the free-standing company none the less faced establishment as well as operating and administrative requirements. Moreover, if the board of directors was to exercise control and to monitor activities, some institutional apparatus was necessary. The required functions were undertaken by the principals in the cluster sets.

One explanation for the many frauds and shortlived ventures was that the promoter abandoned the company after taking a profit from promotion and start-up, leaving minimal revenue-producing assets. Not all failures were

[53] Stillson, 'Financing', p. 592.

[54] Chapman, 'British-based investment groups', p. 246.

[55] The Rothschilds' Exploration Company furnished mining engineers for various Rothschild projects. Spence, *Mining engineers*, pp. 22–3, 137, 265. See also Turrell and Van Helten, 'The Rothschilds'.

[56] Stillson, 'Financing', p. 594, points out that from 1905 to 1914 the bulk of British investment in British-registered companies with Malayan rubber plantations was *not* attracted by agency houses, but rather the British companies were floated by 'London issuing houses'. At one point, Stillson describes the latter as intermediaries between British wealth-holders and promoters (p. 591) and at another as either merchant bankers or promoters themselves (p. 595). The line between the finance house and the merchant bank was often thin, both playing a role in investment banking.

attributable to sharp practice, but a responsible systematic approach to management could avoid disaster. The free-standing company had to find outsiders for this purpose. In addition to the inclusion of professional statements in the prospectus, accountants were asked to make periodic investigations, and at times were involved at the board's request in a quasi-managerial role in the overseas operations, one example of which was the connection between Price, Waterhouse and the British breweries in Chicago.[57] In a similar manner, mining engineers not only offered reassuring information for the prospectus, but stayed on as mine managers, while trading companies acted as 'managing agents'. When a British trading company, such as Balfour, Williamson, invested in U.S. oil production, coal mining, and flour milling, managerial services were provided. In this instance, the trading firm was behaving as a prototype multinational enterprise, investing in diversified operations related to its general trading activities. In some instances trading companies developed industry-specific managerial expertise.[58] Most important, if the free-standing company was generating profits, interested parties sought to remain involved to ensure effective management.

The services rendered to the free-standing companies were often highly profitable to the service sector enterprises; many promoters flourished.[59] In 1909 an observer remarked on overseas business which 'gave a great amount of employment in the city of London and other cities for directors, managers, clerks, solicitors, and accountants, etc.'. Mining finance firms found opportunities for themselves and their friends. Trading houses, extending activities beyond the mere movement of commodities, perceived that the added connections *vis-à-vis* overseas investments not only expanded their commerce but offered important sources of earnings.[60] Merchant banks became involved in marketing metals and through their loose connections with free-standing firms obtained information on the size of reserves and other crucial data affecting present and future prices, the effects of which on some occasions were to stabilize metal prices.[61] In sum, the principals in the clusters might participate both in the initiation and in the continuation of the free-standing companies. The needs of the free-standing company were the basis of the clusters. How service sector individuals and firms were utilized frequently became a way of determining whether the free-standing company proved profitable, how long it lasted, and what became of it.

## III

What happened to the thousands of free-standing companies registered in England and Scotland in the years 1870-1914? Among the approximately 2,000 free-standing companies remaining in existence in 1914[62] the profitable

[57] Wilkins, *History of foreign investment*.

[58] Stillson, 'Financing', pp. 593-4, suggests that in the 1920s and early 1930s the London issuing houses became less important in the financing of Malayan rubber, and the Malayan agencies, which appear to have developed the managerial expertise, relatively more significant.

[59] Not all promoters were successful. See Michie, 'Options, concessions', pp. 154-7.

[60] Crammond, 'Comments'.

[61] On the London Rothschilds see Wilkins, *History of foreign investment*.

[62] See note 12.

ones included those that developed their own in-house managerial organizations, and those still under the aegis of a mining engineering firm or a trading company's management. Those that were unprofitable or earning low returns included numerous companies which never developed effective management, but nonetheless continued to exist.[63] For every company still in existence in 1914 far more had vanished, their termination taking varied forms. In many instances dissolution of a free-standing company left productive assets abroad in the hands of nationals or British expatriates (the British registration had been deemed superfluous). Sometimes the overseas assets went to a multinational enterprise possessing superior managerial resources. Often a dissolved company would be replaced by a differently structured free-standing one, the assets transferred from the first to a second free-standing unit. Sequences of free-standing companies holding the same overseas assets were common, but derived from different circumstances. Sometimes the solicitors felt the articles of association were not broad enough; in some instances the succession related to ownership changes (and was a means of rewarding previous owners); on occasion, promoters believed a new company would be more attractive to the investing public, while at other times restructuring followed bankruptcy of the prior company. At times winding up left no assets and nothing remained to liquidate; many free-standing companies were abortive. While far from precise the evidence suggests that the number of free-standing companies with continuity, flourishing as successful, profitable enterprises, represented a very small percentage of the total number established. The mortality rate of the overseas companies seems to have greatly exceeded that of their purely domestic counterparts.[64]

In view of such a high mortality rate, why were lessons not learned? Why was British investment so readily forthcoming for so many years? Several reasons may be adduced. As some enterprises were profitable, the potential for success existed; free-standing companies were presented in such a way as to generate confidence, even though the prospectus might cloak the reality; nominal, projected returns always looked attractive; and few investors appreciated the managerial difficulties inherent in these ventures.

The character of these firms and their performance through time may be illustrated by examples selected from different industries and countries, providing substance for the earlier generalizations and showing how, in specific terms, the clusters related both to the companies' persistence and to their performance through time. The examples also reveal the managerial

[63] Often, they were formally dissolved years later. Some were lucrative for the managing agent, but *not* for the shareholders.

[64] That these companies had a higher mortality rate than domestic ones is suggested in Payne's study of Scottish companies, at least in regard to overseas mining companies. Payne, *Early Scottish limited companies*, table 23, pp. 101ff. Shannon, 'Limited companies', shows the high mortality rate of *all* registered companies. Between 1875 and 1883, for example, of the 9,551 companies registered, 35 per cent were 'abortive' (p. 382). Of those continuing in business, 34 per cent eventually became insolvent (p. 387)! Shannon separates out some of his data by home, colonial and foreign, but most of his figures are not divided in this manner, so his tabulations do not aid in segregating domestic from overseas business.

dilemma: how did a company established afresh provide adequate management to a business abroad?

In May 1871 the Spanish government offered for sale the Rio Tinto Mines.[65] Why? It wanted to raise monies 'to relieve the state of burdensome obligations'. There was little interest until the German merchant, Heinrich Doetsch, who had extensive trading and mining interests in southern Spain, went to London, seeking out financiers 'with appropriate experience and resources in the promotion of a new venture, to purchase, modernize and operate the Mines'. He met with Hugh Matheson of Matheson & Co., from the same family associated with Jardine Matheson & Co., the large trading company in the China trade. Matheson had taken part in other 'promotions', in Persia for example, and in 1873 he formed a syndicate to raise money to buy the mine, after which the Rio Tinto Company Ltd. was floated on the British market. Respectable 'financiers' and a Member of Parliament were put on the board, though Matheson himself was the key figure. Doetsch, whose firm Sundheim & Doetsch received a cash commission of £80,000 from the new Rio Tinto Company for arranging the flotation, became vice-chairman. Matheson & Co. would act as commercial agents for Rio Tinto throughout the world (except in continental Europe) and receive a commission on sales and purchases; others involved were similarly rewarded for services supplied, for example, Clark, Punchard and Co. received a contract for building railway facilities to the mine.[66]

Matheson & Co. continued to participate in many other business projects.[67] For a long while after its establishment Rio Tinto did not handle its own marketing, and according to Harvey's account, only Doetsch and Matheson were 'willing to devote the greater part of their energies to the handling of Rio Tinto business'.[68] Eventually, however, an administrative organization emerged, enabling the Rio Tinto Company Ltd. to become an entity in its own right.

In origin Burmah Oil was also a free-standing company. The promoter, who connected the opportunity in Burma with the monies in Britain, was the Scottish-born East Indian merchant, David Cargill. The 'concept of its creation' came when Cargill and Kirkman Finlay met at the Rangoon office of Galbraith Dalziel & Co., managing agents of the then Rangoon Oil Company Ltd. (a free-standing company, registered in Edinburgh in 1871).[69] Finlay was one of those roving young Scots, who before going to Burma had been in Angola seeking his fortune overseas. Both Cargill and Finlay were associated with trading companies; they used the existing Rangoon Company as the basis for the search for oil in Burma. Finlay returned to Scotland in 1879 and became Cargill's right-hand man in 'the Glasgow office'.[70] While Corley is not specific, the Glasgow office seems to have been that of Cargill's trading company rather than of the Rangoon Oil Company

[65] What follows is based on Harvey, *Rio Tinto*.

[66] Ibid., pp. 4-11, 26-35, 43, 48n., 49.

[67] Chapman, 'British-based investment groups', p. 235; see also Jones, *Banking and empire*, pp. 11-2.

[68] Harvey, *Rio Tinto*, p. 102.

[69] Corley, *Burmah Oil Company*, pp. 15, 17, 13.

[70] Ibid., pp. 18, 22.

Ltd., though they may have been one and the same. Nothing existed in Glasgow related to the oil business except a head office. For ten years until 1886 the record of oil operations in Burma was a lossmaking one. In that year Cargill established the Burmah Oil Company Ltd., registered in Edinburgh, a typical free-standing company. The goal was to attract outside financial resources to be applied to the potentially profitable opportunity in Burma. A new company would be preferable to the loss-ridden Rangoon Oil Company Ltd.[71] Corley noted that 'in structure the new company was merely one branch of an East India mercantile house, or rather a group of more or less interrelated businesses, and Cargill must have needed much agility of mind to keep separate all the various strands, from tea plantations in Ceylon to oil wells in Burma'. Finlay was alone in the organization, in devoting all of his time to oil, and soon moved from Glasgow to London where he became concerned with the 'marketing, staff and technical aspects from the London office'.[72] Corley has outlined the growth of the business, with the trading company initially taking the lead in getting the concession, starting drilling operations (the trading company had 'no technical expertise to call on'), beginning refining, and all along encountering the problems of staffing the new venture. The company called on Boverton Redwood, the foremost oil consultant in Britain; Ferrier has described him as 'a kind of single-handed oil personnel agency' for the British oil industry.[73] Over time, Burmah Oil Company Ltd. began to form its own managerial organization. By the end of the nineteenth century, the company owned tankers,[74] though trading companies were still employed to handle marketing. As time passed, this free-standing company had to create its own administrative structure in order to survive.

Still another set of free-standing companies was organized by William Knox D'Arcy, the son of an Irish solicitor whose family had emigrated to Australia. While living in Australia in the 1880s D'Arcy had been approached by three Australian brothers to assist them in developing a gold mine in that country. D'Arcy (as promoter) formed a free-standing company in Britain and floated the company, retaining shares in the business, a shrewd decision which by the mid-1890s made him a wealthy man; until 1910 the Mount Morgan Mine was one of the largest gold mines in the world. Returning to England, he served as chairman of the London board of the Mount Morgan Gold Mining Company, Ltd: 'He kept in close touch with his Australian affairs', although the Australian business seems to have been run from Australia.[75]

The United States was host to some successful British free-standing

[71] Ibid., p. 30. This is a good example of sequences of companies. Instead of using the Rangoon Oil Company Ltd., a new company with a more promising future was set up.

[72] Corley, *Burmah Oil Company*, pp. 32-3.

[73] Ibid., pp. 35, 39, and Ferrier, *British Petroleum Company*, I, p. 32. See also Jones, *State and the emergence*, pp. 97-8, on Boverton Redwood.

[74] Corley, *Burmah Oil Company*, p. 49.

[75] On William D'Arcy and the Mount Morgan mine, see Ferrier, *British Petroleum Company*, I, p. 31 (the quoted passage); Western Range Cattle Industry Study Collection (WRCIS), Library of Congress, Acc. 11,090, Reel 22; Spurr, ed., *Political and commercial geology*, p. 251; Hall, *London capital market*, p. 112.

companies. Certain gold-mining companies were very profitable, owing to supervision by mining engineering firms with headquarters in Britain. Most companies associated with Balfour, Williamson's American trading affiliate prospered. One important free-standing company set up by Balfour, Williamson became part of the Royal Dutch-Shell Group.[76] In these cases the clusters provided the early basis for management and for success.[77] Otis Steel Co. Ltd. also did well, but not because it was a free-standing company. In the early twentieth century it was dissolved as a free-standing entity, and the British shareholders became portfolio investors in an American-based enterprise.[78] All those which flourished eventually developed, or took over and used, middle management administrative structures; many gave up their British incorporation, which became superfluous.

Of the formidable number of British free-standing companies investing in the United States (and apparently elsewhere too), shortlived ventures far outnumbered the longlived, healthy ones.[79] For example the American Association Ltd. and its various associated ventures proved a major fiasco. Initially organized in 1887 as a free-standing company to acquire mineral land in the American south, the establishment of the American Association Ltd. was followed by a whole cluster of other British companies. These included the Middlesborough Town Company, Ltd., and its successor the Middlesborough Town Lands Company, Ltd., the Coal and Iron Bank of Middlesborough, Ltd., the Middlesborough Hotel Company, Ltd., the Cumberland Gas Company, Ltd., the Middlesborough Electric Company, Ltd., the Middlesborough Street Railroad Company, Ltd., the Middlesborough Water Company, Ltd., and the Watts Steel and Iron Syndicate, Ltd.

In May 1889, Middlesborough, Kentucky, had 50 inhabitants, rising to 15,000 two years later as a new iron and steel town was formed. Press reports indicated that by 1889 some $10 million in British monies had been subscribed, and the promoters were seeking more. Then came the 1890 Baring Crisis, the U.S. panic of 1893, and the collapse of the whole project. America was left with furnaces and a steel plant; British investors in the free-standing companies lost everything. The American Association Ltd. was bankrupt, as were all the other companies. In November 1893 the *Investors' Review* commented that 'what actual cash capital these various joint-stock ghosts managed to extract from the British public it would be impossible . . . to say'.[80] The promoters of the American Association Ltd. were involved also in other U.S. and foreign undertakings.[81] Some associated

[76] California Oilfields, Ltd.

[77] Wilkins, *History of foreign investment*. The Scottish investment trust companies, which can be called free-standing companies, did very well. See Kerr, *Scottish capital, passim*.

[78] Wilkins, *History of foreign investment*. A British accountant joined the board of the *American* company to represent the British shareholders.

[79] On the numerous failures, see Spence, *British investments*, pp. 230-2. Ashmead, *Twenty-five years*, tells a similar story of lack of success in the United States and worldwide.

[80] Wilkins, *History of foreign investment*, and *Investors' Review*, 2 (1893), pp. 606-8.

[81] Prominently involved, for example, was Dillwyn Parrish of 2 Copthall Buildings in the City. Parrish was not only a participant in numerous American activities from railroads to attempting brewery promotions, to investment trusts, but in 1892 he was a director of the Rothschilds' Exploration Co. Ltd., the Adventurers of Mexico Ltd., the Delagoa Bay and East African Railway Co. Ltd., and the Foreign Pilsen Electric Light and Power Co. Ltd.! For his directorships, see *Directory of directors 1892*.

with this venture seem to have wanted to sell equipment to it, while iron and steel producers planned to make money through construction contracts. British investors in this group of companies suffered severe losses mainly because of inadequate administration of the American Association Ltd., and of the Middlesborough companies.[82]

At much the same time in a different region within the United States a British free-standing company was established to take over the Hammond Company, one of America's leading meat packers. The British company was floated; the promoter prospered; but here again there was virtually no direction or administration from Great Britain; despite the lack of effective governance the company survived but lost rank; then, in time, it returned to American control; the company's properties were purchased by American meat packers, and the free-standing company was dissolved.[83]

In all branches of activity, industrial, mining, or cattle ranching, in numerous instances British free-standing companies doing business in the United States failed to create satisfactory managerial organizations, with the consequence that holders of the companies' securities faced losses. While financial returns were unsatisfactory to their British owners, these enterprises did, however, contribute to American productive resources.[84] Sometimes free-standing companies established in America would go through dissolutions, only to be followed by reconstructed ventures which in turn also failed.[85] Sometimes, the free-standing company was fraudulent from the start,[86] paying no dividend at all—or only one to enable the promoter to sell stock as the price rose.[87] Many were wound up within a few years of formation,[88] and some, failing to raise capital, were aborted before birth.[89]

Paterson has documented the poor performance of British free-standing companies in Canada.[90] He concluded that 'decision-making authority far removed from the area of economic activity was bound to slow down the process of reaching economic decisions. It was also likely to lead to less well-informed decisions, because of unfamiliarity with local Canadian conditions. When this failure to delegate responsibility was coupled with the unwillingness to engage local expert opinion, the results usually led to unprofitability.'[91] All of this is true and legitimate, but it neglects the fundamental difficulty; the free-standing firm could employ engineers to make surveys and could

[82] Wilkins, *History of foreign investment.*

[83] Ibid.

[84] Ibid.

[85] Ibid. See also Spence, *British investments, passim.*

[86] The most famous, or as Spence puts it, 'infamous' free-standing company scandal in America was the Emma Silver Mining Co. Ltd., which from start to finish was fraudulent. Spence, *British investments*, ch. viii.

[87] Wilkins, *History of foreign investment.*

[88] For example, the 'Gold Queen' Ltd., formed in 1888, was wound up in 1892; the Old Lout Mining Co., Ltd., formed in 1888, was wound up in 1894; and the Ni-Wot Gold Mines Ltd., also formed in 1888, was liquidated in 1894. Reel 52, WRCIS. The Mines Intersection Syndicate Ltd. formed in 1897 was wound up in 1898. Reel 64, WRCIS.

[89] The Boulder Valley Collieries Co., Ltd., registered in 1874 did no business whatsoever. Reel 40, WRCIS.

[90] Although he does not use the term 'free-standing companies', the business failures which he documents were almost all of that variety. Paterson, *British direct investment*, pp. 80–103.

[91] Ibid., pp. 101-2 and 112.

use service sector agencies; but it had no real home office to draw on to make the required decisions. The lean governance structure, the absence of home office experience to transfer to Canada, created the principal disability. As Paterson notes, those few ventures which proved successful developed managerial hierarchies, administrative structures.[92]

One more example of 'failure' seems appropriate. McKay has described the activities of Palmer Harding, an English contractor who obtained a concession for a horse tramway line in Rouen in 1877. Harding set up a French company, but failed to get 'administrative approval' to sell the shares to French investors; accordingly, an English holding company (a free-standing firm) was established, with inflated capital, to raise money in Britain. The company languished.[93] Subsequently, the French Thomson-Houston applied its considerable experience and made a success of an electric tramway.[94]

These illustrations suggest that in countries lacking indigenous management, for example in Spain and Burma, British free-standing companies eventually provided the administrative requirement, whereas in other parts of the world the British free-standing firm had no advantage in creating or furnishing management; in Canada, British settlers seem to have run the very few successful, efficiently managed British free-standing companies; likewise, in Australia, the same appears true. Indeed, often the free-standing company became only a means of enriching the promoter. Passive investors tempted by the prospects of profits were incapable of providing management. In the United States and Canada the British contribution was often solely financial; the British free-standing company had no sustained advantage. Americans, especially, either possessed or could obtain the technology, and could run the projects. The free-standing company became an albatross. Why should Americans pay for a board of directors that generated only cost and no benefit to the ongoing business? Moreover, the free-standing form became prey (and this was especially true of mining companies) to the unscrupulous, who gained by providing a 'service' in setting up the company and perhaps selling equipment to it, but retained no interest in its continuing success or failure. In the French example, the British free-standing 'holding company' added nothing except capital. When an experienced French company (an affiliate of an American multinational) took over the venture, it became highly successful.

A distinction has already been drawn between less developed and developed host countries, managerial creation via the free-standing company tending to take place more often in the former. The disappearance of the British free-standing parent company, leaving resources in national hands, so prevalent in the United States seems to have occurred in the case of British

[92] Ibid., p. 103. These ventures were typically run by Britons who settled in Canada. In 1893 the managers of the British Columbia Canning Co., Ltd. and the Anglo-British Columbia Packing Co., Ltd. were both long-time residents in the province.

[93] McKay, *Tramways and trolleys*, pp. 133-4.

[94] Ibid., p. 134. The French Thomson-Houston was an affiliate of the American company, General Electric. See ibid., pp. 127ff. and Wilkins, *Emergence*, pp. 58-9 and 94.

stakes in Russia as well,[95] and by 1870-1914, according to Feis 'In British India the demand that the London boards be abolished increased in firmness.'[96] An important question to consider is whether the British head office developed crucial managerial functions. In the more successful companies this was the case, but in many others it was not, and accordingly the British-registered company was erased, leaving an operating company in the host country with some British portfolio investments. The presence of a shortlived British free-standing company that failed to provide anything beyond capital did not necessarily mean that economic activity abroad was also shortlived.[97]

The British free-standing company concept is useful in dealing with agriculture, banking, and certain railway investments, as well as with those in the economic sectors discussed in the specific illustrations above. While in broad terms free-standing companies participated in every economic sector, such companies tended to be absent from the high-technology industries of this era, notably the electrical and chemical industries. Public utilities and certain low-technology electrical manufacturing industries did attract such companies, but not businesses with the most advanced technology.[98] There was no free-standing company in the car industry. It appears that advanced technology could not be effectively transferred via this type of intermediary and that the lean governance structure was the constraint.[99]

The many free-standing firms in Britain were designed to match abundant British capital, under British management and control, with profitable opportunities. So many proved shortlived because international business involved not only capital export but diffusion of known products and processes and the successful transfer of a management package. The free-standing company with its tiny home office had either to find or to create that package; otherwise it was doomed to dissolution.

## IV

The most typical British direct investment abroad between 1870 and 1914 appears to have been that which began as a free-standing company, a form which proved extremely effective in raising capital in Britain for business overseas. Was the free-standing company equally successful in providing management, technology, and business know-how? American enterprise abroad in the main had no problem in this respect; U.S. businessmen took experience at home and extended it, modifying and making changes as

[95] Based on discussions with V. Bovykin, A.A. Fursenko, and B. Ananyich.

[96] Feis, *Europe*, p. 28.

[97] The evidence on U.S. portfolio investments suggests that as information channels improved, British investors felt less hesitancy in investing in some companies registered abroad.

[98] Eastman Kodak Co., Ltd. was a British free-standing company for a few years, though tax matters changed this. However, the form was not viable for this innovative firm.

[99] It might be argued, however, that British business was generally deficient in high technology industries. None the less, there were British businesses abroad in high technology activities, for instance Marconi in the electrical industry. This took the form of the 'typical' multinational enterprise, not the free-standing company form. In the car industry, which lagged far behind the American industry before 1914, no British foreign direct investment occurred—of either variety.

needed, but developing foreign operations from a given knowledge of both product and process. This was the case with certain British firms as well. Some (not all) British free-standing companies that emerged out of expatriates' or foreign nationals' endeavours had local management in place. Some that arose from a trading company genesis could call on the trading house's managers. But many, and perhaps most, British free-standing companies had no company-specific experience on which to rely. At first, therefore, they had to engage existing service sector individuals and firms that both identified the opportunities and furnished the initial supervision.

At least initially, the service companies were infrequently industry-specific. The trading company, for example, was excellent as a conduit of information on trading conditions, but it lacked ongoing experience in the production of raw materials or manufactured products; that is, a trading company did not, at the start, know how to manage goods-producing units. Accordingly, industry-specific service functions multiplied; trading companies learned and became specialized. Management of productive activities was required if the free-standing company was to generate returns to its shareholders. Some free-standing companies became highly successful; most of these ultimately had to shed their reliance on the outsiders' services and develop their own company-specific managerial expertise. In some instances, service sector firms were able to provide the basis for the transition; in other cases, service sector firms created within their own organizations the needed expertise. Many more free-standing companies failed to find or install competent management, or to exploit service sector companies effectively, and were wound up.

Research on the free-standing company as an operating entity is still in its infancy. The paradigm should provide insights into the establishment, operations, and performance of British cotton textile plants in India, British meat packers in Argentina, and British nitrate firms in Chile.[100] It assists us in understanding much of British overseas banking,[101] and implies a need to rethink the nature of British capital exports that did not go into government loans. Far more research is needed to trace the relationships between the free-standing companies and existing British businesses. What were the competitive and complementary associations? Can the free-standing company be seen as an intermediate solution for some British businesses—between integration and arm's-length alternatives? Was the solution selected because of managerial constraints? Did the free-standing company succeed in activities where the prototype multinational enterprise had no advantage? How do we identify such activities?[102] The free-standing company approach may aid us in learning more about the efficiency of British enterprise overseas and the course of technology transfer. It may also give help in evaluating the costs

[100] It helps, for example, in understanding the behaviour of John Thomas North and his promotion of a battery of Chilean nitrate companies. See Greenhill, 'Nitrate and iodine', pp. 236-7.

[101] The Imperial Bank of Persia is a splendid example of a free-standing company. Jones, *Banking and empire*.

[102] For example, a multinational enterprise producing rubber tyres had a major advantage in doing so worldwide, but no advantage in growing rubber. A free-standing company not only had no advantage in manufacturing rubber tyres, but would be at a disadvantage. However, both types of organization needed to learn afresh about rubber plantations.

and benefits of British overseas business. Little is known about the history of most of these companies after 1914; more information is needed on how they survived during the remainder of the twentieth century.[103]

Likewise, more research is required on the transition and the mix between British-registered companies and those registered abroad (without a British parent). There seem to be systematic patterns relating to British registration and overseas registration, which poses the question why a company should have been registered in England or Scotland rather than only abroad. Tentatively, it seems that overall management from a British head office with no British registration was virtually impossible, although all kinds of specific functional relationships could persist.[104]

The free-standing company concept directs our attention to the institutional dimensions of overseas direct investments and the conduct of operations abroad, to the rationale behind particular business forms, to the nature of the business interconnections that started and maintained British foreign direct investment, and to the critical role of management in determining the success or failure of direct investment. It questions whether the fragmented functional management by various service sector units could be prolonged and could alone provide a basis for continuity.

This analysis suggests that it is the company rather than the investors in the company that should be studied as the principal actor in the foreign direct investment process. Most significant was the finding that fundamental to the free-standing company was its inherently weak managerial structure at origin, causing it to depend on outside providers of services. This initial lean governance structure was responsible for the short life or failure of many of the British businesses operating overseas. Attention should be directed to the company, to the management of its business abroad, and to the development of productive activity overseas within the firm. To be sure, part of the substantial British direct investment abroad in this era was made by traditionally defined multinational enterprises, but far more seems to have been by British-registered free-standing companies. While not entirely unique to Great Britain, this type of institution was certainly far more in evidence there between 1870 and 1914 than in any other country.[105] The reason is obvious. Britain was the world's largest creditor nation—and its nationals chose not to send their wealth abroad unsupervised. Though frequently not up to the task, the free-standing company was designed to provide that supervision. Between 1870 and 1914 the free-standing company

[103] Tignor, *Egyptian textiles*, mentions some free-standing companies operating in Egypt, from the turn of the century into the 1950s.

[104] Lewis suggests that 'Foreign ownership [and] the location of boards of directors in London' enhanced British exports—but that 'externally registered entities' were not a necessary condition for either Argentinian or Brazilian imports. Trade in this context is the 'functional' relationship. Lewis, 'Railways and industrialization', p. 219.

[105] Free-standing companies with headquarters in the United States operated in the sugar industry of Cuba, in mining in Latin America, and in other circumstances. Their relative importance in U.S. direct investment, 1870–1914 was, however, miniscule in comparison with their role in the United Kingdom. Free-standing companies with headquarters on the European continent also existed and require further investigation. Recent research suggests they were nowhere near as important as in the British case.

was not only of major importance in the history of British foreign direct investment, but was central to the history of all British capital exports.

*Florida International University*

**Footnote references**

Ackerman, C.W., *George Eastman* (Boston, 1930).
Ashmead, E., *Twenty-five years of mining, 1880-1904* (1909).
Brayer, H.O., 'The influence of British capital on the western range cattle industry', *J. Econ. Hist.*, Supplement, 9 (1949), pp. 85-98.
Casson, M., *Multinationals and world trade* (1986).
Caves, R.E., 'International corporations: the industrial economics of foreign investment', *Economica*, 38 (1971), pp 1-27.
Caves, R.E., *Multinational enterprise and economic analysis* (Cambridge, 1982).
Chandler, A.D., 'The growth of the transnational firm in the United States and the United Kingdom: a comparative analysis', *Econ. Hist. Rev.*, 2nd ser., XXXIII (1980), pp. 396-410.
Chandler, A.D., *The visible hand* (Cambridge, Mass., 1977).
Chapman, S.D., 'British-based investment groups before 1914', *Econ. Hist. Rev.*, 2nd ser., XXXVIII (1985), pp. 230-51.
Chapman, S.D., *The rise of merchant banking* (1984).
Clements, R.V., 'British-controlled enterprise in the west between 1870 and 1900 and some agrarian reactions', *Agric. Hist.*, 27 (1953), pp. 132-41.
Coram, T.C., 'The role of British capital in the development of the United States, *c.* 1600-1914' (unpublished M.A. thesis, University of Southampton, 1967).
Corley, T.A.B., *A history of the Burmah Oil Comany, 1860-1924* (1983).
Cottrell, P.L., *British overseas investment in the nineteenth century* (1975).
Crammond, E., 'Comments' in *J.R.S.S.*, LXXII (1909), p. 482.
Dahl, A.J., 'British investment in California mining, 1870-1890' (unpublished Ph.D. thesis, University of California, 1961).
Davis, L.E. and Huttenback, R.A., 'The export of British finance, 1865-1914', in A.N. Porter and R.F. Holland, eds., *Money, finance and empire, 1790-1960* (1985), pp. 28-76.
Davis, L.E. and Huttenback, R.A., *Mammon and the pursuit of empire* (Cambridge, 1986).
Dunning, J.H., *American investment in British manufacturing industry* (1958).
Dunning, J.H., 'Changes in the level and structure of international production: the last one hundred years', in M. Casson, ed., *The growth of international business* (1983), pp. 84–139.
Dunning, J.H., *Studies in international investment* (1970).
Dunning, J.H. and Archer, H., 'The eclectic paradigm and the growth of UK multinational enterprise', paper presented at Business History Conference, Wilmington, Dela., 1987.
Edelstein, M., *Overseas investment in the age of high imperialism: the United Kingdom, 1850-1914* (New York, 1982).
Feis, H., *Europe: the world's banker, 1870-1914* (New York, 1965).
Ferrier, R.W., *The history of the British Petroleum Company*, I (1982).
Greenhill, R., 'The nitrate and iodine trades, 1880-1914,' in D.C.M. Platt, ed., *Business imperialism, 1840-1930* (Oxford, 1977), pp. 231-83.
Gruber, W., Mehta, D. and Vernon, R., 'The R & D factor in international trade and international investment of U.S. industries', *J. Pol. Econ.*, 75 (1967), pp. 20-37.
Hall, A.R., *The London capital market and Australia, 1870-1914* (Canberra, 1963).
Harvey, C.E., *The Rio Tinto company* (Penzance, 1981).
Hennart, J.-F., 'Internalization in practice: early foreign direct investments in Malaysian tin mining', *J. Int. Bus. Stud.*, 17 (1986), pp. 131-43.
Hunt, W., *Heirs of great adventure*, 2 vols. (1951, 1960).
Jackson, W.T., *The enterprising Scot: investors in the American west after 1873* (Edinburgh, 1974).
Jefferys, J.B., *Business organisation in Great Britain, 1856-1914* (New York, 1977).
Jones, C., 'Great capitalists and the direction of British overseas investment in the late nineteenth century: the case of Argentina', *Bus. Hist.*, 32 (1980), pp. 152-69.
Jones, C., 'The state and business practice in Argentina, 1862-1914', in C. Abel and C.M. Lewis, eds., *Latin America, economic imperialism, and the state* (1985), pp. 184-98.
Jones, C., 'Who invested in Argentina and Uruguay?', *Bus. Archives* 48 (1982), pp. 1–23.
Jones, G., *Banking and empire in Iran* (Cambridge, 1986).

Jones, G., 'Foreign multinationals and British industry before 1945', *Econ. Hist. Rev.* (forthcoming).
Jones, G., *The state and the emergence of the British oil industry* (1981).
Jones, G., ed., *British multinationals: origins, management and performance* (Aldershot, 1986).
Kerr, W.G., *Scottish capital on the American credit frontier* (Austin, 1976).
Kindleberger, C., *American business abroad* (New Haven, 1969).
Lewis, C.M., 'Railways and industrialization: Argentina and Brazil, 1870-1929', in C. Abel and C.M. Lewis, eds., *Latin America, economic imperialism and the state* (1985), pp. 199-230.
Lougheed, A.L., 'British company formation and the Queensland mining industry, 1886-1890', *Bus. Hist.*, 25 (1983), pp. 76-82.
McFarlane, L.A., 'British investment in midwestern farm mortgages and land, 1875-1900: a comparison of Iowa and Kansas', *Agric. Hist.*, 47 (1974), pp. 179-98.
McKay, J., 'The house of Rothschild (Paris) as a multinational industrial enterprise, 1875-1914', in A. Teichova et al., *Multinational enterprise in historical perspective* (Cambridge, 1986), pp. 74-86.
McKay, J., *Tramways and trolleys* (Princeton, 1977).
Michie, R.C., 'Crisis and opportunity: the formation and operation of the British Assets Trust, 1897-1914', *Bus. Hist.*, 25 (1983), pp. 125-47.
Michie, R.C., *Money, mania and markets: investment, company formation and the stock exchange in nineteenth-century Scotland* (Edinburgh, 1981).
Michie, R.C., 'Options, concessions, syndicates, and the provision of venture capital, 1880-1913', *Bus. Hist.*, 23 (1981), pp. 147-64.
Nash, G., *Herbert Hoover* (New York, 1983).
Nelson, R.R. and Winter, S.G., *An evolutionary theory of economic change* (Cambridge, Mass., 1982).
Nicholas, S., 'British multinational investment before 1939', *J. Eur. Econ. Hist.*, 11 (1982), pp. 605-30.
O'Hagan, H.O., *Leaves from my life*, 2 vols. (1929).
Ostrye, A.T., *Foreign investment in the American and Canadian west, 1870-1914: an annotated bibliography* (Metuchen, N.J., 1986).
Paish, G., 'The export of capital and the cost of living', *Statist* Supplement, LXXIX (14 Feb. 1914), pp. i-vii.
Paish, G., 'Great Britain's capital investments in individual colonial and foreign countries', *J.R.S.S.*, LXXIV (1911), pp. 167-87.
Paterson, D.G., *British direct investment in Canada* (Toronto, 1976).
Payne, P.L., *The early Scottish limited companies, 1856-1896* (Edinburgh, 1980).
Platt, D.C.M., *Britain's investment overseas on the eve of the First World War* (New York, 1986).
Pollard, S., 'Capital exports, 1870-194; harmful or beneficial?' *Econ. Hist. Rev.*, 2nd ser., XXXVIII (1985), pp. 489-514.
Porter, A., *Victorian shipping, business and imperial policy* (Woodbridge, Suffolk, 1986).
Powell, E.T., *The mechanism of the city* (1910).
Remer, C.F., *Foreign investments in China* (New York, 1933).
Rippy, J.F., *British investment in Latin America* (Minneapolis, 1959).
Scott, J. and Hughes, M., *The anatomy of Scottish capital: Scottish companies and Scottish capital, 1900-1979* (1980).
Shannon, H.A., 'The limited companies of 1866-1883', *Econ. Hist. Rev.* 4 (1933), repr. in E.M. Carus-Wilson, ed., *Essays in economic history* (New York, 1966), pp. 380-405.
Simon, M., 'The pattern of new British portfolio foreign investment, 1865-1914', in A.R. Hall, ed., *The export of capital from Britain, 1870-1914* (1968), pp. 15-44.
Spence, C.C., *British investments and the American mining frontier, 1860-1901* (Ithaca, N.Y., 1958).
Spence, C.C., *Mining engineers and the American west* (New Haven, 1970).
Sprague, M., *Money mountain: the story of Cripple Creek gold* (Boston, 1953).
Stillson, R.T., 'The financing of Malayan rubber', *Econ. Hist. Rev.*, 2nd ser., XXIV (1971), pp. 589-98.
Stone, I., 'British direct and portfolio investment in Latin America before 1914', *J. Econ. Hist.*, 37 (1977), pp. 690-722.
Stopford, J., 'The origins of British-based multinational manufacturing enterprises', *Bus. Hist. Rev.*, 48 (1974), pp. 303-45.
Spurr, J.E., ed., *Political and commercial geology and the world's mineral resources* (New York, 1920).
Svedberg, P., 'The portfolio-direct composition of private foreign investment in 1914 revisited', *Econ. J.*, 80 (1978), pp. 763-77.
Tignor, R.L., *Egyptian textiles and British capital, 1930-1956* (forthcoming).
Turrell, R. and Van Helten, J.J., 'The Rothschilds, the Exploration Company and mining finance', *Bus. Hist.*, 28 (1986), pp. 181-205.
Vernon, R., *Storm over the multinationals* (Cambridge, Mass., 1977).
U.S. Federal Trade Commission, *Report on cooperation in American export trade*, 2 vols. (Washington, D.C., 1916).
Wells, L.T., *The product life cycle and international trade* (Boston, 1972).

Wilkins, M., 'Defining a firm: history and theory', in P. Hertner and G. Jones, eds., *Multinationals: theory and history* (Aldershot, 1986), pp. 80-95.
Wilkins, M., *The emergence of multinational enterprise: American business abroad from the colonial era to 1914* (Cambridge, Mass., 1970).
Wilkins, M., 'The history of European multinationals: a new look', *J. Eur. Econ. Hist.*, 15 (1986), pp. 483-510.
Wilkins, M., *The history of foreign investment in the United States to 1914* (Cambridge, Mass., forthcoming).
Wilkins, M., *The maturing of multinational enterprise: American business abroad from 1914 to 1970* (Cambridge, Mass., 1974).
Wilkins, M., 'Modern European economic history and the multinationals', *J. Eur. Econ. Hist.*, 6 (1977), pp. 575-95.
Wilkins, M., 'Multinational enterprises', in H. Daems and H. van der Wee, eds., *The rise of managerial capitalism* (Louvain, 1974), pp. 213-35.
Wilkins, M., ed., *British overseas investments, 1907-1948* (New York, 1977).
Wilkins, M. and Hill, F.E., *American business abroad: Ford on six continents* (Detroit, 1964).
Williamson, O.E., *Economic institutions of capitalism* (New York, 1985).
Wilson, C., 'The multinational in historical perspective' in K. Nakagawa, ed., *Strategy and structure of big business* (Tokyo, n.d. [1976]), pp. 265-86.
Wiman, E., 'British capital and American industries', *North Amer. Rev.*, 150 (1890), pp. 220-34.

# [2]

# The Free-Standing Company Revisited

*Mira Wilkins*

A 'free-standing company' is a firm set up in one country for the purpose of doing business outside that country. The term 'free-standing' was adopted to contrast this type of investment over borders with the more familiar one of today's multinational enterprise that begins with business operations *at home* and *then* moves abroad, building on its competence and needs and generally pursuing a related line of business. With the free-standing company, the individual founders established a new 'free-standing' unit in the home (headquarters) country with the immediate intention of operating outside that headquarters nation.[1] My initial research on the free-standing company concentrated on the history of British-headquartered free-standing companies; quickly, however, it became apparent that other nations also were homes for such companies.[2]

The identification of the free-standing company came from a desire to understand the institutional business structures associated with international capital movements. The importance of the notion rested on its insistence that we ask questions about the essential features of international business firms as they evolve through time, including how they are managed. In my analysis, I focus on the firm. Investors in a firm and the firm itself may be one and the same, or there may be a separation of ownership and control of a firm—as in the modern managerial corporation. To understand the history of international business, I believe the attention must be on the *firm* as the actor rather than on a more generalized approach. In some cases, holders of shares (ownership) of a firm were widows and orphans, or institutional investors on their behalf; in other cases, shareholders were active participants; frequently, there was a mix of passive and active investors. There is a separate literature on British individuals as investors, and I do not attempt to add to that literature here.[3] The originality of the concept of the free-standing company lies in its emergence from an attempt to clarify the business enterprise's characteristics (including the nature of management), behaviour, performance, and influence as the firm expands over borders through time.

Resources (especially capital, technology, and management) often do not move, domestically, or to foreign countries, in arm's-length transactions. The 'visible hand' of business managers is present; business transactions are governed by those who administer the enterprise.[4] To study business across borders, we must look at the business institutions.[5] Research on the free-standing company, a special form of multinational enterprise, helps us to discern and to explain historical patterns of global economic integration and thus to understand an important aspect of global economic history. Some have suggested that such research may contribute insights into aspects of imperialism.[6]

### *Historiographical Background*

Before I revisit the concept of the free-standing company (FSC), some historiographical background is necessary. The identification of and the labelling of the free-standing company as a type of multinational enterprise arose out of my re-examination of British capital exports of the late nineteenth and early twentieth centuries. In that period Britain was by far the world's leading capital exporter; a substantial portion of the nation's total savings was invested abroad.[7] Britain's capital exports in those years have attracted immense attention from economic historians, as well as from contemporary commentators. There are numerous studies of these British capital flows, as well as of subsequent British capital exports. Typically, at least since the 1960s, historians classified the overseas interests of British-registered companies as 'portfolio investments'; students of the capital flows considered the capital as raised in Britain and exported.[8] Many authors assumed that the bulk of British investment abroad in the late nineteenth and early twentieth centuries was passive. Yet, some scholars in the 1920s and 1930s and some writers in the immediate post-Second World War years recognized that, while this was certainly true of British stakes abroad in government bonds and other British holdings of securities, the overseas interests of British-registered companies suggested, in today's usage, 'direct' rather than passive portfolio investments, since the enterprise itself was extending across country borders to control and to manage the operations abroad. Since the 1970s scholars have tried to assemble statistics on the history of British multinational enterprise and consider the portfolio/direct overseas investment ratios. A number, beginning with Tom Houston and John Dunning, explicitly included the British-registered companies—once designated as portfolio investors—as foreign direct investors.[9] I called such British firms free-standing companies (FSCs): they were registered in Britain, had a headquarters there, but had *no operations there in the specified (or in a vertically related) industry*; their overseas business was usually set up in a single foreign country, or a single region. They were free-standing because their international business did not grow out of an ongoing business that operated at home, with the firms seeking to 'internalize' (combine) overseas operations in their existing activities. I identified thousands of British owned and controlled FSCs, with business abroad—in and outside the Empire.

My point of departure was research (beginning in 1959) that I had done on the history of American business abroad. To the surprise of many readers, I had found numerous American companies, from the late nineteenth century onwards, that had started at home and had developed domestic market expertise, and then rapidly became multinational enterprises. American businesses such as Singer Sewing Machine, General Electric, National Cash Register, International Harvester, Aluminum Company of America, and Ford Motor Company, for instance, early in their histories established formidable international operations, which evolved out of their domestic activities.[10] My own research had uncovered the historical pattern of US businesses that began at home and then expanded abroad. At the same time, in the 1960s, students of contemporary multinational corporations, including Raymond Vernon, Charles Kindleberger, Richard Caves, and John Dunning, for example, were all taking the pattern of domestic first and then foreign for granted.[11]

Louis Wells has noted that two concepts are widely held today among researchers on multinational enterprise: '(1) to survive abroad, a firm needs some kind of advantage over local competitors, and (2) a firm must have some reason to internalize that advantage through ownership rather than contracting with another firm [or outside individual].'[12] Wells's apt summation assumes that at the point when it invests abroad the enterprise has already internalized the advantage in its *home* nation. Wells has espoused 'product-cycle theory', which is what Mark Casson (in Chapter 3 below) attacks, but it was not only product-cycle theorists who accepted the notion of a firm's need for competitive advantage.[13] In a 1995 summary of the state of the art on multinational corporations, James R. Markusen discusses at length 'ownership advantages', the knowledge-based assets, which multinationals transfer; like his predecessors, he too takes for granted the existence of these advantages within the company; he also assumes that the advantages have been derived from experiences within the firm.[14]

Research on multinational enterprise, historical and contemporary, initially focused on American companies.[15] When historians of multinational enterprise turned to study the path of British multinationals, they at first applied the 'American model' (derived from the prior research) and they realized that many British industrial enterprises conformed neatly to the 'American' pattern: J. & P. Coats, Lever, Courtaulds, and others began with operations at home, and then went overseas based on their domestic business expertise.[16] From my own research (which had shifted from the history of American business abroad to the history of foreign investment in the USA), I had become aware that many *British* overseas investments carried management and potential for control over borders. Often, however, these British firms investing abroad did not fit the traditional multinational enterprise 'model' that I had previously encountered: frequently, they did not start with domestic business operations and then expand abroad based on the core competencies they had developed at home.[17] The free-standing company—the company that inaugurated foreign business afresh—could not have *at origin* advantages within the firm, since it had no domestic operations on which to base these advantages.

What did this do to the widely accepted theoretical framework? What, if any, advantages did the newly established free-standing company have? By definition, because it had no *operations at origin at home*, to conduct business abroad the company had to engage the talents of outsiders. I identified clusters of individuals and other firms with varying expertise that surrounded an individual free-standing company.[18] Stanley Chapman's research on British-based investment groups had substantial influence on my thinking.[19] Yet, my clusters comprised more than his investment groups. I considered—and debated, particularly with Jean-François Hennart—whether skills in raising capital could be considered an advantage. Owing to the absence of operations in the UK, it seemed to me that, once more by definition *at home* and *at origin*, there was a 'lean governance structure' internal to an individual company. And as I paid special attention to the many British free-standing companies—mining, cattle-ranching, brewery companies, and so forth—in the USA in the late nineteenth and early twentieth centuries, I was impressed with how often these were short-lived activities. I related this, in many instances, to the lack of effective direction and administration at origin, or subsequently.[20] Also, I noted that a number of ventures were 'scams', set up by promoters to tap British capital markets solely to enrich the promoters. In addition, I was impressed with the work of Donald Paterson, who compared British direct investments in Canada with American multinationals there. He found major differences, with the former less successful than the latter.[21] In sum, my identification and definition of the free-standing company emerged from the juncture of four distinct research trails: (1) economic historians' research on British overseas investment, (2) business historians' and economists' work on the growth of the firm, domestically and internationally, (3) economists' studies of and theories of multinational enterprise, and (4) business historians' investigations into the history of multinational enterprise.

As others joined me in exploring the nature and growth of free-standing companies, six sets of questions arose that required further clarification: (1) *Context:* where, exactly, do free-standing companies fit in British economic history? (2) *Definition:* what, more precisely, was to be included under the rubric British 'free-standing company'? (3) *Elaboration:* how do we improve and add to our understanding of British free-standing companies? (4) *Evaluation:* were British free-standing companies associated with British economic decline? Were they 'second-rate' foreign direct investments? (5) *Extension:* were there only British-headquartered free-standing companies? How general—across source-of-capital countries—was this form of doing business abroad? And (6) *Explanation*: why were numerous free-standing companies headquartered in Britain and certain Continental European nations, and why, elsewhere, was the organizational form less evident? Why did so few enterprises survive over the decades *as free-standing companies*? What functions did free-standing companies serve within the evolving world economy? The questions, as posed under the first four headings, all relate to the history of British free-standing companies, but can, by extension, apply to free-standing companies headquartered in other nations. Item 5 specifically makes that extension. And, item 6 takes the extension into account. The matters covered under all six topics are discussed from different angles in the chapters in the present volume. It is those essays along with other critiques that stimulate and inform this introductory chapter, which explores these six broad subjects. I will save for the conclusion of this book some further thoughts on the implications and significance of the research on free-standing companies and address the topic where we go from here: what are the principal unresolved questions?

## *Context*

What is the place of free-standing companies in British economic history? Britain in the late nineteenth and early twentieth centuries was the world's greatest capital exporter. In 1914 over 40 per cent of global foreign investment was from Britain.[22] Under British joint-stock company laws, companies were registered to do business in Britain and abroad; under the relevant joint-stock acts, between 1856 and 1914, 154,817 companies were registered in London and 9,303 in Edinburgh.[23] In addition, within Britain, family firms (often partnerships) existed that did not register; these too engaged in business at home and abroad. Thus, joint-stock companies do not account for all British domestic or overseas business. Nor, for that matter, do they cover, by any means, all long-term foreign investments, for individuals and informal groups purchased securities of companies and governments abroad; most—but not all—of those bonds and stocks were portfolio holdings.[24] Christopher Schmitz counted the Scottish-registered companies and found that 853 were, by his definition, set up to engage in overseas investment; of this number 315 were still active in 1914. The Scottish overseas investors were only a small (albeit important) part of the British total. Schmitz suggests that in the late nineteenth–early twentieth centuries 'perhaps as many as 15,000 or 20,000' companies were formed for foreign business and registered in London.[25] These numbers dwarf those cited by A. R. Hall as registered in England and Scotland and listed in the *Stock Exchange Official Intelligence in* 1914 and as operating mainly or wholly overseas (1,976) that I used in my *Economic History Review* article.[26] The mortality rate of English joint-stock companies, by all reports, was somewhat higher than that of their Scottish counterparts.[27]

If we view, at their origin, companies set up under British joint-stock company laws, five types that were owned and controlled within the UK seem to have participated at the start, or subsequently would engage, in overseas investment:

1. *Domestic companies.* These were basically established to take part in business at home; then, later, they developed business operations abroad that involved making investments. Some of these companies also acquired portfolio investments outside Britain.
2. *Domestic/international companies.* These participated in business at home and began business abroad *before* they were registered, so at the time of registration they were already international (J. & P. Coats is an excellent example). Some were, at origin, international, for different historical reasons (e.g. Borax was a merger of an American and a British company; it was British-controlled and British-headquartered).
3. *Trading and shipping companies.* Many of these connected activities at home with those abroad. They started with a need at home and meshed it with some Anglo-foreign relationship(s).
4. *Investment trusts and certain other financial intermediaries.* These often made sizeable foreign portfolio investments, but had little or no direct investments abroad.
5. *Free-standing companies.* These were organized for the specific purpose of undertaking business abroad, typically in a particular country or region.

All five of these categories of joint-stock companies served as international capital flow conduits. Category 4—investment trusts—excepted, all seem to have had, or in the future would make, more overseas direct than portfolio investments, and all were associated with networks of trade, technology transfer, information dissemination, and managerial extensions abroad. Above and beyond these five categories there were *foreign-controlled* companies (part of foreign multinational enterprises or controlled by foreign individuals) registered in Britain; some of these companies became conduits for outward from Britain foreign direct investments.[28]

Joint-stock companies established under British law were required to keep stockholder lists. They had registered capital. Many remained family or closely held firms. The securities of others were traded, yet still closely held. Recently, William Lazonick has written that the critical transformation in US capital markets, which supported technological innovation, came with the rise of the market for industrial securities in the USA in the 1890s. He argues that the existence of this market meant that owner-entrepreneurs who had built up their firms from new enterprises to major ones 'could now monetize their accumulation of real assets through a transfer of ownership. The old owners could now exit from their enterprises', leaving control in the hands of career managers and easing the transfer to managerial capitalism.[29] As I read that passage, I wondered about its relevance to British-registered companies and, particularly, to British free-standing companies. There were markets in Britain for the securities of the registered companies that participated in overseas business. The British knew how to package companies to sell their securities and raise moneys that would in turn be exported. Many of the registered companies were listed and traded on stock exchanges. Yet the presence of that market in England and Scotland did not necessarily mean a transition to managerial capitalism. There is no question in my mind that all the above categories of registered companies provided conduits for capital export, that only some of the companies were actively traded on the London or Edinburgh (or Liverpool or Glasgow) stock exchanges, and, of those that were, most (at least at origin) did not have broad managerial capabilities within the firm. The fact that they could go to British capital markets (and the existence of active securities markets) did not in and of itself replace the owner-entrepreneur with managerial organizations. Indeed, what turned my initial attention to the free-standing company was that, unlike the classic multinational enterprise, the model for which was derived from empirical research on US-headquartered enterprises, the free-standing company did not first develop a business and managerial structure *at home*, which it could then at low marginal cost transfer abroad.

None the less Lazonick's point is critical. To operate over distance (as these companies did when they made foreign direct investments) required different kinds of managerial capabilities from those of local business. Because of this, the free-standing company at origin was usually associated with clusters of outsiders.[30] Since it lacked at formation competencies internal to the company, it had to obtain them from outside the firm. Britain—and especially the City (the financial district of London)—had an extraordinary 'service' sector capability on which these companies could draw.[31] It has been and will be my argument that, following on the theory of multinational enterprise—as articulated in the earlier quotation from Wells—a firm must have advantages over actual or potential local competitors in order to survive abroad. I believe we need, therefore, to study the nature of that advantage. We cannot assume away management. We need to ask how the production of goods and services over borders was managed and how the managerial structures evolved. We also have to consider how the clusters of outsiders related to that advantage. Does the starting advantage have to be 'internal' to the company? Could that advantage lie exterior to the company, in the financial, commercial, accounting, engineering, and other services accessible to those in the City? Were there available talents in other locales in the UK? Did merchants—whether in London or elsewhere in Britain—engaged in international trade provide the experience and information to serve the new enterprises (at least the ones that survived)? What were the institutional networks associated with these businesses conducted over borders?

A significant part of the context for free-standing companies in Britain is that they proliferated in the most advanced, most capital-rich nation in the world, the country with the most sophisticated stock market. They emerged in a nation that dominated international trade as well as international investment. Free-standing companies furnished the basis—or so it was thought—for residents within Britain to get a better return on capital than could be obtained at home.[32] The investors' belief was that opportunities existed in the newer parts of the world; these opportunities, opened by Britishers (under capable British direction), would bring forth greater rewards than investments in the more mature home economy.[33] Investors knew of these prospects because of Britain's experience in overseas commerce. Founders of free-standing companies, as investors and as mobilizers of capital, understood the premiss of higher returns. Free-standing companies would offer conduits for capital to flow into the freshly identified overseas investment opportunities. But did the companies have sufficient 'advantage', or were they able to obtain sufficient 'advantage', to derive the hoped-for profits? The services of the City might supply the advantage; so, too, might other knowledgeable businesses and businessmen.

Free-standing companies multiplied in number in late nineteenth and early twentieth century Britain, where there was a rising demand for new goods and services as economic growth occurred and incomes increased. They spread in the Age of High Imperialism, when the 'Sun Never Set on the British Empire'. In the mid-nineteenth century, Britain had been the industrial workshop of the world; by the late nineteenth century, with the development of new industrial technologies, the USA and Germany were challenging Britain. The overseas business of free-standing companies has to be considered in the context of both Britain's domestic economy and that country's changing role in the global economy. As noted, throughout the pre-First World War years, the UK remained the world's largest trading nation and the world's greatest international investor. One truly significant group of companies that were free-standing at origin were the British multinational banks. Significance is measured not by the count of companies, but by their impact—and these banks had vast influence. As Geoffrey Jones has shown, these banks did not emerge as extensions of existing British domestic banks; rather they were newly set up with the aim of doing business in a single country or region overseas.[34] There were other major British firms that began as free-standing ones, such as British Petroleum Company and Rio Tinto. While many of the free-standing companies were transient, a number had profound consequences.

Of the $18 billion–$20 billion total British overseas investment on the eve of the First World War (1914), T. A. B. Corley (in his chapter in this volume) has estimated that $8.2 billion was direct investment and $6.6 billion of the direct investment was by free-standing companies.[35] I am not entirely comfortable with these figures, but I believe Corley is, indeed, accurate in his conclusion that the greater part of British direct investment overseas in 1914 was initially established by free-standing companies.[36]

### *Definition*

Many questions have arisen concerning the definition of free-standing companies: which companies qualify and which do not? What began, in my view, as something simple and straightforward is clearly not.[37] The attempts at clarification have served the vital purpose of stimulating more careful analysis of the institutional forms of conducting business over borders. In providing definitions, I do not want to pigeon-hole.

Rather, as we try to delineate the principal characteristics of business over borders, we need to ascertain where or whether the free-standing company 'model' fits the evidence. To do that I must define my terms and recognize where there are ambiguities. I will discuss seven separate definitional matters that have arisen.

There no longer seems to be much—or any—dispute over *a first definitional matter* that once created confusion and controversy, yet the point must be reiterated. An individual who migrates and sets up a business abroad has *not* established a free-standing company.[38] As I have written elsewhere, it is bizarre to call the Scottish-born Andrew Carnegie a 'British investor in the United States'. I follow this rule globally: a Britisher resident in China, who started and ran a business there, and formed a company that had no parent (or headquarters) domiciled in Britain was not to be included as a British overseas investment. The latter required residence in Britain.[39] There are no difficulties in this definition when we consider the USA as a host. On the other hand, the Hongkong and Shanghai Banking Corporation, registered in Hong Kong, but with shareholder lists in both Hong Kong and the UK, does present some definitional quandaries. For consistency, it is probably better to call it a Hong Kong registered company and exclude it.[40] To do so provides the opportunity to compare, for example, cotton textile mills registered in India and run by Britishers with those operating in India and registered in the UK; or diamond mines registered in South Africa and run by Britishers with those South African diamond mines registered in the UK. We want to enquire were there basic differences between those businesses with and without a UK-registered parent? I believe there were.[41] It makes us ask why and when a headquarters in London, or elsewhere in Britain, was established. Whenever there was British registration, there was at least a nominal British headquarters. Note that in host countries—Russia, the USA, and Italy, for example—domestic registration, e.g. incorporation, was required or was the procedure of choice for business operations. The British free-standing company doing business in Russia and, in some cases, the USA held stock in an operating subsidiary.[42] As Peter Hertner's chapter shows, 'foreign companies'—those founded abroad—had to register to do business in Italy.[43] For our purposes, the determinant point was whether there was *a parent* in the UK. To qualify as a British free-standing company, there had to be British registration—that is, at least a nominal British head office. There had to be supervision by—or the extension of—a company domiciled in, resident in, Britain. This is vital, for ours is the study of the operation of business *over borders*. This said, I share the caution of my co-contributors to this volume on the matter of equating registration and headquarters (more on this below).[44]

A *second definitional problem* involved a total misunderstanding by some readers of the crucial distinctions between the 'classic' multinational enterprises—as described above—and the free-standing companies.[45] A *third set of questions* homed in on foreign 'direct investments': are there only two kinds, the free-standing type and the classic multinational, or do a wide variety of forms exist? There were overseas direct investments made by British individuals, for instance in real estate. Individuals and groups of UK residents controlled companies set up abroad. These direct investments do not fit the free-standing company definition, nor do some of them meet the classic multinational enterprise criteria.[46] Several authors in this book make extremely valuable suggestions on different sub-types of free-standing companies.[47] The answer is that there are more than the two forms of foreign direct investments. If, however, we focus solely on joint-stock companies registered in Britain, categories (1), (2), and (3) above would seem to fit as classic multinational enterprises; category (4) did not involve much direct investment (but, to the extent that it did, it would seem to conform to the classic type). Category (5) is the free-standing company case, by definition, and we can expand it to include various subcategories. Were there any joint-stock companies that did not go under any of these five rubrics and yet engaged in overseas direct investments? British-American Tobacco Company (BAT) combined the international business of two firms that were classic multinationals, but it does not belong under heading (2) since it was not British controlled at origin. It was similar to a free-standing company in that it was set up in the UK to do business abroad, yet, because, at origin, it was American controlled and managed, it would not qualify for inclusion in category (5). Over time, the ownership and control of BAT moved to the UK. Did it then become a free-standing company? We will return to the important matters of nationality and of change through time later in our consideration of definitions.

An associated and more challenging definitional problem—*our fourth one*—looks at how we define a firm. If there is a coterie of companies, commonly managed, I have no difficulty in defining the collection as a firm, even if the companies are separately registered.[48] How does this apply to the activities abroad of 'investment groups', so well documented by Stanley Chapman.[49] Some of my colleagues have asked: is an analysis of investment groups and their overseas activities an alternative to a free-standing company type of analysis? I believe the two approaches are entirely complementary. As noted, I had read and admired Chapman's work and was influenced by it when I started to write on free-standing companies. I never perceived the free-standing-company concept as a substitute or rival one, but considered rather that free-standing companies were often part of Chapman's investment groups. Yet, free-standing companies were also associated with other business clusters. These findings led to the broader dilemma of defining the firm. Is 'the firm' the cluster of companies, or the single free-standing one? If one moves away from formal registrations to the business history of enterprises, usually—but not always—the query resolves itself.[50] Jean-François Hennart's, Natalia Gurushina's, Rory Miller's, and Geoffrey Jones's chapters herein—each from different perspectives—capture the various relationships between free-standing companies and the associated clusters.[51] Jones finds the term 'free-standing' a 'misnomer', since these companies were frequently part of wider enterprise groups. In a sense he is right, yet the phrase was adopted solely to differentiate free-standing companies from the classic multinational enterprise; and in that respect, it is not a misnomer.[52] But to return to the investment groups of Chapman. Whereas I had seen the constituent, separately registered in Britain companies within these collectivities, as 'free-standing', Chapman does not like that designation. In his chapter in the present volume, he provides a very convincing story of the growth of British business in India and the East. 'The firm' for him is the cluster, the group of companies associated with the agency house.[53] Robert Greenhill, in 'Investment Group, Free-Standing Company or Multinational? Brazilian Warrant, 1909–1952', posed many of the same issues in a different geographical setting.[54] Greenhill's case study dealt with the evolution of a trading firm. Such 'networked' businesses prompt us to ponder what, in fact, constitutes common management, which is critical to our discussion of the nature of the firm and how business was governed over borders.[55] Chapman's narrative and that of Greenhill seem closer in their descriptions to that of the classic multinational enterprise than to the free-standing company one: the merchant houses (the wider enterprise groups) develop on the basis of internally generated talents; their investments are associated with their 'advantage' in marketing; they have 'advantage' in information; they have appropriate experience and skills. Interestingly, the classic model was to a large extent formulated on the basis of American *industrial* companies; Chapman's and Greenhill's centre firms are merchants. Yet, I have never felt this paradigm need apply only to manufacturers.[56]

The role of the clusters *vis-à-vis* the free-standing company seems crucial. If, at least at origin, the company did not—by definition—have internally generated headquarters expertise then it had to obtain the talents from outside. In the renditions of Chapman, Greenhill, and

Hennart, the cluster has a pivotal firm with minority interests in a collection of satellite free-standing ones (albeit Chapman does not see the satellite units as 'free-standing'). Hennart's theoretical analysis seeks to explain two related phenomena—that of the free-standing company proper and that of the firm that takes the minority stakes. There seems, however, to be an added element in the clusters—that is, the exogenous group of interested parties in any single free-standing company. These clusters of services surround and assist the free-standing company, with no clear centre.[57] Thus, in my 1988 article I wrote of promoters, solicitors, accountants, investment trust company representatives, and so forth, as part of the clusters. Sometimes, these firms (or their principals) had equity interests in the free-standing company, and sometimes not. Gurushina—in Chapter 6—and Reinhard Liehr and Mariano E. Torres Bautista—in Chapter 9—are excellent on interlocking directorates and clusters of companies. The 'business world' in late-nineteenth- and early twentieth-century Britain was small enough for studies of who's who on boards of directors often to be a good start in tracing the networks and nuclei.

*A fifth definitional problem* sprang up apropos of nationality: if I define the British free-standing company as one registered in Britain, under British ownership and control, I must specify the meaning of '*British* ownership and control'. If a company was headquartered in Britain (as nominally it must be under British registration), what percentage of the ownership must be British to call it British owned or British controlled? Are the two identical? Does the size or proportion of ownership necessarily indicate control?[58] Share registers reveal that British-registered companies were often not wholly British owned. As pointed out in other chapters, Bolivian Francisco A. Aramayo participated in the organization of a free-standing company in London in 1906; he held control.[59] In Chapter 6, Gurushina considers the Russian Tobacco Company, set up in Britain by Russians, to invest in Russia.[60] While, formally, such companies looked like *British* free-standing ones, that might not be the case at all. How does the free-standing-company notion fit when an Aramayo (or a group of Russians) makes a 'direct investment' in a company in the UK that, in turn, becomes the vehicle for an investment in Bolivia (or Russia)? Equity investments (in Hennart's discussion) are designed to carry control, but the equity held by the Bolivian (or the Russians) rather than by many (or few) Britishers is the key here in understanding the development of the business activity.[61] If a resident of a host country sets up a company in Britain, which he owns and controls, but which is registered under British law and raises only debenture capital in Britain, is that a British free-standing company? Take the same circumstances and have the firm raise equity as well as debt capital; how much equity must be held in Britain to move the ownership 'control' to that country? Clearly, ambiguities abound.

A number of large German, French, and American investors made third-country investments (in public utilities and mining in Latin America and in the British Empire, for example) through British-registered companies.[62] American multinationals often used British subsidiaries for business abroad. At origin, the British-American Tobacco Company (set up in London) was two-thirds owned by American Tobacco; its key management was American; it was 'American owned and controlled'; as noted, I excluded it at origin as a *British* free-standing company. Likewise, when Singer Sewing Machine administered a major portion of its foreign business through London, I believe this was decentralization within a US-headquartered multinational enterprise and not *British* business abroad.[63] In sum, it is important to establish whether a British-registered entity taking part in overseas investments was ultimately 'British directed', or, in effect, German, French, or American direct investments and not a *British* free-standing company at all.

In brief, a British-registered company need not be British owned and controlled. My definition of a *British* free-standing company has required British ownership and control of the parent and the overseas operations.[64] Exactly what constitutes British ownership and control may be hard to determine.[65] We have to examine the individual firm to establish the actual 'headquarters' and thus the nationality. As a further complication, the nationality of ownership and control (and the headquarters) could change through time.

A *sixth definitional question* arose out of and was linked with the last. It was not only the nationality issue that posed quandaries in the determination of a headquarters. What constitutes a 'headquarters'? Corporate structures (registration) were used for many purposes: raising money, liability, tax, and national rules and regulations. 'Registration' *per se* is not adequate to determine the home office. Yet, I have used British registration merely as a convenient handle, recognizing it as imperfect and well aware that the only way to identify the true head office of an enterprise is to look at the firm's records.[66] Ownership *of the firm*, if concentrated, is linked with control. If not concentrated, control may be separate. When I discuss tiers of ownership and control of the overseas business, the firm is my focus. 'Control' of the firm may be separate from ownership. None the less, as a company extends abroad, it is possible to say that there is 'control', or at least potential for control of the foreign operations. A headquarters is the place from which 'control' or potential control emanates. Jean-François Hennart and Mark Casson in their chapters herein debate some of the highly complex issues of control. When Edith Penrose wrote of the growth of the firm, she focused on the expansion of an administrative core. Yet, administration within the firm can be decentralized. Every student of multinational enterprise knows how murky some of the control issues are.[67] Because a number of free-standing companies were 'brass plates in the City', some authors have assumed that I believed that in the case of free-standing companies control from Britain was always weak.[68] I have never, however, argued that this is the distinction between classic multinational enterprises (where control could be minimal) and free-standing companies (where control could be carefully maintained).[69] Casson suggests that with certain free-standing companies, there was no direct investment at all, that the investment abroad was a 'portfolio one'.[70] In my view, by definition, the free-standing company has a headquarters in one country and extends abroad; by definition, it makes 'direct investments'. What seems crucial is that the free-standing company, at least at origin, confronted *different* choices relating to control and governance from those of the classic multinational enterprise. That accepted, the nature of control and the structure of governance by free-standing companies become important research topics. The spectrum of headquarters control presented by Corley in his chapter herein seems an excellent starting point.[71]

*Our seventh and last set of definitional questions* relate to the time dimension—the evolution of the firm. There appear to be three separate queries. The first two have easy answers; the third is the most problematic. (1) Can a firm through time change its headquarters, its nationality? Yes. (2) Could existing companies over time *become* free-standing ones? Yes, again. A company in a host country could be taken over by a British free-standing company. There was often a sequence of free-standing companies, acquiring the same assets, each better capitalized or more skillfully chartered, each hopefully able to raise new moneys.[72] On the other hand, I would argue that when, for example, the British-American Tobacco Company became British controlled—that is, changed its 'headquarters'—it did not qualify as a free-standing company, since within its organization the basic managerial capabilities had by then been fully internalized. Indeed, at origin, BAT—unlike the typical free-standing company—operated abroad in a number of countries and regions. It had core competencies drawn from American Tobacco *and* from Imperial Tobacco. (3) If a company began as a free-standing one, what characteristics must it maintain to remain in that category? In the past, my answer had been that, if a surviving enterprise internalized managerial capabilities on an international scale, it no longer qualified as a free-standing company. Yet, this response was not precise; it did not address exactly what characteristics a company had to sustain to persist under the label 'free-standing'. By definition, lean governance existed at the start; the firm did not have operations in Britain, at origin, other than those related to the establishment of the head-office. But was lean governance from that small head-office fundamental to my definition of a *continuing* free-standing company? In my 1988 article 'The Free-Standing Company', I wrote: 'The limited size of the typical home office was ultimately the crucial feature that distinguished these companies from contemporary US multinationals.' What I had meant to say was that 'At the start of their overseas business, the limited size of . . .'.[73]

As my colleagues (including the authors of the chapters herein) have pursued research on free-standing companies, I have had to think more carefully about the firms that survived—some for generations. My concern at this juncture focuses on definitional dilemmas. Clearly, individual companies that began as free-standing followed different paths. What is unclear is how long in the course of an individual company's history the term 'free-standing' continues to be meaningful. What does 'lean governance' entail? When, more exactly, can we say managerial capabilities have been internalized? Just how much of a home office *and* overseas corporate administration are required before we drop the designation free-standing?[74] It seems to me that at this point in our research flexibility must substitute for rigidity, and, probably, we must accept imprecision. We need to study the emergence of a broader business (if that occurs), the shaping of administrative structures, and how and what kinds of managerial and technical expertise developed. As in the growth of any business firm, this is a process. A single foreign plant, plantation, or bank office can be administered by a few individuals within the host country or from abroad. Enterprises, however, that come to employ thousands and comprise multiplant, multioffice, multifunctional, multinational activities require administrative hierarchies and the internalization of technical know-how. The British overseas banks (so well described by Geoffrey Jones), which founded and acquired multioffice outlets, had to create managerial organizations and obtain knowledgeable personnel for survival. They had different needs from the single mine, plantation, or jute factory that persisted over time. Some free-standing companies came to be drawn into wider enterprise groups after their origin. This was true of a number of mining ventures and of some of the companies that Chapman describes.[75] As we seek to refine our considerations on what happens over time, our understanding of the realities and the nature of business over borders deepens. Contributors to this volume do not apply the free-standing concept to business through time in the same manner. This is, however, in my view, entirely acceptable, because our purpose is to use the concept as a means of comprehension, of guiding our questioning.[76]

Thus, while it is useful and necessary to try to be reasonably careful in definitions, taxonomy can get tedious and we should try to avoid over-classifying. Premature definitions should not be allowed to divert attention or create blinders. What is central to the research on free-standing companies is that thousands were established, owned, and controlled in the home country, to conduct business abroad through direct investments, generally in a particular host country or region, and that the foreign business of these companies did not evolve out of ongoing business operations *at home*. These companies, therefore, had to develop anew and to find the know-how to run such enterprises abroad if the businesses were to survive.[77] How, when, and where they did so is vital to an analysis of the international business relationships and to the understanding of global economic history.

### *Elaboration*

Elaboration (based on newly assembled evidence) helps with some of the definitional difficulties and puts them into a broad perspective. As noted, Christopher Schmitz has recently scrutinized the 9,303 companies registered in Edinburgh (1862–1914) and identified 853 companies set up for overseas business. Of these, 87 (roughly 10 per cent) were 'investment trusts, general investment'.[78] These probably would not be free-standing companies in my definition, because most had no business operations abroad; typically, they made their foreign investments from their home-base or appointed independent agents to make foreign portfolio-type investments in capital markets outside the UK.[79] Thirty-one were 'general trading, agencies'; I have long classified most trading companies as service multinationals, in keeping with the 'classic' multinational enterprise, since they had a domestic business rationale (to export or import goods), which linked operations abroad with those at home.[80] Thus, they would be excluded from the free-standing company category. There were, however, some trading companies set up to operate solely overseas and not to conduct trade with Britain, which would qualify them as free-standing companies. Most of the rest of Schmitz's 853 would seem—at least on the surface—to fit under the rubric, free-standing companies.[81] Table 1.1 summarizes Schmitz's findings.

One of the most helpful elaborations of the free-standing company concept relates to industries. Schmitz's research confirms Mark Casson's argument that, at least for the Scottish free-standing companies,

Table 1.1. *Scottish-registered companies set up for overseas investments, 1862–1914*

| Industry | % | % | Number | Number |
|---|---|---|---|---|
| Mining | 44 | | 376 | |
| Gold | | 19 | | 163 |
| Copper | | 3 | | 29 |
| Agriculture, ranching | 22 | | 184 | |
| Rubber plantations | | 5 | | 46 |
| Tea plantations | | 4 | | 30 |
| Livestock, ranching | | 2 | | 21 |
| Manufacturing | 4 | | 34 | |
| Jute spinning | | 1 | | 7 |
| Transportation, communication | 2 | | 18 | |
| Services, utilities | 5 | | 42 | |
| General trading, agencies | | 4 | | 31 |
| Investment, real estate | 17 | | 148 | |
| Investment trusts | | 10 | | 87 |
| Mortgage companies | | 3 | | 29 |
| Land, real estate | | 4 | | 31 |
| Miscellaneous | 1 | | 10 | |
| General, unspecified | 5 | | 41 | |
| TOTAL | 100 | | 853 | |

*Source*: C. J. Schmitz, 'Patterns of Scottish Portfolio Foreign Investment 1860–1914', unpublished report to ESRC (1994).

there was a disproportionate share in what Casson calls 'property-related' investments.[82] The paucity of stakes in transportation and communication may be the case with Scotland and not England. British Inland Revenue Department data show a heavy concentration of British companies abroad in railroads and transport in the late nineteenth century.[83] My earlier writings had stated that free-standing companies existed in all sectors—primary products, manufacturing, services; I still hold to that but am prepared to amend the conclusion. Casson has made a major contribution in insisting that the concept is more suitable in analysing economic behaviour in certain sectors than others.[84] Hennart also emphasizes this, arguing that the free-standing form was appropriate in capital-intensive projects where there was little collateral—that is, an inadequate basis for borrowing.[85] Many of the contributors to this volume have noted the free-standing company's viability as a form for new mining ventures, especially when there was high risk, and also because there were active groups of mining engineers and investment bankers in London which were experienced in financing mining ventures. London was the 'premier metal market at that time'.[86] Nowhere was there better information on the market for the output of new mining ventures and on the demand for copper, lead, zinc, phosphates, tin, and other minerals. So, too, the free-standing-company form also became a viable one for plantations, especially those in rubber and tea. In the past, I suggested that the classic multinational enterprise often had no advantage in backward integration over the free-standing company. For example, Ford Motor Company had no knowledge within the firm on the cultivation of rubber. It had to hire specialists. The free-standing companies with their rubber plantations in Malaya probably had an advantage over Ford with its rubber plantations in Brazil. The former were frequently set up or came to be managed by experienced agency houses; they were thus better positioned to draw on outsiders' talents.[87] Geoffrey Jones shows that the free-standing-company form was utilized for British overseas banking.[88] While there were free-standing companies in manufacturing, none was in a 'high-technology' industry that required ongoing complex technical assistance from a parent organization. The complete absence of free-standing companies in high-technology production is one of the most crucial findings of recent research.[89] Likewise, few free-standing companies sold branded, trademarked goods.[90] For high-technology products, the multinational enterprise needed control over research and development and its transmission within the firm. For branded products, there had to be careful governance to promote the good or service and to avoid debasement of the name. Each involved managerial control that seemingly needed to be internalized to be efficient. The manufactured output did not, however, have to be high technology (only new technology) or branded merchandise for the classic multinational to perform better than the free-standing company. As a case in point, there is evidence that Japanese cotton-spinning companies that made direct investments in Chinese spinning (and behaved as American-model classic multinationals) created more efficient operations than British free-standing companies in the identical Chinese industry. Existing theories of multinational enterprise would predict this; the Japanese advantage was managerial.[91]

A principal feature of many free-standing companies seems to lie in their relationship with other companies, with the loose clusters of outsiders.[92] Alice H. Amsden and Takashi Hikino have maintained that 'late-industrializing enterprises . . . pursued strategies of vertical integration and unrelated diversification simultaneously, in unsystematic and complicated ways'. They cite as an example a mid-1980s statement by the chairman of Korea's Lucky-Goldstar Group:

> My father and I started a cosmetic cream factory in the 1940s. At the time, no company could supply us with plastic caps of adequate quality for cream jars, so we had to start a plastic business. Plastic caps alone were not sufficient to run the plastic-molding plant, so we added combs, toothbrushes, and soap boxes. This plastic business also led us to manufacture electrical and electronic products and telecommunication equipment. The plastics business also took us into oil refining which needed a tanker-shipping company. The oil-refining company alone was

> paying an insurance premium amounting to more than half the total revenue of the then largest insurance company in Korea. Thus, an insurance company was started. This natural step-by-step evolution through related businesses resulted in the Lucky-Goldstar group as we see it today.[93]

As I read this statement, I had a sense of *déjà vu*. Balfour, Williamson & Co.'s acquisitions, for example, seem to have been made in much the same kind of natural, step-by-step evolution.[94] A similar pattern can be seen in studies of British investments in South Africa; one investment led to information about other semi-related activities.[95] These added businesses required new capital and different expertise. Often companies were set up separately. If they called for sizeable amounts of capital, they might be registered in the UK. If not, they need not have been. The internalization that the chairman of Korea's Lucky-Goldstar Group described might not exist, although the same kind of cluster sequencing was apparent—principally, but not necessarily, in host late industrializing countries (Balfour, Williamson & Co., which carried on the step-by-step approach, did so not only in Latin America but also in the USA). The notion of 'wider-enterprise' groupings gets us back to the definitional problem of 'defining the firm'.

Geoffrey Jones notes that the British overseas banks—which were unquestionably free-standing, at least at origin—were not part of any broader enterprise collectivity. Yet, John Dunning and E. V. Morgan have included them in 'the financial nucleus' present in the City. Jones would agree. And not only were they linked in a financial network, but these banks had to recruit from outside personnel to administer their banking operations. Until they developed capabilities internal to their organizations, they were forced to turn to banks within Britain for staffing. The overseas banks would apply to their home office for the names of clerks 'able and willing to take up the challenge of banking in colonial or foreign markets'.[96] In time, the British overseas banks that survived provided their own expertise, established their own on-the-job training programmes, and generated their own distinct bank 'culture'. Yet, as Jones argues, they continued to rely on and remain part of London's agglomeration of financial institutions and markets.

A very useful elaboration of the concept of free-standing companies comes when detailed applications are made to different host countries and regions. The chapters in this volume are a wonderful beginning in country and regional treatments, but we need many more such essays for comparative purposes. What is confirmed at this point is that British free-standing companies were in business in Empire and non-Empire host countries. These companies operated in the most developed regions of the world as well as in less developed ones. There is no neat centre–periphery pattern. None the less, there may well be some systematic differences between those within Empire and non-Empire (or between parts of the Empire and non-Empire), relating to British registration.[97] And a major divergence between those in developed and less developed host areas did exist in longevity: all the research finds that the lifespan of British free-standing companies in less developed host countries was longer than in the USA, for example.

Were the 'cluster' patterns similar in each host region? Were the modes of doing business the same or unique? Even though at first free-standing companies were specific to a country or region, there seem to be common features as we survey the global characteristics of British overseas investments. The British merchant groups that Chapman has chronicled operated in a similar manner in various parts of the world.[98] So, too, the overseas banks that Geoffrey Jones has researched appear alike in genesis (if not in continuity) from one region to the next.[99] Yet there were special aspects by geography. Thus, Chapman argues that key London promoters of international companies had no experience with India and the Far East.[100] Another difference lay in staffing. British free-standing companies in less developed countries often hired British expatriates—already settled there—or sent personnel from the UK. In developed countries, nationals within the host countries were fully capable of carrying on activities, which may explain why the domestication of free-standing companies (the elimination of the British headquarters) usually came more rapidly in developed than in less developed countries.

Some businesses in the same industries and same countries, often associated with identical clusters of companies, were established as free-standing ones in Britain, while others had only local registration. Why did this dissimilarity exist? The answers are not yet entirely evident, but, *ceteris paribus*, companies registered in Britain tended to be larger (with greater capitalization) than those in the same industries—in the same cluster—formed in host countries.[101] The high cost of floating a company in Britain (for example, the costs of lining up and paying directors, fees to accountants, charges for British specialists' trips overseas for verification purposes) had to be offset by the capital acquired. Chapman (in Chapter 7) and my own research confirm this high cost. G. D. N. Worswick and D. G. Tipping indicate that, with both a head office in Britain and an operating establishment abroad, 'a fairly large minimum size is therefore pre-supposed'.[102] Hennart, who in Chapter 2 gives his own answers on the different reasons for British rather than host-country registration, points out that some locally incorporated 'Western' tin mining companies in Malaya were reincorporated in London when their capital needs grew. In the same chapter, he hypothesizes that, the more a firm was oriented towards export from a host location, the more likely it would have a foreign registration; he shows, for instance, that, in Ceylon, tea growing was undertaken by both sterling (London-registered) and rupee (locally incorporated) companies; sterling companies specialized in the highest quality tea, which was sold in London, while the generally smaller rupee companies sold most of their produce on the local market.[103] On the other hand, there were many British free-standing companies that did not participate in exporting from the host country.[104] In the case of South Africa, where sometimes there was London registration of diamond- and gold-mining companies and sometimes not, the advantages of *South African* incorporation have been summarized as follows: (1) avoidance of the inconvenience and constraints of English company law; (2) no need to hold annual meetings in London; and (3) no need to provide shareholder registers.[105]

A. R. Hall, in *The London Capital Market and Australia 1870–1914*, studied the relative use of various types of securities issued by companies operating in Australia in 1914, broken down by those companies registered in the UK and those registered in Australia; he found that the bulk of 'Australian securities' in London were issued by companies registered in the UK. 'Most of the ordinary shares of companies registered in Australia were held there, only preference and debentures being issued in London and these made up a relatively small proportion of the resources of the companies concerned.'[106] This coincides with Hennart's more recent findings. R. P. T. Davenport Hines and Geoffrey Jones, in their introduction to a volume on British business in Asia since 1860, discuss London-registered and locally registered 'British' businesses in that region, including in the latter discussion the business of expatriate locally resident Britishers and suggesting that the place of registration gave no consistent guide to sources of capital, 'although as a general rule locally registered companies seem to have drawn at least some of their capital from locally resident Europeans and occasionally Asians'.[107]

The British-registered free-standing company usually sought to tap British capital markets. Lance E. Davis and Robert J. Cull have pointed out that, in 1910, 18.2 per cent of American stock issues were traded on both the New York and London stock exchanges. Davis and Cull found that, in sectors other than railroads, American commercial and industrial firms were traded on both stock exchanges, 'however, the same firms were seldom listed on both exchanges'. They concluded that 'a substantial fraction of American securities traded in London were not even imperfect substitutes for many of the stocks and bonds traded in

New York'. Apparently, British free-standing companies, with their securities denominated in sterling, would *not* be traded in New York.[108]

As noted, there were costs as well as benefits to founders of a business in forming a free-standing company in the UK. When a free-standing company was organized, however, there was some kind of management over borders, no matter how lean the head office. If the purpose of setting up a free-standing company was purely to obtain capital in Britain and if the initiative came from abroad, perhaps the free-standing form was used differently from those cases where the initiative came from the UK. There are not enough studies on whether there were managerial or other systematic differences between companies in the same industry that were registered in a host country (employing foreign capital) and those registered in Britain. Did it matter to management structures as to where the initiative came?

The discussion of British versus local registration of companies dominated by British capital has prompted new research on the functions of a head office. In the administration of business over borders, what does a head office do? At the very minimum, if there was a registered company, the secretary of the company filed reports required by law. In Chapter 4, Corley presents a spectrum, from that of a 'brass plate' to that of a fully operational head office. This is very helpful. Some addenda might be made. First, what were the proportions in each category (which types of head offices were more common)? Secondly, what were the changes through time (were companies once and forever in a set category, or do companies through time move from one category to the next)? Thirdly, how did the nature of the headquarters relate to survival through time? Fourthly, were there systematic industry and host country/region differences in the functions of the British registered company's head office? Finally, as a fifth point, we need more details on those free-standing companies where the head office was or became 'fully operational', 'in regular correspondence', and 'concerned mainly with financial matters'. Corley provides a fine beginning to this elaboration. Geoffrey Jones shows that the head offices of successful British overseas banks played a major role in the provision of financial and recruitment services, while remaining 'lean' in 'size' (in numbers of individuals). I would classify them, however, in Corley's terms, as 'fully operational'. Natalia Gurushina's chapter reveals the complexities of activities of British head offices in dealing with the financing of Russian business.[109]

To conduct a successful business involves a certain amount of know-how; resources do not combine automatically; management matters. If, by definition, a new company is established that does not have within its midst the learning experience, as in the case at origin with free-standing companies, in order for it to continue it must obtain knowledge from outside. This brings us to one of the most significant contributions of the chapters in this volume. Many focus on what happened to free-standing companies over time. What were the patterns? We are back to the time dimension, now summarizing recent findings and adding new insights on the validity of different definitional choices. An individual free-standing company could—even before it started to function or after many years—exit (through failure, full absorption by another company, or abandonment of the British headquarters).[110] In my 1988 *Economic History Review* article, I commented on the high drop-out rate, which I attributed to scams and lean governance (inadequate management from the UK). I believed then, and still do, that many more of these companies were failures than successes.[111] Yet, there were long continuities and success stories.[112] It is thus wise (and necessary) to devote attention to what happened to those companies that began as free-standing and persisted over many years. And, if the business abroad was viable, we need to ask *why* was a foreign (British) head office retained? Assuming no 'exit', the firm's subsequent history could follow one of several paths: (1) the business could remain as a single purpose, single (or occasionally several) facility enterprise within the host country, keeping a separate identity; if so, there was usually no reason to expand the size of the home office; (2) it could be partially absorbed within a wider enterprise group, still maintaining a small head office in Britain; and (3) it could grow into a more extensive enterprise, internalizing within its business organization managerial and technical capabilities. In this third category, some companies continued for many years with lean governance from Britain that proved efficient and appropriate to the business undertaken, while at the same time developing *abroad* an impressive administrative organization. Others that began as free-standing companies created large head offices (and added operations) in Britain and became multifunctional, multiproduct, multioffice, multiplant, multifacility businesses—resembling the classic multinational enterprise. I am convinced that the principal feature of free-standing companies, at origin, was *not* their absence of business in Britain, but rather the lack of business *experience* in Britain, *internal* to the company, on which to draw.[113] How they coped with this deficiency through time tells us a great deal about the microeconomics of economic history.

Mark Casson suggests that free-standing companies were more adept at development of new activities than at maintenance.[114] This requires much more research; it is challenged by Gurushina.[115] Hennart notes that as late as 1967 UK-registered free-standing companies were producing over 75 per cent of Nigeria's tin output; presumably they had their own managerial structures.[116] Rory Miller shows how railroad companies created within their organizations professional management and survived.[117] Did the single purpose tin-producing and railroad companies remain 'free-standing' through the years? This depends on the definition of the free-standing company adopted. If one argues that they persisted as single-activity ventures within a single host country, albeit with a professional management, does that qualify them for continuing free-standing status? At least one contributor to the volume believes that to be the case.[118]

A key set of survivors was a small collection of British overseas banks, whose history Geoffrey Jones has documented. They began as free-standing companies. In response to business opportunities in certain regions they generated banking skills *and* managerial capabilities within their organizations.[119] As these overseas banks expanded, by my original (1988) definitions they were no longer free-standing businesses, for they internalized their managerial talents and did not depend on buying basic services (core competencies) from outsiders.[120] Note, however, it was not the British overseas banks that extended into the USA, Austria, or Italy that persisted, but those that were established in much less developed regions.[121] In the cases of the railroads and overseas banks, the British home office continued to be modest, but served more than a fund-raising function. In Corley's terms, it seems to me (as I have earlier noted in relation to overseas banks), both had head offices that were 'fully operational'. When we discuss 'operations', we must consider production of *services*. These head offices produced important recruiting, purchasing, as well as financial services on an ongoing basis for the overseas activities. The head office also produced other 'client' services. It had access to and the ability to transmit information. The costs of the head office appear to have been offset by the benefits.

One major company that started as free-standing demonstrates vividly the process of transformation over time. Rio Tinto (in the early and mid-1990s RTZ Corporation, briefly RTZ-CRA, and then in early 1997 back to its original name, Rio Tinto) began as a free-standing company, operating a mine in Spain; it became a giant international mining enterprise, with vast expertise internal to its business organization. In 1990 the RTZ Corporation employed 73,612 individuals worldwide, of which 15,459 were in the UK. When, in 1993, RTZ, which had 50 per cent of its operating assets in the USA and Canada, considered reducing its currency exposure by migrating to the USA, its British management rejected the idea, in part because 88 per cent of its shareholders were in the UK but also because, as Sir Derek Birkin, chairman, declared, 'We do think that being British is helpful. There's an image of fair play, of cultural skills.'[122] This company is no longer free-standing by my definition; yet, the exact point that it changed from a free-standing company to a modern multinational enterprise is difficult to determine, but it may not be necessary to make that determination with exactitude.

Another case of transformation through time is Anglo-Persian, now the British Petroleum Company (BP), which began as a free-standing company with an oil concession in Iran; by 1947 it had 14,456 employees in the UK (out of 107,269 worldwide) and was a leading oil multinational.[123] In 1990 it employed 118,050 worldwide, of which 30,693 were in the UK.[124] In this instance as well it is hard to decide exactly when capabilities became internalized. Corley's discussion of the origins of British Petroleum highlights some of the difficulties of the free-standing-company paradigm, but also the concept's value.[125] The origins of BP go back to the D'Arcy Concession of 1901. In 1903 William Knox D'Arcy formed the First Exploitation Company, a prototypical free-standing company.[126] In 1905 Burmah Oil became involved in D'Arcy's venture and a new corporate structure emerged.[127] When, in 1909, the direct predecessor to BP (Anglo-Persian) was formed, we could—following Corley—call that company a part of the multinational, Burmah Oil. The latter provided skills, but they proved to be insufficient; Anglo-Persian used a managing agency with poor results. Burmah Oil's chemists were unfamiliar with the properties of Persian oil. In time, as Corley points out, Burmah Oil could not handle the management. Anglo-Persian increasingly internalized its own managerial needs. We are back to defining a firm.[128] Clearly, for a while, Anglo-Persian was part of a larger multinational enterprise.[129] As Burmah Oil's investment became passive, Anglo-Persian emerged as 'the firm', and, as it internalized its expertise, it behaved as any multinational enterprise would do. The free-standing-company concept seems valuable in dealing with the origins of this company (and in thinking about its subsequent development). We do not want to employ the concept as a strait-jacket. Yet, having the concept as a guide, does show how, as this oil firm's business grew, its needs changed, as did its strategies and its managerial structures.[130] It overcame the limitations of a free-standing company.[131]

Schmitz's research on Scottish companies offers new data on continuity. His study indicates that 764 companies were set up in Scotland before 1914 for business abroad (I have taken his original 853 companies and subtracted 87 investment trusts and 2 other investment companies on the grounds that these would not, at origin, fit my definition of free-standing). Of these, only nineteen were still active in 1992. Schmitz kindly provided me with their names (see Table 1.2). With two exceptions, these companies had begun business within the

TABLE 1.2. *1992 survivors of Scottish-registered companies set up for business abroad, 1862–1914*

| Company name | Date of registration | Primary activity at origin | Primary location at origin |
|---|---|---|---|
| 1. Scottish Assam Tea | 1865 | Tea plantation | India |
| 2. Tharsis Sulphur & Copper | 1866 | Mining | Spain |
| 3. Samnuggar Jute Factory | 1874 | Jute manufacture | India |
| 4. African Lakes Corporation | 1878 | General trading | British East Africa |
| 5. Victoria Jute | 1883 | Jute manufacture | India |
| 6. Titaghur Jute | 1883 | Jute manufacture | India |
| 7. Doloi Tea | 1884 | Tea plantation | India |
| 8. Burmah Oil | 1886[a] | Oil exploration | Burma |
| 9. Dharmai Tea | 1894 | Tea plantation | India |
| 10. Consolidated Tea & Lands | 1896 | Tea plantation | India |
| 11. Amalgamated Tea Estates | 1896 | Tea plantation | India |
| 12. Kanan Devan Hills Produce | 1897 | Agriculture | India |
| 13. Anglo-American Direct Tea Trading | 1898 | Tea, coffee, cocoa plantations[b] | India and Ceylon |
| 14. Shelford Rubber Estates | 1906 | Rubber | Malaya |
| 15. Third Mile (FMS) Rubber | 1906[c] | Rubber | Malaya |
| 16. Anglo-Sumatra Rubber | 1907 | Rubber | Dutch East Indies |
| 17. South Georgia[d] | 1909 | Trading | British Empire |
| 18. Juru Estate[e] | 1910 | Rubber | Malaya |
| 19. Kajang Rubber Estate[f] | 1910 | Rubber | Malaya |

[a] Reconstructed 1902.
[b] The company's name notwithstanding.
[c] This has been subsequently reconstituted as an investment company.
[d] Renamed Christian Salvesen in 1969.
[e] Renamed Dean Park Hotel Group in 1986.
[f] Renamed Inch Kenneth Kajang Rubber in 1933.
*Source*: Data from Christopher Schmitz, 28 Feb. 1994. He had 21 non-financial survivors. I dropped North British Canadian Investment (a land company) and Scottish Trust & Loan Co. of Ceylon (which invested in tea plantations) from the list, considering them investment companies.

British Empire. There are on this survivor list, as I would anticipate, no Scottish companies with business (at origin) in the USA. The roster also suggests the need to consider continuities by industry. It contains three manufacturing facilities, all in jute, and all of which were part of the Thomas Duff & Co. managing agency group. As for the persisting tea companies, nos. 10–13 were part of the James Finlay & Co. group. The earliest of the continuing tea companies, Scottish Assam Tea (no. 1), was in the Williamson, Magor & Co. group. Others of these long-lived companies were either associated with managing agency groups or were no longer free-standing.[132] Hennart argues that 'free-standing companies were created to internalize the international market for equity capital. When this market became more efficient, they lost their *raison d'être* and evolved into domestic companies. Their disappearance was the logical consequence of changed market conditions.'[133] Does this explain these survivors?

Three aspects of the history of free-standing companies over the years require attention. The first, which we have just discussed, deals with the ongoing activities of free-standing companies established before 1914. In this regard, Tamás Szmrecsányi has made the tempting suggestion that the free-standing form could perhaps be seen as transitional.[134] Following this approach, companies that lasted pursued different tracks, but in each case developed workable business organizations. This raises the definitional question of whether we want to reserve the term free-standing for only 'origins' or for firms that remain over time single-function, single-country businesses. Or, alternatively, do we also want to include firms—such as the British overseas banks—that did not develop in Britain 'operations similar to those done abroad'? If the home office came to produce the required services to administer the business abroad, even if the home office stayed small, should we drop the term 'free-standing'? As noted, there were several paths through time. If the firm's economic activity continued on and became domesticated in the host country, it ceased to be a continuing free-standing company; it came to be controlled and managed in the host country. One type of survivor (with a continuing British head office) was a business that maintained the single-core activity and never became part of a large multifunctional, multioffice, many-country operation. Another type of survivor was a firm transformed into the familiar category of multinational enterprise. There also seem to be 'intermediate' survivors—i.e. those with a single-core or single-country (or region) activity, but with a sizeable business; in addition, there were survivors that were for all practical purposes not independent, but closely associated with a wider enterprise group (usually a trading company) so as to have the latter constitute the multinational firm. Writing in 1931 on British overseas investments in 1929, Robert Kindersley noted that 'almost every British company operating abroad [and registered in the UK] maintains an expensive London head office or agency, which absorbs part of the company's capital'. What Kindersley seemed to be saying is that those persisting British free-standing companies established important (or at least costly) head-office activities.[135] Whereas a number of companies did continue on during the inter-war period as basically single-function, single-country enterprises (and probably should still be designated 'free-standing'), such lasting entities dwindled in the decades after the Second World War, as Britain lost her colonial Empire and as Third World countries intensified the process of industrialization, and economic nationalism triumphed. As the world economy changed, the free-standing-company form seemed increasingly inappropriate.

A second approach to the free-standing company over time looks at new British companies organized after 1914. The period prior to the First World War was the heyday of the free-standing company. Hennart observes, however, that free-standing companies were still being floated in the 1990s, yet his list includes none that is British. He found that in the 1920s, in parts of the British Empire (from Malaya to Nigeria) where capital markets were poorly developed, many free-standing companies were floated in Britain for rubber plantations and tin-mining.[136] Other data point to more British free-standing companies in existence in 1927 than in 1909—suggesting that many new companies were established in the 1920s. On the other hand, these same data—based on the 'number of assessments' by the Commissioner of Inland Revenue—show that, as a percentage of the total tally of domestic and overseas company assessments, there was a sharp decline from 1909 to 1927 in the overseas portion. Moreover, an increase in the 'number of assessments' might not necessarily mean more new companies; it could mean existing companies had taxable revenues in 1927 but not in 1909.[137] Rory Miller's research on the west coast of South America, which revealed numerous British free-standing companies before the First World War, found few new ones in that region in the 1920s. Jones's corporate biographies of British overseas banks include less than a handful set up after 1914.[138] My own research on the USA as a host to foreign investment uncovered no new British free-standing companies investing there after 1914.[139] Rory Miller points out that, in the early 1920s, the British government placed restrictions on capital exports and 'raising money [in Britain] for enterprises outside the Empire was particularly difficult'.[140] Once again, Kindersley is also helpful. He wrote that in the nineteenth century 'the British company was the favourite medium for the investment of British capital overseas. The high rate of income tax now [referring to 1929–1930] payable by British registered companies as compared with companies registered abroad, and the rapid industralisation of foreign countries has now left but little scope for the further development of this method of investment . . . '.[141] After 1929–1930, this became ever more true.

A third approach is to consider the changing industry composition of free-standing companies through time. This is virgin territory, but British Commissioner of Inland Revenue figures on 'numbers of assessments' are revealing. Table 1.3 gives the total number of assessments of British overseas companies, broken down by the largest industry categories. What is most striking is the decline in the use of the form in railroads and transport over time. Also there is the confirmation of the data in Table 1.2—i.e. the continuing relative importance of plantation companies. Remember, however, that 'numbers of assessments' reveal nothing about the size of investments, nor the importance of individual investments, only that these were providing profits subject to tax. The sharp 1932 drop in number of assessments of plantations

TABLE 1.3. *British overseas companies, number of assessments, by largest industry category*

| Industry category | 1890/1 | | 1895/6 | | 1909 | | 1927 | | 1932 | | 1938 | |
|---|---|---|---|---|---|---|---|---|---|---|---|---|
| | No. | % | No. | % | No. | % | No. | % | No. | % | No. | % |
| Railroads and Transport | 621 | 33 | 527 | 28 | 410 | 13 | 202 | 6 | 125 | 5 | 104 | 4 |
| Mines | 295 | 16 | 246 | 13 | 614 | 19 | 330 | 9 | 264 | 10 | 231 | 9 |
| Oil concessions | | n.a. | | n.a. | 69 | 2 | 78 | 2 | 60 | 2 | 31 | 1 |
| Land and Mortgage | 281 | 15 | 238 | 13 | 194 | 6 | 273 | 8 | 255 | 10 | 120 | 5 |
| Plantations | | n.a. | | n.a. | 930 | 29 | 1,194 | 34 | 486 | 19 | 1,018 | 40 |
| Public utilities | 59 | 3 | 96 | 5 | 67 | 2 | 82 | 2 | 99 | 4 | 63 | 2 |
| Others | 624 | 33 | 746 | 41 | 919 | 29 | 1,343 | 38 | 1,264 | 50 | 976 | 38 |
| TOTAL | 1,880 | 100 | 1,853 | 100 | 3,203 | 100 | 3,502 | 100 | 2,553 | 100 | 2,543 | 100 |

*Notes*: Percentages may be off due to rounding.
n.a. = not available.

*Source*: G. D. N. Worswick and D. G. Tipping, *Profits in the British Economy 1909–1938* (Oxford, 1967), 93, 146.

might well be explained by the fall in commodity prices and the resulting losses experienced. The number of overseas banks was small (and because of this not included in Table 1.3), yet these were some of the most significant British free-standing companies—significant in their impacts on the trade and banking systems in the regions where they operated. These data do not provide host locations, which might help explain not only the use of the form but also the shifting industrial composition.

## *Evaluation*

The concept of the free-standing company, when introduced, was meant to be descriptive; it was not value-laden, nor normative. I described what I found in my research. Yet the concept stirred a controversy I had not anticipated, albeit perhaps I should have. At the very time the idea was aired, British economic historians were paying attention to the roots of British economic decline and there was a new scrutiny of the history of British corporate performance, both at home and abroad. Alfred Chandler's appraisals of the weaknesses of managerial capitalism in Britain disturbed British economic historians.[142] Geoffrey Jones had written of unsuccessful British manufacturing multinationals.[143] My discussion of the small head office and 'lean governance', my contrasting of the classic multinational that transferred the advantages of its own experiences with the free-standing company that had started anew, my noting that many free-standing companies were short-lived and had a high failure rate, along with the conclusion by many observers that free-standing companies were not in advanced-technology industries, seemed grist to the mill of a literature seeking to explain British inadequacies. It surprised me how easily the 'free-standing-company' idea was incorporated into the British concerns over 'declinology'—that is, explanations of British decline. Charles Jones saw my rendition of the free-standing company as a 'kind of 2nd rate' foreign direct investment; T. A. B. Corley interpreted my discussion as one of looking at 'an inferior' form of foreign direct investment. Casson countered the argument that 'the free-standing company is just an inferior culturally-specific form of multinational enterprise'.[144] With no such intention, my evidence seemed to provide ammunition to students of the roots of British decline and to raise the blood pressure of some serious scholars, who came to the defence of British business enterprise.

The resulting debate has been fruitful. Corley defends the viability of British companies and the monitoring from their home office. He presses us to scrutinize more closely what monitoring was done. Casson sees these firms not as a less entrepreneurial type of multinational enterprise, but rather as playing an important entrepreneurial role. Geoffrey Jones demonstrates clearly that many British overseas banks, which began as free-standing companies and did not develop banking networks at home (at least until very recently), were successful for decades by every criterion—profits, provision of services, and so forth. Chapman finds that surviving free-standing companies had often been initially, or were later folded into, an experienced British mercantile firm, hardly a sign of 'failure'.[145]

The notion of second-rate foreign direct investment has different normative implications when judged in terms of: (1) the firm itself; (2) the home country; and (3) the host countries. These three vantage points for 'evaluation' are conceptually separate. In the concluding chapter of this volume, I will address these three distinct categories. (I will also deal with its success in the facilitation of global integration.) Here we need note only the juxtaposition of research on free-standing companies and that on the competitive advantages of firms and nations.

### *Extension*

Were free-standing companies exclusively British headquartered? In my own writings and above, I have concentrated on British free-standing companies because they were the most numerous of all nationalities and because, when they proliferated and took on importance in the late nineteenth and early twentieth centuries, Britain was the world's largest capital exporter. None the less, I have long been aware that the form was far from confined to British-headquartered enterprises.[146] Students of the history of Dutch, Belgian, and French business abroad, in particular, have found that the concept enriches their research.[147] Harm Schröter has identified a small number of Swiss and German free-standing companies.[148] Gregory Marchildon, in his chapter in the present volume, is wonderful in using the idea to illuminate Canadian business abroad.[149] Miller points out that in the pre-First World War years, Cerro de Pasco, the US-owned company that mined in Peru, fits the mould;[150] certain US sugar producers in Cuba conformed to the pattern.[151] Obviously, there was no British monopoly on the free-standing company form. In addition, for some headquarters countries, leaving aside the UK, the free-standing-company concept may have validity in analysing outward direct investments in the 1920s—and perhaps even later.[152]

All the comments on context discussed above can be considered in relation to the free-standing companies headquartered in European and North American capital-exporting nations. With one exception—the paper by William Hausman and John Neufeld (which deals with the 1920s)—the chapters herein that discuss non-British free-standing companies begin their analyses with the late nineteenth and early twentieth centuries; most extend to a later period as well. This research has opened new horizons. The emerging consensus seems to be that free-standing companies were a principal type of conduit for capital exports for the Netherlands and Belgium.[153] Regrettably, we do not have in this volume a general paper on French free-standing companies, albeit the Hertner and Szmrecsányi chapters cover French companies and my own reconsideration of the data suggests that this form of starting business abroad seems to figure importantly in the French capital export story.[154] The chapters herein confirm preliminary conclusions that free-standing companies were less frequently headquartered in the USA, Germany, Switzerland, and Sweden.[155] Marchildon describes Canadian free-standing utilities in Latin America and the Caribbean.[156] Schröter suggests that countries with empires—Britain, Holland, Belgium, and France—tended to have more free-standing companies than countries with smaller, or without, empires—the USA, Germany, Switzerland, and Sweden.[157] Yet the geographical extension of free-standing companies from imperial countries was far from exclusively within Empire.[158] Moreover, companies from countries with overseas empires were *not* 'more international' than those from nations without or with relatively small empires; thus, there were large outward foreign direct investments by classic multinational enterprises from the USA, Germany, Switzerland, and Sweden in the pre-1914 years. Can it be that, in general, countries with sizeable capital surpluses in the late nineteenth and early twentieth centuries tended to be the most important homes to free-standing companies?

Virtually all the definitional matters posed above in relation to British companies have arisen as the study of free-standing companies has been stretched to include other headquarters countries. The problems of migration are important. A company formed by a German settler (immigrant) in Russia, Guatemala, Brazil, or China does not qualify under the rubric free-standing (or as part of a classic multinational enterprise), if there was no home office.[159] Likewise, a Dutch expatriate in the Dutch East Indies or a French settler in Algeria who initiated a business *with no parent company back home* is not counted as a 'foreign' investor. By definition, a free-standing company required business over borders—that is, registration/residence in a headquarters nation. 'Registration' *per se*, however, might not indicate headquarters. The Suez Canal Company, for example, was 'registered in Egypt', but its administrative head office was in Paris; its *legal domicile* was at its Paris administrative headquarters.[160]

The classic multinational enterprise—with a headquarters and economic activity in continental European countries—had a long history.[161] There were also many 'wider-enterprise' groups that bore strong resemblance to the British ones chronicled by Chapman. There were clusters. Hennart—in Chapter 2—notes, for example, the role of the Belgian Empain group and the Belgian free-standing traction companies associated with it. As Hennart indicates, the clusters of companies domiciled in Belgium pose many of the same kinds of difficulties in defining a firm as were encountered in our examination of the British groups.[162] Some Dutch trading groups, described in Ben Gales and Keetie Sluyterman's chapter, are analogous.[163] Szmrecsányi found hints of a connection between a French sugar *machinery* manufacturer and the large French free-standing sugar producer in Brazil.[164] Thus, with not only British free-standing companies, but European Continental ones as well, we have to reflect on the history of corporate networks, of loose groupings of companies. Marchildon's study of Canadian free-standing utilities is superb on Canadian clusters that helped the utilities overcome the limitations of being free-standing units.[165] Networks and alliances in business history have been studied in the context of cartels; perhaps more important were these clusters of interactions that we saw in British business history and that seem more generally in evidence.

The matter of defining the nationality of a business over borders raised questions when we studied British free-standing companies; the same is true of the non-British counterparts. The first complication lies in what constituted a 'country'. In the British case, we defined all parts of the overseas Empire as 'foreign'. Although wary, we used registration in Britain as a proxy for headquarters. The authors of the chapters herein have adopted that protocol to make our papers consistent. But

Harm Schröter—in his chapter—shows some of the bizarre consequences of following that pattern rigidly in relation to Belgium and the Belgian Congo in the post-First World War years.[166] Moreover, on the European Continent, where borders were redrawn through time, scholars have struggled with how to define 'foreign' business. Is an Austrian company's investment in what became Czechoslovakia in the inter-war years a domestic investment before 1914 and a foreign one after the war; and if we define investments in overseas empires as 'foreign', what do we do about empires that cover contiguous territory (i.e. were not overseas)?[167]

A second matter of nationality related to ownership and control of a firm registered in one country to do business abroad. Ben Gales and Keetie Sluyterman have considered Dutch free-standing companies, adopting the same criteria as I used for British ones. If residents of one country invested back home or in a third country through a Dutch-registered entity, they argued that this was not a *Dutch* free-standing company.[168] This is important. So frequently did foreign individuals and companies use Dutch intermediaries in the pre-First World War years, as well as later, that the Dutch literature had special names for this practice. Gales, writing on the period before the First World War, found that Germans often formed companies in Holland to tap Dutch capital markets for *German* business activities—so-called 'bypass investments'. In addition, he points out that it was very common for French and Belgian investors to set up companies in the Netherlands to invest in the Dutch East Indies—so-called 'transfer investments'. Gales notes that the German 'bypass investments' seemed to have been German managed, while, with the 'transfer investments', the nature of the management varied.[169] Similarly, to operate in Belgian or French colonies, non-Belgian or non-French multinationals registered in, or acquired companies registered in, the mother country.[170] After 1914 the 'nationality' problem takes on much more complexity (see below).

With Canadian-registered public utilities abroad, a third matter of nationality arose. In these cases, the management and direction might well be by Canadians from a Canadian head office, but the majority of the ownership could be American and/or British.[171] With the Canadian public utilities in Latin America and the Caribbean, the clusters on which they relied for talents in many instances extended into the USA. Obviously, we need to look carefully at the business activities and get behind the corporate edifices. Ford Motor Company, for example, for years let its Canadian affiliate own and handle all British Empire business (outside Great Britain); its Canadian affiliate was, however, a part of the Ford Motor Company's multinational business.[172]

One has to sift the evidence to decide where the headquarters of a firm is located, from where the direction of the business arises. As in the British case, this may not be apparent from the place of registration. Especially after the First World War, the location of registration (incorporation) more and more might reflect tax and other considerations. As we pass through time, there is a growing imperative to raise the 'legal veil' and study the nature of the business activity *per se*. The value of the free-standing-company concept is that it presses us to consider the business history of enterprises that operate over borders in terms of strategies and managerial structures. The interest is in the *firm*—its impact and performance—and goes beyond the capital flows.

Research on free-standing companies headquartered on the European Continent and in North America has added substantial richness and depth to what we know of international business history. The industry composition of the involvements of non-British-headquartered free-standing companies provided some surprises. One was the truly heavy participation of Dutch free-standing companies in tropical agriculture (sugar, coffee, tobacco, and rubber).[173] The share seems out of keeping with any other national record on free-standing companies.[174] On the other hand, given the heavy concentration of Dutch free-standing companies in the Netherlands East Indies, the surprise evaporates. Likewise, the use of Belgian companies for investments in tramways seems distinctive. While this has been noted before, it comes out very strongly in the international comparative context and can be understood in terms of learned capabilities within Belgium. So, too, Canadian entrepreneurs' unique way of organizing business in public utilities in Latin America seems to have no global counterpart. Marchildon provides the rationale.

In many Continental European nations, banks played a very different role *vis-à-vis* foreign direct investment than was the case with US or British business abroad. The precise relationships between banks and free-standing companies remains elusive.[175] By contrast, one of the most fruitful outcomes of the research on non-British free-standing companies has been the re-examination—on a global scale—of the nature of business over borders in public utilities. Hausman and Neufeld's excellent chapter is a major contribution. They explore outward .US foreign direct investments in electric power companies in the 1920s. When, years ago, I wrote on the history of American business abroad, I had no difficulty in seeing such stakes as part of the discernible activity of US multinational enterprise. No 'flags' went up then that these investments failed to conform with the pattern I had perceived as general. Indeed, when Hausman proposed this paper for the Milan Conference session on free-standing companies, I nervously agreed. Had I been blind in my previous findings? Hausman and

Neufeld concluded (to my relief) that the free-standing-company paradigm was in general *not* appropriate; in the main, the most important of these investments arose out of the participants' experience in their home enterprises—and built on that knowledge base.[176] The use of the free-standing concept, however, encouraged Hausman and Neufeld to try to answer questions they would not otherwise have asked. In addition, I began to wonder whether there was one large American-based utility that might go under the rubric free-standing: International Telephone and Telegraph Corporation, formed in 1920.[177] The fit is awkward, and, on consideration, I believe that the application of the free-standing-company concept to this public utility does not contribute much to our understanding of its strategies or structure.

Marchildon's chapter finds the concept useful in studying pre-1914 Canadian utilities abroad.[178] Yet, over time, the concept seems to become less helpful. Indeed, when it is applied to the inter-war financing of Latin American (and other) power, light, and telephone companies through Canadian (or, I might add, American, Belgian, or Swiss) holding-company structures, perhaps we need to search for superior models. Yet, here again, as with Hausman and Neufeld's considerations of US investments abroad in this sector and Hennart's treatment of the Empain group (he believes that the free-standing-company concept is applicable at least in the pre-1914 years), research on the free-standing company has spurred a more careful scrutiny of the way business is managed and financed over borders. Reflections on management, along with finance, give us a fresh view of the clusters of companies involved, offering valuable insights into the development of public utilities on a global scale.[179]

Research on non-British free-standing companies seems to confirm their presence in certain infrastructure investments, in plantation agriculture, and in mining. Most important, it verifies their absence in economic activities involving high-technology differentiated trademarked products—in modern *industrial* activities that required management of scale and scope economies.

The geographical spread to host regions or countries of non-British free-standing companies is noteworthy. Gales and Sluyterman's findings for the pre-First World War years (as well as subsequently) on the overwhelming importance of the Netherlands East Indies and the relative unimportance of the Netherlands West Indies and Surinam are of great interest.[180] And, it was not that the Dutch were uninterested in the Western Hemisphere; the USA ranked second (a distant second to be sure) to the Netherlands East Indies as a host to Dutch free-standing companies.[181] Just as in the case of the classic multinational enterprise, so, for free-standing companies, the geographical distribution of outward foreign direct investments varied greatly by home-country nationality.[182] Also the geographical direction of free-standing companies (at origin) and later in their development may have differed (at least in proportions) from that of classic multinationals of the same nationality.[183]

Gales and Sluyterman's study of free-standing companies that operated in the Dutch East Indies shows that, of new companies starting operations there, the ones registered in Holland were far larger than those registered locally. They write, 'Registration in the mother country was preferred if links with the capital market were important.'[184] This coincides with the earlier findings on British free-standing companies within a common industry, within empire. Gales and Sluyterman's research uncovered, however, no connection (by place of registration) between companies in the host country that exported and those that did not—challenging one of Hennart's hypotheses on British free-standing firms. Another of their pertinent discoveries was that, unlike the classic Dutch multinationals where the initiative for foreign direct investments generally came from the parent company, with free-standing companies, more often than not, the initiative came from abroad. I am not, however, prepared to accept this as a general rule for differentiating classic multinationals and free-standing companies—since with the 'classic' American multinationals I know of many instances where entrepreneurs, customers, or agents abroad were responsible for the initiation of foreign investment plans and I am also aware of many instances with British free-standing companies where the initiative came from men in the UK.[185]

The studies of non-British free-standing companies (like those of their British counterpart) seem to emphasize the importance of the use of the form in the pre-First World War period and the decline in its usage as the twentieth century progressed. A possible ambiguity lies in the 1920s and whether, as the USA became a major creditor nation, the form was used more often in the USA in that decade than earlier (and, as noted above, some authors have argued that, in the 1920s, the British—in certain activities and in certain regions—continued to use the form extensively).

In the post-First World War era, as indicated earlier, as taxation became a key issue, the use of corporate structures for tax reasons became commonplace. Foreign-exchange restrictions affected corporate conduits for capital. In my view, the free-standing-company concept fades in significance as these other international considerations loom. The proxy use of 'registration' for headquarters becomes less viable and the requirements of penetrating corporate veils to identify patterns of corporate direction and management become ever more crucial.

Networks of public-utility financing of operations in the 1920s crossed national borders with extraordinary complexity. Yet in the 1920s and well beyond, in some activities, as was the case with British firms, a number of non-British free-standing companies did persist as single-core-function, single-host-country activities with limited head offices.[186] New free-standing companies were organized in the inter-war years and in the aftermath of the Second World War. Still the concept seems to me to have less neatness in fit in the post-First World War years and less explanatory power. Moreover, as we move into the 1920s and particularly into the post-Second World War era, the composition of international direct investments changed; the diffusion of modern industrial process and products could not be done through free-standing companies. What the concept does (and should do), however, is to prompt us to consider more carefully historical *networks of business from different vantage points*: legal, ownership, financial, and managerial structures and at the same time to examine intra- and inter-company trade, technology, and information-transfer structures—as they alter over time and as they are part of and have impact on the changing world economy. As most students of the history of multinational enterprise are aware, these different structures—all linked with business over borders—frequently do not coincide.[187] Clearly, as we decipher the post-First World War forms of business abroad, we need to pay more careful attention to where the true headquarters of a firm is located, since registration often is less useful as a proxy. The headquarters–business abroad relationships merit more careful scrutiny.

### *Explanation*

It is not sufficient to describe free-standing companies. We need explanations. In Chapters 2 and 3, Jean-François Hennart and Mark Casson seek to test existing theories and develop their own. I will leave them to speak for themselves. To their contributions, I want to add, however, several thoughts of my own, focused on explaining *why* pre-1914 free-standing companies were so frequently headquartered in Britain and did not so often have headquarters in the USA;[188] why in certain Continental European nations the form was often adopted and why, elsewhere, it seemed inappropriate; why the form was employed at all; what kinds of free-standing companies survived through time; and what functions such companies served within the evolving world economy.

The explanation for why the headquarters of free-standing companies were so prevalent in Britain and not so apparent in the pre-1914 US environment seems clear. In Britain by the late nineteenth century there was abundant capital, seeking higher returns. At the same time, worldwide, British traders were experienced in handling exports (and imports). British entrepreneurs went abroad, searching for opportunities. Information was abundant. Britain was connected with the rest of the world. As this happened, individuals saw opportunities. An infrastructure developed in London to float companies to raise moneys for the ventures identified by Britishers and by individuals of other nationalities. The British could offer the services. The free-standing company was a superb institutional vehicle to take advantage of perceived opportunities—opportunities for investors, promoters, traders, and shippers of British and of other nationalities. As Hennart points out, for high-risk projects where collateral was lacking and where there was unfamiliarity, for projects that could not borrow, the British-registered free-standing company was a brilliant institutional device.[189] It seemed to provide safety to the British saver (since it was registered under British law and its head office was domiciled in Britain); it was a channel of information; it was a way of mobilizing funds that would not otherwise have been transmitted over borders. It was far from a 'second-rate' kind of foreign direct investment.

In the USA, as the geographically extended market unified by railroad lines grew in size and as population rose, domestic companies emerged in new industries to fill national needs; there was a tremendous demand for capital at home (before the First World War the USA was a debtor in world accounts), so there was no special urge by individual savers to seek financial opportunities abroad; yet, American *companies* quickly became multinational ones, naturally and logically extending their range to world markets (and when necessary seeking sources of supply) as part and parcel of their growth at home. US industry developed differently from that of Britain.[190] Since the pace of development, the industrial composition, the geographically dispersed national market, and America's resource base were unlike that of Britain, it followed that what was reflected abroad would not be identical.[191] There is no difficulty in explaining the separate paths of these two countries which were sources of foreign direct investment: the main differences were based on the extent of opportunities at home, the level and nature of the industrialization process, the characteristics of the domestic market, the amount of capital available in the source nation, and the existing financial infrastructure.

This explains why London and not New York (why Britain and not the USA) was the centre for headquarters of free-standing companies in the pre-1914 years. By extension, one can argue that because, in each Continental European nation, the course of industrialization was different, so too we would expect varying usages of the free-standing form. A comparison of Holland and Germany is instructive—and might well follow a discussion parallel to that of Britain and the USA. The Dutch had a well-developed stock market, abundant capital, a relatively small domestic market (relative to Germany), as well as a long history of international involvements. By contrast, German political unification had opened up a sizeable national market. Like US business, German enterprises' first priority was domestic, and only secondarily international. We would have predicted more free-standing companies headquartered in Holland than in Germany.

The explanations appropriate to the cases of France, Switzerland, Belgium, and Sweden are still being shaped. As noted, the current thinking is that France and Belgium were important homes for free-standing companies, while Switzerland and Sweden were not. Explanations have been offered that deal with France and Belgium as imperial powers, the nature of national legislation (including tax laws), the characteristics of capital markets in these countries, the relationships between banks and enterprises, the stages of development, the domestic industrialization processes, the changing size of domestic markets, and more generally, the business history of firms in these nations. These explanations are as yet tentative and not conclusive. Perhaps, however, most cogent, France and Belgium in the pre-1914 years had capital surpluses; Switzerland and Sweden did not; this was especially true of Sweden.[192]

The free-standing-company form of business was used when it supplied a need. In the late nineteenth and early twentieth centuries, the global economy became integrated as never before in history. Business organizations were required to serve in a world where people, goods, money, and information were crossing borders to an unprecedented extent. Free-standing companies offered many connections. They linked expatriates abroad with home sources of capital. They gave traders (and shippers) ways of taking advantage of newly identified prospects. They seemed to present a fine institutional conduit for available capital to move abroad (for individual savers and for investment-trust companies they seemed to offer a means of reducing risk in investment and gaining a higher return than available domestically—and to do so with low transaction costs). And, most important, with the spread of information, they furnished a form that could capture and employ newly available knowledge in a manner to raise the output of goods and services. They were, to repeat, not an inferior form of foreign direct investment, just different from the form that students of multinational enterprise had been studying.

The free-standing form of business seemed a good way to start up projects or to introduce new capital to existing projects abroad. There would not have been the multiplication of such companies if they were not seen as appropriate. Why, however, did so few companies survive as free-standing ones? I have earlier explained the short-lived companies in terms of scams and lean governance. I maintained that, when managerial competence was internalized, there were survivors (but the term free-standing no longer applied). Hennart has criticized my analysis as being too much based on the experience of high-risk mining firms (which he admits did make up a large proportion of British free-standing firms). Miller has argued that there were not that many scams (especially when one leaves out the mining sector), and that lean governance was a problem but was readily overcome and thus was not the principal reason for lack of survival. Miller claims that quite a number of companies that the west coast of South America hosted lasted over long periods, developing means of coping with lean governance. He suggests that the reasons for the exits lay in British involvements in declining industries (rubber, nitrates, railroads). That there were few new British free-standing companies in Latin America in the inter-war years and that some older ones did not persist was—according to Miller—based on problems in the British capital market, tax considerations, and capital-outflow restrictions.

Miller's reasons for the small number of start-ups after the First World War makes good sense to me (and they also would explain the decline of older ones). Ranald Michie reminds us that between 1914 and 1979 (1925–1931 excepted) the British had foreign-exchange controls.[193] In the 1920s the USA became the centre for cosmopolitan finance.[194] Both Geoffrey Jones and T. A. B. Corley feel there were still a sizeable number of new British free-standing companies in the 1920s. Clearly, however, by this decade, a variety of additional international business forms had developed, some of which were similar to the free-standing company seen in pre-war Britain, but many of which were quite different.[195] Most important, worldwide economic conditions altered, and, as new industries arose, the free-standing company form—once highly suitable—seemed less so.

While I am convinced by the new evidence that, at least for poorer countries, I did in my earlier writings underestimate the longevity of many of the free-standing companies and the foundations for future operations that they established, I am not prepared to abandon the importance of focusing on managerial structures and managerial arrangements for persistence. Every survivor described in the chapters herein (by Hennart, Miller, Marchildon, and Jones) seems to have introduced substantial internalization of administration and technical abilities or at least to have regularized inter-firm connections. The French company studied by Szmrecsányi worked out a way of managing the business that proved satisfactory for years (it was for a while one of the leading sugar producers in Brazil), but it is not clear that this company with its lean governance from Paris was able to make adjustments over the decades; in time its market share declined, and eventually the administration of the business from Paris came to an end.[196]

Explanations of the course of the free-standing company must rely heavily on the study of the growth of the firm. Research that considers when and why vertical and horizontal integration take place and when and why related and unrelated diversification occur is germane. Free-standing firms are no different from other enterprises. Even the starting point is not unique, for, if we turn to purely domestic companies, we recognize that at origin these too have to locate outsiders to run the operations. As the business grows, a company hires and develops its own experienced personnel. Where the free-standing company differs is its extension over borders; in this respect it encounters problems common to all multinational enterprise.

The world economy changed after 1914, which more than anything else accounts for the absence of a proliferation of new free-standing companies. Corporate structures took on a different role. Successful enterprises expanded and became more complex. Taxation became a key influence. Britain's relative decline as a world power meant it no longer had the pivotal place in the international economy of prior years. New modern industries arose where the free-standing form was not adequate (it could not cope with the business requirements). An explanation of the free-standing company and its course through time must be grounded in the history of the world economy.

None the less, in the era of their prominence, free-standing companies played a key role within the evolving world economy. They mobilized business resources; they provided 'connections' between the 'old' world and the rest of the world. The Suez Canal Company was a typical free-standing company. Free-standing companies established railroads, opened mines and plantations, developed resources to make them commercially viable, set up tramways in urban areas, and furnished telephone and power and light services. They offered long-term capital and short-term credit. They transferred more advanced ways of producing goods and services. They did not, however, move 'high technology'. In some cases, they provided the beginnings for activities with long histories within a host country, but that were no longer controlled from abroad. In other instances, they internalized management and served as the launch pad for long-lived important multinational enterprises. Free-standing companies persisted during the inter-war years and after the Second World War, but, as the world economy was transformed, new industries and new needs surfaced. There came to be available far superior business conduits for the spread of industrialization on a global scale. There are still free-standing companies today, yet they are dwarfed in the overall panorama and have been superseded—in the main—by other forms of business over borders.

## NOTES

1. M. Wilkins, 'The Free-Standing Company, 1870–1914: An Important Type of British Foreign Direct Investment', *Economic History Review*, 2nd ser., 41 (May 1988), 259–82.
2. My first three publications that dealt with free-standing companies were in 1986. In 'Defining a Firm, History and Theory' (in P. Hertner and G. Jones (eds.), *Multinationals: Theory and History* (Aldershot, 1986), 80–95, esp. 84–7), while I recognized that the concept had broader implications and advocated more research, I considered only my findings on the history of British companies in the USA. That same year, in 'European Multinationals in the United States 1875–1914' (in A. Teichova, M. Lévy-Leboyer, and H. Nussbaum (eds.), *Multinational Enterprise in Historical Perspective* (Cambridge, 1986), 55–64), I commented on the existence not only of British, but of French free-standing companies. My third 1986 publication was 'The History of European Multinationals: A New Look' (in *Journal of European Economic History*, 15 (Winter 1986), 483–510, esp. 501–3), wherein I noted British, French, and Dutch headquartered free-standing companies. In 1987 (in 'Efficiency and Management: A Comment on Gregory Clark's "Why isn't the Whole World Developed?"', *Journal of Economic History*, 47 (Dec. 1987), 981–3), I used the free-standing-company concept as a handle to consider Clark's appraisal of 'British' textile firms in India, China, and elsewhere. I noted that in 1910 not a single Lancashire cotton textile mill operated as a multinational enterprise in China, India, or Brazil. I employed insights from my work on free-standing companies to evaluate 'British' management of cotton-textile enterprises. The next year, 1988, I wrote on free-standing companies in two more contributions. In one, 'European and North American Multinationals, 1870–1914: Comparisons and Contrasts', *Business History*, 30 (Jan. 1988), 8–45, esp. 14–19, I once more put free-standing companies in the overall context of business over borders. In the second, 'The Free-Standing Company, 1870–1914', published in *Economic History Review*, for the first time I devoted an entire article to the concept, specifically as it applied to British overseas investments, not merely in the USA but worldwide. That article summarized much of my earlier thinking about free-standing companies and was—until now—the only contribution that I have made solely devoted to the topic. Two added 1989 publications of mine are, however, germane. In my lengthy book, *The History of Foreign Investment in the United States to 1914* (Cambridge, Mass., 1989), I discussed the presence of British, French, and Dutch free-standing companies in the USA as part of all foreign investment in that nation. My earlier research for that book was what had in the first place turned my attention to free-standing companies. In 'The Impact of Multinational Corporations' (*South African Journal of Economic History*, 4 (Mar. 1989), 4–20, esp. 7–20), I tried to discern whether the free-standing-company concept would aid in understanding direct investments in South Africa. More recently, in 'Multinational Corporations: An Historical Account', in R. Rowthorn and R. Kozul-Wright (eds.), *Transnational Corporations and the Global Economy* (London, forthcoming), I have sought to fit the impact of free-standing companies into a more general perspective. Meanwhile, many

other authors have been writing on the subject; some of their work will be reviewed as this chapter progresses.

3. That literature is concerned with the savers and asks who in Britain invested (by region, social class, religion, and so forth).
4. The term 'visible hand' comes from A. D. Chandler, *The Visible Hand* (Cambridge, Mass., 1977); I use the phrase in exactly the sense that Chandler does; indeed, Chandler's work has been very influential in my thinking. When Oliver Williamson discusses the governance of firms, he too is talking about the visible hand. On the firm as a transmitter of technology, see, for example, M. Wilkins, 'The Role of Private Business in the International Diffusion of Technology', *Journal of Economic History*, 34 (Mar. 1974), 168–88. In discussing the growth of the firm I have been very influenced by Edith Penrose. See her *The Theory of the Growth of the Firm* (Oxford, 1959; 3rd edn., 1995).
5. Douglass North makes the distinction between institutions (the rules of the game) and organizations (the players). See his 'Economic Performance through Time', *American Economic Review*, 84 (June 1994), 359–68, and his *Institutions, Institutional Change and Economic Performance* (Cambridge, 1990). I use the word 'institution' differently, more as a synonym for organization; as I use the term, I mean a study of the channels, structures, and edifices that frame transactions. My usage involves more than (but also less than) the rules of the game.
6. Several chapters in this volume make that suggestion, either implicitly or explicitly.
7. In this chapter I use the words abroad, overseas, and foreign synonymously to indicate outside the UK. I consider a British investment in a colony to be a 'foreign' investment. A British investment abroad is by my definition one made by an individual or company resident in the UK.
8. On this use of the phrase 'portfolio investments', see H. Segal and M. Simon, 'British Foreign Capital Issues, 1865–94', *Journal of Economic History*, 21 (Dec. 1961), 567–81; M. Simon, 'The Pattern of New British Portfolio Foreign Investment, 1865–1914', which first appeared in J. H. Adler (ed.), *Capital Movements and Economic Development* (London, 1967) and was republished in A. R. Hall (ed.), *The Export of Capital from Britain 1870–1914* (London, 1968), 15–44; and M. Simon, 'The Enterprise and Industrial Composition of New British Portfolio Foreign Investment, 1865–1914', *Journal of Development Studies*, 3 (1967), 280–92. These articles set the stage for the designation of companies that raised money in Britain for capital export as 'portfolio investments'. See also L. E. Davis and R. Huttenback, *Mammon and the Pursuit of Empire: The Political Economy of British Imperialism, 1860–1912* (Cambridge, 1986), and 'Theories of Capital Exports: Lessons from the British Experience', in B. Stallings, *Banker to the Third World: US Portfolio Investment in Latin America, 1900–1986* (Berkeley, Calif., 1987). In some of the even more recent literature, this formulation continues to be maintained. See, for example, C. H. Feinstein, 'Britain's Overseas Investments in 1913', *Economic History Review*, 2nd ser., 43 (May 1990), 289. It is true that in the main the investors in these firms were 'portfolio investors', but the *firm* itself made the overseas investments, extending itself abroad; the firm was responsible for the conduct of the overseas business operations. Since the existing British literature at that time had used the words 'direct investments' to signify those investments overseas by firms that bypassed securities markets in their capital exports, Simon and others—in employing the phrase 'portfolio investments'—wanted to indicate that they were excluding these other overseas investments that were made 'directly'. As far as I can determine, the use of the words 'portfolio investments' to deal with British overseas investments evolved from the work of Simon.

George Paish and Robert M. Kindersley, the most prominent earlier students of British overseas investments, did not use the term 'portfolio investments'. See M. Wilkins (ed.), *British Overseas Investments, 1907–1948* (New York, 1977), for reprints of Paish's and Kindersley's most important papers on British overseas investment. Likewise, neither C. K. Hobson, *The Export of Capital* (London, 1914), nor H. Feis, *Europe: The World's Banker, 1870–1914* (New York, 1965; repr. of 1930 edn.) uses the words 'portfolio investments'.

9. The contemporary distinction between portfolio and direct investments lies in the matter of control. Portfolio investors are passive; direct investors are not. This distinction was not always the norm. The literature on British overseas investments and that on American investments abroad evolved with very different vocabularies and the result has been great confusion. As indicated in note 8, the British spoke of investments made directly as those that bypassed the stock market. In the American literature, covering both US long-term outward and inward investments, there has been since the 1920s the category 'direct investments' (defined by control). The US Department of Commerce came to define a direct investment as 25% or more ownership of a business abroad; in time, it lowered this threshold to 10% (first for US business abroad and then later for foreign business in the USA). In the US literature 'direct investments' carried with them the potential for control. Cleona Lewis in her *America's Stake in International Investments* (Washington, 1938) included British companies that extended into the USA as direct investments. So, too, a 1949 United Nations publication (undoubtedly because of American influence) applied the term 'direct investment'—following American usage—to British companies operating abroad (United Nations, *International Capital Movements during the Inter-War Period* (Lake Success, NY, 1949), 32–3). In the mid-1950s, R. V. Clements specifically challenged what he believed was the prevailing assumption that historically all British overseas investment had been of a passive nature. See, for example, his 'British Controlled Enterprise in the West between 1870 and 1900 and Some Agrarian Reactions', *Agricultural History*, 27 (1953), 137–41. John Dunning's student, T. C. Coram ('The Role of British Capital in the Development of the United States, 1600–1914', M.Sc. (Social Science) thesis (University of Southampton, 1967)), did not understand the difference between the US investments of British immigrants and British residents, but he did perceive that there were many British direct investments in the USA. Coram labelled some of what I would later call free-standing companies, 'syndicate' investments. There were many other historical studies of British investments in the USA—on cattle and mining companies—that discussed these stakes in terms of 'direct investments', although not using that phrase. In the early 1970s, J. M. Stopford, in 'The Origins of British-Based Multinational Manufacturing Enterprise', *Business History Review*, 48 (Autumn 1974), 303–35, was puzzled over how to classify certain British investments, those which he saw as having only a financial 'shell' in Britain; he was not, however, ready to call them direct investments. Indeed, my first thinking about 'free-standing companies' arose from my discussions with Stopford on a preliminary draft of his 1974 paper. Then came T. Houston and J. H. Dunning, *UK Industry Abroad* (London, 1976); D. G. Paterson, *British Direct Investment in Canada 1890–1914: Estimates and Determinants* (Toronto, 1976); I. Stone, 'British Direct and Portfolio Investment in Latin America before 1914', *Journal of Economic History*, 37 (1977), 690–722; D. C. M. Platt (ed.), *Business Imperialism 1840–1930: An Enquiry Based on British Experience in Latin America* (Oxford, 1977); P. Svedberg, 'The Portfolio Direct Composition of Private Foreign Investment in 1914 Revisited', *Economic Journal*, 88 (1978), 763–77; and J. H. Dunning, 'Changes in the Level and Structure of International

Production: The Last One Hundred Years', in M. Casson (ed.), *The Growth of International Business* (London, 1983), 84–139. In the interim, and even earlier, there were many studies that could be reread as works on British managed investments overseas by companies organized in Britain to do business abroad. The American vocabulary—distinguishing portfolio and direct investments in terms of control—is now becoming established in the literature on British capital exports: see, for example, M. Edelstein, 'Foreign Investment and Accumulation', in R. Floud and D. McCloskey, *The Economic History of Britain since 1700*, ii. *1860–1939* (2nd edn., Cambridge, 1994), 173–96.

10. My first book on the history of American business abroad, based on Ford Motor Company archives in Dearborn and worldwide, was M. Wilkins and F. E. Hill, *American Business Abroad: Ford on Six Continents* (Detroit, 1964). This was followed by a broader two-volume study of all American business abroad: M. Wilkins, *The Emergence of Multinational Enterprise: American Business Abroad from the Colonial Period to 1914* (Cambridge, Mass., 1970), and M. Wilkins, *The Maturing of Multinational Enterprise: American Business Abroad from 1914 to 1970* (Cambridge, Mass., 1974). Thus, during the 1960s, when everyone was discussing American multinationals' challenge in Europe, I was pursuing *the history* of US-headquartered multinational enterprises. To write that history involved an immense amount of research and reading and developing a framework of analysis. My framework emerged out of archival evidence, along with the contemporary studies of business history, especially those of Allan Nevins and Alfred Chandler; Edith Penrose's work on the growth of the firm was very helpful; and then there were the highly germane studies of contemporary international business, particularly those of Raymond Vernon, Charles Kindleberger, John Dunning, and, to a far lesser extent, Stephen Hymer. My approach to the evolution of US business abroad took shape after using business archives, reading hundreds of US business histories, numerous inter-war studies of US foreign direct investment (from those of Cleona Lewis to Frank Southard), as well as the huge cartel literature. My research was novel, since I was asking a new set of questions about my findings. My results were also novel: few scholars had realized how quickly in their historical evolution innovative American companies had moved into international business.
11. My own research differed from most of the contemporary studies in the 1960s in that I included backward integration of multinational enterprises into raw material production; I also included service-sector multinationals.
12. L. T. Wells, Jr., 'Mobile Exporters: New Foreign Investors in East Asia', in K. A. Froot (ed.), *Foreign Direct Investment* (Chicago, 1993), 182.
13. In my own research, I was influenced, but not convinced, by product-cycle theory, yet I found fundamental the notion of advantage. All the early theorists, considering multinational enterprise, accepted the notion of 'advantage'. See R. E. Caves, *Multinational Enterprise and Economic Analysis* (2nd edn., Cambridge, 1996), 1–2.
14. J. R. Markusen, 'The Boundaries of Multinational Enterprises and Theory of International Trade', *Journal of Economic Perspectives*, 9 (Spring 1995), 169–89. The point should, however, be made that contemporary scholars differ from earlier ones, and among themselves, on what constitutes 'advantage'. Sometimes these assets are called proprietary assets or firm-specific assets.
15. This was even true of the British leader in studies of multinational enterprise, John Dunning. His first book was on American business in Britain: J. H. Dunning, *American Investment in British Manufacturing Industry* (London, 1958). In Chapter 2 herein, Jean-François Hennart discusses Dunning's 'eclectic

theory' of multinational enterprise; in keeping with the pattern, it too assumes 'advantage'.

16. See, for example, G. Jones (ed.), *British Multinationals: Origins, Management and Performance* (Aldershot, 1986).
17. When, at the start of the 1970s, I turned from studying American business abroad to do research on the history of foreign investment in the USA, my plan was to turn the coin over and write on the history of foreign multinationals in the USA as I had previously written on US business abroad. (Raymond Vernon's big project at Harvard Business School had begun with US business abroad and then turned to non-US headquartered multinationals.) To understand foreign direct investment in the USA (inward investment), I read the immense general historical literature on international capital flows; I came across many direct investments that were not like those of the US multinationals that I had come to know so well. I asked, were these specific only to the host USA or more general? And, since I was reading the capital-flow literature, I decided to write on *all* foreign investment in the USA: the outcome was my earlier cited *The History of Foreign Investment in the United States to 1914*, published in 1989; a second volume is in process.
18. See my 'The Free-Standing Company'.
19. S. D. Chapman, 'British-Based Investment Groups before 1914', *Economic History Review*, 2nd ser., 38 (May 1985), 230–51.
20. Wilkins, 'European and North American Multinationals'; Wilkins, 'The Free-Standing Company'; Wilkins, *The History of Foreign Investment*. Note that many that invested in the USA were short-lived as British free-standing companies, but some became the basis for very viable and sustained American-headquartered enterprises.
21. See D. G. Paterson, 'The Failure of British Business in Canada, 1890–1914', in H. Krooss (ed.), *Proceedings of the Business History Conference* (Bloomington, Ind., 1975), and his *British Direct Investment in Canada*.
22. Depending on the source, the percentage varies, but it was clearly huge. See Wilkins, *The History of Foreign Investment*, 145, for one set of numbers. On the importance of British overseas investment, see M. Edelstein, *Overseas Investment in the Age of High Imperialism: The United Kingdom, 1850–1914* (New York, 1982).
23. C. J. Schmitz, 'Patterns of Scottish Portfolio Foreign Investment 1860–1914', unpublished report to ESRC (1994), 2 n.6; see also Davis and Huttenback, *Mammon*. Schmitz uses the term 'portfolio foreign investment' in the traditional manner (as applied to the British data).
24. Portfolio investments, as I am using the term in this chapter, are those wherein the outward foreign investor is not planning to (not able to) influence the outcome of the investment; there may be intervention, but only when something goes wrong. Investments in foreign government securities are portfolio ones; likewise, most British investments in American railroads were portfolio ones. Foreign portfolio investments can be in debt or in equity. They can be made by firms or individuals. I am discussing here long-term foreign portfolio investments, not short-term bank deposits or other short-term 'portfolio' assets (these are sometimes designated as 'portfolio investments' and sometimes not). By contrast, I use the following definition of direct investments: foreign direct investments are those where the investor has control or potential for control and/or the investment relates to the business operations (that is, it is integrated with a business *operations* strategy). Some British-resident individuals made direct investments; many of the investments of the 'investment groups' so

well described by Stanley Chapman did not go through companies registered in the UK, but were clearly direct investments.

25. Schmitz, 'Patterns', pp. i, 3 n.7. Companies could be registered in London or in Edinburgh. London-registered companies might, however, have a 'registered head office' in Liverpool. See Rory Miller, Chapter 8 herein, on 'Liverpool-registered' companies.
26. Wilkins, 'The Free-Standing Company', 262 n.12. Companies could be traded in London, in Edinburgh, on provincial exchanges, or *not* traded at all. The numbers of 'registered' companies far exceeded those listed in stock-exchange manuals.
27. T. A. B. Corley, Chapter 4 herein. Some have suggested that the reason for this lay in managerial ability. Thus, W. G. Kerr (*Scottish Capital on the American Credit Frontier* (Austin, Tex., 1976), 2), writes that 'British [Scottish and English] ranching interests by the mid-1880s spread from Montana and Wyoming range south to . . . Texas'. Most of the investment failed, mainly 'because the British investors knew nothing about ranching on the western plains. [While Kerr does not say so, some of the few successful ones were Scottish.] Such was not the case with Scottish mortgage companies organized to do business in Texas, the South, the Midwest, the Pacific Northwest, and the plains states. The directors of these companies knew their business and their investments prospered.' The ranching companies and the mortgage companies were both direct investments.
28. Note that this approach to classifying the registered companies results in an inevitable lack of synchronization between my findings and the data assembled by George Paish, Herbert Feis, Matthew Simon, Lance Davis, and others. They were trying to determine capital flows, while I have been studying business over borders. Paish's careful 1909, 1911, and 1914 articles (and discussions on his September 1909 and 1911 papers) on British overseas investments are in Wilkins (ed.), *British Overseas Investments*. They are and have been over the years a primary source for anyone doing research on British overseas investments before 1914. Paish indicated in 1909 that in his estimates of overseas investments he had not included the 'private investments of mercantile and banking houses'. In his totals he made informed allowances for these investments. As noted earlier, Paish never used the words 'portfolio investments'; he never actually used the phrase 'direct investments' either, as far as I can establish. It was Feis, *Europe: The World's Banker*, 15n., interpreting Paish, who in 1930 would employ the term 'direct investment', as that investment, which did not leave 'traces in the form of securities issue'. What the literature on British capital exports came to call direct investment (after Feis and Simon) was what Paish referred to as 'private capital employed abroad' by banking houses, 'branch manufacturing, mercantile, and trade undertakings, &c., &c.'. (See his 1911 article, 'Great Britain's Capital Investments in Individual Colonial and Foreign Countries', *Journal of the Royal Statistical Society*, 74/2 (1911), 187, repr. in Wilkins (ed.), *British Overseas Investments*). The reason for lack of synchronization in the current research with prior studies lies in the different (and new) questions being asked. Paish, Feis, Simon, Davis, *et al.*, were all considering the amounts of British overseas capital. The student of free-standing companies seeks to understand, to repeat, the nature of and the investments made in the course of conducting British *business over borders*. They are not identical. Paish and his contemporaries were well aware that some British overseas investment was passive and some carried control, but they made no attempt to quantify this particular distinction. The same was true of Feis, *Europe: The World's Banker*, 29 (Feis writes, for example, that in 1914, 'Almost all of the mine properties financed by British capital were held under

British control and management. . . . The gold and diamond mines of South Africa and West Africa were almost entirely under British management . . . ').
29. W. Lazonick, 'Learning and the Dynamics of International Competitive Advantage', in R. Thomson (ed.), *Learning and Technological Change* (New York, 1993), 187.
30. Wilkins, 'The Free-Standing Company'.
31. This suggestion was made by an anonymous reviewer of the manuscript for this book, and it is, of course, crucial to the storyline. On the services of the City, see R. C. Michie, *The City of London: Continuity and Change, 1850–1990* (London, 1992), and J. H. Dunning and E. V. Morgan, *An Economic Study of the City of London* (London, 1971).
32. Jean-François Hennart has made this point in a number of different articles.
33. This is consistent with the traditional view (the textbook rendition) that, *ceteris paribus*, investors seek the highest return on their money. See Edelstein, *Overseas Investment*, and Sir Alec Cairncross, *Home and Foreign Investment, 1870–1913* (Cambridge, 1953), for more on British capital exports in this era.
34. G. Jones, *British Multinational Banking, 1830–1990* (Oxford, 1993), 9–10, and Jones, Chapter 13 herein.
35. On the accepted $18 billion–20 billion figure, see Wilkins, *The History of Foreign Investment*, 145, 156. These are stock figures. For Corley's estimates, see Chapter 4 herein.
36. My discomfort lies in a concern over the underlying data; it lies in the fact that foreign-direct-investment data and 'capital' of free-standing companies represent statistics collected in divergent manners. I do, however, greatly admire Corley's efforts to make these estimates.
37. Part of my before-noted reservations over Corley's numbers are associated with the definitional questions: if we do not have uniform definitions, how can we put exact numbers on the categories? In this chapter and in the following chapters in the present book many definitional issues surface. Likewise, in articles published elsewhere on free-standing companies, the phrase has been interpreted in diverse ways.
38. None of the contributors to this volume has included the companies of immigrants or expatriate (locally resident) investors under the rubric 'free-standing company'. We are unanimous in that regard.
39. This means that books such as C. F. Remer, *Foreign Investment in China* (New York, 1933), must be used with special care; he included the businesses of expatriates. Indeed, very frequently in much of the literature on British investments in Asia (and elsewhere), no differentiation is made between the Britisher resident in the host country *and* the British enterprise with a home office in the UK. There needs to be a 'home office' in the UK for there to be a business investment over borders, a foreign direct investment.
40. Geoffrey Jones includes it as a British overseas bank, basically because its behaviour pattern was completely in keeping with the other British overseas banks registered and definitely headquartered in the UK. He, however, is very clear in noting its place of residence. As indicated in note 7 above, we defined 'foreign' to include colonies. Reinhard Liehr and Mariano E. Torres Bautista, Chapter 9 herein, seek to justify the inclusion of Canadian-registered companies in Mexico as a special type of British free-standing company. Their argument is that these were, in reality, British companies. I have strong doubts, but their chapter addresses the same problem of economic activity within an empire and wherein lies the 'headquarters'.
41. This is true at least in the cases of cotton textiles and diamond mines. See the section on 'Elaboration' for more on this matter.

42. Natalia Gurushina, Chapter 6 herein, on Russia; the US generalizations are based on my own research on foreign investments in the USA. (In the USA domestic registration was not required, but for tax, liability, and other reasons it was often the procedure of choice.)
43. Peter Hertner, Chapter 5 herein.
44. There could be a British head office *without* British registration. There needs to be studies of how frequently this was the case of new firms set up to do business abroad. My research indicates that, at least in the period before 1914, this was not the norm. A firm might have a London representative, or a London office that pursued specified functions (related, for example, to finance, purchasing, and staffing), but that did not provide overall administrative direction. For some of my earlier thoughts on the firm established abroad, with no UK registration, that attracted both British capital and management, see my 'European and North American Multinationals', 16–18. Clearly, this matter has to be addressed. Thus, Rory Miller, going through *Stock Exchange Yearbooks* for the 1890s, found British-owned Chilean-registered railway companies with twice-yearly shareholders' meetings in Liverpool, obviously dominated by Liverpool merchants (Miller to Wilkins, 10 Mar. 1995). Geoffrey Jones also warns about the problems of 'registration' (Jones to Wilkins, 15 Dec. 1995). Later in this chapter I elaborate on some of the problems. By the early twentieth century, the British Inland Revenue Department had separated out three groups of 'identifiable income from abroad'. The first group consisted of portfolio investments (as we would define the term today). The second group included the profits of British companies operating abroad. The third group involved British firms doing business mainly at home but also overseas. The second category—those of businesses typically registered in the UK—appears to coincide quite closely (albeit not exactly) with our free-standing companies; on the other hand, Worswick and Tipping, in dealing with British companies (with British headquarters) operating abroad, identified a number that were 'non-corporate' (presumably without British registration under British joint-stock company laws): G. Cassel *et al.*, *Foreign Investments* (Chicago, 1928), 126, 140–1, and G. D. N. Worswick and D. G. Tipping, *Profits in the British Economy 1909–1938* (Oxford, 1967), 86, 93, 116, 118. I am indebted to T. A. B. Corley for directing me to this last reference.
45. Some early commentators, who had not read the literature on multinational enterprise, failed to comprehend the basic distinction. I can only refer them to the authors cited in notes 10, 12, 13, and 14 above, and particularly to the Wells and Markusen formulations as given in the text of the present chapter. Some chapters in the present volume contrast the free-standing company and the multinational enterprise; I believe the more appropriate contrast is between the free-standing company and the *classic* or traditionally conceived multinational enterprise. As I earlier wrote, 'I view them [free-standing companies] as a type of MNE' (Wilkins, 'Defining a Firm', 86).
46. Some family and individual investments, however, fit very well into the traditional multinational-enterprise category. Thus, the early international activities of the Coats family firm, J. & P. Coats (before it was incorporated), conform nicely with the model of the classic multinational enterprise. Likewise, the international business of Lipton and Beecham (see T. A. B. Corley, 'Britain's Overseas Investments in 1914 Revisited', *Business History*, 36 (Jan. 1994), 73–4) fit, in my mind, easily into what to me was the familiar 'American' model. On this matter, I totally agree with Corley. I would also put the trading companies that were *not* registered in Britain yet had managing partners there in the category of the classic multinational enterprise. On the other hand, as noted,

Group 2 of the British Inland Revenue Department categories (see note 44 above) contains income from operations abroad not linked with free-standing companies. See Worswick and Tipping, *Profits*, 88.

47. Gurushina, Chapter 6, Miller, Chapter 8, and Jones, Chapter 13 herein, for example. Gurushina's chapter differentiates between the functions of 'core' and intermediary free-standing companies. Miller and Jones show other different types of free-standing companies.
48. Multinational enterprises are typically a group of separate corporations commonly managed. We drop the corporate veils as we discuss the nature of the 'enterprise'.
49. S. D. Chapman, *Merchant Enterprise in Britain* (Cambridge, 1992).
50. See my 'Defining a Firm', for some of the fundamental issues. Alfred Chandler has recently written, 'As a historian who has spent a career in examining the operations and practices of business firms, I have not given much thought to precise definitions of the firm. I have had little trouble locating information on literally hundreds of individual enterprises' ('Organizational Capabilities and the Economic History of the Industrial Enterprise', *Journal of Economic Perspectives*, 6 (Summer 1992), 79–100, esp. 79). While I generally agree with Chandler, I do think there are often problems in defining the multinational firm (and firms within firms). Yet, at the same time, I do believe that the business history of enterprises often resolves these problems. Chandler never puzzled, for example, at the time Du Pont had major interests in General Motors, whether he was talking about one firm or two. The data seemed to resolve the issue. Interesting insights on these questions come from R. H. Coase, 'The Nature of the Firm', *Economica*, NS 4 (Nov. 1937), 387–9; Penrose, *The Theory of the Growth of the Firm*; and G. B. Richardson, 'The Organisation of Industry', *Economic Journal*, 82 (Sept. 1972), 883–96.
51 See their chapters herein.
52. Jones, Chapter 13 herein. See also Mark Casson, Chapter 3 herein, who agrees with Jones.
53. Chapman, Chapter 7 herein. Chapman sees truly free-standing companies as ones floated in London, but *not* associated with the agency houses. These—at least the ones with operations in India—were, he believes, 'on the margins of the system'.
54. R. G. Greenhill, 'Investment Group, Free-Standing Company or Multinational? Brazilian Warrant, 1909–1952', *Business History*, 37 (Jan. 1995), 86–111.
55. M. Casson, *The Organization of International Business* (Aldershot, 1995); see also Casson, Chapter 3, and Hennart, Chapter 2 herein. See Wilkins, 'Defining a Firm', 90, on 'firms within firms'.
56. See also Hennart, Chapter 2 herein, for his views on this. Chapman—in his discussion—sees no importance in the place of registration for the companies within the group, aside from commenting on the expense of setting up companies in the UK. In the introduction to the 1995 3rd edn. of her *The Theory of the Growth of the Firm*, p. xviii, Edith Penrose discussed the metamorphosis of the firm in the 1980s and 1990s in terms of core firms and networks. She felt that the firm as she had described it in her earlier work has in recent years become less coherent. Yet, as one studies the growth of certain groupings of overseas businesses in the late nineteenth and early twentieth centuries, one sees the same kind of rough edges in the conception of the firm. Later in this chapter, I mention the 'free-standing' companies in the USA in which Balfour, Williamson & Co. played a pivotal role. The loose cluster—with minority interest but attention to management—was a clear form of doing business.

Unlike Chapman, I do see a difference between those companies registered and not registered in Britain.

57. Neither the service provider nor the free-standing firm is the centre. The service firms assist other unrelated companies, as the need arises.
58. For more on the matter of ownership and control, nationality aside, see Casson, Chapter 3 herein, and my 'Defining a Firm'.
59. Miller, Chapter 8, and Hennart, Chapter 2 herein. To complicate matters, Aramayo was apparently *resident* in Paris.
60. Gurushina, Chapter 6 herein.
61. J.-F. Hennart, 'International Financial Capital Transfers: A Transaction Cost Framework', *Business History*, 36 (Jan. 1994), 51–70, and Hennart, Chapter 2 herein. The 'entrepreneurial activity' in these cases was Bolivian and Russian.
62. Rory Miller reports that by 1913 the Chilean Electric Tramway & Light Co. Ltd., London, was German owned. The Lagunitos Oil Co. Ltd., London, in business in Peru, was by 1913 American, owned by a group associated with Herbert Hoover. Miller, Chapter 8 herein; William J. Hausman and John L. Neufeld, Chapter 14 herein; and Wilkins, *The Emergence of Multinational Enterprise*, 185. Germans and Frenchmen used British companies as instrumentalities for South African investments (Wilkins, 'The Impact of Multinational Corporations').
63. Wilkins, *The Emergence of Multinational Enterprise*, 42–4.
64. See above. Rory Miller asks: can a free-standing company have a *shared* home? On the west coast of South America, Aporama Goldfields Co. and Corocoro United Copper Mines (both registered in London) had considerable French interests on their boards. Presumably, French businessmen could visit London 'to look after their interests'. Would this count as a 'shared' home? (Miller to Wilkins, 14 Oct. 1996). Is a 'shared' home tantamount to shared ownership and control?
65. The US Department of Commerce faced this problem in its studies of foreign direct investment in the USA. Its solution was to label the first foreign parent the foreign direct investor, and then to go beyond that and ask further questions on the UBO—ultimate beneficial owner.
66. A business could be registered abroad and owned and controlled from Britain (see note 44 above for more details). When one consults business archives, usually it is possible to determine 'headquarters' and the allocation of responsibilities within the firm. While British registration is far from a perfect proxy for 'a headquarters', when it was absent—as indicated—often the British 'headquarters functions' were hard to maintain.
67. A splendid introduction to the complexities of ownership and control can be seen in D. K. Fieldhouse, *Merchant Capital and Decolonization: The United Africa Company 1929–1987* (Oxford, 1994). Fieldhouse's book is on the United Africa Company (UAC), a subsidiary of the multinational enterprise Unilever. UAC was itself a multinational, within the larger Unilever. It was fully owned, yet potentially but only partially administratively controlled by Unilever. It was a separate administrative entity within the large multinational, Unilever. UAC in turn had a range of affiliates that it administered with different degrees of decentralization. Caves (*Multinational Enterprise*, 1) calls what constitutes control a 'judgmental issue'.
68. Corley, 'Britain's Overseas Investments in 1914 Revisited', 74. This is not the view Corley takes in the chapter included in this volume.
69. In my studies of the history of traditional multinational enterprises, I have found many instances where parent companies did not exercise strong control over subsidiaries. Amount of control unquestionably varies by company,

function, time, and many other variables. Within single multinationals, it was not strange to find subsidiaries that had autonomy for years. The contemporary literature on multinationals is filled with survey articles whose authors asked subsidiary managers, 'how much autonomy do you have?' On control by free-standing companies, see Wilkins, *The History of Foreign Investment*, 306.

70. Casson, Chapter 3 herein.
71. Corley, Chapter 4 herein.
72. Gurushina, Chapter 6 herein, is wonderful on this. See also Liehr and Torres Bautista, Chapter 9 herein, on the sequence of companies that began with United Mexican Mining Co. Ltd. My own research has found similar sequences of free-standing companies.
73. Wilkins, 'The Free-Standing Company', 264; also 279, wherein I state that the lean governance structure 'at origin' was responsible for many failures of free-standing companies.
74. Jones, Chapter 13 herein, for example, sees the British overseas banks as continuing through time as free-standing. They were, we all agree, set up as free-standing firms, yet they developed a lean but entirely adequate home office and abroad an extensive professional management. Chandler, in *The Visible Hand* and in his *Scale and Scope: The Dynamics of Industrial Capitalism* (Cambridge, Mass., 1990), considers the evolution of overall administration and the relationship between a central staff office and corporate administration. His insights are helpful in this regard.
75. Chapman, Chapter 7 herein; see also R. T. Stillson, 'The Financing of Malayan Rubber, 1905–1923', *Economic History Review*, 2nd ser., 24 (1971), 589–98. And we are back to the fourth definitional problem on what constitutes a firm.
76. Perhaps, as Miller and Jones, Chapters 8 and 13 herein, suggest, we need different typologies in dealing with free-standing firms as they evolve through time.
77. Both Corley, Chapter 4, and Miller, Chapter 8—exempting mining companies—see a higher survival rate than I do; I do not think we should exempt mining companies. The US evidence seems clear on a very high mortality rate; other evidence I have seen seems to confirm this. I am, however, convinced by all the authors in this volume that it is very important to pay much more attention to what happened to companies through time; see the section of the present chapter on 'Elaboration'.
78. Schmitz, 'Patterns', 11.
79. Many investments trusts (more the English than the Scottish ones) made domestic investments in free-standing companies, which, in turn, made the overseas investments. If an investment trust made an investment in American railroad securities, for example, usually that investment could be made in the UK and did not involve any activity by the investor in the USA. Some investment trusts invested in dollar securities within the USA and to do this they usually used an agent—banker or broker—and did not have an office, a direct investment, in the USA. See Wilkins, *The History of Foreign Investment*. See also R. Kindersley, 'British Foreign Investments in 1929', *Economic Journal*, 41 (Sept. 1931), 371, repr. in Wilkins (ed.), *British Overseas Investments*; Kindersley wrote on the problems of 'double counting' of British overseas investments, which was true before 1914 as well as later.
80. See, for example, Wilkins, *The Emergence of Multinational Enterprise*, and M. Wilkins, 'Japanese Multinationals in the United States: Continuity and Change, 1879–1990', *Business History Review*, 64 (Winter 1990), 585–629. My view of trading (and shipping) companies is consistent with that adopted by the British Inland Revenue Department, which classified such companies in Group 3

rather than Group 2. See note 44 above for the groups and Worswick and Tipping, *Profits*, 86, for the classifications.

81. Once again it is to be noted that there is an absence of full synchronization between what I call 'free-standing companies' and the overseas companies discussed by Paish, Simon, Davis, and most recently Schmitz. All the companies discussed by them were not necessarily free-standing ones by my definition. Also, I become increasingly wary of lists. The more one goes beneath the surface, the more apparent it becomes that especially over time seemingly 'free-standing companies' may often be anything but.
82. M. Casson, 'Institutional Diversity in Overseas Enterprise: Explaining the Free Standing Company', *Business History*, 36 (Oct. 1994), 96.
83. Paish's figures—14 Feb. 1914 (in Wilkins (ed.), *British Overseas Investments*)—and Corley, 'Britain's Overseas Investments in 1914 Revisited', 80, which uses them, deal with transactions rather than numbers of companies; they do indicate important British involvements in overseas tramways, telephones, and telegraph. Miller, Chapter 8 herein, notes heavy British concentration in railroads in the host countries that he considers. Schmitz's work provides paid-in capital by 1913 ('Patterns', 12); these are the figures that are used by others for 'accumulated stock'; they do not indicate sizeable Scottish stakes in this sector. Worswick and Tipping (*Profits*, 146), contains data showing the relative importance of 'railroads and transport' in the late nineteenth century. See also Table 1.3. There needs to be more research on the use of the free-standing company form in railroads.
84. Casson, 'Institutional Diversity', 96; Corley, Chapter 4 herein, also makes this point.
85. Hennart, Chapter 2 herein.
86. See Hennart, Chapter 2, Hertner, Chapter 5, Gurushina, Chapter 6, Miller, Chapter 8, and Liehr and Torres Bautista, Chapter 9 herein. It has often been noted that mining projects were speculative ones, which perhaps is another way of saying high-risk ones. The quotation in the text is from Michie, *The City*, 63. For a splendid article on the role of the City in mining projects, see C. E. Harvey and J. Press, 'The City and International Mining, 1870–1914', *Business History*, 32 (July 1990), 98–119.
87. It could be argued that Ford Motor Co.'s 'advantage' was that it had an assured market for the rubber produced. But the experienced merchant firms that were associated with the free-standing companies in the rubber business had a comparable advantage in commodity markets. Moreover, the rubber-plantation companies that were set up and managed by agency houses might not be considered free-standing at all. It should be noted that Ford was very unsuccessful in its efforts to grow rubber. Wilkins and Hill, *American Business Abroad*, ch. 8.
88. G. Jones, *British Multinational Banking*.
89. I did make this point in Wilkins, 'The Free-Standing Company', 277. For some companies that started in industries (oil, for example) where new technologies were essential, the firm found it needed to have within its own organization the asset-specific talents—that is, the companies developed managerial structures and hired their own engineers.
90. Most of the typical 'American-model' multinationals sold trademarked products. On this, see M. Wilkins, 'The Neglected Intangible Asset: The Influence of the Trade Mark on the Rise of the Modern Corporation', *Business History*, 34 (Jan. 1992), 66–95. There were some free-standing companies, which had branded goods. Pillsbury-Washburn Flour Mills Co., Ltd. in the USA in the late nineteenth century was a British-owned free-standing company, floated in

London in 1889 (Wilkins, *The History of Foreign Investment*, 320–2). Also, some of the breweries abroad that were owned by free-standing companies had beers with trade names. But read Wilkins, *The History of Foreign Investment*, on the baneful experience of Pillsbury when it was a British free-standing company.

91. Wilkins, 'Efficiency and Management', 982.
92. I emphasized this in Wilkins, 'The Free-Standing Company'.
93. From A. H. Amsden and T. Hikino, 'Borrowing Technology or Innovating', in Thomson (ed.), *Learning and Technological Change*, 256.
94. Miller, Chapter 8 herein. See also W. Hunt, *Heirs of Great Adventure: The History of Balfour, Williamson and Company Limited* (2 vols.; London, 1951, 1960).
95. Based on the research I did for Wilkins, 'The Impact of Multinational Corporations'.
96. See Jones, Chapter 13 herein, and his *British Multinational Banking*. Dunning and Morgan, *An Economic Study*, 156 (these comments are for a later period but are applicable for earlier times). The quotation is from E. Green, 'Export Bankers: The Migration of British Bank Personnel to the Pacific Region, 1850–1914', in O. Checkland, S. Nishimura, and N. Tamaki (eds.), *Pacific Banking 1859–1959* (London, 1994), 82. Green looked at personnel records of British domestic banks and showed that the latter were recruiting grounds for the overseas banks.
97. Within parts of the Empire, there were special issues on British registration that did not prevail elsewhere. Otherwise, it seems remarkable how few differences there were between Empire and non-Empire stakes.
98. Chapman, *Merchant Enterprise*.
99. G. Jones, *British Multinational Banking*.
100. Chapman, Chapter 7 herein.
101. This was true only *vis-à-vis* the *identical clusters*. Thus, Otis Steel (a British free-standing company in the USA) was far smaller than US Steel. The British free-standing breweries in the USA did not consistently have larger capitalization than the US-owned ones.
102. Chapman, Chapter 7 herein, and Wilkins, *The History of Foreign Investment*, 493–4. Worswick and Tipping, *Profits*, 88: the context of this comment lay in comparing the 'supposed' capitalization of the average overseas company with the average British domestic one.
103. Hennart, Chapter 2 herein.
104. Hennart's suggestion that sizeable exports from the host country made British registration more appropriate than local registration might apply to mines and plantations (and jute factories), but it did not apply to American cattle companies or American mortgage companies that were set up as free-standing, or for that matter to British free-standing breweries in the USA, South Africa, and Peru.
105. R. V. Kubicek, *Economic Imperialism in Theory and Practice: The Case of South African Gold Mining Finance 1886–1914* (Durham, NC, 1979), 88.
106. A. R. Hall, *The London Capital Market and Australia 1870–1914* (Canberra, 1963), 97–8.
107. R. P. T. Davenport Hines and G. Jones (eds.), *British Business in Asia since 1860* (Cambridge, 1989), 10. Rory Miller, Chapter 8 herein, suggests that merchant groups used local registration when they did not need the resources of the London stock market and 'for reasons of commercial confidentiality'.
108. L. E. Davis and R. J. Cull, *International Capital Markets and American Economic Growth, 1820–1914* (Cambridge, 1994), 66, 71. When I wrote *The History of*

*Foreign Investment*, it did not occur to me to compare the American stock issues traded in New York and London. Yet, the matter is extremely germane to the history of free-standing companies. Davis and Cull see the lack of synchronism as based on British capital flows being targeted at 'economic activities that lay outside the scope of the still embryonic American financial market'. See Davis and Cull, *International Capital Markets*, 71. Perhaps there were institutional explanations as well. Americans wanted to trade in dollar issues. Britishers were willing to buy dollar-denominated American railroads and large industrials such as US Steel, but were not prepared to invest in many of the less familiar 'commercial and industrial' firms. Americans were not interested in trading in sterling-denominated companies. The free-standing companies were sterling-denominated.

109. Corley, Chapter 4 herein, puts the banks' head offices in the category of 'maintaining regular correspondence'. See Gurushina, Chapter 6 herein, on the head offices of British free-standing companies in Russia.
110. Hertner, Chapter 5 herein, notes a huge British free-standing bank in Italy—of which he found no further trace: also a typical exit. If a company was replaced by another free-standing one, the first company is considered as an 'exit'. If the company continues on within the host country with no London head office, we can consider this to be the end to a British business abroad, i.e. an exit.
111. There is a problem in defining success: see the section on 'Evaluation'. The research of Reinhard Liehr and Mariano E. Torres Bautista on Mexico (see Chapter 9 herein) confirms the short-lived characteristics of many of these ventures.
112. The point is made by a number of contributors to this volume.
113. See earlier discussion on the third query under the seventh definitional problem: if a company began as a free-standing one, what characteristics must it maintain to remain in that category?
114. Casson, 'Institutional Diversity', 96, and Chapter 3 herein.
115. Gurushina, Chapter 6 herein.
116. Hennart, Chapter 2 herein. Many of these may well have been only nominally free-standing. See Jones, Chapter 13 herein, for an indication that in the 1930s at least some of these may have become part of the London Tin Corporation group. The London Tin Corporation appears to have been a multinational enterprise, with interests in Malaya, Nigeria, Thailand, and Burma (J.-J. van Helten and G. Jones, 'British Business in Malaysia and Singapore since the 1870s', in R. P. T. Davenport-Hines and G. Jones, *British Business in Asia since 1860* (Cambridge, 1989), 168–70, 184–5.
117. Miller, Chapter 8 herein.
118. Miller, Chapter 8 herein, thinks it legitimate to call these ongoing, continuing free-standing companies. He argues that they did not become classic multinationals (at least by conventional definitions), and, if they did not remain free-standing companies, we need another category of foreign direct investments (Miller to Wilkins, 14 Oct. 1996).
119. G. Jones, *British Multinational Banking*, and Jones, Chapter 13 herein.
120. Miller, Chapter 8 herein, accepts my view and does not include, for example, the Anglo-South American Bank (ASAB) as a free-standing company. By 1913 Miller notes that the ASAB operated (or at least had offices) in several countries in Latin America, in the USA, and in Europe. Miller sees the geographical expansion (along with the internalization of management) as creating 'a more or less' classic multinational in the financial service sector. Like other British overseas banks, it had, however, he agrees, started as a free-standing company

(the Bank of Tarapacá & London in 1888) and—in Miller's view—remained free-standing until 1900, when it expanded into business in Argentina (Miller to Wilkins, 14 Oct. 1996).

121. I do not think that the failure to survive in the USA was based on regulatory restrictions, which did exist, but instead was based on the absence of a need for overseas banks (US banks could suffice). On Anglo-Austrian's two incarnations as a British bank, see G. Jones, *British Multinational Banking*, 228–9. On the exit of a British overseas bank from Italy, see Hertner, Chapter 5 herein. In Canada, the longest lasting British overseas bank was the Bank of British North America, founded in London in 1836; it had first-mover advantages and had a long history. In 1918, however, its assets were taken over by the Bank of Montreal. There was by that time no need for an overseas bank in Canada. When R. Cameron and V. I. Bovykin were planning their edited volume *International Banking 1870–1914* (New York, 1991), I tried to push contributor Ian Drummond to deal with overseas banking in Canada; he argued that locally incorporated banks did the largest share of the business, and that portion increased in the period under study (p. 192). By 1913 the Bank of British North America had a mere 3.9% of the commercial banking assets in Canada (ibid.). In Australia, it is true that the British role lasted longer and was more important. Yet, Australia was far less developed than the USA or Canada. On the role of British banks in Australia, see G. Jones, *British Multinational Banking*, 57, 98. By contrast, in some less developed countries, these banks were truly important. By one estimate, in 1914, British overseas banks controlled a third of the deposits in the Brazilian banking system and over a quarter of those in Argentina and Chile (G. Jones, *British Multinational Banking*, 56). The role of the Imperial Bank of Persia was even more substantial, although comparisons should be made with great care, since there existed an active pre-modern banking business—in bazaars (see G. Jones, *Banking and Empire in Iran*, i. *The History of the British Bank of the Middle East* (Cambridge, 1986), 205, 235). Yet, after 1929, in Iran the domestic Bank Melli increasingly took market share from its foreign competitors (ibid. 236).
122. This firm became RTZ-CRA at the end of 1995 and then readopted the name Rio Tinto in 1997 (*Financial Times*, 21 Dec. 1995 and 28 Feb. 1997). On its earlier history, see C. E. Harvey, *The Rio Tinto Company: An Economic History of a Leading International Mining Concern, 1873–1954* (Penzance, Cornwall, 1981); J. M. Stopford, *Directory of Multinationals* (1992), 1168–70; and *Financial Times*, 11 Aug. 1993.
123. J. H. Bamberg, *The History of the British Petroleum Company*, ii (Cambridge, 1994), 268. On its early history, see R. W. Ferrier, *The History of the British Petroleum Company*, i. *1901–1932* (Cambridge, 1982), and T. A. B. Corley, *A History of the Burmah Oil Company 1886–1924* (London, 1983).
124. Stopford, *Directory*, 220.
125. See Corley, *A History*, and an earlier draft of his chapter published herein.
126. Ferrier, *The History*, 53.
127. Ibid. 70.
128. See Wilkins, 'Defining a Firm', 90, where I puzzled over this same case. My rendition now is slightly different from that one.
129. Corley is an expert on Burmah Oil and I have to agree with his analysis here.
130. In this regard, we could spend time tracing it from its origins and show how different its experiences were from say Standard Oil of New Jersey (now EXXON) or Shell. What the free-standing-company concept does is push us to look closer at the course of the business history of particular enterprises. It provides an analytic frame of reference.

131. The phrase is borrowed from the title of Gregory Marchildon, Chapter 15 herein.
132. Data from Geoffrey Jones and Stanley Chapman on the managing agency groups. We need more business histories. Burmah Oil, for example, was no longer free-standing; it is doubtful that Tharsis would so qualify. Survivors and paid-up capital data from Christopher Schmitz, 28 Feb. 1994.
133. Hennart, Chapter 2 herein. Hennart also points out that some existing free-standing companies survived after their *raison d'être* had disappeared.
134. The suggestion was made in discussions in Milan, in October 1994. He made this suggestion as a way of considering the differing paths of surviving companies. He did not make it in the same context as Casson, who refutes those who argue that the 'free-standing company may be just a transitory phenomenon . . . called into being by speculative bubbles on the stock exchange . . .' (Casson, Chapter 3 herein).
135. Kindersley, 'British Foreign Investments in 1929', 376, repr. in Wilkins (ed.), *British Overseas Investments.* (Kindersley was arguing that part of the capital of these companies was employed at home and should not be included as a capital export.) For more details on expenses of home offices, see Kindersley, 'British Overseas Investments, 1938', *Economic Journal* 49 (Dec. 1939), 687–8.
136. Hennart, Chapter 2 herein.
137. Worswick and Tipping, *Profits*, 137. The percentage of total number of assessments was less than 1%, dropping from 0.76% in 1909 to 0.33% in 1927. Worswick and Tipping believed the increase in foreign assessment numbers 1909–27 was 'barely significant' (p. 88).
138. Miller, Chapter 8 herein, and G. Jones, *British Multinational Banking*, 403–13. The Anglo-Austrian Bank (in its second reconstruction) was a post-First World War creation, as was its successor the Anglo-International Bank (1926) (Jones, *British Multinational Banking*, 228–31). There were others post-1914, but they were few and far between.
139. This research is as yet unpublished.
140. Miller, Chapter 8 herein.
141. Kindersley, 'British Foreign Investments in 1929', 378. Kindersley pointed out that most of the British-registered companies still operating abroad had been set up in an earlier era. Michie (*The City*, 131) has a fine summary of the role of the City in overseas investment 1913–79, which provides a good context for the decline in the use of the British free-standing company.
142. On British decline, see W. P. Kennedy, *Industrial Structure, Capital Markets and the Origins of British Economic Decline* (Cambridge, 1987); Kennedy believed overseas investment substituted for domestic investment. This was *not* a new idea but was now given new currency. In 'The Growth of the Transnational Industrial Firm in the United States and the United Kingdom: A Comparative Analysis', *Economic History Review*, 2nd ser., 33 (1980), 410, Chandler wrote: 'The British failure to participate fully in the growth of the new industries and to meet competition from the United States and the continent has often been explained as entrepreneurial failure. A better term may be managerial failure: that is the continuing existence of the family firm helped to deprive Britain of a class of trained managers and sets of technological and managerial skills that became increasingly essential, not only to technically advanced industries but also to the operation of modern urban, industrial economies.' In *Scale and Scope*, 235–7, Chandler wrote of the inadequacies of British 'personal management' and the absence of managerial hierarchies in modern industries. For criticisms, see, for example, L. Hannah, 'Delusions of Durable Dominance OR The Invisible Hand Strikes Back: A Critique of the New Orthodoxy in

Internationally Comparative Business History 1980s', manuscript (1994); see also G. Jones, 'Big Business, Management and Competitiveness in Twentieth Century Britain', in A. D. Chandler, Jr., F. Amatori, and T. Hikino (eds.), *Big Business and the Wealth of Nations* (Cambridge, 1997).

143. G. Jones (ed.), *British Multinationals.*
144. In the initial draft of C. Jones, 'Institutional Forms of British Foreign Direct Investment in South America', *Business History*, 39 (1997), 21–41; Corley, Chapter 4, and Casson, Chapter 3 herein. Ben P. A. Gales and Keetie E. Sluyterman, Chapter 11 herein, also interpreted my rendition as describing a form 'inferior' to the US multinational enterprise.
145. Chapters of Corley, Casson, Jones, and Chapman herein. The experienced mercantile firms in India, in particular, provided on-the-spot management for both sterling and rupee companies. These wider enterprise groups within India had under their jurisdiction many companies and vast numbers of employees (in 1913 Andrew Yule & Co. provided managerial services to some sixty companies with 200,000 employees, while in 1939 James Finlay & Co. had under its supervision 139,260 employees). See Chapman, *Merchant Enterprise*, 125, and C. Jones, *International Business in the Nineteenth Century* (Brighton, 1987), 195.
146. I have discussed, albeit briefly, free-standing companies from other nations in a number of places, including my *The History of Foreign Investment*.
147. On non-British free-standing companies, see Chapters 2, 3, 4, 5, 10, 11, 12, 14, and 15 herein, but especially Gales and Sluyterman, Chapter 11, and Harm Schröter, Chapter 12 herein, which are the first attempts to treat systematically Continental European free-standing companies. Tamás Szmrecsányi, Chapter 10 herein, considers the history of a French free-standing company. In addition, see B. P. A. Gales and K. E. Sluyterman, 'Outward Bound: The Rise of Dutch Multinationals', in G. Jones and H. G. Schröter (eds.), *The Rise of Multinationals in Continental Europe* (Aldershot, 1993); and H. G. Schröter, *Aufstieg der Kleinen: Multinationale Unternehmen aus fünf kleinen Staaten vor 1914* (Berlin, 1993).
148. Chapter 12 herein; see also Hertner, Chapter 8 herein.
149. Gregory P. Marchildon, Chapter 15 herein.
150. Miller, Chapter 8 herein.
151. Corley, Chapter 4 herein, using Cleona Lewis's data, wants to push the US free-standing company share of total US outward foreign direct investment to some 18% in 1914.
152. Hennart, Chapter 2, Schröter, Chapter 12, Szmrecsányi, Chapter 10, and Marchildon, Chapter 15 herein—for such suggestions.
153. Gales and Sluyterman, Chapter 11, Schröter, Chapter 12, Hertner, Chapter 5, Corley, Chapter 4, and Hennart, Chapter 2 herein.
154. Szmrecsányi, Chapter 10, and Hertner, Chapter 5 herein. Corley, Chapter 4 herein, gives an estimate of free-standing companies as 10% all French foreign direct investment. I think that has to be low. Years ago, R. Cameron (in *France and the Economic Development of Europe 1800–1914* (Princeton, 1961)), insisted that French investment abroad was far from passive; recent research confirms this. I have found that there were not only many French multinational enterprises of the classic model sort, but numerous French free-standing companies with direct investments abroad.
155. At least that is the way I interpret the data. This does not exactly correspond with Corley's conclusions, Chapter 4 herein.
156. Marchildon, Chapter 15 herein.
157. Germany did, however, have colonies before the First World War.

## 62 Mira Wilkins

158. But see the striking conclusions of Gales and Sluyterman, Chapter 11 herein, on the relative importance of the Dutch East Indies, and Schröter, Chapter 12 herein, on the special role of the Belgian Congo in Belgium's investments abroad.
159. There were sizeable German immigrant and expatriate communities in many parts of the world. These were often linked with German multinational enterprise, providing employees, markets, and information. See, for example, Wilkins, *The History of Foreign Investment*, for Germans in the USA.
160. Schröter, Chapter 12, and Gales and Sluyterman, Chapter 11 herein, deal with some of the special problems of including colonies as 'foreign'. On the Suez Canal Co. (which I would call a free-standing company), see E. H. Tuma, 'Suez Canal: Another Dimension in the European Network', *Journal of European Economic History*, 24 (Winter 1995), 626.
161. See, for example, L. G. Franko, *The European Multinationals* (Stamford, Conn., 1976), and Jones and Schröter (eds.), *The Rise of Multinationals in Continental Europe*.
162. Hennart, Chapter 2 herein. On Belgian banks and free-standing companies, see also Herman Van der Wee and M. Goosens, 'Belgium', in Cameron and Bovykin (eds.), *International Banking*, 122–7.
163. Hennart, Chapter 2, and Gales and Sluyterman, Chapter 11 herein.
164. Szmrecsányi, Chapter 10 herein.
165. Marchildon, Chapter 15 herein.
166. Schröter, Chapter 12 herein.
167. My solution to reflect realities would be to call the contiguous Austro-Hungarian Empire the political unit and business outside it would be 'foreign'. After the break-up, the new nations are the political entities and some business that was once domestic becomes, by definition, 'foreign'.
168. Gales and Sluyterman, Chapter 11 herein.
169. B. Gales, 'In Foreign Parts: Free-Standing Companies in the Netherlands around the First World War', unpublished paper prepared for the Milan Conference (1994). Just as American multinationals used British intermediaries to do business in certain parts of the world, so too they used Dutch intermediaries to do business in the Netherlands East Indies—in Gales's term, transfer investments. Thus, Standard Oil Company (New Jersey) in 1912 formed N. V. Nederlandsche Koloniale Petroleum Maatschappij (NKPM) to operate its new concession in the East Indies (I. H. Anderson, Jr., *The Standard-Vacuum Oil Company and United States East Asian Policy 1933–1941* (Princeton, 1975), 205).
170. When the British Lever Brothers wanted to do business in the Belgian Congo, in 1911 it set up La Société Anonyme des Huileries du Congo Belge. In French West Africa, Lever Brothers bought what appears to have been a typical French free-standing company, Compagnie Propriétaire du Kouilou Niari (and, like many free-standing companies, it turned out not to live up to expectations) (C. Wilson, *The History of Unilever* (3 vols.; New York, 1968), i. 168, 179).
171. Marchildon, Chapter 15 herein, treats these companies as Canadian free-standing ones, while Liehr and Torres Bautista, Chapter 9 herein, consider them as 'British'.
172. None of this had anything to do with free-standing-company activities (Wilkins and Hill, *American Business Abroad*). Ford's Canadian affiliate in its early decades had an immense degree of managerial 'autonomy'. This was a case of a multinational enterprise, where administrative 'control' from headquarters was minimal, albeit the Canadian company gained from being part of a

multinational enterprise in what was transferred from the parent *vis-à-vis* product and production knowledge.

173. Gales and Sluyterman, Chapter 11 herein.
174. At least this is the tentative conclusion from the present state of research. The British had many free-standing companies in agriculture (but not the *share* that the Dutch had); none the less, the new data in Table 1.3 on Britain does show the importance of plantation companies in the inter-war period. Interestingly, although the Germans had few free-standing companies, in terms of numbers Schröter found those in agriculture were pre-eminent (Chapter 12 herein). We do not have any industry distribution figures on French-headquartered free-standing companies. Our one case study of a French business abroad is in sugar (milling and plantations) (Szmrecsányi, Chapter 10 herein).
175. Cameron and Bovykin (eds.), *International Banking*, contains numerous useful insights in this regard. In some cases banks were clearly central to the clusters surrounding free-standing companies. See, for example, J. Thobie, 'European Banks in the Middle East', in ibid.
176. Hausman and Neufeld, Chapter 14 herein.
177. See T. Abo, 'ITT's International Business Activities, 1920–1940', *Annals of the Institute of Social Science*, 24 (1982–83), 104–28.
178. Marchildon, Chapter 15 herein.
179. This new research set me thinking about multinational enterprise and the establishment of infrastructure within the world economy (Wilkins, 'Multinational Corporations').
180. Interestingly it was a Dutch multinational, the Royal Dutch Shell group, that made the largest pre-war investment in Curaçao (in the Dutch West Indies), in a refinery there, designed to process crude oil from its new Venezuelan oil properties. Royal Dutch Shell, of course, had large investments in the Dutch East Indies as well.
181. Gales and Sluyterman, Chapter 11 herein.
182. Wilkins, 'European and North American Multinationals', for differences in direction.
183. Our evidence here is weak.
184. Gales and Sluyterman, Chapter 11 herein.
185. See also Marchildon, Chapter 15 herein, where, in the case of the Canadian free-standing public utilities abroad, some (but not all) of the initiative came from Canada. F. S. Pearson—an American entrepreneur—was important in many of the Latin American investments. I found a number of third-country entrepreneurs would participate in British free-standing companies. That, however, fits the notion of Gales and Sluyterman that the initiative came from abroad.
186. Szmrecsányi, Chapter 10, discusses a French company in Brazil, a less developed country where the arrangement was entirely viable.
187. I cannot overemphasize this when dealing with the history of the classic multinational enterprise. One can look at multinational enterprises and draw charts; depending on the structure that one is trying to document, the charts look entirely different. The research on free-standing companies brings forth comparable conclusions.
188. Corley, Chapter 4 herein, suggests that they represented 80% of British outward compared with roughly 20% of US outward foreign direct investment at the eve of the First World War.
189. Hennart, 'International Financial Capital Transfers', and Hennart, Chapter 2 herein.
190. Chandler, *Scale and Scope*, makes this point. The paths to economic

development were different. On US business abroad, see Wilkins, *The Emergence of Multinational Enterprise.*

191. Wilkins, 'European and North American Multinationals'.
192. See Schröter, Chapter 12 herein, for his very useful explanations on why Belgium was particularly attractive as a headquarters locale for free-standing companies. He throws important light on these questions.
193. Michie, *The City*, 106.
194. M. Wilkins, 'Cosmopolitan Finance in the 1920s', in R. Sylla, R. Tilly, and G. Tortella (eds.), *The State, the Financial System, and Economic Modernization* (Cambridge, forthcoming).
195. M. Wilkins, 'The History of Foreign Investment in the United States from 1914', manuscript in process.
196. Szmrecsányi, Chapter 10 herein. I will admit that it did have quite a long life.

# [3]

*Geoffrey Jones and Judith Wale*

## Merchants as Business Groups: British Trading Companies in Asia before 1945

Merchants formed an important component of British foreign direct investment before 1945. Locating in parts of Asia, Latin America and other developing economies, they often diversified into non-trading activities, including the ownership of plantations. This article examines three such British firms active initially in Asia, though with operations also in North America, Europe, and Africa. Often regarded as handicapped by managerial failings, especially from the early twentieth century, the authors cast these firms as more entrepreneurial and possessing greater managerial competencies than has been suggested. The article argues that their business strategies continued to evolve in the interwar years and that, when viewed as business groups, their organizational forms were robust, though considerable diversity in the performance of the three British firms can be observed. This evidence is shown to have implications for wider debates about the competencies of British management as a whole.

British foreign direct investment (FDI) was much larger than that of the United States before 1945, and its organizational composition was very different. According to the widely-cited estimates of John H. Dunning, Britain accounted for 45 percent of total world FDI

GEOFFREY JONES is professor of business history in the economics department of the University of Reading, U.K.

JUDITH WALE is lecturer in accounting, University of Warwick Business School; visiting research fellow at the Centre for International Business History, University of Reading; and visiting research associate in the Business History Unit at the London School of Economics.

The authors would like to thank two anonymous referees for their helpful comments on an earlier draft of this article, as well as participants of seminars held at the universities of Lancaster, Kobe, Reading, and Uppsala. Duncan Gilmore of James Finlay plc. kindly made available the published accounts of that company. Monica Clough was a font of information about the company. Many thanks are due to Andrew Riley for his guidance on the content and structure of the records of Harrisons & Crosfield (hereafter H & C), which are deposited at the Guildhall Library, London (hereafter GL).

*Business History Review* 72 (Autumn 1998): 367-408. 

in 1914 and 40 percent in 1938, compared to the share of the United States of 18 percent and 28 percent respectively.[1] However the management of the international activities of U.S. and British business differed sharply. U.S. FDI primarily took the form of a company with pre-existing domestic business establishing a subsidiary in a foreign country, over which it exercised management control. In the classic Chandlerian model, as modern industrial enterprises emerged they both diversified their product range and expanded abroad.[2] British manufacturing companies made investments of this nature from the 1860s also.[3] However, the majority of British FDI was undertaken by many thousands of separately quoted British companies which invested in overseas mines, ranches, plantations, utilities, and many other activities. Typically they invested in a single overseas country and in a single activity. They were established in order to undertake that activity and they did not grow out of a pre-existing domestic business. However their boards of directors were usually located in Britain and exercised some form of managerial control over the overseas business. In a classic study, Mira Wilkins termed such firms "free-standing" companies and argued that they comprised a major component of British FDI.[4]

Again in contrast to the United States, merchants played an important part in the growth of British FDI. From the late eighteenth century British merchants settled in the ports of Asia, Latin America, and later elsewhere to take advantage of the spectacular growth of British foreign trade and the new opportunities arising from the abolition of government restrictions and monopolies. Once established, these merchants often became interested in the export of local commodities as well as the import of British goods, and eventually engaged in other

[1] John H. Dunning, "Changes in the Level and Structure of International Production: The Last 100 Years," in *The Growth of International Business*, ed. Mark Casson (London, 1983), 84-139; Geoffrey Jones, *The Evolution of International Business* (London, 1996). T. A. B. Corley, "Britain's Overseas Investments in 1914 Revisited," *Business History* 36 (1994): 71-88, suggests that British FDI was higher than Dunning's figures.

[2] Alfred D. Chandler, Jr, *Scale and Scope* (Cambridge, Mass., 1990), 38-45.

[3] S. Nicholas, "British Multinational Investment before 1939," *Journal of European Economic History* 11:3 (1982): 605-30; Geoffrey Jones, ed., *British Multinationals: Origins, Management and Performance* (Aldershot, U.K., 1986); Geoffrey Jones, "British Multinationals and British Business since 1850," in *Business Enterprise in Modern Britain*, eds. M. W. Kirby and Mary B. Rose (London, 1994).

[4] Mira Wilkins, "The Free-Standing Company, 1870-1914: An Important Type of Foreign Direct Investment," *Economic History Review*, 2nd series, 41 (1988): 259-85. See also Mira Wilkins, "Defining a Firm: History and Theory," in *Multinationals: Theory and History*, eds. P. Hertner and Geoffrey Jones (Aldershot, U.K., 1986), 80-95; and Mira Wilkins and Harm Schröter, eds., *The Free-standing Company in the World Economy, 1830-1996* (Oxford, 1998).

related business activities, such as acting as shipping and insurance agents. In many developing regions, the lack of infrastructure and of local entrepreneurship meant that British merchants could not rely upon others to create the complementary business needed for their trading houses. This led them to invest in infrastructure, and later in mines and plantations.[5] This process intensified from the 1870s in response to a variety of factors, including the impact of transportation and communications improvements. Another factor was the adoption of limited liability legislation in Britain, for in many cases diversification was achieved by promoting new joint-stock companies on British capital markets, where they took their place among the many other "free-standing" companies engaged exclusively in overseas business. The merchants often retained some of the equity of the new firms, or placed directors on their boards, or remained linked to them in other ways.[6] The numerous free-standing companies identified by Wilkins were in fact "clustered" around various interest groups, of which merchant houses or trading companies (the two terms are used interchangeably in this article) formed one major component.[7]

In a crude sense, U.S. business expanded abroad from the nineteenth century using "hierarchy," while much though not all British overseas business was organized into atomistic units linked by "networks." There are obvious contrasts to be made, but much remains unclear about these British "networks." The most systematic attempt to describe the networks organized around merchants was undertaken by Stanley Chapman, who termed them "investment groups." He identified thirty leading British-based investment groups active before 1914 divided into regional specialists in Asia, Latin America, Russia and South Africa. Chapman argued that their main function was financial. "There can be no serious doubt," he concluded, "that the investment group was primarily a device to maintain the wealth and

[5] J. S. Fforde, *An International Trade in Managerial Skills* (Oxford, 1957), 115-17.

[6] The expansion of British merchants is documented in Charles A. Jones, *International Business in the Nineteenth Century* (Brighton, 1987); Stanley D. Chapman, "British-Based Investment Groups before 1914," *Economic History Review*, 2nd series, 38 (1985): 230-51; and Chapman, *Merchant Enterprise in Britain* (Cambridge, U.K., 1992). Although not expressed in modern concepts of FDI or the multinational enterprise, the work of earlier generations of economic historians identified and documented the diversification of merchant houses into other activities in the nineteenth century. See especially G. C. Allen and A. G. Donnithorne, *Western Enterprise in Far Eastern Economic Development: China and Japan* (London, 1954) and *Western Enterprise in Indonesia and Malaya: A Study in Economic Development* (London, 1957); D. C. M. Platt, *Latin America and British Trade, 1806-1914* (London, 1972); D. C. M. Platt, ed., *Business Imperialism, 1840-1930* (Oxford, 1977); and F. E. Hyde, *Far Eastern Trade, 1860-1914* (London, 1973).

[7] Wilkins, "Free-Standing."

power of the family (or families) that constituted the particular business."[8] Chapman demonstrated that these investment groups sometimes reached a formidable size—running counter to the Chandlerian view that the problem with British business from the late nineteenth century was its inability to create larger units. However, in other respects, Chapman supported the Chandlerian critique of "personal capitalism." The majority of these enterprises retained a strong family influence and, at least before 1914, the partnership form. Chapman found a series of examples of managerial failure and other adverse "managerial consequences of British business nepotism" even before 1914.[9] Chapman's study ended in 1914 with the impression that the British merchants were running out of steam, in part because of the consequences of "nepotism," and that new opportunities were being lost, though Chapman was also careful to stress the diversity of the performance of these firms.[10] There are parallels in this argument with the Wilkins critique of British free-standing companies, handicapped—she argued—by a lack of managerial hierarchies and, in most cases, fated for extinction.[11]

Subsequent debate on Chapman's "investment groups" has been muted. Robert Turrell and Jean-Jacques van Helten argued that Chapman had confused matters by using the same term for merchants and South African mining groups.[12] The "investment groups" were rather amorphous in character, with permeable boundaries, and many (though not all) subsequently disappeared. Consequently the identification and composition of particular mercantile groups is not easy. Charles Jones has added a further number of British mercantile "investment groups" active in Latin America to Chapman's original list.[13] Latin American specialists like Jones have also questioned the managerial weakness hypothesis. It has been suggested that managerial structures and strategies of the "investment groups" in Latin America were by no means as weak or inadequate as sometimes supposed, and that it is far too narrow to define their role in financial terms.[14]

[8] Chapman, "British-Based," 243.

[9] Chapman, "British-Based," 244.

[10] Chapman, *Merchant Enterprise*, 292, 309.

[11] Wilkins, "Free-Standing."

[12] R. Turrell and J.-J. van Helten, "The Investment Group: The Missing Link in British Overseas Expansion before 1914," *Economic History Review*, 2nd series, 40 (1987): 267-74; Chapman, "Investment Groups in India and South Africa," *Economic History Review*, 2nd series, 40 (1987): 275-80.

[13] Charles A. Jones, "Institutional Forms of British Direct Investment in South America," *Business History* 39:1 (1997): 21-41.

[14] Jones, "Institutional Forms"; Robert G. Greenhill, "Investment Group, Free-Standing Company or Multinational? Brazilian Warrant, 1909-52," *Business History* 37:1 (1995): 86-111.

This article re-examines the issues surrounding "investment groups." It focuses on three such groups active initially in Asia identified by Chapman: James Finlay, Harrisons & Crosfield, and the Borneo Company.[15] It begins by describing the chronological, geographical, and managerial evolution of each enterprise. It then discusses their structures, competencies and capabilities. It concludes that the concept of an "investment group" is too narrow to describe the scope and significance of such enterprises. The alternative of "business group" is proposed.

## Three British Merchant Houses

James Finlay, Harrisons & Crosfield, and the Borneo Company all established the main features of their business in the decades between the 1870s and 1914, though in two cases their history reached further back. The Scottish merchant firm of Finlays was founded about 1765 by James Finlay, and then grew rapidly under his son Kirkman Finlay, who established cotton mills in Scotland at the beginning of the nineteenth century and opened branches in Germany and the United States to trade in textiles and buy cotton.[16] By the 1830s Finlays was buying its raw cotton from India and had closed its U.S. branches. In 1862 a branch of the firm was opened in Bombay, followed by one in Calcutta in 1870. Once established in India the firm began to trade in many commodities other than cotton, and it developed a business as agents for insurance and shipping companies. It also moved into non-trading activities, floating "free-standing" companies, mostly on the Glasgow Stock Exchange, in which it usually retained a minority share of the equity. In the early 1870s Finlays entered the fledgling Calcutta jute industry by establishing jute mills, recruiting two Dundee jute manufacturers to the venture to provide technical expertise. In the 1880s the firm began trading in tea and within two decades had come to control very large tea plantations in India amounting to 270,000 acres by 1901. These were owned by four large British-registered "free-standing" tea companies: Consolidated Tea & Lands, Amalgamated Tea Estates, Kanan Devan Hills Produce, and Anglo-American Direct Tea Trading. The latter firm integrated forwards by

[15] In the case of the Borneo Company, Chapman identifies the founding merchants—the Hendersons—rather than the Borneo Company as the core of the investment group. See below.

[16] J. Brogan, *James Finlay and Company Limited* (Glasgow, 1951), provides an outline history of Finlays.

*Jones and Wale / 372*

establishing tea distribution companies in the United States, Canada, and Russia. In the same period Finlays acquired shareholdings in tea blending, tasting, and warehousing companies in London. During the 1900s cotton textiles manufacture was begun in Bombay, and the firm built a sugar refinery in the United Provinces in India in 1913. Both operations supplied the domestic market. These ventures were also placed in partly-owned companies. Among the British "managing agencies" in India, Finlays were unusual in having operations in both the Calcutta and Bombay areas.[17]

Throughout the nineteenth century the Glasgow-based firm was organized as a partnership. However over the course of the century the original family were replaced as owners by John Muir, who joined the firm in 1849, and who by 1883 had become the sole proprietor. Muir died in 1903 and was succeeded by his son, Sir (Alexander) Kay Muir, who in 1909 converted the proprietary company into a private limited company, wholly owned by family members. Under British law, private companies were allowed the benefits of limited liability but there was no obligation to disclose accounts, and shares were not quoted or tradable on the capital markets. In 1924 Finlays converted into a public company, which meant that shares became dispersed among a larger number of holders, who had access to the accounts. However the Muir family retained a controlling shareholding until the 1950s. When Sir Kay retired from the chairmanship in 1926, he was succeeded by his younger brother, James Finlay Muir, who was chairman for a decade before being replaced by a non-family member.

During the interwar years Finlays continued to evolve. In India, it reacted to Japanese cotton textile competition by installing new machinery at its cotton mills which enabled them to change their production from coarse to fine grade cottons. It also built another sugar factory in Bihar, India, in the 1930s, which however was almost immediately destroyed by a severe earthquake.

More radically, the firm opened tea plantations in East Africa. In 1926 land was purchased in Kenya and, using staff transferred from its Indian tea operations, Finlays planted around 5,000 acres of tea by 1933, at which time the International Tea Agreement stopped further development. This venture involved extensive infrastructure development, including the building of hydro-electric facilities and schools, as

[17] Rajat K. Ray, *Industrialization in India* (Delhi, 1979), 263. "Managing agent" was the name used to describe British merchant houses in India. They were more usually known as "agency houses" in Southeast Asia.

well as modern tea factories.[18] Less successful was an attempt to enter sugar refining in South Africa during the First World War. Before 1914 Finlays had acquired a shareholding in merchant firms trading with, and in, South Africa, and during the war this led to an involvement in a government-inspired project to develop the sugar lands of Zululand. A new company was formed—the St. Lucia Sugar Company—but the region was subject to flooding, and the refinery and sugar cane lands were duly flooded. In 1923 the St. Lucia company was liquidated, and Finlays withdrew entirely from South Africa in 1931.[19]

In addition, Finlays used its affiliate, the Anglo-American Direct Tea Trading Company, to expand its tea distribution facilities. In 1912 a New York subsidiary was incorporated, followed in 1924 by a Canadian incorporation. During the interwar years the firm opened branches in Chicago, Philadelphia, and San Francisco. As U.S. demand expanded for "green" tea, as opposed to the "black" tea purchased by Finlays in South Asia, Anglo-American opened a buying office and tea factory in Taiwan in 1927. This investment was lost during the Second World War, while the U.S. business was sold to its local management in 1944.[20]

Table 1 summarizes the organization of the Finlay "group" around 1938. The Glasgow headquarters presided over wholly-owned branches in London, India, and Ceylon and partly-owned affiliated companies registered either in Britain or India. The rationale behind this structure will be examined further below.

Harrisons & Crosfield originated in 1844 as a Liverpool merchant house engaged in tea trading, buying tea in India and China and selling it in Britain and elsewhere. This business was conducted without any overseas branches. From the 1890s, by which time the partners had moved to London, there were radical changes of strategy. Between 1895, when the first overseas branch was opened in Colombo, and 1911, a network of offices was opened in India, Malaya, the Dutch East Indies, the United States (New York), Canada (Montreal), Australia (Melbourne), and New Zealand. These branches were usually established to trade in tea, but soon acquired a wider range of import and export trade, as well as acting as agents for insurance and shipping companies.[21] Meanwhile the tea trading interests

[18] Undated memo c.1945, Finlays archives, University of Glasgow (hereafter UGD) 91/413/2.

[19] Brogan, *James Finlay*, 77-79; J. F. Muir to Gatheral, 22 Sept. 1945, UGD 91/413/I.

[20] "The Anglo Story," *Finlays House Magazine* 1 (1964), UGD 91/377.

[21] All the insurance company principals were British, as were nearly all the shipping companies. The exceptions in shipping were mainly Dutch.

# Jones and Wale / 374

## Table 1

## James Finlay "Group" c.1938

| *Wholly-owned branches* | *Date opened* | *Principal activities in addition to import shipping, and insurance (including Lloyds) agencies* |
|---|---|---|
| *United Kingdom* | | |
| Glasgow | 1765 | Head office: secretarial services to plantation and other companies |
| Catrine and Deanston | 1801/1806 | Textile mills |
| London | 1871 | Secretarial services to plantation companies |
| *South Asia* | | |
| Bombay, India | 1862 | Textile mill management |
| Calcutta, India | 1870 | Jute mill management |
| Karachi, India | 1890 | Cotton ginning management |
| Chittagong, India | 1901 | |
| Vizagapatam, India | 1932 | Manganese ore exports |
| Colombo, Ceylon | 1893 | Plantation management; warehouses |

| *Principal affiliates* | *Date started /acquired* | *% of equity held* | *Place of registration* | *Principal activities* |
|---|---|---|---|---|
| Golabarry Co. | 1872 | 95% | India | Calcutta jute milling |
| Champdany Jute Co. | 1873 | 95% | India | Calcutta jute milling |
| Consolidated Tea and Lands Co. | 1896 | ?30%* | Glasgow | Indian tea plantations |
| Amalgamated Tea Estates Co. | 1896 | ?30%* | Glasgow | Indian tea plantations |
| Kanan Devan Hills Produce Co. | 1897 | ?30%* | Glasgow | Indian tea plantations; rice milling |
| Anglo-American Direct Tea Trading Co. | 1898 | ?30%* | Glasgow | Indian tea plantations; tea distribution in Canada and USA; office in Taiwan |
| Swan Mill | 1908 | ?30% | India | Bombay textile mills |
| Finlay Mills | 1908 | ?30% | India | Bombay textile mills |
| United Provinces Sugar Co. | 1912 | ?30% | India | Sugar refining in United Provinces |
| Belsund Sugar Co. | 1932 | 100% | India | Sugar refining in Bihar |
| African Highlands Produce Co. | 1926 | 100% | Glasgow | East African tea plantations |
| P.R. Buchanan & Co. | 1894 | ?30% | London | Agents for Indian tea plantations; tea warehousing in U.K.; selling agents for coffee, cocoa and other products |
| George Payne & Co. | c.1900 | ?30% | London | Packing and blending of tea, coffee, cocoa in U.K.; chocolate manufacture in U.K.; offices in Colombo (Ceylon), Calcutta (India), Durban (South Africa) |

* The Tea companies also held cross-shareholdings in one another.

Source: J. Brogan, *James Finlay & Co. Ltd.* (Glasgow, 1951); James Finlay Archives, University of Glasgow.

led to the purchase of tea estates in Ceylon beginning in 1899 followed by further estates in South India, and the development of distribution facilities in consuming countries. In the 1900s Harrisons & Crosfield entered the new rubber plantation industry in Malaya. Harrisons & Crosfield's first rubber plantation investment was in 1903, which made it one of the first movers, and by 1914 it had established a considerable number of rubber plantations in what had become the world's biggest rubber producing country, as well as in the Dutch East Indies.[22]

During the interwar years Harrisons & Crosfield extended its activities into timber and invested in manufacturing. In 1920 Harrisons & Crosfield acquired a logging business in North Borneo (now Sabah, Malaysia) in a joint venture with the British North Borneo Company, the chartered company which formed the colonial administration of North Borneo until 1946. The subsequent logging operations of the British Borneo Timber Co. became substantial—with the production of timber under their concession increasing from 1.1 million cubic feet in 1919 to 4.9 million cubic feet in 1937—with large sales being made to the Chinese and Japanese markets as well as in Europe. Diversification into manufacturing arose from the firm's rubber interests. Harrisons & Crosfield established factories on its Malayan rubber estates to process liquid latex into marketable form (ribbed smoked sheet at this date) and then at the end of the 1920s it became involved in manufacturing a new product—Linatex—from latex. A factory was established in Malaya to manufacture Linatex, and in 1938 a small plant opened in Britain which aimed to incorporate Linatex into other products.[23] In addition, Harrisons & Crosfield's Canadian branches, initially established to sell tea, diversified into chemicals distribution. Harrisons & Crosfield acquired a Canadian chemicals distribution company in 1935, and followed this up by the acquisition of the Canadian subsidiary of the American Cyanamid and Chemical Company in 1938.[24]

[22] J. H. Drabble, *Rubber in Malaya, 1876-1922* (Kuala Lumpur, 1973).

[23] Records of British Borneo Timber, Wilkinson Process Rubber and Wilkinson Rubber Linatex companies, Harrisons & Crosfield archives, GL; G. Nickalls, ed., *Great Enterprise: A History of Harrisons & Crosfield* (London, 1990). Linatex was a thick rubber sheet which was valuable because of its abrasion-resistant properties. It appears to have been almost alone before 1945 as a sophisticated product manufactured from raw rubber. Finding large scale uses and hence markets for Linatex was a significant problem which was compounded by early quality control difficulties in production. Its first large scale use was in wartime, as a cover for fuel tanks in ships and aircraft, but its main post-1945 use was as belting for conveyors in mining (for the movement and sorting of coal and ores), though it also came to be used in pumps and valves.

[24] Harrisons & Crosfield appears to have exported some chemicals from Canada before 1920, though such activities were moribund from 1921. In the 1930s Harrisons & Crosfield in Canada gained experience of importing industrial raw materials and intermediate goods

*Jones and Wale / 376*

Rubber Plantation, c. 1920s. Latex transport on the Begerpang estate of the United Serdang (Sumatra) Rubber Plantations, Ltd., Dutch East Indies (Indonesia). This company was managed by Harrisons & Crosfield. Harrisons & Crosfield archives, Guildhall Library. (Photograph reproduced courtesy of Elementis plc.)

Copra Factory, 1921. Bagging copra at the factory, Straits Plantations, Ltd., Malaya. This company was managed by Harrisons & Crosfield. It was normal for rubber companies to diversify by cultivating and processing small quantities of another crop, such as coconuts. Harrisons & Crosfield archives, Guildhall Library. (Photograph reproduced courtesy of Elementis plc.)

Table 2 summarizes the organizational structure of the Harrisons & Crosfield "group" in the late 1930s. As in the case of Finlays, the British headquarters presided over wholly-owned branches in Asia and elsewhere, together with a large number of affiliated companies registered in various places and in which Harrisons & Crosfield held various degrees of equity. Like Finlays also the firm had abandoned its partnership structure. In 1908 it became a limited liability company with its preference shares publicly quoted, and the founding family influence had gone altogether by the time of the First World War.

The Borneo Company's origins can be traced to the establishment of a branch of a Glasgow merchant firm in Singapore in 1846. It became closely linked with the Brooke family (the "White Rajahs") which established itself as the rulers of Sarawak in Borneo (now a state of Malaysia). The venture was given extensive privileges by the White Rajahs as a vehicle to develop the economy, and in order to take advantage of this opportunity the London-registered Borneo Company was founded in 1856, although the company remained very Scottish in its recruitment. A Glasgow merchant firm—R. & J. Henderson—which traded in India and elsewhere were closely involved in the finance and management of the company, and it is this firm which Chapman identifies as the "investment group" rather than the Borneo Company itself. Certainly through to the 1890s Hendersons provided substantial credit to the Borneo Company, though thereafter the Borneo Company took on a more independent existence.[25] In Sarawak, the Borneo Company performed a wide spectrum of functions ranging from import/export business and banking—it was the only banker until after the Second World War—to growing commodities and mineral exploitation and development. In Singapore a large import and export business was developed and other activities—notably brick manufacture—were initiated. The firm was one of a handful of merchant houses which formed a collusive and profitable shipping cartel—the Straits

through large scale importing from Europe of steel products. Threat of war in Europe was one of the factors behind the move into distribution within North America. Harrisons & Crosfield seized the opportunity to acquire successively two companies which together allowed them to distribute a wide range of products for a number of important chemicals manufacturers. H. J. Williams, typescript history of Harrisons & Crosfield in Canada (1961), Harrisons & Crosfield archives, GL. These two moves belonged to a strategy common to many trading companies by the late 1930s: that of acquiring specialized manufacturers' agencies. Agencies for Canadian and U.S. manufacturers were an exception to the general rule that Harrisons & Crosfield acted as overseas sales agents for British manufacturers. The other exception was in Australia and New Zealand, where the company held agencies for local foodstuffs and other manufacturers.

[25] R. J. Henderson to Borneo Company, 28 Dec. 1898; letter to Mr. Grenfell, 2 Mar. 1919, MS 27235, Borneo Company archives, GL.

## *Jones and Wale / 378*

### *Table 2*

### Harrisons & Crosfield "Group" c.1938

| *Wholly-owned branches* | *Date opened* | *Principal activities in addition to import shipping, and insurance (including Lloyds) agencies* |
|---|---|---|
| *United Kingdom* | | |
| London | c. 1845* | Head office: secretarial services to plantation companies |
| *Southeast Asia* | | |
| Kuala Lumpur, Malaya†, ‡ | 1907 | Rubber export, plantation management |
| Singapore† | 1917 | Rubber export, plantation management |
| Medan, Sumatra, Dutch East Indies‡ | 1910 | Rubber export, plantation management, engineering workshops |
| Batavia, Java, Dutch East Indies‡ | 1911 | Tea and rubber export, plantation management |
| Sandakan, British North Borneo‡ | 1918 | Timber export, forest management |
| *South Asia* | | |
| Colombo, Ceylon‡ | 1895 | Tea and rubber export, plantation management |
| Calcutta, India‡ | 1900 | Tea export, plantation management |
| Quilon, India‡ | 1912 | Tea and rubber export, plantation management, engineering workshops |
| *Elsewhere in Asia* | | |
| Shanghai, China | 1917 | Tea export |
| Kobe, Japan | 1917 | Textiles export |
| *Elsewhere* | | |
| New York, USA | 1904 | Tea import and distribution |
| Montreal, Canada‡ | 1905 | Tea and rubber import, chemicals distribution |
| Melbourne, Australia | 1910 | Tea and rubber import, general distribution |
| Wellington, New Zealand | 1910 | Tea and rubber import, general distribution |

| *Principal affiliates* | *Date started /acquired* | *% of equity held* | *Place of registration* | *Principal activities* |
|---|---|---|---|---|
| c. 40 plantation companies | 1903-30 | <1%-25% | London§ | Rubber and tea plantations |
| Rubber Plantations Investment Trust Ltd. | 1908 | >50% | London | Holding shares in plantation companies |
| British Borneo Timber Co. Ltd. | 1920 | 41.7% | London | Hardwood logging and milling |
| Twining Crosfield & Co. Ltd. | 1916 | ?50% | London | U.K. tea trading |
| Irwin Harrisons Whitney Inc. | 1914 | ?20% | New York | U.S. tea trading |
| Davenport & Co. Ltd. | 1927 | 100% | India | Managing tea plantations |
| Wilkinson Process Rubber Co. Ltd. | 1926 | ?7% | Kuala Lumpur | Linatex production |
| Wilkinson Rubber Linatex Ltd. | 1930 | 100% | London | Linatex production |

* The first office was opened in Liverpool in 1844, but the partnership early established a second office in the city of London, which soon became the center of the firm's operations.

† The Singapore branch represented a British-controlled company which Harrisons & Crosfield acquired. In 1922 the Kuala Lumpur and Singapore branches were merged to form Harrisons, Barker & Co. Ltd. (which was renamed Harrisons & Crosfield [Malaya] Ltd. in 1946).

‡ In these countries Harrisons & Crosfield had branch offices in a number of locations in addition to the main offices listed here.

§ In the case of several companies with plantations in Java, the London-registered company was merely a holding company for a wholly owned and locally-registered operating company.

Sources: *One Hundred Years as East India Merchants: Harrisons & Crosfield 1844-1943* (the company, 1944); Harrisons & Crosfield, "Sphere of Operations in 1949" (privately printed); annual reports and board minutes of individual plantation companies; Harrisons & Crosfield lists of shareholdings in "secretarial" companies; all in Harrisons & Crosfield archives, Guildhall Library, London.

Homeward Conference—which handled a substantial proportion of Singapore's exports to the West.[26] In Thailand, the Borneo Company opened an office for trading in Bangkok immediately after the country was opened to trade with the West in 1856. After the Treaty of Chiengmai in 1883 opened the way for Western firms to cut trees rather than buy them from indigenous foresters in northern Thailand, the Borneo Company moved into teak production.[27]

A distinguishing feature of the Borneo Company was that it was organized as a public company from its inception in 1856. It was one of the very first companies formed under the provisions of the Companies Act of that year. However its shares were closely held, and it was not until 1922 that the firm even obtained a Stock Exchange quotation. The Borneo Company also ventured into a "new" industry in the interwar years when it used its extensive knowledge of Southeast Asian markets to enter automobile distribution. In the early 1920s it began importing and selling cars into Singapore and Malaya, and its subsidiary Borneo Motors Limited eventually became one of its most important activities.[28] Borneo Motors secured the right to distribute certain types of vehicles in specified markets from various leading manufacturers, including General Motors and Austin. Table 3 summarizes the organizational structure of the Borneo Company around 1938, indicating the other principal affiliates as well as the wholly-owned branches.

It is not an easy matter to capture satisfactorily the size and importance of these three British firms in a comparative context. As their ordinary shares were not quoted before 1914 and not widely traded before the Second World War, net assets rather than market capitalization seems a more appropriate measure. Table 4 shows the net assets of the three firms in 1913 and 1938. It shows comparative figures for three large British overseas banks active in Asia in this period, and for two of the largest British merchant houses specializing in Latin America, Antony Gibbs, and Balfour Williamson.[29]

[26] W. G. Huff, *The Economic Growth of Singapore* (Cambridge, U.K., 1994), 128-33.

[27] H. Longhurst, *The Borneo Story* (London, 1956); Stephanie Jones, *Two Centuries of Overseas Trading: The Origins and Growth of the Inchcape Group* (London, 1986), 19-21, 196-211; Rajeswary A. Brown, *Capital and Entrepreneurship in Southeast Asia* (London, 1994), 72-5; Borneo Company archives, GL.

[28] Borneo Company board minutes, 31 Oct. 1923, MS 27178/17; annual reports of Borneo Motors, MS 27373, GL. Huff, *Economic Growth*, 263, mistakenly observes that the only British merchant house in automobile distribution was Guthries.

[29] On British overseas banks, see Geoffrey Jones, *British Multinational Banking, 1830-1990* (Oxford, 1993). The figures for Antony Gibbs are estimates. The firm was organized

## Jones and Wale / 380

### Table 3

The Borneo Company "Group" c.1938

| *Wholly-owned branches* | *Date opened* | *Principal activities in addition to import shipping and insurance agencies* |
|---|---|---|
| *United Kingdom* | | |
| London | 1856 | Head office; secretarial services to affiliated companies |
| *Southeast Asia* | | |
| Kuching, Sarawak | 1856 | Plantation management; banking; timber extraction |
| Singapore | 1856 | Regional head office |
| Bangkok, Thailand | 1856 | Rice milling; wharves and warehouses |
| Chiengmai, Thailand | 1884 | Teak forests in Thailand |
| Batavia, Java, Dutch East Indies | 1856 | |
| Penang, Malaya | 1920 | Tin company and plantation management |

| *Principal affiliates* | *Date started /acquired* | *% of equity held* | *Place of registration* | *Principal activities* |
|---|---|---|---|---|
| Alexandra Brickworks Ltd. | 1899 | ?80% | Singapore | Brick manufacture in Singapore and Penang |
| Sarawak Rubber Estates | 1910 | 99% | London | Rubber plantations |
| Haboko Tea Company | 1914 | 100% | Dutch East Indies | Tea plantations and tea factory in Dutch East Indies |
| Borneo Motors Ltd. | 1925 | 80% | Singapore | Automobile retailing in southeast Asia |
| Masters Ltd. | 1930 | 11% | Singapore | Advertising agents |

Source: Henry Longhurst, *The Borneo Story* (London, 1956); Stephanie Jones, *Two Centuries of Overseas Trading* (London, 1986); Borneo Company archives, Guildhall Library, London.

### Table 4

The Net Assets of James Finlay, Harrisons & Crosfield and the Borneo Company: Some Comparisons, 1913 and 1938 ($m)*

| | *1913* | *1938* |
|---|---|---|
| James Finlay | 7.3 | 22.1 |
| Harrisons & Crosfield | 6.0 | 15.2 |
| Borneo Company | 2.1 | 5.5 |
| Antony Gibbs & Sons | 7.3 | 9.8 |
| Balfour Williamson & Co. | 9.7 | 9.8 |
| Hongkong Bank | 22.3 | 40.9 |
| Chartered Bank | 14.6 | 29.3 |
| Mercantile Bank of India | 3.0 | 10.4 |

* Sterling data are converted at the rate of £1 = $4.86 in 1913 and £1 = $4.89 in 1938.

The problem with the data in Table 4 is that until the 1948 Companies Act British firms did not have to publish "consolidated" balance sheets. This means that the many partly-owned companies in their orbits are not captured in the net asset figure. For example, while Harrisons & Crosfield had net assets of £2.8 million ($9.9 million) in 1932, the "group" as shown in Table 2 had total net assets of around £16.5 million (nearly $58 million). This made the enterprise as a whole comparable with U.S. consumer goods firms such as Quaker Oats and Coca-Cola measured by assets.[30] Using the random non-financial measures which are available, the three British companies appear large and complex enterprises. In the early 1950s Harrisons & Crosfield was ranked as one of the "top five" agency houses in Malaya controlling 226,000 acres of rubber alone, the largest of any group.[31] The Borneo Company was, among many other things, the second largest teak producer in Thailand.[32]

The British employed a rather small staff . It is unlikely that the head office staff at Finlays and the Borneo Company exceeded fifty in the interwar years, though the Harrisons & Crosfield head office was larger—over three hundred in 1952—largely as a result of the administrative work generated by the numerous plantation companies under its control.[33] The British expatriate staff at the various branches and in affiliates was also modest. Harrisons & Crosfield's Asian branches—excluding Singapore—employed just over one hundred in 1924.[34] On the other hand, a very much larger labor force was employed on plan-

---

as a number of interlocking partnerships. This estimate attempts to capture the overall size on the basis of data in the Antony Gibbs archive, GL. The figures for Balfour Williamson are also estimates, since the first set of published accounts relate only to 1949. The estimates rely on these accounts and on a substantial amount of financial data for 1900-38 in Wallis Hunt, *Heirs of Great Adventure: The History of Balfour Williamson & Co. Ltd., Volume 2* (London, 1960).

[30] The assets of the trading companies as revealed in Table 4 reflected the tendency to own a significant amount of property merely because of the companies' needs, integral to their activities, for offices, warehouses and housing for their European employees. Harrisons & Crosfield at least however did not undertake investments in real estate on a significant scale either before or after 1945. On the contrary, these avoided owning plantations and associated processing facilities through having only very small shareholdings in plantation companies. In this article, sterling has been converted into dollars at the contemporary average exchange rate for each year, using B. R. Mitchell, *British Historical Statistics* (Cambridge, U.K., 1988), 702-3. During 1920-21 and 1931-32 sterling was much weaker in relation to the dollar than in other years.

[31] J. J. Puthucheary, *Ownership and Control in the Malayan Economy* (Singapore, 1960), 26-8,58.

[32] Brown, *Capital*, 69-74.

[33] List of London head office staff in 1952, Harrisons & Crosfield archive, GL.

[34] Staff lists, Harrisons & Crosfield archive, GL. No data exists on employment in the U.S., Canada and Australia operations.

tations and in teak forests. In 1945 James Finlay calculated its total world-wide employment as at least 150,000.[35]

Despite the complexities of measuring the size and significance of the firms, it is evident that the Chapman view of them as primarily financial devices to "maintain the wealth and power" of families hardly does justice to their complexity and durability. They appear before 1914 as dynamic and entrepreneurial enterprises developing new sources of supply of resources such as tea, rubber, and teak, establishing markets for these commodities and for other products, and even pioneering modern industrialization, especially in India. They and firms like them served as important agents integrating Asia into the world economy. The firms were constantly evolving, but it is evident that long term investments were made. In tea in particular, the companies pursued extensive international vertical integration strategies from plantation to consumption. These companies were not merely perceiving opportunities for trade intermediation, but in some instances creating the trade itself.[36] Once established in a country, they acquired and utilized local knowledge and information which reduced the costs of diversification into other activities. Knowledge and information emerge at the heart of the capabilities of these firms.

Nor is it evident that, as suggested by Chapman, the entrepreneurial drive of the firms disappeared after 1914. The research of many regional specialists on South and Southeast Asia in the interwar years has tended to support a critical view of the strategies and competencies of British trading companies. They are generally cast as building their businesses in the privileged conditions of a nineteenth century colonial environment, where they were able to establish and sustain a variety of monopolistic practices. In the more difficult economic and political conditions of the interwar years, their organizational and other failings became liabilities. In interwar India many of the British agency houses remained focused on their traditional areas of jute, coal, and tea, rather than participating in the new industries developing behind tariff barriers.[37] Maria Misra has ascribed this fail-

[35] Calcutta to Glasgow, 17 Sept. 1945, UGD 91/413/1. It has proved impossible to reach a similar employment figure for Harrisons & Crosfield and the Borneo Company.

[36] This more dynamic view of British merchants/trading is found in some of the existing literature, including Fforde, *International Trade*, and—in the case of Russia—Fred V. Carstensen, "Foreign Participation in Russian Economic Life: Notes on British Enterprise, 1865-1914," in *Entrepreneurship in Imperial Russia and the Soviet Union*, ed. Gregory Guroff and Fred V. Carstensen (Princeton, N.J., 1983).

[37] B. R. Tomlinson, "Colonial Firms and the Decline of Colonialism in Eastern India," *Modern Asian Studies* 15:3 (1981): 455-86.

ure to a lack of organizational flexibility stemming from the retention of the partnership form.[38] Greg Huff found the agency houses in Singapore conspicuous by their lack of participation in interwar industrialization.[39] Ian Brown has suggested also that by the 1930s the British agency houses were being damaged by innovative Japanese business practices in their traditional business involving the export of Southeast Asian tropical commodities.[40] However the theme of decline, or at least lost opportunities, is not uniformly supported in the literature. Rajeswary Brown agrees that the import of British goods, especially Lancashire textiles, was of declining importance for the British agency houses in interwar Southeast Asia, in part because the Asian middlemen who had formerly distributed these goods developed direct links with western—and Japanese—manufacturers. However she places this story in the context of the shifting strategies of the agency houses and their growing involvement in commodity production and the provision of services to the numerous free-standing companies which they had promoted.[41]

The extent to which these three firms "missed opportunities" in the interwar years is debatable. Certainly James Finlay and Harrisons & Crosfield were supportive of and involved in the collusive international commodity cartels of the 1930s. However a focus on the overall strategies of the firms suggests continued evolution rather than mere recourse to cartels. Harrisons & Crosfield and the Borneo Company entered the "new" industries of the period, and the former company at least began to develop technological capabilities. In at least two cases the search for new opportunities took the companies into new regions. Finlays invested in Africa while Harrisons & Crosfield laid the foundations of an industrial manufacturing and distribution business in the developed world. The interwar diversifications of the three firms were built on their core competencies and appear well judged. Finlays transferred its considerable tea expertise to another continent. The Borneo Company built on its well-established agency business for western manufacturers when it entered automobile distribution. Harrisons & Crosfield's rubber plantation interests led on to rubber manufacturing, but also provided a link into chemicals, for its

[38] Maria Misra, "Entrepreneurial Decline and the End of Empire" (unpublished D.Phil. thesis, University of Oxford, 1992).

[39] Huff, *Economic Growth*, 187-8, 222-3.

[40] I. Brown, "The British Merchant Community in Singapore and Japanese Commercial Expansion in the 1930s," in *International Commercial Rivalry in Southeast Asia in the Interwar Period*, eds. S. Shinya and M. C. Guerrero (New Haven, 1994).

[41] Brown, *Capital*, 190-2.

*Jones and Wale / 384*

Southeast Asian branches were major importers of fertilizers and pesticides in the interwar years. Moreover the firm's interest in chemicals also arose out of a desire to absorb the shock of competition from synthetic rubber by becoming distributors of synthetic rubber products. The diversifications were also successful in risk-reduction—in the late 1930s, for example, Borneo Motors became an important source of income for the Borneo Company—and proved important foundations for the post-1945 development of all three companies.

## Business Groups

Critics of the British merchant houses in Asia have pointed to their organizations which appear both complex and riddled with conflicts of interest.[42] Writers who have focused on industries rather than on the British merchant houses have frequently criticized the costs involved in the "managing agency" system (which is discussed further below). This view is frequently expressed in the literature on the Malayan rubber industries.[43] This section reconsiders the organizational forms employed by these three firms and argues that they should be treated as being more than mere devices to capture rents.

All three British companies were organized as firms which operated within the context of a wider business group. This concept seems far more appropriate than "investment group," for it is evident that these diversified and durable enterprises were more than the primarily financial devices implied by the latter term. Finlays, Harrisons & Crosfield, and the Borneo Company can be regarded as multinational firms headquartered in Britain and with branches in foreign and colonial countries. In so far as firms and organizations can be distinguished, they were in the latter category, as they had an administrative apparatus, employment contracts, and repeated and general procedures and practices.[44] Activities were internalized within these firms when to be successful they required either a large knowledge base on the part of the firm, or maintenance of a good reputation among actual or potential clients. These activities included trading operations and their roles as agents for manufacturing, shipping, and insurance com-

[42] J. H. Drabble and P. J. Drake, "The British Agency House in Malaysia: Survival in a Changing World," *Journal of Southeast Asian Studies* 12:2 (1981): 308-9.

[43] P. T. Bauer, *The Rubber Industry* (London, 1948), 11; Huff, *Economic Growth*, 188.

[44] R. N. Langlois and P. L. Robertson, *Firms, Markets and Economic Change: A Dynamic Theory of Business Institutions* (London, 1995).

panies. By the interwar years these services were undertaken by wholly-owned overseas branches. This was the case from the beginning for the Borneo Company, but Harrisons & Crosfield and Finlays initially operated abroad through partnerships, and it was only in 1908 and 1909 respectively that these partnerships were replaced by wholly-owned branches. The overseas branch networks remained modest for two of the companies; in 1938 the Borneo Company had five overseas branches and Finlays had six branches. Harrisons & Crosfield, on the other hand, had at least twenty significant branches.

In these activities there were strong internalization incentives. Shipping companies depended on the local knowledge and reputations of their agents to generate flows of cargo and passengers. It was very important that malpractice or incompetence did not damage relationships with the shipping companies.[45] There were similar considerations with insurance companies. In the case of Finlays, for example, commission from insurance was one of the more important sources of income of its Calcutta branch in the 1900s. The firm acted as Calcutta agents for one life, four fire, and eight marine insurance companies. But the business was highly competitive and there were risks of opportunistic behavior by the numerous "native" canvassers used to sell policies. Excessive losses led to investigations by the insurance company concerned.[46] Given the close interlinking of trade, shipping and insurance business—the company typically arranged the shipping, and insurance of the goods they imported and exported—it was unsurprising that all three activities were fully internalized.

There were also strong internalization incentives for certain non-trading activities which were wholly-owned by the overseas branches. The Borneo Company's teak business, which was owned and managed by its Chiengmai branch, provides an example. This was a case of vertical integration motivated especially by the need to maximize the quality and reliability of teak supply. Teak was a long-term and capital-intensive business. Teak trees chosen for felling were "girdled," and thereafter the trees had to stand for at least three years so that they dried out and seasoned sufficiently to become floatable. The hilly terrain made elephants, and in some cases buffalo, the only means to transfer the logs to a river. In the 1890s the Borneo Company owned a herd of six hundred elephants to do this work. During the annual rainy season single logs were then floated down the rapids to collecting

[45] Gordon Boyce, *Information, Mediation and Institutional Development: The Rise of Large-Scale Enterprise in British Shipping, 1870-1919* (Manchester, 1995), 64-5.

[46] L. Hay to R. V. Mansell, 4 Apr. 1910, UGD 91/193.

*Jones and Wale / 386*

Borneo Company elephants in Thailand, c. 1910. An elephant team hauling teak through the Thai jungle, MS 27460, Guildhall Library. (Photograph reproduced courtesy of Inchcape plc.)

points in calmer waters, and then bound into rafts to be floated down to the Borneo Company sawmill in Bangkok. But the rains were unpredictable so teak supplies could fluctuate sharply, locking up large amounts of capital for several years. The high asset-specificity of felled trees, herds of elephants, and sawmills encouraged internalization.

There were much weaker internalization incentives in other areas of the business of the British trading companies such as plantations and manufacturing. Here alternative arrangements were adopted designed to secure access to trade flows and to information, while avoiding the risks involved in dealing in, say, tropical commodities where output and prices were unpredictable because of seasonal and cyclical fluctuations. The solution developed in the late nineteenth century was to place most non-trading activities into separately incorporated entities, with their own boards of directors, which were seldom wholly-owned. Frequently an overseas branch would secure a concession for plantation land or for a mine, and a separate company would then be formed to undertake this business. Alternatively a new business line, such as motor vehicle distribution, would be developed by an overseas branch and then, at a certain point, spun off into a separate company. Many of these new companies would be floated on the British equity markets—thus becoming "free-standing" companies—but some would also be registered in the country of operation. In both cases, the reputation for competence and honesty of the parent trading company was used to attract outside stockholders into investing in the new companies.

The share of the equity retained by the merchant house in these separately incorporated entities varied widely from a substantial percentage to sometimes as little as 1 percent or even less. There were several reasons for this. The parent firm sought income from commission and the provision of management services rather than dividends, so the general rule was that sufficient equity was taken to tie the affiliate to the parent. However in some cases new companies would be floated on the market and interest in the issues would be less than expected. Throughout the period the three companies also traded in the shares of affiliates, sometimes selling to make profits if prices were high, and buying if prices seemed cheap. There were inter-firm differences also. Harrisons & Crosfield often had very small shareholdings in the tea and rubber plantation companies in its orbit, though in a few cases the share of the equity reached 25 percent. Finlays took higher stakes on the whole. Its large Southeast Asian tea plantation interests were held in the four Glasgow-registered companies formed

*Jones and Wale / 388*

in the 1890s shown in Table 1 in which Finlays held a little less than one-third of the equity. These companies also held cross-shareholdings in one another.

It is hard to establish systematic patterns behind these shareholding percentages. There is some evidence of the British trading companies taking a higher percentage of the equity in the interwar years, perhaps reflecting declining new investment opportunities. The Borneo Company took more than three-quarters of the equity of the Singapore-registered Borneo Motors Ltd. in 1926. Harrisons & Crosfield held 41.7 percent of the issued capital of the British Borneo Timber Co. when it was formed in 1920. It also continued to hold small stakes only in some, though not all, of its new interwar plantation companies.[47]

In some respects debt was more important than equity within the business groups. The parent merchant house sometimes made substantial loans to affiliates and, conversely, affiliates with surplus cash would deposit them at the overseas branches. Within Finlays, debt was used as much as equity to finance overseas operations. During the 1900s a substantial proportion of the total assets of the James Finlay partnership, which amounted to just over £2 million ($9.7 million), consisted of advances to affiliate companies. These stood at around £500,000 ($2.4 million) in 1903 and 1904, had climbed to almost £600,000 ($2.9 million) by 1906, and then fell back to £455,000 ($2.2 million) by 1908. Over 90 percent of these advances were to the four Finlay tea companies which had been plunged into unprofitability by a major depression in India tea between 1900 and 1911.[48] Affiliates also borrowed large sums from English, Scottish, and overseas banks which were guaranteed by the trading company parent in return for a commission. In 1906, for example, only £40,000 ($194,000)—or 7 percent—of total Finlay advances was to the Champdany Jute Company, which owned Finlays' jute manufacturing enterprise. But this company, whose total capital was £200,000 ($970,000), had additional loans of £122,600 ($595,000) from banks guaranteed by Finlays. Throughout the period 1895 to 1916 Champdany's debt to Finlays and the banks under Finlay guarantee was at least 50 percent of its issued capital, and often much higher, reaching 120 percent of its capital in 1907 and 1908.[49]

[47] Records of British Borneo Timber Co. and list of shareholdings in "secretarial" companies, Harrisons & Crosfield archives, GL.

[48] Files on accounts, UGD 91/28/1,2,4.

[49] Champdany reports and accounts, UGD 91/162.

The affiliates within the business group were linked to the parent by cross-directorships. The directors of the parent would be well represented on the boards of all the London and Glasgow-registered companies, without regard for the size of the shareholding. In the interwar years each plantation company in the Harrisons & Crosfield group had a board of directors of whom the greater proportion were also members of the Harrisons & Crosfield board or had served as senior Harrisons & Crosfield managers in the East. This in turn led to most Harrisons & Crosfield directors holding directorships in multiple plantation companies, and a few held more than ten simultaneously for a long period of years.[50] In the case of locally-registered companies, senior managers at the overseas branches of the trading companies would typically provide several of the directors.

Most importantly, parents and affiliates were joined by management contracts. These were of two types. The trading companies would be appointed secretaries and/or "agents" to almost all affiliate companies regardless of the size of the equity shareholding. Typically the appointment would occur simultaneously with the creation and flotation of a limited liability company. The agreements made the parent merchant house the exclusive buying and selling agents for the companies. The secretarial function was performed in Britain. It involved the provision of full management support to the boards of directors of individual companies, the administration of the accounting and other information systems, and the issue and transfer of shares. Very often this function included the provision by the trading company of a boardroom in London or Glasgow where the directors of the affiliates could meet. Each agreement between Harrisons & Crosfield and a plantation company stipulated that Harrisons & Crosfield would put one (or in some cases two) of its own directors on the plantation company's board.[51] The agency function was based overseas and involved the management of the business on the spot. The duties were wide-ranging and included everything from securing staff and materials, to day-to-day management, to selling the output. In general, the agency function involved collecting, processing and transmitting to individual company boards in Britain all relevant information to assist decision-making.

Agency and secretarial agreements were for a set number of years, which could vary from one to fifteen years. They were typically

[50] Annual reports of Harrisons & Crosfield and plantation companies, Harrisons & Crosfield archives, GL.

[51] Agency agreements, Harrisons & Crosfield archives, GL.

## *Jones and Wale / 390*

renewed, but terms were modified from time to time. In the case of Harrisons & Crosfield's secretarial and agency agreements with plantation companies, the fundamentals of the agreements did not change at renewal, nor did the basic selling commission of 1.5 percent on gross proceeds, or the buying commission of 2.5 percent on imported and local purchases for the companies. However, agreements on the annual secretarial fee, the annual fee per acre, and the handling and shipping fee per pound of produce were modified from time to time.[52] It was most unusual for agreements not to be renewed once a relationship was formed.

In a commodity such as tea, different modes were employed at different stages. In both Harrisons & Crosfield and Finlays the plantations were in the hands of separately affiliated and partly-owned companies. This made sense in terms of risk-sharing, as tea production is a risky business because of seasonal fluctuations in yields and price movements. The wholly-owned branches were involved at the stage of selling and moving the produce, on which they earned various types of commission, as well as in providing management services, for which they received a fee.

At the marketing stage, capital requirements and the need for local information and contacts encouraged separate incorporation and part-ownership. However, there was considerable organizational experimentation, and differences persisted between Finlays and Harrisons & Crosfield. After experimentation with distribution through its own branches, Harrisons & Crosfield opted around the time of the First World War to merge its operations in consuming countries with local partners. In 1916 its U.K. distribution operation was merged with that of the old-established tea importer R. Twining as Twining Crosfield & Co. Ltd., and in the United States there were amalgamations with two leading importers and distributors in 1914 and 1924 to form the partly-owned Irwin-Harrisons-Whitney Inc, one of the largest tea importers in the United States in the interwar years.[53] Finlays had more control over its tea distribution venture, the Anglo-American Direct Tea Trading Company, than Harrisons & Crosfield had over its marketing affiliates, and it seems that the equity was closely held by Finlays and the other Finlay tea companies. In Britain, too, Finlays appear to have sought a higher level of ownership and control over its

[52] Ibid.

[53] Harrisons & Crosfield, *One Hundred Years as East India Merchants: Harrisons & Crosfield, 1844-1943* (London, 1944), 35-6; records of Irwin-Harrisons-Whitney, Harrisons & Crosfield archives, GL.

tea business, controlling its own warehouses, brokers, tasters, and packers. Neither firm sought to brand their teas, though Harrisons & Crosfield experimented with their own brand, "Nectar," before 1914.[54]

The organizational structure of the three British companies can be described as a business group consisting of the core trading company surrounded by a cluster of non-wholly-owned firms which engaged in repeated transactions with one another. Contracts formed a very important component of the links between the parent and the affiliated firms, but the parent was more than a market provider of consulting, distribution, and financial services, because there were also ties of equity and cross-directorships, and because the contracts were repeatedly renewed.

The boundaries of these business groups were permeable in a number of respects. As new activities were spun off into separate companies, there was an on-going process of new firm creation. Also, at the "outer edges" of the group, there were other activities with which repeated transactions were made. Banks were the most important category. The trading companies had long-term relationships with certain British domestic and/or overseas banks, and the credit facilities provided by these banks were important sources of funds, and at times critical. The Borneo Company, for example, had strong ties with the main British overseas banks in its region, Hongkong Bank and, especially, Chartered Bank. During the early 1930s, when the Borneo Company's fortunes were at such a low ebb that it could not pay dividends, bank overdrafts were critical for the company. Chartered provided a central overdraft facility, and the Borneo Company could choose whether it was utilized in London or at one of the overseas branches.[55] These commercial relationships were reinforced at board level. In the 1920s a director of the Borneo Company joined the board of Chartered Bank. Finlays were represented continuously on the board of the National Bank of India from 1895, and between 1936 and 1945 they shared the same chairman.[56] This Scottish company also had long-standing relations with members of the Scottish financial establishment, especially the Royal Bank of Scotland.

Harrisons & Crosfield also had a long-term relationship with a bank—the English clearing bank, Barclays. This relationship did not

[54] Harrisons & Crosfield's "Nectar" brand was mainly exported from the U.K. Within the U.K., before tea activities were hived off into Twining Crosfield, Harrisons & Crosfield undertook blending and packet labeling for named distributors. Harrisons & Crosfield, *One Hundred Years*, 15-16.

[55] Borneo Company board minutes, 19 Dec. 1934, MS 27178/20, GL.

[56] G. Tyson, *100 Years of Banking in Asia and Africa, 1863-1963* (London, 1963), 101.

extend to cross-directorships, but it was durable. It is possible that the connection originated in Quaker networks, since the original Harrisons & Crosfield partners were Quakers and Barclays and its predecessor banks were also strongly linked to the Quakers. Barclays overdrafts were important for Harrisons & Crosfield during its rapid expansion between 1910 and 1913, and even more so during the slump of 1921-2. Barclays were normally appointed bankers when Harrisons & Crosfield established a new company and became its secretaries and agents, although when Harrisons & Crosfield was not yet the agent in a plantation company's early years, the initial bankers were often retained.

The core trading companies had much to gain from the way the business groups worked. The income earned by them under agency and secretarial agreements for their services often provided a substantial proportion of their total income and was especially valuable as a source of income in that it was not linked to profits or dividends. Under the terms of most agreements, the agent earned commission on sales turnover or—in the case of plantations—planted acreage. Secretarial and agency fees were fixed amounts which did not vary either with profitability or turnover. During the early 1930s the relative importance of Harrisons & Crosfield's secretarial fees within its total income increased considerably since they were fixed while commission from sales of rubber and tea and from purchases for the estates fell because of declining activity.[57] At each stage of the production and associated activity of a tropical commodity, the trading company would derive its income. This included not only buying inputs for and selling outputs by plantations, but also commission on both shipping and insurance. Commission earned from insurance was often considerable. Each plantation company, for example, needed fire insurance for its products, premises, and fittings, as well as marine insurance for its products. Further commission was earned from guaranteeing bank loans to affiliated companies.

These arrangements help to explain the robustness of the core trading companies in the face of the external shocks of the interwar years. Figure 1 gives comparative data on return on capital employed (ROCE) between 1909 and 1941. In the case of Finlays, profit figures are missing for 1912 and 1921-22, while capital employed figures for 1910-20 are close estimates derived from various sources rather than actual data.[58]

[57] Harrisons & Crosfield ledgers, Harrisons & Crosfield archive, GL.
[58] Return on capital employed (ROCE) is profit after tax as a percentage of capital

*Figure 1*

Comparison of Return on Capital Employed after Tax: Harrisons & Crosfield, the Borneo Company and James Finlay, 1909–41

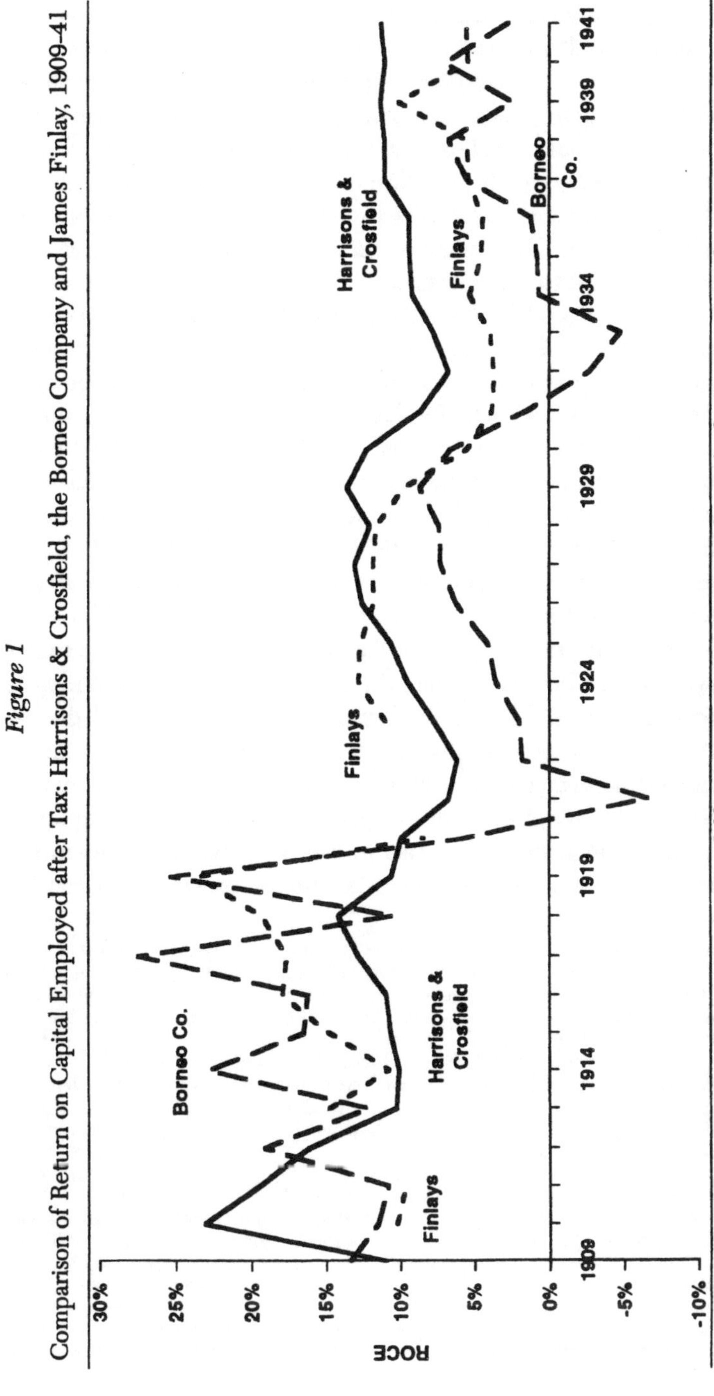


Source: Company Annual Accounts: GL for Harrisons & Crosfield, Borneo Co. (MS 27200, 27185 for BCL); The Company for Finlays. Note on Finlays: actual profits but estimated capital employed for 1910-11 and 1913-20; no data available for 1912 or 1921-2.

*Jones and Wale / 394*

The pre-war years emerged as highly profitable for all three firms, and during the First World War profits soared. In contrast, the 1920-21 recession was a major shock. However the three firms recovered well in the later 1920s. Harrisons & Crosfield's average ROCE between 1921 and 1941 was 9.8 percent and the dividend on its deferred ordinary shares ( which ranked behind larger issues of 6 percent preference and 10 percent preferred ordinary shares) averaged nearly 16 percent. Finlays' experience was not too dissimilar. The firm suffered major losses in the early 1920s—its four large Indian tea companies lost £458,000 ($1.68 million) in 1920 and its Indian piecegoods business lost over £160,000 ($615,000) in 1921—but there was subsequently a sharp recovery and in 1924 the same four tea companies earned profits of over £1.75 million ($7.72 million). ROCE after tax averaged 7.3 percent for 1924-41.[59] The Borneo Company's performance was much less impressive. The company paid no ordinary dividend for 1921-2, or 1932-40, while arrears of preference dividend accumulated between 1933 and 1936; these were paid by 1941. Losses were incurred in 1921 and 1932-3. The average ROCE for 1921-41 was only 2.7 percent.

Careful interpretation is needed of such return on capital calculations. They are based on published accounts, at a time when accounting conventions and lack of legislation in Britain permitted the existence of undisclosed reserves. There are for these companies no surviving internal accounts which might be more revealing of the reserves position. On the other hand, a recent extensive scrutiny of British company balance sheets, internal as well as published, demonstrates that by no means all companies used secret reserves in this period.[60] At

---

employed. Capital employed is share capital (ordinary + preference) + reserves (including profit and loss balance) + debentures + any other long term loans. ROCE has been a standard measure of company performance since the 1950s. It is applicable to the published accounts of earlier periods, given that there has been no fundamental change in the way in which such accounts are prepared. Its retrospective application can be further justified by the fact that contemporaries could have calculated ROCE if they had wished to do so; they had the necessary information. Knowledge of the meaning and usage behind the terminology appearing besides the various numbers on the credit side of balance sheets allows the historian to identify with reasonable accuracy those numbers which comprised the company's reserves.

[59] For Finlays' misfortunes in the early 1920s, see Brogan, *James Finlay*, 107, and "A Few Dates, Facts and Figures in the History of James Finlay & Co.," n.d., UGD 91/413/10.

[60] A. J. Arnold, "'Publishing Your Private Affairs to the World': Corporate Financial Disclosures in the U.K., 1900-24," *Accounting, Business & Financial History* 7:2 (1997): 162. If secret reserves did exist, ROCE figures would be slightly lower than those calculated from the published accounts. There is evidence that contemporaries regarded the accounts as a worthwhile source of information. The banks which granted trading companies (and other companies) overdrafts for their head offices in Britain and for their overseas branches were eager to receive the accounts each year for the purpose of assessment of creditworthiness.

any rate, over a sufficiently long timespan it is plausible to argue that the main performance trends can be discerned from the published accounts and, in particular, that inter-firm differences can be identified.

The range of outcomes in return on capital employed in Harrisons & Crosfield, the Borneo Company, and Finlays in the interwar years can be explained in a number of ways. An important factor was the fate of the commodities in which the three firms dealt. The Borneo Company was badly damaged by falling teak prices after 1929, and especially by the introduction of Imperial Preference in favor of teak from India and Burma.[61] The other two companies were greatly affected by the price falls in tea and rubber. After the disastrous fall in tea prices in 1920, Finlays was hit again by declining tea prices from the late 1920s until the International Tea Agreement took effect in 1933. Harrisons & Crosfield benefited from the boom in rubber prices in the mid-1920s, but was then hit by the decline in rubber prices before the industry was "stabilized" under the International Rubber Regulatory Committee from 1934. The terms of the restrictive agreements in rubber may not have—as has often been argued—explicitly favored the British-owned rubber plantations as against the Malay smallholders, but at the very least it protected them from pressures to invest in technological change.[62] This linkage illustrates the extent to which the incomes of the British trading companies were sustained by international cartels, commodity quotas and other collusive arrangements. However, the diversified nature of these business groups—and the near-impossibility of identifying the profitability of different activities from surviving archival records—means that the correlation between their profitability and individual commodity prices is not complete. While the fortunes of Finlays were heavily dependent on tea prices, for example, the Finlay group were also cotton goods manufacturers in Scotland and India, jute and sugar manufacturers in India, and insurance and import agents.

The varied performance of the firms could also be related to differences in management quality, although this variable is unquantifiable. However there is good evidence that in the late 1920s the Borneo Company's difficulties were compounded by managerial fail ings. Its wholly-owned Haboko Tea Company in the Dutch East Indies suffered from poor, and allegedly fraudulent, management as well as the problem of heavy losses. In 1931 the Borneo Company took

[61] Longhurst, *Borneo Story*, 77.

[62] J. H. Drabble, *Malayan Rubber: The Interwar Years* (London, 1991), 304-5.

*Jones and Wale / 396*

the unusual step of appointing Harrisons & Crosfield as the managing agents of this company.[63] The Borneo Motors affiliate experienced a downward trend of profits from the date of its formation as a public company in 1926 and paid no dividends between 1929 and 1933, a sustained recovery only occurring from the mid-1930s.[64] In 1932 the Borneo Company's chairman resigned, and there were a number of in-house investigations trying to identify unprofitable parts of the business which could be closed down.[65] There is no parallel suggestion of managerial problems in the other two companies and, indeed, their interwar diversifications into East African tea, rubber manufacture, and chemicals distribution suggest a more confident as well as competent management.

The ability of the core merchant house to withstand the interwar fluctuations in primary commodities, and in two of the cases earn quite high returns on capital employed, might also be seen as resting on the outside shareholders in the affiliated companies.[66] They paid in a variety of ways for the services of the trading company and the fees of the directors placed on their boards. Harrisons & Crosfield managed by far the largest number of such companies and it also earned the highest return on capital employed. However, although the costs might be high, so were the services provided wide-ranging, and they extended to more than "merely" managing. An important feature of many agency agreements of plantation companies were provisions to enable the quality of products to be monitored and in some cases improved. Harrisons & Crosfield, for example, provided specialist technical services for its affiliated plantation companies. In 1925 it purchased the Prang Besar Estate which had been created in 1921 as a new estate in Malaya designed to produce high-yielding rubber trees. The techniques developed at Prang Besar were diffused to the other rubber companies in the business group and led to productivity improvements.

However there were self-evidently potential conflicts of interest within the business groups. Commission incomes based on sales provided an incentive to promote growth through retained earnings, and thus to suppress the distribution of profits to the shareholders of affil-

[63] Borneo Company board minutes, 19 and 26 Nov. 1930, 3 and 31 Dec. 1930, 14 Jan. 1931, MS 27178/19, GL; Agreement between Haboko Tea Co. and Harrisons & Crosfield, 22 Apr. 1931, MS 27357, GL.

[64] Borneo Motors Ltd. annual reports, MS 27373, GL.

[65] Borneo Company board minutes, 27 May 1931, MS 27178/19, and 11 Jan. 1933, MS 27178/20, GL.

[66] Annual reports and accounts of Harrisons & Crosfield (GL), Finlays (the company), and the Borneo Company (MS 27185, GL).

Borneo tea estate, c. 1900. The Borneo Company's Haboko tea estate in the Dutch East Indies (Indonesia), MS 27447, Guildhall Library. (Photograph reproduced courtesy of Inchcape plc.)

Jute Mill in Calcutta, 1940. View of James Finlays' jute mill in Calcutta (Photograph reproduced courtesy of James Finlay plc.)

iated firms. Certainly the system could deliver anomalous outcomes. When Finlay Muir in Calcutta was appointed agent of Champdany Jute Company on its formation in 1873, it received a 5 percent commission on the amount of sales. As Champdany's performance was not very good in the two decades before the First World War and profitability was far more volatile than sales, this was a satisfactory arrangement for Finlays. Between 1897 and 1900 no dividends were paid to the ordinary shareholders, but Finlay Muir earned £41,000 ($198,000) in commission over the four-year period.[67] These conflicts of interest were made transparent when seven outside shareholders in the Champdany Jute Company took legal action against Finlays in the Scottish courts in 1895. Two of the four separate accusations made against Finlays related to the interest paid on Finlay loans to Champdany and the level of commission income earned by Finlays.[68]

The legal action was finally dropped in 1899 before a final judgement, but it had significant repercussions. In a complex reorganization of the capital structure in 1897, a scheme was launched whereby one-half of the ordinary shares could be converted to preference shares with a 5 percent dividend on their nominal value—provided the shareholder gave no support for the on-going legal action—while Finlays agreed to buy back the new preference shares at a price around double the market rate for the ordinary shares.[69] Finlays thereby allowed the minority shareholders to realize one-half of their shareholdings at a reasonable price. The scheme reduced the voting power of the minority shareholders, whose number fell over time. Initially only 40 percent owned by Finlays, by 1920 less than 5 percent of the stock was not controlled by Finlays or the Muir family. Despite this shift in ownership, greater care was also taken in the formal relationship between Finlays and Champdany. In the 1900s James Finlay in Britain and Finlay Muir in Calcutta continued to receive commission on the range of services they provided for Champdany—including the buying and selling of jute, insuring the properties, and guaranteeing bank advances—but the formal board minutes always recorded that the

[67] "Statements, Figures, Accounts of More than Passing Interest," UGD 91/168. This situation was not unique. See Chapman, *Merchant Enterprise*, 301.

[68] Ross E. Stewart, "Scottish Company Accounting, 1870 to 1920: Selected Case Studies of Accounting in its Historical Context" (unpublished Ph.D. thesis, University of Glasgow, 1986), 327-50. There is also an excellent final year undergraduate dissertation on the Champdany case by Alistair Smith, "The Champdany Jute Company Ltd., 1873-1921," Department of Economic History, Glasgow, Oct. 1988.

[69] The shareholders would consequently fall into two distinct groups: those who exited from the company by taking advantage of the selling price offered, and those who decided to remain with the company and who would have an interest in future dividends and future movements in return on capital employed.

Finlay directors abstained from voting.[70] This practice also became the norm in the affiliate companies of Harrisons & Crosfield and The Borneo Company.[71]

The striking thing about the Champdany Jute case was its rarity. The case had originated in special circumstances. The company had been launched with less than 50 shareholders—most of them related to Finlays or the Muir family in some fashion—and, although a limited liability company, it initially resembled more closely a private company. However a number of factors broke down the atmosphere of trust. As some of the original shareholders died, their estates came into the hands of trustees who had fiduciary obligations to seek the maximum value of their investments. Champdany's shares were listed in the Glasgow Stock Exchange in 1889. Just as the shareholder profile changed, tensions grew. Champdany's dividend performance was consistently poorer than the average for the Calcutta jute industry. From the late 1890s, however, the transfer of share ownership into Finlay hands diminished the grounds for conflict.

The rarity of the Champdany case might suggest that the trading companies seldom sought to pursue their interests to such an extent that outside shareholders were blatantly disadvantaged. In part this was because the merchant houses were themselves shareholders, so dividends were also of concern to them. But the boards of affiliated companies retained some autonomy and legal responsibilities to all their shareholders. Typically they would negotiate the level of agency and secretarial fees, authorize capital expenditure recommended by the agents, and request and receive information on production and sales. The trading companies also sought to encourage confidence in their integrity by postponing, reducing or forgoing commissions when corporate performance was very bad.[72] Given that the creation of new affiliates continued at least up to the 1920s, maintaining a reputation for honesty and good management was essential for raising further outside capital. However it is also evident that the shareholdings of many companies were closely held, often it would seem by people linked in social or familial networks, and for the most part these people were not ones to complain or even to sell their shares to secure a higher return.

The three British trading companies faced a number of classic agency problems to which they responded with alternative institutional and contractual arrangements. Certain activities subject to high

[70] Champdany board minutes, 1899-1914, UGD 91/178/5.
[71] Board minutes of plantation companies, Harrisons & Crosfield archives, GL.
[72] Ibid.; Stewart, "Scottish Company Accounting," 261.

transaction costs were fully internalized, while in other cases coordination was achieved without full ownership and control. The managements of the parent companies were undoubtedly concerned with longevity and sought to use funds generated in one activity to fund new opportunities elsewhere. This may offend against contemporary Anglo-American expectations of managerial behavior, but the system helped the firms to survive a period of considerable economic turbulence, and to some extent funded innovation, as in the case of Harrisons & Crosfield's research on high-yielding rubber.

## Management Systems

Many of the criticisms of the quality of the management of the British merchant houses—and British "personal capitalism" in general—have centered on the problems of family ownership and the partnership form. However, Finlays was the only one of the three companies in which a family influence persisted into the interwar years, and its financial performance was notably better than that of the Borneo Company. The issue of managerial competencies is however wider than debates about "personal capitalism," and it is important to establish the nature of the management systems operated by the companies.

In all these cases the heart of the management was the board of directors in London or, in Finlays' case, Glasgow. The boards were small—that of Harrisons & Crosfield usually consisted of up to nine persons—and made executive decisions at (usually) weekly meetings. The directors made overall strategic decisions, but also concerned themselves with a vast range of other issues from the selection of staff to approving small items of expenditure, despite the small size of their head office staff.

The directors made entrepreneurial decisions, but few modern heroic figures stand out, though a number of individuals were especially important. Sir John Muir was the dominant influence on Finlays between the 1860s and his death in 1903. He was primarily responsible for the key diversification into India and tea. In the mid-1920s his son Sir Kay Muir took the decision to diversify into Kenya, while his younger brother James Finlay Muir, who replaced him as chairman in 1926, vigorously supervised the growth of the East African business. At Harrisons & Crosfield, Arthur Lampard, appointed as director in 1894, was largely responsible for the establishment of overseas branches and the development of rubber plantations in Malaya.[73] In general, however, the directors functioned as teams, as they did at the Borneo Company. One writer in 1951 concluded that the "secret" of Harrisons & Crosfield's success lay "in the collective ability of the board rather than the brilliance of any one director."[74]

This "collective ability" rested on access to knowledge and information which permitted effective decisions to be taken. Most directors had served with their companies overseas for long periods and accumulated considerable regional product-specific experience. At Harrisons & Crosfield, the normal route to a directorship was through long service abroad, culminating in a senior managerial position overseas, such as branch managing director. Each tended to become a specialist, so that at any given time Harrisons & Crosfield's London board included experts in rubber, tea, timber, general trading, etc. It was the norm at Harrisons & Crosfield and the other companies for directors to spend months overseas at a time, during which they would inspect operations in detail and report to the rest of the board. Conversely, senior staff when they came back to Britain on leave would visit head office and provide directors with up-to-date information.

The accumulation of information and decision-making at board level had the potential to become excessive and lead to overload. Harrisons & Crosfield's rapid growth before the First World War led to precisely such an outcome, and the result was a clarification of directors' duties and an administrative reorganization. Three main functions of directors were identified: to monitor essential facts only; to supervise specific parts of the business; and to plan future strategies. Each director was given a specific aspect of operations to be in charge of, and three advisory committees of directors were formed to cover plantations, trading, and general administration. A major aim of the reorganization was to devolve far more administrative work to supporting head office staff, who were in turn organized into a departmental committee structure which mirrored that of the directors and their committees.[75] This system stayed in place in the interwar years.

The centralization of control at the head office was combined with the delegation of other decisions to different layers within the wider group. These included the directors of affiliated companies, but also

[73] Harrisons & Crosfield, *One Hundred Years*, 20-9.

[74] K. M. Stahl, *The Metropolitan Organization of British Colonial Trade* (London, 1951), 92.

[75] Report of the Organization Committee, 18 July 1919, Harrisons & Crosfield archives, GL.

*Jones and Wale / 402*

overseas branch managers and managers of estates. This delegation enabled the head offices to function without large bureaucracies but, more significantly, it was the best means of conducting businesses engaged in trade and commodities, where up-to-date information and knowledge of local circumstances were vital. An important consequence of this system was that the information on which decisions were taken was spread quite widely within the enterprise.

Chandler has described at length how "the personal ways or culture of British management differed from the managerial ways or culture of American and German firms."[76] For the most part, British enterprises lacked the extensive managerial hierarchies and the organization charts which were found in the modern industrial enterprises of the two other countries. It is evident that this "personal" style is mirrored in the administration of these three firms with, for example, the central role of directors, their personal visits of inspection to overseas branches, and so on. Yet the degree of amateurism or lack of system should not be exaggerated. All three firms had management information systems in place. Information flows in and out of London and Glasgow were very large, both as regards the number of communications by telegram, letter and report, and as regards the detail of reporting. Overseas branches reported at regular intervals to their head offices, invariably providing detailed financial information and analysis of all aspects of the business.

The delegation of some decision-making to overseas managers made their quality, reliability and motivation of central importance. Staff were recruited often as the result of personal recommendation or acquaintance with directors. At Finlays, potential employees were extensively questioned on their family backgrounds, their family's position in society, and the occupations of their relatives.[77] The upshot was that the trading companies sought respectable, privately educated young British men for their management cadres. This was the convention for British overseas business at the time, but at least two of the firms showed an interest in recruiting university graduates. Harrisons & Crosfield was actively recruiting graduates by at least the end of the First World War,[78] though over time the company shifted towards recruiting people with special technical skills, especially accounting and engineering. Finlays also recruited graduates from this period,

[76] Chandler, *Scale and Scope*, 242.
[77] Stewart, "Scottish Company Accounting," 218.
[78] Report of the Organization Committee, 18 July 1919, Harrisons & Crosfield archives, GL.

especially from Glasgow University, as well as employing Chartered Accountants. However other British trading companies, such as Swires in East Asia, were recruiting a much higher percentage of graduates (mostly from Oxford and Cambridge) by the interwar years, and none of the British companies matched the large-scale employment of graduates undertaken by large Japanese trading companies such as Mitsui Bussan from the early twentieth century.[79]

Once recruited, staff were socialized into strong corporate cultures. Finlays and the Borneo Company were very Scottish in their ethos and recruitment, and their corporate cultures drew on "traditional" Scottish values of moral probity as well as financial acumen. As one of the greatest threats to a trading company was from unauthorized speculative dealing, corporate cultures tended to include ritual denunciations of such activity. "We intend to adhere to what has been the rule of our Firm in the past," Finlays' Calcutta branch affirmed in 1910, "and to go in as little as possible for business of a speculative nature. We prefer to do a small business on safe lines rather than a large one on speculative lines."[80] The result was the creation of a managerial cadre which could be relied upon not to act opportunistically, while long service overseas gave them extensive tacit knowledge of their region of operation. In all three companies there were incentives and expectations for managers to learn local languages such as Malay and Tamil.

In their overall recruitment strategy and use of socialization strategies, the British merchant houses were similar to the British overseas banks of the period.[81] However the trading companies had a more commercial culture. On the other hand, they did not rely entirely, or even primarily, on corporate cultures to monitor or incentivize their managers. Although there was an expectation of lifetime employment, managers were appointed on three to five year contracts which were not renewed automatically. At Finlays, at least before the First World War, as each contract neared expiry, there would be a negotiation about terms and conditions of the next one, if one was to be offered.[82] The performance and behavior of individual staff were discussed at board meetings, and monitoring was reinforced by periodic visitations from

[79] Shin'ichi Yonekawa, "General Trading Companies in a Comparative Context," in *General Trading Companies: A Comparative and Historical Study*, ed. Shin'ichi Yonekawa (Tokyo, 1992), 8-32. For Swires, see London staff ledger, Swire archives, School of Oriental and African Studies, London, JSS I/5/1.

[80] J.F. Calcutta to J.F. Bombay, 11 Feb. 1910, UGD 91/447/6/I.

[81] Jones, *British Multinational Banking*, 49-51.

[82] Correspondence in UGD 91/447/2/1.

*Jones and Wale / 404*

directors and head office staff. Before 1914 such on-the-spot investigations had an ad hoc nature. At Finlays, the autocratic Sir John Muir made regular visits to India during which offending staff would be harangued or dismissed.[83] In the interwar years more regular procedures were put in place. Harrisons & Crosfield had two branch traveling inspectors charged with visiting every branch and affiliated company once a year. The criteria employed to judge staff were implicit, but the financial performance of the branch or activity in which the staff member was involved would be the leading criterion of "success" or "failure." Evidence of the energetic pursuit of business was also well regarded, provided it took place within the accepted norms of the firm and did not take the form of "speculation." Given the importance of flows of information to the London and Glasgow head offices, the most highly regarded managers in all three companies were good communicators who took the initiative of keeping the head office informed of new opportunities as well as providing clear accounts of existing activities and problems. Behavior which was unorthodox or unacceptable to the expatriate community was very badly regarded.

An important element of the employment contracts of managers was their entitlement to commission. As a broad generalization it can be said that from the late nineteenth century many trading company managers were paid by a combination of a fixed salary and a commission on profits, as well as sometimes receiving bonuses, though some staff were paid entirely by a fixed amount, while others were paid solely on commission with guaranteed minimum. An examination by Ross Stewart of 620 employment contracts offered by Finlays showed growing numbers of overseas employees receiving commission. The use of commission meant that accounting practices within the organization had to be transparent. At Finlays there was a broad trend for the basis of the commission to get more tightly defined over time. In the late nineteenth century commission was paid on sales figures at overseas branches or on the basis of cash remitted to the head office. Subsequently rather more specific definitions of "profits" were employed with specific provisions about what items should be charged to the profit and loss account before commission was paid.[84] Given the importance of inter-branch trading and the diverse activities of the trading companies, there was room for considerable tensions to arise between branches and affiliates as to who had the rights to particular

[83] Minute book of managers of Finlay Muir, Calcutta, 1895-1900, UGD 91/110.
[84] Stewart, "Scottish Company Accounting," 186-217.

business and commission. Harrisons & Crosfield, which had the largest number and spread of branches and affiliates, went furthest in addressing this problem in 1920 when it issued detailed rules on inter-branch trading, which established the procedures to be followed, and basis of commission to be charged, in all possible circumstances that could arise between an exporting branch and an importing branch.[85]

A potential problem with the payment of commission to staff was that it might give the wrong incentives, leading towards, for example, excessive or artificial short-term maximization of profits. The use of four or five year contracts was one safeguard against this eventuality. Moreover, these contracts were binding. At Finlays, in the instances where employees terminated their contracts for reasons other than ill-health, employees were required to pay a fine equivalent to their annual salary.[86] Moreover, unwelcome behavior was checked both by the various monitoring systems and by moral corporate cultures. When Arthur Lampard introduced a system of payment of plantation superintendents by results, fears were expressed that they would maximize tapping in the short term to the detriment of the long-term future of the plantations. However Lampard expressed his "confidence" in the plantation managers, and "even were [they] capable of such a short-sighted policy," he felt there was a system of visiting agents to act as a check "which would immediately put a stop to anything of this kind."[87]

## Conclusion

This article has examined the strategy, organization, and management of three British multinational merchant groups from the late nineteenth century to the Second World War. Rather than being regarded as primarily financial in function, they have been cast as entrepreneurial enterprises which used their knowledge of countries and products to search for new opportunities for trade. They set up organizational systems and flexible organizations to exploit these opportunities. These characteristics were most evident in the expanding world economy before 1914, but still evident in the interwar years, when the companies deepened their involvement with their host regions while also

[85] Harrisons & Crosfield, Regulations in regard to Inter-branch Trading adopted by the Board on 6 January 1920, Harrisons & Crosfield archives, GL.

[86] Stewart, "Scottish Company Accounting," 214.

[87] A. Lampard to V. Ris, 24 Feb. 1911, Harrisons & Crosfield archives, GL.

*Jones and Wale / 406*

searching for opportunities elsewhere. These three companies, and their counterparts, were important components of British FDI in this period. The financial performance of at least Harrisons & Crosfield and James Finlay has been shown to be reasonable in the interwar context in so far as it can be measured and compared to others, and bearing in mind that it rested in part on collusive agreements. As for whether opportunities were "missed," the three companies might or might not have benefited from greater involvement in interwar India or Southeast Asia in industrialization through import substitution. The diversifications which they did undertake, however, built on existing core competencies and proved, with hindsight, well judged.

The article has suggested that the organizational structures employed by these British firms to control their diversified operations should be seen as more than devices to capture rents. They functioned as "business groups" rather than "investment groups" in which different modes were employed in response to different cost structures and to achieve different goals. They internalized activities with high transactions costs. In other cases they avoided the costs of full internalization by using contracts, minority equity stakes, and cross-directorships to secure access to trade flows and information, and to monitor quality. This worked to the financial benefit of the core concern, but it is not evident that outside shareholders were exploited in any meaningful sense, though undoubtedly the overall emphasis of the system was towards survival rather than short-run dividend maximization.

The core competencies of the British trading companies lay in knowledge and information, and their internal management structures reflected this. The centralization of decision-making at the level of the directors worked in part because of the tacit knowledge these persons possessed of commodities and countries, and because of personal links into other business networks. Despite the central coordinating and monitoring of boards, decision-making was also spread within the network. Overseas branch managers and plantation managers took routine decisions, negotiated contracts, and received and generated information. The system entailed potentially acute agent/principal problems, but these issues were both identified and often addressed by the trading companies. They developed effective monitoring procedures, staff recruitment policies, incentive structures, and management information and accounting systems, none of which were static. Especially from around the time of the First World War, the introduction of more formalized control procedures and the appointment of more formally qualified staff is observable.

*Merchants as Business Groups / 407*

Compared to contemporary developments in the United States, the managerial competencies of these three firms look fragile. U.S.-style managerial hierarchies and information systems were far from evident. The British model involved management from Britain by directors who possessed considerable tacit knowledge of regions and products, who controlled their managerial staff by recruiting from specific social networks and then motivating them by commission payments. It was not a system that would have sustained a modern industrial enterprise in chemicals or automobile manufacture. However, it worked well for these complex business groups based around trade and resource exploitation in developing countries. Even during the interwar years—hardly an auspicious time for firms engaged in international trade and primary products—they survived, continued to evolve and, with the exception of the Borneo Company in the 1930s, paid dividends to shareholders.

Self-evidently, the managerial competencies of these British firms, residing in information and knowledge, suggested that they functioned best within a relatively narrow range of activities. They were capable of innovation—such as improving crop yields—but were unlikely to be pioneers of radical new technologies or processes. On the other hand, the continued ability of their management to evolve was striking. They survived the Second World War, the end of commodity cartels, and decolonization.[88] In 1967 the Borneo Company merged into the international trading and shipping firm Inchcape. At the end of the 1970s Inchcape and Harrisons & Crosfield —by then European-style *sogo shosha* (general trading companies)—were ranked 19th and 91st largest U.K. companies by turnover, and James Finlay 448th. Twenty years later these firms still continued in existence and were still evolving. Inchcape and Harrisons & Crosfield were restructuring as international automobile distribution and speciality chemicals companies respectively, while James Finlay after a period of diversification had become once more an international tea trader and owner of plantations.

In a wider context, the material presented here contributes to the continuing debate about British management as a whole before the Second World War. The "personal" style of management, so heavily critiqued by scholars making comparisons with U.S. managerial capitalism, was without doubt important in explaining British failures at

[88] For a study of the Borneo Company after the Second World War, see Nicholas J. White, *Business, Government, and the End of Empire: Malaya, 1942-1957* (Kuala Lumpur, 1996), chapter 6.

*Jones and Wale / 408*

various times in capital-intensive manufacturing activities. However, this style worked better than might have been expected in some other activities, including the management of a truly formidable amount of FDI spread round the world.[89]

[89] This argument is explored in Geoffrey Jones, "Great Britain: Big Business, Management and Competitiveness in Twentieth-Century Britain," in *Big Business and the Wealth of Nations*, eds. Alfred D. Chandler, Franco Amatori, and Takashi Hikino (Cambridge, Mass., 1997).

# [4]

*By Kwang-Ching Liu*
GRADUATE STUDENT AT
HARVARD UNIVERSITY

# Financing a Steam-Navigation Company in China, 1861-62[1]

*Russell & Co., the Boston partnership which had long been prominent in the China trade, found its business as commission agent in a state of serious decline by 1861. Therefore Edward Cunningham, a junior partner resident in Shanghai, conceived the idea of founding a steamship line to operate up the Yangtze River. This venture would require a capital far exceeding that used by Russell & Co. in its commission business. The head of the firm, Paul Sieman Forbes, who lived in New York and Newport, spurned the project in favor of more lucrative and secure investments in the United States. Cunningham then showed his promotional abilities by raising the necessary capital in China. Not only was the resultant Shanghai Steam Navigation Company profitable in itself, it also brought much commission business to Russell & Co. This article, based mainly on the manuscript records of the Forbes family, contributes to a more realistic estimate of the amount of American capital in the Far Eastern trade and to a greater appreciation of the administrative problems and methods involved.*

The old China trade is still in the memory of New England and stands as a record of this country's relations with the Far East. The extensive activities of American agencies and commission houses in China typify the expansion of mercantile capitalism. A forgotten episode in this story is the steam-navigation enterprise established by Russell & Co. in 1861–62 and successfully operated by this firm until 1877, when it was sold to a Chinese company. This enterprise had at one time a fleet of 18 steamers, magnificent American steamboats of the Hudson or Charleston types – larger

[1] This study represents the first attempt to use the Forbes Collection at Baker Library, part of an extensive donation to Harvard by Mr. W. Cameron Forbes (see Robert W. Lovett, "The Collection of W. Cameron Forbes," *Harvard Library Bulletin*, Vol. 5 [Autumn, 1951], 381–5). Other sources in Baker Library concerning Russell & Co. are discussed in "China and Foreign Devils," *Bulletin of the Business Historical Society*, III (Nov., 1929), 9–19, and "Perkins & Co., 1803–1827," *ibid.*, VI (March, 1932), 1–5. Printed papers of the Shanghai Steam Navigation Company – the original collection of Henry Sturgis Grew – can be found in Widener Library. (On H. S. Grew, see the biographical note in his *Letters from China and Manila, 1855–1862* [privately printed, 1927].)

in its time than the steam fleet of any British firm in China. From 1867 to 1872, this American fleet had a virtual monopoly of the steam traffic on the Yangtze River, while enjoying a dominant position also in some lines on the China coast. As Robert Bennet Forbes recalls in his brief history of Russell & Co., it was this steam enterprise which kept that old commission house going in the last years of the maritime expansion of Massachusetts: [2]

> Throughout this period of steam prosperity the house flourished also, making up for the decay of the general trade by local business brought in by the control of the steam company. Their income was as large as their most prosperous years. . . .

Today this story should be of interest to the historians of the American steamboat, for this is the first time, as it were, that American and British steamers of river and coastal types were brought to a contest. In the very years when Britain was taking away from the United States her lead in ocean steam, American steamboats – the low-draft sidewheelers perfected in America's own internal waterway expansion – proved to be far superior in these distant waters of China. (These were boats between 500 and 2,000 tons; some of them were "knocked down" and sent to China in sailing vessels, to be set up there.) No better testimony to their superiority can be given than this from a British official report from Hong Kong dated 1861: [3]

> As far as river navigation is concerned, our attempts to compete with Jonathan are simply absurd, as those who own English steamers here at present, must, ere this, have discovered to their cost. But, even in sea-going steamers, if "the proof of the pudding be in the eating," we should wish to know where the British steamers are, which are as swift, as safe, as commodious, as serviceable or as economical in expenditure of fuel as *Yangtze* or *Peiho*?

As late as 1865, the Commissioner of Customs at Shanghai reported: [4]

[2] Robert B. Forbes, *Personal Reminiscences*, 2nd ed. rev. (Boston, 1882), 366. In 1876, on the eve of the sale of the Russell fleet to the Chinese-government-sponsored China Merchants' Steam Navigation Company, it had a total of 16 steamers (a total of 11,204 tons); among the rival companies in China, the China Navigation Company (Butterfield & Swire & Co., agents) had six steamers, the China Coast Steam Navigation Company (Jardine, Matheson & Co., agents) had six, while the China Merchants' Steam Navigation Company had just overtaken the American fleet by having 17 steamers (a total of 11,706 tons). (Imperial Maritime Customs, *Report on Trade at the Treaty Ports*, 1877 [Shanghai, 1878], 76–77; also references in *North-China Herald*, Shanghai, hereafter *NCH*.)

[3] Quoted in Fred E. Dayton, *Steamboat Days* (New York, 1925), 375–82. The date of this report is determined by its mention of the American-built steamer *Yangtze* (owned by Dent & Co.) as having run for nearly three years.

[4] Imperial Maritime Customs, *Report on Trade at the Treaty Ports*, 1865

The Americans at Shanghai are as in the case everywhere else [in China], in the ascendant as regards shipping; it is impossible to compete with their steamers, except by opposing them with others of the same kind, and built on the same model. On the Yangtze line, seven steamers out of nine are American; the others are distributed on the Ningpo, Hongkong and Japan routes. . . .

From the point of view of business history, however, what is perhaps more significant than the American technological triumph represented by this enterprise is the triumph of American entrepreneurship, for the difficult practical question was: how was Russell & Co. to find the capital to buy American steamboats? A commission house in the China trade, Russell & Co. had acted mainly for constituents and had very little capital of its own. How then did it solve the problem of its transition to the industrial age? Was it possible at the time to get fresh capital from the United States?

The noteworthy aspect of Russell & Co.'s steam-navigation enterprise, as the following pages will show, is the fact that it did *not* rely on the capital of the commission house itself, nor on investment from the United States. Chiefly as a result of the efforts of a younger China merchant, Edward Cunningham (1823–89) of East Milton, Massachusetts,[5] capital for the enterprise was organized locally in China, among subscribers mainly composed of Chinese compradormerchants and British traders residing in China. The story of this enterprise is therefore primarily that of a *tour de force* in the work of promotion – in the unique setting of China's treaty ports.

From the point of view of business institutions, the arrangement by which local capital was brought into the enterprise is also of interest, for this arrangement was in fact an extension of a time-honored practice of commission houses, which frequently acted as agents for owners of vessels. The capital of Russell & Co.'s steam-

(Shanghai, 1866), 133. After 1871, primarily because of the lower cost of building in Britain, Russell & Co. itself ordered all its new steamers from Glasgow – furnished with English machinery, but built on American models. (See Cunningham to P. S. Forbes, 18 and 20 April, and Cunningham to Russell & Co., Shanghai, 18 May 1871, Forbes Collection – hereafter FC.) Of Russell & Co.'s 16 steamers in 1876, six were such English-built American models. (U.S. Congress, *House Miscellaneous Documents*, 45th Cong., 2nd sess., no. 31, "Testimony taken before the Committee on Expenditures in the State Department" [Washington, D. C., 1878], part 2, pp. 230–1.)

[5] Edward Cunningham was clerk with Russell & Co., 1845–49, and partner, 1850–57, 1861–63, and 1867–77. In 1850–54, he was very active in his capacity as American Vice-Consul in Shanghai. (Tyler Dennett, *Americans in Eastern Asia* [New York, 1922], 210 and 217 ff.) Cp. Cunningham's own essay, *Our Political and Commercial Relations with China* (Washington, D. C., 1855); copy in Massachusetts Historical Society.

navigation enterprise was organized on a joint-stock basis, under the Shanghai Steam Navigation Company. However, Russell & Co. was to serve as "permanent agents and treasurers" of this company – actually to manage and control its entire business. Russell & Co. was thus, in the full role of the modern entrepreneur, operating a large-scale transport service.

In the years 1861–62, when Edward Cunningham was working on the creation of this enterprise, John Heard, of the rival American house Augustine Heard & Co., was still in Shanghai. In his memoirs (written in 1891), he writes: [6]

> An attempt was made about this time to get up a steamer company. Russell & Co. were the promoters and after some vicissitudes, it was successful, under the name of the Shanghai Steam Navigation Company. We had a plan of the same kind under consideration but I gave it up. I still think we were right in doing so, for although Russell & Co. were very successful, for a long time it had the effect of merging the house – the mercantile house – into a steamer agency.

From the point of view of the mercantile tradition, "steamer agency" was perhaps a less dignified business. Yet it was surely more in step with the industrial age, which Western traders were at this time ushering into Asia.

## The Commission House and the Steam Fleet

Russell & Co.'s opportunity to enter into the steam-navigation business in China came at a time when its traditional commission business in trade had declined, as a result of the new speculative tendency in the China trade and British competition in imports to the United States. Edward Cunningham analyzed the situation as of early 1861 as follows: "I see all our business gone & I look around to find who has it. Not Heards, or any house on commission. It is being done by parties on their own account. . . . The business has become too complicated to be done by agents. Distant principals fall off and trade falls into the hands of those who will operate themselves on the spot." [7]

[6] John Heard, III, "Diary, 1891," Heard Collection (at Baker Library, hereafter HC), FP-4, pp. 139–40. Heard & Co. operated normally one and sometimes two steamers on the Yangtze River in the period 1861–67, but did not set up a large project like Russell & Co.'s. Cp. Mary Gertrude Mason, "Aspects of the Trade between China and America, 1840–1870," *Bulletin of the Business Historical Society*, X (April, 1936), 24–28.

[7] Cunningham to P. S. Forbes, 4 June 1861, FC. (Cunningham in this letter overstates the case, since the commission business of Russell & Co. continued for many years after 1861; see below, p. 180. For further description of

For the new term of partnership 1861–63, two important partners were sent over to China: Edward Cunningham, to return to his former post in Shanghai, and Warren Delano, Jr.,[8] an old China merchant of the Canton factory days, to the senior house at Hong Kong. While the two men had the responsibility for devising ways to revive the house's fortunes, they were also presented with a new opportunity. As a result of the new treaty settlement between China and the powers in 1858–60, three ports on the Yangtze River and three on the North China coast were opened for the first time to foreign navigation and trade.[9]

How was Russell & Co. to profit from this situation? Within a few weeks of his return to Shanghai after an absence of three years, Edward Cunningham proposed that the firm enter the steam-navigation business in China, starting with a small line of three steamers on the Yangtze River. The volume of trade and of passenger traffic on this river, from whose banks the Taiping rebels were about to be cleared, was believed to be "incalculable." Moreover, Cunningham was convinced that the low-draft steamboat of the Mississippi type was best suited to navigation on the Yangtze. As he wrote to Paul Sieman Forbes, the head of the house residing in the United States: [10]

> For such work & such a river there are no boats in the world that can compete an hour with the boats that navigate the Western rivers of America. . . .
> The only rivals, supposing them once established, they have to fear, are American boats like themselves. There is no one likely to establish a *line* among the Americans and the English are so infatuated with their own boats that they are not likely to attempt American boats until compelled to do so.

Cunningham estimated that a line of three steamers in regular

---

the difficulties encountered by China merchants who were trying to act on a commission basis for distant principals, see S. G. Checkland, "An English Merchant House in China after 1842," *Bulletin of the Business Historical Society*, XXVII [Sept., 1953], 162–9.) Russell & Co.'s exchange business in China's treaty ports, which had been very large in the late 1840's and early 1850's, had by this time also declined. (Forbes, *Reminiscences*, 359–61.)

[8] Warren Delano, Jr., was partner of Russell & Co. in 1840–46 and 1861–66. On his unsuccessful industrial ventures in the United States in the 1850's, see J. M. Forbes to P. S. Forbes, 8 Nov. and 7 Dec. 1857, "Letters of John Murray Forbes, 1843–1867" (typewritten volume at Baker Library – hereafter LJMF); also Daniel W. Delano, Jr., *Franklin Roosevelt and the Delano Influence* (Pittsburgh, 1946), chap. 9.

[9] This is the so-called second treaty settlement – the result of the treaties negotiated in 1858 and the two conventions of 1860 at the conclusion of the Anglo-French expedition to Peking. Hankow, Kiukiang, and Chinkiang on the Yangtze River and Newchang, Tengchow (Chefoo), and Tientsin in the Gulf of Pechihli area were opened.

[10] Cunningham to P. S. Forbes, 1 Feb. 1861, FC.

semiweekly service between Shanghai and Hankow (a distance of about 600 miles) would yield an annual gross profit of $342,000.

But how was Russell & Co. to finance a steam line? A glance at the capital account of the house shows clearly that it was not prepared for this enterprise of the industrial age. Three sidewheelers – "fully 300 feet long" – were estimated to cost a total of $480,000. For the term 1861–63, the partners of Russell & Co. had put up a total capital of only $400,000, which, together with some other credits, made up a working capital given at $460,000.[11]

It must have been obvious to Cunningham, therefore, that Russell & Co. could not in any case put up the *entire* capital for the three boats. Subscriptions would have to be solicited from individuals to supplement the house's investment, in a manner not unlike that by which sailing vessels had sometimes been financed in the past. However, Cunningham asked, in view of the good profits the steamers would bring, should the house not try to put up the main part of the capital required? Since commission business in trade was declining, was it not best to stake the house's future on the steam enterprise?[12]

As it happened, these ideas of Cunningham's were to meet with opposition from the other important partner in China – Warren Delano, Jr. – who had superior authority over the affairs of the house in China and was in actual control of the firm's funds.[13] Delano's opposition indicates the reluctance of a commission house, even in its declining days, to abandon its customary form of business. His main reason for opposing Cunningham's suggestion was that Russell & Co. should not give up its commission business in trade, but should, on the contrary, muster its resources to try to revive it. Since his return to China in 1860, Delano had decided on a policy for Russell & Co.: namely, to give out advances more liberally to prospective constituents with a view to encouraging

[11] Delano to P. S. Forbes, 18 Sept. 1861; cp. Cunningham with P. S. Forbes, 28 June 1863, annex. Russell & Co.'s only other assets were real estates in China valued in 1861 at $260,000. Referring to another business project (shipping rice for the Chinese government) Cunningham wrote in June, 1861: "The only real difficulty was the want of money, . . . times having changed since we could depend on Houqua for a floating balance of 2 or 300,000 and an extra 200,000, in case of great need." (Cunningham to P. S. Forbes, 14 June 1861, FC.)

[12] Cunningham's proposal is discussed in Delano to P. S. Forbes, 14 and 27 Feb. and 1 and 16 March 1861; see also Cunningham to P. S. Forbes, 4 June 1861, FC.

[13] Delano's superior authority is discussed in Delano to Nelson Marvin Beckwith, 4 Dec. 1860. Delano was also in control of the credits supplied to Russell & Co. by Baring Brothers & Co., London. (Cunningham to P. S. Forbes, 15 May 1861, FC.)

business. In February, 1861, at the very time when Cunningham was urging him in repeated letters to make appropriations for the immediate ordering of steamers, Delano was engaged in carrying out this policy. As he reported to P. S. Forbes: "Our capital is *all* out and at work at 9% interest and turning in commission at not very long intervals." [14]

Delano also had a steamer project of his own: a line of three steamers to run from Hong Kong and Canton to the other coastal ports of China. However, that Delano's chief concern was still the firm's traditional commission business can be seen in the fact that, even for this scheme of his own, he did not propose that the house should commit large capital. He hoped that the project might be financed mainly, if not entirely, by individual subscribers, with Russell & Co. itself in the role of agent. As he wrote to P. S. Forbes: "These steamers, however, are becoming a necessity upon the coast and if we can get them up and secure control and management of them without having to invest too much in them, we must try to do it." [15]

Only after Delano had found it difficult to get subscriptions for this project (and also after Cunningham had demonstrated his ability to get subscriptions in Shanghai for the Yangtze project) did he suggest to P. S. Forbes that the house might invest $100,000 in the coastal line – this being the largest amount he thought the house could spare for steamers. As he wrote to P. S. Forbes on 31 March 1861: [16]

> With regard to the subscription papers for the two lines, I cannot say I think there is much chance in our getting up the two lines. I have however little doubt about the Yangtze river line if E. C. [Edward Cunningham] can depend on his "Chinese partners" [who] will join in the enterprise in the shape we place it. The coast line I think may be got up if R. & Co. will assume $100,000 – and *you* can place with *cash* subscribers $100,000 more in New York, Boston &c. Native and other friends in Canton, Hongkong, Foochow & Shanghai may I think be depended upon for $200,000 – perhaps a little more.

Cunningham, meanwhile, had proceeded to organize some subscriptions from individuals in Shanghai – believing that there was great urgency for action, since the Yangtze River was expected to

[14] Delano to P. S. Forbes, 1 March 1861. "The experience of the past six months proves to me that we can use here a large capital in advances upon merchandise securing both interest and commissions and thereby making up a portion of our loss by the withdrawal of our distant constituents." (Delano to P. S. Forbes, 18 Sept. 1861, FC.)

[15] Delano to P. S. Forbes, 16 March 1861, FC.

[16] Delano to P. S. Forbes, 31 March 1861, FC.

open in June and there was the prospect of spectacular profits for steamboats in the first months after the opening. As early as the middle of March, Cunningham succeeded in getting some "Chinese friends and constituents" to join him in a small project: the purchase of an old steamer (193 tons) known to be available at San Francisco and costing some $45,000. As Cunningham recalled later in a letter to P. S. Forbes: "After strenuous, honest efforts to do the thing through Delano, perfectly willing he should have the credit if he would only do it, I found that I must try other ways or R. & Co. would be left lagging behind. So I organized our own little company, & sent for the *Surprise*." [17] Documents of this period show that it was after hearing of the step taken by Cunningham that Delano for the first time expressed to Cunningham his approval of the Yangtze steamer project.

Delano was in fact greatly vexed by the manner in which Cunningham had taken the matter into his own hands, for Cunningham, as a protest against Delano's lack of co-operation, had sent the order for the *Surprise* directly to San Francisco, by-passing the Hong Kong house. Nevertheless, on 26 March Delano wrote Cunningham for the first time giving his approval to the Yangtze plan, on condition, however, that the house itself make no investment in it. As Delano put it: "I shall send you herewith the draft of a paper to which our friends hereabouts subscribe for the purpose of building three boats or less for the Yangtze. . . . Russell & Co. as a firm can take no interest — but the individual partners may do so to the extent of their wishes & means outside of the house accounts. . . . I quite approve of your clerks having interest in the steamers, as you see, *ours* have." [18] These ideas Cunningham was constrained to accept, although, as his letters to P. S. Forbes show, he felt much "aggrieved" at Delano's attitude.[19]

[17] Cunningham to P. S. Forbes, 4 June 1861. See also Delano to Cunningham, 26 March, and Delano to P. S. Forbes, 26 May 1861, FC.

[18] Delano to Cunningham, 26 March 1861, FC.

[19] Cunningham to P. S. Forbes, 15 May and 4 and 14 June, FC. On 4 June, Cunningham wrote: "I claim distinctly that I am altogether the aggrieved party. Aggrieved because Delano would not treat my suggestions for business with sufficient consideration. . . . The facts are that as soon as I found out what an important matter the steam navigation of the Yangtze was to be, I lost no time in giving him every information and pressing upon him the necessity of immediate action. I was so prompt that we could have been two months *before* everyone, instead of two months behind. He treated my suggestions with a sort of lofty superciliousness, hard to bear from a man whom I had already found out to be not supernaturally clever. . . . He also came near shutting up any chance of joint action in Yangtze steam, for, in my indignation I, at first, so

As it was worked out in the months of April and May, through a very strained correspondence between Cunningham and Delano, a subscription plan of $320,000 was set up. (It was still hoped that three sidewheelers of a smaller size could be bought with this sum.) Of the total, $170,000 was subscribed in Shanghai, about $75,000 in Hong Kong, and about $75,000 reserved for partners not in China – P. S. Forbes and Robert Shaw Sturgis. As indicated in Cunningham's letter to P. S. Forbes dated 14 June 1861, much of the allocation for Shanghai was filled by "old Chinese friends" – Cunningham himself having taken only about $20,000. (Another important American subscriber was Thomas Walsh, Russell partner in Shanghai from 1858 to 1860. In 1861 he was with a new firm in Nagasaki.) Orders for new steamers were sent to P. S. Forbes in New York as early as April, 1861.[20]

Delano once suggested that the subscribers to the project should form an "association."[21] It appears that what was actually formed was some kind of organization based on "subscription papers," an association which would have no clear existence outside of Russell & Co.'s books. Deliberations among subscribers, who were either members of Russell & Co. itself or their Chinese friends, were probably held only informally. Russell & Co. was in any case to serve as agent for the project. The *Surprise,* which arrived at Shanghai late in July, 1861, was operated by Russell & Co. as its own boat,[22] although doubtless under a separate account.

For its agency Russell & Co. was to receive regular commissions. Moreover, Russell & Co. would benefit from trading and other opportunities in connection with the control of the steamers. However, Edward Cunningham regretted that the house itself could not own a large share of the steamers outright, and thus reap a great part of the direct profit of the enterprise. As he remarked to P. S. Forbes in his letter dated 4 June 1861 (in connection with a general discussion of the policies of the house): "Meantime our policy this

---

wrote. But, reflecting that he is not the house, I destroyed my letter, drew up a proper subscription list, and determined to unite."

[20] Delano to P. S. Forbes, 26 May 1861; and Cunningham to P. S. Forbes, 15 May, 14 June, and 11 July 1861, FC.

[21] "In the ownership of the vessels spoken of, I think each individual interest should extend through all the vessels – which [*sic*] working for a common fund would avoid any jealousy or preference of one over another, and would simplify accounts and the management generally. . . . The proprietors should be an association – but avoid anything like incorporation and a charter." (Delano to P. S. Forbes, 16 March 1861, FC.)

[22] Shipping intelligence, *NCH,* 27 July 1861; Delano to P. S. Forbes, 14 Oct. 1861, FC.

term should have been to make our living by steamers & to have slid easily & without loss into the new order of things. This great line on the Yangtze, that we throw into the hands of a multitude of subscribers, should have been mainly kept in the house, & helped out our profits."

## The Role of the Head of the House in America

At this point it is necessary to ask: what was the attitude of Russell & Co.'s "head of the house," Paul Sieman Forbes,[23] toward this enterprise in China? Residing most of the time in New York and Newport since his return from China in 1853, P. S. Forbes still put up a large part of Russell & Co.'s capital. His account in the house in February, 1861, stood at $288,000 to his credit, of which $165,000 was loaned to partners of the firm in China.[24] Would P. S. Forbes consider further investment in China – in a new steam-navigation enterprise?

In considering P. S. Forbes's attitude, however, we must see him not only as an investor in the China trade, but also as a businessman in the United States, for like the senior China merchant, J. P. Cushing, P. S. Forbes had been attracted since his return by the opportunities for investment at home. Since the early 1850's, we know that he had made large purchases of securities through his cousin John Murray Forbes, particularly those of the railroad projects which the latter promoted. For instance, in January, 1855, P. S. Forbes purchased a total of $200,000 of the Military Tract stocks and bonds and the Aurora (Chicago, Burlington & Quincy Railroad) bonds. In January, 1856, he is known to have asked J. M. Forbes to make for him another investment of $100,000 in the

[23] P. S. Forbes was partner of Russell & Co., 1844–73, and was its head from 1846 until his retirement. (For the phrase "head of the house," see partnership agreement on the admission of T. Walsh, appended to Cunningham to P. S. Forbes, 12 Oct. 1856, FC.) R. B. Forbes was partner, 1839–44 and 1849–54. J. M. Forbes was partner, 1834–38, although in the late 1850's he still retained rights of "good will" – rights which he held jointly with P. S. Forbes. On the term 1861–63, J. M. Forbes wrote P. S. Forbes: "Co-partnership terms same in other respects with the present one by which the entire *good will* of the House practically reverts to you at the end of the term." (J. M. Forbes to P. S. Forbes, 15 Nov. 1859, LJMF.)

[24] Beckwith to P. S. Forbes, 14 Feb. 1861 (cp. Delano with P. S. Forbes, 18 Sept. 1861). Articles of Co-partnership for the term 1855–57 show that P. S. Forbes received from 2/16 to 3/16 of the firm's division of profits. As head of the house, P. S. Forbes gave wide responsibility to his partners in China. "Someone was destined to wear the mantle & I know of few who would have spread it more widely over others than I am doing." (P. S. Forbes to R. B. Forbes, 15 July 1858, FC.)

Hannibal & St. Joseph Railroad (a branch of the Chicago Central System).[25] By March, 1861 (at the time when Cunningham was working on the steamer project in China), P. S. Forbes is known to have owned about $200,000 of this railroad's bonds as well as a "large interest" in stocks.[26]

Personally P. S. Forbes was a "steam enthusiast" – in the tradition of the Forbes family's fondness for things nautical.[27] In the 1850's, often in co-operation with R. B. Forbes, P. S. Forbes had built several steamers for Russell & Co.'s use in China, including the composite steamer *Antelope* (named after the famous clipper ship) and the *Min*. However, that P. S. Forbes had to weigh investments of this type against the surer prospects of securities in the United States is indicated by a letter he wrote in February, 1858, during a short visit to China, to R. B. Forbes. P. S. Forbes wrote in the tone of a chastened hobbyist: [28]

> I have always had a horror of having anything to do with steam & if I had not, the *Antelope* & *Min* would have cured me – they beat your losses by steam, that is some 100,000$. The *Antelope* is now being used by Uncle Sam [in China] for 6 mos on a fair charter – but we shall sell her as soon as we can find someone green eno to buy her. I beg therefore you won't suggest any more steam operations – there is only one more possible for R. & Co. & I don't know what we shall do about it. The *A.*'s model wanted rather more hollow lines forward, but she is a good seaboat & her engine should have been more amidship – If I were you I would send no credit to China for investment, but would be content to get my 10% on Hann. & St. [Hannibal & St. Joseph] Bonds.

On this trip to China, P. S. Forbes sent home a credit of $128,000 to be invested in securities in the United States, including a further investment in the Hannibal & St. Joseph Railroad.[29]

[25] "Your engagements standing thus far about 60,000$ for Mil. Tract Bonds & Stocks and 50,000 for Aurora Bonds. I am negotiating for a further lot of Mil. Tract Bonds and Stocks which will about use up the 90,000 remaining." (J. M. Forbes to P. S. Forbes, 21 Jan. 1855.) "You asked whether you can have 100,000 instead of 50,000 of the Mo. Bonds. You misunderstood me. The Bonds we propose to sell are not Missouri *State* Bonds – but Hannibal and St. Jo. R. Road Bonds. . . ." (J. M. Forbes to P. S. Forbes, 21 Jan. 1856, LJMF.)

[26] J. M. Forbes to P. S. Forbes, 5 March 1861. J. M. and P. S. Forbes jointly owned at this date $400,000 of the Third Mortgage and Convertible Bonds issued by this railroad, under an arrangement by which each took half (see same to same, 19 July 1858 and 3 Feb. 1860, LJMF).

[27] See the frequent mention of the steamboat in P. S. Forbes's letters to R. B. Forbes throughout the 1850's. P. S. Forbes once thought of taking out a patent for his invention of a new instrument of propulsion – "a wheel placed obliquely to its axis" – an idea which does not seem to have worked. (P. S. Forbes to R. B. Forbes, 23 June 1857 [illustrated], FC.)

[28] P. S. Forbes to R. B. Forbes, 13 Feb. 1858, FC.

[29] J. M. Forbes to P. S. Forbes, 23 Feb. and 14 March 1858, LJMF. P. S.

In 1861, when the partners of Russell & Co. in China conceived of the new project of steam lines in China, how did P. S. Forbes react to the idea? In April, 1861, the Civil War in the United States broke out. How did this event affect P. S. Forbes's attitude?

As is clearly reflected in the letters from Delano and Cunningham to P. S. Forbes in the year 1861 (P. S. Forbes's own letters of this period unfortunately not having been preserved), the head of the house at home showed no interest whatsoever in making any investment in the new project. In the dispute between Cunningham and Delano on the financing of the Yangtze River project, P. S. Forbes came out in favor of Delano's idea that the house itself should avoid committing funds. In his letters to Cunningham written in the months of April and May, after he had received Cunningham's February and March letters, P. S. Forbes advised "conciliating" Delano. This mortified Cunningham so much that in a letter dated July, 1861, he offered to resign from his post in Shanghai – to go and live in Europe! [30]

In the months that followed, P. S. Forbes was to show that he not only did not favor the house's making investments in the project, but also that he personally had no inclination to bring fresh funds to China – and in this he was to disappoint Delano as well as Cunningham. As we have seen, as early as 31 March 1861, Delano had written Forbes suggesting that a part of the capital of the coastal line should be raised in the United States. In his letter dated 26 May, Delano also informed Forbes that about $75,000 under the Yangtze plan was reserved for him and for R. S. Sturgis (partner of Russell & Co., 1850–57). Another letter of Delano's dated 14 October 1861, indicates that P. S. Forbes had made no response to these suggestions. On this date we find Delano writing to Forbes – in rather tactful language: [31]

I see R. S. Sturgis is in America and from him you must have received

---

Forbes did build another steamer in 1859, the *Peiho,* which cost about $200,000 and was partly financed by Russell & Co. itself (see Beckwith to P. S. Forbes, 8 Aug. 1859, FC). J. M. Forbes gave the following advice when the vessel was being fitted out: "Take *another* figure. You can always in China get 9 to 12% for money, or today can buy undoubted Western mortgages & R. Rd. Bonds that will give you equal to 10% interest – at which rate her [*Peiho's*] yearly interest on her cost on arrival will be say $21,000. If you cannot do better there, I would consider carefully before refusing an offer of a little under her cost." (J. M. Forbes to P. S. Forbes, 2 May 1859, LJMF.) Although P. S. Forbes did not heed this advice in 1859, he approved the sale of the steamer in China in early 1860 (see Delano to P. S. Forbes, 7 April 1860, FC).

[30] Cunningham to P. S. Forbes, 11 July 1861, FC.

[31] Delano to P. S. Forbes, 14 Oct. 1861, FC.

sometime since the particulars of the subscriptions for the two lines: I doubt if he will take any and if he does not there will be quite as much left as you will want, I think. Still, he may want all he can get and complain of not having enough assigned to him.

Meanwhile, the $320,000 Yangtze plan had been realized in China, and Delano eventually had to give up his plan for a coastal line.

Was P. S. Forbes, then, not interested in this enterprise in China at all? As a member of Russell & Co., he was to help the enterprise in a very important way: namely, by undertaking to supervise the purchase and building of steamboats in the United States. As early as April, 1861, J. M. Forbes observed that P. S. Forbes was "dabbling in steam" again,[32] having contracted for Russell & Co.'s future use a coastal steamer, the *Flambeau* (850 tons). After June, 1861, when orders for the Yangtze steamers had reached the United States, P. S. Forbes was to keep himself busy by supervising their construction. (Before the end of the year two sidewheelers were contracted for: the *Kiangse*, first called *Khechong*, 514 tons, and the *Huquong*, 1,339 tons. P. S. Forbes's favorite steamboat-builders were Henry Steers of Brooklyn and Thomas Collyer of New York; among his engine builders was Allaire Works of New York.[33] J. M. Forbes found it necessary to warn P. S. Forbes not to be swayed too much by the "zeal for science" of the engineers!) It should be noted that in this work, P. S. Forbes, Russell & Co.'s head partner, was actually in the capacity of an agent. The construction costs were to be met by remittances from China, and P. S. Forbes was to receive a commission for advancing funds. These facts can be seen, for instance, in a letter from Delano to P. S. Forbes: [34]

I note that you were pushing the work upon the *Flambeau* in the hope of having her ready for sea in all August: I shall give you until after 20 September to complete her — and shall look for her here in the first week of December. We shall try to send you *some* money on account of her by the outgoing mail — and still more by the succeeding — but the rate of exchange is very adverse and to a certain extent upsets the calculations as to the amo. which the $320,000 subscribed in China will place in New York. . . .

I note that in consideration of your advancing the money for the two boats now in hand, you propose to dispense with the assistance of the J. M. F[orbes] & Co. and to save for yourself the commission they would charge: this suits all here well enough.

Given the inclination of P. S. Forbes to keep his capital at home,

[32] J. M. Forbes to P. S. Forbes, 14 April 1861, LJMF.
[33] Delano to P. S. Forbes, 5 and 14 Oct. 1861, FC; Dayton, *Steamboat Days*, 379, 393.
[34] Delano to P. S. Forbes, 7 Aug. 1861, FC.

the outbreak of the Civil War in the United States was to provide another reason for his doing so, for, as far as P. S. Forbes was concerned, the war brought forth another possible use of his capital at home, also in connection with steamboat building, but for another purpose. Because of the urgent need for naval vessels, the Union Government had asked businessmen familiar with problems of shipbuilding to supply new gunboats. In 1863, P. S. Forbes was to join R. B. and J. M. Forbes in fitting out two boats for the Government – the *Cherokee* and the *Meteor*. It must have been also in 1863 that he embarked on a major lone venture, the 2,638-ton sloop-of-war *Idaho*, which involved a capital outlay of $550,000.[35]

In 1861 all this was still in the future. However, as early as May, 1861, P. S. Forbes already had knowledge of the Government's need for steamboats: hence, the possibility of the extension of his contracting activities. On 16 May 1861 we find J. M. Forbes writing to P. S. Forbes as follows, after R. B. Forbes had had a talk with Secretary of the Navy Gideon Welles: [36]

> Bennet is nearly crazy to buy or build something. . . . We have assurances from the Secy. of Navy and from some of the Senators that any vessel we build will be favorably considered. In short, all the encouragement possible short of promising to buy her. . . . If the war ends suddenly & we cannot sell her to the Gov., how would ours do as a mate to yours? Why don't you strengthen yours enough to make her available for guns? Then possibly I might, if things change in China, get yours off the Government under the encouragement from the Secretary.

As it happened, this steamer of P. S. Forbes's to which J. M. Forbes referred, the *Flambeau*, was not sent over to China but was sold to the Navy for $100,000.[37]

It should be noted that selling steamers to the Government was not more profitable than selling them to Russell & Co.'s project in China. In November, 1861, P. S. Forbes sent over to China, in the place of the *Flambeau*, a smaller boat discharged from the "volunteer navy of Massachusetts," the *Pembroke* (300 tons). R. B. Forbes, who owned one-fourth of this vessel, recalls that in her sale to Russell & Co.'s project in China, his share realized a net profit of $13,354 – one of his very few business successes during

[35] Forbes, *Reminiscences*, 266–9, and appendix table of vessels; *Letters and Recollections of John Murray Forbes*, Sarah Forbes Hughes, ed. (Boston and New York, 1899), II, 71–72; U.S. Navy Department, *Official Records of the Union and Confederate Navies in the War of Rebellion* (Washington, D.C., 1894–1922), series 2, Vol. I, pp. 55, 107.

[36] J. M. Forbes to P. S. Forbes, 16 May 1861, LJMF.

[37] U. S. Navy Department, *Official Records*, 84.

the Civil War.[38] However, it was one thing to sell steamers to China – or to contract for the building of steamers for China – but quite another to invest funds there permanently, particularly since the war had brought forth new opportunities at home.

## Further Promotion Efforts in China's Treaty Ports

Russell & Co.'s steam-navigation enterprise did not end here. The $320,000 plan having been set up, and the three steamers having been ordered, Edward Cunningham in Shanghai was still not satisfied that the business opportunity had been fully realized. In fact, Cunningham had become more convinced that in order to make the enterprise a permanent one, it was necessary to have more boats and also to set up lines between the coastal ports. He now hoped to set up a fleet of five river and five coastal steamers and also a warehouse system at the various ports in connection with the steamer business.

Cunningham's achievement was that he found the means to accomplish this expansion. Left to his own devices, Cunningham was able to show what an energetic entrepreneur could do in these new trading centers in the East. In the months between August, 1861, and March, 1862, he succeeded in raising further capital of about a million U. S. dollars – mainly from two groups in the mercantile community of China's treaty ports. On 27 March 1862, the Shanghai Steam Navigation Company was founded with a capital of Tls. 1,000,000 (the *tael* being the local Chinese currency), or the equivalent of $1,358,000.[39]

How then did Cunningham accomplish this feat? His success lies in the fact that he could persuade his "Chinese friends and constituents" to make further investments – and, moreover, in his effective promotional effort among the foreign community in Shanghai, which was dominated by the usually unco-operative British merchants. Cunningham's work is all the more remarkable, because in the same period other firms in China had failed in such

[38] Forbes, *Reminiscences*, 264, 277.

[39] Warren Delano, Jr., took little part in the preparation of this enlarged plan, and is known to have attempted to stop Cunningham from purchasing waterfront properties at the Yangtze ports for the steam enterprise. In February, 1862, after Delano had been informed of recent purchases of this kind made by Cunningham, he wrote to a former Russell partner: "You may imagine with what degree of patience I take this news – at the same time, I hope to get rid of the whole thing by and through the means of E. C.'s 'grand consolidated coast of China and river steam navigation, lightering and warehousing association.'" (Delano to Beckwith, 20 Feb. 1862, FC.)

plans. John Heard's letters written in this period show that Augustine Heard & Co. had contemplated a similar project, but could not find the necessary capital. (A similar British project likewise failed. Throughout the year 1862, W. R. Adamson & Co. advertised in the Shanghai newspapers for subscriptions for a "China and Japan Steam Navigation Company" – a project which was never realized.)[40] There is in fact no better testimony on Cunningham's work than that of John Heard himself, who wrote to a partner on 20 February 1862, after learning of Russell & Co.'s imminent success in "floating" its steamer company:[41]

> Our plan for a Company has always been to get Chinese interested, and this we tried to do, but could not to any considerable extent. It never occurred to us that it would be possible to do anything with the foreign community – and it is they as well as Chinese who supported R. & Co.

On 3 March, John Heard wrote another partner:[42]

> They have wiped our eyes regularly. There is no disguising the fact. I think, however, they would have made more money had they kept their boats to themselves. We have often thought of the same scheme in connection with *Chinese*, but have never been able to obtain sufficient encouragement. It never occurred to us that the foreign community would assist, and that is where R. & Co. have got the windward of us, by enlisting all the small houses in their favour.

With regard to the Chinese, it should be pointed out that Cunningham, who had been with Russell & Co in Shanghai from 1850 to 1857, could rely on his friendship with Chinese compradors and merchants, personal relationships being so important even among the treaty-port Chinese. When Cunningham succeeded in raising funds for the *Surprise* in March, 1861, Warren Delano, Jr., had written him: "You claim Chinese whom [*sic*] we supposed were the friends & constituents of R. & Co. to be your particular constituents, upon whom R. & Co. have no influence except thro' you! I do not mean to say this is not exactly so. . . ."[43] Of the Chinese who made subscriptions to the Shanghai Steam Navigation Company as it was finally organized, we know the names of nine: Ahyune, Chongfat, Koofunsing, Chan-yeu-chang, Ahkai, Hupkee, Lyungchong, Wong-yong-yee, and Ahyou.[44] The first

[40] *NCH*, 1862 and 1863 (copy in British Museum).
[41] John Heard's letter book, HC, FL–7, p. 197.
[42] *Ibid.*, p. 210.
[43] Delano to Cunningham, 26 March 1861, FC.
[44] These were present in the S. S. N. Co.'s shareholders' meetings in 1863 and 1864. See "Minutes of a General Meeting of the Shareholders of the S. S.

four on this list are known to have been one-time compradors of Russell & Co. who had developed independent business in Shanghai. Koofunsing's silk firm was one of the largest in that port.[45]

However, even in persuading his "old Chinese friends" to co-operate in the enterprise, would Cunningham not have to think of concrete ways to demonstrate its advantages? In making purchases of waterfront sites at the various ports for the steamer business – which he insisted on doing in spite of the frequent protests of Delano – Cunningham decided to choose properties situated near the Chinese business sections. (The Kin Lee Yune wharfage site at Shanghai, which became the main base of Russell & Co.'s steamer business, was chosen because it was right next to the Chinese city; it proved to be one of the S. S. N. Co.'s great attractions from the point of view of native shippers.)[46] Around August, 1861, we know that Cunningham took another step designed to foster the interest of his Chinese friends in the steamboat business. At a time when the freight rates on the Yangtze River were spectacularly high, Cunningham arranged to have his Chinese friends share the ownership of an immediately profitable steamer, which he himself undertook to bring up from the Canton River and have repaired. Concerning this boat, the *Williamette* (413 tons), Cunningham later remarked: "Though I took the risk myself, I took none of the profits, dividing her up, as soon as she was safely running, among our Shanghai Chinese, in order to induce them to enter upon the grander scheme of the SSN [Shanghai Steam Navigation] Company."[47]

Having thus assured the support of the Chinese, Cunningham next took the imaginative step of appealing to the British-dominated foreign community in Shanghai. How then did it occur to Cunningham that Russell & Co. could secure the co-operation of

N. Co.," 10 Feb. 1863 and 18 Jan. 1864, and "Minutes of a Special General Meeting," 3 Oct. 1864.

[45] Ahyune, Chongfat, and Koofunsing are known to have been Cantonese compradors of Russell & Co. who had followed the firm to Shanghai. See Cunningham to John Murray Forbes, Jr., 24 April, 14 May and 4 June 1868, Russell & Co., Canton Papers (at Baker Library). Chan-yeu-chang does not seem to have become Russell & Co.'s comprador until 1865, but before that date he is known to have made large shipments of his own between Shanghai and Hankow on the S. S. N. Co.'s steamers. (Delano to P. S. Forbes, 19 Aug. 1864; George Tyson to P. S. Forbes, 24 March 1865, FC.) The silk quotations of the "chop" of Koofunsing (Koo-foong-sing or Kukee) appear frequently in *NCH*.

[46] Cp. Forbes, *Reminiscences*, 364–6.

[47] Cunningham to P. S. Forbes, 10 Nov. 1865; shipping intelligence in *NCH*, 27 July 1861.

the British – as it never occurred to John Heard? From the Prospectus of the Shanghai Steam Navigation Company, issued by the Shanghai house of Russell & Co. around January, 1862, and distributed, at first confidentially, among the company's non-American business friends,[48] we know that Cunningham had counted chiefly on one fact: namely, that the small British houses in Shanghai which did not own steamers or warehouses themselves had in the past been dependent on large British houses (such as Dent & Co. and Jardine, Matheson & Co.) for such facilities. Could some of these houses, then, be persuaded to see the advantages of making investments in an American-British-Chinese steam-navigation and warehousing company? As Cunningham boldly declared in the Prospectus:

> The principle upon which it is proposed to found this Company is of the soundest nature. It is the protection of the houses of moderate means, by whom the bulk of the foreign business of the country is transacted, and who, collectively, are the strength of the community, against the monopoly and concentration of the larger houses, who naturally turn to their own advantage, their individually greater resources.

The question here was perhaps not one of insight – for the needs of the small houses must have been equally apparent to Augustine Heard & Co. – but one of the actual ability to work out arrangements attractive to prospective subscribers. Judging from the Prospectus, Cunningham had emphasized one very tangible advantage of his plan: on the basis of the favorably situated waterfront properties Russell & Co. had already procured for the enterprise, it was possible to build an extensive godown (warehouse) system at all the ports.[49] As the Prospectus envisages, the S. S. N. Co.'s warehouses were to be made available to the shareholders of the company under a special arrangement of pro rata return of profits – which would help the shareholders to reduce the cost of their trading activities between the ports. Thus the Prospectus points out:

[48] "Prospectus of a Joint Stock Company for Steam Navigation of the Chinese Waters, and the Establishment of a Warehouse System in Shanghai" (undated); cp. John Heard, III's letter book, HC, FL-7, pp. 145, 155–6.

[49] The Kin Lee Yune site at Shanghai's French Concession was convenient for the foreign merchants as well as for the Chinese. As a correspondent of the *NCH* described it: "The premises of the [S. S. N.] Company are upon the French Concession, and under the walls of the native city, so that they are very favorably situated for every description of merchandise, and for laying down teas under preparation for shipment. They will accommodate, when completed, from 30,000 to 35,000 tons of cargo." (*NCH*, 29 March 1862, 50.)

By this system, for the warehouse, the actual cost of warehouse and shipping expenses will be paid by each shareholder and no more, and he will stand in that respect on a much better footing than if he transacted his business in godowns far from the water at excessive cost of carriage, labor and rent.

This practical advantage had probably disposed the Shanghai merchants to consider actively the possibilities of the steam-navigation business. Cunningham estimated that five river and five coastal steamers would yield an annual net profit of Tls. 500,000.

It is indicative of the effectiveness of Cunningham's planning – and also no doubt of Russell & Co's prestige in the community – that the project was greeted with enthusiastic response. At least 15 members of the foreign community, not counting members of Russell & Co. itself, are known to have become the S. S. N. Co.'s early subscribers, among whom eight can be identified as British merchants associated with a moderate-sized trading firm. Others included continental Europeans and two known Americans not of Russell & Co. – one of them George F. Heard.[50] When, therefore, the Shanghai Steam Navigation Company was formally created on 27 March 1862 – as reported in the *North-China Herald*[51] – at a shareholders' meeting held at Russell & Co.'s hong at the Bund, it was an occasion unprecedented in the annals of the treaty ports. British, American and Chinese merchants gathered to drink champagne and talk about the Yangtze River!

As it was finally worked out, of the total capital of Tls. 1,000,000 (in 1,000 shares of Tls. 1,000 each, the total to be paid up before 30 June 1862), the foreign community in Shanghai exclusive of members of Russell & Co. can be judged as having subscribed Tls. 300,000–400,000.[52] From the words of Cunningham himself (quoted

[50] The following are members of the foreign community (exclusive of members of Russell & Co.) who were present at the shareholders' meetings in 1863 and 1864. Those who can be identified as associating with British firms are Nichol Latimer and Robert Richard Westall (both Smith, Kennedy & Co.), J. Broadthurst Tootal (Ellisen & Co.), W. Thorburn (Jarvie, Thorburn & Co.), Thomas Hanbury (Bower, Hanbury & Co.), A. J. How (Johnson & Co.), James Whitlow (Holliday, Wise & Co.), J. Wheatley (Reiss & Co., for executor of A. Fincham). The other known American is A. Overweg (Olyphant & Co.). Other foreign shareholders are Francis Loureiro (Shanghai shipbroker), Thomas Vincent (commander, receiving ship *Emily Jones*), G. W. Schwemann and Rudolph Heinsen (both Siemssen & Co.), José Loureiro (Nagasaki agent for Dent & Co.). See above, note 44; identification is based on *China Directory for 1863* (Hong Kong, 1863) and references in *NCH*.

[51] *NCH*, 20 March 1862, 50 51.

[52] The share list of the S. S. N. Co. cannot be found. It was kept at the Shanghai house of Russell & Co.; even clerks of the house were not allowed

below, see note 63) it is further known that members of Russell & Co. together with the Chinese owned a majority of the shares, probably Tls. 600,000–700,000. There is also evidence that the Chinese shareholding was larger than that of American members of Russell & Co. itself. In 1878, this question came up incidentally in a Congressional hearing concerning the American consulate in Shanghai. Walter Scott Fitz, who was the Hankow agent of Russell & Co. in the 1860's, was asked who owned the Shanghai Steam Navigation Company: [53]

> *Q.* Principally Russell & Co.? – *A.* Not principally Russell & Co. Russell & Co. and their friends own the principal part of it.

Thomas Francis Burr, chief officer and captain of the S. S. N. Co.'s steamers in the 1860's, testified:

> *Q.* Were Russell & Co. the largest owner in the concern? – *A.* No; I think the Chinese were.
>
> *Q.* Did Russell & Co. own as much as one-third of it? – *A.* No; they did not own as much as one-third of it. They may have represented more than that.

Among members of Russell & Co. who took shares, Edward Cunningham was the largest subscriber, having raised for the purpose about Tls. 150,000 – largely, it seems, by converting some of his Shanghai real estate, purchased in the early 1850's.[54] Two

access to copies (Frank Blackwell Forbes to Cunningham, 11 Feb. 1871, F. B. Forbes's Letter Books [family collection], hereafter FBFLB. Lacking a copy of the share list, we can nevertheless make some deductions from the following facts: (1) In the Prospectus, which envisages a total capital of Tls. 1,200,000, it was stated: "Of the 1,200 shares into which the capital is divided it is understood that Messrs. Russell & Co. will take 700. There remain 500 shares, of which it is proposed to leave 100, for the present, for other ports. Of the remaining 400, 150 have already been applied for." (2) It is known that Russell & Co. as a firm had taken only a token subscription of a few shares; see below, note 58. (3) It is further known that individual members of Russell & Co. themselves had to rely on their Chinese friends to muster the votes of over 500 shares in the S. S. N. Co.'s shareholders' meeting: members of Russell & Co. themselves – as one source indicates – did not own even one-third of Tls. 1,000,000; see below, notes 53 and 63. It can be deduced, therefore, that when the Prospectus says that Russell & Co. planned to take 700 shares, it means that this quantity was reserved for members of Russell & Co. *and their Chinese friends.* As worked out in March, 1862, the stock capital of the S. S. N. Co. was not Tls. 1,200,000 but Tls. 1,000,000; see the "Constitution and Deed of Settlement, Shanghai Steam Navigation Company," March, 1862, and "Report of the Board of Directors for the General Meeting," 18 Jan. 1864. It can be assumed, therefore, that adjustments had been made in the allocation as stated in the Prospectus.

[53] U. S. Congress, *House Misc. Docs.*, part 1, pp. 885, 224.

[54] In June, 1863, Cunningham wrote P. S. Forbes the following concerning his contribution to the house's capital for the next term: "I have already ex-

other partners in China, George Tyson and H. S. Grew, also took shares. (Tyson and Grew came to China in 1853 and 1856 respectively, starting as clerks in the firm.) Frank Blackwell Forbes (the up and coming young man of the house destined to play a very important role in the affairs of the Shanghai Steam Navigation Company) was also an original subscriber.[55]

Did P. S. Forbes himself make any subscriptions to this enlarged plan? His investment at this time, if any, was at most Tls. 100,000 – a minor part of the stock capital of the Shanghai Steam Navigation Company. In all the Russell & Co. documents that we have read, the first mention of P. S. Forbes's shareholding refers to the year 1870, when he owned a total of Tls. 100,000.[56] (It is possible that P. S. Forbes made this investment in 1867, since after that year the Shanghai Steam Navigation Company proved very profitable, yielding a minimum annual dividend of 12 per cent.) P. S. Forbes's attitude in 1862 is probably stated accurately in a letter written to him by J. M. Forbes, commenting on a steamer which had been ordered in the name of P. S. Forbes but which was now being transferred to Russell & Co. for the Shanghai Steam Navigation Company: "With my views about steam I should prefer to see the risk of the enterprise remain where it now does, spread over a number instead of concentrating on your shoulders. . . . I don't see why the present situation is not just what you want, giving R. & Co. the benefit of having a fast steamer with only a part of the risk in their hands."[57] It should be noted that when J. M. Forbes referred to the part of the risk in Russell & Co.'s hands, he was thinking of the Shanghai Steam Navigation Company's shares owned by various individual members of the firm. As shown in a statement entitled "Ways and Means As They Will Stand on 1

hausted myself upon capital. . . . By organizing the Yangtze [Insurance] Co., I helped you to about Tls. 150,000, which will always continue if business is profitable. By the S. S. N. Co., if that prospers, you will have another Tls. 150,000. With the above my resources are finished. Personally I cannot do anything except to allow my surplus rents to accumulate, & there will be none unless the SSN Co. pays dividends when I can lay up what my shares give – perhaps [Tls.] 10 or 15,000 a year." On Cunningham's inability to supply capital from the United States, see Cunningham to P. S. Forbes, 21 Jan. 1859, FC.

[55] For data on various partners, see Forbes' *Reminiscences*, appendix table. Among clerks of the firm who took shares were F. W. Sauermann, J. W. Leembruggen, and F. E. Foster. (See above, note 44.)

[56] Henry Hughes Warden to P. S. Forbes, 25 Aug. 1870; Russell & Co., Shanghai, to P. S. Forbes, 5 April 1871, FC. The shares of the S. S. N. Co. were reset at Tls. 100 a share in 1868.

[57] J. M. Forbes to P. S. Forbes, 6 Dec. 1862, LJMF.

January 1864," sent to P. S. Forbes by Cunningham, the total value of the stocks of the Shanghai Steam Navigation Company and of the Yangtze Insurance Association held by Russell & Co. was only $60,000.[58]

As for J. M. Forbes – a China merchant in his youth but now a full-fledged industrial capitalist – he showed no interest at all in this new enterprise in China. J. M. Forbes declared to P. S. Forbes that he was "a confirmed *croaker* as to steam in China." [59] His attitude towards investment in the stocks of the steam-navigation company in China is indicated in a letter to P. S. Forbes, in which he discussed the possible sale of two steamers originally belonging to the Michigan Central Railroad: [60]

> But if you will consent to forego *building* & make this like ours a mere speculation in the two old boats, we will put them into common stock – with the clear understanding that they shall be sold for money or something that can be turned into money at once – so as not to involve us in putting them on as part of anybody's steamers, taking out pay in stock or any such long-winded modes of sales; we will gladly do so & join you in offering to R. & Co. one of them *positively*. . . .

## The Commission House As Entrepreneur

It remains to describe the institutional arrangement by which capital in China's treaty ports was brought into Russell & Co.'s steam-navigation project. By whom was this enterprise to be managed – now that it was owned by a large body of shareholders? How was Russell & Co. to retain its control of the enterprise? [61]

The Shanghai Steam Navigation Company, to be sure, was organized as a joint-stock company with its ownership based on transferable share certificates.[62] However, from the very beginning it was the shareholders' understanding that Russell & Co., the promoter of the enterprise, was also to manage its entire business. The Prospectus of the Shanghai Steam Navigation Company named Russell & Co. as "managing agents," who were to "take charge and

[58] Cunningham to P. S. Forbes, 28 Jan. 1863, annex, FC.

[59] J. M. Forbes to P. S. Forbes, 6 Dec. 1862, LJMF.

[60] J. M. Forbes to P. S. Forbes, 25 Jan. 1863, FC.

[61] In the following pages, an attempt has been made to describe the "institutional arrangements" made at the time of the creation of the enterprise, with only incidental references to its later history. The writer is preparing a study of the 15-year story of this American enterprise in China, with emphasis on policy and management and including an analysis of profit and service.

[62] It should be noted here that the S. S. N. Co. was never incorporated or chartered; Cunningham described it as a "private co-partnership." (U. S. Congress, *House Misc. Docs.*, part 1, p. 886.)

become responsible for the entire current business." In the Shanghai Steam Navigation Company's Constitution and Deed of Settlement — to which the shareholders acceded at the creation of the company — the status of Russell & Co. was defined in Article X:

> The house of Russell & Co. will act as permanent agents and treasurers of the Company. Their duties will be to take charge of all the current business of steamers and warehouses, including appointment of officers, providing supplies and coal, ordering new boats and machinery at the requisition of the Directors, disbursing for expenses and receiving all dues, and they shall be responsible to the Company for proper management, for clear and correct accounts of receipts and expenditures, which shall be made up semi-annually on 31st December and 30th June, and for balance of profit. . . .

How does this arrangement differ from the traditional practice of the commission house acting as agent for the owners of vessels, which, as we have seen, was the basis of the $320,000 subscription plan as conceived in 1861? Of course, Russell & Co. now undertook to manage a much more complicated business. Instead of taking care of single vessels or the business of single voyages, the commission house was to be regularly in charge of a modern steam-navigation company, commanding a fleet of steamers and serving eight or nine ports of China. However, this was still an *agency* arrangement. The Shanghai Steam Navigation Company, as such, was a mere *ownership organization*: it had no managerial arm of its own. Russell & Co. was to furnish all the managerial personnel and the offices for the Shanghai Steam Navigation Company.

However, as a joint-stock organization, was the Shanghai Steam Navigation Company not to have control over policy-making functions, as distinct from managerial functions? As provided in the Constitution and Deed of Settlement, control over policies was retained in the annual General Meeting of Shareholders and the "President and the Board of Directors," with the General Meeting itself keeping the authority for major decisions. Articles VII and VIII read:

> The building or purchase of new boats or of additional premises, and reserves for repairs, additions and insurance funds, shall only be made at General Meeting, which shall also determine the half yearly dividend to 31st December of each year.
>
> The President and Board of Directors shall determine upon the details of construction and ordering of new boats, when determined upon by the shareholders; upon repairs of the old; upon the line of employment of the various boats, changing from one to the other as circumstances render advisable; and may at any time in the year require a detailed statement from the agents upon any point over which they may wish to exercise supervision. . . .

The question is, however, who was to be in actual control of this ownership organization?

Of the capital stock of the Shanghai Steam Navigation Company, as we have seen, the British and the Chinese together held a large bulk, probably 70 or 75 per cent. However, from the point of view of control of the enterprise, one other fact stands out: members of Russell & Co., together with the Chinese subscribers, still held a majority of the total stocks, probably 60 to 70 per cent. This is indeed the basic fact upon which Cunningham relied for the control of the enterprise. As Cunningham himself recalled in 1870, referring to the question of Russell & Co.'s hold on the Shanghai Steam Navigation Company's agency: "Russell & Co. really holds in their own hands this question of the agency. They have only to keep the capital stock as it stands, and hold the shares they command, and manage with average success and ability, and they will have a sufficient following of Chinese to insure permanency." [63]

However, since the foreign community in Shanghai outside of Russell & Co. held a great number of shares, Russell & Co. had to admit an important check on its control of the enterprise, in the persons of the members of the Board of Directors, usually English, who were called in Russell & Co.'s correspondence "outside directors." From the very beginning, probably as the result of an informal agreement, it became the practice to elect two of the normal four directors from among the foreign shareholders who were not members of Russell & Co.; in 1862–63, these were N. Latimer and F. Loureiro, and in 1863–64, N. Latimer, J. B. Tootal, and T. Vincent.[64] While these men were in general sympathetic toward the Russell management, they nevertheless represented the shareholders' concern for larger immediate dividends, a view not necessarily identical with Russell & Co.'s idea of what would contribute to the enterprise's long-term well-being.

However, in its role as the actual manager of the enterprise, could Russell & Co. not exert an influence on the outside directors? Russell & Co. itself was not without a voice in the directorate ("the President and the Board of Directors"). It became customary for the managing partner of Russell & Co. in Shanghai always to be elected President of the Shanghai Steam Navigation Company (in

[63] Cunningham's memorandum, "Scrip Dividend of the S. S. N. Co. for 1870," FC. According to the provision of the Constitution and Deed of Settlement, a majority vote in the General Meeting of Shareholders decides in all cases, although the Prospectus proposes that the vote of 700 shares is necessary for the change of agency.

[64] See the Board of Directors' reports for the various years.

1862–64, Edward Cunningham), and for at least one other member of the firm to be chosen as a director (in 1862–63, H. S. Grew, and in 1863–64, F. B. Forbes). All available documents show that the directors' meetings, which were regularly held twice a year, always went very smoothly. That the outside directors were disposed to follow the suggestions of the Russell management even on major issues is indicated by the solution of a problem which arose in December, 1870 – one of the most controversial questions in the history of the Shanghai Steam Navigation Company. Because the Shanghai Steam Navigation Company's business in the preceding three years had brought very large returns, some shareholders of Shanghai's foreign community had demanded at the end of 1870 a larger cash dividend for the year than the usual 12 per cent. Henry Hughes Warden, Russell & Co.'s managing partner at Shanghai, believed, however, that the profits should be retained as reserves; he proposed to issue, instead of an extra cash dividend, a "scrip dividend," representing 20 per cent of the company's capital. (In 1872, this "scrip dividend" was converted into the company's stock, again at Warden's suggestion.) That Warden could with little difficulty win over the outside directors to his view may be seen in the following excerpts from his letters to P. S. Forbes: [65]

> The S S N Directors have agreed to issue scrip to represent the Reserves of the Co. I am almost sure to put that through. (21 December 1870)
>
> The Directors have decided to present to the General Meeting our project to issue say 20 per cent of scrip based upon the savings of the Co. now standing at credit of Ins. and Dep. a/c [Insurance and Depreciation account]. . . . We keep the money and hope at the same time to satisfy the stockholders. (16 February 1871)

In the last analysis, since the Russell management controlled the majority vote in the General Meeting of Shareholders, it could always invoke this final authority. While a showdown between the Russell management on the one hand and the outside directors on the other does not seem to have ever occurred, it is known that at least on one occasion, the managing partner of Russell & Co. in Shanghai (in this case, George Tyson, who succeeded Cunningham) did contemplate using the firm's control over shareholders to change a decision of the directors. In June, 1866, when the S. S. N.

[65] Warden to P. S. Forbes, 21 Dec. 1870 (postscript) and 16 Feb. 1871, FC; "Minutes of a General Meeting," 4 March 1871 and 20 Feb. 1872. Cunningham criticized Warden for the form of the scrip issue; see Cunningham to P. S. Forbes, 11 May and 28 Aug. 1871, FC. However, Cunningham had assumed that the mistake was Warden's and that the Board of Directors could be brought to agree with whatever form of scrip Russell & Co. might propose.

Co. purchased a new steamer, the *Plymouth Rock* (2,397 tons), the question arose whether appropriations should be made from reserve funds or from current profits. Tyson reported to P. S. Forbes: [66]

> I think the terms of sale are very favorable to the [S. S. N.] Company, though I should have preferred the Insurance and Depreciation Funds should be retained. But the outside directors would not assent to other terms – it is always however in the power of the shareholders to change it.

As it happened, Tyson worked out a way to pay for the steamer without touching the reserves.

* * *

To delve briefly into the later history of the Shanghai Steam Navigation Company, it may be stated that under the management and control of Russell & Co. the enterprise proved very successful. After a few years of poor profits under conditions of acute competition, the Russell fleet emerged after 1866 as the leader in the steam-navigation field in China. Between 1867 and 1872, the Shanghai Steam Navigation Company enjoyed virtual monopoly of the steam traffic on the Yangtze River (and on the short coastal line between Shanghai and Ningpo), while at the same time it was in a dominant position on the North China line (between Shanghai and the ports of the Gulf of Pechihli area). In the eight years from 1867 to 1874, the average annual dividend was no less than 18.75 per cent upon capital stock. When, in February, 1877, after two years of a mere 7 per cent dividend, it was decided to accept the offer of the China Merchants' Steam Navigation Company to purchase the entire fleet and properties of the company, there was available for division among shareholders a sum of over Tls. 2,650,000. (It should be noted that in the 15 years of its existence the Shanghai Steam Navigation Company made only one reissue of stocks – Tls. 250,000 in 1867, partly as payment to the partners of Dent & Co. for its Yangtze steamers. Otherwise, the expansion of the enterprise was entirely through the conversion of profits to stocks – Tls. 625,000 in 1868 and Tls. 375,000 in 1872. After 1868, an active market for securities of local enterprises grew up in Shanghai. The "S. S. N." was a leading item in the local share-

[66] Tyson to P. S. Forbes, 22 June 1866, FC. The problem was finally solved by applying to the *Plymouth Rock* the indemnity received from underwriters in London for the steamer *Huquong* (sunk Aug., 1866); see "Report of the Board of Directors," 18 Jan. 1867.

brokers' bulletin and was always quoted above par until 1874.)[67]

While the shareholders of the Shanghai Steam Navigation Company had undoubtedly profited from the enterprise, how did Russell & Co. itself benefit from it? Russell & Co. received, for its agency, a regular commission of 5 per cent upon gross receipts. In the prosperous years of the enterprise, this commission amounted to an annual total of about Tls. 100,000.[68] (Russell & Co.'s *net* gain from the Shanghai Steam Navigation Company's business in the year 1870 was estimated by F. B. Forbes to be about Tls. 50,000. Russell & Co.'s total net profit for the same year was a little over Tls. 200,000.)[69] Moreover, the control of the steamers had given Russell & Co. other advantages: the commission charged for the procurement of steamers and supplies, the use of the Shanghai Steam Navigation Company's cash assets at a low 5 per cent interest,[70] and the trading facilities between the Chinese ports. In June, 1862, Cunningham founded the Yangtze Insurance Association — for which Russell & Co. served as "secretaries and agents." This association obtained most of its business by underwriting cargoes shipped in the Shanghai Steam Navigation Company's steamers.[71]

While specialization in the steam-carrying business thus aided Russell & Co.'s still diverse activities in China, it also indirectly helped the house's foreign trade — a business which Russell partners always hoped to revive. (In the 1860's and 1870's, Russell & Co.'s foreign trade was still mainly on account of constituents, although now and then it invested directly in tea and silk shipments on a moderate scale. The house also entered into a joint-account arrangement with J. M. Forbes & Co. of Boston and the firm of

[67] Data for this paragraph are taken from the Board of Directors' reports of the various years and from *NCH*.

[68] The Constitution and Deed of Settlement provided that after 30 June 1863 Russell & Co.'s commission was to be reduced to 3½ per cent upon gross receipts; however, a decision of the General Meeting of 18 Jan. 1864 made the 5 per cent rate permanent. The gross receipts of the S. S. N. Co. for the three years 1868, 1869, and 1870 are known to be, respectively (in round numbers), Tls. 1,983,000, Tls. 1,890,000, and Tls. 1,938,000 (F. B. Forbes to David King, Jr., 1 July 1871, FBFLB).

[69] F. B. Forbes to P. S. Forbes, 29 Nov. 1870, FBFLB. The total net profit of Russell & Co. itself for the year 1869 is known to have been about Tls. 176,000, and for 1870 over Tls. 200,000. (Warden to P. S. Forbes, 11 Aug. 1870 (postscript), FC; F. B. Forbes to James Murray Forbes, 21 Nov. 1870, FBFLB.)

[70] This arrangement was provided for in the Constitution and Deed of Settlement, Article X.

[71] Delano to P. S. Forbes, 23 June 1862, FC; F. B. Forbes to W. M. Clarke, 19 July 1869, FBFLB.

Cordier in Paris.)[72] In the period 1871–76, Russell & Co. deposited Tls. 500,000–600,000 worth of the Shanghai Steam Navigation Company's reserve funds with Baring Brothers & Co., London, in the form of U. S. Government Bonds. This deposit was used as security for a "revolving credit," which had benefited Russell & Co.'s exchange operations in connection with the tea and silk trade.[73]

The present article has described merely the promotion and financing of Russell & Co.'s steam-navigation enterprise, which gave the old China-trade commission house a new lease on life. But my evidence suggests a broader hypothesis on the overseas expansion, especially in the Far East, of American capitalism. In this enterprise, the export of capital from the United States played little or no part. That portion of the capital of the Shanghai Steam Navigation Company which was supplied by the Americans, and by the British, must be regarded as the reinvestment in a lucrative transport service of profits derived from China's foreign trade. The sidewheeler on the Yangtze was an American export, but it was not sent to China by forces within the United States. The chief contribution of Russell & Co. was entrepreneurship, which, by utilizing the financial resources accumulated in the treaty ports of China, effected a technological innovation in the domestic transport of that country.

[72] These facts emerge from a study of FBFLB for the years 1866–71. The following are typical references to Russell & Co.'s foreign trading activities during this period. Concerning the silk shipments of the season of 1870, F. B. Forbes wrote Cunningham: "You can see that our own risk is only 68,000 taels – the loss of which, at the extreme figure of 20% would be Tls. 13,600 – while our commissions on Tls. 495,000 at an average of 3% are Tls. 14,850." (12 Sept. 1870.) In Nov., 1871, F. B. Forbes noted that the firm had shipped 261 packages of tea to J. M. Forbes & Co. – one of the very few tea shipments which the house made in that year. "This shipment is not on a j/a [joint account] but for a/c of Russell & Co. 1871, and we drew for it under Baring credit No. 2" (to Samuel Wyllys Pomeroy, Jr., 22 Nov. 1871).

[73] Directors' reports, 1871–76. One reason why it was decided to invest the S. S. N. Co.'s reserves in U. S. Government Bonds was that the local banks were unwilling to give more than 6 per cent interest for deposits. See Warden's reply to a shareholder in the General Meeting of 1870 ("Minutes of a General Meeting," 5 March 1870). Concerning the arrangement of the "revolving credit," see Warden to P. S. Forbes, 22 March 1871, with annex, FC; F. B. Forbes to H. H. Warden, 27 June 1871, FBFLB. The last reference reads: "French mail in this morning brings a revolving credit from Barings for £25,000 to commence when our securities are in their hands. Cm$^{n}$ [commission] ¼%."

# Part II
# Entrepreneurial Networks and Diasporas

# [5]

# Entrepreneurial Networks in International Business

**Mark Casson**

*Department of Economics*
*University of Reading*

Entrepreneurship is widely recognized as a key factor in economic growth [Leibenstein, 1968]. Historical studies of commercialization and industrialization suggest that the speed of "take off" is higher when entrepreneurs in related lines of activity work well together [Grassby, 1995]. In the aggregate, entrepreneurs may work better as a cooperative network than as a collection of competitive individualists. Unfortunately, attempts to develop the idea of an "entrepreneurial network" encounter the difficulty that both "entrepreneur" and "network" are somewhat nebulous concepts. Using economic theory, however, it is possible to define them in a rigorous manner. This paper elucidates the concept of an entrepreneurial network, distinguishes different levels of entrepreneurial network, and shows how these different levels interact with each other to promote growth in the international economy.

## An Economic Approach to Networks

Until recently, economists assumed that competitive markets could handle information in a costless manner, failing to recognize that, whatever kind of institution is involved, information processing incurs substantial costs. Moreover, to explain why people compete so readily, economists assumed that material greed was the dominant human motive. Recent research has sought to remedy these weaknesses [Casson, 1995]. Information costs have been incorporated into decision making using the theory of teams [Carter, 1995], and ethical constraints on greed have been introduced using theories of altruism [Collard, 1978] and "self-control" [Thaler and Shefrin, 1981]. In line with these trends, this paper emphasizes information costs, and stresses the social and ethical dimension of behavior too.

Within this new theoretical framework, networks emerge quite naturally as coordinating mechanisms. Coordination can also be effected through firms and markets. Networks have been commended as alternatives to firms on the grounds that their decision making is more democratic and their outcomes more equitable. It has been said that networks are preferable to markets because they involve more social contact and encourage information to be shared; they are said to be more cooperative and less competitive, and to

*BUSINESS AND ECONOMIC HISTORY,* Volume Twenty-six, no. 2, Winter 1997.
 ISSN 0894-6825.

reinforce the sense of mutual obligation on which society depends [Best, 1990]. The new theoretical perspective shows that networks are often more efficient too. Communication may be richer and more reliable within a network than within either a firm or a market. The question is no longer whether networks are required for coordination, but simply under what conditions they work best.

The choice between firm, market, and network may be analyzed using the principle that the most efficient arrangement will survive and less efficient arrangements will not. Individual members of a network face the alternatives of trading impersonally in a market or becoming ordinary employees of a firm. If the gains from belonging to the network are less than the gains they anticipate from these alternatives, then they will quit the network. If everyone behaves the same way then the network will disintegrate. Conversely, if people believe that they would be better off within a network than within a firm or market, then they will quit to join the network instead. In the long run the arrangement used under any given set of circumstances has a tendency to be the efficient from the private individual's point of view.

What is efficient in one industry, however, or in one location, may not be efficient in another. Thus different institutional arrangements may coexist in different parts of the economy. The role of network theory is to identify the factors which govern which arrangement is used under which circumstances. As circumstances alter, the balance of advantages may change over time; thus a successful network may start to decline if a shift in technology or a change in the structure of demand creates new problems with which firms or markets can deal more easily.

Given that networks are widely used, it would be surprising if they all took the same form. Historical evidence clearly points to diversity. For example, the networks of the Northern Italian textile districts [Bull, Pitt and Szarka, 1993] have always been very different from the networks of the merchant community of a great metropolis like London [Brenner, 1993]. There are differences across function (manufacturing, banking, scientific research), across industries (between mining and metal fabrication, for example), over space and over time. Within the general concept of a network, therefore, different types of network need to be identified. The failure, so far, to develop an adequate typology of networks is one of the major obstacles to further advance in the field. Without an adequate typology it is impossible to explain how the form of the network adapts to the specific coordination problems that it used to solve.

The importance of distinguishing different kinds of network is underlined by the way that membership of different kinds of network overlaps. Some people belong to only local networks, based in small regions such as industrial districts or rural "shires." These people include self-employed artisans, leading farmers, local dealers, and so on. In each region, though, there will be a few people who belong to national networks too. These middle-level entrepreneurs include local wholesale merchants, and other leading local employers. Within a national network there will be some who belong to an international network. These high-level entrepreneurs include major export and import merchants, managers of large industrial concerns, bankers, and so on.

A feature of entrepreneurial networks is that members of a high-level network specialize in belonging to several lower-level networks. Thus members of the international network will deliberately keep in contact with several national networks, while members of a national network will deliberately keep in contact with several local networks. The higher-level entrepreneurs maintain a presence in lower-level networks so that they can promote trade and investment between people in different lower-level networks. At each level they use their own network to share information that is surplus to their own requirements, and receive similar information in return. Each member may have knowledge of some local network that they cannot put to any further use themselves, but which may still be valuable to other people. Each member thereby derives advantage from information that others cannot use. Through the network they can also club together to advance their mutual interest in free trade, cheap transport, and security of property.

**Basic Concepts and Definitions**

An adequate definition of a network must be sufficiently general to accommodate the diversity noted above, yet specific enough to form the basis for rigorous analysis. For the purposes of this paper a network may be defined as a set of high-trust relationships which either directly or indirectly link together everyone in a social group. A linkage is defined in terms of information flow between two people. It is a two-way flow in which both individuals send messages and receive them. The individual linkage is the basic element from which a network is built up. Different configurations of linkage create different kinds of network. In a dense network almost everyone can communicate directly with everybody else, whereas in a sparse network people often have to communicate indirectly through someone else instead. The geometry of the linkages is one of the dimensions on which a typology of networks can be based .

Networks play an important role in synthesizing information. Most economic decisions – in particular, investment decisions – are sufficiently complex that they cannot be taken using only information from a single source. It is necessary to pool information from several sources. Thus an employer seeking to expand production needs to know about product prices and raw material prices, as well as the cost of machinery and the latest technology embodied in it. While he could research these issues for himself, it is often cheaper to get information and advice from other people instead. "Who you know" is often more important than "what you know" because the *people* that you know can plug the gaps in *what* you know. This, of course, depends on knowing the *right* people. Sometimes the right people are those who know a lot of facts, but more often they are people are simply know a lot of other people who in turn know useful facts. These people can act as brokers, linking the decision maker who demands the information to the person who ultimately knows the facts.

It is important to note that the flows of resources that the network is used to coordinate may also constitute a network, though not a network of the kind described above. They form a network in the sense that different factories within an industrial district may be connected to one another by intermediate product flows, as when leather soles and leather uppers are passed to an assembly line in which they are sewn together to make up shoes. Products may be transported over networks too; thus goods destined for export may be transported over a railway network, passing through various railway junctions (nodes) on their way to a port. Here they may be loaded onto liner ships, which follow a network of routes to different parts of the world. The difference between these networks and the type of network defined above is the network defined above is concerned with information flow, and not with the flow of material products themselves. The material flows are the objects of coordination and the information flows are the means by which they are coordinated. The subject of this paper is information flow, but to understand why different structures of information flow are used in different circumstances it is, of course, necessary to understand the structure of the product flow as well. This is illustrated by the modeling of international trade flows at the end of this paper.

## The Quality of Information

Considered as a commodity, information faces serious problems of quality control. Information may be false, and acting on false information can be very costly indeed. Information may be incorrect because of the *incompetence* of the person who supplies it – for example, his observations may not be correct. It may be due to a *failure of communication* – language difficulties or cultural differences may lead to a message being misconstrued. Finally, the error may be due to *dishonesty*. The source of the information may not bother to check it properly because he knows that someone else will suffer the consequences. More seriously, he may deliberately distort the information to influence the recipient's behavior to his personal advantage. Networks can improve the quality of information by diffusing competence, in the form of best-practice techniques, by standardizing language and culture to reduce communication costs, and by encouraging honesty between members [Casson, 1997].

Dishonesty is a particular problem for information embodied in contracts. Contracts may be offered purely to lure people into situations where they can be taken advantage of. Dishonesty can be controlled in various ways. If there is a prospect of further trades, then enlightened self-interest may suggest to a potential cheat that the cheating should be postponed until further trades have taken place. If there is always a prospect of future trades, so that no one is sure when the last trade will take place, then honesty may be sustained indefinitely. Repetition can be encouraged by breaking down one-off large-value trades into recurrent low-value trades. This may also help to reduce inventory costs, though transport costs will almost certainly increase as a result. There are many instances, though, such as the supply of indivisible durable goods and infrastructure, where this is not practicable.

An alternative approach is to invest in reputation mechanisms. While people may not trade with the same person again, they may well expect to trade with people who are known to them. If they cheat one person then word may get around to other people and future trades will be lost as a result. This discourages cheating at the outset. Because networks facilitate such information flow, they can play an important role in strengthening reputation mechanisms.

The logic of this argument has a weakness though. However enlightened, the logic of self-interest is that the decision to cheat represents a finely tuned response to the circumstances that prevail at the time. The fact that a person cheated one trading partner does not necessarily mean that they will cheat another, because the material incentives may be different in the second case. To transfer experience from one encounter to another in a relevant form, the reputation mechanism must convey a large amount of information on the situation in which the cheating took place.

A further weakness of the reputation mechanism is that it only works if the cheat is caught. While it may discourage some people from cheating, it may simply encourage others to put more effort into devising more subtle forms of fraud. Finally, the assumption that reputation is of purely instrumental value has a number of counter-factual implications. For example, not only will businessmen start to defraud their customers shortly before they plan to retire, but they will maximize the value of their final transactions in order to maximize their fraudulent gain. This is because, by assumption, they care nothing for their reputation in its own right.

This is where the high-trust nature of the network relationship becomes important. In a high-trust relationship both parties can trust each other even though they each face a material incentive to cheat. Because by definition a network is high-trust, the chances of being cheated are much lower when trading within a network than when trading outside it.

The basic idea behind a high-trust network is that people people face emotional incentives as well as material ones, and that emotional incentives of an appropriate kind can outweigh material incentives that would otherwise induce people to cheat. If each person knows that the others face an emotional incentive of this kind, then each will believe that the others will not cheat. This belief is warranted because the supposition is correct. No one cheats, predictions are borne out, and so a high-trust equilibrium is sustained.

**Entrepreneurship: Judgmental Decision-Making in a Volatile Environment**

The key to understanding entrepreneurship is to recognize that decisions are taken in a volatile environment. This reflects the fact that the economy is in a constant state of flux. In the absence of volatility the economy would settle down into a permanent state of equilibrium. Most economists assume that the primary function of the entrepreneur is to organize production. This is a mistake. Schumpeter [1934] distinguished five types of innovation, of which only two have to do with production. Yet self-styled Schumpeterians of today emphasize technological innovation in production to the exclusion of the other three forms. Two of the other three forms are concerned with developing new markets – for exports of finished goods, and for raw materials from new sources of supply.

Most markets are created because an entrepreneur – or in some cases a group of entrepreneurs – decided to set them up. Markets are institutions devised to overcome a series of obstacles to trade. To overcome these obstacles, markets tend to take a specific form. The entrepreneur acts as an intermediator, buying from sellers, reselling to buyers, and covering his costs by a margin between the buying and selling prices. Ordinary buyers and sellers are happy to pay this margin because the process of trade is greatly simplified for them.

There are four main obstacles to trade. The first is ignorance of who to trade with, which is overcome by setting up a market at a convenient central place. The intermediators have a regular presence there. Sellers bringing their goods to market therefore know that there will always be someone willing to buy, while buyers know that there will always be someone willing to sell. To guarantee this situation, the intermediators need to hold stocks of goods to offer to the buyers, and stocks of money to offer to the sellers.

The mention of money leads to the second obstacle to trade that intermediators help to overcome. This is the difficulty for the trader of specifying exactly what he wants to buy, and describing what he has to offer in return. This is overcome by inspecting goods that are on display – or at least examining a sample of them – and by holding money as a convenient means of payment to offer in exchange. The display consists of the goods that the intermediator holds in stock to satisfy immediate demand. Indeed, the intermediator may have notified the buyers in advance of the goods he has for sale by advertising them to the buyer in his home.

Next is the problem of negotiating price. This is simplified when there are several people to haggle with, since the presence of competitors encourages everyone to offer their best price at the outset. The presence of several intermediators dealing in the same good at the same place gives the buyers and the sellers confidence that the price quoted by each intermediator is a competitive one. The ease of searching for the best price ensures that all the prices are the best, and therefore obviates the need to actually shop around.

Finally, there is the problem of enforcement of contracts. Because of their constant presence in their market, intermediators quickly acquire a reputation. Once they have acquired a good reputation, it becomes a valuable asset which they have a strong incentive to maintain. It pays to be honest with everyone, because word of their default will quickly get around. This is the customer's guarantee of quality, and the supplier's guarantee that he will get paid. If the buyer and the seller were to try to deal with each other directly, then because of their sporadic appearance at the market, and their consequent lack of reputation, neither can fully trust the other. Use of an intermediator therefore creates a chain of trust. The buyer pays in advance, and the seller pays in arrears. The intermediator thereby eliminates the risk from trading with people of no repute, while the people of no repute can trade because they both trust the intermediator.

## Entrepreneurial Networks and the Growth of International Trade

From a historical point of view the most dramatic impact of entrepreneurial networks has almost certainly been in the development of international trade. So far as Western European history is concerned, it is the Age of Discovery, and the subsequent Commercial Revolution, which testifies most vividly to their impact. However, the impact is so pervasive that it can be seen throughout the second millennium [Britnell, 1993; Snooks, 1995].

The obstacles to trade that were overcome were not simply those of transport costs, tariffs, and the difficulty of operating in foreign jurisdictions. International relations were unstable. Where trade was possible, the interests of political leaders lay mainly in levying taxes and tolls. There was popular dislike of merchants who exported local foodstuffs, driving up the prices of necessities such as corn in local markets, or "forestalled" local consumers altogether by buying wholesale at the farm gate [Chartres, 1985]. There was also suspicion of import merchants, who were accused by the puritanical of creating a socially wasteful demand for novelties, and by the working classes of destroying local artisans' jobs.

The role of entrepreneurial networks in supporting international trade is illustrated schematically in Figure 1. It shows two industrial districts, located in different countries. In each industrial district there are three upstream plants connected to two downstream plants. Each plant is indicated by a square. Because the optimal size of plant is different at each stage, vertical integration is discouraged. It is therefore supposed that each plant is owned and managed by an independent self-employed entrepreneur. Flows of intermediate product from an upstream plant to a downstream plant are indicated by thick lines. The arrowhead indicates the direction of material flow. Any upstream plant can supply any downstream plant within the same district.

Information flows are indicated by thin lines. Information connects people – who are denoted by circles – rather than plants. Information flow is a two-way affair, so there are arrowheads in both directions. In each district a merchant, M11, M21, specializes in handling information. He acts as an information hub. In contractual terms, he buys output from the upstream producers and "puts it out" for downstream processing. He negotiates prices and quantities with the producers, using the information he has gathered from the upstream producers to inform his negotiations with the downstream producers, and *vice versa*. The information he processes is mostly encoded in price quotations.

**Figure 1:** *International Trade – Entrepreneurial Networks*

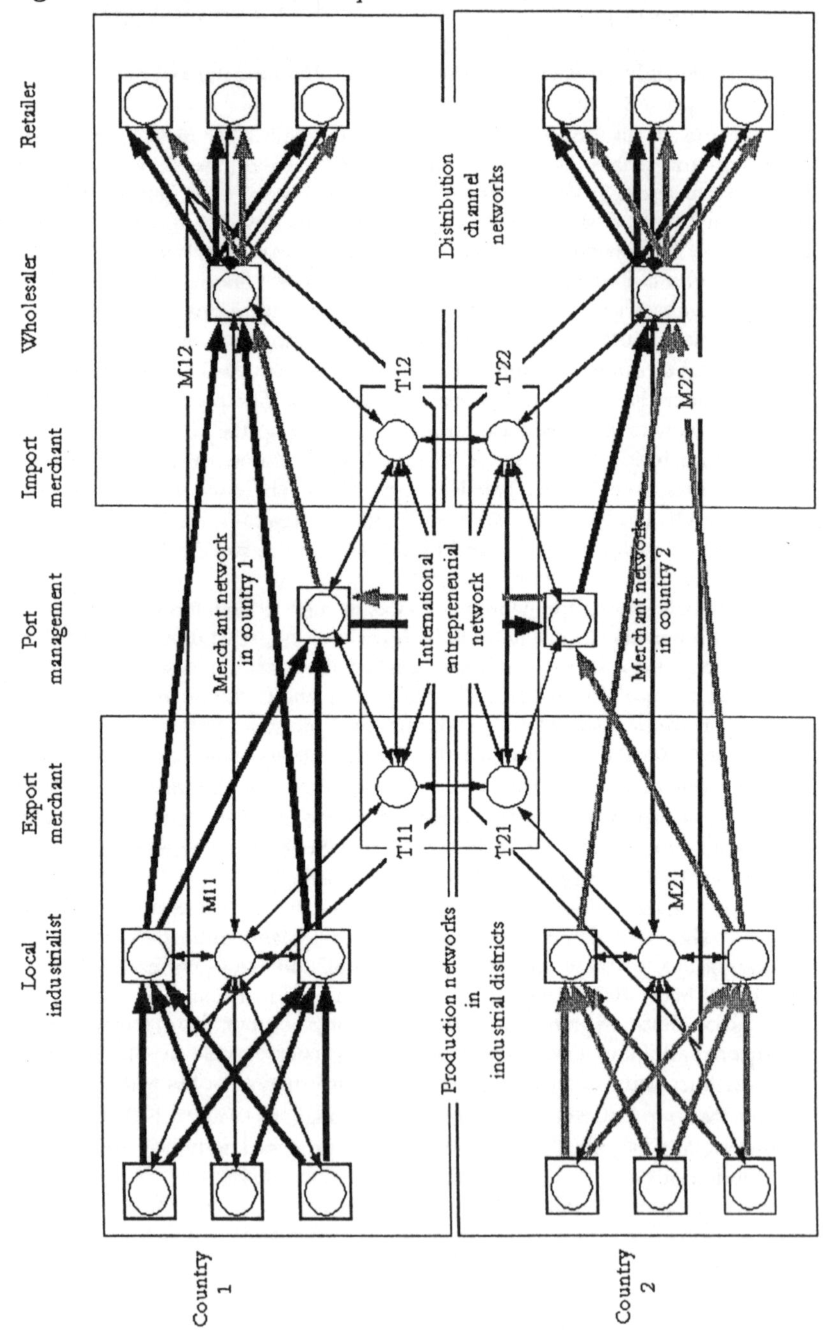

Notice that information flows exhibit a different pattern from product flows. The information flows are intermediated by the merchant, whereas the product flows are not. The merchant handles the information and acts as a nexus of contracts between the producers, but he does not physically handle the product. The product is transported directly from the upstream producers to the downstream producers. The merchant simply gives instructions as to what product is to be delivered where. Because the merchant handles only information, the circle that represents him is not associated with any square.

Now consider the rest of the figure. It is assumed that the two districts produce different variants of the same type of product. Both products are consumed in both countries. Some consumers prefer one variant, and others prefer another. The two variants may differ simply in design, having the same quality of workmanship and selling for roughly the same price. Alternatively, one product may be distinctly superior to the other in terms of quality, and sell for a premium price. Nevertheless, some consumers are always prepared to switch to the other variant if there is a significant fall in its price. To this extent the different varieties are substitutes for each other. Flows of the first variety, produced in country 1, are indicated by thick black lines, and flows of the second variety, produced in country 2, by thick grey lines.

Goods for the home market are consigned directly to a domestic wholesale distributor, whereas goods for export are sent to the nearest port. This is also the port through which the other variety is imported. Goods are consigned from this port to the domestic wholesaler, who then combines the two varieties of good in the proportions requested by local retailers, and dispatches them together.

The diagram shows only one merchant in each industrial district, and only one wholesaler in each domestic market. In practice there are likely to be several merchants of each type, and these merchants may constitute a group in their own right. Potentially they compete with one another, but in practice they can collude as well. Thus the merchants within an industrial district may seek to impose customary prices for putting out when demand is buoyant, while reserving the right to cut prices further when times are bad. On the more positive side, they may organize an apprenticeship system in conjunction with a local college, and encourage "on the job" training by collectively outlawing the "poaching" of staff.

The figure shows four merchants specifically engaged in international trade. There are two in each country – one organizing exports and the other organizing imports. Like their domestic counterparts, these merchants do not handle the product whose flow they coordinate. Each export merchant buys from the merchant in his local industrial district and sells into the foreign distribution channel, setting a margin between his buying price and his selling price to cover his administrative costs. These costs include the charges levied at the ports, the cost of shipping, and the cost of transport to and from the port. Thus in country 1 the export merchant T11 buys from the merchant M11 and sells to the merchant T22, who in turn sells on to the wholesaler M22. The import merchant T12 buys from the merchant T21 and resells to the wholesaler M12. Similarly in country 2 the export merchant T21 buys from M21 and sells to T12, while the import merchant T22 buys from T11 and sells on to the wholesaler M22.

Note that intermediation by the merchants involves more than just a single stage. The domestic market involves two merchants, the putter-out and the wholesaler, while international marketing involves no less than four stages. Linking the putter-out to the wholesaler are the export merchant in the home country and the import merchant in the foreign country.

The justification for all these stages is that each intermediator overcomes some obstacle which the two adjoining intermediators would encounter if they tried to "cut him out" and do business directly. In domestic markets it is the difficulty that ordinary people face in negotiating large deals, where fine judgement is required in fixing a suitable quantity and price. Collecting reputational information on quality of workmanship, and on reliability in payment and delivery, is also important. In the international context, combining knowledge of two different countries, and keeping this knowledge up-to-date, is the key advantage. Certainly, if critical information must be collected face-to-face then a good deal of time-consuming travel may be involved. It could, of course, be something as simple as a language difference. The export merchant may speak the foreign language, for example, whereas the domestic merchant does not. This can only explain one additional stage of intermediation in an international context, though. There must be another factor too, such as a special knowledge of local customs and laws needed to enforce contracts.

The structure of networks that supports international trade is also shown in the figure. There is a hierarchy of networks with interlocking membership. Each network is indicated by a box, enclosing the individual members of the group. The highest-level network comprises the international merchants. The figure illustrates additional horizontal and vertical links within this group. These links will tend to arise naturally from chance meetings at conferences and international trade fairs. Such events are a traditional method of setting up business deals in foreign markets. The fairs allow export merchants from different countries to share their experiences of other countries with merchants in non-competing lines. They also allow export and import merchants from the same country to share information relating to the prospects for the domestic industry as a whole. More generally, everyone can form an assessment of how well everyone else is doing, and therefore benchmark their own performance against that of their competitors with greater accuracy.

There are two middle-level networks, comprising the merchants of each country. Half the members of each network belong to the high-level international network, and the remainder belong to low-level domestic networks. The figure shows that there are two main types of low-level network: one concerned with production and the other with distribution. Within the production network the role of the putter-out is dominant. As indicated earlier, there will normally be a group of putters out. They will form a local business elite, and socialize with each other. They also form the dominant group within the wider network that includes the artisan entrepreneurs. The self-employed artisans are the lowest level of entrepreneur in the system in the terms of the overall significance of the strategies they pursue. There is a similar distinction between the wholesalers and the retailers within the distribution network. The wholesalers are essentially the "channel leaders," dictating terms to the retailers because of their superior access to information through their backward links into production.

It should be emphasized that from an economic point of view the links between entrepreneurs at different levels are maintained largely on the initiative of the higher-level entrepreneurs, who find the high-trust network links a cost-effective way of maintaining control. If the international merchants did not socialize with the domestic merchants then they might have to integrate backwards into production, or integrate forward into distribution, to achieve the control they require. Similarly if the putters out did not socialize with the artisans then they would have to integrate into production themselves and take on the artisans as employees. This would require a detailed knowledge of craft production methods which they do not have. Again, if the wholesalers did not socialize with the retailers then they might have to integrate forwards into retailing themselves, and take on the retailers as their employees. The costs of employee supervision are such that it is cheaper to invest in a few "handshakes" and some friendly hospitality instead.

## The Geometry of Networks

The geometry of the network at each level is different. In general, the lower the level of the group, the greater is the focus on supporting routine operations and the stronger is the consequent incentive to channel information through a hub.

The local merchant, or putter out, is the hub of communications in the industrial district. Coordination is effected by communication between merchant and artisan, and not between one artisan and another. The artisans defer to the judgement of the merchant in setting the price because he has a wider view of the situation than they possess.

In the high-level network the hub is replaced by a dense web of communications which allows all the members to communicate directly with each other. The network is democratic and collegial. This reflects the dispersion of expertise within the group. Everyone knows something which could conceivably be important to any of the others, and so there is active socialization.

The middle level network resembles a chain, in which each element is connected only to adjacent ones. Putters out are in touch with wholesalers and export merchants; wholesalers are in touch with putters out and import merchants, and so on. This structure reflects the fact that the linkages are focused on maintaining channels of distribution.

**The Location of High-Level Entrepreneurial Networks**

Entrepreneurs tend to be relatively footloose. High-level entrepreneurs in particular are willing to pursue profit opportunities wherever they may lead. In international business entrepreneurial ideas may be stimulated by foreign travel on military service, diplomatic service, scientific survey work or engineering work. Historically, travelling could be connected with the itinerant trade of the pedlar, drover, or the latter-day sales representative [Pirenne, 1925; Fontaine, 1996]. Entrepreneurial attitudes are characteristic of many migrants. Many entrepreneurs seem to grow up in relatively open societies where immigration is common, outside influences are strong, and the force of purely local custom and tradition is relatively weak. The strong commercial links of these communities with the outside world make ambitious young people aware of the opportunities that exist elsewhere.

Given that entrepreneurs are mobile, the regions that are most successful in the long run will be those that are most attractive to entrepreneurs. The most obvious attraction is that the region is an information hub. It is here that the kind of wide-ranging synthesis of information that is required for major innovations can most readily be effected. Since a large amount of commercial information is encoded in the form of prices, and prices are set in markets, the range of markets is a crucial factor.

Furthermore, an existing market center is the obvious place for an entrepreneur to develop a new market for an innovative product. By creating a new market where existing markets can be found, the entrepreneur simplifies the shopping process, since on a single visit an ordinary customer can accomplish several trades. This agglomeration economy is reinforced by other economies too. In any given market, the intensity of competition and the degree of liquidity are both important in guaranteeing customers reasonable prices when trading at short notice. By simply joining an existing market an entrepreneur can give that market greater "depth." By reducing customers' information costs, this greater depth makes the market center an even more attractive place to trade. In aggregate terms, this generates increasing returns to market size, as measured by the volume of trade [Krugman, 1991].

To facilitate the enforcement of contracts a market center requires an efficient and honest legal system which is well adapted to resolving potentially complex legal disputes. People must be free to enter markets, and to incorporate companies. Business and government must network effectively, and obviously taxation and the risk of expropriation must be low. The local culture should be welcoming to entrepreneurial immigrants, and conducive to networking. Networking amongst entrepreneurs not only improves their overall quality of service to the customer, but also facilitates the collective financing of strategic investments designed to increase the volume of trade.

A highly competitive and impersonal culture is not appropriate, because it presumes too much self-interest and breeds distrust in matters that inevitably remain inadequately covered by the law. In the long run the most successful central places are those whose culture engineers high levels of trust among entrepreneurs.

## References

Best, M.H., *The New Competition: Institutions of Industrial Restructuring* (Oxford, 1990).

Brenner, R., *Merchants and Revolution: Commercial Change, Political Conflict and London's Overseas Traders, 1550-1653* (Cambridge, 1993).

Britnell, R.H., *The Commercialisation of English Society, 1000-1500* (Cambridge, 1993).

Bull, A. et al., *Entrepreneurial Textile Communities: A Comparative Study of Small Textile and Clothing Firms* (London, 1993).

Carter, M.J., "Information and the Division of Labour: Implications for the Firm's Choice of Organisation," *Economic Journal*, 105 (1995), 385-397.

Casson, M.C., *Studies in the Economics of Trust* (Aldershot, 1995).

Casson, M.C., *Information and Organisation: A New Perspective on the Theory of the Firm* (Oxford, 1997).

Chartres J.A., The Marketing of Agricultural Produce, in J. Thirsk, ed., *The Agrarian History of England and Wales V: 1640-1750, II Agrarian Change* (Cambridge, 1985), 406-502.

Collard, D.A., *Altruism and Economy* (Oxford, 1978).

Fontaine, L., *History of Pedlars in Europe*, trans. V. Whittaker (Oxford, 1996).

Frank, R.H., *Passions within Reason: The Strategic Role of the Emotions* (New York, 1988).

Grassby, R., *The Business Community of Seventeenth Century England* (Cambridge, 1995).

Krugman, P.R., *Geography and Trade* (Cambridge, MA, 1991).

Leibenstein, H., "Entrepreneurship and Development," *American Economic Review*, 58 (1968) 72-83.

Pirenne, H., *Medieval Cities: Their Origins and the Revival of Trade*, trans. F.D. Halsey (Princeton, NJ, 1925).

Schumpeter, J.A., *The Theory of Economic Development*, trans. R. Opie (Cambridge, MA, 1934).

Snooks, G.D., "The Dynamic Role of the Market in the Anglo-Norman Economy and Beyond, 1086-1300," in R.H. Britnell and B.M.S. Campbell, eds., *A Commercialising Economy: England 1086 to c.1300* (Manchester, 1995), 27-54.

Thaler, R.H., and H.M. Shefrin, "An Economic Theory of Self-control," *Journal of Political Economy*, 89 (1981), 392-40.

# [6]

# *Diaspora Entrepreneurial Networks in the Black Sea and Greece, 1870-1917**

**Ioanna Pepelasis Minoglou**
Panteion University

**Helen Louri**
Athens University of Economics & Business

## Introduction

The few studies that have been written about the Greek diaspora from Russia have either concentrated on the 'golden age' (from the end of the XVIIIth century until the Russian-Turkish War of 1877-78) of Odessa, or they have focused on the role of Greek shipping in the Black Sea in connection to maritime networks in Western Europe.[1]

The process of 'early' decline in Odessa, the rise of the Greek entrepreneurial interest in the 'newer' eastern ports of the Black Sea and the Sea of Azov, and the eventual demise of Greek

* We thank Dr. Gelina Harlaftis for her expert comments throughout the writing of the paper. We also thank the participants of the staff research seminar of the Economic History Department (L.S.E.).
An earlier draft of this paper appeared (in September 1994) under the title «Greek Diaspora Merchant Communities of the Black Sea and the Sea of Azov and Greek-Russian trade: 1870-1917». This initial draft was financed by the Economic Research Center of the Athens University of Economics and Business and it was written in collaboration with Olga Sokolowskaya, who collected and translated the Russian material used.

[1] See: G. Harlaftis, *A History of Greek owned Shipping: The Making of an International Tramp Fleet, 1830 to the Present Day* (London 1996). This book has an excellent account of the development of Greek shipping in the Black Sea. Also, G. Harlaftis, "The Role of the Greeks in Black Sea Trade, 1830-1900", in L.R. Fischer and H.W. Nordvik (eds), *Shipping and Trade, 1750-1950: Essays in International Maritime Economic History,* (Ponterfract 1990). Also P. Herlihy, 'Greek Merchants in Odessa in the 19th Century' *Harvard Ukrainian Studies* III/IV (1979-1980).

entrepreneurs during the second decade of the XXth century are main themes of this paper. It examines Greek entrepreneurial networks from the stand-point of the Black Sea and the Sea of Azov. This is the first time a systematic attempt has been made to explore Greek-Russian trade and its interconnections with the diaspora. The material used is largely Russian. This is a novelty for up to now scholars who have done research in the field have largely worked with British archival material. The study of new material on an unresearched time period can only provide 'conclusions' that must be treated at this stage merely as preliminary and hypothetical. In short, the main hypotheses made regarding the features of the Greek merchant diaspora in the Black Sea are the following:

I. The Greek entrepreneur of the Black Sea was a mobile creature, following the trade routes and showing versatility in adapting to new situations. He had a multi-business orientation, often spreading risks by participating in different ventures, combining commerce with banking, and shipping. (Less often, a merchant would simultaneously interweave commercial activities with manufacturing and land cultivation). Also, he was keen on conducting business on credit. In addition, he operated within the framework of a cosmopolitan network. To put it simply, the Greek merchant communities in the Black Sea were an integral part of a larger whole, i.e., the international commercial Greek diaspora spreading from the Black Sea (and the Danube) throughout the Mediterranean and reaching up to Northern Europe and Britain. However, it should also be underlined that Greek merchants went into joint ventures with local businessmen and cooperated with the branches of locally established foreign firms, often without necessarily relinquishing their 'privateer' status.

II. Greek decline in the Black Sea area began almost half a century after the overall demise of the merchant activities of the Greek diaspora. Although from the 1870s both Odessa and its Greek merchants may have suffered a decline, it is also clear that: a) the decline of Odessa was relative as it remained a large port[2] and b) Greek merchants, following the shifts in the grain trade routes, moved eastward along to other increasingly important Black Sea and Sea of Azov ports.[3] The growth of these ports after 1870 coincided with a more obvious Greek presence. The process of decline of the Greek interest in the wider area of the Russian Black Sea came after 1905.

III. The thesis that the Greeks succumbed to the penetration of British and French joint-stock companies around the 1850s (either by becoming middlemen or by departing) cannot be generalized.[4] It is of some relevance only for Odessa and not the other ports of the area. (Some of the other factors which had a negative influence on the Greek merchants of Odessa were: the increasing support of the Russian government towards native entrepreneurs and the rise of local and Jewish middlemen after the emancipation of the serfs in 1861.)

IV. The decline in Russian Greek trade brought about during the Balkan wars and World War I. had a devastating impact on the Greek diaspora in Russia, although trade with Greece was but a small part of their activities.

In sum, our research introduces both new information and hypotheses while simultaneously it confirms some of the observations made in the literature that the Greek merchant of the diaspora was 'polytropos' (i.e. a man of many resources) and that Greek merchants in the Sea of Azov played an important part in the transition of Greek shipping from sail to steam.[5]

[2] For the assumption that the overall decline of the merchant activities of the Greek diaspora started in the 1850s see: H. Hadziiossif, «Greek Merchant Communities and Independent Greece: Interpretations and Problems», *Politis*, 1983, pp. 28-34 (in Greek). Also, Odessa remained the largest port in terms of population but not of the export trade.

[3] Grains were the main export item of southern Russia. Before 1900, the Sea of Azov exported a third of the wheat exported from south Russian ports. By 1910 it exported over half.

[4] A. Kitroeff, 'The Greek Diaspora in the Mediterranean and the Black Sea as Seen through American Eyes' (1815-1861), in S.Vryonis, Jr., *The Greeks and the Sea*, (New York 1994).

[5] G. Harlaftis, *Greek Seamen and Greek Ships on the Eve of World War I*, (Athens, 1994), (in Greek).

In terms of methodology, the material at our disposal posed two basic problems. First, how to integrate the general picture (the macro-facts, such as the figures for Russian trade with Greece) with the rich micro-information on the network of Greek firms in the Black Sea. The second difficulty has to do with the nature of the material. Chronologically there are gaps in the data available and thus it has not been possible to present long and complete time series. If, at times, we appear to be offering 'snapshots' and not the flow (dynamic) of economic events, it is not out of choice but only because there was no other option!

Finally, we wish to note that the names of the Russian Greeks mentioned in the text have been written exactly in the same way as we found them in the Russian archives. We have thus faithfully copied them in order to convey the degree to which Greeks adjusted culturally to their host country (i.e. Russia).

This paper has largely been based on Russian material which was collected and translated by Olga Skolovskaya (Russian Academy of Sciences, Institute of Slavic and Balkan Studies). It has made extensive use of Russian bibliographical sources of the early XXth century. However, the bulk of the material employed has been drawn from Russian primary sources - both published and unpublished. The primary published material largely consists of statistical surveys of the Russian government from 1870 to 1916. These included the annual surveys of the foreign trade of Russia, the bulletins of the Russian Ministry of Trade and Industry, surveys based on Consular Reports, Customs Reports, the regulations of Trade Committees etc. Extensive use was also made of the contemporary Russian press (journals and newspapers).

A few words are necessary on the attitude of the bureaucracy of Imperial Russia towards the diaspora Greeks and Greece. The documents available reveal that Russian officials had mixed feelings about Greek entrepreneurs. On the one hand they admired them for their commercial talent and their 'devotion' to Greece. On the other, they resented the fact that although they were Russian subjects they continued to live as Greeks (for example donating to

Greek charities and the Greek government) and were adept in evading taxes.

Although Russia as a great power applied political and economic coercion over Greece, the attitude of its officials towards their Greek counterparts does not appear to have been as condescending as that of Germany or Britain. An interesting example of how Russian officials empathised with the plight of Greece is the following: in 1898, the 'protecting' powers (including Russia) created an 'international' body for the supervision of Greek state finances. It was named the International Financial Commission (I.F.C.) and apparently some important Russian officials, including the Minister of Finance S.J.Vitte, disapproved of the 'financial subjugation' which this commission entailed for Greece.[6]

## The general economic background: the Black Sea and the Sea of Azov Ports

Historically, the presence of Russia in world trade did not match the size of its economy.[7] Russian producers were basically geared towards the home market. Although the latter grew fast throughout the XIXth century, requiring an increasing amount of resources, from the 1870s onwards Russia managed to become a major exporter of raw materials as well. For instance, grain exports before World War I. represented almost one third of world grain exports. Russian grain was almost exclusively exported from the ports of the South. These ports were surrounded by the 11 most important grain-growing regions of the country. Russia at the time was also a major producer and exporter of petroleum

6 State Russian Historical Archive in St. Petersburg (SRHA), S.Vitte to S. Mouraviev, 4 December, 1897, Fond 560, Inventory 22, File 195, pp.197-199.

7 Archive of Foreign Affairs of the Russian Empire (AFARE), Fond Greek Table, File 555, pp.2-3.

8 Kerosene accounted for around 80 percent of all petroleum product exports of Russia prior to 1910. Thereafter, and up to the outbreak of World War I., kerosene exports fell to about 50 percent of the exports of petroleum products. The main importers of Russian petroleum goods were Turkey, Britain, Germany, Belgium, France and Holland.

products among which kerosene was the most important.[8] Petroleum products were mostly exported from Batoum and Novorosiisk.[9]

**TABLE 1 : Russian Imports**
*(in thousand roubles)*

| *Years* | Bulgaria | G.Britain | Germany | Greece | Romania | Turkey | France |
|---|---|---|---|---|---|---|---|
| *1892* | 31 | 101,177 | 101,653 | 1,029 | 1,457 | 9,671 | 18,491 |
| *1894* | 39 | 132,758 | 142,976 | 2,411 | 1,933 | 7,185 | 28,123 |
| *1896* | 31 | 111,309 | 190,169 | 2,598 | 1,704 | 6,100 | 23,411 |
| *1898* | 79 | 115,294 | 202,197 | 722 | 1,873 | 6,867 | 27,110 |
| *1900* | 386 | 127,144 | 216,852 | 760 | 1,589 | 7,705 | 31,445 |
| *1902* | 107 | 99,224 | 208,471 | 921 | 1,600 | 7,544 | 26,883 |
| *1904* | 58 | 103,390 | 228,154 | 900 | 1,996 | 7,368 | 26,548 |
| *1906* | 340 | 105,725 | 298,421 | 1,143 | 4,843 | 7,826 | 28,717 |
| *1908* | 38 | 120,285 | 348,426 | 1,344 | 2,756 | 7,452 | 36,287 |
| *1910* | 56 | 153,847 | 449,794 | 1,587 | 2,311 | 10,836 | 60,972 |

*Source*: M.V.Dovnar-Zapolskii, *Russian Exports and the World Market* (Kiev 1914).

Foreign trade was the main livelihood of the 40,000,000 people living in the South on the eve of World War I.[10] In 1912 the value of Russian exports in total was equal to 1,500,000 milliards of roubles and 60 percent (i.e. 900,000 milliards) went through the ports of the Black Sea and the Sea of Azov.[11] Most industrial exports of Russia left from the North.[12] The few industrial exports of the South were directed mostly to the Balkans and Turkey. They consisted of wood, glass, cotton, metals and rubber articles.

Odessa, the most important port of the Black Sea throughout the XIXth century, was founded in 1786. From then and up to 1857

[9] During 1885-1900 the total exports of kerosene was equal to 78 percent of the total petroleum exports of Russia

[10] This figure is for 1913. Source. 'About measures in developing imports trade of Odessa port.' Kiev, 1914

[11] Alaverdov E.G., 'Russian Export Through the Port of the Black and Azov Seas', (Rostov-via-Donu), 1975

[12] K.V. Kozmin, *Russian Grain Exports,* St.Petersburg 1912. Also, *Russian World,* 16 October, 1913.

it was a free port.[13] By the middle of the XIXth century Odessa's main business was the exporting of grain (basically soft wheat). Navigable rivers such as the Dniestr and Dnieper carried cargo for export down to Odessa. Railways connected Odessa with the grain growing regions of Bessarabia. By the end of the XIXth century, due to the quickening of the pace of exports of hard wheat grown in the south-east regions, the relative importance of Odessa declined. Other ports on the Black Sea and the Sea of Azov increased in importance. On the eastern Black Sea the rising ports were Nikolaev and later Novorossisk. The one that flourished most was Novorosiisk, especially after the closing down of Sevastopol which became a military base of the Imperial Navy. The ports of the Sea of Azov which came to rival Odessa were Rostov, Taganrog, Mariupol, Berdiansk and Yeisk. They were all 'late developers'. By the end of the XIXth century, forty percent of all the grain exports of the South went through the Azov ports.[14]

Navigation was difficult in the Sea of Azov, especially during

**TABLE 2 : Russian Exports**
*(in thousand roubles)*

| *Years* | Bulgaria | G.Britain | Germany | Greece | Romania | Turkey | France |
|---|---|---|---|---|---|---|---|
| *1892* | 196 | 118,523 | 138,239 | 6,812 | 4,943 | 15,910 | 35,109 |
| *1894* | 330 | 175,303 | 147,866 | 4,687 | 7,726 | 16,089 | 56,160 |
| *1896* | 461 | 160,902 | 184,004 | 5,278 | 7,691 | 14,399 | 58,203 |
| *1898* | 510 | 139,906 | 179,436 | 9,653 | 12,675 | 14,477 | 68,594 |
| *1900* | 479 | 145,576 | 187,635 | 8,733 | 5,276 | 18,516 | 57,449 |
| *1902* | 626 | 189,100 | 203,154 | 9,113 | 15,852 | 15,847 | 55,143 |
| *1904* | 723 | 230,423 | 234,843 | 7,471 | 9,617 | 25,300 | 61,782 |
| *1906* | 307 | 225,447 | 284,674 | 10,391 | 17,583 | 15,241 | 76,505 |
| *1908* | 458 | 220,513 | 278,991 | 10,800 | 12,823 | 22,764 | 64,625 |
| *1910* | 211 | 315,475 | 390,640 | 18,331 | 15,049 | 27,859 | 93,646 |

*Source* :M.V.Dovnar-Zapolskii, *Russian Exports and the World Market* (Kiev 1914).

[13] Presumably this was the only *porto franco* in Russia. .

[14] The main exports in order of importance from the Sea of Azov were grain, flax, wool, fat, butter, caviare, leather and iron.

the colder months of winter and the hottest days of summer. In addition, the waters were almost always low and swampy. Transportation to the Sea of the Azov from the hinterland-producing regions was basically effected via rivers. For example, in Mariupol, grain which was the main export staple of the Sea of Azov, was first transported in sacks to the river Kalmeus. Then, the sacks were loaded on boats, rafts and barges. The *schlepts* took the sacks on board and transfered them to the sea-going ships.[15]

Regarding the Greek presence in the area, migration to Russia (Moscow, Kiev, St. Petersburg, Nerchinsk, Vladivostock, and Podolsk) dates back to the Byzantine Empire. An indication of the dispersion of Greeks throughout Russia is the fact that the Greek government had representation in twenty 'cities'. However, most Greeks settled in the South around the shores of the Black Sea.[16] The largest migratory wave towards this area took place under Ekaterina II [the Great], who attracted settlers to this area by granting them special advantages (such as, for example, free land and no obligation to pay taxes). Many of the settlers originally came from the Ionian islands which were at the time a Russian Protectorate.[17] Moreover, Greeks from the Crimea set up on the sparcely populated shore of the Sea of Azov the town of Mariupol and twentyfour villages.[18]

By the mid XIXth century many Greek merchants in the Black Sea had become wealthy, largely as a result of their involvement in the grain trade. The Russians came to resent their prosperity and eventually measures were taken to curtail their preferential status. A good example is the case of the flourishing communities of the Nezine Greeks. In 1883, the Senate abolished the 'independent Greek Estate of Nezine' and one year later their special privileges in trade were also withdrawn. The Greeks

[15] Colonel M. Zolotariev, 'Historical Essay', report prepared for the government.

[16] SRHA, Fond 23, Inventory 11, File 1303, AFARE, Fond Greek Table, File 205, p.2, also File 558, p.3.

[17] Harlaftis, 1990 (*ibid*).

[18] In 1775 they were given special advantages with regard to trade and they paid no taxes to the Treasury.

complained to the Czar, but they were unable to effect a return to their previous status. In an effort to protect all its subjects in the same way, the Russian government on 2 November 1909 signed a declaration stating that Nezine Greeks in Russia would have no special rights as in the past.[19]

## The social 'fabric' and network of the Greek diaspora of southern Russia

There was some degree of social assimilation of Russian Greeks. For example, some served in the diplomatic service of Russia. A certain A.G. Konstandinidi worked as a Russian Vice-Consul in Piraeus (1913). One of the members of the Russian State Council at the time was a A.I. Vergopoulo. Greeks also sat on a number of trade committees and societies. For instance, A. Pecatoros was on the special commission for grain exports of the Merchant and Exchange Committee.[20] Another Greek, E. Panafidin of St. Petersburg worked in the Department of Trade and Industry of Russia and was the chairman of the consulting committee of the Russian Trade Exhibition organized on the ship "Emperor Nickolai II".[21]

Greeks were also active as members of societies representing the interests of local entrepreneurs and merchants. For example, a Greek, N.I. Papadopoulo, was the chairman of the association of tobacco plantations in the Kubanski Ekaterinodanki region. Also, in 1907, in Odessa a Society of South Russian exporters was set up largely by Greek interests.[22] In 1916, a Chamber of Commerce was established. It had a capital of 1,000,000 rubles. Among the Jews

[19] The same was to hold for Russians in Greece.

[20] Greek merchants became members of the nobility. In addition to Rodocanaki who became (through the initiative of Sergei Vitte) a member of the Russian nobility in 1896, there is also the case of Konstantin Vasilievich Targoni who was in the petroleum business. Also see: SRHA,Fond 23, Inventory 11, File 919; also, Fond 20, Inventory 2, File 1164, pp. 1-3. Also, Vestnik Torgovo-promishlennogo siezda, I, Odessa, 1910.

[21] AFARE, Fond 'Mission in Athens', File 1482, p.54. Also, SRHA, Fond 20; Inventory 7; File 129.

[22] Y.K. Mazaraki from Odessa was on the Board of the South-West Export Trade Chamber founded in 1912 in Kiev. Another Greek, P.A. Sakelaridi, was a member of the Taganrog Trade and Manufactures Committee.

and Russians who were members of this Chamber, two well-known Greeks participated: A. Anatra and A.R. Hari.[23] Moreover, Greek merchants often acted as consultants to the government and in particular to the Department of Trade and Manufactures.[24]

Aside from assimilation, the 'socio-political' network developed by the Greek diaspora in Russia depended largely on attaining some degree of 'internal cohesion' through a web of charitable foundations. Besides strengthening ties among nationals, charity was a good business move, as in 1879 the Ministry of Finance allowed charities to import tax-free goods to up to 5,000 rubles a year. Such charities set up by Greek merchants can be found in Odessa, Sevastopol (1893), Taganrog (1895).[25]

In addition to financing charities in Russia, many Greeks of the diaspora cultivated social links with the homeland by making large donations to the Greek state. A notable example is that of Averov who, although amassing a huge fortune in Russia and Egypt, lived a frugal life and upon dying in Alexandria in 1899 left 18,000,000 drs to the Greek state.[26] Sometimes, it was the Greek state that approached the diaspora community for funds. For example, in July 1914 the Greek government created a committee for securing funds from diaspora Greeks in order to build a new dreadnought.[27]

In the last analysis not all migrants were a 'permanent' loss in human capital for Greece. We have no data on the flow of emigrant funds from Russia to Greece. With about 600,000 Greeks established in Southern Russia in the first decade of the twentieth century, they could have not been insignificant in size. Also, it was usual for emigrants, after having lived for many years in Russia and

23 SRHA, Fond 23, Inventory 11, File 919.

24 SRHA, Fond 20, Inventory 7, File 129, pp. 15-16.

25 AFARE, Fond GA, II-8,1893, File 4, Inventory 45; GA 11-8, 1895, File 2.

26 For this and the fact that the developed social-humanitarian consciousness of the Greeks impressed Russian officials see: AFARE, Fond Greek Table, File 203, p. 6.

27 The committee which was headed by Admiral Coundouriotis sent a letter on this subject to (Grivas) the Greek Consul at Sevastopol on 10 July 1914. Presumably, such letters were sent to other cities where the diaspora element was prominent. Source: AFARE, Fond Greek Table, File, 2846.

becoming Russian subjects, to return to Greece where, of course, they spent the 'fortunes' they had amassed.[28] Finally, it should be noted that during the Balkan wars Greeks from Russia went to Greece as volunteers. Most were from the Black Sea area.[29]

## The cosmopolitan networks and multi-business character of Greek entrepreneurs

The diaspora entrepreneurs of Russia were not merchants as they have been known in the traditional sense. They had two notable characteristics. First, they developed a cosmopolitan business network based on family (kinship) ties which extended all over central Europe, Italy, France and Britain. For example, it was typical for a merchant in Odessa exporting grain to Greece and Britain to have branch offices in Athens and London headed by some relation, a brother or a cousin or a son-in-law.

Second, the Greek merchants in the Black and Azov Seas' trading firms were no simple traders (middlemen) solely buying and selling grain. Greeks could be found in a number of different activities, such as, for example, in the soda, oil, and sugar trade, in mineral water production, in the extraction of marble and in stockbroking.[30] Greeks were also prominent in the processing and distribution of petroleum products in Kuban.[31] They were also active in the tobacco industry which was an important sector in the south of Russia.[32]

The biggest factory of this kind in the southwest region was the tobacco and cigarette factory of P.S. Spilioti in Kiev which was established in 1883.[33] It started off as a humble enterprise with one

[28] Unfortunately we do not have data on this movement of population.

[29] For the fact that Russia supported the Greek war effort by supplying goods and money for Greek soldiers and by decorating Greeks of Russia for their heroism in transporting these goods see: AFARE, Fond Greek Table, File 555, *Rech*, 29 September, 1912.

[30] *New Odessa Courrier*, 1909.

[31] For Targoni and the fact that he founded a petroleum company in 1909 see: SRHA, Fond 23, Inventory 25, File 393, Inventory 11, File 919.

[32] In 1912, there were approximately 500,000 firms in the tobacco trade which had an annual turnover of 183,000,000 rubles.

[33] Other Greeks in the tobacco trade were: N.I. Bostanjoglo; Chilikidi; Y.B. Karaki; K.&D. Mavroidi; K. Mesaksudi; H.&K. & A. Papa-Ilia and P. Persidi.

machine. In three months it had 23 machines and in six months it acquired a drying iron system. By the end of the century, this factory dried 600 *puds* of cigarettes every day and employed about 120 workers. Also, its annual turnover was 600,000 rubles (in 1901 its capital was 200,000 rubles). Spilioti had large pieces of land (a total of 1,020 *sazhen*, 1 *sazhen*=2.13 metres) and five houses in the Kiev region. He, like other rich Greeks, diversified his activities: he published newspapers and books. His firm went bankrupt in 1910 and was sold out to his Jewish creditors.[34]

**TABLE 3: Russian Imports of Currants: 1895-1905**

| Years | *In general to Russia* | | *From Greece* | |
|---|---|---|---|---|
| | **in puds** | **in roubles** | **in puds** | **in roubles** |
| 1895 | 1,465,835 | 1,117,304 | 1,361,387 | 994,219 |
| 1897 | 427 | 1,205 | - | - |
| 1899 | 14,630 | 444,64 | 2,756 | 4,907 |
| 1901 | 6,302 | 3,948 | 612 | 2,742 |
| 1903 | 4,256 | 10,979 | 740 | 1,855 |
| 1905 | 2,408 | 6,699 | 202 | 577 |

*Source*: State Russian Historical Archive in St. Petersburg, Fond 22, inv. 3, File 58, p. 54.

Greeks were men of many talents. Most started off as middlemen (i.e pure traders) in one basic export staple of Russia (for example either grain, caviare, butter or petroleum goods). Many became producers (landowners or manufacturers) while often going also into banking and shipping. For example, the famous merchant Marazlis was also involved in the bottling and distribution of mineral water from which he made huge profits.[35]

It was, in general, typical for the merchant of the Greek diaspora to be in many lines of trade (business) simultaneously. Consequently, we would like to advance the hypothesis that the

[34] SRHA, Fond 23, Inventory 11, File 239, pp. 15-22.
[35] SRHA, Fond 23, Inventory 25, File 393.

**TABLE 4**

**Russian Exports to Greece: 1892-1893**
*(in thousand drachmas)*

| | 1892 | 1893 |
|---|---|---|
| Grain | 13,090 | 15,358 |
| Caviare | 726 | 524 |
| Animals | 1,114 | 126 |
| Butter | 98 | 116 |
| Cheese | 23 | - |
| Different flours | 36 | 190 |
| Timber | 135 | 90 |
| Vegetables | 16 | 5 |
| Leather goods | 35 | 23 |
| Agricultural products | 6 | - |
| Flax and woollen yarn | 32 | 10 |
| Fat | 26 | 3 |
| Fish | 3 | 25 |
| Tea | 3 | 2 |
| Other goods | 11 | 100 |
| Total | 15,355 | 15,524 |

**Russian Imports from Greece: 1892-1893**
*(in thousand drachmas)*

| | 1892 | 1893 |
|---|---|---|
| Olive oil | 915 | 534 |
| Olives | 371 | 99 |
| Wine-figs | 152 | 217 |
| Grapes | 136 | 1,163 |
| Fruit | 5 | 36 |
| Tobacco (in leaf) | 85 | 63 |
| Wine | 332 | 165 |
| Other goods | 93 | |
| Total | 2,089 | 2,277 |

*Source:* State Russian Historical Archive in St. Petersburg, Fond 20, inv. 7, File 129, p. 38.

Greeks in the Black Sea were so ahead in their business practices, that probably they were the most important and vital force in the world-wide Greek diaspora network. The Greek merchant firm in the Black Sea was a 'primitive' multinational as it had an almost global reach and was involved in a number of activities. This advanced specimen of diaspora entrepreneurship disappeared after World War I. We will try to explore why this happened. It will be argued that the final death blow may have been dealt with the 1917 revolution, but the fact is that the Greek merchant communities were operating in an increasingly hostile environment after the last part of the XIXth century.

**Important Greek firms**

The regulations which existed in Russia before 1914 for the operation of firms were very abstract. The absence of corporate law led to corruption and excess profits. Most big export and industrial firms, organized as corporations, belonged to Germans who were the largest foreign minority in Russia. Greek firms compared to them were usually not large and they had a personal or family character.[36]

The Greek merchants in Odessa were the first Greeks to make large fortunes in Russia. However, in the 1870s the Odessa Jews pushed the Greeks out of the grain trade and in the 1890s they succeeded in displacing them from other activities too. The Jews were better organized both in the national and the world markets, supported by Jewish diaspora business networks. The Greeks decided to move up to the 'difficult' ports on the Azov Sea. The family structure of their business helped their versatility. The archival material gives us a relatively large list of names of Greek merchants in the area. This is done in a'snapshot' manner as the dates concerned are: the 1850s (10 names), the end of the XIXth century (37 names) and 1909-1911 (45 names). Most of the names refer to merchants who had their firms (or at least the headquarters

[36] *Trade and Manufacturing in Odessa*, 9 July, 1914.

of their firms) in Odessa.

Odessa's livelihood depended on foreign trade and banking. In both fields the Greeks were pioneers. Notably, the only (known) warehouses in XIXth century Odessa were of Greek ownership. Usually, they were part of their owners' mansions. The few such facilities that existed were basically built in the Greek street, Police street and the Polish street (in the house of Voutsina) and the Jewish street. As noted above, most large Greek merchants were exporters who owned the cargoes they exported. The main importing firms were Rodocanaki and the Petrokokino Brothers.[37] The latter was a fairly old trading-house founded by Evstrati and Dimitri Mihailovich Petrokokino. This firm which in 1857 had an annual turnover of 1,000,000 rubles largely imported luxury manufactured goods (such as, for example, dresses, toys, household goods) from France, Germany, England and the U.S.A.[38]

The most famous Greek firm operating in the south of Russia after the 1870s was that of F.P. Rodocanaki based in Odessa. The founder of the family empire was Fedor P. Rodocanaki who besides being the Greek 'Consul for Commerce' in Odessa[39] was an important guild merchant. His entrepreneurial activities began in the 1820s and his enterprises, which spread all over the Novorosiisk area, had an annual turnover of around 5,000,000 rubles. Besides owning large tracts of land (3,600 *desitins*) which was cultivated under 'modern methods', this company had a wide range of activities. In addition to being in the export trade, it was also involved in banking (see below). Moreover, this company processed rice and manufactured a variety of goods, such as champagne, flour, cloth, paint and paper. Reportedly, the factories of Rodocanaki at one point employed "several thousands of

37 Other such examples were: N.&A. Diamanti, S.A. Ksido, Kollaro, D. Kuloglou, N. Shivas, S.F. Melissarato, M.&D. Pandaki, Panas Co., Hadji, Zarifi M.S. Source: *Inquiry of World Trade*, Odessa ,1911.

38 *Trade and Manufacturing in Odessa*, 9 July, 1914.

39 B.V. Ananiich, *Bankers Houses in Russia, 1860-1914* (Leningrad 1991), p.8.

labourers and craftsmen" [40] and the flour steam-mills it owned in Novorossisk and Sevastopol produced daily up to 6,500 *puds* of flour of the highest quality. In addition, F.P.Rodocanaki played a pivotal role in the development of shipping in the Black Sea and it had 'stations' in six ports. The firm reached its peak under Perikl Rodocanaki, the son of the founder.[41] With the initiative of Sergei Vitte (Minister of Finance) Perikl was proclaimed a member of the Russian nobility in 1896.[42] A. Anatra was another famous Greek merchant of Odessa.[43] He was called a millionaire and he had shares and stocks in factories, ships and other large enterprises. As president of the Black-Sea Yacht club, and protector of the clandestine Greek schools he developed wide social activities in the Greek community.[44] At the beginning of the XXth century the most famous tobacco factory in Odessa was that of V.O. Stamboli. He sold his goods all over Russia. He was also a publisher of newspapers and active in philanthropic work in the Greek community.[45] Another famous Greek family, which although based in Athens had strong connections in Odessa, was Recanati. Reportedly, together with a Russian Greek from Odessa, B.Zacharoff, and Alexander Gelfand, a famous Russian Jew, he headed the grain 'mafia' of Odessa.[46]

The information available on the activities of Greek merchants in the Sea of Azov ports from the Russian archives is less detailed. However, the sources support the well-known fact that the most important Greek grain merchant-cum-shipowner of the region was Maris Vagliano who had started his career as a simple skipper. They

[40] Namely, during the second generation when it was run by Perikl the son of the founder.

[41] According to one source, the annual turnover of the Rodocanaki firm was 1,200,000 rubles, but unfortunately we do not have a date for this figure. For this and the other information on this firm see: SRHA, Fond 20, Inventory 2, File 1164, pp. 1-3.

[42] Ananiich, *op.cit.*, pp.8, 56, 70, 13, 134.

[43] More than one Member of this family was a Merchant. Source: SRHA, Fond 23, Inventory 11, File 1023, pp. 1-2.

[44] *Trade and Manufacturing in Odessa*, July 9, 1914.

[45] *New Odessa Courrier*, 1909.

[46] Colonel M. Zolotariev, 'Historical Essay', report prepared for the government.

also provide us with one detail which may prove significant: in 1869 Vagliano with two other Greek merchants named Kalogera and Kouppa sent abroad in total at least one sixth of all the exports of Taganrong, Mariupol and Berdiansk.[47]

**Russian Greek trade**

Throughout the XIXth century the most important trade partners of Russia in order of importance were Germany, Great Britain, France and the Netherlands. Russia basically exported to these countries raw materials and imported from them industrial goods. (Tables 1 and 2). Trade with Greece was a different story. Despite the enormous presence in the Black Sea of Greeks basically in the export-import trade with Western Europe, there was an ongoing Greek-Russian trade. This has received little attention. This trade, small in the scale of total Russian exports, was extremely significant for the small Greek state.

Apparently, from the 1870s onwards the total value of imports from Russia to Greece increased much faster than the total value of Greek exports to Russia. For the years 1892-1910 see tables 1 and 2. The goods Russia imported from Greece and exported to her, as can be seen from Table 4, were mostly food supplies, raw materials and a small part consisted of manufactured goods.[48] The main products that Greece imported from Russia were: cereals, (wheat, rye, corn, oat), flax, butter, sugar, wood, coal, paper, red and black caviare, livestock products, hoops, and kerosene. Greece exported to Russia: currants, metals and minerals (lead, silver, ore, iron ore, manganese), wine, tobacco in leaf, olives, olive oil, silk, cocoons, leather, sponges, lemons and oranges.

In consequence, the two most important features characterizing trade relations between Greece and Russia were: i) the more or less permanent imbalance established between the two partners. Trade with Greece, as already noted, was of minor importance to Russia

47 *Ibid.*
48 *Russian Trade in the Balkans* (Moscow 1890). Also, *Bulletin of Inquiry of the Ministry of Trade and Industry* (St. Petersburg 1913).

whereas, for Greece, Russia was a major trading partner. It rivalled Britain. For example, in 1904 Russian exports to Greece were 30,800,000 drs whereas British exports to Greece were 28,700,000 drs.[49] ii) Moreover, Greece exported to Russia far less than what she imported from her. Greece had a permanent deficit in the balance of trade with Russia, the value of imports from Russia being consistently around ten times larger than the value of Greek exports to Russia.[50]

This picture was obscured towards the second decade of our century with the Balkan Wars and World War I. seriously interrupting trade in the region and with the October Revolution giving the final blow to the merchant communities of the area.

Moreover, it should be underlined that Russian-Greek trade relations were untypical in one more way. Unlike Britain and France, Greece's other two major trading partners and political 'supervisors', Russia was not an important direct source of foreign capital for Greece. However, indirectly, capital flowed from the Greek diaspora members of the Black Sea in various ways (as for example bequests). There were no important foreign direct investment of Russia in Greece. The one exception we know of is that in 1912 Russian firms were building the port of Candia and they were also interested in the concession for the building of an electric tram-way in Chania. Russian trade with Crete was significant in the end of the XIXth century and the beginning of the XXth century and apparently the Russian Consulate had established warm relations with the business world of Crete.[51]

Finally, a few words on the merchants involved in Greek Russian trade. They were basically not Russians. Throughout the XIXth century most of the export trade was in the hands of Jews

[49] *Demb*, St. Petersburg 11 October, 1912.

[50] 1 October, 1912, *Novoe Bremie.*

[51] For these attempts at F.D.I. and the involvement of a Greek by birth Russian diplomat by the name of Argyropoulos see: archival material of the Department of Foreign Trade of the Ministry of Foreign Affairs of Russia found in: SRHA, Fond 23, Inventory 8, File 34, pp.12,17.

and Greeks. The locals (i.e. the Russian merchants), had in their hands only the domestic trade network. They started to show an interest in the international market only in the 1890s, pressing the government to take some measures to help them reach the international market.[52]

**Trade diplomacy: treaty negotiations and the currant crisis**

In theory, Russian export trade was based on the principle of free trade. However, in practice customs were levied and Greek-Russian trade relations were regulated on the basis of the trade and navigation treaty Traktat of 12 July 1850. This treaty was based on the principle of the most-favoured-nation clause.[53]

Apparently, at the end of XIXth century the Greek government made repeated attempts to modify the treaty, in the hope that Greece would be able to increase its exports to Russia. First, in 1877, Athens appealed to St. Petersburg to lower its customs on figs and tobacco. Then, in 1885, 1888 and 1889 appeals were made for Russia to reduce its custom duty on olives. These appeals were ignored by the Russian government as the tariffs on Greek products were already lower than the tariffs on imports from other countries.

However, such pressures on Russia mounted with the 1893 currant crisis. The story was as follows: in October 1893, the Greek Minister to St. Petersburg announced that his government wished to open negotiations for the conclusion of a new treaty. The date was not coincidental: at the time France, which was a large consumer of sultanas - Greece's most important exportable item - had just raised her tariffs and Greece was searching for other outlets in order to avert a major crisis.[54] Russia was a good market to search out.[55] (See Table 3) Not only was she a significant trading partner of Greece, but she also had consulates in Zante, Cefalonia, Patras

[52] AFARE, Fond Greek Table, File 555, p. 3.

[53] It was signed by the King of Greece and the Czar and was applied from December 25, 1850 onwards. Regarding shipping, Greek vessels could freely carry and store their own products in all Russian ports without any tariff or other charges, as was the case with Russian vessels.

which, together with Ithaca and Korinth, were Greece's main currant-producing areas.[56] Thus, Athens declared to St. Petersburg that, if Russia agreed to abolish its customs on currants and reduce them on currant alcohol, the Greek government would be willing to: i) reduce its tariffs on Russia's main exports to Greece (i.e. caviare and cereals); and ii) purchase from Russia all of its lamp oil (kerosene) which was a state monopoly in Greece.[57]

The Russian Minister of Finance initially turned down the Greek proposals. Tariffs were an important source of income for the Treasury. In addition, he feared that Greek merchants in Russia would come to control the distillery business and thus hurt Russian distillers.[58] Russian officials, however, became more compliant when in 1894 the King of Greece - King George - arrived in Russia personally in order to boost Greece's negotiating position. King George was directly related to the Russian imperial family as his wife Queen Olga was a Russian princess. Under mounting pressure from the Greek government and Russian diplomats[59] the government set up in 1895 a committee to study the Greek demands. The committee quickly prepared a report in which it more or less assented to the changes desired by Athens without

[54] Greece's main markets up to 1893 had been France, Britain and the U.S.A. had also been important consumers.

[55] For the significant size of Russian imports see Table 1.

[56] AFARE, Fond Greek Table, File 519, pp.106-107.

[57] Though currants were the main 'Greek' item laid on the negotiating table, the Greek government also demanded that the Russians also reduce the customs on one *puds* of olive oil from 1 ruble 98 copeks to 60 copeks and that they abolish totally the tariff on olives and figs. Source: SRHA, Fond 20, Inventory 7, File 129.

[58] For example the Russian Treasury had an annual income of 1.5 milliard to 2 milliard rubles a year only from the customs on olive oil, olives and figs. The Russian government agreed to reduce its customs on black olives by 25% i.e. from 2 rubles to 1.5 rubles for one puds. Source: AFARE, Fond Greek Table, file 579, pp.20-21, 88.

[59] All along, since the time of the first appeals of the Greek government regarding the Trade Treaty, Russian diplomats had tried to convince the Ministry of Industry and Trade to be more compliant for political reasons towards Greek demands. Sources: V.R. Lamzdorf, *Diaries 1894-1896* (Moscow 1991). Also, SRHA, Fond 40, Inventory 1, File 47, p.187.

abolishing the 1850 treaty.[60] Namely, it proposed that up to 1903: i) the export of Greek currants to Russia be duty free and ii)the customs on figs, olives and olive oil be reduced by Russia by 50 percent. Peculiarly, no mention was made regarding the lifting of Greek taxes on grain although grain was Russia's major export to Greece. However, this report took it for granted that for this time period Greece would buy all its kerosene in Russia and it would lower by 50 percent its customs on butter, caviare and wood imported from Russia and would place fixed tariffs on imported sheep and rams.[61]

In the end, no new convention was signed as the distillers of southern Russia (mostly Georgians and Moldavians) mounted pressure on the Minister of Finance. The only compromise made by the Russian government was that it agreed to hand all of the customs revenues from Greek currants to Queen Olga for her charitable work. Reportedly, with these funds she built a hospital for sailors (in Pireaus).[62] Russia, in spite of the lack of success of the negotiations - at least temporarily - was able to absorb Greece's sudden currant surplus. It arrived through the Black Sea and the Azov Sea ports and was sold at very low prices.[63]

Among the local markets which absorbed large quantities of

[60] Ever since the time of the first appeals of the Greek government regarding the trade treaty, Russian diplomats had tried to convince the Ministry of Industry and Trade to be more compliant for political reasons towards Greek demands. In particular M. Onu, the Russian Ambassador to Athens proposed a compromise solution to Vitte largely on political grounds: i.e. he was particularly sensitive to the fact that Greece and Russia had strong religious ties and that the Greek royal family was related to the Czar. Sources: Lamzdorf, *passim*. Also, SRHA, Fond 40, Inventory 1, File 47, pp.187-188.

[61] This compromise solution was made at some point in the beginning of the negotiations. Vitte had suggested that the 1850 Treaty remain intact and that a convention be added to it referring to currants, with the understanding that Greeks would give preferential treatment to Russian grain and would also reduce customs regarding butter, caviare, flour and vegetables. AFARE, Fond Greek Table, File 519, pp.20-21 and 101.

[62] The annual income from the customs on currants was reported as being 600,000 rubles. However, no date is given for this figure. Source: J. Soloviev, *Memories of a Diplomat* (Moscow 1959), p.125.

[63] Around 1894 the prices recorded are 80 copeks for 1 *puds*. Source: AFARE, Fond Greek Table, File 519, p.88.

Greek currants were: Warsaw (Poland was part of Russia at the time), Moscow, Kovno, Grodno, Vilna, Dvinsk, Berdichev, Elisavetgrad, Kiev, Vinnicha, as well as some other towns in Russia.[64] However, by the beginning of the twentieth century England and the U.S.A. became the main markets for Greek currants.

Before closing this section it should be underlined that the failure of Greece to attain a new trade agreement with Russia is testimony to two facts. First, to the limited political power of the Greek diaspora in Russia from the end of the XIXth century onwards.[65] Second, to the relations of unequal dependence which existed between Greece and Russia. For Greece, Russia was its most important source of grain, but for Russia Greece was just a minor trading partner. Thus, although Greece raised its customs duties on grain and flour at least twice (once in the late XIXth century and again in 1905), Russia (to our knowledge) did not issue any protest to the Greek government.

Another example which portrays Greece's dependence on Russia is that Greece, although no new trade agreement was signed, began in 1903 to buy all of its kerosene from Russia. The story was as follows. In 1885 H. Trikoupis established a state monopoly in kerosene. This monopoly purchased all the kerosene it supplied to the Greek Government from the Greek firm Ralli Bros. which had its headquarters in London. Ralli Bros. acted as a middleman. It bought the kerosene it delivered to the government from the U.S.A. firm Atlantic Co. of Philadelphia. In 1903 the Government did not renew its annual contract with Ralli Bros.[66] Instead, it decided to accept bids from various sources. Offers were made from the Atlantic Co.; a Romanian firm Steana and Aurora

[64] *Ibid.*

[65] The word 'onwards' is used with reserve for it is not certain whether the Greek diaspora in Russia at any time (i.e. even during its economic peak) had political power in Russia.

[66] This state monopoly gave to the Greek Treasury an annual income of 7,000,000 drs. Source: SRHA, Fond 23, Inventory 24, File 99, p.39.

and three Russian companies: Caspian and Black Sea Petroleum Trade Co; L.I. Arvanitidi Co. and P.A. Sideridi Co. In the last two Russian companies Greek Black Sea merchants had an important stake.[67] From 1903 up to 1908 the Greek state monopoly bought all its kerosene from the Russians.[68] It has been argued that this change in policy and the decision to buy all the kerosene from the Russian bidder was due to the pressure the Russian representative in the I.F.C. had been levying on the Greek government over the years.[69]

**Greek merchant bankers**

Odessa, from its inception in the late XVIIIth century, was a credit market for the entire Black Sea and the Azov Sea region and partly even for Moscow and St Petersburg. Its first banks were usually merchant banks - i.e. banks that sprang from trading houses and as a result their operations were intimately linked with trading activities. At first, banking was in the hands of Greek and Italian merchants, but eventually they were ousted by Jews and local Russians.

It is generally difficult to find archival material, other than registration documents, regarding the activities of the first banks in Russia. However, the scant evidence available allows us to gain a general picture of Greek banking. Probably the most important Greek bankers of Odessa were the Rodocanaki family. By the time Fedor P. Rodocanaki, the head of the family empire, died in 1889

[67] The firm of Arvanitidi was established in Constantinople and that of Sideridi in Alexandria. Both of these entrepreneurs were Russian subjects and they sold Batoum kerosene which they transported from Baku. Source: SRHA, Fond 22, Inventory 3, File 58, p.108.

[68] At first all the kerosene was purchased from the Caspian Co. But from 1904 business with the Caspian Co. was stopped because of the internal political upheaval in Russia. Thus, from 1905 till 1908 the suppliers of kerosene to Greece were the Russian firms of Arvanitidi and Sideridi. Source: SRHA, Fond 24, Inventory 3, File 58, p.104.

[69] From 1909 onwards Greece started to buy kerosene from the U.S.A. and Romania again. But from 1914 onwards the U.S. firm Standard Oil Co. became the only supplier of kerosene to the Greek Government. SRHA, Fond 22, Inventory 3, File 58, p.108 and Fond 23, Inventory 24, File 991, pp.78-79.

he had founded a number of banks in the South and also in St. Petersburg. These were: The Bank of Odessa; the Azovsko - Donskoi Bank ; the Bank of Kiev; the Postov- na - Donu Bank; the Berdichev Bank; the Bank of Herson; the St. Petersburg International Commercial Bank and the Russian Bank for Foreign Trade. Rodocanaki set up some (if not all of these banks) together with Greek and foreign capitalists. Notably, the St. Petersburg International Commercial Bank was a joint partnership with foreign banks, F. Mavrocordato of Odessa, and Scaramanga a banker from Taganrog. As a rule, Greek merchant bankers had tight links with foreign banks often through their commercial networks and bank offices in northern European countries.[70]

Also, most Greek merchant bankers had financial interests outside banking or trade. One such case was that of the banker F.I. Petrokokino, whose brother D.I. Petrokokino was the director of the Ribinsk - Bologovskoi railway. (As already mentioned in the text, the Petrokokino family was one of the most important and oldest merchant families in Odessa).[71] Some Greek bankers in Odessa branched out into other areas. For example, as mentioned in the text, F. Maurocordato, who owned a merchant bank in Odessa, also co-founded the St. Petersburg International Commercial Bank.[72]

Not all Greek merchant bankers were centred in Odessa. A famous Greek merchant and banker outside the Odessa area was D.E.Bernardaki. His son N.D. Bernardaki who succeeded him in 1870, besides being a prominent banker in Moscow, founded the Kiev Private Commercial Bank, the Kiev Industrial Bank, the Siberian Trade Bank, the Nishinovgorod Bank and the Vilen and

[70] Such was the case of the banker M.V.Efrussi, who was reportedly a Greek and the son of an Odessa guild merchant. He set up banks in Paris and Vienna. A Russian subject, he became a member of the Portuguese nobility after having failed to become a member of the Russian nobility. For the fact that Efrussi was awarded the order of St. Vladimir (4th value) for the large donations he gave to soldiers wounded during the Russo-Turkish war of 1877-1878 see Ananiich, *op.cit.* pp.8-9, 19.

[71] Another example is that of M.V.Effrussi who had an important stake in various agricultural and industrial enterprises in the Novorosiisk region Ananiich, *op.cit.*, pp.8, 136.

[72] Ananiich, *op.cit.* p.133.

Don Land Bank.[73] Another such case was I.E. Kondojanaki the owner of a well-known merchant bank in St.Petersburg.[74]

In the 1870s the ruble joined the gold standard. This led to a remarkable increase in foreign capital flows to the south of Russia. An expansion took place in private banking which was marked by the demise of the Greeks and the rise of the Jews. At first the Jews infiltrated Greek banks. Notably, by the 1880s Jews infiltrated the operations of Rodocanaki.[75] Nevertheless, despite of tough competition Greek bankers were not totally eclipsed.[76]

**Greek shipping**

Russia had the largest river fleet and the longest railway network, but it lacked a substantial and modern sea-going fleet. In terms of the number of ships and their tonnage, Russia held the 11th position in the world. For instance, in 1909 it had 2,533 vessels and only 834 steamers.[77] (It should be noted that many of these ships belonged to Greeks who made use of the Russian flag).[78] Coastal shipping in the southern ports of Russia was by 1880 primarily in the hands of ROPIT - the Russian Society of Steamship lines and Trade - which was founded in the midst of the Crimean war in 1857 and was subsidized by the Russian government.[79]

Russian exports, being mostly raw and semicultivated products, were exported in bulk 'mass loads' in large part by British and

[73] For Bernadaki see: I.F. Gindin, *State Banks and the Economic Policy of the Tzarist Government, 1861-1892* (Moscow 1960).

[74] Ananiich, *op.cit.* pp.49, 133-134.

[75] Such was the case of Rafailovich who became a partner of the Efrussi family in 1880. Gindin, *op.cit.* pp.55-56.

[76] Another Greek banker in Odessa mentioned in the archives was I. Ksidias in the beginning of the XXth century. Source: SRHA, Fond 20, Inventory 2, File 1164.

[77] SRHA, Fond 265, Inventory 4, File 7.

[78] One example was that of the ship Volga whose owner was a Greek who was a Russian subject by the name of Raftopoulo, AFARE, Fond Greek Table, Inventory 497, 1914, File 501, p.2.

[79] It was founded with a capital of 10,000,000 rubles and such was its commercial success that the prices of its shares doubled. Source: SRHA, Fond 265, Inventory 4, File 7, pp.46-47.

Greek flags. For example in 1913 exports going under the British flag were 389,711 *puds*; Russian 79,904 and Greek 42,755.[80] Foreign flags also dominated the Russian import trade.[81]

Grain exports through the Sea of Azov ports of Tangarog and Rostov, regardless of destination, were basically carried by ships which were either Greek-owned or chartered by Greek merchants.[82] According to one source, 80 percent of grain was carried in such a manner.[83] The most famous grain merchants in the Azov Sea, who were also big shipowners, were the Vagliano brothers. Marinos was in the Azov, Andreas in Marseille and Panaghi in London. The Vagliano had an extensive network of trading houses all over the Sea of Azov and collaborated closely with other Greek merchants in the area such as, for example, R.A.Negreponte, Mussuri, Ambanopoulo. From the late 1870s they had steamers. This was not peculiar, for Greek grain merchants who were in shipping were among the first to make the transition from sail to steam.

Greek shipowners were, indeed, prominent in the steamship business. The steamship company of Rodocanaki had so much leverage that, in 1882, it appealed to the administration of the Zakavkaszskaya railways and managed to sign a convention regarding the loading lines that were connected with the ports of the Black Sea of Marmora and the Mediterranean seas. It also established a special consulting board at the Russian Department of Railways.

The Greek shipowners in the Sea of Azov were largely financed by Greek merchant banks. In Rostov we know of Greek steam barges and ships. The following vessels are mentioned with Greek flags: Peter, Constantine Zvoronos, Haralampios Negreponte. (The

[80] Kozmin, *passim*.

[81] 'Short survey on the reports of Imperial Russian Consulars...', vol.2, St. Petersburg 1909, pp.105-106.

[82] Interview with chairman of the Council of the Representatives of trade and commerce, member, of the state council of Russia, N.C. Avdakof. B.V. 26 September 1912. Source: Interview of 'Birjevie Vedomosti'.

[83] *Russkoe Slovo*, 15 October, 1913.

Lloyd's Register of shipping mentions a substantial fleet owned by companies established in Russia from 1870 to 1914). Russian officials in Rostov were annoyed with the fact that Greek shipowners had taken control of the transit trade in the area. In 1910, they complained that Greek shipowners did not pay attention to the fact that they were Russian subjects and, ignoring Russian traditions and rules, they put Greek flags on their ships with the excuse that they were not of Russian origin.[84] Apparently, long after Greeks lost their preeminence as merchants in the Black Sea they remained a strong force in shipping in the Sea of Azov.

**The response of Greek entrepreneurs to changing conditions**

Greek entrepreneurs in Odessa started to face competition from the Jews in the 1870s. In addition, by the turn of the XXth century, some of the market share of the Greeks was lost to Russian merchants, as the latter had gained some strength - in part because they had attracted the interest of the Russian government. But Greek merchants east of Odessa and in the ports of the Sea of Azov were still a formidable economic force. The final blow to Greek merchants came in three stages: the first Russian revolution (1905-1907), the Balkan wars (1912-1913) and W.W.I.

The exact dimensions of the repercussions of the first Russian Revolution (1905-1907) are not known. However, Greek merchants suffered (in particular, those who were involved in petroleum extraction and distribution in Baku). Probably, more important was the fact that Greek merchants were in a state of uncertainty about their fortunes. Testimony to this is that in 1905, with the outbreak of the revolution, 15 Greek businessmen appealed to the Greek ambassador, Argiropoulo, to protect their property. Their names were: Abattielo, Aleferaki, Evasena, Frangopoulo, Karageorgis,

[84] For the companies established in Russia from 1870-1914 see: Harlaftis *op.cit* (1995) chapter 3. For Russian complaints against Greek shipowners see: memo prepared by the Department of Trade and Ports in Postov-na-Donu for the Ministry of Foreign Affairs on 17 of July 1910. See: AFARE, Fond Greek Table, Inventory 486, File 23, pp.1-3.

Koutana, Lagada, Lalechopoulo, Lokos, Manezi, Maseramati, Panousa, Recatoro, Rigi, Rossolimo.[85]

Nevertheless, Greek traders continued to remain an important force in the Sea of Azov even after the first Russian Revolution (1905-1907). An indication of the fact that business was still lively for the Greeks and that Russia continued to receive immigrant Greeks is that as late as 1909, a Greek native, Victor Magoula, opened an 'information Bureau' providing services to Greek merchants who did not know Russian with information on Russian laws, customs and Greek firms in Russia.[86]

Yet, these were difficult times for Greek merchants. The crisis hit also the larger old firms such as that of Evriviadi S. Sklavo. In fact, these older establishments often amalgamated in order to face up to increasing competition. A notable case where large and old Greek firms went into joint partnerships was that of Vasiliu, Yenni and Pinandu who set up a joint venture in 1913.[87]

Greeks also made joint ventures with Jewish and Russian entrepreneurs.[88] For example, it is known that A.A.Alexandraki who traded in grain and oil was in partnership with Armavir; P.S. Palli a sugar merchant was in partnership with Brailov.[89] Other examples are the following. In 1911 the broker Y.Kary (a Greek from England) set up an export-import trading firm and went into partnership with the Russian noble N.Govorov and Ivan Alexandrovich Zarifi, a Greek merchant who had trade houses in Bordeaux and in Nice.[90] Also, in the same year A.P.Kriona who had a leather factory went into partnership with S.M. Rubinstein, the

[85] The first Russian Revolution was centred on St.Petersburg and Moscow. However, it totally destroyed the kerosene trade in Bacoum; hence the fear of Greek entrepreneurs about its repercussions. For the names of those Greeks who asked for protection see: AFARE, Fond Greek Table, File 2718.

[86] Reportedly, the Russian Ministry of Trade and Industry looked on this firm with a favourable eye. Source: SRHA, Fond 1284, Inventory 188, File 115, pp.1 2.

[87] SRHA, Fond 23, Inventory 11, File 1239.

[88] Greeks as owners of a firm would often cooperate or combine with Jews, Russians or Ukrainians, but Jewish firms never sought out Greek, Russian, or Ukrainian partners.

[89] *Inquiry of World Trade* (Moscow 1912).

[90] The capital of this firm was 4,000 rubles.

son of a Jewish merchant.[91] In spite of these partnerships, many Greeks were not able to escape bankruptcy in 1913. For example, this was the case of Collaro, who set up in 1912 a trading house in wood products with the Russian nobles K.G. and E.K. Bernatovich and the Belgian O.P. Miller. This firm was closed down by its owners in 1914, soon after the beginning of World War I.[92]

By the time of the outbreak of the Balkan wars, most of the firms registered in Odessa were Jewish.[93] However, even as late as during World War I, the Greek presence was still significant. Testimony to this is that in 1916 a Chamber of Commerce was established in Odessa. Among the Jews and Russians who were members of this Chamber, two well-known Greeks participated, A.Anatra and A.R. Hari.[94] The last Greek firm to be mentioned in the archives to be registered in Odessa was the trading house of M.F. Avgerino and I.M. Michalakis. It was set up in 1917 and its purpose was to deal in the fish trade. Its capital was a mere 20,000 rubles.[95]

Finally, it should be underlined that throughout this final phase of decline, the Greek merchants in the newer ports (i.e. Novorosiisk) and the Sea of the Azov lost less of their market share than the Greek merchants of Odessa. For example, in 1912, out of 17 foreign firms in Odessa dealing in the grain trade only one Y.E.Ekonomidi was Greek; the others were Jewish.[96] By contrast in Novorasiisk about half of the firms conducting foreign trade were Greek in 1912. Also, at about the same time out of 90 trading firms

[91] SRHA, Fond 23, Inventory 11, Fond 1023. For other examples of Greek Jewish partnership see SRHA, Fond 23, Inventory 11, Fond 1023, p.155

[92] For the limitation of banking credits see *Rech*, 13 Oct. 1992. For the timber trade see SRHA, Fond 23, Inventory 24, File 1237, p.1, 28.

[93] SRHA, Fond 23, Inventory 11, File 1023, p.155.

[94] It had a capital of 1,000,000 rubles. Source: SRHA, File 23, Inventory 11, File 1023.

[95] All the other new firms registered in March 1917 were Jewish (Levinshtein, Rozenbaum, Mendel, Rabinovich, etc.). Source: SRHA, Fond 23, Inventory 11, File 1459. p.1, 29.

[96] *Inquiry of World Trade*, (Odessa 1911, 1912). This same journal, referring to 1911, notes that out of 150 trading firms less than 15 were Greek. Most of the other firms were Jewish.

in Rostov 11 were Greek.[97] Moreover, one cannot overlook the fact that by World War I. certain industries in which Greeks were prominent were experiencing a crisis, e.g. the tobacco industry.

**The final blow: the war embargoes and their impact on Greek business in the area and Greek-Russian trade**

Before the Balkan wars the Black Sea and the Sea of Azov exported usually around 400,000,000 *puds* of grain.[98] But war brought disruption. Turkey closed the straights during the larger part of 1912 (at some points for all foreign ships and at other points only for Bulgarian and Greek ships).[99] The economy of the Azov Sea suffered more than that of the Black Sea, for 75% of Azov exports were served by Greek ships.

The grain trade shrank in volume. For example, the port of Herson had exported in 1912 (up to the month of April) 1.5 million *puds* of grain whereas in 1910 during the same period it had exported 10 million *puds*. A panic overcame the grain market as prices plummeted.

The negative repercussions of the embargo were far reaching: Many small and medium firms in the grain trade closed down in Odessa, Rostov, Herson, Taganrog, Mariupol, Batum, Novorosiisk, Ekaterinodar. Barges and tug boats (which incidentally were mostly owned by Greeks) lay idle without work. Labourers connected with the grain trade (many of whom were Greek) began to starve.[100] Greek shipowners also suffered great losses. Some freights were totally lost and a large quantity of spoiled goods was thrown into the sea.[101] Moreover, delays imposed a heavy burden

[97] Reportedly these Greeks were all Russian subjects. Also, it should be noted that in 1910 Kaluta (A.T.) was vice-consul of Greece to Rostov. Source: *Inquiry of World Trade*, (Odessa 1912).

[98] *Vechernee Vriemie*, St. Petersburg, 12 September, 1912.

[99] It should also be noted that the Dardanelles were also closed during 1911 as a result of the Italian-Ottoman War. During May 1912 when the blockade was temporarily lifted in two days, 14-16 May, a total of 18 Greek Russian steamers entered Russian Black Sea ports. Source: *Rech*, 18 May, 1912.

[100] *Novoe Vremie*, 1 October, 1912.

[101] *Rech*, 18 May, 1912.

as they usually cost up to 300-400 rubles a day.[102] In Nickolaev, just in April 1912, there were losses of 2,000,000 rubles and in Odessa 300,000 rubles.[103] This embargo on Greek ships gave a boost to Russian shipping lines. Most of the grain trade by then flew under the Russian flag as Greek merchants freighted Russian steamships under terms that were considered extremely favourable to their owners.[104]

The impact of the closing of the straights for the Greek economy was detrimental, for on the eve of the Balkan wars it was recorded that Greece still depended on Russia for two thirds of its grain imports. The lack of Russian grain led to severe starvation. Deaths were reported from starvation in Evia, for example, and bakeries were stormed in Volos.[105] Notably, after the end of the Balkan Wars and during the peace negotiations between Turkey and Greece, one of the first issues placed by Athens on the negotiating table was the free passage of Greek ships through the Dardanelles.[106]

In short, during the Balkan wars the grain trade between Greece and Russia suffered a severe blow. Notably, the Bank of Athens, which had played an important role in developing Russian exports to Greece, stopped all credits. The only export item of Russia which appeared to continuously increase in volume was wood for the railway network and rebuilding the villages and towns destroyed by the wars.[107] The fall in trade was reflected in the declining customs' revenues from wheat imported from Russia.[108]

[102] *Novoe Vremie*, 28 April, 1912.

[103] *Ibid.* Also, In 1913 Turkey decided every day for a few hours to allow free passage of ships of neutral countries. Source: *Den*, Oct. 5, 1913.

[104] *Bulletin of Inquiry of the Department on Foreign Trade of the Ministry of Trade and Industry*, (St. Petersburg, No. 52, 1913).

[105] See the report of the agent of the Russian Ministry of Trade and Industry from Athens in 1913, SRHA, Fond 23, Inventory 9, file 718.

[106] SRHA, Fond 23, Inventory 9, File 271, p.153.

[107] For the rise in timber imports in general and from Russia in particular see: the same source as for reference 104.

[108] For this and the concern of Russian civil sevants over the fall in Russian exports to Greece and the high duties placed on grain imports see: AFARE, Fond Greek Table , File 555, p.544.

The closing of the straights had a negative impact on Greek merchants and shipowners in the Black Sea regardless of whether they were doing trade with Greece. Above all, the Balkan wars dealt a blow to Greek-Russian trade. From the point of view of scholarship, the Balkan wars reveal the intricate and tight interrelationship which existed between Greece and Russia prior to World War I.

With World War I. Greek shipping and Greek-Russian trade suffered further. In August 1914, Turkey confiscated some Greek steamers carrying grain and dry products from Russia and Romania.[109] Apparently, part of the Russian sea trade with Greece was diverted from sea to land transportation.[110] For example, Greek olives from 1915 onwards were exported to Odessa by railway through Romania. Due to the war, both Russia and Greece imposed trade restrictions.[111] For example, Greek and other foreign merchants no longer had the same rights to buy Russian grain as Russian merchants.[112] Olives were no longer exported in large quantities to Russia as the Greek government periodically forbade its export.

Russian-Greek trade (and Greek shipping in the Black Sea) did not suffer only because of the closing of the straights by Turkey and mutual trade restrictions posed by the two governments. One more 'negative' factor was at work: the blockades imposed by the *Entente* on the southern ports of Greece periodically prior to Greece's going to the war in 1918. In January 1916 the *Entente* Powers established an International

[109] Nevertheless, some steamers under the Greek flag were allowed to proceed; the Greek ship 'Katina Andreadis' with grain (15 September, 1914) and the steamer 'Preveza' on 9 October, both going to Marseille.

[110] 'Report of the Odessa Committee on Trade and Manufactures', (Odessa 1915). The Greek ministry gave Russian merchants the use of three railway waggons per day for conducting this import-export business. The Russian Minister of Railways, through the Russian Ambassador, asked Mr. Diamantidi to increase the number of railway waggons available to the Russian merchants because three were not enough for their consignments.

[111] From the beginning of World War I, the Greek government tried to organise a food supply system and to struggle with high prices.

[112] In February and March 1915, 5,000 sacks were imported from Greece (1,000 sacks = 6 thousand *puds*).

Food Commission. A laisser-passer covering the ports of Greece for grain was given only for one month.[113]

During World War I. many Greeks abandoned their houses and closed down their business in Russia. We know about several Russian state initiatives to exclude Greeks from Sevastopol, Novorossisk, Yalta, and some other military ports. The ex queen of Greece, Olga, who lived in Russia during the whole period of World War I (1914-1918) tried to help Greeks and delay their departure.[114] After the closing down of the Dardanelles, Greek shipowners moved from the Black Sea to Greece and London. Instead of moving cargoes from Taganrog to Hull or Rotterdam, they began to carry cargoes from Buenos Aires to Northern Europe.

## Conclusions

Using new sources and information largely of Russian origin we have introduced new hypotheses and explained those prevailing about the role and the evolution of the Greek diaspora in southern Russian ports, especially with reference to Greek-Russian trade from 1870 to 1917, a period of demise for the diaspora. To our knowledge this area has not been explored before in the literature. Before presenting the main findings we would like to stress again the fact that the quantitative data at our disposal suffered from gaps which reduced our ability to draw more definite conclusions. Given the turbulent history of Russia at the end of last century and the beginning of this one, this was to be expected.

Prior to World War I. Russia was an important source of basic goods for Greece, such as cereals, wood and kerosene. The Greek diaspora in the Black Sea and the Sea of Azov played a major role

[113] In June 1915, Greek shipowners decided to appeal to the great powers of the Entente to abolish strict measures against Greek shipping, and sent a report to the Greek government, showing the great losses for Greek trade arising from the blockad of the Greek coast and ports. The Entente's authorities organised in Athens a special commercial committee which controlled trade activities and gave permissions to the merchants.

[114] Central State Archive of Russian Federation. Moscow, Fond 686, Inventory 1, File 62a.

in developing Greek-Russian trade. In fact, Greek merchants were an active force in the growth of the foreign trade network of southern Russia. At first, they flourished in Odessa. Later in the 1880s, due to the decline of Odessa as a port as well as the increasing competition of the Jewish and Russian firms, Greek merchants moved to the difficult sea of Azov and controlled a large part of the grain, kerosene and wood trade and its sea transportation. It should be underlined that the trade deficit of Greece in terms of its trade with Russia grew after the 1870s.

This study has sketched the socio-economic aspects of the Greek entrepreneurial network in southern Russia. It has also uncovered the diplomatic weakness of Greece and its diaspora *vis-à-vis* Russia as expressed in the inability of Greece to convince Russia to absorb its currant surplus from the 1890s onwards. The multi-dimensional character of Greek merchants and the close links established between the Greek trade, banking and shipping network has been confirmed. Often Greek merchants were simultaneously in all three lines of business in addition to being industrialists and landowners.

The exact dimension and nature of the contribution of the diaspora to the Greek economy is difficult, if not impossible, to assess.[115] Nevertheless, given on the one hand, its economic success and its close links with Greece (established through emigrant remittances, capital repatriation, shipping and trade) and on the other, the relatively small size of the recently independent Greek state in terms of both population and economy, its impact could not have been negligible. At this point we would like to suggest that one more factor be taken into account: it is probable that part of the profits originating in the Black Sea area reached Greece via the foreign government loans raised in the international capital market. The Greek entrepreneurs of south Russia had close

[115] For original work on the role of the diaspora in Greece see G.B. Dertilis and K. Kostis (eds), *Issues in Modern Greek History (18th-20th Century)* (Athens 1992), (in Greek).

links with Greek international bankers (mainly located in Paris, London and Vienna) and the latter played an important part in the floatation of Greek loans prior to World War I.

Finally, regarding the decline of the diaspora this paper has shown that it was a long drawn-out process which began in Odessa in the 1870s and spread to the eastern ports shortly prior to the Balkan Wars and World War I. Thus, it has been shown that the decline of the Greek presence in southern Russia predated the October revolution of 1917.

REFERENCES

Ananiich, B.V., *Bankers Houses in Russia, 1860-1914*, (Leningrad 1991).

Dertilis, G.B., and Kostis, K., (eds), *Issues in Modern Greek History (18th-20th Century)*,(Athens 1992), (in Greek)

Dovnar-Zapolskii, M.V., *Russian Exports and the World Market*, Kiev, 1914.

Gindin, I.F., *State Banks and the Economic Policy of the Tzarist Government, 1861-1892*, (Moscow 1960).

Harlaftis, G., *A History of Greek-owned Shipping: The Making of an International Tramp Fleet, 1830 to the Present Day*, (London 1996).

__, *Greek Seamen and Greek Ships on the Eve of W.W.I.*,(Athens 1994), (in Greek).

__, "The Role of the Greeks in Black Sea Trade, 1830-1900", in L.R. Fischer and H.W. Nordvik (eds), *Shipping and Trade, 1750-1950: Essays in International Maritime Economic History*, (Ponterfract 1990).

Herlihy, P, «Greek Merchants in Odessa in the 19th Century» Harvard Ukranian Studies III/IV, 1979-1980.

Hadziiossif, H., «Greek Merchant Communities and Independent Greece: Interpretations and problems», *Politis*, 1983, pp. 28-34 (in Greek).

Kitroeff, A., «The Greek Diaspora in the Mediterranean and the Black Sea as Seen through American Eyes» (1815-1861) in S.Vryonis, Jr., *The Greeks and the Sea*, (New York 1994).

Kozmin,K.V. *Russian Grain Exports*, (St.Petersburg 1912).

Lamzdorf, V.R., *Diaries, 1894-1896*, (Moscow 1991).

Soloviev, J., *Memories of a Diplomat*, (Moscow 1959).

# [7]

## Indian and Arab entrepreneurs in Eastern Africa (1800-1914)

William Gervase CLARENCE-SMITH

Economic life in colonial Africa was stereotypically divided into three spheres. At the top were Western firms, modern, efficient, Weberian, highly capitalised, and organised on the joint-stock principle. In the middle were 'Asiatic' intermediaries, often compared to Jews. Their funds came from 'usury', and their modest prosperity was attributed to close knit community bonds, based on family, religion, caste and similar 'pre-modern' social structures. At the bottom of the social heap were 'natives', ignorant, simple-minded, living for the moment, and incapable of rational economic behaviour. Officials thus took it upon themselves, as part of the 'civilising mission', to protect both 'natives' and Western firms from 'Asiatic' wiles. One can smile at the crudity of such a picture, and yet it is remarkable how much of this mind-set still survives in non-governmental organisations, ministries, and even universities.

The reality was quite different. 'Asiatics' were not simply intermediaries, but were to be found at the top and bottom of society. A select few were fabulously wealthy, acting as creditors of last resort for Western firms.[1] Tarya Topan was even knighted by the British in 1890, for services rendered to suppress the slave trade.[2] Among the poor were Asian 'coolies' from non-mercantile communities, much less upwardly mobile than legend has it. 'Communities of trust' of a 'pre-modern' kind were not limited to Indians and Arabs, but were central to the operations of many Western firms, notably Scots and New Englanders. Conversely, Indians and Arabs made much use of modern techniques. Indeed, Asian businesses may have been more economically beneficial to Africa than Western firms, as they relied less on official protection.

### 1. Communities of trust

In the risky economic conditions of the western Indian Ocean, the problem of agency attained a rare degree of urgency. In the absence of any more than sketchy foundations of the rule of law, the difference between a business prospering and collapsing often depended on who could be trusted, and how far. The ultimate sanction for those in breach of trust was expulsion from tight knit communities, equivalent to 'social death'.[3] In the eighteenth century, Hindu Vania (Banians) formed the hegemonic Indian community, notably those from the Kathiawar or Saurashtra peninsula of Gujarat.[4] One group of Vania, based in the Portuguese colonial capital on Mozambique Island, dominated much of the Swahili coast.[5]

---

[1] Clarence-Smith 1989 ; Ewald and Clarence-Smith 1997.

[2] Naseem 1975 : 102.

[3] Dobbin 1996 ; Austin and Sugihara 1993.

[4] *Gazeteer* : IX-1, 74, and VIII, 148.

[5] Alpers 1975 : 89-94, 144, 147-9.

Another group played a similar role in the Red Sea and Gulf of Aden, from bases in Yemeni ports, Massawa and Suakin.[6] Competition came mainly from Omani and Hadhrami Arabs, together with Maghribi Arabs settled in Cairo.[7]

The nineteenth century witnessed the rise of merchants from Kutch, a semi-autonomous state in the far west of Gujarat, sandwiched between Sindh and Kathiawar.[8] Hindu Bhatia, claiming Kshatriya or warrior status, prevailed in the Omani empire.[9] By the 1840s, they had spread into Mozambique, competing with Vania merchants.[10] Nizarian Ismaili Muslims, known as Khoja, came with the Bhatia, but were initially less wealthy. Some Khoja refused to follow the Aga Khan from the 1850s, becoming regular 'Twelver' Shi'ites or Ithnashari, especially in Oman and Mauritius.[11] Sunni Muslim Memon first went to Mauritius, and became one of the wealthiest communities south of the Zambezi from the 1870s. They were also of some significance in East Africa.[12] A common Kutchi identity acted as a bridge between these varied communities, and the Kutchi dialect of Gujarati is still widely spoken in eastern Africa to this day. Thus the fortunes of Tarya Topan, an Ismaili, were intimately linked to business relations inherited from his father with the Bhatia customs farmer, Jairam Shivji.[13]

From around the 1870s, other Gujarati began to immigrate in greater numbers. Zoroastrian Parsi, of Iranian origins, had been present as traders in eastern Africa from at least the eighteenth century.[14] However, their energies had largely gone into Far Eastern trade up to the 1860s.[15] By 1880, a 'temple of fire' existed in Zanzibar, and their numbers increased.[16] They gained a particularly prominent position in Aden and South Africa.[17] Jains went especially to Ethiopia, but also to Mombasa.[18] Daudi Bohora, Mustalian Ismaili of Yemeni origins, were concentrated in Madagascar and the Horn of Africa.[19] The Surti were Jafari Bohora, that is converts to Sunni Islam from Ismailism, and from Mauritius they spread to Réunion, South Africa, and British Central Africa.[20] Hindu Patel (Patidar) from the Charotar Plain, tax collectors and village headmen of Sudra or peasant status under the Mughals, remained small traders in British East Africa before 1914.[21] Goan Catholics were displaced in the Zambezi valley by immigrant Gujarati from the 1870s.[22] Goans

---

[6] Das Gupta 1979 : 69-72, 164, 288.

[7] Ewald 1989 ; Ewald and Clarence-Smith 1997 ; Bhacker 1992.

[8] Rushbrook Williams 1958.

[9] Dobbin 1996, ch. 5 ; Pocock 1955 : 71-2.

[10] Caldeira 1852-53 : II, 106.

[11] Morris 1968 : 66-8, 78 ; Brown 1971 : 178-82 ; Mangat 1969 : 13 ; Walji 1974 : 72-4, 85, 136 ; Emrith 1967 : 71 ; Swan 1985 : 3, 41, 70 ; Robert 1977 : 53 ; Landen 1967 : 140-2.

[12] *Gazeteer* : IX-2, 50-7 ; Emrith 1967 : 24, 71 ; Swan 1985 : 3, 10 ; Dotson 1968 : 42, 139-40 ; Brown 1971 : 167.

[13] Bhacker 1992 : 72, 175 ; Naseem 1975 : 73.

[14] Jackson Haight 1967 : 137.

[15] Dobbin 1972 : 2-3, 9-16.

[16] Brown 1971 : 160.

[17] Mangat 1969 : 83 ; Swan 1985 : 6-7, 10 ; Bhana and Pachai 1984 : 24-6.

[18] Janmohamed 1986 : 586 ; Bharati 1972 : 60-3 ; personal communication C Schaefer 4.10.1987.

[19] Frere 1873 : 101 ; Robert 1977 : 53.

[20] Misra 1964 : 22-4, 69, 122-5 ; Emrith 1967 : 24-5, 75-6 ; Robert 1977 : 65-6 ; Swan 1985 : 147 ; Dotson 1968 : 139-41.

[21] Morris 1968 : 92-100.

[22] L. White, personal communication, 30 April 1987.

remained in one niche, however, selling alcohol, which neither pious Muslims nor 'twice-born' Hindus would touch.[23]

The stereotype of the penniless 'coolie' making a fortune in Africa is highly misleading, for most traders came as agents of firms in India.[24] At the least, they had a recommendation to a kinsman, a member of the same religious community, or somebody from the same village.[25] Young men disembarking in Africa may well have seemed poor, but their commercial and credit connections with India were crucial advantages.[26] This explains why free Muslim Gujarati immigrants, arriving in Natal from the 1870s, were rapidly able to sweep aside the few former indentured labourers who had set up in trade.[27]

Partnerships were the most common form of organisation in the early nineteenth century. In the Red Sea area in the 1840s, partners received a share of profits proportional to their investment. Each man specialised in some activity within a clearly defined hierarchy, in which the treasurer was the senior partner.[28] Young men were sent out to Africa as apprentices for some ten years, and either became partners or set up their own businesses. Muslims had the advantage of bringing wives and families, whereas Hindus almost always came as single men.[29] Accounts were kept in Gujarati or Kutchi by double entry, « with the proverbial neatness and clearness of a Guzerat accountant ».[30]

Larger firms were transnational in scope and organisation, and were usually based in India, increasingly in Mandvi (Kutch), Bombay or Karachi. They had branches, associates and agents all over the Indian Ocean and the China Sea, from Yokohama to Cape Town.[31] Entrepreneurs who made fortunes in Africa usually moved their headquarters to India.[32] Thus, Jairam Shivji left for Bombay in 1853, followed by Tarya Topan, who ended up with more capital engaged in the China trade than in Africa.[33]

That said, few Indian communities broke out of the Indian Ocean on any scale. Parsi merchants took up Western education precociously, and established branches in Britain by the middle of the century.[34] The Aga Khan Ismaili were a little slower off the mark, but by the 1890s they had developed strong business connections in Europe, the United States and Australia.[35] Tarya Topan owned a business in London in which 'he had considerable sums invested', and, from the turn of the century, a British educated Aga Khan put great pressure on his followers to adopt Western education and customs.[36] A. M. Jivanji, a Bohora who set up a branch

---

23 Brown 1971: 163-5.

24 Bhacker 1992 : 70-6 ; Alpers 1975 : 92 ; Guillain 1856-57 : III, 372-3.

25 Frere 1873 : 101-2.

26 Vail and White 1980 : 65.

27 Swan 1985 : 3-4.

28 Pankhurst 1974 : 190-1.

29 *Gazeteer* : IX-1, 74 ; Frere 1873 : 101-2 ; Brown 1971 : 181 ; Naseem 1975 : 82.

30 Frere 1873 : 101.

31 Bhacker 1992 : 160, 242 ; Dobbin 1996 : 113 ; Jackson Haight 1967 : 79, 143 ; Landen 1967 : 134 ; *Gazeteer* : V, 121.

32 Sheriff 1987 : 105.

33 Naseem 1975 : 85, 94, 108 ; Bhacker 1992 : 175-7.

34 Dobbin 1972 : 53-64 ; Vicziany 1979 : 187.

35 *Gazeteer* : IX-2, 44 ; Dobbin 1972 : 154.

36 Dobbin 1996 : 117, 122-3.

of his Karachi firm in Mombasa in 1891, had an agency in Adelaide, Australia.[37] In contrast, Bhatia travelling to Europe still faced complete exclusion from their caste in the 1870s.[38]

Indian firms moved some way beyond the narrow limits of communities imposed by birth. The concentration of leading families in the Fort district of Bombay brought capitalists together to a greater extent than ever before, fostering not only economic partnerships, but also personal friendships and a common sense of Gujarati identity in this non-Gujarati city. The adoption of the joint-stock principle from the 1830s allowed members of other communities, including Europeans, to be brought onto company boards, although founding families usually kept a majority of shares.[39] In Africa, Indians not only provided credit to Arabs, but at times also employed them or became their business partners.[40] At the very least, Arab and African traders were seen as essential links in commercial chains that stretched to the heart of the continent.[41]

Arab business communities went through a period of flux in the nineteenth century. The Omani rulers favoured their own people, many of them Ibadi Muslims.[42] However, the Omanis never entirely managed to push aside their Hadhrami neighbours from South Arabia, who shared Sunni Islam of the Shâfi<sup>c</sup>î legal school with the overwhelming majority of coastal African Muslims.[43] As early as the 1880s, some 2000 of the estimated 60 000 permanent inhabitants of Zanzibar town in the 1880s were from Hadhramaut, equal in number to resident Omanis.[44] As Omani political power waned from the 1880s, the Hadhrami grip tightened, and they left Omani traders far behind.[45] The Hadhrami also pushed out Maghribi traders from the northern Red Sea from the mid-nineteenth century.[46] However, the Hadhrami community was itself divided into rival social strata. *Sayyid* descendants from the Prophet, *shaykh* religious specialists and *qabîlî* members of major tribes were at loggerheads, but all lorded it over their *maskîn* compatriots.[47]

The 'scramble for colonies' posed considerable problems to Indian and Arab communities at the end of the nineteenth century. The decline in Omani power was a blow not only to Omani Arabs but also to many Gujarati merchants, notably those of the Bhatia caste.[48] German, French, Italian, Portuguese, Egyptian and Ottoman officials favoured their own nationals, especially in the upper reaches of the import-export trade.[49] Although the metropolitan British state remained well disposed towards 'Asiatics', especially those from India, 'men on the spot' were often more hostile. Moreover, every advance towards settler self-government in British colonies

---

[37] Mangat 1969 : 53-5, 75. He seems to have been a Daudi rather than a Jafari Bohora.

[38] Frere 1873 : 100.

[39] Dobbin 1972 : 20-5, 227 ; Dobbin 1996 : 88, 91.

[40] Guillain 1856-57 : III, 372-4 ; Sheriff 1987 : 112 ; Naseem 1975 : 104

[41] Landen 1967 : 134.

[42] Bhacker 1992 : 95, 120, 123, for prominent families.

[43] Le Guennec-Coppens 1997.

[44] Bricchetti 1899 : 27.

[45] Le Guennec-Coppens 1997 : 166-72 ; Ingrams 1937 : 151 ; Salim 1973 : 135 ; Cooper 1977 : 107, 146 ; Strobel 1979 : 135 ; Willis 1993 : 96, 139-40, 210-1.

[46] Ewald 1989.

[47] el-Zein 1974 : 129.

[48] Allen 1978.

[49] Vail and White 1980 : 132-4 ; Deschamps 1961 : 280, 299 ; Walji 1974 : 124-8, 137 ; Pankhurst 1974 : 209 ; Ewald 1989.

was accompanied by anti-Asian legislation.[50] Nevertheless, it was estimated in 1905 that four fifths of 'capital and business energy' in British East Africa still lay in Indian hands.[51]

Another significant result of the opening of the Suez Canal in 1869, and the 'colonial peace' that spread from the 1880s, was the growth of rival commercial communities. Greeks were formidable competitors in the Red Sea and Gulf of Aden, together with Armenians, Persians, Oriental Jews, Syrians (including Lebanese and Palestinians), Egyptian Copts, Ethiopian Muslims, and Somali.[52] Greeks and Syrians were also to be found further south, while Chinese traders were active in Madagascar, the Mascareignes and South Africa.[53] A few Hindu Tamil Chettiars followed the 'coolie frontier' to Mauritius and Natal.[54] Lithuanian Jews spread all over South Africa and British Central Africa, and beyond.[55] Even European corporations might be more properly analysed as commercial communities, such as the Scots of the McKinnon Group or the Moroccan Jews who controlled the main Portuguese shipping company.[56]

**2. Trade trends**

The commercial supremacy of Indians was legendary, and yet this was often described as an intermediary trade. Sir Bartle Frere expressed it thus in 1873 : « Everywhere, wherever there is any foreign trade, it passes through the hands of some Indian trader ; no produce can be collected for the European, American or Indian market, but through him ; no imports can be distributed to the natives of the country, but through his agency... It is difficult to convey to those at a distance an adequate idea of the extent or completeness of the monopoly. »[57]

This portrayal fails to reflect the position of Indians at the very summit of trading structures.[58] While Frere admitted that a « Banian ... sometimes stands to the foreign firm in a relation more like that of a partner than a mere broker, agent or go-between », he was unwilling to admit that some Western firms were subordinate to Indian ones. Frere also downplayed the role of Arabs. Thus, in the 1830s, the London firm of Newman, Hunt & Christopher went into partnership with an Omani Arab, ᶜAmir b. Saᶜîd al-Shaqsî.[59]

Indian commerce initially focused on 'legitimate' products, traded on the coast.[60]. Cotton cloth was by far the most important manufactured commodity brought to the region, and the Indian import business survived a switch from Indian to Western sources of supply.[61] Moreover, Indians dealt in non-traditional products imported from the West. Tarya Topan made great profits from American kerosene,

---

50 Ghai 1983 ; Swan 1985 ; Bhana and Pachai 1984 : 30.

51 Gregory 1971 : 66.

52 Pankhurst 1968 : 51-65, 359-60, 410-30 ; Bidwell 1983 : 22, 66 ; Manzoni 1884 : 357-9 ; Monfreid 1961 : 141.

53 Thompson and Adloff 1965 : 269-74 ; Swan 1985 : 8.

54 Bhana and Pachai 1984 : 9-11 ; Beejadhur 1935 : 65 ; Schérer 1985 : 73-4.

55 Saron and Hotz 1955 : ch. 19

56 Blake 1956 ; Clarence-Smith 1985 : 96.

57 Frere 1873 : 101-2.

58 Dobbin 1996 : 114.

59 Bhacker 1992 : 161-2.

60 Frere 1873 : 102.

61 Emrith 1967 : 25 ; Pankhurst 1974 : 210 ; Cattelani 1897 : 134 ; Istituto Geografico de Agostini 1913 : 191, 207.

and considered Russia as an alternative source of supply.[62] Ivory was the most important single export to the 1880s. It was at first sent to Bombay, partly for re-export to China and the West. However, Bombay's re-exports to the West largely ceased from the 1870s.[63]

The slave and ivory trades in the interior of Zanzibar's sphere of influence were initially a closely guarded Omani preserve.[64] The rare Indians who ventured far into the interior before the 1880s were usually from poorer communities, notably Ismaili Khoja.[65] However, the slave trade across the Indian Ocean was shared between Omani and Hadhrami Arabs.[66] The Hadhrami were especially active from their base in the Comoros, outside the Omani empire and politically dominated by Hadhrami *sayyid* lineages.[67] Similarly, slave trading accounted for much of the Hadhrami prominence in the Red Sea, again outside the Omani empire.[68] Some Kutchi Indians were involved in slaving, but on a minor scale, due in part to British pressure.[69]

As colonial authority and railways spread into the interior from the 1880s, Gujarati traders came with them.[70] One legendary Ismaili, Allidina Visram, had a commercial network all over German East Africa and British East Africa by the time he died in 1916, extending into the Belgian Congo, the Sudan and Ethiopia. He also owned a fleet of dhows and a small steamer on Lake Victoria.[71] However, this remained a risky business : an Ismaili who built up a similar commercial empire, Sewa Haji Paroo, was murdered in 1897.[72] Established Battier firms moved from old centres, such as Zanzibar, Bagamoyo and Lamu, to ports where new railways began, such as Mombasa and Dar-es-Salaam, but they were more cautious about going into the interior.[73]

Although Indians increasingly became agents or suppliers of Western firms after the opening of the Suez Canal and colonial conquest, it remains unclear how much autonomy they retained in the era of the telegraph and the steamer. Indians certainly took to the new technology 'with a vengeance' in the case of Omani date exports.[74] In Mozambique Island around 1914, « a few of the more prosperous [Indians] import their own goods from Bombay or Lisbon ».[75] Niche trades were also important. Thus, Hadhrami control of flows of coffee from Yemen to Egypt remained solid.[76] Another lucrative activity was gun running in the Red Sea, especially in the 1910s, when the Ottoman-Italian war and the First World War provided rich pickings

---

62 Naseem 1975 : 87.

63 Sheriff 1987 ; Bennett 1978: 14, 52.

64 Burton 1860 : I, 328.

65 Gregory 1971 : 35;.

66 Kelly 1968 : 413 ; Douin 1936-41 : III-1, 265-6 ; Gavin 1975 : 156-7, 161.

67 Campbell 1989 ; Shepherd 1980 ; Hafkin 1973 : 54-7.

68 Toledano 1982 : 58 ; Ewald 1989.

69 Bennett 1978 : 74-5.

70 Naseem 1975 : 136, 177 ; Vail and White 1980 : 64-5.

71 Mangat 1969 : 47-53, 77-81; Dobbin 1996 : 120-1.

72 Dobbin 1996 : 120.

73 Janmohamed 1986 : 585-8, 596.

74 Allen 1978 : 166-8.

75 Great Britain 1920 : 303.

76 Laërne 1885 : 429-30 ; Ingrams 1937 : 161.

for Hadhrami merchants.[77] Similarly, gun running by Indians established in Masqat came to the fore from 1890.[78]

**3. Shipping moves**

Sail navigation was one of the rare economic activities in which Arabs were considered more important than Indians in the nineteenth century.[79] The golden age of Omani shipping was in the early nineteenth century, due to neutrality in European wars. Major shippers in their own right, the lords of Masqat aggressively expanded the Omani merchant fleet. They purchased large square rigged ships seized by the British as prizes, and had others built for them in Bombay. In Cochin, Bombay and Arabian ports, they also bought *baghla*, ships made of Malabar teak, two masted, lateen rigged, and of 70 to 100 tons burden.[80]

Other communities remained active in shipping. Hadhrami Arabs concentrated on areas outside the Omani empire, or on its periphery, notably the Red Sea, Lamu, the Comoro Islands and southern India.[81] Indians sold some ships to Omanis in the early nineteenth century, but Masqati vessels tended to pass into Indian hands after 1815, in payment of debts. Nevertheless, one Zanzibar Arab owned a 400 ton Indian-built ship in the 1840s, for trade with Arabia and India, and it was estimated that Omani-owned ships still carried over half the trade of the Gulf in 1854.[82] In Mozambique, Indians owned sailing vessels of up to 400 tons early in the century.[83] One Indian of Mozambique Island had a ship built for himself in Angoche, further down the coast, in 1811.[84]

The coming of the steamer had a contradictory impact. The Red Sea was turned from backwater to shipping artery, first by the use of steamers from India from 1829, and then by the opening of the Suez Canal in 1869. However, the number of large sailing ships initially increased, criss-crossing the Red Sea in an auxiliary role to steamers. Hadhramis dominated this coasting business from the 1850s, limiting the Gujaratis and pushing out Maghribi rivals from the northern Red Sea.[85]

Indians and Arabs also sought to gain a foothold in the new technology. William McKinnon set out to destroy this competition, with the aid of mail subsidies granted to his British India Steam Navigation Company, but he did not enjoy complete success.[86] In the 1890s, Dada Abdullah & Co., of South Africa, had two steamers regularly plying the route from Bombay to Durban.[87] A. M. Jivanji, the Bohora entrepreneur of Karachi and Mombasa, operated steamers from Bombay to Jiddah and Mauritius in the 1900s. Steamers of the famous Parsi firm of Cowasjee Dinshaw, based in Aden, played an important role in East Africa's coastal navigation.[88] Muslim Indian companies in Mauritius also owned two companies for

---

[77] Hogarth 1978 ; Cornwallis 1976.

[78] Allen 1978 : 156-66 ; Landen 1967 : 152-4.

[79] Landen 1967 : 133.

[80] Nicholls 1971 ; Bhacker 1992 ; Benjamin 1976 ; Fattah 1997.

[81] Ewald and Clarence-Smith 1997 ; Clarence-Smith, forthcoming.

[82] Sheriff 1987 : 22-3, 104 ; Landen 1967 : 118, 133.

[83] Jackson Haight 1967 : 79.

[84] Hafkin 1973 : 173.

[85] Ewald and Clarence-Smith 1997.

[86] Munro 1987 ; Blake 1956.

[87] Swan 1985 : 6.

[88] Mangat 1969 : 82-3.

docks, lighterage and stevedoring from the 1870s.[89] At least one Arab firm, belonging to the Hijazi-Hadhrami al-Saqqâf family, brought Southeast Asian pilgrims by steamer from Singapore to Jiddah before 1900.[90]

**4. Finance markets**

The financial tap root of the western Indian Ocean lay in India in 1800, and the position had not changed as much as might be thought by 1914. Surat had been the nerve centre of Gujarati banking under the Mughal emperors, and the city retained a strong financial role long after much of its trade, ship-building and manufacturing had shifted to Bombay.[91] Gujarati bankers, often Vania by caste and Hindu or Jain by religion, benefited hugely from exports of raw cotton and Malwa opium to China from the late eighteenth century. A number of joint-stock Gujarati banks developed from the 1830s, with Parsi bankers in the vanguard. A further boost came from exports of raw cotton to the West, cut off from its main supplier by the American Civil War in the 1860s.[92] The movement of funds around the western Indian Ocean was facilitated by the use of bills of exchange (*hundi*), although these attracted quite high interest rates.[93]

Conditions in Gujarat became more difficult after the banking crash that followed the bursting of the 'cotton bubble' in 1866. This was worsened by late nineteenth century British 'debt settlement' programmes, which cancelled debts of wealthy landowners for which insufficient documentary evidence could be adduced.[94] However, the great Gujarati bankers adapted to the situation, taking up deposit banking and turning more resolutely to joint-stock companies.[95] The Industrial Commission reported during the First World War that Indian financiers in Bombay 'have throughout shown themselves little, if at all, inferior to the English in enterprise, and usually in command of more capital'.[96]

Although the availability of credit from India was significant, trade and local financial operations were vital to capital accumulation, especially tax farming. The collection of customs duties on behalf of the state secured favourable treatment for one's own ships, or those of commercial allies, and the practice was especially important in the sultanates of Oman and Zanzibar.[97] However, this was a risky speculation, for which it was easy to bid too much, as Tarya Topan found to his disgust in the late 1870s.[98] Customs farming was also reported in Mombasa prior to the establishment of Omani rule.[99] Even the Portuguese in Mozambique Island may have farmed the customs in the 1840s.[100] Indian traders in Masqat also provided marine insurance for Arab shippers.[101]

---

[89] Emrith 1967 : 24, 27.

[90] Clarence-Smith 1997 : 300.

[91] Nightingale 1970 : 171 ; *Gazeteer* : II, 183.

[92] Dobbin 1972 : 18-20.

[93] Landen 1967 : 139.

[94] Dobbin 1972 : 154-6 ; *Gazeteer* : IX-1, 96.

[95] Desai 1978 : 204-8 ; *Gazeteer* : II, 185.

[96] Desai 1978 : 183.

[97] Sheriff 1987 : 126-7 ; Allen 1978 : 109-13, 133 ; Naseem 1975 : 39-40.

[98] Bennett 1978 : 106.

[99] Mangat 1969 : 3.

[100] Marinho 1847 : 147.

[101] Naseem 1975 : 31.

Money changing and the lending of funds were widely practised specialities.[102] Although there are few details on banking operations proper, Frere noted in 1873 that north of 14 degrees, « hardly a loan can be negotiated, a mortgage effected, or a bill cashed without Indian agency ».[103] In 1886, Indians had a quasi-monopoly of banking and money-lending in Massawa.[104] Interest rates varied in terms of risk and trust, and did not merit the label of 'usurious' which was often attached to them. In Merca, on the Somali coast, Indian merchants lent to each other at 1.5% in the 1890s, to Arab traders at 10%, to coastal Somali traders at 20%, and to unreliable suppliers of gum from the interior at 200%.[105] Currency arbitrage was also important, especially between gold and silver based currencies.[106]

Although Arabs were generally financially subordinate to Gujarati merchants, Hadhramis were increasingly successful in challenging Gujarati financial pre-eminence in the Red Sea towards the end of the nineteenth century, in part by relying on Ottoman and Egyptian support.[107] Arabs also played a role as moneylenders at a more modest level in East Africa, for example in Lamu.[108]

Loans to Western traders formed an important part of Indian financial operations, at times leading to control over Western firms. Already in the eighteenth century, Portuguese traders in Mozambique were heavily dependent on advances of trade goods from Vania merchants.[109] Although Indians borrowed short term from American merchants in the 1830s, in trade goods and cash, the flow of credit was soon reversed, with the customs master Jairam Shivji as a major lender. By the 1860s and 1870s, many Western firms depended on credit from the great Indian financiers of Zanzibar, who also discounted bills of exchange.[110] Jairam Shivji lent at a standard rate of 9 % a year, while Tarya Topaņ generally lent to Westerners at 7,5 % to 9 %. By the 1870s, United States and French firms owed hundreds of thousands of dollars to Indians. German firms were in much the same position a decade later, although they also made small loans to Indian retailers.[111] In 1873, the Jairam Shivji family business had £140 000 outstanding in loans and mortgages to Europeans and Americans, and Indians were partners in European firms.[112] In 1906, one Indian partner even bought out the American company of W.J. Towell & Co., exporting dates from Masqat.[113]

Credit over long periods was essential to maintaining the flow of ivory from the heart of the continent, and it was provided by both Indians and Arabs. Rates of interest on trade goods were high, reflecting insecurity in the interior, the risk of default, and long periods before loans were repaid, sometimes amounting to several years. Caravan leaders usually contracted to sell their ivory and other goods at favourable rates to their creditors, in effect a form of interest payment.[114] When the

[102] Pankhurst 1968 : 63, 360 ; Pankhurst 1974 : 208-11 ; Cattelani 1897 : 20, 73, 97 ; Naseem 1975 : 32, 68, 132 ; Hafkin 1973 : 86 ; Vail and White 1980 : 65 ; Deschamps 1961 : 280 ; Swan 1985 : 9.

[103] Frere 1873 : 102.

[104] Pankhurst 1968 : 360.

[105] Cattelani 1897 : 20, 73, 97.

[106] Naseem 1975 : 132 ; Pankhurst 1974 : 208-11.

[107] Douin 1936-41 : III-1, 257 ; Ewald 1989 : 82-3.

[108] el Zein 1974 : 89-92.

[109] Alpers 1975 : 92 ; Jackson Haight 1967 : 81.

[110] Dobbin 1996 : 114, 117 ; Naseem 1975 : 84-7.

[111] Sheriff 1987 : 96, 107, 112 ; Mangat 1969 : 8-11.

[112] Frere 1873 : 101-2.

[113] Allen 1978 : 124, 138-9, 143-4.

[114] Naseem 1975 : 51-3, 121-3, 133-4 ; Jackson Haight 1967 : 77-9 ; Cooper 1977 : 42.

famous Arab caravan leader, Tippu Tib, brought a law suit against his creditor Tarya Topan, the judge ruled that high rates of interest were justified by the risks involved.[115]

Care was taken to conceal investment in commerce seen as illegal by the British authorities, notably the trade in slaves. Indians owed a great deal to British protection, and could ill afford to alienate their patrons. Nevertheless, it was estimated that about half the slave trade of Zanzibar in 1873 was financed by Indians.[116] In Mozambique, the financing of the slave trade was almost entirely in Indian hands in the 1840s, the last decade of exports to Brazil.[117]

Arabs and Indians loaned money or supplies to obtain pearls and mother-of-pearl from the Red Sea and the Persian Gulf. Advances were made at the beginning of the season, on the security of the catch, and at interest rates of 10-25 % per diving season by around 1900. As with the ivory trade, profits were bolstered by preferential purchasing arrangements.[118] Indian moneylenders in pearling settlements on the African shores of the Red Sea area were occasionally attacked and robbed.[119] By the end of the century, Arabs dominated this business, although Indians retained a share.[120]

Loans to farmers were nothing new, as Indians had long financed Yemeni coffee growers.[121] Cloves in Zanzibar and Pemba became a major attraction in the nineteenth century, and credit was increasingly secured on the plantations themselves, rather than on the harvest. By 1860, four fifths of Zanzibari clove estates were said to be mortgaged to Indians. However, contrary to tenacious stereotypes, Indians preferred not to foreclose on land, but rather to buy the harvest at preferential rates.[122] The same was true of Mauritian sugar, where much land fell into the hands of Indian creditors during the 1880s sugar crisis. Such land was often sold on by Indian financiers to foremen of Indian work gangs, who owned about a third of the island's cane lands by 1910.[123] Other lands fell into Indian hands through debt in the cape pea zone of southwestern Madagascar, and in the coconut groves opposite Mozambique island.[124]

Slave worked plantations were an Omani speciality, notably for cloves and coconuts in Zanzibar and Pemba, sugar in Pangani, and grain on the Kenya coast.[125] Wealthy Indians, such as Jairam Shivji and Tarya Topan dabbled in cloves, but were badly affected when British Indians were forbidden to own slaves in 1859.[126] Hadhramis were the owners of the largest numbers of slaves in Zanzibar in 1876, but this was probably because they were labour contractors, hiring out slaves for urban and port work.[127] A sharp decline of plantation agriculture set in from the 1890s,

---

115 Sheriff 1987 : 108.

116 Frere 1873 : 103-7.

117 Marinho 1847 : 147 ; Jackson Haight 1967 : 266.

118 Kunz and Stevenson 1908 : 89-90, 98-9, 143, 154 ; Lorimer 1908-15 : I-2, 2227, 2233, 2236 ; Miles 1919 : II, 415-6 ; Pankhurst 1968 : 366 ; Pankhurst 1974 : 198-9.

119 Monfreid 1961 : 108-9, 114-5.

120 Lorimer 1908-15 : I-2, 2236.

121 Bidwell 1983 : 19-23.

122 Cooper 1977 : 139-43; Bennett 1978: 69, 108.

123 Beejahdur 1935 : 83-4 ; Emrith 1967 : 24-7.

124 Thompson and Adloff 1965 : 275, 357 ; Vail and White 1980 : 64-5 ; Moreira Junior 1905 : I; 209.

125 Cooper 1977 ; Glassman 1995 : 97 ; Beachey 1976 : 203.

126 Sheriff 1987 : 53, 65, 205-6 ; Cooper 1977 : 139.

127 Ingrams 1937 : 155 ; Bhacker 1992 : 140 ; Cooper 1977 : 184-5.

caused by restrictions on slavery, the rejection of land claims, and a lack of comparative advantage in a context of falling world prices. This contributed greatly to overall Omani economic decline.[128]

While urban properties were sometimes acquired as an unintended by-product of financial activities, Arabs and Indians came to specialise in this form of investment.[129] Indeed, real estate was a sector in which Arabs were often considered more important than Indians, with Hadhramis to the forefront.[130] Indians had already acquired many buildings in Mozambique Island by the 1830s, and most of the waterfront of Masqat had fallen into their hands by 1900.[131] The firm of Visram owned urban properties scattered around Kenya by 1916.[132]

**5. Manufacturing developments**

The precocious nature of Indian investment in African manufacturing has rarely been properly recognised, and much remains to be discovered about it. Links, if any, to the rise of manufacturing in India itself need to be explored. However, it does appear that Indian traders were pioneers in exploring the potential of industrialisation, often seizing opportunities before Western entrepreneurs. Their role in Madagascar is mentioned, but details are lacking.[133] An even greater gap in the picture is South Africa.

Much Indian industry was export processing in nature, a sensible option in poorly developed economies, where economies of scale were otherwise hard to obtain. As early as 1835, Indians in Mauritius owned a sugar factory, and their involvement in this industry grew over time.[134] An Indian aloe fibre factory existed in the island in the 1890s.[135] Camel-driven presses were used to extract coconut oil in Zanzibar in the 1840s.[136] As the interior of East Africa was opened up, the firm of Visram invested heavily in cotton ginneries, as well as saw-mills, soda plants, and mills to extract oil from sesame seeds and copra.[137] A sugar factory was initiated by a Gujarati entrepreneur near Kisumu, in Kenya, around 1910.[138] The First World War gave a new boost to Indian cotton ginneries, of which there were about 100 by 1925, as East Africa came to supply Indian rather than Lancashire mills.[139]

Indians also ventured into production for local consumption. The Atchia brothers set up a hydro-electric plant in Mauritius in 1900, and their company was in business for half a century. Another Indian firm was involved in the electricity sector, and Indians opened the first cinema on the island in 1915.[140] As for Visram, he had

[128] Salim 1973 : 66-76, 100-5, 111, 113-5, 123-5, 132-3 ; Iliffe 1979 : 130-2 ; Cooper 1980 : 199-200, 212.

[129] Mangat 1969 : 53 ; Naseem 1975 : 107.

[130] Landen 1967 : 133 ; Ingrams 1937.

[131] Alexandre 1979 : 86 ; Allen 1978 : 115-6.

[132] Naseem 1975 : 78.

[133] Deschamps 1961 : 280.

[134] Benedict 1961 : 26.

[135] Emrith 1967 : 26.

[136] Cooper 1977 : 63.

[137] Mangat 1969 : 78-9.

[138] Bharati 1972 : 107.

[139] Dobbin 1996 : 122.

[140] Emrith 1967 : 26-8

furniture factories in Kampala and Entebbe in Uganda, as well as a soap factory in Mombasa, by the time he died in 1916.[141]

**Conclusion**

Indian and Arab commercial communities came under considerable pressure after 1914. Colonialism entered into a neo-mercantilist phase, which was only slowly and partially reversed after 1945, and racist discrimination against 'foreign Asiatics' was stepped up. Independence was even worse, as attacks on alien minorities culminated in the savage massacres of the 1960s in Zanzibar. Indians and Arabs both suffered from the expulsions decreed by Idi Amin in Uganda, and from similar, if less extreme, policies throughout the region. Socialist policies also closed economies and brought them to their knees. When the Somali state imploded into anarchy, the plight of Arabs and Indians was intense.

Signs of renewal are apparent, despite the survival of xenophobic and racist prejudices. Old ties are slowly being repaired or forged anew, as the generation of independence fades into the background. Economic liberalisation has tempted some South Asians and Arabs back to Africa, notably to Uganda and Tanzania. A Hadhrami-Ethiopian entrepreneur, Muhammad b. Husayn al-ᶜAmûdî, has played a key role in the recent economic recovery of Ethiopia.[142] This renaissance is still fragile, but these diasporas have been in this kind of situation before. Their tenacity and flexibility allows them to rise again, like the phoenix from its ashes.

*** References**

- Alexandre, V. (1979), *Origens do colonialismo português moderno*, Lisbon, Sá da Costa.
- Allen Jr., C. H. (1978), *Sayyids shets and sultans : politics and trade in Masqat under the Al Bu Said, 1785-1914*, PhD Thesis, University of Washington.
- Alpers, E. (1975), *Ivory and slaves in East Central Africa*, London, Heinemann.
- Austin, G., and Sugihara, K., eds. (1993), *Local suppliers of credit in the Third World, 1750-1960*, London, Macmillan.
- Beachey, R. W. (1976), *The slave trade of eastern Africa*, London, Rex Collings.
- Beejahdur, A. (1935), *Les Indiens à l'Ile Maurice*, Port Louis, M. Gaud.
- Benedict, B. (1961), *Indians in a plural society : a report on Mauritius*, London, HMSO.
- Benjamin, N., (1976), « Arab merchants of Bombay and Surat, c. 1800-1840 », *The Indian Economic and Social History Review*, 13, 1, pp. 85-95.
- Bennett, N. R. (1978), *A history of the Arab state of Zanzibar*, London, Methuen.
- Bhacker, M. R. (1992), *Trade and empire in Muscat and Zanzibar : the roots of British domination*, London, Routledge.
- Bhana, S., and Pachai, B., eds. (1984), *A documentary history of Indian South Africans*, Cape Town, David Philip.
- Bharati. A. (1972), *The Asians in East Africa : Jayhind and Uhuru*, Chicago, Nelson Hall.
- Bidwell, R. (1983), *The two Yemens*, London, Longman.
- Blake, G. (1956), *B. I. centenary, 1856-1956*, London, Collins.
- Bricchetti, L. R. (1899), *Somalia e Benadir ; viaggio de esplorazione nell'Africa Orientale*. Milan, C. Aliprandi.
- Brown, W. T. (1971), *A precolonial history of Bagamoyo, aspects of the growth of an East African coastal town*, PhD Thesis, Boston University.

[141] Mangat 1969 : 78-9.

[142] *Financial Times*, 2.3.1998.

- Burton, R. F. (1860), *The lake regions of Central Africa*. London : Longman Green Longman and Roberts.
- Caldeira, J. (1852-1853), *Apontamentos d'uma viagem de Lisboa á China e da China a Lisboa*, Lisbon, J. Lavado.
- Campbell, G. (1989), « Madagascar and Mozambique in the slave trade of the western Indian Ocean, 1800-186 », in W. G. Clarence-Smith, ed.,*The economics of the Indian Ocean slave trade in the nineteenth century*, London, Cass.
- Cattelani, G. (1897), *L'avvenire coloniale d'Italia nel Benadir*, Naples, F. Giannini e Figli.
- Clarence-Smith, [W.] G. (1985) *The third Portuguese empire, 1825-1975, a study in economic imperialism*, Manchester, Manchester University Press.
- Clarence-Smith, W. G. (1989), « Indian business communities in the western Indian Ocean in the nineteenth century », *The Indian Ocean Review*, 2, 4, pp. 18-21.
- Clarence-Smith, W. G. (1997) 'Hadhrami entrepreneurs in the Malay world, c. 1750 to c. 1940', in U. Freitag and W. G. Clarence-Smith, eds., *Hadhrami traders, scholars and statesmen in the Indian Ocean, 1750s-1960s*, 297-314, Leiden : Brill.
- Clarence-Smith, W. G. (forthcoming), « The rise and fall of Hadhrami Arab shipping in the Indian Ocean, c1750-1940 », in David Parkin and Ruth Barnes, eds., *Ships and the development of maritime technology across the Indian Ocean*, London, Curzon.
- Cooper, F (1977), *Plantation slavery on the East coast of Africa*, New Haven : Yale University Press.
- Cooper, F. (1980), *From slaves to squatters ; plantation labour and agriculture in Zanzibar and coastal Kenya 1890-1925*. New Haven, Yale University Press.
- Cornwallis, K. (1976). *Asir before World War I : a handbook*, Cambridge and New York, Oleander Press and Falcon Press.
- Das Gupta, A. (1979) *Indian merchants and the decline of surat, c1700-1750*, Wiesbaden, Steiner.
- Desai, N. (1978), *Social change in Gujarat, a study of nineteenth century Gujarati society*, Bombay, Vora.
- Deschamps, H. (1961), *Histoire de Madagascar*, Paris, Berger Levrault.
- Dobbin, C. (1972) *Urban leadership in western India : politics and community in Bombay city, 1840-1995*, London: Oxford University Press.
- Dobbin, C. (1996), *Asian entrepreneurial minorities : conjoint communities in the making of the world-economy, 1570-1940*, Richmond, Curzon.
- Dotson, F. and L. (1968) *The Indian minority in Zambia, Rhodesia and Malawi*, New Haven, Yale University Press.
- Douin, G. (1936-1941), *Histoire du règne du Khédive Ismail*, Rome and Cairo, Société Royale de Géographie d'Egypte.
- Emrith, M. (1967), *Muslims in Mauritius*, Port Louis [no publisher].
- Ewald, J. J. (1989), « The Nile Valley system and Red Sea slave trade », in : W. G. Clarence-Smith, ed., *The economics of the Indian Ocean slave trade in the nineteenth century*. London, Cass.
- Ewald, J. & Clarence-Smith, W. G. (1997), « The economic role of the Hadhrami diaspora in the Red Sea and Gulf of Aden, 1820s to 1930s », in U. Freitag and W. G. Clarence-Smith, eds., *Hadhrami traders, scholars and statesmen in the Indian Ocean, 1750s-1960s*, pp. 281-296, Leiden, Brill.
- Fattah, H. M. (1997) *The politics of regional trade in Iraq, Arabia and the Gulf, 1745-1900*, Albany, State University of New York.
- Frere, B. (1873), « Memorandum by Sir B. Frere regarding Banians or natives of India in East Africa », *British Parliamentary Papers*.
- *Gazeteer of the Bombay Presidency* (1896-1904), Bombay, Government Central Press.
- Gavin, R. J. (1975)*Aden under British rule, 1839-1967*, London: C. Hurst.

- Ghai, Y. and D. (1983) *The Asian minorities of East and Central Africa*, London : Minority Rights Group.
- Glassman, J. (1995) *Feast and riot ; revelry, rebellion, and popular consciousness on the Swahili Coast. 1856-1888.* London : J. Currey.
- Great Britain (1920) *A manual of Portuguese East Africa*, London : Naval Intelligence Division.
- Gregory, R. G. (1971) *India and East Africa, a history of race relations, 1890-1939*, Oxford, Clarendon Press.
- Guillain, C. (1856-1857), *Documents sur l'histoire, la géographie et le commerce de l'Afrique Orientale*, Paris, A. Bertrand.
- Hafkin, N. J. (1973), *Trade, society and politics in northern Mozambique, c.1753-1913*, PhD Thesis, Boston University.
- Hogarth, D. G. (1978) *Hejaz before World War I: a handbook*,.Cambridge and New York: Oleander Press and Falcon Press.
- Iliffe, J. (1979). *A modern history of Tanganyika.* Cambridge : Cambridge University Press.
- Ingrams, W. H. (1937) *A report on the social, economic and political conditions of the Hadhramaut*, London, HMSO.
- Istituto Geografico de Agostini (1913), *L'Eritrea economica*, Novara.
- Jackson Haight, M. V. (1967) *European powers and south-east Africa, 1796-1856*, New York, Praeger.
- Janmohamed, K. K. (1986) 'The emergence of Mombasa as the chief commercial centre of East Africa, 1895-1914', in G. Liesegang et al., eds., *Figuring African trade*, pp. 571-96, Berlin: D. Reimer.
- Kelly, J. B. (1968). *Britain and the Persian Gulf 1795-1880*, Oxford : Clarendon Press.
- Kunz, G. F., and Stevenson, C. H., 1908, *The book of the pearl : the history, art, science and industry of the queen of gems* [no place of publication or publisher].
- Laërne, C. F. van Delden (1885) *Brazil and Java: report on coffee-culture in America, Asia and Africa*, London, W. H. Allen & Co.
- Landen, R. G. (1967). *Oman since 1856.* Princeton, Princeton University Press.
- Le Guennec-Coppens, F. (1997), « Changing patterns of Hadhrami migration and social integration in East Africa », in U. Freitag and W. G. Clarence-Smith, eds., *Hadhrami traders, scholars and statesmen in the Indian Ocean, 1750s to 1960s*, Leiden, Brill.
- Lorimer, J. G.(1908-15) *Gazeteer of the Persian Gulf, Oman and central Arabia*, London: no publisher indicated.
- Mangat, J. S. (1969), *A history of the Asians of East Africa, c1886-1945*, Oxford, Clarendon Press.
- Manzoni, R. (1884) *El Yèmen, tre anni nell'Arabia Felice*, Rome, [no publisher].
- Marinho, J. Pereira (1847) *Treze meses de administração geral da provincia de Moçambique*, Lisbon, M. de J. Coelho.
- Miles, S. B. (1919) *The countries and tribes of the Persian Gulf*, London, Harrison & Sons.
- Misra, S. C. (1964). *Muslim communities in Gujarat*, London, Asia.
- Monfreid, H. de (1961) *Les secrets de la Mer Rouge*, Paris, Le Livre de Poche.
- Moreira Júnior, M. A. (1905) *Relatorio referente ás provincias ultramarinas e ao districto autonomo de Timor*, Lisbon, Imprensa Nacional.

Morris, H. S. (1968) *The Indians in Uganda*, London, Weidenfeld and Nicolson.
- Munro, J. F. (1987), « Shipping subsidies and railway guarantees: William McKinnon, eastern Africa and the Indian Ocean, 1860-1893 », *Journal of African History*, 28, 209-30.
- Naseem, A. W. (1975) 'Nature and extent of the Indian enterprise along the East African coast and subsequent role in the development of Kenya, 1840-1905', PhD Thesis, St. Johns University, New York.

- Nicholls, C. S. (1971) *The Swahili coast, politics, diplomacy and trade on the East African littoral, 1798-1856*, New York, Africana Publishing Corporation.
- Nightingale, P. (1970) *Trade and empire in Western India, 1784-1806*. Cambridge, Cambridge University Press.
- Pankhurst, R. (1968) *Economic history of Ethiopia, 1800-1935*, Addis Ababa, Haile Selassie I University Press.
- Pankhurst, R. (1974), « The "Banyan" or Indian presence at Massawa, the Dahlak islands and the Horn of Africa » *Journal of Ethiopian Studies*, 12, 1, 208-11.
- Pocock, D. (1955), « The movement of castes », *Man*, 55, pp. 71-2.
- Robert, M. (1977), « Les musulmans à Madagascar et dans les Mascareignes » *Revue française d'études politiques africaines*, 138-9, pp. 46-71.
- Rushbrook-Williams, L. F (1958), *The black hills: Kutch in history and legend; a study in Indian local loyalties*, London, Weidenfeld and Nicolson.
- Salim, A. I. (1973),*Swahili-speaking peoples of Kenya's coast, 1895-1965*, Narobi, East African Publishing House.
- Saron, G., and L. Hotz, eds. (1955), *The Jews in South Africa : a history*, London, Oxford University Press.
- Schérer, A. (1985), *La Réunion*, Paris, Presses Universitaires de France.
- Shepherd, G. (1980), « The Comorians and the East African slave trade », in J. L. Watson, ed., *Asian and African systems of slavery*, Oxford, Blackwell.
- Sheriff, A. (1987), *Slaves, spices and ivory in Zanzibar. integration of an East African commercial empire into the world economy, 1770-1873*, London, J. Currey.
- Strobel, M. (1979), *Muslim women in Mombasa, 1890-1975*, New Haven, Yale University Press.
- Swan, M. (1985), *Gandhi, the South African experience*, Johannesburg, Ravan Press.
- Thompson, V., and Adloff, R. (1965), *The Malagasy Republic*, Stanford, Stanford Uniersity Press.
- Toledano, E. (1982), *The Ottoman slave trade and its suppression*, Princeton : Princeton University Press.
- Vail, L., and White, L. (1980), *Capitalism and colonialism in Mozambique, a study of the Quelimane district*, London, Heinemann.
- Vicziany, M. (1979), « Bombay merchants and structural change in the export community, 1850-1880 » in K. N. Chaudhuri and C. J. Dewey, eds. *Economy and society: essays in Indian economic and social history*, 163-96, Delhi : Oxford University Press.
- Walji, S. R. (1974), « A history of the Ismaili community in Tanzania », PhD Thesis, University of Wisconsin.
- Willis, J. (1993), *Mombasa, the Swahili and the making of the Mijikenda*. Oxford, Clarendon Press.
- el-Zein, A. H. M. (1974), *The sacred meadows : a structural analysis of religious symbolism in an East African town*, Evanston, Northwestern University Press.

# [8]

## 'After Shaking his Hand, Start Counting your Fingers'

### Trust and Images in Indian Business Networks, East Africa 1900-2000

*GIJSBERT OONK**

### Introduction[1]

In this study, I examine how 'ethnic' trading networks are created and re-created, but may also fracture and fall apart. This occurred among some Indian groups in East Africa, who initially strengthened their economic and cultural ties with India by maintaining intensive trade relations and taking brides from the homeland. However, after just one generation, their economic focus was on East Africa, Japan and the UK. Many of today's well-off Indian businessmen in East Africa show little economic interest in India. In fact, Gujarati businessmen in East Africa created new, rather negative images of their counterparts in Gujarat. During the last century, their overall image of Indians in India was transformed from one of a 'reliable family or community members' to one of 'unreliable, corrupt and, untrustworthy 'others'.

In the literature on 'diasporas', there is a tendency to explain the economic success of Chinese, Indian or Jewish businessmen in terms of 'trust' based on ethnic background and trading networks. The major aim of a 'network' is the circulation of capital, credit, information, goods and produce, men and women. Generally speaking, an ethnic network does not trade inside information and does not exchange women with other networks. Nevertheless, trade, credit, and information may be bought from other networks. More often than not, networks are seen as a rather static informally organised system, which is used as a tool by its various members. On the whole, we assume that notions of the same religion, language, and regional background reinforce concepts of 'trust', mutual aid and shared values among migrant traders and businessmen. Within these networks, there is a strong emphasis on an ethic of hard work, the moral and economic support of each other, and the gift of a superior 'business mind'. In most literature the system, itself is not questioned, reservations are expressed about how the members of a business community take advantage from it. As a rule, this type of literature tends to emphasise the 'success stories' in migrant business communities.[2]

This is particularly true for the literature on South Asians in East Africa where the economic and political contributions of Indians to the East African countries account for many pages in this vast and growing literature. Despite its prolixity, this literature provides a poor explanation of the success of Indian business communities in East Africa. Most of it stresses the importance of hard work, long hours of labour, community support in setting up new businesses or in providing credit, and the so-called entrepreneurial skills of South Asian traders and industrialists in East Africa.[3] Recently, the long list of these often teleological explanations has been extended by the 'diasporic' argument, in which the economic success of diasporic groups is seen to result from the mutual pooling of resources, the transfer of credit, the investment of capital, and the provision of services among family, extended kin network or members of the same group. The decisive argument within 'diaspora studies' seems to be the role of the 'motherland', which is often seen as an endless source of capital, labour and a reference for the maintenance of the ethnic identity.[4] In many definitions or descriptions of the concept of 'diaspora', the homeland, motherland or *heimat* is considered to be of overwhelming importance to the migrants in diaspora. The relationship with the motherland is described as a cultural bond experienced by almost all migrants. Many studies emphasise that the religious, cultural, and often economic orientation towards their country of origin plays an important role in the identity of migrants in a foreign country. As Clifford has put it, 'the language of diaspora is increasingly invoked by displaced peoples who feel (maintain, revive, invent) a connection with a prior home [...].'[5] Robin Cohen assumes 'a collective memory and myth about the homeland' and the 'development of a return movement' to be among the common features of a diaspora.[6] In this concept, institutions that endeavour to control everyday activities, like for example religious practices, the education of children, and the organising of marriages reinforce diasporic notions.[7] In this research, however, I found that the homeland is becoming less and less important to some Asian Africans, either as an economic source or as a cultural point of reference. The images of the homeland may be important to many overseas migrants, but not for Hindu Lohanas in East Africa. Cogently, this diaspora literature fails to see the shifting loyalties of kinship, caste, and community, and in particular, the shifting importance of the role of the native soil, or homeland.[8]

The Indian government also tends to overestimate the importance of Indian 'diasporic feelings'. In its recently published Report of the High Level Commission, it states that 'Since India achieved Independence, overseas Indians have been returning to seek for their roots and explore new avenues and sectors for mutual beneficial interaction from investment to transfer of economic skills and technology, to outright philanthropy and charitable work. This trend has become more marked in the last decade, as the Indian economy has opened up, giving rise to a new range of opportunities for emerging generations.'[9] This is, in fact, far from true and the consequence of wishful thinking. The main aim of the commission is to explore the possibilities of improving the relationship between India and 'Persons of Indian Origin' [PIO] and 'Non Resident Indians overseas [NRI]'. This is, of course, the result of the disappointment felt by Indian Government in the role played by PIOs and NRIs, so far.

In this article, I argue that there is a need to study 'the importance of the motherland' as a local 'bottom-up' process. Local, in the sense of a well defined geographical and historical area and 'bottom-up' in the sense that I choose to take the perspective of the 'agent', the one who creates, experiences and mythologises the motherland, or not. By taking this perspective, we may build up a view of how the 'motherland' is defined by the *creators* of ethnic networks themselves. This may provide us with insights into the economic and cultural agenda of individuals as well as groups in a fast changing economic and cultural environment. This research was based on the life histories of twenty Hindu Lohana families who have lived in East Africa for three or more generations.[10] The results of this research are particularly opposite for those families who settled between the 1880s and the 1920s in East Africa.[11] Most interviews were conducted in Dar es Salaam, the Coastal Region, and Nairobi. The focus is on two interrelated successful Gujarati business families who made their wealth in East Africa, the Hindu Lohana families of Sunderji Nanji Damordas and Keshavji Anandji.[12] Within these two families, there has emerged a remarkable change in their social and economic relations with India. India used to be the most important economic business partner and supplier of brides to the male members of these families, but after Indian Independence India had become economically insignificant for these families, while at the same time they developed a marital preference for Indian women who were raised in East Africa.[13] As the picture presented is representative of the Hindu Lohana business community in East Africa as a whole, it is by no means a definitive picture of the South Asians in East Africa.[14] The Muslims (including Ithnasheries and Khoja Ismailis) especially, have followed a different pattern which is beyond the scope of this article.

Below, I describe how the economic focus of Gujarati businessmen in East Africa changed from an orientation towards India to an orientation towards East Africa, Japan, the UK, Canada, and the US. Many well-off Indian businessmen in East Africa show little economic interest in India. The once favoured Indian counterparts in Gujarat have had to cede their place in the minds of Indians in East Africa. Gujarati businessmen in East Africa have created new, rather negative images of their former partners in Gujarat. The overall image has been transformed from one of 'reliable family or community members' to one of 'unreliable, corrupt, and untrustworthy others'. Simultaneously, the image of India changed from that of 'the beloved motherland' to one of an 'overcrowded, stinky and unorganised and underdeveloped country'.[15] Most significantly, the growing preference of Gujarati businessmen for marrying Gujarati women raised in East Africa and, at the same time, an increasing economic orientation towards the West have cut off the economic and kinship bond with India.

The transformation of images and notions of trust within the Gujarati business network has to be seen within the broader perspective of social, economic, and political change. The growth of the Indian settlement in East Africa was strongly related to the British Empire. Following the Independence of India (1947) and of the East African countries (1960-61), it is said that South Asians had to make up their minds and 'choose' to where they 'belonged'. In fact, I argue, by then they had already made up their minds and tended to focus on the West, especially the UK. Most informants argued that after the 1960s, they had no emotional (family) or economic bonds with India and therefore they tended to focus on the UK. This may be true for many, but they had hardly any more business or family relations with the UK or the West. In other words, the change of orientation from India to the West was a choice which had to be legitimised. And the emergence of negative images of India and towards Indian businessmen in India has to be seen within this framework.

The article is built on four sections. First, we introduce the general migration history of Indians in East Africa. In this section, the focus will be on the absence of Hindu women in East Africa. This is followed in the second section of the life histories of early Lohana migrants who settled in East Africa between 1880 and 1920. Here, the main aim is to show how Indian families literally lived in two worlds; India and Africa. This, dual life, changed in the period after the 1920s, when increasingly Indian businessmen settled with their wives and families, the theme of the third section. In the period between 1920 and 1960, we see a shift in economic and social orientation of Hindu Lohanas from India to Africa and the UK. In the fourth and concluding section, we provide some possible explanations for this shift and the changing attitude of Hindu businessmen in East Africa towards their counterparts in India.

## Migration and Settling of Indians in East Africa

In the nineteenth-century trade between South Asia and East Africa was constrained by the rhythm of the monsoons. From November to March the well-known beautiful dhows sailed from West India to East Africa, and from April to October the return journey was made. The trade in cotton textiles, ivory, and spices was profitable, but dangerous. Many traders did not return home safely. The rough sea, pirates, and various diseases claimed the lives of many traders and early adventurers.

It was only in the late nineteenth century that some Indian traders started to settle in Zanzibar and on the East African Coast. These early Indian settlers are nowadays seen as the pioneers of many South Asian family business houses in East Africa, such as that of Nanji Damordas, who came accompanied by his father at the age of ten, to look after some business opportunities in Zanzibar. Most of these early migrants were asked to join the flourishing family businesses or to assist in the businesses of community members. Initially, they travelled back and forth to India, but slowly they settled in East Africa and invited their brothers and sisters, wives and children to join them.

The general migration history of Asian East Africans is well documented. Long before East Africa was 'discovered' by Europeans, Zanzibar and the East African Coast were well-known trading destinations for Arabs and South Asians. These trading relations were strengthened during the establishment of the British Empire in East Africa. In the period between 1880 and 1920, the number of South Asians in East Africa grew from about 6,000 to 54,000. These included Hindus (among them well-known business families like Patels, Lohanas, and Shahs), Muslims (especially Ithnasheries, Bohras, Ismailis), Sikhs, Goans and others.[16]

The various Asian business communities that arrived in the late nineteenth century developed far more intimate social and economic relationships with each other than they had done in India. These linkages resulted in new business habits, marriage policies, and forms of capital accumulation. Their shared knowledge of the Gujarati language and their minority status (never more than two per cent of the total population in East Africa, somewhat higher in the main trading ports) in a new society played an important role in this process. Despite the development of intimate socio-economic links, inter-caste marriages and marriages between Hindus and Muslims were still uncommon.[17]

The Muslims settled with their families earlier than the Hindus owing to the Hindu taboo on travel overseas.[18] Upper-caste Hindu men considered Africa to be 'alien' and 'unsafe' for women, and believed that women would be better cared for if they stayed behind in their own extended households in India. Owing to the economic and social uncertainty in East Africa, most Hindu women remained behind in India to look after their parents-in-law, children, and property, and to supervise of their children's education.[19] The unmarried Hindu men generally went back to India to marry, and their wives stayed behind from the beginning with the men making frequent trips back and forth. Otherwise, the women came to the East African Coast for a few years, returning to India for childbirth, where they generally remained for ten to twenty years until their children had finished their education.[20]

The Sultan of Zanzibar, Seyyid Bargash, must have been aware of this as he encouraged Hindus to bring their wives to his realm. In the early 1880s he is reported to have sent his private vessel to welcome the first Hindu woman in Zanzibar and gave her a reward of Shs 250/–. As a pledge of his good intentions, he promised to turn Zanzibar's Old Fort into a residence for the wives of merchants and offered to equip it with water pipes fitted with silver taps to ensure that Hindu women need never appear in public.[21] This occurred precisely at the time the Hindu community in Gujarat revolted successfully against Brahmin priests and religious customs which were cramping their mercantile activities and making overseas commerce difficult.[22] All these activities paved the way for Hindu migrants and settlers in the late nineteenth and early twentieth centuries. A new (in fact very old) world was to be discovered.

## Marriage, Money, and Markets, 1880-1920

The migration history of Sunderjibhai follows the well-trodden pattern migration history of Hindu Lohanas in East Africa. In 1916, at the age of ten, he arrived in Zanibar with his father, Nanjibhai Damordar. They were asked to look after a shop of a relative, Kesawji Dewanji, whose sons did not want to settle in East Africa and had returned to India.[23] At an earlier stage, one of Nanjibhai's younger sisters had already married a Lohana Indian (same jati) in Uganda.[24] He traded in 'everything where money could be made'.

At the beginning of the twentieth century, the main goods in which South Asians traded included textiles, garments, ivory, gold, and foodstuffs such as maize, beans, and grains. Textiles and garments were imported from India, whereas ivory and gold were sold in India. Most foodstuffs were bought and sold locally. In addition, some relatively well-off families were involved in a form of banking. Most goods sold to (mainly Indian and Arab) traders up-country were sold on a 90 or 120 day credit, with an interest of between six to nine per cent per annum. Thus, the profits of these traders included a profit on sales as well as a profit on the advancement of money. Some bigger families exchanged 'hundis' (bills of exchange) with traders in Bombay, Zanzibar, Muscat, and Dar es Salaam.[25] This is often seen as an early and sophisticated way of banking. Keshavji Anandi [99 years, Hindu Lohana], the grand old man of the Anandji family, recalled:

> My grandfather had all kinds of connections with Bombay, Porbandar and Muscat. In Porbandar we had some relatives who looked after the interest of my grandfather. In the same way, he had his brother-in-law in Bombay, who looked after the family business interest at that place. Now, whoever cashed the hundi in say Dar es Salaam, they could travel to Bombay or Porbandar and got the money there and then. Within the family trust, we would arrange the balances. That went on for a long time. In fact, we made a lot of money on the commission of writing and cashing hundis next to our trading activities.[26]

The most important point here is that the family business was represented by family members in various cities in various parts of the world. These networks existed because of the thriving active communal relations and marriage patterns. Some family members had migrated to East Africa, whereas others did not leave India and looked after the 'Indian' part of the business interest, including real estate and land. The family and community relations were reinforced by the activities of traders and messengers who often made a trip once a year in the name of the family eldest to inform themselves about the family business. However, after settling with their wives many Hindu Lohana in East Africa were very reluctant to make the journey to India once again.

In those days, some migrants visited India 'when it was really necessary', for example to attend marriages or funerals or because of the immediate health problems of family members. Many of my elderly informants in East Africa do not recall their fathers and grandfathers visiting India often, except for the following reasons: to find a suitable bride; to get medical treatment; to retire and to have a peaceful life back home; and have his ashes scattered above the Ganges.[27] Most elderly Hindu migrants recalled, 'We seldom went back, but we had good business relations with India.' This is evidence that the typical Indian family networks emerged, which supported the international trade relations between South Asia and East Africa. In this network, the business is ideally centred on the family eldest and/or his brothers. The business activities are usually divided geographically and therefore separated. The profits of the family are usually ploughed back into the family and each male member gets his share of the family profits.

Far from home, the family structure of Indians in East Africa changed from a 'joint family' to a 'nuclear family'. Because of the overseas business connections, it was impossible to live under one roof. Therefore, the traditional business-structure in which the family income was to be divided among the male family members had to be altered. The ideal of a joint patrilineal family business was not supported by 'Hindu law' in East Africa. In the Mithakshara school of Hindu law, which applies in Gujarat, all agnatically related males born into the family have an equal undivided share in the family business, which is mostly headed by the family eldest. In East Africa, the only accepted basis for the division of property was by legally registered shares in a partnership or company. As a result, the familial 'sharing' of business amongst the brothers and their (grand) father remained an Indian sentiment but was replaced by more individual forms of ownership. Besides breaking the old pattern, the Indian family members in Africa started to do some business on their own account.[28]

Although the economic scene was changing, the social scene tended to follow familiar ways. Successful Lohana business families built typical 'extended family' houses in order to reproduce Indian culture as far as they could. Though these houses were meant for the extended families to live in, most of the family members who were spread all over East Africa and developed more nuclear units.[29] Even in the face of inevitable change, those pioneers who decided to stay in East Africa rather than retire in Gujarat did everything to reproduce their 'Gujarati culture' in their homes in East Africa. In the case of Sunderjibhai, this consisted in a typical extended family house in Mombasa. In his house there is a large living room with colonial furniture and a traditional Gujarati rocking couch (which can still be seen in many Gujarati houses in East Africa). The portraits of his parents have a prominent place and are decorated with fresh flowers. Except for some small pieces of traditional African art, the living room exudes on the air of Gujarat.

Next to the living room is the kitchen. The house is a typical one-kitchen house, where the extended family lives and shares its meals. There are various apartments were couples with their children have their bedrooms. The whole family, however, shares the living room and kitchen. There is no table in the kitchen, which means that the women sit on the floor while preparing the vegetables, cutting the fruits, and cooking the meals. They are assisted by a Gujarati Brahmin (woman) cook.[30] Next to the kitchen is the dining room where there is a big family dining table where the meals are shared. We have to take off our shoes before entering the dining room. Men and women eat separately. In this house neither liquor nor meat is consumed. This family has maintained their Gujarati tradition of being vegetarian and non-drinkers. Sunderji wears his Nehru (Hindu) cap and dhoti or pyjama with pride.

Within the process of migration and the re-inforcement of Gujarati culture in East Africa, the idea of the joint family relation has remained important. The Mombasa business of Sunderji and his father, for example, flourished as they made use of the advantages of running an informally organised family business. Not only did they use their family network in Zanzibar and India, they also witted colonial law. In the 1920s a person was not allowed to be both a broker and a trader. So, Nanjibhai applied for the broker's licence, while his son Sunderji acquired the trading licence. In this way, the family was able to provide both services to their clients. By law, these firms were separate.

In short, the first generation of Indian businessmen was born in India and maintained a strong economic and social bond with India. They sought their wives in India; they had property and business there and they chose to retire in Gujarat or like Nanji Damordar to reproduce their 'Indian' style in East Africa. Though Indians in East Africa did not visit India very often, their homeland was still an important point of reference. It is interesting to note that the cultural and charitable relations with India were not necessarily explored within the joint family, but via community ties. The heads of nuclear families tried to improve their status by charity. Some Indian pioneers in East Africa made generous charity contributions to the Indian villages from which they came. The Anandji family built a hospital, the family of Damordas built a small school and an orphanage, and the well-known Madhvani and Mehta families contributed to similar projects in Gujarat. These examples show that India was still in the hearts of these businessmen, even when they were not able to visit India in person.

## Marriage, Money and Markets: 1920-1960

In the second period two major changes occurred. First, there was the emergence of a preference for marrying Hindu women brought up in East Africa, instead of Lohana women brought up in India. Consequently, caste boundaries were crossed to find partners [mainly Patels and Shahs]. The fact that Hindus allowed the constraints of caste boundaries to be broken illustrates the change which took place as the Indian community became socially more oriented towards East Africa. To be more precise: they were more oriented towards Indians in East Africa. Initially, however, the demand for (Lohana) Hindu women from India was still great as there were twice as many Hindu men as Hindu women in East Africa.[31]

Second, India became less important as the business partner of the Indian settlers in East Africa. They tended to focus more on East Africa, the UK, and Japan. India lost out the international competition in the textile industry to Japan and, to a lesser extent to Europe. Its general market share in East

Africa diminished dramatically and it became less important as a major export destination.[32] This was the result of two major economic developments. India lost its economic momentum toward becoming a major industrial nation, whereas East Africa took its initial promising steps towards industrialisation, in which Indians played an important role.[33] East Africa tried to produce its own textiles.

In this period, a growing number of Asians in East Africa were educated in so called 'Indian schools' in East Africa, where teaching up to fourth standard was in Gujarati and after that in English.[34] Therefore, a growing number of Asian East Africans were fluent in Gujarati as well as in English. For them, the step towards further education in the UK was relatively small. A number of well-off students attended colleges and universities in the UK. This meant that they developed a strong sense of the English language and European culture, while remaining 'Indian' in outlook and religion. Ultimately, this shift towards the West is reflected in the images these businessmen developed about businessmen in India.

Bharat is a typical example of a Hindu Lohana who did not marry within the Lohana community.[35] He was born in Dar es Salaam and studied in the UK. He then fell in love with a Patel woman and proposed to her. He was the first male member of his family to break the Lohana chain that is to marry outside the Lohana community.[36] He explained his preference for a 'locally raised Indian woman' in terms of her knowledge and experience of the East African way of life. This included general attitude such as the 'slow pace of life', and knowledge of the Swahili language, of how to train African servants, and of how to cook Gujarati food, which by then had already undergone changes in East Africa. It was less spicy, milder, sometimes with coconut milk, and the use of ghee was declining. In his view, it was better to marry outside the community, but within East Africa, than within the community with a Lohana raised in India, who 'would not know anything about Africa'.

Nevertheless, it was not an easy task for the young man to convince his father that he wanted to marry outside his caste.

> It took me a year to convince my father. Though, I have to admit that he was pretty cool about it. In the sense that, of course, he told me that I was the first one of the male heritage of Nanji Damodar, to break this particular tradition. I said, but to me an Indian is an Indian. I must say there was some resistance more from some of my brothers. They are more traditional, I would say. My father was pretty open-minded about this once you talk with him, even to the extent of accepting marrying an non-Indian or a Muslim. My youngest brother is married to a Muslim. So he accepted this.[37]

What was the argument that convinced him?

> Well basically I said, give me one reason, besides the argument that I am breaking any particular traditional pattern, that I should not marry this woman. If I were to marry another Indian then I could understand. But there is no change in the religion, there is no change

> in the tradition even. We both speak Gujarati. I could understand, I can accept his argument, if it were a different religion, different race, then fine, then you have to think about what happens to the offspring. But he was not able to present such an argument. I think he finally, he saw my point of view without admitting it. But we had various discussions about this thing.[38]

In spite of his argument, something did happen to his offspring. His two daughters do not consider themselves Lohanas (born of a Patel), but Hindus. The perceptions of his elder brothers did not change. Some still wanted to see their own children marry within the same caste. Bharat: 'However, I don't think their children will face the same resistance I had. So if they show up with another Hindu, this would be "acceptable".'

Thus, some of the male members of the family developed a preference for Hindu females raised in East Africa, even when this meant marrying outside their caste.[39] The main explanation given for this was that they knew 'East African culture'. This preference for Indian women raised in East Africa ultimately led to deteriorating social and family relations with India. India became less and less important as a source for finding marriage partners. This was especially true of those families who migrated before the beginning of the twentieth century. They lost their family ties with India and, therefore, the urge to visit India for family reasons.

Not only was the demand for Indian women raised in India declining, some offspring of pioneer families mentioned a remarkable change in the quality of products coming from India. Broadly speaking, most agreed that the quality of Indian produce deteriorated, especially after the Second World War. This process of deterioration started in the 1930s. It is especially well illustrated by the case of textiles. Khangas, shirts, saris, and cloth once were imported from India, from the 1930s, the Japanese textile producers took over the East African market. Most of the informants recalled that the Japanese were able to offer better quality textiles at a cheaper rate. Their products were better finished, dyed, and manufactured than products from India. Another plus point was it was said that the Japanese were 'very ambitious', whereas the Indian industrialists had become too 'arrogant and unreliable'.[40]

The above [p. 75] mentioned firm of Keshavji Anandi closed its (Indian) Porbandar firm around 1935. From that moment, the business bond with India was broken. This coincided with the opening of Keshavji Anandi's trading firm in Japan. In the words of one among his offsprings:

> In Mombasa we imported textiles from India in the late 1930s. Now, in the late 1930s there was a man who was employed in our firm. This man was very ambitious and very enterprising. He said, you are a good company and you deal with Japan, why don't you let me open an office there and buy locally and export to East Africa, because we know exactly what is required here. So it was in the middle of the 1930s that a company in Japan was opened in the name of Devani

> & Company. And he bought goods from manufactures and exported them here, to Mombassa and Dar es Salaam. Now again, there was also a partnership firm in the name of Devani brothers in Dar es Salaam. They also dealt with retail business. So there were three main companies importing from Japan. The family company from Mombassa, the family company from Dar es Salaam, and Devani & Co in Japan. Japan was prospering during the War, but the office was taken over as 'enemy property' in the War.[41]

Indian East African firms went to Japan and the Japanese were ambitious enough to have at least three trading companies in Mombasa and Dar es Salaam: Japan Cotton Trading Company, Washo Kibushik Kaisja, and Tokio Kibushik Kaisja.[42]

The gradual economic separation from India was a consequence of the cutting of social ties evidenced by the growing preference for marrying Indian women raised in East Africa and – in the words and memory of the informants – the deterioration of economic relations. Another reason was the growing importance of formal banking, which meant there was less need to re-enforce informal (family) banking networks. The importance of the 'Hundi system' declined in favour of formal banks. In other words, those family members who stayed in India – and did not move to East-Africa – grew less and less important as economic and social capital.

Nevertheless, statistics reveal no dramatic decline in the figures for imports and exports from and to India. On the contrary, my general impression is that India remained East Africa's second largest export destination after the UK.[43] Confronted with this evidence, many second-generation Indians in East Africa replied that these trade activities must have been conducted by 'new Indian migrants', especially those who came after the Second World War.[44] Therefore, it appears plausible that the 'old migrants' needed to legitimise their changing economic focus in the face of the 'new migrants'. One way to do this was to create negative images of India and its inhabitants.

The second generation Indians in East Africa started to focus on new ventures in the UK. Pertinently, the Indian Government changed its policy towards Indians after Indian Independence in 1947. Before Independence Indians overseas played a crucial role for Nationalists like Gandhi in their fight against discrimination in colonial societies. After Independence, the new policy of Nehru and others may be characterised as 'studied indifference'. Overseas Indians were advised to identify with the place in which they resided and not with India.[45] The change in India's policy and the new economic focus of East African Indians on the UK may have fuelled the growing social en economic distance between India and Indian East Africans.[46]

In my view, it is not surprising that Asian businessmen in East Africa developed a new image of India and businesses men in India in this period. Almost without exception, informants spoke negatively of India, and in one way or the other, they sought legitimation for the fact that Asian East Africans do not want to do business with India. They do not want to retire or settle there and, they do not trust an Indian from India.[47] Many of these views are the consequence of experiences. For example, as one Hindu informant stated,

> There is very little honesty in India. They cheat, they send you excellent samples, and if you buy, they send an inferior quality. Or when a shipment of them arrives, you will find out that they have sent less, than you had agreed on. At the same time, when we want to do export there, there are so many amendments. You get tired. We don't have this with other countries, like South Africa, England, and Canada and America. We stopped trading with India. In life, you have to avoid unnecessary headaches don't you?

In a second interview, he added,

> You see, my parents and grandparents had family members in India. So, we knew there was someone to rely on. Someone who took care of the 'Indian' side of the business, but now Bwana, we have no one there. Who can you trust if you have no one there?[48]

The changing social orientation (in terms of family and marriage patterns) towards East Africa reinforced the idea that the 'Gujarati Community' in East Africa was different from the Gujarati community in India. This is in sharp contrast to the previous period during which Indian imports in East Africa were still important, and most Indian families in East Africa had some family members to look after their businesses overseas.

Despite the fact that family and community ties with West India were weakening, some Indian Africans continued to deal with businessmen in India. But over the years they realised that 'something' had changed. A Gujarati from India was no longer the same as a Gujarati from East Africa. Eventually this became the difference between chalk and cheese.

One other informant told me that,

> I am more comfortable do business with a Gujarati from East Africa than a Gujarati in India. Especially when we talk on the phone. As a rule, I would take someone's word for it. Normally eight out of ten times this doesn't go wrong, nevertheless with Gujaratis in India eight out of ten times this goes wrong. [...] For example, we dealt with various business houses in India and also with houses owned by Gujaratis. There was one case in which there were certain deals which could not be documented, and basically we had a verbal agreement. And in the end there was a difference on what we agreed to. This would not happen with most of the Gujaratis from East Africa. There would be unwritten, unspoken understanding of mutual trust.[49]

Many Lohanas felt that Gujaratis from East Africa were more civilised, more reliable, and more exposed to modern life. This was often attributed to the higher standard of education East African Gujaratis enjoyed in East Africa and the UK. They experienced more transparency among Indian East Africans than among Gujaratis from India during the various rounds of consultations before finalising a deal. Of course, there may be other reasons for this that have nothing to do with education. However, in the interviews differences in education were mentioned by many, often in conjunction with 'civilisation', as a main cause of difference. See for example the following:

> You see, they don't know how to speak properly. They, in India, are crude, rougher than we are. When our parents arrived in East Africa, we were with the British; and they educated us. So we learned how to speak, how to dress. This is lacking there, especially in the villages.[50]

Alongside the role of education and the exposure to a more 'Western lifestyle', another argument arose. In India, there is more competition, so Indian businessmen are more competitive than their Indian African counterparts; they are sharper and faster in their dealings. Eventually, this led to a 'lot of mistrust' towards Indians from India in the Indian East African community.

> Our Indian African culture is different. Indians in India are more competitive; they are sharper, better equipped in the negotiation process. They have to be, because of the bigger population. When we do business with them, we get screwed. There is a lot of mistrust in our community against Indian Indians. You know, we have a saying that if you make a deal with an Indian Indian, and shake hands with him, you better start counting your fingers...[51]

This is undeniable evidence that, the second-generation Indians show a remarkable change in their perceptions of Gujaratis in India. They have constructed an image of a dissimilar overseas community, which they perceive as no longer a part of their own community. Gujaratis in India are seen as 'untrustworthy', 'unreliable', and 'uncivilised'. At the same time, they have adjusted to a more 'Western' life style. This is reflected in their 'suit-tie' western dress, written business agreements in English and the discontinuation of the practice of reading Gujarati newspapers and magazines. Bharat, for example, did not subscribed to any of the Gujarati newspapers or magazines. His English was fluent and he kept his business correspondence in English. However, sometimes, when he wrote to his father, he made the effort to formulate at least a few sentences in Gujarati. Like other Gujarati businessmen of his generation, he spoke Gujarati, sometimes infiltrated by a few English words. At home, he spoke Gujarati with his wife and children, while his wife would answer him in Gujarati, his children might answer in English. India has become a foreign nation to them. Indeed, they have visited India only once, as tourists.

## Conclusion

The literature on diasporas tends to highlight the importance of the motherland. This is seen as the migrants' umbilical cord to their homeland. It would seem to be unthinkable that migrants would cut off this relationship, but this is exactly what happened in the case of the Hindu Lohanas in East Africa who migrated and settled in East Africa before, say the 1930s. Initially, India was primarily important as a source of business connections and served as a pool for new recruits for East African firms. Furthermore, it was an important reservoir for marriage partners, which served as an important marker of purity within the Indian network. Nevertheless, the image of the Indian Subcontinent changed between 1880s and the 1960s, from being the beloved 'mother' to an alien other.

In this article I have shown that Indian Africans do not trust Gujarati businessmen from Gujarat. They are seen as 'unreliable', 'uncivilized' and 'untrustworthy'. This change in image can be explained by two interrelated causes: indubitably, Gujaratis in East Africa developed a preference for Indian marriage partners raised in East Africa, who know 'their culture'. Consequent with this shift in attitude, their interest in doing business with India diminished. They were educated in East Africa and Europe, and developed an interest in a European life-style. As a trading minority, they were exposed to African and European culture, more than to that of Gujarat. Therefore, it may not come to surprise to observe that, after a while, India became less civilised in their minds. However, there is no denial of the fact that their cultural roots emerged from Gujarat. But the cultural, and more important, economic interest in India declined.

These conclusions raise questions about the importance of the concept of the 'diaspora', especially in respect of the meaning of the role of the 'motherland'. In my view, the notion of the motherland loses its importance (whether invented, imagined or real) if it is not reinforced instrumentally. By taking a 'bottom up' approach in which we follow the informants' arguments it becomes clear that migrants, more easily than is thought in the diaspora literature, discontinue thinking about their roots as a source of recognition, identification, and appreciation. This is ultimately shown by the fact that Indian Africans refuse to do business with 'fellow Gujaratis' in India, who are not seen as members of the same community. There is no 'ethnic' business network or 'natural trust' in this trading diaspora. In other words, ethnic trading networks are created, but may also fall apart. Concepts of trust and mutual aid within these networks are constructed, and have to be earned by experience. Within these networks a 'good name' is just as easily lost as gained.

## Bibliography of Works Cited

**Unpublished Sources**

Honey M., *A History of Indian Merchant Capital* (PhD thesis, University of Dar es Salaam, 1982).

Sheriff A., *The Rise of a Commercial Empire* (PhD thesis, London School of Economics, 1971).

**Published Sources**

Bagchi, A.K., *Private Investment in India, 1900-1939* (Oxford, 1972).

Bannerjee, D., *Colonialism in Action: Trade Development and Dependence in Late Colonial India* (London, 2000).

Burton, R., *Zanzibar: City Island and Coast* Vol. 1 (London, 1872).

Cohen, R., *Global Diasporas. An Introduction* (London, 1997).
Dobbin, C., *Asian Entrepreneurial Minorities. Conjoint Communities in the Making of the World-Economy, 1570-1940* (Richmond, 1996).
Gregory, R.G., *India and East Africa: A History of Race Relations within the British Empire 1890-1939* (Oxford, 1971).
- *South Asians in East Africa. An Economic and Social History 1890-1980* (Boulder, 1993).
- *Quest for Equality. Asian Politics in East Africa 1900-1967* (New Delhi, 1993).
Himbara, D., *Kenyan Capitalists, the State, and Development* (Nairobi, 1994).
Indian High Level Commission, *Report on the Indian Diaspora* (Delhi, 2000).
Kotkin, J., *Tribes: How Race, Religion, and Identity Determine Success in the New Global Economy* (New York, 1992).
Lal, M.C., *India's Missed Opportunity with the Non-Resident Indians* (Aldershot, 2001).
Mamdani, M., *From Citizen to Refugee: Uganda Asians come to Britain* (London, 1973).
Markovits, C., *The Global World of Indian Merchants 1750-1947. Traders of Sind from Bukhara to Panama* (Cambridge, 2000).
Oonk, G., *Ondernemers in Ontwikkeling. Fabrieken en Fabrikanten in de Indiase Katoen-Industrie 1850-1930* [Entrepreneurs in Development. Mills and Mill Owners in the Indian Cotton Textile Industry] (Hilversum, 1998).
Pearce, F.B., *Zanzibar, The Island Metropolis of Eastern Africa* (London, 1967 [1920]).
Playne, Sommerset, *East Africa (British): Its History, People, Commerce, Industries, and Resources* (London, 1908/1909).
Ramchandani, R.R., *Uganda Asians. The End of an Enterprise* (Bombay, 1976).
Tinker, H., *Separate and Unequal. India and the Indians in the British Commonwealth 1920-1950* (St. Lucia, 1976).
- *The Banyan Tree: Overseas Emigrants from India Pakistan and Bangladesh* (Oxford, 1977).
Vertovec, S., *The Hindu Diaspora. Comparative Patterns* (London, 2000).
Voigt-Graf, C., *Asian Communities in Tanzania. A Journey Through Past and Present* (Hamburg, 1998).

**Articles and Essays**

Butler, Kim D., 'Defining Diaspora, Refining a Discourse', *Diaspora* 10/1 (2001), 189-219.
Clifford, J., 'Diasporas', *Cultural Anthropology* 9 (1994), 302-338.
Morris, H.S., 'The Indian Family in Uganda', *American Anthropologist* 61 (1959), 779-789.
Honey, M., 'Asian Industrial Activities in Tanganyika', *Tanzania Notes and Records*, 75 (1974), 55-69.
Nagar, R., 'The South Asian Diaspora in Tanzania: A History Retold', *Comparative Studies of South Asia, Africa and the Middle East'*, 16/2 (1996), 62-80.
Oonk, G., 'The Changing Culture of the Hindu Lohana community in East Africa', *Contemporary Asian Studies* 13/1 (2004), 7-23.
Rudner, D., 'Banker's Trust and the Culture of Banking among the Nattukottai Chettiars of Colonial South India', *Modern Asian Studies* 23/3 (1989), 417-458.
Safran, W., 'Comparing Diasporas: A Review essay', *Diaspora* 8/3 (1999), 255-291.
Schnapper, D., 'From the Nation-State to the Transnational World: On the Meaning and Usefulness of Diaspora as Concept', *Diaspora* 8/3 (1999), 225-254.
Tölöyan, K., 'Rethinking Diaspora(s): Stateless Power in the Transnational Movement', *Diaspora* 5/1 (1996), 3-37.

## Notes

* Gijsbert Oonk studied in Rotterdam. At present he is an Associate Professor of Non-Western History in the History Department of the Erasmus University. He has published on the history of the cotton textile industry in West India as well as on the Indian diaspora in East Africa. He can be reached at Oonk@fhk.eur.nl. His scholarly website is: www.goonk.nl.

1 This research was made possible by the *Netherlands Foundation for the Advancement of Tropical Research* (WOTRO) in collaboration with the History Department of Erasmus University Rotterdam, The Netherlands. In addition, the Vereniging Trustfonds Erasmus Universiteit Rotterdam, The Netherlands, and the History Department of the same university made available the necessary funds for attending the Association of Asian Studies conference in New York, March 2003. An earlier version of this paper was also presented at the Posthumus Institute, Utrecht, 28 November 2003. I would like to thank Ferry de Goey, Ned Alpers and Ned Bertz for discussing their ideas and insights with me.

2 Kotkin, *Tribes: How Race, Religion, and Identity Determine Success.* Recent studies on the 'success of the Indian diaspora' include: Dobbin, *Asian Entrepreneurial Minorities.* See for more studies endnote 4. In his recent study, Claude Markovits makes a strong argument against these 'ethnic' notions of trust. He emphasises that local networks, whether ethnic or not, play a crucial role in determining the 'success' or 'failure' of business communities/groups. In his view, this is not - the result of sharing secrets or specific business attitudes, but due to the fact that a 'good name' and reputation is easily gained or lost within these business networks. Markovits, *Global World of Indian Merchants.*

3 Gregory, *India and East Africa,* and his *South Asians in East Africa.* Ramchandani, *Uganda Asians*; Voigt-Graf, *Asian Communities in Tanzania.*

4 Steven Vertovec overvalues this argument in his otherwise interesting study. Vertovec, *Hindu Diaspora,* 25. Cohen sees the relation with the homeland as an important key for identity questions of diasporic groups. Cohen, *Global Diasporas.*

5 Clifford, 'Diasporas', 310.

6 Cohen, *Global Diasporas,* 26. See for a critical review of this book: Safran, 'Comparing Diasporas', 255-291.

7 For a critical analyses of these concepts, see: Schnapper, 'From the Nation-State', 225-254.

8 Butler emphasises rightly the 'historical' dimension of the diaspora; its existence over at least two generations. Butler, 'Defining Diaspora', 189-219. Khachig Tölöyan argues that: 'More problematically [...] the project of re-articulating the nation-state seems also to require the option of dis-articulating it. Tölöyan: 'Rethinking Diaspora(s)', 12.

9 The Indian High Level Commission, *Report on the Indian Diaspora.* See also: Lal, *India's Missed Opportunity.*

10 These families include more than 200 people of whom 78 were interviewed between 1999 and 2003. Extended fieldwork and archival research took place from June 2002 to July 2003. Information on occupation, knowledge of languages, and, for example, nationality is available for almost all the family members. Seven or eight key informants were interviewed three or four times or more often. Besides such formal methods, the researcher attended informal meetings, dinner parties and celebrations of holidays.

11 Those who settled after the 1930s tend to have stronger emotional and physical relations with India. This however does not mean that they produce a more positive image.

12 Hindu Lohanas in East Africa come from the rural districts of Cutch and Kathiawar (Gujarat, West India). They were traditionally labourers, masons, husbandmen, shopkeepers, and traders. It is said that their history is related to that of one of the Kshatria (warrior) castes, which in ancient times was called Lavan. The plural form of this was Lavanam and, over a period of time it changed first to Lavana and finally to Lohana. In the nineteenth century, many turned to weaving and textile trading. Those in Kathiawar were especially well established as maritime traders and many were doing business in Oman. When the Sultan of Oman moved

his headquarters from Musquat to Zanzibar (1832), Lohana traders quickly followed him and set up shops there. From there, they spread to the mainland from 1885 onwards.

13 The focus on (Lohana) Hindus is a consequence of my personal network of Asian businessmen. They form the majority of Hindus in East Africa. It was estimated that, in 1995, there were 3,000 Lohana Hindus among 10,000 other Hindus in Tanzania. Among the other Hindu communities were Bhatias, Patels, Vanias, Brahmins, and 'others'. None of these other Hindu *jatis* had more than 800 people each. In addition, the number of South Asian Muslims was estimated at 26,000 in 1995. Voigt-Graf, *Asian Communities in Tanzania*, 53.

14 Those businessmen who are active around Hindu (Lohana) temple activities tend to relate more strongly to India. Nevertheless, they have diminished their business activities with India as well.

15 In this article, I use the terms 'South Asian' and 'Indians' as synonyms. Formally, it would be more correct to use 'South Asians', because South Asia was split into India and West and East Pakistan after the Partition in 1947. Nevertheless, colonial sources refer to 'India' and 'Indians' and many 'South Asians' in East Africa refer to themselves as Indians, or recall that they went to 'Indian' schools.

16 Gregory, *South Asians in East Africa;* Idem, *Quest for Equality.*

17 Literature on this subject includes: Gregory, *India and East Africa;* Mamdani, *From Citizen to Refugee*; Ramchandani, *Ugandan Asians*; Tinker, *Separate and Unequal;* Idem, *The Banyan Tree.*

18 According to the 1887 census, there were 4,866 Muslims and 1,022 Hindus/Jains in Zanzibar.

19 Diverging concepts of purity and impurity made it rare for Hindu merchants to take their wives out of India, while Muslim merchants generally travelled with their families, especially to Muslim countries. Little is known about the Hindu taboo on crossing the seas. There is evidence that Hindus have been crossing the seas without compunction for many centuries, but the kind of ritual penances which had to be performed on their return are obscure. In some communities, such as that of the Gujarati Vanias of Porbandar during Gandhi's time, we know that these rituals took place, but we lack information on other communities. One hypothesis that seems plausible is that the generalised taboo on the voyage of women represented a kind of substitution. The fact that the woman of the household did not travel beyond the seas seems to have been sufficient to ensure the continuing purity of the household. However, questions remain about what happened when Hindus decided to take their wives and children to East Africa. Markovits, *Global World of Indian Merchants*, 27; Nagar, 'The South Asian Diaspora', 62-80.

20 The inter-relationship between social ties and business is clearly seen from various family histories. The eminent Muslim firm of the Karimjis was established in Zanzibar in the early 1800s as general importers and export merchants. The founding father of the Karimji family was Jivanji Buddhaboy. He had three sons: Pirbhoy Jivanjee; Karimji Jivanji and, Esmailji Jivanji. They carried on their father's business under the name of Pirbhai Jivanji until 1861. By then, the brothers separated. Karimji Jivanji started his own business while the other two brothers worked jointly. Alibhai Karimji Jivanji followed Karimji Jivanji. In the late 1800s, he went to India for the marriage of his only son, Alibhai. As he had separated from the family business and because of the considerable sum he had to pay towards the marriage, he invested in buying goods in India to bring them to Zanzibar to trade. The sailing ship in which he was returning on the way to Zanzibar after the marriage of his son ran into a storm on the way and the whole cargo had to be jettisoned. Karimji Jivanji thus landed on shores of the Zanzibar with his investments lost, no capital of his own, and debt to others. Source: family archive Dar es Salaam.

21 Contemporary sources on the position (and absence) of Hindu women in East Africa include: Burton, *Zanzibar: City Island*, 329-35; Pearce, *Zanzibar*, 257. See also: Honey, *History of Indian Merchant Capital*, 74.

22 Sheriff, *Rise of a Commercial Empire*, 354.

23 We actually know very little about those families which went back to India. If we assume that the reasons were business

failure, bad management, or the like, we also may assume that this is why stories of those who settled in East Africa have become (mainly) success stories.

24 Child marriages were quite common in those days. This kind of marriage also shows that the chain migration had many of side effects. Not only did Sunderji's father have friends who went overseas, he also married one of his daughters to an Indian man who lived overseas.

25 There is still very little known of the importance and functions of 'hundis'. The most detailed information, related to the notion of trust among Chettiars in South India, can be found in Rudner, 'Banker's Trust and the Culture', 417-458.

26 Interview Dar es Salaam, October 2002. This oral evidence is supported by Sommerset Playn's business directory of 1909. Here we find, for example, the family of Lalchund Moolchund which had business branches in Zanzibar, Mombasa, Dar es Salaam, Bombay and Hyderabad. The father lived in Hyderabad and the son looked after the East African branches. Playne, *East Africa (British)*, 113.

27 Martha Honey stated: 'India was, there fore, primarily important as a source of business connections, rather than a source of capital. India served as a reservoir for new recruits for East African firms and as network of business contacts which could utilised by the East African traders'. Honey, *History of Indian Merchant Capital*, 63.

28 Morris, 'Indian Family in Uganda', 779-789. Interviews with Bharat in October 2002. He stated that the idea of a family trust was still very much alive. They shared family capital and family-managed businesses. However, there was a growing interest in doing business on their private account.

29 One family, which I met in Nairobi, decided to live under one roof again after being separated in East Africa for some twenty years. This show, that there is no 'natural' tendency towards a more nuclear family.

30 This reflects a typical Indian tradition in which there used to be a strong notion of purity and impurity in relation to food and the acceptance of food from others. One cannot accept food from everyone. The food restrictions are not so strongly observed in East Africa, but, even so, it is Brahmins who operate the many vegetarian restaurants and sweet shops. See for an extended history in the change in food habits of South Asian Africans, Oonk, 'Changing culture of the Hindu', 7-24.

31 The Tanganyika Census of 1931 counted 5,162 Hindu men and 2,600 Hindu women: *Report on the Non-native Census* (26 April 1931), 38. Note that the issue here was not where the people were born. In fact many of these men and women were born in India as it was the practice of Hindu women to have the delivery of their babies – whenever possible – at their mothers' places. Often, this was in Gujarat, India. After the delivery, mother and child would go back to East Africa where the child was raised.

32 Imports from India in East Africa rose from 679 (1901) to 2,313 x £ 1,000 (in 1921); after which it declined to 658 x £ 1,000 (in 1938). In the same period, the exports from East Africa to India grew from 136 to 3,500 x £ 1,000 (1900-1938). Despite of this, the 'old Indian migrants' have been more involved in exports to the UK, which showed the same growth in this period. Imports from Japan were insignificant in 1900-1910, and rose from 171 to 1,763 x £ 1,000 in the period 1920-1938. See, Gregory, *South Asians in East Africa*, 51.

33 The causes of India's economic decline are part of a long dispute among Marxist, Nationalist and European scholars. A few excellent studies are: Bagchi, *Private Investment in India* and, more recently, Bannerjee, *Colonialism in Action*. For the role of Indians in the industrialisation process in East Africa, see Honey, 'Asian Industrial Activities in Tanganyika', 55-69. See also Himbara, *Kenyan Capitalists*.

34 Oonk, 'Changing Culture', 7-23.

35 For an extensive version of the case of Bharat see, Oonk, Ibid.

36 Two of his elder sisters had already married outside the community, and that they married within the Hindu community was considered 'good enough'.

37 Bharat in Dar es Salaam June 1999.

38 Bharat in Dar es Salaam June 1999.

39 See footnote 32.

40 The problem of the quality of the Indian products and the growing competition with Japan was also felt in India.

41 Manilal Devani in Dar es Salaam October

2002.

42 Nanji Damordar in Mombasa June 1999. The issue of the Japanese Competition is also discussed in the annual reports of the Bombay Millowners Association. The Indian millowners were especially concerned about the China market and to a lesser extent the East African market. See Oonk, *Ondernemers in Ontwikkeling.*

43 See footnote 33. The annually published 'bleu books' on British East Africa include a rich variety on statistical material related to the import and export various products.

44 It was not only Hindus who decided to focus on East Africa to a growing extent. From the personal archives of some of my Muslim informants, it became clear that Indian Muslims had written several requests to the Indian Government asking to sell their land and property in India and transfer huge sums of money from India to East Africa in order to re-invest this there. These kind of transfers were often refused or took so long that most informants kept some family member to look after the property oversees. Obviously, the partition of British India in India and Pakistan in 1947 may well have accelerated the process of losing contact with India-for Muslims.

45 Lal, *India's Missed Opportunity.*

46 In my interviews it was difficult to highlight the importance of '1947', this event seemed to be overshadowed by the aftermath of the Independence of East African nations in the early 1960s. After the 'Africanisation' projects in the late 1960, it became clear that Indian Africans could not easily apply for Indian Passport. Some present day Indian Africans still feel that they were 'left alone by their mother', others mentioned that by then, they were already 'cut off' from India and the Indian Indians.

47 These negative images were repeated with some hesitation. In my introduction to this research, I told many informants about my earlier research in Gujarat. Many informants tried to convince me that Indians in East Africa were more 'modern' and educated then Gujaratis from Gujarat.

48 Interview Dar es Salaam November 2002. This is not to say that family members are per definition reliable. This informant was cheated by two of his half-brothers and lost a huge part of his business in the early 1980s. In the late 1950s, Morris noted that the Indian African said: 'Do not go into partnership with your brother. He is sure to cheat you.' Morris, *Indian Family in Uganda*, 785.

49 Interview December 2003.

50 Anonymous informant February 2001.

51 Anonymous informant March 2003.

# Part III
# Political Economy and Patterns of Global Entrepreneurship

# [9]

# Capitalist Dreams: Chile's Response to Nineteenth-Century World Copper Competition

WILLIAM W. CULVER

*State University of New York, Plattsburgh*

CORNEL J. REINHART

*Clinton Community College*

The rapid increase in the produce of the mines of Cuba and Chili cannot be looked upon by the British miner otherwise than as a total annihilation of the mining interests of this country. . . .
———"[Editorial: Foreign ores]," *Mining Journal*, 11:287 (February 20, 1841), 60.

[Copper mining in Michigan] is an interest in which more than fifty million dollars of capital is engaged, an interest that is being crushed by foreign competition—the competition of convict raised ores in Chili.
———U.S. Senator Zachariah Chandler, *The Congressional Globe*, Pt. 1, 40th Congress, 3d sess. (January 18, 1869), 416.

As the produce of the Chili mines now regulates the price of copper all over the world, and all speculation as to its future price must depend on the probable future yield of these mines, their condition is a subject of prime importance to all interested in the copper trade.
———James Douglas, "II. The Copper Mines of Chili," *Quarterly Journal of Science, and Annals of Mining Metallurgy, Engineering, Industrial Arts, Manufactures and Technology*, 9 (1872) 159.

Chili is still, though a smaller producer than the Peninsula [Michigan], the apparent arbiter of price, and Chili Bars the standard of value.
———[Editorial], "The Movement of Copper in England and France in 1886," *Engineering and Mining Journal*, 42:4 (January 22, 1887), 56.

Hernando de Soto's recent book, *The Other Path*, argues that capitalism has not failed in Peru and Latin America, rather, it has not been tried.[1] Basing his case on the observation that Latin American economies are strangled by arcane policies and regulations, de Soto goes on to bolster his point by

The authors are grateful for research support in Chile from the State University of New York, University Awards Committee, and from the National Science Foundation.

[1] Hernando de Soto, *El otro sendero: la revolución informal* (Bogotá: Editorial Oveja Negra, 1987; English ed., *The Other Path: The Invisible Revolution in the Third World*) (New York: Harper & Row, 1988).

0010-4175/89/4525–2832 $5.00 

providing a fresh and powerful look at the undeniable reality of the large "informal," and thus unregulated, economic sector in Peru.[2] As with any such generalization, how strongly does its explanatory value remain when measured against specific events, over long periods of time? This article seeks just such a perspective. It examines the impact of such regulations as mining codes and mineral taxation on the efforts of Chilean copper entrepreneurs to compete worldwide in the nineteenth century. De Soto may be correct in his contention that today's highly regulated economies keep Latin Americans from being as productive as their resources justify, but to extend this view into the past ignores earlier productive accomplishments, as well as significant efforts at different times and places to cast off Latin America's mercantile legacy.

Nineteen-century copper production in Chile provides a prime case to investigate this key issue of political economy. Chilean copper was a leading world industry for several decades, gradually sliding into stagnation and eventual collapse, while major ore deposits remained untouched. Can this instance of industrial degeneration be attributed to state regulation? Perhaps, but then how can the long earlier expansion under the same regulations be explained?

Capitalism rarely exists as unregulated entrepreneurial activity. As practiced in the real world, the question that concerns us involves entrepreneurship amid governmental regulation of varying degrees and objectives, with some level of tax burden.[3] Chilean copper entrepreneurs have earned a key place in any consideration of nineteenth-century Latin American productive activity, since they had expanded their enterprise continually for sixty years under an unreformed eighteenth-century mining code. The memory of this Chilean success, however, faded following their competitive loss to their counterparts in Michigan and Montana. Why this failure occurred focuses our attention here. We contend that after the middle of the nineteenth century certain key structural innovations pursued in North America were not duplicated in Chile. In the United States following the Civil War, the state became the firm ally of entrepreneurs. In Chile it did not.[4] This made a crucial difference. While copper serves as the industrial focus of this article, political obstacles to an ever-evolving modern capitalism form its central theme.

The full significance of Chile's colonial regulatory legacy emerges only when its copper trade is placed in a broad perspective, the kind envisioned by

[2] "Informal" refers to the unregistered, unregulated, and illegal shops, services, and production operating alongside the formal and regulated economy. De Soto estimates 50 percent of Peru's economy falls into the informal sector.

[3] Charles W. Anderson, *Politics and Economic Change in Latin America: The Governing of Restless Nations* (Princeton, New Jersey: D. Van Nostrand Company, Inc, 1967). Chapter One, in particular, influenced the authors' thinking on this topic.

[4] Anderson, *Politics*, 9.

Charles Tilly.[5] For copper, this means examining the metal's mining, smelting, and sale in Great Britain, Chile, and the United States—sequentially the world's leading producers during the last century. Coupled with the extraordinary international surge in demand for copper products during the latter decades of the nineteenth century,[6] such an examination gives rise to a series of questions. Why did Chile's leading market position, founded on earlier successful competition with English copper entrepreneurs working mines in Cornwall,[7] result in the eventual denationalization of the best of Andean mines? What prevented a continuing expansion of copper production, utilizing new, mining methods for low-grade ore? Can we find specific evidence of strangulation by antiquated policies? What were the Chilean entrepreneurs, who built and managed the industry, doing to meet American competition? Indeed, how aware was the Chilean mining community of its competitive weakness in the 1880s and their impending collapse?[8] Was Chile's forty years as the world's leader in copper production simply an illusion?

If rigid mercantile regulations did not stop Chilean entrepreneurs from competing with, indeed closing, the copper mines in Cornwall, England, or later, smelters in Swansea, Wales, why then did Chilean mining entrepreneurs later find these same regulations hindering their competition with producers in the United States, leading to the denationalization of Chilean copper after 1900. Finally, why was the wave of state-supported mining reform that swept the world in mid-century resisted and delayed in Chile? We believe the answer to this last question provides the key to understanding Chile's loss of competitiveness. Unable to find a political consensus in a Congress dominated by agricultural interests, the copper industry remained stalemated between traditional miners, who conceived of their efforts as a speculative adventure, and modern mining engineers wanting to transform copper into a business. This split in the copper industry itself led to a political failure that echos down through Chilean history to the present.

Chile's copper market position in the last century was based on an ability to raise increasing amounts of ore at a cost lower than all other producers from a

[5] Charles Tilly, *Big Structures, Large Processes, Huge Comparisons* (New York: Russell Sage Foundation, 1984).

[6] Every issue of the *Engineering and Mining Journal* of the 1880s contained editorial commentary and news on the swelling world copper demand. The *EMJ* gave copper an especially prominent role from 1882 to 1884 as overall United States production began to total more than any competitor. See Merwin L. Bohan and Morton Pomeranz, *Investment in Chile: Basic Information for United States Businessmen* (Washington, D.C.: U.S. Government Printing Office, 1960), 87, for a typical business observation about this period of increasing copper demand.

[7] See R. O. Roberts, "Development and Decline of the Copper and Other Non-Ferrous Metal Industries in South Wales," *Transactions of the Honorable Society of Cymmrodorian* (South Wales, 1956); and T. C. Barker and J. R. Harris, *A Merseyside Town in the Industrial Revolution: St. Helens 1750–1900* (London, 1959), 240–446, for a British interpretation of this process.

[8] Clearly, twentieth-century copper politics in Chile has generated a considerable interest. An excellent and thorough analysis of the post-World War II era is found in Theodore H. Moran, *Multinational Corporations and the Politics of Dependence* (Princeton, New Jersey: Princeton University Press, 1974).

seemingly inexhaustible supply of ore,[9] yet these immense Chilean ore reserves, centered in the northern provinces of Coquimbo and Atacama, were not sufficient to protect the Chilean industry from stagnation in the face of North American competition. The magnitude of the relative and absolute decline of nineteenth-century Chilean copper can be shown. In 1852 the United States placed far behind Chile with less than 1 percent of the world's copper production (see Table 1), while Chile in that same year produced more than 40 percent. By 1900 the United States had vaulted to first place, extracting 56 percent of the world's copper; Chile had fallen to fourth with only 5 percent of the world's ore coming from Chilean mines.[10] Both vein and porphyry Chilean copper ore never gave out. In fact, during the 1920s, under North American industrial control, Chile again became a leading producer.

Copper mining flourished world-wide after the 1850s as demand for copper expanded at unprecedented rates. Entrepreneurs in Chile and the United States, simultaneously astonished and eager in the face of new levels of copper consumption created by industrial expansion (especially steam engines and electrical use), invested in numerous mining and smelting projects. These individuals risked their capital in search of substantial personal gain. At the same time, they believed their efforts to be patriotic, promising new levels of material prosperity for their respective countries; yet as investment increased production, it correspondingly increased competition. Expansion of production meant lower costs, and producers unable to compete successfully were "left by the wayside." Little time or energy was wasted on regrets over failed competitors; survival went to the "strongest and fittest," failure to the "weak and defective."[11] This was believed to be as true for countries as it was for individuals.

[9] Chile still holds approximately 40 percent of the world's copper reserves, both as vein and porphyry coppers. Reserves are estimated on the basis of ore that can be mined "economically" (where the cost of production is below a given market price). Early copper mines were based on veins (cracks in other rocks filled with concentrations of the metal); in the late nineteenth-century porphyry deposits (very low concentrations of the metal dispersed throughout a huge area) became the mainstay of the industry. See A. B. Parsons, *The Porphyry Coppers* (New York: American Institute of Mining and Metallurgical Engineers, 1933); Victor Hollister, *Geology of the Porphyry Copper Deposits of the Western Hemisphere* (New York, 1978); and Alan M. Bateman, *Economic Mineral Deposits* (New York: John Wiley and Sons, Inc. 1981), 482. Given unlimited free energy, most metal reserves are limitless, as mineral distribution in very small quantities is vast, especially if ocean bottom nodules are considered. For an overview of the nodule aspect of copper, see Robert Bowen and Ananda Gunatilaka, *Copper: Its Geology and Economics* (New York: John Wiley and Sons, 1977).

[10] Nicol Brown and Charles Turnbull, *A Century of Copper* (London: Effingham Wilson, 1906), 20–21.

[11] This type of social Darwinist thinking and language is found in the mining journals of all countries. Mining journals were read not just by mining engineers and investors, a conservative lot to this day, but also by the investing public. For most of the last century the leading journal in the United States has been the *EMJ* and in England, the *Mining Journal* of London. Both had an informational role like the contemporary *Wall Street Journal*. *The Mining Journal*'s original title at its founding in 1835 was *The Mining Journal, Railway and Commercial Gazette; Forming a Complete Record of the Proceedings of All Public Companies*.

TABLE 1:

*Production from Selected Copper Mining Countries and Percentage as a Part of World Total, 1810–1900 (in tons of 2,000 lbs.)*

| | *Great Britain* | | *Chile* | | *United States* | | *World* | |
|---|---|---|---|---|---|---|---|---|
| *Year* | *Tons* | *Percentage* | *Tons* | *Percentage* | *Tons* | *Percentage* | *Tons* | *Percentage* |
| 1810 | 6,400 | 35 | 1,653 | 9 | 0 | | 18,200 | 100 |
| 1820 | 8,377 | 44 | 1,653 | 9 | 0 | | 18,850 | 100 |
| 1830 | 12,235 | 45 | 3,004 | 11 | 0 | | 27,350 | 100 |
| 1840 | 12,346 | 34 | 7,114 | 20 | 0 | | 36,445 | 100 |
| 1850 | 13,228 | 27 | 13,607 | 28 | 728 | 1 | 49,381 | 100 |
| 1860 | 17,967 | 24 | 37,602 | 51 | 8,064 | 11 | 73,907 | 100 |
| 1870 | 8,046 | 7 | 48,724 | 42 | 14,112 | 12 | 114,934 | 100 |
| 1880 | 3,662 | 3 | 43,628 | 31 | 30,240 | 21 | 142,374 | 100 |
| 1881 | 4,340 | 2 | 42,547 | 23 | 35,840 | 20 | 181,342 | 100 |
| 1882 | 3,880 | 2 | 48,058 | 24 | 45,323 | 22 | 202,036 | 100 |
| 1883 | 2,934 | 1 | 46,031 | 21 | 57,763 | 26 | 224,306 | 100 |
| 1884 | 3,752 | 2 | 46,646 | 19 | 72,473 | 30 | 245,005 | 100 |
| 1885 | 3,106 | 1 | 43,120 | 17 | 82,938 | 33 | 253,120 | 100 |
| 1886 | 1,648 | 1 | 39,228 | 16 | 78,882 | 33 | 241,089 | 100 |
| 1887 | 436 | 0 | 32,648 | 13 | 90,739 | 36 | 250,538 | 100 |
| 1888 | 1,680 | 0 | 34,989 | 12 | 113,180 | 38 | 294,803 | 100 |
| 1889 | 1,014 | 0 | 27,160 | 9 | 113,388 | 39 | 291,018 | 100 |
| 1890 | 1,047 | 0 | 29,254 | 10 | 129,882 | 43 | 305,334 | 100 |
| 1895 | 650 | 0 | 24,724 | 7 | 190,307 | 52 | 368,963 | 100 |
| 1900 | 870 | 0 | 28,784 | 5 | 303,059 | 56 | 545,439 | 100 |

SOURCES: C. E. Julian, *Summarized Data of Copper Production* (Washington, D.C.: Superintendent of Documents, 1928), for Great Britain, United States and the world; Guillermo Yunge, *Estadistica minera de Chile en 1906* (Santiago de Chile: Imprenta Litografía i Encuadernación Barcelona, 1909), for Chile; and the *Engineering and Mining Journal* (New York), for years 1880–1890 in the United States and world.

Chilean mining entrepreneurs, more so than their counterparts in the United States, produced for world markets. Chile, of course, did not possess the domestic market potential of the United States. Interestingly, every mineral product produced in Chile for the world market, with the one exception of natural nitrate, was also produced or potentially produced after 1848 in the United States.[12] As both countries had people who were able and willing to respond to the growing industrial world economy, the two countries naturally became trade competitors. Moreover, most of their pre-1870 trade competition centered on supplying copper to the domestic market in the United States. The ultimate consequence, however, of the integration of Chile into the commercial and industrial life of the world was not the progress Chilean entrepreneurs expected.[13] By the twentieth century, failed dreams were the rewards for Chile. Chile was left by the wayside.

Some observers are not surprised. For them certain nationalities of entrepreneurs were, and still remain, culturally unable to organize and adapt to meet competition.[14] Applied to Chile, this perspective minimizes the extent of national economic achievement in the nineteenth century and ignores forty years of competitive success in the world copper market. From the vantage point of scholars in the United States, the belief that serious competition from Chilean entrepreneurs never existed is easy to hold: The footprints of Chilean

[12] 1848 refers to the date after which the United States had fall access to the lands of the West—lands that had earlier been a part of Mexico.

[13] The best summary on the role of idea of progress in Latin America is E. Bradford Burns, *The Poverty of Progress: Latin America in the Nineteenth Century* (Berkeley: University of California Press, 1980). The authors have also been influenced by John Stanley's introduction to Georges Sorell, *The Illusions of Progress*, John and Charlotte Stanley, trans. (Berkeley: University of California Press, 1969).

[14] A prominent version of this argument is made by Seymour Martin Lipset: "The evidence presented thus far would seem to indicate that, regardless of the causal patterns one prefers to credit for Latin American values, they are, as described, antithetic to the basic logic of a large-scale industrial system." See his "Values, Education, and Entrepreneurship," in *Elites in Latin America*, Seymour Martin Lipset and Aldo Solari, eds. (New York: Oxford University Press, 1967), 32. Lipset develops this position as an outgrowth of the ideas of Max Weber on the requisites of economic development. "Structural conditions make development possible; cultural factors determine whether the possibility becomes an actuality" (p. 3).

An earlier holder of this view is Thomas C. Cochran, "The Legend of the Robber Barons," *The Pennsylvania Magazine of History and Biography*, 74 (July, 1950). Cochran puts forward the position that "comparative studies need to be made of the place of entrepreneurship in varying national cultures. There seems little doubt that such studies will go further toward explaining the economic progress of different regions than will any assessment of potential natural resources. It is these cultural elements, to a very large extent that determine who will become entrepreneurs, a culture with feudal standards of lavish living or the support of elaborate ceremonial organizations of church and state will obviously not have the capital to invest in economic development that will be available in a culture where frugal living, saving, and work are the custom" (pp. 320–1).

Another very recent expression of this view is found in Michael Novak, "Why Latin America is Poor," *The Atlantic* (March, 1982). Novak extends the present into the past when he writes, "Why, then, didn't Latin America become the richer of the two continents of the New World? The answer appears to be in the nature of the Latin American political system, economic system, and moral-cultural system. The last is probably decisive" (p. 67).

efforts have been largely erased. To the extent that important nineteenth-century productive efforts in Chile are acknowledged, those efforts are typically characterized as aberrations at best or at worst incompetent efforts by culturally inferior entrepreneurs.[15] How is it known that the business decisions of these Chilean capitalists were defective? The implicit answer seems to be that the fact of failure itself proves Chilean incompetence; such explanations, however, leave much unexplained.

The scholarly origins of the belief in the Chilean inability to marshal the resources necessary for industrial projects can be traced to the historiography concerning nineteenth-century economic life in the United States. American scholars began searching for the secrets of economic growth in the period in which that country was an industrial success. N. S. B. Gras' pioneering work of the 1920s and 1930s on business history posited a stage analysis of economic evolution. For Gras, the late nineteenth century could best be understood as the period of the rise of industrial capitalism in which new technology and power machinery were employed to produce low-cost products.[16]

The 1950s saw the emergence of an entrepreneurial approach to industrial

[15] Most influential on this point is Clark Winton Reynolds, "Development Problems of an Export Economy: The Case of Chile and Copper," in *Essays on the Chilean Economy*, Markos Mamalakis and Clark Winton Reynolds, eds. (Homewood, Illinois: Richard D. Irwin, Inc., 1965). Reynolds draws a number of observations from secondary sources about nineteenth-century Chilean copper to conclude that Chilean entrepreneurs were outdated and backward in their outlook. "[T]here were few men in Chile at the turn of the century who had contacts with the large investment consortia and who were aware of the developments in copper technology and their potential application in Chilean mining" (p. 212). While these comments were directed at the years in which porphyry copper was just being developed, the statement implies, incorrectly, a chronic condition.

Less prominent but also significant in the downgrading of Chilean entrepreneurial ability is Leland Pederson's *The Mining Industry of the Norte Chico, Chile* (Evanston, Illinois: Northwestern University, 1966). A geographer, Pederson looks at silver, gold, and copper from the Conquest to the present, providing a broad historical perspective. A view similar to Reynolds is expressed: "The vast majority of Chile's mining entrepreneurs were incapable of adopting more than the simplest of the new techniques, such as oil lamps as a replacement for tallow candles" (p. 193). Again there is a blurring of the decades. Still other studies repeat these notions: Joseph Sumwald and Philip Musgrove, *Natural Resources in Latin American Development* (Baltimore: Johns Hopkins University Press, 1970), 167; Robert Cortes Conde, *The First Stages of Modernization in Spanish America* (New York: Harper & Row, Publishers, 1974), 69–71; Lawrence MacDonnell, "The Politics of Expropriation, Chilean Style," *Quarterly of the Colorado School of Mines*, 68:4 (October, 1973), 195–6; and Moran, *Multinational Corporations*, 20–22.

These studies assume a lack of effective nineteenth-century entrepreneurship in Chile. They ignore the years prior to the 1880s. The studies are also strongly influenced by the bitter twentieth-century copper analyses that appeared in Santiago as Chileans debated how to respond to the dominance of United States capital in the Chilean copper industry. The classic Chilean study is Francisco A. Encina, *Nuestra inferioridad económica, sus causas y sus consequencias* (Santiago: Imprenta Universitaria, 1912); also important is Santiago Macciavello Varas, *El problema de la industria del cobre en Chile y sus proyecciones económicas y sociales* (Santiago: Universidad de Chile, 1923). Macciavello Varas is a key source for Reynold's position on the nineteenth century. The weakness of all of these studies, from our point of view, is their lack of discrimination about the decades from the 1840s to the 1880s.

[16] N. S. B. Gras, *Business and Capitalism* (New York: F. S. Crofts and Co., 1939).

development. For the group of scholars at Harvard under the Research Center in Entrepreneurial History, America's great leap forward in the 1870s, 1880s, and 1890s is best understood as a product of the entrepreneurial genius of individual business leaders.[17] Perhaps the most important scholar of the entrepreneurial school, Thomas Cochran, significantly recast the debate over industrial growth by arguing that entrepreneurs act only within a certain set of fairly well-defined economic and social values.[18] Specifically, his study of late nineteenth-century railroad industry leaders found that these men sought approval and acted within the parameters established by other East Coast business leaders.[19]

Alfred Chandler, Jr. shared this sociological perspective but emphasized bureaucratic organization.[20] For Chandler, the thirty years between 1870 and 1900 saw major changes in the economic life of the United States. The creation of a national rail network and the attendant growth of urban markets created the conditions necessary for business innovation and indeed brought "Big Business" to the United States. In industry after industry the processes were the same. The dominate economic unit was one "which integrated within a single business organization the major economic processes: production or purchasing of raw materials, manufacturing, distribution, and finance."[21] Thus, for Chandler, the basic economic innovation during the last half of the nineteenth century was not technological but rather the creation of new forms of organization and new ways of marketing. These innovations were vital for survival in the face of intense competition.

We believe one consequence of this train of thought concerning the dynamics of industrial growth was the suggestion in the North American literature treating Chilean copper that nineteenth-century Chileans did not achieve anything of industrial significance.[22] Chilean literature on the same subject and period has been silent, focusing instead on the decades when nationalization was at issue. Still, the question raised by the entrepreneurship center is important. What were Chilean copper entrepreneurs doing in the last century? This problem is best approached with a comparative examination of international competition in the copper industry over time.[23]

Nowhere was nineteenth-century international competition more intense

[17] A useful summary of the older literature is found in Louis Galambos, "American Business History" (pamphlet, The Service Center, American Historical Association, n.d.).

[18] Cochran, "The Legend," 320.

[19] Cochran, 320–1.

[20] Alfred D. Chandler, Jr. "The Beginning of Big Business in American Industry," *The Business History Review*, 33 (Spring, 1959), 6; and argued subsequently in *The Visible Hand: The Managerial Revolution in American Business* (Cambridge, Massachusetts: Belknap Press, 1971).

[21] Chandler, "the Beginning," 9.

[22] See n. 15 for a review of this literature.

[23] Influential in forming this approach has been Charles Tilly, *Big Structures*.

than in the copper industry.[24] In the early decades of the century, copper producers in Chile challenged and then largely eliminated their counterparts in Great Britain.[25] From the 1840s, the Cornish–Welsh copper dominance had collapsed, so mining and smelting of the red metal became one of the first industries characterized by price competition for a uniform commodity with many potential producers. While production of copper took place in numerous regions of the world and trade of the metal was widespread, most of the world's copper (specifically from 1845 to 1890) came from mining regions in either the United States or Chile.[26] Copper production in both countries rose in industrial quantities to supply the unmet demands for the metal—first in Great Britain and then in the East Coast industries of the United States.[27]

[24] Most historical studies of the copper industry focus on just one country or mining district. There are, however, several studies that take a comparative perspective on copper from a technical point-of-view: Brown and Turnbull, *A Century;* Parsons, *The Porphyry Coppers;* Bowen and Gunatilaka, *Copper;* ; Hollister, *Geology of the Porphyry Copper Deposits;* and Otis Herfindal, *Copper Costs and Prices: 1870–1957* (Baltimore, Maryland: Johns Hopkins University Press, 1969). One popular description of copper mines is both interesting and useful: Ira B. Joralemon, *Romantic Copper: Its Lure and Lores* (New York: D. Appleton Century Co., 1934).

Among the many monographs and articles on Welsh and Cornish copper, the work of R. O. Roberts stands out. Especially important is his article cited above in n. 7: "Development and Decline." For the United States regions, see William B. Gates, Jr., *Michigan Copper and Boston Dollars: An Economic History of the Michigan Copper Mining Industry* (Cambridge, Massachusetts: Harvard University Press, 1951); F. E. Richter, "The Copper Industry in the United States, 1845–1925," *Quarterly Journal of Economics*, 41 (February and August, 1927), 236–91, and 684–717; Angus Murdock, *Boom Copper: The Story of the First U.S. Mining Boom* (Calumet, Michigan: Brier and Doepel, 1964); and C. B. Glasscock, *The War of the Copper Kings* (New York: Grosset and Dunlap, 1935).

For Chile, in addition to those works previously cited, see Benjamin L. Miller and Joseph T. Singewald, *The Mineral Deposits of South America* (New York; McGraw-Hill Book Company, 1919); Markos Mamalakis, *The Growth and Structure of the Chilean Economy: From Independence to Allende* (New Haven: Yale University Press, 1976); C. M. Sayago, *Historia de Copiapó* (Copiapó: Imprenta de "El Atacama," 1874); and James M. Little, *The Geology and Metal Deposits of Chile* (New York: The Bramwell Company, 1926).

Two studies specifically investigate the causes for the decline of Chilean copper, and the conditions that allowed for the takeover of the Chilean industry by United States capital. See Joanne Fox Przeworski, *The Decline of the Copper Industry in Chile and the Entrance of North American Capital, 1870–1916* (New York: Arno Press, 1980); and Juan Alfonso Bravo, "United States' Investment in Chile: 1904–1907" (Masters thesis, Department of History, American University, Washington, D.C., 1980).

[25] The *MJ*, from 1838 through 1848 in weekly chronicles, followed the Chilean pressure on the copper mines of Cornwall. The best contemporary review of this crisis is found in *United Kingdom, House of Commons [Select Committee on Copper], British Sessional Papers*, "Copper Ore: Copies of all Memorials and Petitions Presented to the Board of Trade, and to the Chancellor of the Exchequer, Respecting the Duty on Copper Ore, and Copies of the Answers Sent to the Applications Since January, 1849" (March 15, 1847).

[26] Copper production statistics before 1880 are not always reliable, but they do provide a general production range useful for comparison. The mining regions listed in Table 1 constitute, each in its turn, the leading pre-1900 world producers.

[27] T. Egleston, "The Port Shirley Copper Works," *School of Mines Quarterly*, 7:4 (July, 1886), 1–25; and "Commerce and Progress of Chile", *Merchants Magazine and Commercial Review*, 13 (1845), 325–6.

The major difference between ore production in Chile and the United States was in Chile's initial lead, which was based on extensive expansion of the existing colonial mining industry by entrepreneurs. The United States had no such traditional mining. Chilean production expanded as new mines opened to ship high-grade ore and smelted metal to Swansea, Liverpool, Baltimore, and Boston. Chile from the start was export oriented. Production in the United States similarly began with an orientation towards the Swansea smelters and, as in Chile, soon developed a smelting capacity of its own.[28] By 1870, however, only small quantities of copper from the United States left the East Coast ports. In the 1880s copper producers in Michigan and the western United States once again become interested in exports and began to compete with Chileans for control of the European markets. In 1882 producers in the United States began a practice that was to last for years. They dumped surplus copper in Europe at prices well below their production costs. Table 2 illustrates the dimensions of the turnabout in the copper industry.

Contrary to the implications of the historiography of United States industrial development and of the existing literature on Chilean copper, the authors believe the failure of Chilean entrepreneurs to build the basis for their continued industrial prosperity was not in their lack of ability to bring together technology, resources, and transportation in new organizations to take advantage of market opportunities. Indeed, as long as competition hinged solely on technical, organizational, and commercial ability, strong Chilean-based competition was a reality. During the latter part of the century, however, as world competition heightened and became characterized by United States dumping of surplus production, successful United States entrepreneurs had the state at their side—developing and implementing policies favorable to extractive, commercial, and industrial projects.[29] In short, those states that collaborated with or were captured by entrepreneurial interests gave specific industries an incomparable competitive edge. Benjamín Vicuña Mackenna, largely ignored by others looking at this issue, held that the failure of progressive Chilean copper entrepreneurs was primarily political in nature.[30] Their inability to overcome the power of traditional landed interests, which were indifferent to

[28] Gates, *Boston Dollars*, 9–10.

[29] John D. Leshy, *The Mining Law: A Study in Perpetual Motion* (Washington, D.C.: Resources for the Future, Inc., 1987). The entire book develops this theme, but chapters 1–3 are especially useful. This is the best overview of United States mining law and the law in mining history.

[30] Benjamín Vicuña Mackenna, *El libro del cobre y del carbón de piedra en Chile* (Santiago: Imprenta Cervantes, 1886). The views of Vicuña Mackenna are further supported by correspondence from industry leaders, which arrived too late for inclusion in this classic book—correspondence stored in the Archivo Nacional de Chile, Fondo Benjamín Vicuña MacKenna. In preparation for *El Libro de Cobre*, he wrote to all of the leaders in copper asking for their recollections and recommendations for the industry. Most helpful were letters from Juan Mackay, Guillermo C. Biggs, and Enrique Sewell.

TABLE 2

*New York Copper Price Per Pound and Copper Production from Chile and the United States, 1810–1900*

| | Chile | | United States | | Copper Price (New York) |
|---|---|---|---|---|---|
| Year | Tons | Percentage (World) | Tons | Percentage (World) | Cents/Pound |
| 1810 | 1,653 | 9 | 0 | | 43 |
| 1820 | 1,653 | 9 | 0 | | 29 |
| 1830 | 3,004 | 11 | 0 | | 22 |
| 1840 | 7,114 | 20 | 0 | | 24 |
| 1850 | 13,607 | 28 | 728 | 1 | 22 |
| 1860 | 37,602 | 51 | 8,064 | 11 | 22.25 |
| 1870 | 48,724 | 42 | 14,112 | 12 | 22.625 |
| 1880 | 43,628 | 31 | 30,240 | 21 | 20.125 |
| 1881 | 42,547 | 23 | 35,840 | 20 | 18.125 |
| 1882 | 48,058 | 24 | 45,323 | 22 | 18.5 |
| 1883 | 46,031 | 21 | 57,763 | 26 | 15.875 |
| 1884 | 46,646 | 19 | 72,473 | 30 | 13.875 |
| 1885 | 43,120 | 17 | 82,938 | 33 | 11.125 |
| 1886 | 39,228 | 16 | 78,882 | 33 | 11 |
| 1887 | 32,648 | 13 | 90,739 | 36 | 11.25 |
| 1888 | 34,989 | 12 | 113,180 | 38 | 16.75 |
| 1889 | 27,160 | 9 | 113,388 | 39 | 13.75 |
| 1890 | 29,254 | 10 | 129,882 | 43 | 15.75 |
| 1895 | 24,724 | 7 | 190,307 | 52 | 10.875 |
| 1900 | 28,784 | 5 | 303,059 | 56 | 16.625 |

SOURCES: C. E. Julian, *Summarized Data of Copper Production* (Washington, D.C.: Superintendent of Documents, 1928), for Great Britain, United States and the world; Guillermo Yunge, *Estadistica minera de Chile en 1906* (Santiago de Chile: Imprenta Litografía i Encuadernación Barcelona, 1909), for Chile; and the *Engineering and Mining Journal* (New York), for years 1880–1890 in the United States and world.

industrial development, at a time early enough to make a difference, hampered their industry's evolution more than anything else.[31] Landed interests could not identify industrial development with their own concerns and ignored calls for policy reforms which were crucial for modernizing the copper industry.[32]

The early success of the Chilean mining community's production of copper

[31] Two sets of Chilean Congressional debates chronicled the position of landed agricultural interests in the face of calls for mining code reform. In both the Chamber of Deputies and the Senate, see the *Boletín de las sesiones ordinarios de la Camara de Diputados* and the same for the *Senado* for 1872 to 1874; and again for 1882 through 1888.

[32] The Congressional debates of the 1870s and 1880s are a topic in and of themselves. Mine code reform implied restricting the rights of surface land owners. For a characteristic exchange, see *Boletín de las sesiones ordinarios del Senado*, 24 July 1872, 102–6.

in industrial quantities took place under an eighteenth-century mercantilist mining code. The code conceived of minerals in terms of state revenue; this conceptualization led to regulations aimed at organizing mining to provide maximum tax receipts and to prevent tax fraud by mining interests.[33] That Chilean copper thrived under a considerable tax burden is a credit to Chilean entrepreneurship. It is this restrictive mining code that ultimately distinguishes the copper industries of Chile from those of the United States. As late as the 1860s, mining in Chile was technologically the same as that in Michigan, Montana, and Arizona. During mid-century, in Chile and the United States, production was expanded extensively rather than intensively. Competition was based on exploiting resources at more points, not by increasing the sophistication of technology at given points.[34]

It was only in the 1870s, as interregional domestic competition heightened, that intensification of production appeared in the United States; and it is at this time that mining and smelting methods can be differentiated between Chile and the United States. Still, the change was a gradual one. Hand-held drills, picks, and shovels coexisted alongside newer industrial methods. Clearly technological change, especially the application of gigantic power machinery financed by capital outside of the mining industry, set the stage for expansion and market domination by the United States, but economic expansion in copper was not a simple application of machinery, however inventive, by "daring" entrepreneurs grappling with new organization methods to better exploit natural resources. If copper expansion required nothing more than the application of new ideas, Chile would have stayed with Michigan, Montana, and Arizona stride for stride.[35] Each region possessed extensive reserves. Entrepreneurs in each region were aware of new large-scale applications of steam and electricity.[36] They all understand the role of railroads, increased scales of production, new drills, and lighting systems. Capital was readily available for all;[37] skilled labor was at hand.[38] The crucial catalyst for the

[33] Luz María Mendez Beltrán, *Instituciones y problemas de la minería en Chile, 1784–1826* (Santiago: Universidad de Chile, 1979), 16–26; and Vicuña MacKenna, *El libro del cobre*, 495.

[34] John D. Davis, *Corporations* (New York: Capricorn Books, 1961), 262. In his last chapter, focusing on the modern corporation, Davis presents an interesting discussion of the role of corporations in the shift from extensive to intensive expansion. He sees a direct correlation between corporate organization and industrial growth.

[35] Eujenio Chouteau, *Informe sobre la provincia de Coquimbo* (Santiago de Chile: Imprenta Nacional, 1887). His introduction is an expression of belief in inevitable progress, cast in terms of a strong copper industry needing a new impulse of modernization.

[36] For example Carlos Cousiño and Marcial Gatica were importing the latest copper smelting equipment in 1884. Minister of Hacienda Barros Luco, in *Boletín de las sesiones ordinarios del Senado*, 7 October, 1884, 575.

[37] Thomas O'Brien, in tracing the movement of Chilean capital into the Chilean nitrate mines, clearly shows that capital was available in Chile during this period, but he does not look into the copper industry's problems, in "The Antofagasta Company: A Case Study of Peripheral Capitalism," *Hispanic American Historical Review*, 60:1 (1980), 1–31.

[38] "The native 'baretoris' or miner is a skillful workman, unsurpassed by the miner of any other country in the mere handicraft of his calling, more enduring and more expert in the handling

factors of production to be combined into an efficient mine operation became a national agreement on the importance of industrial progress, with debate centered on the best *means* for that progress, as opposed to debate over the *ends* of industrial growth itself. Debate regarding the means of industrial progress in the United States led to supportive public policy. In Chile such a public debate stalled, and the search for coherent modern industrial and mining policy was prolonged into the twentieth century.

Chile and the United States both had civil wars in mid-century that can be interpreted as a part of a national debate over industrial progress.[39] In the United States the Civil War helped to provide a consensus by eliminating a significant conservative perspective from the economic debate. After 1860, with elimination of social debris of the past from Congress and creation of a new national goal to include a vast internal market, a national rail network, and protective tariffs, the United States had achieved the essential institutional and political consensus needed to stimulate profound reorganization and internal growth in every phase of American economic life.[40]

In the copper industry of the United States this national direction translated into two important developments. The first was the legislating of a 1861 tariff on smelted copper, which was raised further in 1864.[41] Michigan politicians argued that higher profits and wages in the mines of the United States would ensure the development of Michigan and the West. In its hearings on the copper industry in 1865, the United States Revenue Commission heard testimony that only a tariff of six to eight cents a pound, at a time when the price for smelted copper hovered just twenty cents (see Table 2), could reverse the

---

of his tools than a Cornishman. . . . The Chilean miner . . . handles both hammer and drill, a mode of mining known as singlehand drilling, which is growing in favor in some of the mining districts of the United States." J. D., Jr., "Chili, Her Mines and Miners—II," *EMJ*, 38 (July 26, 1884), 55.

[39] Maxwell Whiteman, *Copper for America: The Hendricks Family and a National Industry, 1755–1939* (New Brunswick, N.J., 1971), 207–8. Also see Maurice Zeitlin, "Class, State, and Capitalist Development: The Civil Wars in Chile (1851 and 1859)," in *Continuities in Structural Inquiry*, Peter M. Blau and Robert K. Merton eds. (Beverly Hills, California: Sage Publications, 1981), 121–64.

[40] Support for this interpretation of the role of the American Civil War is somewhat controversial. The authors follow the case made by Barrington Moore, Jr., *Social Origins of Dictatorship and Democracy Lord and Peasant in the Making of the Modern World* (Boston: Beacon Press, 1966), especially 141. The same argument is made in a novel but very useful manner by Major L. Wilson, "The Concept of Time and the Political Dialogue in the United States, 1828–1848," *American Quarterly*, 19 (1907), 619–44. Wilson observes the South's insistence on clinging to the past, represented by slavery, as distorting the national debate over economic development and forcing the debate towards conflict between the parties of the "past" and the "present." Also useful is Eugene Genovese's several works on the Southern mind, especially his *The Political Economy of Slavery* (New York: Pantheon Books, 1965), ch. 1. William R. Taylor makes much the same argument with different sources in his classic, *Cavalier and Yankee: The Old South and American National Character* (Garden City, New York: Doubleday and Company, 1961).

[41] U.S. Revenue Commission, *The Copper Crisis in the United States* (Washington, D.C., 1866), 11, 13, 15, 17 and 19. See also *Congressional Globe*, 40th Cong., 3d sess. (January 18, 1969), 416.

low profits caused by stiff Chilean competition.[42] Michigan's two U.S. Senators complained of low-cost Chilean copper, which was supplying upwards of one-third of the United States market and thus depressing Atlantic seaboard prices.[43] Additional arguments held that Chileans hurt the United States by their refusal to buy New England manufactures, preferring instead to spend their copper dollars in Great Britain.

The issue of national security was raised with the assertion that the United States, by importing Chilean copper concentrates and ore, had allowed itself to become dependent on a foreign supply of a vital war materiel.[44] The political campaign for ever higher copper tariffs did not peak until 1869. Pressing new moral arguments, the "Copper Senators" proclaimed, falsely, that Chilean copper should be banned via a tariff because Chilean mines relied on forced convict labor.[45] These debates over the Copper Act of 1869, which placed a five-cent a pound tariff on refined copper, revealed a deep hostility towards Chilean involvement in the market of the United States.[46]

While intended to protect and develop only Lake Michigan copper, the high profits generated by the tariff induced new mines to open in Montana and Arizona during the 1870s. The result of the new mines was a domestic price war.[47] The high prices that tariff protection secured for copper producers within the United States stimulated production and ultimately led entrepreneurs to engage in competition in foreign markets. In the early 1880s Western and Michigan surplus copper started arriving in Europe priced below production costs,[48] thus driving down the price of the "Chili bar."[49] This use of foreign markets was raised to the level of economic principle by Andrew

[42] U.S. Revenue Commission, *Copper*, 12.

[43] During this time the American copper industry split over struggle between smelting interests in Maryland and mines in Michigan and Tennessee. The seaboard smelters wanted low-cost, tariff-free Chilean ore. See proceedings of Congressional debates on HR1460, "To Regulate the Duties on Imported Copper and Copper Ores." The debate extended throughout the 40th Congress, Third Session, from December 1868 to February 1869. See also the Second Session debates in the *Congressional Globe; EMJ*, 4 (July 25, 1867), 56; and 7 (January 2, 1869), 2.

[44] U.S. Revenue Commission, *Copper*, p. 15.

[45] *Congressional Globe*, 40th Cong., 3d sess. (January 18, 1869). During the session Senator Zachariah Chandler of Michigan spoke endlessly about Chilean copper. His emotional pleas included a mixture of exaggerated and mistaken claims. "Copper is an interest that is absolutely being crushed by foreign competition—the competition of convict raised ores in Chile" (p. 416).

[46] *Congressional Globe*, 40th Cong., 3d sess. (January 18, 1869), 416.

[47] The Montana–Michigan copper price war is thoroughly reviewed in K. Ross Toole, "A History of Anaconda Copper Mining Company: A Study in the Relationships Between a State and Its People and a Corporation, 1850–1950" (Ph.D. Thesis, Department of History, University of California at Los Angeles, 1954).

[48] A typical comment of the era is found in the *EMJ*, 35:22 (June 2, 1883): "But yet a glance at the figures which illustrate the excessive growth of copper production will show the careful student and speculator that our American markets can no longer stand the tension of such burdens as are heaped upon them by the ambitious operators of mines. And so we are confronted by a new question: Are we ready to try to experiment the problem of shifting the battle from home to foreign fields, where we come into competition with the pauper labor of Spanish-speaking people and the inexhaustible beds of Chile, Africa, Portugal, Spain, and Australia?" (p. 313).

Carnegie in his "Law of Surplus," which held that it was cheaper for large industrial enterprises "to run a loss for a ton or a yard than to check . . . production" during times of oversupply. "In order to keep running in hard times" and "in order to hold the market in good times," Carnegie argued that American industrialists must exploit foreign markets.[50]

The 1866 revamping of the mining code in the United States began the other major development supporting the dramatic shift in the structure of the world copper market towards control by producers in the United States. This reform allowed mineral property claims to be made and held with a minimum of bureaucracy, and it offered complete title security to the claim holder, without taxation.[51] The 1866 Mineral Lands Act constituted a formal rejection of minerals as a source of public revenue either through their sale or by taxation, and secure full possession of a mining property was made possible for individuals, corporate or corporeal, through a simple claim process.[52]

This policy approach, reaffirmed in the Mineral Development Act of 1872, was a formulation intended to meet the needs of new corporate organizations.[53] The 1872 law made investments even more secure than the 1866 law and made possible the consolidation of many small claims into one large property. Financiers believed that consolidation was obligatory to insure large processing plants would be fed sufficient ore over a long period of time at a planned rate and at a predictable price. Only consolidated mineral properties could justify the huge investments required by new efficient plants. Planning and predictability were absolutely critical for financing to be available for ever larger installations. It was widely believed that "nothing but steady, unavoidable losses will force a mine into suspension, and therefore, the period leading to the survival of the strongest is usually much longer than is generally believed."[54] Well-financed mines, secure in their mineral property ownership, could wait out competitive losses and thus prevail in the end.

As the copper industry in the United States underwent the transformation to ever larger scale processing of ore, it required far more capital than had

[49] Since the 1840s, Chilean smelted copper was exported in bars 6×2×2 inches. In Europe and North America this "Chili bar" became the international standard for forward copper trading due to its consistent high quality and dominating abundance. Each bar was stamped with the name of the smelter of origin (interview with Sr. Claudio Canut de Bon Urrutia, July 17, 1980, Museo de Antropología de La Serena, Chile). Old Chili bars from several smelters are on display in the museum in La Serena.

[50] Dumping of surplus production was standard procedure for North American industry during the era. See Edward D. Crapol and Howard Schonberger, "The Shift to Global Expansion, 1865–1900," in *From Colony to Empire: Essays in the History of American Foreign Relations*, William Appleman Williams, ed. (New York, 1972), 186.

[51] The legislative fight was led by William Stewart of Nevada. See the *Congressional Globe*, 39th Congress, 1st sess. Senate Bill 157, 3548.

[52] *Ibid.*

[53] William Doherty, *Minerals Conservation in the U.S.: A Documentary History* (New York: 1971), 542–55. See also Leshy, *The Mining Law*.

[54] "Foreign Copper and Lead Mines", *EMJ*, 37 (1884), 456.

previously been available to the industry. Those mining and smelting capitalists able to secure stable financing outside the mining industry became the survivors. This trend was noticed in 1876 by Abram S. Hewitt, president-elect of the American Institute of Mining Engineers, who observed in an address to his fellow mining engineers that the industry had gone through many stages of leadership: from pioneer to mine engineer, from mine engineer to mechanical engineer, and lastly towards control by corporate financiers.[55] As Hewitt looked back on the previous decade, he also noted that meagerness of government supervision characterized the relationship between government and mining in the United States and that this had allowed progress to continue unimpeded. He pointed out that this condition was to be contrasted with the complicated mining codes of Spain, Mexico, or Chile, which may have enriched the coffers of the state but had also tied the hands of the new class of mining entrepreneurs.[56] Hewitt concluded his address by reaffirming that industrialists and financiers, freed of state control, needed to continue to forge the most important development of the century: the industrial corporation. He innocently believed that this development would be the outgrowth of a new and beneficent principle: that "the practical association of diffused capital, through the agency of corporate organization, with labor, for the promotion of economy, [worked] for the improvement of processes, and for the general welfare of mankind."[57]

The appearance of the corporation indeed constituted a momentous innovation in business organization. This new form did not just happen; it was the conscious result of involvement of the state in the nineteenth-century social economy. The granting of the legal rights of a person to a paper entity, the corporation, and then limiting the liability of this fictitious person to the amount of capital invested must be seen as a major intervention. Limiting liability resolved the greatest fear of mining investors—that continual calls would be made for more capital, which, if not paid, would lead to forfeiture of ownership rights. Limited liability also opened the door for a major change in the United States economy: the concentration of dispersed capital into a few hands. Hewitt's hope for the general welfare, however, turned out to more closely resemble general warfare in the copper industry during the last years before the combined mining regions in the United States displaced Chile as the world's leading copper producer.

During the 1880s, the mining press in the United States continually studied "how our competitors are bearing up under the strain."[58] In 1881 the San Francisco *Bulletin* carried a report on copper ore shipments from Arizona and editorialized that, with the railways now in place, Arizona could "compete

[55] Abram S. Hewitt, "A Century of Mining and Metallurgy in the U.S.," *EMJ*, 21 (1876), 609.

[56] Hewitt, "A Century of Mining," 612. [57] Ibid., 614.

[58] "Foreign Copper and Lead Mines", *EMJ*, 37 (1884), 456.

successfully with Chile in supplying the English demand. . . . The future of the Arizona copper mines is bright and full of promise, and now that avenues of transportation are open by which products can reach tidewater, we ought to be able to undersell every other copper country.''[59]

Warming up to the copper contest, the *Engineering and Mining Journal* took an even more dramatic line in its editorials in 1884. The editors wrote that ''it seems to be a mighty struggle now between the producers in all parts of the world.''[60] The same editorial went on to analyze the capacity for Chilean copper miners to continue production, noting that as the mines remained under Chilean control, ''they are probably capable and willing, with that faith which is at the same time the blessing and curse of mine ownership, to struggle at least for years to come.''[61]

The North American copper mining industry felt proud and boastful, ready to take on any and all challengers. With this truculent attitude, mining capitalists in the United States were determined to force not just their counterparts in foreign copper regions but each other as well to the wall. The tactics used with foreign competitors were not more ruthless than those used with domestic ones. For Western producers, ''in every case it comes to be a struggle for existence and the law of survival of the fittest applies in industry as in physical existence.''[62]

As the 1880s ended New York-based copper corporations, working deposits in Montana and Arizona, along with their Boston competitors who were working the Michigan deposits, constituted a dominating influence on world copper markets. This dominance, grounded in supportive legislation at the regional and national levels,[63] had its strength in promotion of access to the financing necessary to change copper mining from a family-run, small-scale, cottage speculation to a highly developed, large-scale, mechanized business.[64] From the 1860s onward, once Southern opposition was eliminated, the United States Congress created a uniform and standardized national market. Important for the growth of the copper industry in the United States were railroad expansion, joint-stock corporations, and limited liability; but the copper tariffs and a modern mining code based on private property stand out as absolutely critical. In short, copper in the United States was able to become an aggressive, efficient, and competitive industry because the state provided the necessary legal, physical, and economic infrastructure.

[59] ''Copper—Arizona's Place Along the Producing Regions,'' the *San Francisco Bulletin*, reprinted in *EMJ*, 32 (1881), 22.

[60] ''Foreign Copper and Lead Mines'', *EMJ*, 37 (1884), 456.

[61] *Ibid.* [62] ''The Copper Question,'' *EMJ*, 47 (1889), 452.

[63] See Toole, ''A History of the Anaconda,'' for a detailed analysis at the state level; and Frank William Tausig, *Some Aspects of the Tariff Question* (Cambridge: Howard University Press, 1915), 161–70, for an analysis of federal copper politics.

[64] Walter H. Voskuil, ''Copper,'' *Minerals in World Industry* (Port Washington, N.Y., 1930), 226–7; and Alfred D. Chandler, ''The Beginning,'' 28–31.

The story of copper in Chile during this period contrasts sharply with what occurred in the United States. As the 1870s began Chile outproduced all other countries in copper,[65] yet the leaders of the Chilean copper industry were concerned about the future—and rightly so. While the Chilean copper region still had the world's lowest prices and the highest output, they saw the recent North American tariffs, as well as other changes in the United States, as potential threats. The progressive Chilean copper leadership began to press for legislation to rationalize Chilean mining along lines taken by the United States through its reforms of 1866 and 1872.[66]

Chilean mining reforms in 1874, however, actually made the situation worse for the copper industry. The reformed mining law strengthened surface agricultural land rights against those of entrepreneurs trying to discover, claim, and operate mines.[67] Despite the so-called reforms of 1874, Chilean mining continued to be organized under an eighteenth-century mining policy, while the competition in the United States operated under a modern capitalist code. Chile had a mining policy of state revenue; the United States had one of economic growth. There is no evidence that the world mining community of the 1870s appreciated the full implications of the difference, nor how bad the Chilean copper situation was, nor how good was that of the United States. Whatever these policy differences meant to society in general, they had critical implications for the copper regions involved in a struggle for survival.

The Chilean method of copper taxation had specific unfortunate consequences. The tax policy established in 1810 set a rate of two pesos per pound of copper when the market price was eight to ten pesos.[68] The tax basis remained the value of production, not profit. After mid-century, when copper prices began to fall, the tax became proportionally higher and harder to pay. As the tax was on volume, not profits, it had to be paid even during periods in which the market price fell below the cost of production. Mining resentment against this difficult tax levy, combined with antagonism over the inadequate mining code, lay somewhat behind the unsuccessful Civil War of 1851 and was instrumental in the succeeding Civil War of 1859.[69]

These civil wars have traditionally been viewed in Chile as "anarchist" rebellions,[70] but were in fact based on policy in the North. Mining operators

[65] Chouteau, *Informe*.

[66] Benjamín Vicuña Mackenna, *Libro del cobre*. Vicuña Mackenna expressed this view clearly (authors' translation): "All we ask of the country, that is of government, or the legislators and of the people, is three things, simple and indispensable, urgent and lifesaving: 1. Abolition of the copper tax; 2. Reform of the mining code; and 3. A railway uniting the entire north" (p. 604).

[67] "La cuestión minera," *Boletín de la Sociedad Nacional de Minería—Revista Minera*, 1:2 (January, 1884), 9–10 [hereafter *Boletín*.]

[68] Vicuña Mackenna, *Libro de cobre*, 513–7.

[69] This is implied through numerous references in Pedro Pablo Figueróa, *Historia de la Revolución Constituyente, 1858–1859* (Santiago, 1889). See also an important analysis of these wars taking a somewhat different view in Zeitlin, "Class, State, and Capitalist Development."

[70] Francisco Encina, *Historia de Chile desde la prehistoria hasta 1891* (Santiago, 1940), 52.

claimed their taxes supported government projects only beneficial to urban and agricultural interests, while mining had unmet needs for roads, port facilities, and other infrastructure. In the 1859 Civil War a government was formed in the North in Copiapó. One of its first acts was to suspend the copper production tax and replace it with a lower export tax.[71] The civil wars were lost by the copper interests, yet the other factors of production (principally abundant ore) were so favorable that production continued and even expanded in the 1860s despite the antagonistic policies.

The decades of the 1860s and 1870s indicate a buoyance for Chilean copper that was misleading on account of these favorable factors of production. The United States virtually dropped out of the European market after the American Civil War. Chilean mining, while strained by increasing shortages of high grade ore, still seemed blessed. The key Chilean mining centers enjoyed all of the fruits of nineteenth-century industrial progress: electricity, gas street lights, iron structures (Alexandre Eiffel was contracted to build a church in Coquimbo), and expansion of railroads.[72] Progress in Chile's north seemed real and irreversible but was shortly revealed to be fragile.

Michigan and Western copper producers became jubilant in 1883. They used the detailed production statistics reported in the *Engineering and Mining Journal* to proclaim the copper superiority of the United States.[73] What the Chilean mining community had seen coming for years had now happened. The United States began to sell its copper in Europe, and the relatively strong position of Chilean copper in terms of skills and abundant ore, which had postponed the crisis, was now acute. Although Chilean mines were strained to their fullest capacity to produce the copper extracted in 1883, most mines lost money. Only the hope of better prices and the fear of losing a mining property under the existing code kept more mines from suspending operation. The crisis brought renewed demands for mining reform.

About the time when Chile lost its first place for copper output, mining leaders met in Santiago to create a national mining society, the *Sociedad Nacional de Minería* (SONAMI).[74] SONAMI leadership consisted of mine owners and engineers from the North, with close connections to Liberal Party members of the Chamber of Deputies and the Senate.[75] This new professional organization seems to have been a part of the world-wide rise of a middle class seeking to secure its status through organizational life.[76] SONAMI was not, however, an interest group in a pluralist sense. Born through presidential sponsorship and financed by public monies, SONAMI led the campaign for reform through intensive efforts to convince a majority of the Chamber of

[71] Figueróa, *Historia*, 31. [72] Chouteau, *Informe*, 2.
[73] "Annual Review of the Metal Markets for 1882," *EMJ*, 35 (January 20, 1883), 27–28.
[74] *Boletín*, 1:12 (30 April, 1884), 94. [75] See all issues of *Boletín*, 1 (1883–1884).
[76] For an analysis of this process in the United States, see Robert H. Wiebe, *The Search for Order, 1887–1920* (New York, 1967).

Deputies to legislate a mining policy more favorable to the industry. SONAMI argued that copper prosperity was directly linked to the country's underlying mining policy and that the key to future national economic prosperity was not agriculture but a strong copper industry.[77]

*Boletín,* the SONAMI journal, strenuously pushed for major changes in the existing mind code. Issue after issue, its pages carried the argument that the code was the principle cause of the copper industry's stagnation, which had resulted from a lack of new investment on a scale required to compete with the United States.[78] The copper mining leadership understood that their antiquated mining code sought to provide state revenue, not promote new investment. The code's logic presumed miners would not mine unless forced to do so, and it allowed anyone to claim an existing mine property, if work at that property were suspended, even for a short time.[79]

The mining conditions resulting from the old code were seen as contrary to what was necessary for the Chilean industry to compete with United States producers. The nature of United States competition called for ever larger scales of production as did falling ore grades in Chile. Both conditions, large-scale production and low-grade ores, required consolidation of mining properties, but this was particularly difficult for Chilean producers as their code mandated the individual working of each small claim. When consolidation was attempted, it required a team of lawyers to fend off claim challenges.[80] Such insecurity was not conducive to obtaining the capital necessary for large-scale mine development complete with steam machinery and vast smelting capacity. Thus the existing claim system was believed to be the root cause for Chilean investment funds going elsewhere, particularly into nitrates, as well as Bolivian and Peruvian copper, which had higher ore grades and more favorable codes.[81]

SONAMI's primary goals became twofold: (1) to change the mine claim system to that of the patent system used in the United States; and (2) to abolish the copper tax in favor of an annual patent fee on each claim.[82] The mining leadership did not believe that Chilean copper could both compete world-wide and further capitalize itself if it was also expected to be the prime contributor to the state treasury.[83]

Not until 1888 did the Chilean Congress finally approve a new code.[84] This reform emerged after five years of legislative debate. Towards the end of the debate, curiously, the main opposition came from coal and nitrate mining interests as well as from agriculture. Under the colonial code in force until 1888, metal mining properties could be claimed by anyone, on any proper-

[77] *Boletín*, 1 (1883–1884), all issues.
[78] *Boletín*, 1:1 (15 December 1883), 1–2; and 1:2 (1 January 1884), 9–10.
[79] *Ibid.* [80] *Ibid.* [81] Bravo, "U.S. Investment," 53. [82] *Ibid.*
[83] *Boletín*, 1:12 (1 June 1884), 101–2; and *Boletín*, 3:49 (15 December, 1885), 389.
[84] *Boletín*, 5:4 (31 October 1888), 15; and 6:7 (31 January 1889), 193–208.

ty—a right resented by landowners, who feared reform would strengthen and expand claiming rights to all minerals, not just metals. The coal and nitrate interests resisted reform for the same reason; they were unregulated by the colonial code that only conceived of metal mines.[85] So far as the old code was concerned, nitrate and coal did not exist; surface landowners could claim all subsurface coal and nitrate, free from any outsider's claims, keeping the minerals in reserve. This reserve advantage became one of the central goals of the copper reformers. In the final compromise creating the 1888 reforms, coal and nitrate were given exceptional status and continued as unregulated.[86]

With that legislative success behind it, SONAMI began to push its other proposals: northern rail consolidation, a mining college, and the holding of an international mine exposition.[87] Liberal President José Manuel Balmaceda, who provided essential support for passage of the reform in 1888, initiated efforts to rationalize the railroad situation in the copper region and thus supposedly reduce the rates for copper ore transportation. His program, which called for rail nationalization, was cut short by the Revolution of 1891. SONAMI supported Balmaceda but suspended its meetings, once the revolution broke out. After Balmaceda lost power, SONAMI was conciliatory toward the new agrarian-backed government.[88]

The SONAMI legislative successes of 1888 grew out of its close relations with the president and Liberals in the legislature, but the realignment of power in 1891 dissolved the willingness of both the Chamber of Deputies and the Senate to go along with further reforms. Ministerial budgets allowed for such activities as the International Mine Exposition of 1894 in Santiago, but no legislative measures in support of mining can be found until the end of parliamentary dominance in 1925.[89]

During the 1880s Chilean copper interests advocated mining code reforms which were twenty years old in the United States; they hoped to achieve what miners in Michigan and the American West had already received: legislation that bolstered capitalist practices. United States mineral policy was drafted by mining industry representatives and was aimed at rapid economic growth based on huge quick profits to individuals. One good mine fulfilled the career ambitions of a prospector, an engineer, or an investor. This was in great

[85] There is some confusion in existing writing on various minerals and their regulations in nineteenth-century Chile. For example, in his study of the Chilean economy Markos Mamalakis touches on nineteenth-century copper at several points, making the familiar argument about the incapacity of the copper sector to modernize, but he makes an additional important reference to government policy: "If true laissez-faire ever came close to existence in Chile, it was in nitrate and copper mining" (p. 40). While he is correct in pointing to policy as a factor to be examined, the two minerals, nitrate and copper, were produced under wholly different legal bases prior to 1888. Copper was highly regulated, nitrate not at all.

[86] "Código de Minería," *Boletín*, 6:7 (31 January 1889), 194.

[87] *Boletín*, Serie 2:9 (31 March 1889), 237.

[88] *Boletín*, Serie 2:37 (1 July, 31 October 1891), 190–2.

[89] *La Riqueza Minera de Chile*, 1:1 (September, 1921), 29.

contrast with the Chilean copper mining industry, which had been structured under a code based on Spanish colonial goals of creating revenues for the state in the mining of precious, not industrial, metals. The Chilean reforms, both out of competitive crisis, had the intent of increasing efficiency by allowing for the large-scale, highly capitalized mining as practiced in the United States after the 1870s.

Had reform been realized earlier in Chile, there is no guarantee that Chilean copper would have prevailed in competition with the United States. Given the predatory nature of the New York-based copper mining corporations—specifically the dumping of surplus production below cost while relying on domestic earnings created by a high tariff—it is still possible that Chilean reforms would only have delayed their submission to American industry.

The period of Congressional dominance in Chile (1891–1925), from the point of view of copper, complicated a bad economic situation. The reforms in the 1880s were too little, too late. The Revolution of 1891 simply postponed any further attempt to rationalize and modernize Chilean mining for thirty-five years. Despite the 1888 code reforms, overall mining policy during the years of Congressional dominance remained indifferent to the needs of a failing copper industry. It is ironic that the reforms of 1888, while too late to revitalize Chilean copper, provided the foundation for United States capital to enter Chile. Without these reforms there would have been no large-scale foreign investment in mining.[90] Consolidation of mine holdings would have been too insecure.

During the 1890s United States copper tariffs were dropped; the Western copper industry was unquestionably preeminent worldwide. New technology had brought forth new possibilities at century's end for copper corporations in the United States. As the industry came to depend on the now workable, dispersed, low-grade copper ore (porphyry) properties, scouts from giant American copper corporations searched the planet for porphyry deposits. Since Chile had many of these deposits, mining capital from the United States moved into Chile—the same country that forty years earlier had provided the competitive excuse to build a copper tariff around the United States.

It may be that any industry structured around a given set of regulations becomes, in a sense, comfortable with those regulations. Change means uncertainty and is acceptable only in a crisis. In Chile the mid-century civil wars were based on policy in the North; their focus was limited to lowering the rate of taxation. The copper mining prosperity encountered during the 1860s and 1870s through extensive working of Chilean deposits postponed the crisis necessary to overcome entrenched antimetal mining interests. In Chile the power of agrarian and nonmetal mining interests was such that the needs of

[90] Santiago Macciavello Varas, "Breve estudio," *La Riqueza Minera de Chile*, 3:28 (January, 1925), 509.

industrial copper were not taken seriously by a Congressional majority until too late. Even the reforms of 1888 meant little in the face of Congressional indifference to copper after the overthrow of Balmaceda in 1891, when interests hostile to metal mining settled in for years of governance.

As the nineteenth century closed, with a great American productive capacity in place and Chilean competition demoralized, United States producers began to respond to the dangers of excessive competition. An era of combinations followed, "intended to lessen the rigors of the struggle for existence by uniting the strength and interests of many individuals in a company or association or 'trust.' "[91] There was even an occasional expression of concern for the foreign competitors in the industry press: "The sooner the foreign producers appreciate the ability of our mines to supply the world with cheap copper, the sooner will they cooperate with ours in effecting some reasonable 'working basis' for marketing the large stocks, now in the country."[92] Predatory marketing, supported by tariffs favorable to mining capital, and mining codes written by mining industry representatives, combined to support a copper success in the United States only dreamed of in Chile.

Industrial mining and smelting of copper prospered in the nineteenth century not because of free enterprise, but precisely its opposite, which was the extent and quality of government intervention. Had government not regulated the distribution of subsurface minerals, had mining not been freed of the obligation to contribute to general state revenues and social well-being, had transportation not been subsidized, had limited liability corporations not been legislated into existence, had tariffs not been passed, the United States copper industry would still have emerged—the ore was there; but it would have been a very different industry and perhaps not the world's aggressive dominant copper producer. Unlike the natural change of seasons, competition is not inevitable in its results. As Chilean and United States copper entrepreneurs found in their years of competition, public policy—not their individual entrepreneurial talents—was the ultimate factor in industrial success or failure, and in their nation's economic development.

The case of Chilean copper prior to 1880 suggests that Hernando de Soto is partly correct in his hypothesis that arcane policies and regulations held back economic development in Latin America. An entire industry collapsed and was denationalized in Chile due to circumstances and policies. Had the policies been more supportive of competition with the United States, would circumstances still have held back the copper industry? Perhaps not.

[91] "The Copper Question", *EMJ*, 47 (1889), 452. [92] *Ibid.*, 473.

# [10]

*Journal of African History*, **28** (1987) pp. 119–140
*Printed in Great Britain*



# BIG BUSINESS IN AFRICAN STUDIES

BY A. G. HOPKINS

## ACADEMIC ENTERPRISE AND BUSINESS HISTORY

TEN years ago entrepreneurial history was an obscure branch of African studies, the preserve of a handful of scholars who were principally interested in indigenous enterprise.[1] Today, the subject has grown both absolutely and relative to other branches of historical enquiry. Weighty evidence of this expansion is provided by the appearance of two large volumes containing fifty-nine detailed studies covering nearly 1,200 pages;[2] and supporting testimony can readily be found in other recent publications.[3] It is impossible to summarize these numerous and diverse contributions in the space of one essay, but a modest service can be performed by advertising their existence,[4] and a more ambitious one can be attempted by comparing the state of the art as it now stands with how it was a decade ago.

But tribute must first be paid to the entrepreneurial qualities of our French colleagues, and especially to Catherine Coquery-Vidrovitch and Alain Forest, who organised the Paris conference and then moulded the papers into a coherent publication. Anyone who has attempted a similar task will know not only how difficult it is, but also how idealistic aspirations are traded, in the bourgeois sphere of exchange, for the currency of reality as the time between conception and publication elapses. Editors of volumes of conference papers can afford to smile when they read the earnest criticisms of reviewers who observe that the evidence for one contribution might have been more detailed, and that the analysis of another ought to have been strengthened, for they know that it is a miracle that anything appeared at all, given the mixture of waywardness, mischance and double booking with occurs whenever more than two or three academics are gathered together with productive purposes in mind. Editors are like waiters: their job is to present the chef's creation to its best advantage while also concealing the secrets of the kitchen from the clientele.

The efforts of the editors have been matched by their contributors. All the essays reach an acceptable scholarly standard, and this is a considerable

[1] This essay takes as its starting point the two articles I published in this journal a decade ago: 'Imperial business in Africa. Part I: sources', and 'Imperial business in Africa. Part II: interpretations', in *J. Afr. Hist.*, XVIII (1976), 29–48 and 267–90.

[2] Laboratoire 'Connaissance du Tiers-Monde', ed., *Entreprises et entrepreneurs en Afrique* (*XIX et XX siècles*) (Paris, 1983), 2 vols. This publication arose out of a conference held in Paris in December 1981.

[3] For example the special issue of *African Economic History*, XII (1983), edited by W. G. Clarence-Smith and entitled 'Business empires in Equatorial Africa'. The articles in this issue were originally prepared for a workshop held at the School of Oriental and African Studies in May 1982.

[4] The studies presented to the Paris and London conferences and published in the sources given in notes 2 and 3 above are listed in an appendix to this article. Six of the papers published in *Entreprises et entrepreneurs* (see note 2) were also published in the *Canadian Journal of African Studies*, XVI (1982), 279–359, and specialists will need to compare the two versions as there are some differences between them.

achievement for a project of this scale and diversity. A few are rather slender statements of larger projects, though no less interesting for that, but the majority are solidly based and independently researched case studies which will be of great value to regional specialists as well as to those interested primarily in entrepreneurial history. The volumes have been organised chronologically, and fall into four parts, each prefaced by a brief introduction. The first part contains twelve chapters dealing with indigenous entrepreneurship, mainly in the nineteenth and early twentieth centuries; the second part consists of fifteen studies of expatriate enterprise during the colonial period; the third part complements this theme by treating, in sixteen chapters, the relationship between firms, colonial governments and entrepreneurship; and the final part (also sixteen chapters) examines indigenous and foreign enterprise in the period since independence. Three introductory chapters offer guidance on some of the analytical problems raised by the study of entrepreneurship and colonial enterprise, and a reflective conclusion traces the evolution of private and state entrepreneurship in the twentieth century.[5] Not surprisingly, the presentation of the volumes reflects their Gallic origins: the characteristic whiff of the coarse paper conjures up (improbably) happy memories of visits to France, and the tables of contents remain resolutely at the back of each book.

It is evident from the size of these volumes alone that our knowledge of entrepreneurship in Africa has advanced greatly during the past decade. This is particularly true of the study of expatriate enterprise. Historians avoided this subject ten years ago, and the suggestion that foreign firms ought to attract research commensurate with their importance was regarded in some quarters as an anachronistic attempt to resurrect the history of colonial rule.[6] Since the early 1970s colonial history, albeit of a new kind, has indeed been revived, and it now both runs parallel to and interacts with the study of African history. This development has been made possible partly by the acceptance and rapid spread of research into Africa's economic history, and partly by radical approaches to the past which have reopened, for a new generation of researchers, the problem of the relationship between external influences and economic development. Yet these essays include liberal as well as radical perspectives, and they emphasize content rather than theory. The term 'dependence' does not appear in the title of a single chapter, and though there is one small 'articulation' even that does not apply to a mode of production. The current mood, as judged by these essays, is less confident that it was ten years ago but also more open, and it expresses itself in a form of new empiricism which is neither antiquarian nor the slave of dogma.

A further attribute of these volumes is their geographical scope, which encompasses most of the countries of tropical Africa and extends to north

[5] These chapters, which are not listed in the appendix, are: Hélène Verin, '"Entrepreneur", "entreprise", quelques remarques historiques pour leur définition'; Jacques Marseille, 'L'investissement privé dans l'empire colonial: mythes et réalités'; and Philippe Hugon, 'Essai de typologie des entreprises africaines', all in vol. I, 25–42, 43–60 and 61–76; and René Gallissot, 'De la colonisation à l'indépendance, les métamorphoses du couple "entreprise privée-Etat"', vol. II, 607–34.

[6] My article on 'Imperial business' attracted criticism on this score when it was given as a seminar paper in 1975. It is interesting to find that what was then considered to be out of date has now become modern – at least for a time.

Africa and Madagascar. Almost three-quarters of the studies deal with francophone Africa, and hence with west, west-central and north Africa. This bias scarcely needs explanation, given that the conference was held in Paris and benefited mainly from French funding. But the location is significant because it also symbolizes the way in which academic power has moved during the past decade or so, as French intellectual influences and government support have elevated African studies in France, and as chauvinistic insularity and public expenditure cuts have eroded them in the Anglo-Saxon world.[7] The merits of this shift are evident in the way in which the economic history of large parts of francophone Africa has been rescued from undeserved obscurity. At the same time, it is important to recognize that this development might alter the map of African studies by reducing the scale of sizeable parts of anglophone Africa. Southern Africa, for example, is not represented in these volumes. The imperial connexion may have helped to promote African studies, but it also conspires to confine scholarship – in Britain as well as in France.

## THE MARKET FOR KNOWLEDGE

Comparing these volumes with the state of the subject a decade ago prompts three general reflexions. The first concerns source materials, a subject that was touched upon but not examined systematically at the Paris conference. Despite the expansion of business history, there is still no readily accessible list which matches firms to the sources for studying them. Producing a list of this kind poses difficulties where indigenous firms are concerned, but ought to be straightforward in the case of the major European concerns.[8] Yet it is still not easy even for specialists to know whether prominent firms have historical records and are willing to release them. Specific mention ought also to be made of the importance of recording oral testimony from businessmen trading in and to Africa in the twentieth century, and of the need to do so without further delay as far as the colonial period is concerned. Given the lack of written evidence on numerous aspects of the history of the expatriate firms, it is curious that Africanists have not made greater use of interviews (and not only with senior management). Where testimony of this kind has been set down, it has added vitality as well as new information to the story that would otherwise be told.[9]

Ideally, what we now need is a business records project to identify and preserve written and oral evidence about the expatriate firms in Africa. Is it too late to place this item on the agenda in the hope that it might appeal to the entrepreneurial enterprise of the University of Paris VII, the African Studies Centre at Leiden, and the Business History Unit at the London

[7] A glimpse of the impressive range of research currently under way in France (in one discipline alone) is provided by the lists published regularly in the *Revue française de science politique*. Sir Peter Parker has reviewed the position in Britain for the University Grants Committee: '"Speaking for the future": a review of the requirements of diplomacy and commerce for Asian and African languages and Area Studies' (February 1986). See also A. G. Hopkins, 'From Hayter to Parker: African Economic History at Birmingham University, 1964–86', *African Affairs*, LXXXVI (1987).

[8] For a preliminary survey see Hopkins, 'Imperial business', 29–48.

[9] For such material, see P. N. Davies, *Trading in West Africa* (London, 1986).

School of Economics? Failing this, a practical recommendation which suggests itself is that one or two leading journals might publish regular bulletins of information about sources for business history in Africa.

The second, and related, reflexion concerns the persistence of imperfections in the market for knowledge, even when original sources have been found and used successfully. Like Marshall's non-competing wage groups, Africanists have not yet succeeded in dismantling a number of traditional barriers to the movement of skills and information. There are certainly signs of change: an interest in multinationals and capital flows, for example, has taken historians across regional and political frontiers, and has greatly improved our understanding of these subjects.[10] But numerous anomalies remain which are hard to explain, even when allowance has been made for selective perception and regional specialization. For example, Fieldhouse's study of Unilever is not discussed in any of the contributions to the Paris conference, despite its apparent relevance to several of the papers presented there; nor is it cited in the published version of the S.O.A.S. conference on Equatorial Africa.[11] Since Fieldhouse presents a considerable amount of evidence about one of the most important foreign firms and also offers a clear interpretation for discussion, it is difficult to see how the omission of his book can be defended. Gaps of this size are not confined to these conference papers. Swainson's study of the evolution of modern manufacturing in Kenya contains valuable information about firms such as Baumann, Mitchell Cotts, Brooke Bond and Bata, but her interpretation is weakened by a failure to consider work previously produced by scholars such as Kilby, who presents a comparable argument from a different standpoint.[12] Similarly, Shenton's recent book on Northern Nigeria presents a good deal of useful material on the Niger Company, but discusses it without citing Newbury's central article on this subject.[13] These examples refer to the omission of recent publications. But there is still a tendency to overlook studies of high quality produced in the 1940s, 1950s and 1960s, even though their merits have now been advertised.[14]

These imperfections in the market for knowledge are symptomatic of inefficiencies in the operation of the academic firm. They appear to derive partly from long-standing cultural barriers, notably between francophone and anglophone scholars, and partly from a lack of managerial rigour. Until existing assets are fully used, the final product will have difficulty competing in world markets.

The third general observation concerns the conceptual and analytical

[10] The papers presented to the SOAS workshop (see n. 3 above) are particularly helpful in this regard, as is Gervase Clarence-Smith, 'Business empires in Angola under Salazar, 1930–1961', *African Economic History*, XIV (1985), 1–13.

[11] D. K. Fieldhouse, *Unilever Overseas: The Anatomy of a Multinational, 1895–1965* (London, 1978).

[12] Nicola Swainson, *The Development of Corporate Capitalism in Kenya, 1918–1977* (London, 1980); Peter Kilby, *Industrialization in an Open Economy: Nigeria, 1945–66* (Cambridge, 1969).

[13] Robert W. Shenton, *The Development of Capitalism in Northern Nigeria* (London, 1986); Colin Newbury, 'Trade and technology in West Africa: the case of the Niger Company, 1900–1920', *J. Afr. Hist*, XIX (1978), 551–75.

[14] Hopkins, 'Imperial business', 29–48. See also A. D. Roberts, 'The earlier historiography of colonial Africa', *History in Africa*, V (1978), 153–67.

problems of studying entrepreneurship. It is evident from the conference papers that the term has elastic properties: some authors employ it to refer to innovation; most apply it to business activities in general; and a few regard it as being an attribute of the bourgeoisie. Each of these uses has its justification (though the third one is less easily accepted by a generation which read *Peddlers and Princes*),[15] and had every author embarked upon a definition of his theme the result would no doubt have been arid and repetitive. At the same time, the majority of the contributions appear to lack an overt organizing principle of the kind supplied, for example, by theories of the firm or indeed by more general interpretations of entrepreneurship.[16] A consideration of the origins and application of the concept of entrepreneurship may help to explain why this seemingly obvious gap should exist in studies of business history in Africa.

The term 'entrepreneur' arose in the sixteenth century, when it was used mainly to describe leaders of military expeditions; after 1700 it was applied more widely to government contractors.[17] The early association of the term with government, defence and services has particular interest for Africa today, given the size of the public sector and the extent to which private enterprise is conditioned by official action. Cantillon drew attention to the term in the mid-eighteenth century and linked it to risk-bearing activities, which he defined generously to include most social groups except princes, landowners and salaried employees. At the close of the eighteenth century, Say added a second entrepreneurial function, that of uniting the means of production. Thus, by the beginning of the nineteenth century two of the most important features of the entrepreneurial behaviour, accepting uncertainty and managing an enterprise, had been identified, though in ways which left the relationship between capital and entrepreneurship unresolved. English and Scottish writers employed different terms: the word 'adventurer' was inherited from medieval times, 'projector' was used by Defoe, and 'undertaker' by Smith and, later, by Marshall. In the event, the local vocabulary proved unpersuasive and the French word was gradually adopted. However, entrepreneurs were not given a prominent place in the economic systems described by either Smith or Marx. Smith, viewing a world composed predominantly of small firms, probably felt justified in treating profits as returns to capital rather than as a separate reward for specific entrepreneurial qualities. Marx, too, seems to have regarded the capitalist as encompassing entrepreneurial functions, and he was also suspicious of 'vulgar economists' who concentrated on the epiphenomena of prices and profits and neglected the fundamental laws of motion which shaped society.[18]

It was not until the close of the nineteenth century, following the development of general equilibrium theory by Walras and the rise of the large

[15] Clifford Geertz, *Peddlers and Princes: Social Development and Economic Change in Two Indonesian Towns* (Chicago, 1963).

[16] This sentence is intended to convey a general impression; there are also authors who know more about the theory of the subject than I do.

[17] Two helpful guides are Fritz Redlich, 'The origins of the concepts of "entrepreneur" and "creative entrepreneur"', *Explorations in Entrepreneurial History*, I (1949), 1–7, and Bert F. Hoselitz, 'The early history of entrepreneurial theory', *ibid.*, III (1951), 193–220. See also Hélène Verin, *Entrepreneurs, entreprises: histoire d'une idée* (Paris, 1982).

[18] Verin, '"Entrepreneur", "entreprise"', 28–31 (cf. n. 5).

firm (particularly in the United States), that entrepreneurs achieved academic prominence. Walras was dissatisfied with definitions which reduced the entrepreneur to the status of a manager, but he did not accept the view of the classical economists (and Marx) that entrepreneurs could simply be identified with capitalists. Walras saw entrepreneurs as profit maximizers who played a crucial role in the economy by moving markets towards competitive equilibrium. Accordingly, he suggested that the entrepreneur should be regarded as a separate, and fourth, factor of production.[19] Subsequent developments in the theory of entrepreneurship occurred principally in the Anglo-Saxon world, where two parallel themes emerged: Schumpeter's emphasis on the innovative function of the entrepreneur; and a renewed interest, stimulated by studies of imperfect competition and managerial capitalism, in the entrepreneur as a coordinator of large and long-term operations.[20] In more recent years, the theory of the firm has been developed in a literature of daunting size and complexity.[21] The preoccupation with innovation, and hence with the production of innovators, has produced a number of wide-ranging studies of the psychological and social conditions which were said to favour the appearance of innovators, and these evoked much debate in the 1960s, when discussion of the underdeveloped world was dominated by 'modernization theory'.[22] At the same time, continuing interest in what Pareto termed 'the persistence of aggregates' has prompted a number of analytical refinements, ranging from utility maximizing and 'satisficing' motives to the behaviour of oligopolies and the theory of mergers.[23]

The application of these ideas to economic history was led by scholars in the United States and took place within 'orthodox' economics. Schumpeter's presence provided powerful support for business history, and so too did the close ties which existed between the business community and the academic world. The most eminent example is to be found in the Harvard Business School's post-war programme, which led to the foundation of *Explorations in Entrepreneurial History* in 1949.[24] Business history also

[19] A useful summary, which has an eye on the African context and also comments on Marxist approaches, is E. Wayne Nafziger, *African Capitalism : A Case Study in Nigerian Entrepreneurship* (Stanford, 1977), 6–14 and 14–17.

[20] J. A. Schumpeter, *The Theory of Economic Development* (Cambridge, Mass., 1934); Joan Robinson, *The Economics of Imperfect Competition* (London, 1933); E. H. Chamberlin, *The Theory of Monopolistic Competition* (Cambridge, Mass., 1933); A. A. Berle and G. Means, *The Modern Corporation and Private Property* (New York, 1932); R. Marris, *The Economic Theory of 'Managerial' Capitalism* (London, 1964).

[21] Guides include: C. J. Hawkins, *Theory of the Firm* (London, 1973), G. C. Archibald (ed.), *The Theory of the Firm* (Harmondsworth, 1971), and Mark Casson, *The Entrepreneur : An Economic Theory* (Oxford, 1982).

[22] This literature is surveyed in Peter Kilby (ed.), *Entrepreneurship and Economic Development* (New York, 1971).

[23] O. E. Williamson, *The Economics of Discretionary Behaviour* (Englewood Cliffs, 1964); *idem*, *Corporate Control and Business Behaviour* (Englewood Cliffs, 1970); H. A. Simon, *Models of Man* (New York, 1957); R. M. Cyert and J. G. March, *A Behavioural Theory of the Firm* (Englewood Cliffs, 1963); Sam Aaronovitch and Malcolm C. Sawyer, *Big Business : Theoretical and Empirical Aspects of Concentration and Mergers in the United Kingdom* (London, 1975).

[24] The journal changed its name to *Explorations in Economic History* in 1969; but that is another (interesting) story.

established a strong base in Britain, and acquired its own outlet, the journal *Business History*.[25] An equivalent development appears not to have taken place in France, where liberal orthodoxy met a stronger radical tradition, certainly in studies of the underdeveloped world, and where links between 'le monde des affaires' and the universities were weaker than in the U.S.A. The intellectual environment and its cultural boundaries were thus less receptive to these developments in economic theory and history. In the case of modernization theory this was perhaps no great loss, but the study of entrepreneurship has been hampered by the reluctance to make use of the full range of analytical tools which are now available.

Radical approaches to African history have been particularly powerful and stimulating during the past decade, but they have made only a muted contribution to what might be called, generically, business history, principally, it would seem, because Marx did not develop a theory of entrepreneurship. These subjects have been dominated by liberal scholars, whose compositions are often regarded on the left as hymns to capitalism written within the confines of 'orthodox' economics and divorced from political realities. This stereotype is not without foundation. There is an array of blithely uncritical official histories of firms, and even studies written by professional historians can easily exhibit a subtle bias in failing to ask uncomfortable questions of their material.[26] Moreover, business historians often find themselves in methodological difficulties because they wish to elevate the importance of their subject but also to deny any hint of mono-causality or determinism, which they often regard, mistakenly, as being the preserve of Marxism. Marxist historians, on the other hand, deal with entrepreneurs by subsuming them under portmanteau descriptions, such as the bourgeoisie or capitalism, which are too broad to yield testable propositions about the occurrence of innovation or the behaviour of the firm. This treatment is superficially satisfying because it assimilates an awkward social phenomenon into a grander theme, and enables the subject to be treated with a degree of hostility that is at once vague and comprehensive. In this way both sides can use history, and scholarship, to express ideological affiliations while simultaneously appealing to scientific neutrality.

The main point to be emphasized at this juncture is that subjects merit attention by virtue of their importance as well as their attractiveness. If it is agreed that 'the bourgeoisie, historically, has played a most revolutionary part'[27] then Marxist historians ought to devote as much attention to the entrepreneurial wing of that social group as they do to the emergence of a working class. By the same token, liberal historians ought not to feel obliged, even obliquely, to defend the record of the entrepreneurs they study against all comers. From this it follows that our understanding of entrepreneurship would be greatly improved if Marxists made a more serious attempt to master 'orthodox' theories of entrepreneurship, and if liberals resolved to investigate the social consequences as well as the causes of entrepreneurial actions.

[25] *Business History* was founded in 1958, largely as a result of the initiative of Professor J. R. Harris, and was intended to complement the American journal, the *Business History Review*.

[26] Some examples are given in Hopkins, 'Imperial business', 267–74.

[27] Karl Marx and Frederick Engels, *Manifesto of the Communist Party* (reproduction of the English edition of 1888; Moscow, n.d.), 46.

## HISTORICAL ACCOUNTING IN AFRICA

The foregoing comments are symptoms of an early stage in the growth of a new subject. They are not judgements on the final product, but possible openings for future research. It is evident that our knowledge of entrepreneurship in Africa has increased greatly since 1976, and the extent of the advance can clearly be seen by looking at the main historical divisions treated by the Paris conference: pre-colonial, colonial and post-colonial.

Research undertaken during the 1960s showed that pre-colonial Africa had a plentiful supply of indigenous entrepreneurs and had developed complex commercial organizations to sustain distributive systems which both spanned and survived political divisions.[28] The papers presented to the Paris conference deal only with the period after 1850, but they confirm the validity of these generalizations while also offering a more differentiated view of the experiences of indigenous entrepreneurs under the influence of imperialism. Although it is still too early to attempt a synthesis of 'the rise and fall of whole classes' during this period, the evidence indicates that indigenous entrepreneurs, like indigenous crafts, had a much better survival rate than was once thought.[29] However, generalizations on this subject tend to lose their accuracy once they aspire to continental, rather than regional, validity. And within regional units there is a danger of confusing the fortunes of those African entrepreneurs who were directly involved in the import–export trades with those who operated in the domestic economy, and to use the former as proxies for the latter (about whom far less is known). Those directly involved in the import–export sector appear to have passed through a three-stage sequence of rise–decline–rise, beginning in the mid-nineteenth century with the emergence of profitable openings in international trade, continuing under colonial rule with a phase of relative and (in the 1930s) possibly absolute decline, and ending after 1945 with a new set of opportunities which arose during the terminal period of colonialism. Ten years from now it ought to be possible to specify this historical undulation with greater accuracy and to distinguish its economic and political causes more clearly.

The interest of this subject lies in the prospect of learning more about the interaction between two forms of capitalism, indigenous and introduced, and hence in being able to improve our judgement of the extent to which colonial rule altered the course of African history (and, conversely, how far African history altered the course of colonial rule). However, the answer to these questions requires the solution of an anterior problem, namely the role and importance of indigenous entrepreneurs in pre-colonial Africa. Forms of commercial capitalism existed, as did large and prestigious merchants, but no indigenous bourgeoisie emerged. Why was this? Historians interested in

[28] Today, it is scarcely necessary to document this statement. Evidence remains fullest for West Africa but supporting case studies are now plentiful throughout the continent.

[29] It would require more space than is available here to list the extensive literature which has now been produced on this subject. Two recent studies worth citing are H. Laurens van der Laan, 'Modern inland transport and the European trading firms in colonial West Africa', *Cahiers d'études africaines*, XXI (1982), 547–75, which has some perceptive comments on 'the decline of the middlemen' on pp. 571–2, and Ifeanyi Anagbogu, 'The history of the indigenous leather industry in Sokoto and Kano, Northern Nigeria, 1903–1960' (unpub. Ph.D. thesis, University of Birmingham, 1986), which distinguishes between the fortunes of the various craftsmen-entrepreneurs who made up the industry.

class formation in Africa have devoted more time to tracing the appearance of class consciousness among wage-earners and 'peasants' than they have to considering why a middle class failed to arise before the coming of European rule. Future investigation of this formidable problem will have to consider the economic constraints to entrepreneurial success, the institutional checks to the consolidation of entrepreneurial power (the difficulties of entailing commercial goodwill and wealth, and the extent to which the horizontal integration of the large firm via family and lineage also hampered the development of class relationships), and the interactions between merchants and governments. Examples can be found of theocratic states which sought to subordinate merchant enterprise, of states which were so closely identified with commercialism that they developed a form of pre-industrial corporatism, and of states (like Asante in the nineteenth century) in which the need to encourage but also to control commercial wealth became a central and persistent issue of political debate. At present, we can glimpse the diversity of these relationships, but not the central tendency – if there was one.

A satisfactory analysis of this problem will need to place indigenous entrepreneurs in the wider context of the opportunities open to them in pre-colonial Africa. This will involve a consideration of the availability and price of factors of production, the state of technology, and the level of demand. But it will also need to take account of the political environment, the sources of state power, and the degree of encouragement offered to business enterprise.[30] A programme of this order will require a new history of Africa, one that unites economic and political divisions of the subject while managing to master both.

The main weight of new research, as shown by the Paris conference and other recent publications, has been on the colonial period and on expatriate enterprise in particular. Impressive advances in knowledge have occurred along a wide front since 1976.[31] A good deal of well-researched evidence about the large commercial firms has now been published, though full histories of the major French houses in particular have still to be written.[32] Further work

[30] An example of a recent case study which is moving in this direction is Edward A. Alpers, 'State, merchant capital, and gender relations in southern Mozambique to the end of the nineteenth century: some tentative hypotheses', *African Economic History*, XIII (1984), 23–55. A valuable overview which has relevance for both pre-colonial and colonial Africa is John Lonsdale, 'States and social processes in Africa: a historiographical survey', *African Studies Review*, XXIV (1981), 139–225. Reference should also be made to the special issue of the *Revue française d'histoire d'outre-mer*, LXVIII (1981) entitled 'Etat et société en Afrique noire'. A brief attempt to sketch the long-run relationship between resources and state power is made in A. G. Hopkins, 'The World Bank in Africa: historical reflections on the African present', *World Development*, XIV (1981) 1473–87.

[31] The illustrations which follow are examples of important work published during the last ten years (other than the items listed in the appendix), and are not comprehensive. If injustices of omission (a particularly cruel academic fate) have occurred, I shall be happy to receive corrections and to make amends on a future occasion.

[32] Examples of work completed in the last decade are: Régis Robin, 'La Grande Dépression vue et vécue par une société d'import-export en A.O.F.: Peyrissac (1924–1939)', *Revue française d'histoire d'outre-mer*, LXIII (1976), 544–54; Roger Pasquier, 'La compagnie commerciale et agricole de la Casamance: prélude au régime concessionnaire du Congo?', in J. Vansina *et al.* (eds.), *Études africaines : offertes à Henri Brunschwig* (Paris, 1982), 189–207; Paula Jones, 'The United Africa Company in the Gold Coast/Ghana, 1920–1965' (Ph.D. thesis, University of London, 1983); Newbury, 'Trade and technology'; and van der Laan, 'Modern inland transport'.

has been carried out on expatriate involvement in rural production, ranging from the concessionaires of East Central Africa to the estates of Kenya and Southern Rhodesia.[33] The mining companies have continued to attract the attention of historians, and this has been linked, in the case of the British companies, to new research on the City of London.[34] Relatively little has been published since 1976 on banking in Africa, but knowledge of the other arm of commercial services, shipping, has been greatly improved, especially in the case of East Africa where, arguably, information was most lacking.[35]

[33] Leroy Vail, 'Mozambique's chartered companies: the rule of the feeble', *J. Afr. Hist.*, XVII (1976), 389–416, and the discussion in *J. Afr. Hist.*, XVIII (1977), 283–6; Leroy Vail and Landeg White, '"*Tawani, machambero!*": forced cotton and rice growing on the Zambezi', *J. Afr. Hist.*, XIX (1978), 239–63; *eidem, Capitalism and Colonialism in Mozambique* (London, 1980); B. Jewsiewicki, 'Le colonat agricole européen au Congo Belge', *J. Afr. Hist.*, XX (1979), 559–71; I. R. Phimister, 'Meat and monopolies: beef cattle in Southern Rhodesia, 1890–1938', *J. Afr. Hist.*, XIX (1978), 391–414; Ian Spencer, 'Settler dominance, agricultural production and the Second World War in Kenya', *J. Afr. Hist.*, XXI (1980), 497–514; Paul Mosley, *The Settler Economies: Studies in the Economic History of Kenya and Southern Rhodesia, 1900–1963* (Cambridge, 1983), and the discussion between Choate and Mosley in the *Economic History Review*, XXXVII (1984), 409–16; Robin Palmer, 'The Nyasaland tea industry in the era of international tea restrictions, 1933–1950', *J. Afr. Hist.*, XXVI (1985), 215–39; *idem*, 'White farmers in Malawi: before and after the depression', *African Affairs*, LXXXIV (1985), 211–45; Jonathan S. Crush, 'Settler-estate production, monopoly control, and the imperial response: the case of the Swaziland Corporation Ltd', *African Economic History*, VIII (1979), 183–97. The substantial literature on South Africa is best approached through the *Journal of Southern African Studies* and with the assistance of Timothy Keegan, 'Crisis and catharsis in the development of capitalism in South African agriculture', *African Affairs*, LXXXIV (1985), 371–98. Two valuable articles which draw attention to the importance of financial speculation are J. Forbes Munro, 'Monopolists and speculators: British investment in West African rubber, 1905–1914', *J. Afr. Hist.*, XXII (1981), 263–78, and *idem*, 'British rubber companies in East Africa before the First World War', *J. Afr. Hist.*, XXIV (1983), 369–79.

[34] See B. W. E. Alford and C. Harvey, 'Copperbelt merger: the formation of the Rhokana Corporation, 1930–1932', *Business History Review*, LIV (1980), 330–58; Bill Freund, *Capital and Labour in the Nigerian Tin Mines* (London, 1981); Peter Richardson and Jean-Jacques van Helten, 'The development of the South African gold-mining industry, 1895–1918', *Econ. Hist. Rev.*, XXXVII (1984), 319–40; Duncan Innes, *Anglo American and the Rise of Modern South Africa* (London, 1984); Peter Greenhalgh, *West African Diamonds, 1919–83: An Economic History* (Manchester, 1985); Andrew Roberts, 'The Gold Boom of the 1930s in eastern Africa', *African Affairs*, LXXXV (1986), 545–62; Jean-Luc Vellut, 'Les bassins miniers de l'ancien Congo Belge. Essai d'histoire économique et sociale (1900–1960)', *Les Cahiers du CEDAF*, VII (1981), 1–70. The most recent research on the City of London is cited in P. J. Cain and A. G. Hopkins, 'Gentlemanly capitalism and British expansion overseas. II. New imperialism, 1850–1945', *Econ. Hist. Rev.*, XL (1987), 1–26.

[35] Lionel Zinzou-Derlin, 'La Banque de l'Afrique occidentale dans la crise', *Revue française d'histoire d'outre-mer*, LXIII (1976), 506–18; P. N. Davies, *Sir Alfred Jones: Shipping Entrepreneur Par Excellence* (London, 1978); Stephanie Jones, *Two Centuries of Overseas Trading: The Origins and Growth of the Inchcape Group* (London, 1986); A. N. Porter, *Victorian Shipping, Business and Imperial Policy: Sir Donald Currie, the Castle Line and Southern Africa* (London, 1986); Robert L. McCormack, 'Airlines and empires: Great Britain and the "Scramble for Africa", 1919–1939', *Canadian Journal of African Studies*, X (1976), 87–105; *idem*, 'Man with a mission: Oswald Pirow and South African Airways, 1933–1939', *J. Afr. Hist.*, XX (1979), 543–57; Andre Huybrechts, *Transports et structures de développement au Congo: étude du progrès économique de 1900 á 1970* (Paris, 1970). Important research on Mackinnon and the East African shipping

The evidence presented in these studies addresses a wide range of detailed and frequently unrelated topics, and it would be misleading to suggest that it offers a ready-made formula for achieving spontaneous synthesis. However, at least one theme – the relation between firms and governments – is a sufficiently distinctive feature of the recent literature to deserve special mention here. The subject owes its prominence mainly to a revival of interest in the economic functions of what has become known as the 'colonial state', and is associated particularly with a route to history by way of political economy, though established approaches (derived, for instance, from the theory of pressure groups) have also contributed to our understanding of this topic. This perspective has the great merit of breaking down barriers between specialisms, and in doing so of revealing the sterility of an exclusively 'business' or 'political' viewpoint. The main defect of the approach is to be found in a certain looseness of terms and, as noted earlier, in an unwillingness to consider the historical applicability of theories of the firm. The term 'colonial state', for example, is commonly used in an all-embracing and ill-defined way (as is the term 'peasant'), and tends to be employed as a substitute for more precise concepts, such as government and administration, which it contains but ought not to supplant.

The question which has interested most authors is how far colonial governments can be seen as 'agents of capital'. This problem first appears during the period of partition, and has prompted some investigation of the influence of business pressure groups on metropolitan governments. The most intensive research has been conducted on the French colonial lobby, though it is still not entirely clear whether business interests had greater influence than used to be thought or whether French imperialism was, after all, inspired by a spirit of 'la gloire' which was largely independent of French capitalism.[36] The initial presumption that the newly established colonial governments served as the executive arm of expatriate business is now acknowledged to be over-simple. Quite apart from the problem of demonstrating that the influence which the firms sought to exercise was, in practice, an effective cause of official action,[37] recent research has revealed a kaleido-

interest is being undertaken by Dr J. Forbes Munro, Department of Economic History, University of Glasgow, I am grateful to Dr Munro for allowing me to benefit from reading two of his papers on this subject; see 'Shipping subsidies and railway guarantees: William Mackinnon, East Africa and the Indian Ocean, 1860–93', *J. Afr. Hist.*, XXVIII, ii (1987).

[36] Leyland C. Barrows, 'The merchants and General Faidherbe', *Revue française d'histoire d'outre-mer*, LXI (1974), 236–83; C. M. Andrew, 'The French colonialist movement during the Third Republic', *Royal Historical Society Transactions*, XXVI (1976), 143–66; C. M. Andrew and A. S. Kanya-Forstner, 'The French "colonial party"; its composition, aims, and influence', *Historical Journal*, XIV (1971), 99–128; *iidem*, 'The *Group Colonial* in the French Chamber of Deputies', *Hist. J.*, XVII (1974), 837–66; *iidem*, 'French business and the French colonialists', *Hist. J.*, XIX (1976), 981–1000; *iidem*, *France Overseas: The Great War and the Climax of French Imperial Expansion* (London, 1981); C. M. Andrew, P. Grupp and A. S. Kanya-Forstner, 'Le mouvement colonial français et ses principales personnalités, 1890–1914', *Revue française d'histoire d'outre-mer*, LXII (1975), 640–73; L. Abrams and D. J. Miller, 'Who were the French colonialists? A reassessment of the *Parti Colonial*', *Hist. J.*, XIX (1976), 685–725; S. M. Persell, *The French Colonial Lobby, 1889–1939* (Stanford, 1983); see also now Jacques Marseille, *Empire coloniale et capitalisme française* (Paris, 1984). Oddly, a literature of comparable prosopographical detail has yet to be produced for Britain, the 'nation of shopkeepers'.

[37] Some of these difficulties are apparent in Josephine F. Milburn, *British Business and Ghanaian Independence* (Hanover, New Hampshire, 1977).

scope of relationships which do not readily yield statements of continent-wide applicability. As in the pre-colonial period (a comparison which is surely worth pursuing), examples can be found of colonial governments which restrained expatriate enterprise, which promoted it, and which sought to combine business and administration in a form of colonial corporatism. Improved information has thus created a problem: bad data sustain simple theories of a complex world; good data inhibit easy generalization.

A successful solution to this problem will first need to define the character of colonial capitalism. British capitalism, French capitalism, Belgian capitalism and Portuguese capitalism were all very different animals, and it is unhelpful to suppose that the species can be adequately described simply by repeating the name of the genus. Assuming that the capitalist qualities of the metropolitan economy and society can be established, it is then necessary to see whether these qualities also characterized the colonial presence. This is not a simple inference. The boundaries of expatriate enterprise were not coterminous with those of the colony, and 'national capitalism' was modified abroad by foreign influences: British investment made its presence felt in the Belgian Congo, for example, and Belgian capital played a significant role in Angola.[38] Indeed, it may be necessary to consider the relationship between two maps of colonial Africa: one, already available, of political boundaries; and the other, imperfectly perceived, of the way in which the continent was partitioned by the expatriate firms.[39] In this connexion, it is perhaps rather strange that the concept of informal influence, which has been vigorously debated in the context of the nineteenth century, should disappear at the point when formal empire was acquired, because the exercise of power in the period following partition cannot be comprehended by focusing exclusively on the visible political instruments of colonial authority.

Even where the firms which dominated a colony were those of the colonizing power, it is important to establish whether they represented atavistic or capitalist forces, and in the latter case to specify the type of capitalism they expressed. Moreover, it is unlikely that the result of this enquiry will be valid for the whole of the colonial period because the structure of expatriate enterprise changed with the passage of time. Two main phases may be suggested, though these are not intended to be more than tentative guides for future discussion.[40] Initially, foreign enterprise was dominated by

[38] This theme is developed in Gervase Clarence-Smith, 'Business empires in Angola under Salazar, 1930–1961', *Afr. Econ. Hist.*, XIV (1985), 1–13. Despite the excellent work carried out in recent years on Belgian colonialism in the Congo, notably by Bogumil Jewsiewicki, Jean-Luc Vellut and Jean-Philippe Peemans (following the lead set by Jean Stengers) there still remains considerable scope for evaluating the relationship between the colonial presence and the structure of metropolitan society: did Leopold represent atavistic forces, was he a tool of emerging industrial and financial interests, or was he a modernizing autocrat who saw empire as a means of enabling the monarchy to adapt to the demands of the twentieth century?

[39] Hopkins, 'Imperial business', 274–9; W. G. Clarence-Smith, 'Business empires in Equatorial Africa', *Afr. Econ. Hist.*, XII (1983), 3–4.

[40] This suggestion is developed at slightly greater length in Hopkins, 'Imperial business', pp. 279–82. In 'Business empires', pp. 5–6, Clarence-Smith sets out an interesting threefold division between 'robber colonialism', mature colonialism and reformist colonialism. These categories may be particularly apt when applied to Equatorial Africa, but they prompt two questions of a conceptual kind: first, whether the term

white 'hunters and gatherers', who were certainly profit-oriented but whose activities were not conspicuous for long-term planning or for a capacity to postpone present consumption. From about the 1920s (though considerably earlier in the case of South Africa), a more settled view prevailed. The innovators were replaced by imitators, and a form of managerial capitalism (corresponding, in Weberian terms, to bureaucratic leadership) was installed. This phase was associated with the rise of the large firm and with a business strategy which covered the long term, but it was also characterized by the growth of imperfect competition, by a quest for security, and by the appearance of 'satisficing' aspirations. The period after 1945 saw renewed innovation (most strikingly in the spread of modern manufacturing) and keener competition, but these developments occurred within the structure of managerial capitalism, and the large firm continued to expand – to the point where transnational status was acquired or further enlarged. Evidently, discussion of 'the agents of capital' will rapidly become circular unless it identifies the precise form taken by 'capital', avoids reification, and anchors analysis to a secure historical base.

A similar set of questions needs to be asked of the political representatives of the colonial power. Following the interest, stemming from French intellectual influences, in the 'semi-autonomy of the state' (by which is usually meant the bureaucracy, or what old-fashioned liberals used to call the administration), it is apparent that colonial governments cannot simply be regarded as epiphenomena whose actions can readily be deduced from general propositions about 'the penetration of capital'.[41] The relationship between governments and firms was complementary and competitive: officials needed the expatriate firms to generate revenue and hence to pay salaries and pensions, but they also feared the disruptive consequences of unrestrained private enterprise; business interests looked to government to maintain civil order because it underpinned confidence and credit-worthiness, but they resented the regulations and taxes which accompanied the spread of civil authority and were critical of the limited support they received, whether in providing infrastructure or in responding to 'unfair' competition. The need to evaluate the precise balance of these forces by placing them in the context of a particular colony at a specific historical moment presents serious obstacles to generalization until additional research has been completed.

The current state of knowledge nevertheless prompts two comments which may be worth further consideration. In the first place, the evolution of economic policy in the colonies suggests an analogy with the history of expatriate business to the extent that official attitudes also passed through stages of innovation and managerial control. As in the case of the expatriate

'mature colonialism' has sufficient precision to describe the structure and strategy of the expatriate firms; and secondly, whether the organic analogy is wholly appropriate, since maturity is more likely to be followed by senility than by reform! However, there is now sufficient interest in the business history of Africa to suggest that these issues will be taken up rather than put aside – as happened ten years ago.

[41] Recognition of this proposition has led to a reappraisal of the intricate relationship between economic interests and colonial policy. For two rather different examples see: Elisabeth Rabut, 'Le mythe parisien de la mise en valeur des colonies africaines à l'aube du XXe siècle: La Commission des Concessions Coloniales, 1898–1912', *J. Afr. Hist.*, xx (1979), 271–87, and John Lonsdale and Bruce Berman, 'Coping with the contradictions: the development of the colonial state in Kenya', *ibid.*, 487–505.

firms, the managerial phase was one of 'caretaking' during the inter-war years followed by 'building' after World War II. Right from the outset of the colonial period, governments found themselves more closely involved with the economy than they had anticipated. This situation arose partly from the need to invest in projects (such as the creation of an infrastructure) which often failed to attract expatriate firms, partly from the wish to avoid the disruptive social and political consequences which frequently accompanied unfettered private enterprise, and partly from a paternalist ideology which justified official intervention as the approved means of achieving orderly progress. In its colonial manifestations, the liberal state promoted public enterprise abroad much earlier than it accepted it at home, and its actions helped to sustain hybrid bodies such as the British Cotton Growing Association after its capitalist progenitors in Lancashire had lost interest in their creation.[42] In the 1940s the conversion of colonial officials to the development ideal was demonstrated by deep immersion in new planning procedures, and interventionist zeal was recharged by the prospect of reviving the colonial mission. It is interesting to observe that 'administered trade', which Polanyi regarded as being a feature of pre-colonial Africa, may not have entered upon its highest stage of development until the close of the colonial period.[43] And, by a strange translation of reality into ideology, this stage was reached at a time when individualism was being pitted against state enterprise in the doctrinal battles of the Cold War.

The second comment concerns the capitalist nature of economic policy in the colonies. Colonial governments were more independent of expatriate business than some formulations allow; they intervened in the economy; and they justified their actions by appealing to an ideal, however vague, of improvement. Yet these characteristics apply to a command economy as well as to a capitalist one, and future researchers will need to establish a clearer categorization of policy than exists at present and then relate it to particular regions and periods rather than to Africa as a whole. At one extreme it is possible to envisage policies which, though interventionist, restrained development in the interests of political stability and concentrated on meeting the fiscal needs of the state.[44] Examples of this type of policy, which constitute what might be termed 'the African mode of redistribution', can be found before the advent of colonialism as well as during and after it. At the other end of the spectrum, where capitalist policies can clearly be seen, it is still

[42] The authoritative study is W. A. Wardle, 'A history of the British Cotton Growing Association, 1902–39, with special reference to its operations in Northern Nigeria' (Ph.D. thesis, University of Birmingham, 1980).

[43] Karl Polanyi, *Dahomey and the Slave Trade: An Analysis of an Archaic Economy* (Seattle, 1966). The debate over Polanyi's interpretation was at its height during the 1960s. For an interesting recent discussion (and additional references) see Paul E. Lovejoy, 'Polanyi's "ports of trade": Salaga and Kano in the nineteenth century', *Canadian Journal of African Studies*, XVI (1982), 245–77.

[44] Cyril Ehrlich, 'Building and caretaking: economic policy in British tropical Africa, 1890–1960', *Econ. Hist. Rev.*, XXVI (1973), 649–67. Some of the caretakers became warders. See B. Jewsiewicki, 'The Great Depression and the making of the colonial economic system in the Belgian Congo', *Afr. Econ. Hist.*, IV (1977), 162–72. For a recent case study see D. M. P. McCarthy, *Colonial Bureaucracy and Creating Underdevelopment: Tanganyika, 1919–1940* (Ames, Iowa, 1982), and also the perceptive review by C. C. Wrigley in *J. Afr. Hist.*, XXV (1984), 486–7.

necessary to specify the brand on offer. Some governments opted for minimal intervention which merely 'opened the way' for the expatriate firms. Others adopted policies which promoted particular types of capitalist enterprise. In the British case, for instance, there are grounds for supposing that economic policy favoured the interests of finance and commercial services rather than industry, a bias which was reinforced by the social background and education of officials – in Whitehall as well as in Africa.[45]

Whatever the validity of this thesis, the point to be stressed is that colonial capitalism ought not to be regarded simply as an extension abroad of the interests of metropolitan industry. The moral is evident: colonial officials may not have been 'agents of capital', and even if they were their franchise was larger and more varied than stereotyped references to 'capital' and 'capitalism' indicate.

One function which all colonial systems undertook, irrespective of their capitalist or non-capitalist character, was the defence of trade. The momentous organizational innovation of the seventeenth century, by which the large trading companies internalized the costs of protection,[46] was replaced in the late nineteenth century by a new division of labour which ensured that governments had a monopoly of coercive power. The cost of policing the colonial system, internationally and within individual colonies, was a crucial element in the formulation of policy, and it played an increasingly weighty part in the story of the demise of empire. This huge theme is worthy of consideration in its own right. Its interest in the present context lies in its possible relevance to the role of neutrals – firms which had access to the colonies of other powers while making only a minimal contribution to the overhead costs of running the imperial system. Private traders took advantage of the protection afforded by the East India Company in India in the eighteenth century, and the United States gained from the global order sustained by Britain during the first half of the twentieth century before adopting, in turn, the costly role of policing the world. Did firms from countries without empires have a cost advantage, however indirect, over their rivals or was this offset by the direct benefits which the colonial system offered to the home country and its representatives? This question can only be raised and not answered here, but its value lies in directing attention to the external determinants of the performance of expatriate firms operating in the colonies, and in underlining the distinction made earlier between capital flows and colonial boundaries.[47]

[45] Cain and Hopkins, 'Gentlemanly capitalism', part II, pp. 1–26.

[46] Neils Steensgaard, *Carracks, Caravans, and Companies: The Structural Crisis in the European-Asian Trade in the Early Seventeenth Century* (Copenhagen, 1972).

[47] Examples of 'neutrals' and minority groups operating in the colonies of foreign powers include: S. E. Katzenellenbogen, 'British businessmen and German Africa, 1885–1919', in B. M. Ratcliffe (ed.), *Great Britain and Her World* (Manchester, 1975), 237–62; H. L. van der Laan, *The Lebanese Traders in Sierra Leone* (The Hague, 1975); J. J. van Helten, 'German capital, the Netherlands Railway Company and the political economy of the Transvaal, 1886–1900', *J. Afr. Hist.*, XIX (1978), 369–90; *idem*, 'La France et l'or des Boers: some aspects of French investment in South Africa between 1890 and 1914', *African Affairs*, LXXXIV (1985), 247–63; and Margaret Gannon, 'The Basle Mission Trading Company and British colonial policy in the Gold Coast, 1918–1928', *J. Afr. Hist.*, XXIV (1983), 503–15. The Lebanese community in Senegal is the subject of a Ph.D. thesis currently being researched by Said Boumedouha at the Centre of West African Studies, University of Birmingham.

A consideration of performance involves an assessment of profitability, a topic which enters into the perennial debate over the costs and benefits of colonial rule.[48] Consequently, it is strange to find that no sustained investigation of the profitability of the expatriate firms was presented to the conferences held in Paris and London. This omission can be explained partly by the familiar problem of defective data. But it is hard to avoid the conclusion that it is also the product of a self-imposed handicap. There are hints in some of the Paris conference papers, for example, that quantitative analysis is associated with the unacceptable face of bourgeois economics, 'marginalism', and is therefore to be avoided. This justification may pass as shadow-boxing, but it will hardly stand up in a serious academic contest. An explanation which probably has wider applicability is that, for all its merits, the approach to business history from the standpoint of political economy (at least as the term is currently understood) is rarely accompanied by the training needed to handle accounting data. Yet this drawback ought not to be insuperable. Valuable work on the profitability of expatriate business in Africa has been undertaken from a variety of perspectives, and sets an example which should encourage future research into this difficult but incontestably important subject.[49]

Analysis of the post-colonial period has focused upon three groups of entrepreneurs: transnational corporations; state agencies; and indigenous firms in the private sector. Wide differences of opinion about the roles of these groups in economic development continue to exist, but the literature of the past decade also reveals an interesting degree of convergence which, being less publicized, is worth noting.

The transnational companies aroused considerable controversy in the 1970s, when they were seen as agents of 'late capitalism' charged with the task of perpetuating neo-colonialism and spreading underdevelopment.[50] The term 'late capitalism' suggests that the terminus was in sight, but it is hard to see how this judgement can be sustained, since it requires more knowledge of the future than historians can reasonably claim to have of the past. The argument about neo-colonialism became caught up with attempts to measure dependence, and yielded ambiguous results: large firms could dominate small countries, but they could also imprison themselves by making long-term fixed investments. In both cases indices of dependence turned out

[48] Hopkins, 'Imperial business', 284–9.

[49] See Catherine Coquery-Vidrovitch, 'L'impact des intérêts coloniaux: S.C.O.A. et C.F.A.O. dans l'Ouest Africain, 1910–1965', *J. Afr. Hist.*, XVI (1975), 595–621; *eadem*, 'Investissements privés, investissements publics en A.E.F., 1900–1940', *Afr. Econ. Hist.*, XII (1983), 13–31; Fieldhouse, *Unilever*, 560–76; Greenhalgh, *West African Diamonds*, ch. 5; and H. Laurens van der Laan, 'Trading in the Congo: The N.A.H.V. from 1918 to 1955', *Afr. Econ. Hist.*, XII (1983), 241–59.

[50] The volume of research on the transnational companies is too large to be listed here. An example of work undertaken in the 1970s is Carl Widstrand (ed.), *Multinational Firms in Africa* (Uppsala, 1975). An important case study is Richard Sklar, *Corporate Power in an African State: The Political Impact of Multinational Mining Companies in Zambia* (Berkeley, 1975); a recent work is Kanyana Mutombo, 'Les sociétés transnationales en Afrique: forces centripètes, forces centrifuges. Le cas de L'Union Minière et d'autres sociétés au Katanga' (Ph.D. thesis, University of Geneva, 1985); and an introduction to the subject is provided by P. Hertner and G. Jones (eds.), *Multinationals: Theory and History* (Aldershot, 1986).

to be poorly correlated with stages of increasing underdevelopment.[51] More recently, it has been suggested from both the right and the left (though for different reasons) that Africa's problem is not that it has experienced too much capitalism but that it has had too little.[52] Political scientists also regarded trans-national companies as couriers of a new international order, one that would dissolve the boundaries of the nation state, redistribute the sources of power, and redefine the terms of global negotiation.[53] This vision has not been abandoned, but it has been dimmed by the realization that co-operation between nation states and multinationals has frequently reinforced political boundaries rather than caused them to wither away.

The growth of public enterprise is generally agreed to be a legacy of the late colonial era, though it is worth pointing out that it also represents a reversion to forms of state trading which were widespread in pre-colonial Africa. Recognition of the crucial part played by governments in initiating economic development led to a debate about the relevance of Schumpeter's theory of entrepreneurship to the circumstances of the Third World, though this discussion has long since slipped, by a process of collective forgetfulness, into academic limbo.[54] In the last few years attention has focused less on the innovative role of the public sector than on its function as a redistributive agency. When they established the marketing boards, the colonial rulers discovered a means of taxing rural output which had eluded their African predecessors; its absence had restricted the resource base and size of the pre-colonial state. The leaders of independent Africa, though anxious to shake off the yoke of colonialism, have expanded the tax-gathering institutions they inherited with the result that the apparatus of state has become a resource in itself, giving access to connexions and contracts and serving as a vehicle for recycling revenues for political as much as for economic purposes. Yet discussion of this theme now shows signs of returning to its starting point: if governments are to innovate they will have to display Schumpeterian qualities; and if they are to manage their affairs efficiently they will need to conform more closely to Weber's ideal of bureaucracy than to his concept of patrimonialism.

Indigenous entrepreneurs have occupied a relatively modest place in the literature published during the past ten years, principally, it would seem, because they appear to have a subordinate role in economies which are dominated by entrepreneurial states and transnational corporations. There are signs, however, that local firms may be given greater prominence in the near future, both in the academic literature and in policy recommendations.

The performance of indigenous entrepreneurs has impressed commentators both by its durability in the face of seemingly irresistible forces and by

[51] A helpful survey of the current literature can be found in Colin Kirkpatrick and Frederick Nixson, 'Transnational corporations and economic development', *J. Modern African Studies*, XIX (1981), 367–99.

[52] Much of the impetus behind this discussion was provided by Bill Warren, *Imperialism: Pioneer of Capitalism* (London, 1980).

[53] See Samuel P. Huntington, 'Traditional organisations in world politics', *World Politics*, XXV (1973), 333–68.

[54] For a lucid and still highly relevant assessment see Douglas Rimmer, 'Schumpeter and the underdeveloped countries', *Quarterly Journal of Economics*, LXXV (1961), 422–50.

its flexibility in responding to new demands.[55] Current disillusion with the entrepreneurial record of state agencies, whether 'socialist' or 'capitalist', has shifted attention to the potential of small-scale and low-cost firms; indigenization programmes, combined with commercial specialization by the large expatriate firms, have created more opportunities for local enterprise; and the World Bank's emphasis on 'getting prices right' will reinforce these tendencies by improving incentives in the private sector – assuming of course that its recommendations are implemented. These trends suggest that the research produced during the 1950s and 1960s ought now to be retrieved from obscurity. It is unnecessary, of course, to revive the discussion of achievement needs; but studies of rural innovation, management, technical change and factor proportions remain illuminating and are still relevant.[56] This literature can be developed by adding new themes, two of which ought to be mentioned here: the activities of female entrepreneurs (a curious omission from the conference papers), and the role of the service sector, which has begun to attract the attention of development economists.[57]

If a comprehensive history of Africa is to be written 'from below', it must tell the story of small businessmen and artisans as well as of 'peasants' and wage-earners, and it must do so with a similar degree of empirical care and historical empathy. The art of the historian's science is not only style but understanding.

## CONCLUSION

It is apparent that the study of business history in Africa has made significant progress during the past decade. The weight of empirical information has greatly increased, and so too has our grasp of the important issues. Moreover, the contribution made by historians of Africa has merits which are not always displayed by established branches of the subject in Britain and the United States. Business history in Africa has remained part of the mainstream of historical studies and has not become a narrow sub-specialism. Consequently, researchers have shown a keen awareness of the political context of business activities; they have explored the wider social implications of entrepreneurial decisions; and they have been concerned to relate historical research to current development issues. However, in its present state the

[55] The literature on this subject is too vast to be listed here. But, in addition to the illustrative case studies cited in n.29 above, particular mention must be made of the valuable studies contributed to the Paris conference by Alpers and Berry, which between them capture the diverse shades of continuity and change affecting two very different societies. (For full references see the Appendix to this article.)

[56] The following examples, chosen from one country – Nigeria – were all researched during the 1960s, even though (with one exception) they were not published until the 1970s: Peter Kilby, *African Enterprise: The Nigerian Bread Industry* (Stanford, 1965); Nafziger, *African Capitalism*; Sara S. Berry, *Cocoa, Custom and Socio-Economic Change in Rural Western Nigeria* (Oxford, 1975); and Jan S. Hogendorn, *Nigerian Groundnut Exports: Origins and Early Development* (Zaria, 1978).

[57] An introduction to the history of women in Africa is no longer needed, but the service sector has yet to attract the attention which, arguably, it deserves. For an interesting discussion of the conceptual issues see Jagdish Bhagwati, 'Splintering and disembodiment of services and developing nations', in *idem*, *Essays in Development Economics*, I (Oxford, 1985), 92–103.

subject also exhibits defects which are more pronounced than in entrepreneurial studies dealing with Britain and North America. The market for knowledge remains imperfect; the conceptual apparatus tends to be vague and is sometimes misleading; and there is a reluctance to take advantage of the analytical possibilities suggested by the theory of the firm.

The persistence of these distinctive emphases in the study of business history is supported by custom and in some cases by ideology, but it is not well grounded in principle because both the scope of enquiry and the techniques adopted can be expanded without prejudging the outcome of the investigation. The treatment of historical themes ought to be determined by objective measures of their importance as well as by the instincts and affiliations of individual researchers. It will be interesting to see whether, during the next ten years, scholars can remove some of the barriers which they have erected in the course of their quest for truth. If they can, then the study of entrepreneurship will make a further advance, and the benefits of academic innovation will be felt not only among the relatively small group of shareholders, but by a much wider constituency of historians and economists interested in the relationship between Africa's past and its future.

SUMMARY

This article surveys research into the business history of Africa completed during the past decade, taking as a point of departure the author's previous essays, 'Imperial business in Africa', in this *Journal* (XVII, (1976), 29–48 and 291–305), and using as a point of reference the published proceedings of two conferences held in Paris and London in 1981 and 1983. It is apparent that knowledge of indigenous and expatriate business in the nineteenth and twentieth centuries has expanded considerably during the past ten years, and also that the studies produced by specialists on Africa have particular strengths: they remain integrated with other branches of history; they have illuminated the relationship between business enterprise and official policy; and they have been concerned to explore the wider social consequences of business activities and to relate historical research to current development issues. The literature reveals some characteristic weaknesses too, quite apart from limitations of source materials: the market for knowledge remains imperfect, and specialists often fail to incorporate work which is available; and their analysis is frequently limited by a reluctance to make use of theories of the firm and of accounting techniques. An explanation of these characteristics is offered, and it is concluded that once the present deficiencies have been recognized they can be overcome, and that the quality of research will improve still further as the subject continues to grow during the next decade.

## APPENDIX

This Appendix lists the case studies presented to the conferences held in Paris and London, and published in the volumes referred to in notes 2 and 3 above.

### 1. Paris Conference (Dec. 1981): Vol. 1

Edward A. Alpers, 'Futa Benaadir: continuity and change in the traditional cotton textile industry of Southern Somalia, c. 1840–1980', pp. 77–98.

Moncef M'Halla, 'Apparition d'entreprises capitalistes en milieu artisanal: le cas du tissu de la soie à Tunis', pp. 99–122.

David Birmingham, 'A question of coffee: black enterprise in Angola', pp. 123–8.

Philip D. Curtin, 'African enterprise in the mangrove trade: the case of Lamu', pp. 129–40.
Roger Pasquier, 'Les traitants des comptoirs du Sénégal au milieu du XIXe siècle', pp. 141–63.
Odile Goerg, 'Les entreprises guinéennes de commerce: destruction ou adaptation (fin XIXe siècle à 1913)', pp. 165–79.
Jean-Marc Bellot, 'Commerce, commerçants du bétail et intégration régionale: l'exemple de l'Ouest du Niger', pp. 181–204.
Jean-Jacques Beaussou, 'Genèse d'une classe marchande au Niger: continuité ou rupture dans l'organisation sociale?', pp. 205–20.
Faranirina Esoavelomandroso, 'Un marchand de produit à Tananarive dans les années 1930', pp. 221–33.
Christopher Fyfe, 'Charles Heddle: an African "merchant prince"', pp. 235–47.
J.-R. de Benoist, 'Les missionnaires catholiques du Soudan française et de la Haute-Volta, entrepreneurs et formateurs d'artisans', pp. 249–63.
Charles Geshekter, 'Entrepreneurs, livestock, and politics: British Somaliland, 1920–1950', pp. 265–83.
Denise Bouche, 'Un mythomane, l'Américain Parrish et les mines d'or du Bambouck', pp. 297–304.
Barrie M. Ratcliffe, 'Cotton imperialism: Manchester merchants and cotton cultivation in West Africa in the mid-nineteenth century', pp. 305–22.
J. Forbes Munro, 'British rubber companies in East Africa before the First World War', pp. 323–34.
Babacar Fall, 'Une entreprise agricole privée du Soudan français: la société anonyme des cultures de Diakandape (Kayes), 1919–1942', pp. 335–50.
Mohamed M'Bodj, 'Un essai d'implantation agro-industrielle coloniale au Sénégal: la conserverie de Lyndiane (Sine-Saloum), 1912–1919', pp. 351–65.
Jan Cabot, 'Des entreprises cotonnières en Afrique équatoriale', pp. 367–76.
Bill Freund, 'Nigerian tin mining and imperialism: from the Niger Company to ATMN', pp. 377–93.
A. D. Roberts, 'Notes towards a financial history of copper mining in Northern Rhodesia (Zambia)', pp. 395–409.
Yves Person, 'La crise de l'exploitation du diamant dans la région de Séguéla (Côte d'Ivoire), 1855–1952', pp. 411–22.
W. G. Clarence-Smith, 'Les investissements belges en Angola, 1912–1961', pp. 423–41.
André Nicolai et Claude Origet, 'Electricité et Eaux de Madagascar: un service public dans un contexte colonial, un contexte colonial au service d'une entreprise', pp. 443–61.
Albert Ayache, 'Monographie d'une entreprise coloniale: la Compagnie Sucrière Marocaine (C.O.S.U.M.A.), 1929–55', pp. 463–75.
Laurent Gbagbo, 'Les entreprises coloniales en Côte d'Ivoire à la veille de la Seconde Guerre mondiale', pp. 477–87.
Chantal Chanson-Jabeur, 'Entreprises et travailleurs des transports en Tunisie au lendemain de la seconde guerre mondiale', pp. 489–501.
Abderrahim Taleb, 'Essai de recension des entreprises dans l'Algérie coloniale', pp. 503–24.

2. Paris Conference (Dec. 1981): Vol. II

Romain H. Rainero, 'Note sur une entreprise italienne à charte en Somalie: la "Società anonima commerciale italiana del Benadir" (1898–1905)', pp. 17–24.
Jean-Pierre Chrétien, 'La fermeture du Burundi et du Rwanda aux commerçants de l'extérieur (1905–1906). Une décision de l'administration coloniale allemande', pp. 25–47.

Jean-Luc Vellut, 'Articulations entre entreprises et Etat: pouvoirs hégémoniques dans le bloc colonial belge (1908–1960)', pp. 49–79.
Bogumil Jewsiewicki, 'Capitalisme par procuration et industrialisation sans entrepreneurs: la petite entreprise au Congo belge (1910–1960)', pp. 81–100.
Monique Lakroum, 'Le jeu de l'argent et du pouvoir dans une entreprise coloniale: la Compagnie du Chemin de Fer de Dakar à Saint-Louis', pp. 101–22.
André Prenant, 'Le bâtiment et les travaux publics en Algérie: du secteur refuge à la croissance en marge de l'entreprise publique', pp. 123–48.
Bouziane Semmoud, 'Croissance du secteur industriel privé en Algérie dans ses relations avec le secteur national', pp. 149–64.
Hélène d'Almeida-Topor, 'Un aspect des rivalités impérialistes: la liquidation des firmes allemandes au Dahomey pendant la Première Guerre mondiale', pp. 165–77.
André Nouschi, 'Paradoxes et stratégies: du B.R.P. à la SONATRACH', pp. 179–91.
Claude de Miras, 'De la bourgeoisie d'Etat à l'avènement d'un milieu d'entrepreneurs ivoiriens?', pp. 193–211.
Bruce J. Berman, 'Encourage and constrain: the state and local enterprise in colonial Kenya', pp. 213–27.
Pierre Kipré, 'Grandes sociétés et entreprises individuelles dans la ville coloniale en Côte d'Ivoire à la veille de la Seconde Guerre mondiale', pp. 229–40.
Patrick Manning, 'L'Affaire Adjovi: la bourgeoisie foncière naissante au Dahomey, face à l'administration', pp. 241–67.
Bellarmin C. Codo et Sylvain C. Anignikin, 'Pouvoir colonial et tentatives d'intégration africaines dans le système capitaliste: le cas du Dahomey entre les deux guerres', pp. 269–86.
Janet Macgaffey, 'Business and class formation in Kisangani', pp. 287–300.
Bonnie K. Campbell, 'Etat et développement du capitalisme en Côte d'Ivoire', pp. 301–14.
R. E. Grupp, 'Transposition en Afrique noire de méthodes commerciales modernes: l'entreprise succursaliste "Châine Avion" en Côte d'Ivoire', pp. 353–67.
H. Laurens van der Laan, 'The European trading companies in West Africa: their withdrawal from up-country (1945–1980)', pp. 369–84.
Messan Adimado Aduayom et Ayélé Kponton, 'Place des revendeurs de tissus dans l'économie togolaise', pp. 385–400.
Philippe Hugon, 'Le développement des petites entreprises à Antananarivo: l'exemple d'un processus involutif', pp. 401–20.
Sara S. Berry, 'From peasant to artisan: motor mechanics in a Nigerian town', pp. 421–49.
Régine Nguyen van Chi-Bonnardel, 'Quel avenir pour les artisans sénégalais?', pp. 451–68.
Made B. Diouf, 'Migration artisanale et solidarité villageoise: le cas de Kanèn Njob au Sénégal', pp. 469–78.
Alain Morice, 'Les petites entreprises du travail du métal et la caste des forgerons à Kaolack (Sénégal)', pp. 479–91.
Alfred Schwartz, 'L'entreprise industrielle togolaise en 1980. Un contre-plaidoyer pour une industrialisation de l'Afrique à l'échelle nationale', pp. 493–506.
Albert Engonga-Bikoro, 'L'impact des groupes industriels sur les pays sous-développés: le cas de Elf au Gabon', pp. 507–17.
Jean Suret-Canale, 'Quelques données sur les entreprises en République populaire du Congo (1970–1971)', pp. 519–34.
Lucile Rabearimanana, 'Une entreprise coloniale d'après la seconde guerre mondiale à Madagascar: la Société Sucrière de la Mahavavy', pp. 535–51.

Abiola Félix Iroko, 'Les Forgas et Ateliers d'Adjaha: une entreprise béninoise post-coloniale née en France', pp. 553–69.
Jean-Pierre Durand, 'Conscience de classe et efficacité de l'entreprise dans l'Algérie d'aujourd'hui', pp. 559–69.
Jean Peneff, 'Les chefs d'entreprise en Algérie', pp. 571–85.
Etienne le Roy, 'L'Etat africain et l'entreprise nationalisée. Contribution à une lecture anthropologique de l'entreprise africaine à travers l'exemple de la SIACONGO, agro-industrie congolaise', pp. 587–604.

3. London Workshop (May 1982)

Catherine Coquery-Vidrovitch, 'Investissements privés, investissements publics en AEF, 1900–1940', pp. 13–31.
Georges Courade, 'La constitution d'empires agro-industriels étatiques depuis l'indépendance au Cameroun: politique de développement rural et/ou national?', pp. 33–48.
Richard Derksen, 'Forminière in the Kasai, 1906–1939', pp. 49–65.
Bruce Fetter, 'The Union Minière and its hinterland: a demographic reconstruction', pp. 67–81.
Peter Geschière, 'European planters, African peasants, and the colonial state: alternatives to the *mise en valeur* of Makaland, southeast Cameroun, during the interbellum', pp. 83–108.
A. Guimarães, 'Le chemin de fer de Luanda à Ambaca', pp. 109–24.
Robert Harms, 'The world Abir made: the Maringa-Lopori Basin, 1885–1903', pp. 125–39.
Barbara J. Heinzen, 'The United Fruit Company in the 1950s: trusteeships of the Cameroons', pp. 141–56.
Bogumil Jewsiewicki, 'Raison d'état ou raison du capital: l'accumulation primitive au Congo Belge', pp. 157–82.
Simon E. Katzenellenbogen, 'Financial links between the Congo and its southern neighbours', pp. 183–93.
Herman Obdeijn, 'The New Africa Trading Company and the struggle for import duties in the Congo Free State, 1886–1894', pp. 195–212.
Ulrich Sturzinger, 'The introduction of cotton cultivation in Chad: the role of the administration, 1920–1936', pp. 213–25.
Adelino Torres, 'Le role du capital bancaire dans les colonies portugaises de l'Angola et de St. Tomé de 1864 au début du XXe siècle', pp. 227–40.
H. Laurens van der Laan, 'Trading in the Congo: the NAHV from 1918 to 1955', pp. 241–259.
H. Laurens van der Laan, 'A Swiss family firm in West Africa: A. Brunnsweiler & Co., 1929–1959', pp. 287–97.

# [11]

*By Vincent Ponko, Jr.*
DEAN, SCHOOL OF HUMANITIES
CALIFORNIA STATE COLLEGE, BAKERSFIELD

# The Colonial Office and British Business before World War I: A Case Study

*❡ As Great Britain expanded its economic sphere at the turn of the century, what was the nature of the relationship between the imperial government and private firms seeking profits within the free trade empire? Was there a "well-planned and consistent program directed from the top," or was the government's so-called "high policy" toward business actually the result "of* ad hoc *compromises among various departmental heads" buried three and four levels deep in the Colonial Office? The experience of the Tanjong Pagar Dock Co. of Singapore suggests that the opportunities for British firms to exploit the resources of British controlled territories could be seriously circumscribed by the "arbitrary paternalism" of "crusading bureaucrats."*

One of the most debated problems in the history of Great Britain in the late nineteenth and early twentieth centuries revolves around the causes for British expansion during that period. Positions in this argument have ranged from strict economic interpretations to broad political views. In recent years, however, an ecological approach, in which economic and political reasons are interrelated with institutional and other factors, has won increasing favor. Instead of trying to reduce the phenomena of British imperialism to a single or simple causal explanation, emphasis is now being placed on how the British empire operated on all levels of its existence; how its variables meshed together to give it life. Insights into the "what" and "why" of Great Britain's world position in the late nineteenth and early twentieth centuries are, thus, secured from the reality of the phenomena's individual attributes and not from speculative overviews of why it came into historical existence.[1]

*Business History Review*, Vol. XLIII, No. 1 (Spring, 1969). 

[1] For a broad political view of imperialism as differentiated from an economic interpretation, see W. R. Louis, *Great Britain and Germany's Lost Colonies, 1914–1919* (Oxford, 1967), 155–60. The ecological approach and the shift in emphasis from origin to activity is reflected in such recent works as R. J. Hammond, *Portugal and Africa, 1815–1910: A Study in Uneconomic Imperialism* (Stanford, 1966), and Robert Heussler, *The British in Northern Nigeria* (London, 1968).

For the student of business history this approach to a very important historical problem has great pertinency. Instead of being swamped by vast generalizations, the relationships of business units to the imperial position and to the imperial government become important in their own right, and the role of case studies in the development of knowledge about such questions assumes increasing importance. What, for example, were the opportunities for British business units in the expanding British state, and how well did businessmen use these opportunities? In a free trade empire was British business free to exploit the resources of territories under British domination? What view did the imperial government have toward British firms in the empire and what power did the government have to implement its position?

It is in relation to the last question that this case study hopes to offer some light. Through an investigation of the attitudes and activities of the Colonial Office toward one business unit in the empire, the Tanjong Pagar Dock Co. of Singapore, this study reinforces previous suggestions by this author and others that the institutional structure of the imperial government was not above pursuing an arbitrary paternalism toward British business. The Colonial Office did so on the premise that British businessmen were so selfishly concentrated on the pursuit of profits that they had to be controlled by duly constituted governmental authority in the interests of the empire as a whole.

In addition, the expropriation of the Tanjong Pagar Dock Co. by the government shows that, within this paternalistic attitude, the Colonial Office could also operate with what might be called bureaucratic crusading fever: the optimum and final solution to a complex management problem involving the position of a private company in the empire was, in this case, to abolish the private firm to the extent that its operations could be assumed by governmental officials. Moreover, the records used in the preparation of this paper reveal that this spirit found its roots in the third and fourth levels of the Colonial Office's organizational structure, and that the specifics of the expropriation process were the results of *ad hoc* compromises among various departmental heads rather than an adherence to any well-planned and consistent program directed from the top. Thus, the Secretary of State for the Colonies was faced with the problem of either implementing the conclusions of his subordinates or defying the system of which he was a part. And, since he had almost complete power over all activities in and of the non-self-governing colonies, private enterprise on a unit basis in the British Empire before World War I thus existed at the mercy of the prevailing organizational structure in the Colonial Office.[2]

The fact that the position of private industry within the empire could be so precarious is historically significant in itself. Of equal importance, however, is the revelation that the Colonial Office felt no need to define a policy for itself and/or publish general rules and regulations under which it considered forceful action appropriate on its part. In the memoranda written by the staff of the Colonial Office advocating activity against a particular enterprise, one may find reasons for a particular position – extravagant expense to the government and/or the threat of Germany, for example – but it is clear from the process itself that most of the staff considered that the chance to exercise the Colonial Office's expropriating power was its own justification and that reasons for such action need only be advanced on an *ad hoc* basis in relation to particular circumstances. In the case of the Tanjong Pagar Dock Co., this attitude was rationalized ultimately under the label "high policy."

Before World War I, it is reasonable to say that the British government was dedicated to free trade principles, and at the same time concerned about its world trading position. It seems fair to say also that during this period there occurred an expansion of governmental control over those aspects of individual and business activity deemed clothed with the public interest. Legislation was passed granting the central government and local governing bodies the right to regulate individual and business activity considered to be in the realm of social welfare. The departments to whose lot it fell to implement this legislation were not always happy or enthusiastic about doing the work which accompanied their new responsibilities. In spite of this reluctance, however, the administrative structure of the state grew roughly in proportion to the demands placed upon it.

But what caused this new and almost revolutionary extension of governmental service and bureaucratic activity? A satisfactory answer would seem to hinge on the availability of case studies "distinguishing among different patterns of governmental growth, and

[2] For a contemporary account of the legal superiority of the Secretary of State in relation to the non-self-governing colonies, see Sir Henry Jenkyns, *British Rule and Jurisdiction Beyond the Seas* (Oxford, 1902), 91–104, 122. The importance of studying this institutional factor in relation to the limitations of discretionary activities within the empire by individuals and groups is employed by Robert I. Crane, review article of *Morley and India, 1906–1910*, by Stanley A. Wolpert (Berkeley and Los Angeles, 1967), in *American Historical Review*, LXXIII (February, 1968), 883–84. See also Vincent Ponko, Jr., "Economic Management in a Free-Trade Empire: The Work of the Crown Agents for the Colonies in the Nineteenth and Early Twentieth Centuries," *Journal of Economic History*, XXVI (September, 1966), 363–77.

the need to clarify the social and administrative ingredients in nineteenth-century statecraft." [3]

As far as the organizational structure of the Colonial Office was concerned, this tension between *laissez-faire* and collectivism gave rise to a cavalier attitude toward the sanctity of private investment within the empire. Despite the dedication of the government to free trade, and in spite of its worry over Great Britain's trading position, British business in the imperial territories under Colonial Office control not only had to battle foreign competition but prejudice on the part of a governmental department as well. Thus, in terms of what can be ascertained about the general relations between the imperial government and British business in a period when the British were becoming anxious about their world trade position, as well as in relation to what may be learned about the implications of personal, intradepartmental, and interdepartmental factors in the process of extending governmental authority over a business unit, an investigation of the takeover of the Tanjong Pagar Dock Co. serves as a needed and significant case study.

## I

In the early days of Singapore, most shipping using the port anchored in the pool or the open roads at the mouth of the Singapore River. Proposals to improve this situation by the construction of jetties and docks in the narrow channel forming the entrance to Singapore harbor from the west were made as early as 1846, but it was not until 1859 that work on the first dock was commenced by a company subsequently known as the New Harbor Dock Co. After this start, other firms were formed for the same purpose, including the Tanjong Pagar Dock Co.[4]

On September 1, 1863, the promoters of this enterprise, mostly well-to-do businessmen of Singapore, issued a prospectus calling for the raising of a capital sum of $125,000 (Straits Dollars) in 1,250 shares of $100 each, with power of increase. The next year another prospectus was issued wherein it was proposed that the capital of the company be increased to $200,000, split into 2,000 shares of $100 each. This proposal was favorably received locally and on Septem-

[3] Roy M. MacLeod, "Social Policy and the 'Floating Population': The Administration of the Canal Boats Acts, 1877–1899," *Past and Present* (December, 1966), 104. The first part of this article contains a summary of the conflicting positions taken by various historians regarding the administrative developments in Great Britain during the nineteenth century.

[4] Great Britain, Colonial Office, Straits Settlements. Eastern No. 98. Confidential. *Expropriation of the Undertaking of the Tanjong Pagar Dock Company by the Government of the Straits. Settlements. Instructions for Brief and Counsel to Advise upon Evidence* (August, 1905), 2–3.

ber 29, 1864, the company was registered in the office of the Registrar of Joint Stock Companies under Indian Act No. XIX of 1857 (An Act for the Incorporation of Joint Stock Companies and other Associations).[5]

Even before official birth of the Tanjong Pagar Dock Co., work had begun to construct the facilities it intended to operate at a profit. Moreover, year after year, the size of these facilities increased through an expansion program involving the company's holdings and the absorption of other firms organized for the same business purpose, including the New Harbor Dock Co. By the turn of the century, the Tanjong Pagar Dock Co. virtually controlled the wharfage and docking operations of Singapore harbor.[6]

As the Tanjong Pagar Dock Co. increased in physical size, it also grew bigger in terms of capital and found it necessary to change its controlling apparatus to meet the demands of shareholders not residents or near-residents of Singapore. Perhaps the group most vocal in its request for modification of the company's managerial structure consisted of shareholders who had once been active in the company's affairs in Singapore but had returned to England. This group wielded power in the fact that it included senior partners in firms doing business in Singapore, whose representatives, or junior partners, in Singapore held seats on the board of directors.[7] A willingness to promote the interest of this type of shareholder had not been absent from the company's policy in its early days and so moves in the direction desired by these men were not looked upon as extraordinary. For example, Clause II of the company's original articles of association provided that: [8]

> shareholders who have influenced business to the Company shall be entitled to have divided between them in proportion to the amount of business they have contributed such proportion of one-tenth of the net profits of the Company as the aggregate income from the amount of business contributed by them bears to the total business of the Company.

Since those shareholders most likely to help the company in its initial

[5] The Tanjong Pagar Dock Co. was the first of its kind in Singapore to be organized on a joint stock basis. Since no local authority existed under which it could be incorporated, its promoters had recourse to Indian legislation for this purpose. To make this legislation more effective, the government appointed a local Government Registrar in May 1864. George Bogaars, "The Tanjong Pagar Dock Company (1864–1905)," *Memoirs of the Raffles Museum, No.* 3 (December, 1956), 121.

[6] Colonial Office, Great Britain, Straits Settlements. Eastern No. 96. Confidential. *Correspondence [November 18, 1903, to July 13, 1906] Respecting the Expropriation of the Tanjong Pagar Dock Company, Limited* (July, 1906), #1, "Acting Governor Taylor to Mr. Lyttelton, November 18, 1903," pp. 1–2; Eastern No. 98, p. 3; Bogaars, p. 191–201. An expurgated version of this confidential series of documents is in Great Britain, Parliamentary Papers, LXXVIII (Accounts and Papers, XIV), Cmd. 3249, 1906, pp. 78–287.

[7] Eastern No. 98, pp. 8–9; Bogaars, 166–67, 173.

[8] Eastern No. 98, p. 20.

quest for business were those who had the opportunity of influencing shipping interests (that is, representatives of firms in Singapore using or providing ocean transport), and since such firms were usually represented on the board of directors in one way or another, this provision was intended originally to benefit the early supporters of the company in Singapore. However, this clause was retained in subsequent articles and during the course of the company's life considerable sums were paid to such "contributory shareholders," who continued to be either members of the Board or businessmen active in the company's affairs.[9]

Therefore, when the question of representation on the Board of Directors from shareholders in England came to be raised, it was not long before an agreement was reached settling such a problem to the company's satisfaction. Through a special resolution passed on March 16, 1883, and confirmed on April 6, 1883, a body known as the London Consulting Committee was brought into the management of the Company. In August 1899, the Tanjong Pagar Dock Co. was reconstructed and the London Consulting Committee was provided for as follows in the new articles of association. It became obligatory for the directors of the company to consult the committee on any alteration in the articles of association; or any increase in the capital of the company, or the issue of any unissued shares of the authorized capital of the company; or the borrowing at any one time of any sum exceeding $50,000 on mortgage or other security; or any proposed expenditure beyond $50,000, or any proposed sale or purchase of landed property for upwards of $50,000. The distribution of shares between persons resident in England and those in the Singapore area was as follows: shareholders in England 21,346 shares; local shareholders 8,654 shares.[10]

In the beginning, the formation of the London Consulting Committee did not change the company's operations or its financial policy to any appreciable extent, except that increasing emphasis began to be placed on the necessity of appropriating an acceptable dividend each year. The company had never stinted in this regard, having paid a dividend each year from the year 1870; but after 1883, it gradually became accepted that a dividend of not less than 10 per cent was to be declared each year notwithstanding the need for capital expenditures or the accumulation of reserves. Thus dividends

[9] Eastern No. 98, pp. 20–21; Bogaars, 169.

[10] Eastern No. 98, pp. 8–9; Bogaars, 170–71. Some individual shareholders, however, disliked the arrangement from the beginning and quarrels about the vote played by the London Consulting Committee were not absent from the company's affairs in the nineteenth century.

of 10 per cent were paid from 1885 to 1892; 14 per cent in 1894, 1895, and 1896; 14 per cent plus a bonus of $2 per share for the first half year and $3 per share for the second half year in 1897; dividends from 10 to 14 per cent with bonuses from 1898 to 1903; and dividends of 6 per cent and 20 per cent for the first and second half years respectively of 1905. Moreover, in 1899, the assets of the company were sold to a new company at the rate of one share in the old company to two in the new one. The share capital was at once converted from $1,500,000 to $3,000,000 without any further capital being subscribed.[11]

This dividend record was not challenged in any serious way before 1900 by either the governing authorities in Singapore or London. During the last quarter of the nineteenth century, the company's profits were ample enough to pay such a dividend, provide for depreciation of existing equipment, and at least up to 1885, to build or acquire new facilities in such a way as to meet the growing needs of the port. After 1885, the Company met its responsibilities to the increasing volume of traffic using the port, in which the proportion of bigger ships became the most significant factor, by a flexible but almost around-the-clock operational schedule.[12]

Such a mode of operation, however, strained the company's resources to such an extent that it became impossible to provide a reserve against unforeseen upsurges in business. Beginning around 1897, for instance, the number of ships visiting Southeast Asia began to increase at a rapid rate and this movement was accelerated further by the Boxer Rebellion. Moreover, the largest warships of Western Europe now started to take up stations in the area and to look to Singapore as a port-of-call. As a result of such circumstances, the operations of the Tanjong Pagar Dock Co. broke down and complaints of chaotic conditions at Singapore began to be voiced in alarming fashion. Because by 1900 the company held a virtual monopoly of the wharfage and docking facilities of the port, such complaints were impregnated with the accusation that the company had been derelict in its duty to provide for bigger and better facilities when such expansion was necessary for the health of the port and the security of the British Empire. It was at this point that the

[11] Eastern No. 98, pp. 3–16; Walter Makepeace, et al. (eds.), *One Hundred Years of Singapore, Being Some Account of the Capital of the Straits Settlements from its Foundation by Sir Stamford Raffles on the 6th February 1819 to the 6th February 1919* (2 vols., London, 1921), I, 18; Bogaars, 191–215. Subsequent critics of the company claimed that the 1899 reconstruction was intended to disguise the high dividend rate paid on the formerly smaller number of shares.

[12] In 1899, the Tanjong Pagar Dock Co. purchased the New Harbor Dock Co., but since these two firms had been operating on a joint purse basis since 1881 this action did not add to the Tanjong Pagar Dock Co.'s facilities absolutely. Bogaars, 192–99.

company's dividend record began to come under attack and suggestions began to be made relative to a government take-over of the company's plant along with provisions for government operation.[13]

Faced with this threat, the company decided to develop new plans for the expansion and modernization of its port facilities. In 1904, the managing director of the company, J. R. Nicholson, submitted a report which recommended an expenditure of some $12,000,000 for extensions and improvements of the company.[14] This scheme almost immediately ran into opposition from the London Consulting Committee, for the expenditure of such a sum seemed to pose a threat to the continuation of the now traditional dividend. Therefore, the London group stopped the circulation of the report "unless it could be accompanied by a statement showing how the Works recommended could be financed without endangering a dividend of 12 per cent." [15]

The reaction of the London Consulting Committee to the commitment of company funds for the enlargement and modernization of its facilities produced in turn a counter-reaction from the chairman of the board of directors, John Anderson. Anderson resigned his office as chairman and his position on the board of directors in protest against the action of the London Consulting Committee; and, at a general meeting held in March 1904, he made a long speech bitterly attacking the London Consulting Committee for putting the 12 per cent dividend before the welfare of the port and the British Empire, and for interfering with the board of directors in the management of the company.[16] This attack was made public, and although the London Consulting Committee attempted to refute Anderson by saying it was not against modernization as long as it was a balanced process in which all interests were protected, the end result was to place the London Consulting Committee in the position of being parsimonious protectors of selfish interests.[17]

[13] Eastern No. 98, p. 29; Eastern No. 96, "Acting Governor Taylor to Mr. Lyttelton, November 18, 1903," p. 1; Bogaars, 202, 215–17, 240.

[14] Eastern No. 96, Enclosure A in #5, "Acting Governor Taylor to Mr. Lyttelton, March 30, 1904," pp. 116–18.

[15] Eastern No. 98, p. 15; Bogaars, 223. As a result of this opposition, Nicholson returned to England to consult with the engineering firm of Coode, Son & Matthews. In October 1904, a combined report was issued which called for an expenditure of around £1,500,000 or $15,000,000 (Straits Dollars), an increase of some $3,000,000 over Nicholson's first estimate. See *Tanjong Pagar Dock Co., Ltd., Singapore, Report on Proposed Reconstruction of Wharves and Extension of Dock Accommodation by Messrs. Coode, Son and Matthews and J. R. Nicholson* (London, 1904).

[16] Eastern No. 96, Enclosure D in #5, "Acting Governor Taylor to Mr. Lyttelton, March 30, 1904," pp. 10–31.

[17] In a letter dated March 30, 1904, Acting Governor Taylor wrote to Lyttelton that "it is proper that the Consulting Committee should desire that when placing this report in the hands of the shareholders the directors should, if possible, show how the necessary capital was to be obtained; but the reference to the condition that a dividend of 12 per cent. was not to be endangered appears to justify those who are not, for one reason or

As a result of being placed in such a disunited position, the company found itself severely handicapped in its efforts to establish new facilities and in this manner sidetrack any proposals for governmental control. While he was still chairman of the board, John Anderson had supported a proposal suggesting that the Federated Malay States lend the company $10,000,000 at 3 per cent.[18] After his resignation from the chairmanship and from the board, Anderson continued to support the idea of governmental financial assistance in confidential letters and memoranda to the Secretary of State for the Colonies. In his communications with the Colonial Office, Anderson stressed the conclusion that the health of Singapore and sound management of the Tanjong Pagar Dock Co. were insolubly linked. Thus, he promoted the idea of governmental assistance to the company as a contribution to colonial welfare. Although he opposed the idea of direct governmental control, as through a port trust, Anderson strongly suggested that the government couple financial assistance with the abolishment of the London Consulting Committee and the acquisition of enough power to decide the membership of the Board of Directors or to veto decisions the government thought detrimental to the public welfare. Oddly enough, however, Anderson advised that the government deal with the London Consulting Committee as the real power in the company's affairs in the matter of financial assistance rather than with the board of directors. The Govenor of the Straits Settlements, Sir John Anderson, concurred generally with this position and advanced his views to the Colonial Office in related confidential letters and memoranda.[19]

Perhaps as a result of these suggestions by the two Andersons, Colonial Secretary Sir Alfred Lyttelton, in September 1904, turned to the London Consulting Committee rather than to the board of directors for an explanation and vindication of Tanjong Pagar Dock Co. policy. By means of a letter dated September 2, 1904, the Colonial Office asked the London Consulting Committee the following:

other, supporters of the Consulting Committee, in considering the action of the Committee as influenced by regard for dividends rather than by prudence in the matter of expenditure." Eastern No. 96, #5, "Acting Governor Taylor to Mr. Lyttelton, March 30, 1904," p. 6. See also Eastern No. 96, Enclosure D in #5, "Acting Governor Taylor to Mr. Lyttelton, March 30, 1904," p. 6, 31–34.

[18] Eastern No. 96, Enclosure A in #5, "Acting Governor Taylor to Mr. Lyttelton, March 30, 1904," pp. 7–8; Eastern No. 96, Enclosure C and D in #11 "Mr. J. Anderson to Colonial Office, August 17, 1904," pp. 62–66.

[19] Eastern No. 96, #6, "Governor Sir J. Anderson to Mr. Lyttelton, June 15, 1904;" pp. 34–37; Eastern No. 96, #8 "Mr. J. Anderson to Colonial Office, August 7, 1904," with enclosed memorandum, pp. 38–50; Eastern No. 96 #11, "Mr. J. Anderson to Colonial Office, August 17, 1904," with enclosed memoranda, pp. 59–68. Mr. J. Anderson had both a personal and financial interest in the advice he gave to the Colonial Office. He felt that the consulting committee had bypassed him while giving instructions to the Board's subordinates for the purpose of undermining his leadership; this he took as a personal affront. In ad-

(1) Whether it has been finally decided to carry out the contemplated extensions and improvements, and, if so, within what period and beginning at what date?

(2) What is the sum which the Directors of the Company have come to the conclusion must be borrowed for this purpose?

(3) Whether the Directors would welcome Government assistance in the matter of raising the money?

Furthermore, the Colonial Office offered to discuss the matter informally with the London Consulting Committee if the latter so desired before any more written communication took place.[20]

Such a meeting was duly held. When it responded to the Colonial Office's letter of September 2, 1904, therefore, the London Consulting Committee did so with the feeling that the road had been built for satisfactory governmental support. In a letter dated October 14, 1904, the committee suggested that the government help the company by purchasing some 8,000 shares remaining unissued of the company's authorized capital at $300 a share (a premium of 200 per cent) and, subsequently, lend to the company against debenture bonds at 3 per cent "up to the extent it might find it necessary to be assisted." In return, the committee promised that all such monies would be used for the work of development, that such work could start in six months time and be completed in ten years, and that the company would accept two representatives of the government on the board of directors and one on the London Consulting Committee.[21]

In accordance with Colonial Office procedure, this letter, plus the memoranda of Mr. John Anderson and Governor John Anderson, as well as previous documents on the subject, came under the scrutiny of and were minuted on by various clerks, departmental heads, and the Permanent Under-Secretary of State for the Colonies, before a reply received the approval of the Secretary of State.[22] It is interesting that of these subordinate officials, only the Permanent Under-Secretary voiced the opinion that if the committee's proposals were unacceptable, the government had an obligation to make counter-proposals before any decision involving expropriation was reached. The other civil servants grasped the opportunity presented by the

dition, he owned shares in the company to the value of £4,000. Moreover, for "patriotic" reasons he wanted only people from Great Britain to be on the board of directors.

[20] Eastern No. 96, #12, "Colonial Office to The Tanjong Pagar Dock Company, Limited," pp. 68–69.

[21] Eastern No. 96, #13, "The Tanjong Pagar Dock Company, Limited, to Colonial Office, September 6, 1904," p. 69; Eastern No. 96, #16, "The Tanjong Pagar Dock Company, Limited, to Colonial Office, October 14, 1904," pp. 70–73.

[22] P.R.O. CO 273/306. P.R.O. 885/5, Conf. Print Misc. 65; P.R.O. 885/8, Conf. Print. Misc. 154.

fact that the committee's program was not in accord with that advocated by the two Andersons and urged immediate expropriation. It was assumed by this group of minute writers that such a divergence, however unintentional, indicated that the company was not willing to forego high profits, that it was not going to reduce its dividend demands even in the face of what seemed to be an emergency situation. To these people, the company, or at least the London Consulting Committee, was interested solely in making as much money as possible out of Singapore and, therefore, public interest would always come second in the management of the company, particularly as long as the London Consulting Committee retained its power. The conclusion to this observation was inescapable: a situation where men thousands of miles away, who could not be trusted to put imperial welfare above private profit, were able to determine the destiny of a British possession could not be tolerated.[23] Moreover, it was specifically noted that the very existence of the company as it was then constituted posed a threat to the security of the empire. It was pointed out that two members of the board of directors were representatives of German firms doing business in Singapore and this logical extension of free trade principles was advanced as a danger that, if the company was allowed to live, German capital could gain control of the port for the benefit of the German Empire.[24]

Thus, expropriation was urged on the Secretary of State not for economic reasons but for the purpose of replacing a private operation with a public body on the basis that simply because it was public the replacing body would do a better job for Singapore and the empire as a whole. It was on the strength of this argument that Secretary of State Sir Alfred Lyttelton, after a meeting with his staff, during which both views were aired, chose to take over the company. Thus, on November 4, 1904, Lyttelton informed Governor Sir John Anderson that he had decided to expropriate the company instead of helping it by some form of governmental financial assistance.

In his letter, Lyttelton claimed that the company's offer was so out of line with what Sir John had been supporting as to offer no basis of further negotiation. Sir John at one point had urged that the

[23] This position was also reflected in the letter of Sir John Anderson. "The suggestion that there should be upheld a system giving control, direction, and the power or right of veto to a group of retired merchants 7,000 miles away from the scene, over the working of machinery on which more than one-half of Singapore's whole volume of shipping trade is dependent, is one that I most earnestly hope will never be adopted." Eastern No. 96, #6, "Governor Sir J. Anderson to Mr. Lyttelton, June 15, 1904," p. 35.

[24] P.R.O. CO 273/306. John Anderson had previously voiced the opinion that the existence of two Chinese members on the board of directors constituted a possible security leak and, therefore, a threat to the defense of the port in times of trouble.

government purchase enough shares to control the Company at $200 per share; to Lyttelton an offer to sell at $300 seemed to indicate that the company was not really serious in its proposal. Furthermore, the Colonial Secretary claimed that the purchase of the said 8,000 shares would only bring 500 votes with it, and, therefore, such an offer came close to being a trick. In addition, alternatives to the share purchase arrangement which would give the government a controlling voice in the company in return for substantial pecuniary assistance were brushed aside by Lyttelton with the observation that the London Consulting Committee would not agree to any projects of that sort "and we have no power to compel them to do so." Lyttelton's position, however, was most clearly stated in his observation that expropriation "on grounds of high policy of a Company occupying such an exceptional position and dominating such great public interests stands in no need of justification." [25]

Lyttelton's move to expropriate the Tanjong Pagar Dock Co. caught both the Governor of the Straits Settlements and the London Consulting Committee by surprise. Moreover, both Mr. and Sir John Anderson as well as the London Consulting Committee considered that Singapore was not being served in the best way by the decision. Sir John Anderson, for instance, even tried to change Lyttelton's mind by forwarding in a telegram a new proposal which would save the private nature of the firm, allow for the continuation of a dividend at around 4 per cent, while at the same time give the government a clear majority of voting power and effective control through the purchase of a sufficient number of shares. This scheme was turned down with the observation: "I know no reason to suppose that the Company would accept the offer which you propose and in any case such an arrangement would not give us the kind of control which I regard as necessary." [26] With this refusal, notice was also given that a draft ordinance of expropriation and management prepared in the Colonial Office was being sent to Anderson for introduction into the Legislative Council of the Colony.[27]

The London Consulting Committee objected to Lyttelton's action on the basis that it represented a misunderstanding of the company's willingness as well as its financial ability to expand and modernize its plant in Singapore. As a paying concern, it claimed that it could obtain funds from sources other than the government and that it had

[25] Eastern No. 96, #19, "Mr. Lyttelton to Governor Sir J. Anderson, November 4, 1904," p. 75; Eastern No. 96, #4, "Mr. Lyttelton to Governor Sir J. Anderson, April 22, 1904," p. 5; Eastern No. 96, #6, "Governor Sir John Anderson, June 15, 1904," p. 36.
[26] Eastern No. 96, #29, p. 91.
[27] *Ibid.*

sought governmental assistance because it was more desirable, not because it was the only source for funds. Moreover, it stated that Lyttelton was acting in accordance with inaccurate advice and pointed to the fact that under provisions incorporated in the articles of association during 1904, the purchase of 8,000 shares would provide 10,000 votes, not 500, as specific indication of such bad advice. Furthermore, it pointed to the fact that expropriation without any sort of public or judicial hearing was a forced deprivation of the Company's "future potentiality" and advanced doubts about the Government's ability to do a better job in the future than had been done by the Tanjong Pagar Dock Co. in the past.[28]

## II

On the basis of available evidence, it seems reasonable to assert, also, that the Colonial Secretary had only a hazy idea of what his recourse to "high policy" signified in relation to the process and aftermath of expropriation. The precise extent to which Lyttelton acted only because of the advice of his staff and other "experts" outside the Colonial Office and therefore did not analyze his own justification for expropriation is uncertain, but it seems reasonable to suggest that the Colonial Secretary was at least triggered by the majority view of his staff and that they were affected by Sir John and Mr. John Anderson's tirades against the London group. These people, however, did not present the Secretary of State with a clear-cut program as to what would and should happen after expropriation had been decided. What did happen may be viewed as evidence that it was *ad hoc* bias on the part of the organizational structure and not through analysis of the whole problem which determined expropriation.[29]

The two Andersons and other "experts" outside of the Colonial Office consulted by Lyttelton, for example, took the position that a department of government would not be flexible enough in its personal policies to handle the rapid and sometimes unexpected wharf-

[28] The Federated Malay States held 2,931 shares in the Tanjong Pagar Dock Co. and this plus the offered 8,000 would give the government 10,000 votes under the revised articles. Eastern No. 96, #30, "The Tanjong Pagar Dock Company, Limited to Colonial Office, December 15, 1904," p. 81–82; Eastern No. 96, #47, "The Tanjong Pagar Dock Company to Colonial Office, January 25, 1905," pp. 99, 102.

[29] Governor Sir John Anderson thought Lyttelton unduly influenced by Mr. John Anderson. "I am afraid that the statements in the late Chairman's speech at the General Meeting of the Company in March last may have induced you to take an unduly pessimistic view of the actual value of the Company's property and business, and of the strength of its position as regards the future." Eastern No. 96, #34, "Governor Sir John Anderson to Mr. Lyttelton, December 8, 1904," p. 87. In his letter of November 4, Lyttelton also presented expropriation as "a course which he has reason to believe, has already presented itself to the minds of the Committee as a possible solution." Eastern No. 96, #28, "Colonial Office to The Tanjong Pagar Dock Company, Limited, December 9, 1904," p. 80.

age and docking problems of Singapore. In addition, they claimed that the managers of the Tanjong Pagar Dock Co. would have to be retained if the government took over the Company because their experience could not be replaced and, therefore, the assumption of direct control by the government would mean nothing except added expense and work for the government. Lyttelton's staff did not accept the conclusion of these advisors, but they did use their case to convince Lyttelton that governmental control would be both efficient and feasible. Lyttelton agreed that after expropriation the Tanjong Pagar's facilities would be run by a board and staff consisting of the company's former board of directors and other appropriate personnel. Although ultimate responsibility for its operations would rest with the governor, this board was to operate as a commercial enterprise, as it had in the past.[30]

What seems not to have affected the thinking of the Colonial Office was the idea that the expropriation of a company which had not abdicated its work and was in a sound financial condition was not only of doubtful value or need but would also be an involved and costly affair. Moreover, the view that a board would not be able to push the modernization of the docking and wharfage facilities of Singapore any faster than the private company seems to have escaped the Colonial Secretary.[31] Thus, the expropriation process was entered into with what might be called a bureaucratic crusading fever: the best solution to a complex managerial problem involving business in the Empire was to place it in the hands of duly constituted governmental authority whatever the cost.

This view that the Colonial Office opted for expropriation without really understanding the problems associated with the implementation of such a decision gains support from the way in which the Secretary of State set up the methods and arguments for compensating the shareholders as well as from the structure and operations of the agencies set up in place of the Tanjong Pagar Dock Co.

For example, in the ordinance of expropriation Lyttelton provided for a court of arbitration to determine the amount of compensation

[30] Eastern No. 96, #19, "Mr. Lyttelton to Governor Sir J. Anderson, November 4, 1904," pp. 76–77. In a subsequent telegram Lyttelton stated to Anderson that "a letter was sent last night to the London Committee, giving notice of the intention to expropriate. You should consider the advisability of making a confidential communication to the Board outlining future policy and hinting at intention to make use of them and of their staff in the management of the business, though without committing yourself to retaining the whole of the present Board." Eastern No. 96, #29, "Telegram Sent 11:43 A.M. December 10, 1904," p. 81. One other "expert" was Sir Frank Swettenham, who first opposed a government board and then turned around and approved Lyttelton's arrangement. Eastern No. 96, #14, "Colonial Office to Sir F. A. Swettenham, September 9, 1904," p. 69.

[31] This point was brought out by a member of the Singapore Legislative Council in the debate on the expropriation ordinance. Bogaars, 241.

if no agreement could be reached between the company and the government. Since the government offered a price based on $240 a share and the company asked for something like $700 a share, a two way agreement was not possible and arbitration was necessary.[32] In preparing its case for the court, the government found problems and was forced to develop arguments either not considered by Lyttelton or contrary to his justification for expropriation. One such consideration was the degree of monopoly exercised by the company over the docking arrangements at Singapore. Lyttelton had argued that the company exercised a monopoly, and since it could not be expected to utilize this monopolistic position rightfully, it had to be expropriated. After expropriation, in order to counter the company's argument that its monopolistic role enhanced its value, the government sought evidence that such a monopoly could not be held for long. In other words, the government undercut one of the original considerations leading to expropriation by claiming that rising competition in Singapore, as well as in an area wide enough to include Japan, meant that the company could not for long maintain its position of monopoly. Therefore, "there would appear to be considerable justification for saying that the Company's income from its dock work is not well secured and that there should be a good chance of having applied to it, a small number of years' purchase." [33]

In other instances, the government could not arrive at such a clear-cut conclusion. Because little thought had been given to such problems beforehand, questions such as whether or not shareholders in the company had to be compensated for possible loss and cost of reinvestment, or whether or not the company's existing debentures had to be paid off immediately, and even the problem of what principle to follow in compensating the company, all became the subject of much discussion and uncertainty.[34]

In order to prepare the government's case, moreover, the Colonial Office found it necessary to employ a host of functionaries otherwise not part of the Colonial administration, including a high-priced English counsel and a similarly high-priced arbitration umpire, both of whom considered their fee to be too small. To coordinate this multitude, hundreds of letters and telegrams had to be sent, scores of meetings arranged, many investigations made, all of which cost money. Even this array failed to prevent the court from awarding an amount of compensation to each shareholder far in excess of what

[32] Eastern No. 98, p. 27.
[33] *Ibid.*, p. 22.
[34] Eastern No. 98, pp. 22–24. Later the English counsel and the firm of solicitors used by the Colonial Office recommended that the income approach be used. Eastern No. 96, #233, p. 239. See also Eastern No. 96, #237, pp. 243–44.

the officials of the Colonial Office had confidently expected. In his opposition to the expropriation process, Governor Sir John Anderson had warned that the cost of such action would be high, perhaps too excessive in relation to the objective. His reasoning was based on the analogy of costs involved in expropriating private gas and water companies in the London area a few years before under the authorization of Parliament. This view was rejected by the Colonial Office on the grounds that the gas and water companies' precedent was not pertinent, that Anderson's figures were exaggerated in any case, and that if more realistic figures were used the cost was reasonable in terms of the benefits of governmental control. As we have noted, these officials were thinking in terms of $240 (Straits Dollars) per share. The award of the court, however, came out to $880 per share.[35]

It is to be noted also that in preparing its brief, the government allowed insinuations that the Tanjong Pagar Dock Co. was neglectful of its duties and responsibilities to the empire to be considered as arguments for a low expropriation price. To secure a 12 per cent dividend, ran this train of argumentation, the managers of the company allowed their facilities to deteriorate and permitted narrow considerations of profit to obscure their vision of the future of Singapore and the Empire. In this spirit, for instance, the failure of the company to build a graving dock large enough to hold the biggest units of the British fleet in the area was used to attack the integrity of the company. The facts of the matter were, however, that the company had attempted from about 1885 to 1900 to reach an agreement with the government concerning the construction and operation of such a dock. During 1897, for example, plans and specifications were developed for a large graving dock estimated to cost £305,000. Because the dock was expected to service even the largest units of the British Navy in Asian waters the company decided to ask the Admiralty to contribute 85 per cent of the cost of construction. The British Treasury considered the proportion to be

[35] The arbitration award was based on a valuation of the Straits dollar at 2 shillings, which had been more or less standard for several years, but just before the award was announced the government revalued the dollar at 2 shillings, 4 pence. On the basis of this figure the award comes out to something like $880.00 per share. *Great Britain, Parliamentary Papers*, LXXV (*Accounts and Papers*, XI), Cmd. 2684, 1904, "#502 Straits Settlements Report for 1905," pp. 32–33; Sir Frank Swettenham, *British Malaya: An Account of the Origin and Progress of British Influence in Malaya* (London, 1907), 334, 334n; *One Hundred Years of Singapore*, 14. The share price had risen steadily from around $240 per share at the time of expropriation; in May 1905, shares were selling at $400. After the governor, Sir John Anderson, received Lyttelton's letter of November 4, 1904, he began to buy shares selling under $250 per share. Lyttelton stopped this activity on the ground that it would prejudice the government's case at arbitration. Eastern No. 96, #24, 25, 26, pp. 78–79. As noted the Federated Malay States held 2,921 shares. For the problems arising out of the procedure of arbitration see Eastern #96, #20–355, pp. 77–319.

paid by the government excessive under this proposal; although negotiations continued until 1899 no agreement was reached.[36] In preparing its case for arbitration the government ignored the company's position that the many years of negotiation with the government over this problem had contributed to modernization plans being held in abeyance until the government made up its mind and contended that it would: [37]

> surely be admitted as intolerable that between Colombo and Hong Kong on one line and between Calcutta and South Australia on the other, there should continue to be no dock large enough to take any British ship afloat. As Tanjong Pagar did not propose to provide it, some other agency must have done so, and then the Company would have had to permanently lose the docking of the warships of the largest mercantile vessels, and so many of the smaller merchant vessels as would be attracted by a modern and well equipped dock not necessarily working for "12 percent," but glad to accept profitable work to reduce its outlay on works of necessity provided and maintained for emergencies. . . . Apparently, therefore, the British Navy and the New Mercantile Marine may sink or swim for twenty years to come, but it must be without help from the first-class coaling station of Singapore, where the Company held such a strong position for affording such accommodation.

It was this condition that government ownership was supposed to correct.

From this point of view it is curious that Lyttelton requested that the directors of the company, who had failed to build such a dock, remain on the board which was established to run the facilities formerly owned by the company and that the managing director of the company be retained as the managing director of the Tanjong Pagar Dock Board.[38] Moreover, because the expropriated company was to be run as a commercial enterprise according to commercial principles, the Admiralty was denied representation on the board, even though neglect of its needs had been cited as proof of the company's mismanagement. Under government direction, even the Admiralty was to be treated as just another customer.[39]

[36] Bogaars, 203–205; *One Hundred Years of Singapore*, 9–10.

[37] Eastern No. 98, p. 27. The company's attitude toward this affair is summarized in Eastern No. 96, #47, "The Tanjong Pagar Dock Company, Limited, to Colonial Office, February 9, 1905," p. 101.

[38] Only two of the sitting members were dropped. Mr. John Anderson was added to fill one of these places. Eastern No. 96, #270, "Governor Sir J. Anderson to Mr. Lyttelton, August 23, 1905," pp. 262–63.

[39] Eastern No. 96, #207, "Colonial Office to Admiralty, August 4, 1905," pp. 222–23; Eastern No. 96, #287, "Governor Sir J. Anderson to Mr. Lyttelton, November 2, 1905," pp. 273–75; Eastern No. 96, #306 with enclosure, "Admiralty to Colonial Office," pp. 284–85. It is also curious that in view of the use made of the neglect of the company to build a dock large enough to take the most massive units of the British Navy Lyttelton could state in the House of Commons in answer to a question that he was "not aware that the admiralty contemplated any alteration in the existing naval arrangement with regard to Singapore." Winston Churchill as Under Secretary also stated that "the proposal for the

These provisions contributed after 1905 to the fact that the Tanjong Pagar Dock Board encountered many if not more of the problems of its predecessor, and that it failed for many years to provide the service and expansion which the government claimed the Tanjong Pagar Dock Co. could not and would not provide. It was not until 1908, for instance, that work began on the improvements planned in 1904 and not until 1917 that the bulk of these improvements were completed. By this time, the board had become involved in a legal quarrel with one of its contractors, which traveled all the way to the courts in London before settlement was reached in 1912, and in September 1913 it had become absorbed in the larger Singapore Harbor Board. It is interesting, however, that despite periods in which there was a lessening of the number of ships using its facilities, which in itself indicates that the emergency moves of the government to meet an expected even increase in volume were unneeded, the board, like the company, made enough money to meet its financial obligations and still show a profit.[40]

## III

It seems fair to conclude that in expropriating the Tanjong Pagar Dock Co., the government paid for the privilege of sponsoring an operation which conducted itself much the same as before expropriation took place and which could not accomplish modernization miracles any more than could the Company. Only an organizational structure permeated by the spirit of bureaucracy superiority to the point where its decisions are ultimately based on feeling and internal compromise rather than well-founded analysis would seem to be capable of such action.

In the early twentieth century, British businessmen confronted such an agency in the form of the Colonial Office. This situation is revealed not only by the evidence herein presented concerning the expropriation of the Tanjong Pagar Dock Co., but it is also not contradicted by the general correspondence between the Colonial Office and the Admiralty or the internal policy development during this period within the Colonial Office itself. In this regard, moreover,

acquisition of the docks did not originate with the Committee of Imperial Defense". Great Britain, *Parliamentary Papers* (*House of Commons Debates*, 151, 160), 1905, 254–55, 869.

[40] Great Britain, *Parliamentary Papers*, LXIX (*Accounts and Papers*, VIII), Cmd. 3729, 1908, "#582 Straits Settlements Report for 1007," pp. 7–12; LVIII (*Accounts and Papers*, X), Cmd. 6007, 1912, "#750 Straits Settlements Report for 1911," pp. 3–5; LVIII (*Accounts and Papers*, IX), Cmd. 7050, 1912, "#789 Straits Settlements Report for 1912," pp. 4–5. It is interesting in this regard to note that the financial health of the colony as a whole during these years depended to a great extent on the revenue derived from the growing and marketing of opium and that this period seems to have been a profitable one as far as this product was concerned.

it has been shown elsewhere that British overseas territories under control of the Colonial Office were required to place their supply and financial problems which could not be handled within their own boundaries or those of an adjacent British area in the hands of an office in London known as the Crown Agents for the Colonies. This body operated in part on the general principle of suspecting the motives and intentions of British businessmen with regard to the internal economic development of the Crown Colonies. Thus, this office followed procedures which subjected the operations of those British businessmen engaged in colonial activity to considerations not strictly in accord with the best economic allocation of resources as seen by the business unit itself or colonial officials on the spot. The economic requirements of the dependent empire were managed in a spirit of political as well as economic paternalism with the objects, as various colonial officials and businessmen complained, of making the Crown Colonies "virtuous and wealthy" even against their will.[41] This spirit, of course, partook of the same posture that is revealed by the case of the Tanjong Pagar Dock Co.; the government and its officials rather than private business, should dominate the colonial economic stage because governmental administrators were less likely to be selfishly corrupted, presumably, by the profit motive.

From this point of view it must be noted that the Crown Agents for the Colonies were under the control of the Secretary of State for the Colonies and that their operations received the outspoken support of the Colonial Office staff, to such an extent that it seems not unreasonable to say that in this area the attitude of the Crown Agents was just an extension of that of the Colonial Office.[42] The view that the Tanjong Pagar Dock Co. case was not an isolated incident determined by the strategic importance of Singapore can also be seen in the way the Colonial Office handled applications for economic concessions in the Crown Colonies. Generally, deliberations concerning a request for such a concession took place on the fourth and third levels of the Colonial Office's organizational structure before they reached the Secretary of State of the Colonies for a decision (if his decision was needed). These deliberations can be said to have been

[41] Ponko, *op. cit.* 363–75. However, selected British business units in Great Britain benefited from the operations of the Crown Agents for the Colonies in the procurement of supplies for the dependent empire as well as in the financing of Crown Colony operations.

[42] For example, see Great Britain, *Parliamentary Papers*, XVI (*Reports from Commissioners, Inspectors, and Others, VIII*), Cmd. 4473, 1909, "Crown Agents Enquiry Committee Report to the Right Honourable the Earl of Crewe, K.G.P.C., etc., etc., Secretary of State for the Colonies," in *Report of the Committee of Enquiry into the Organization of the Crown Agents Office with a Despatch hereon from the Secretary of State for the Colonies*, i.

marked by an absence of economic guidelines and by the acceptance of the spirit that action need only be advocated on an *ad hoc* basis in relation to prevailing circumstances. Thus, opportunity was given to those engaged in such discussions to exhibit what might be called a paternal bias in support of governmental control over private enterprise with regard to the economic management of the empire. The view that a British business unit would seek to selfishly exploit the economic opportunities of a particular colony to the detriment of that colony or the empire as a whole if not checked or dominated by the apparatus of the Colonial Office was not lacking. Control over the internal economic development of the empire was seen ultimately as an extension of Colonial Office's general position and not in relation to the satisfying of any criteria set up to help keep decisions about concessions from becoming arbitrary.[43]

Thus, when placed in relation to the work of the Crown Agents for the Colonies, the manner and form of granting concessions in the Colonies, as well as in terms of the general development of the Colonial Office and its correspondence with the Admiralty, the case of the Tanjong Pagar Dock Co. may be said to be "representative" of the attitude of the Colonial Office toward British business before World War I. The evidence concerning the expropriation of the company, supported as it is by other sources, indicates that the opportunities of the business unit to internally exploit the resources of British controlled territories could be circumscribed by the *ad hoc,* uneconomic, somewhat overbearing manner in which the Colonial Office exercised its power and responsibilities.

[43] Colonial Office, Great Britain, Miscellaneous No. 269. Confidential. *Report of the Concessions Committee with Regard to the System of Dealing with Concessions in the Crown Colonies and Protectorates,* 1–9.

# [12]

# A Railroad For Turkey

## The Chester Project, 1908–1913

*There was an interlude when enchantment with Dollar Diplomacy overcame the reluctance of Washington to become involved in Near East politics. The Chester project, however, was defeated by German imperialism, lack of popular support for business ambitions abroad, and vacillation by the promoters themselves. The time for effective alliance between the State Department and American businessmen was not yet at hand.*

*by John A. DeNovo*

ASSOCIATE PROFESSOR OF AMERICAN HISTORY
AT THE PENNSYLVANIA STATE UNIVERSITY

Early in the twentieth century, Admiral Colby M. Chester and associates developed a gigantic program for railroad and mining ventures in Asiatic Turkey. They were beguiled by a vision of great commercial and industrial possibilities for Americans in the Ottoman Empire, a mirage similar to that which had already fostered great expectations for American economic enterprise in Latin America and the Far East. In all three instances, the advocates were optimistic about foreign markets for American industrial surpluses.[1]

Had the ambitions of the Chester syndicate materialized, they might well have altered the course of American relations with the Middle East, and even the course of Turkish history. Although the project turned out to be a colossal and embarrassing failure, the active support of the Taft administration for the American enterprisers comprises a revealing chapter in American diplomatic and business history. In assisting the Chester interests the Department of State departed drastically, but only temporarily, from traditional noninvolvement in the international politics of the Eastern Question.

When Admiral Chester first became interested in the possibilities for economic undertakings in the Ottoman Empire, American interests there were still largely humanitarian, consisting of churches and schools nurtured by missionaries and educators.[2] Strategic interests on the part of the United States were nonexistent, business investments negligible, and trade during the nineteenth century was modest in volume.[3] Precisely because the United States had a humanitarian record not compromised by any vital political stake or ambition in Turkey, American prestige was high among the Turks, who were receptive to expanding commercial and financial ties with American businessmen.

Chester's plans were taking shape at a time when American businessmen found sympathy and support in Washington for their foreign enterprises. President William H. Taft and Secretary of State Philander C. Knox were proud to use the resources of government to promote Dollar Diplomacy, an ambiguous concept with invidious connotations, at least for later generations. As Knox expressed it, "Today diplomacy works for trade, and the Foreign Offices of the world are powerful engines for the promotion of commerce of each country. With the expansion of American commerce it

[1] By a Diplomatist [Lewis Einstein], *American Foreign Policy* (Boston and New York, 1909), pp. 146–147, 155–156; J. Fred Rippy, *The Caribbean Danger Zone* (New York, 1940), p. 135; Charles S. Campbell, Jr., *Special Business Interests and the Open Door Policy* (New Haven, 1951), Chap. 1 ("The Bogey of the Surplus"). As early as the 1880's, prominent Americans thought Latin America might serve as a market for industrial surpluses of the United States. See Russell H. Bastert, "James G. Blaine and the Origins of the First International American Conference" (Ph.D. thesis, Yale University, 1952), Chap. 8.

[2] Leland J. Gordon, *American Relations with Turkey, 1830–1930: An Economic Interpretation* (Philadelphia, 1932), pp. 221–251; Nasim Sousa, *The Capitulatory Régime of Turkey: Its History, Origins, and Nature* (Baltimore, 1933), Chap. 7.

[3] William C. Askew and J. Fred Rippy, "The United States and Europe's Strife, 1908–1913," *Journal of Politics*, Vol. IV (Feb., 1942), pp. 68–69, 73–74; Samuel E. Morison, *The Maritime History of Massachusetts, 1783–1860* (Boston and New York, 1921), pp. 181, 277, 291–293; Gordon, *American Relations with Turkey*, Chaps. 3 and 4; Sousa, *The Capitulatory Régime*, pp. 252–253; Charles M. Pepper, *Report on Trade Conditions in Asiatic Turkey* (Washington, 1907), *passim*, especially p. 28. Pepper was a special agent of the Department of Commerce and Labor.

became imperative that American exporters should have equally efficient support from their government." [4]

When it came to Turkey, both the policy-makers in Washington and American businessmen exhibited dilettantism. At best, they comprehended only vaguely the nature of Great Power politics in the Ottoman setting. For several decades the Ottoman Empire, already stereotyped as the "sick man of Europe," had been in the throes of disintegration. As the Empire fell apart, the desire of each of six European Powers (Great Britain, France, Germany, Italy, Austria-Hungary, and Russia) to prevent a competitor from improving its position enabled the Ottoman Empire to survive a little longer by playing off one rival against another.[5] These rivals did not welcome the appearance of the United States.

Not so with the Young Turks who had gained power in the revolution of July, 1908, when they forced the Sultan to institute a parliamentary regime full of bright but unrealized promise for a better Turkey. Among their plans for modernizing their country, the Young Turks placed economic development high on the list with proposals for extensive railroad and highway construction, port development, irrigation projects, public utilities, and mineral exploitation. Turkey's appalling lack of native capital and managerial skill for her own economic development required her to look abroad for assistance. While the Turks did not lack bids from Europeans anxious to pour capital into the country, they suspected that the motive was to advance the financial and political interests of the European financial groups and their governments at the expense of Turkey. Because the American position was unique in its relative freedom from similar suspicions, many Turks saw an opportunity to use American capital as a possible counterweight for European political ambitions.[6]

* * *

[4] [Philander C. Knox], Memorandum on the State Department [March, 1909], Philander C. Knox MSS (Division of Manuscripts, Library of Congress), Vol. VI, p. 949. See also copy of an address given in Baltimore by Huntington Wilson on Dollar Diplomacy, May 4, 1911, Knox MSS, Vol. XIV, pp. 2,313–2,315, and Henry Pringle, *The Life and Times of William Howard Taft, A Biography* (2 vols.; New York and Toronto, 1939), Vol. II, pp. 678–699, *passim*. The dual nature of Dollar Diplomacy is stressed in Julius W. Pratt, *America's Colonial Experiment: How the United States Gained, Governed, and in Part Gave Away a Colonial Empire* (New York, 1950), pp. 131–132. See also Rippy, *Caribbean Danger Zone*, pp. 134–136.

[5] Ernest E. Ramsaur, Jr., *The Young Turks: Prelude to the Revolution of 1908* (Princeton, 1957), pp. 140-143; Edward Mead Earle, *Turkey, the Great Powers, and the Bagdad Railway: A Study in Imperialism* (New York, 1923), *passim*, especially pp. 3–8, Chaps. 2 and 9.

[6] Milo A. Jewett (Consul at Trebizond, Turkey) to the Assistant Secretary of State, April 10, 1909; Jewett (on leave in Washington) to Assistant Secretary of State, June 23, 1909, both Department of State Archives (National Archives, Washington, D. C.), file 5012/16–18 and /19–20; Lewis Einstein (Chargé d'Affaires, Constantinople), to Knox, No. 1045, confidential, July 15, 1909, Department of State Archives, file 20784/–; Einstein

Admiral Chester's belief that Turkey afforded great opportunities for American entrepreneurs had begun to crystallize as early as 1900 when, as a captain commanding the U.S.S. *Kentucky*, he was sent officially to press for payment of damage claims to American property resulting from the Armenian massacres of the previous decade.[7] Several years later the Admiral's views were reinforced by the enthusiasm of C. Arthur Moore, Jr., whose visit to Turkey in 1906 impressed him with the possibilities of a railroad from Aleppo to the Mediterranean coast near Alexandretta. Moore persuaded his brother-in-law, Colby M. Chester, Jr., son of the Admiral, that the project had possibilities, and the two gained the support of their fathers for the Aleppo-Mediterranean project.[8] The younger Moore's father, a partner in the company of Manning, Maxwell, and Moore, an established firm dealing in railroad supplies, possessed the business standing necessary for enlisting financial support in their project. At this time, the younger Chester was serving as treasurer of Manning, Maxwell, and Moore. The Admiral's other son, Commander Arthur Chester, was designated to assist in the preliminary surveys for the contemplated line.[9]

The available records, though leaving some obvious questions unanswered, are sufficient to delineate the origins of the syndicate.[10] In the summer of 1908, the Admiral represented the United States in Geneva at the Ninth International Conference of Geographers. With the benediction of the State and Navy Departments he then journeyed to Constantinople for the express purpose of investigating American commercial possibilities in the Ottoman Empire. On this mission he represented not only the Chester and Moore interests, but was acting also as an agent of the Boston and New York Chambers of Commerce and the New York State Board of Trade.[11] Since

to Knox, No. 1065, very confidential, July 29, 1909, file 5012/21. Hereafter, all citations to the Department of State Archives will be designated "DS" followed by the file number. All Department of State records cited are in Record Group 59. See also Gordon, *American Relations with Turkey*, pp. 252–256, 264; Earle, *The Bagdad Railway*, pp. 13, 19.

[7] *Papers Relating to the Foreign Relations of the United States, 1901* (Washington, 1902), pp. 514–515; Allan Wescott, "Colby Mitchell Chester," in Allen Johnson *et al.* (eds.), *Dictionary of American Biography* (22 vols.; New York, 1944–1958), Vol. XXI, p. 171; Lloyd C. Griscom, *Diplomatically Speaking* (Boston, 1940), pp. 169–173.

[8] Laurence Shaw Mayo, "The Chester Concession under Fire," *Asia*, Vol. XXIII (July, 1923), p. 521. The elder Chester had retired from the Navy as a Rear Admiral in 1906.

[9] James M. Laidlaw to Knox, Nov. 24, 1909, DS 5012/31–32. Arthur Chester retired from the Navy in 1905.

[10] The business records of the Chester syndicate are in the possession of Mr. Henry Woodhouse of New York City, but he has not made them available to scholars. (Correspondence of the writer with Mr. Woodhouse between 1952 and 1957 and an interview in 1955.)

[11] C. A. Moore (President of Manning, Maxwell, and Moore) to Secretary of State Elihu Root, Oct. 14, 1908; Root to V. H. Metcalf (Secretary of the Navy), Oct. 20, 1908; both DS 16251/–; Robert Bacon to Diplomatic Officers of the United States in Europe, April 8, 1908, DS 2793/11A.

the Admiral's original contacts were with Sultan Abdul Hamid, the Americans had to reopen negotiations with the new Young Turk regime after the revolution of 1908–1909.

The original plan for an American-built railroad from Aleppo to the Mediterranean ran into trouble when German interests protested that the line would traverse an area already assigned to their Berlin to Baghdad project.[12] Encouraged, however, by the cordial reception the Young Turks had given the Admiral's overtures, the Chester interests in the next few months enlarged their original plans into a more ambitious program of railroad building and mineral development.

By the late summer of 1909 the Chester syndicate had applied for concessions to cover lines eastward from Sivas in central Anatolia by way of Harput, Arghana, Diabekir, Mosul, and Kirkuk to Sulaimaniya near the Persian border. Branch lines were projected from the main line to the Black Sea port of Samsun, to the Mediterranean *via* Aleppo, and to Van *via* Bitlis.[13] These lines, comprising at least 2,000 kilometers, would have entailed expenditures estimated at more than $100,000,000.[14] These projected routes ran through areas reputedly rich in minerals, which the enterprisers intended to exploit along the railroad rights of way. A major attraction for some of the participants lay in the prospects for the sale of railroad construction equipment and rolling stock.

Actually, the Chester associates were not the first Americans to express interest in railroad lines projected for Asia Minor. Dr. Bruce Glasgow, representing the Anglo-American firm of J. G. White and Company, had applied earlier (July, 1909) for most of the same lines. Glasgow, furthermore, had filed his claims with the American Embassy in Constantinople and received diplomatic assistance from embassy officials, who reported that the White Company was making good progress with the Turks during the summer.[15]

Under these circumstances, the pique of embassy officials with Arthur Chester, Constantinople agent of the Chester interests, is

[12] Lewis Einstein (Chargé d'Affaires, Constantinople) to Knox. No. 1045, July 15, 1909, DS 20784/–.

[13] During the course of protracted negotiations wtih Turkish officials the exact lines to be included in the Chester Project underwent frequent revision. Henry Janes (Chargé in Constantinople) to Knox, No. 126, April 1, 1910, DS 867.602 Ot 81/13. Russia objected to the invasion of her sphere in northern Anatolia by the Sivas-Samsun branch, which the Ottoman government eventually withdrew from the Chester Project. There was extended controversy over the Mediterranean terminal with the syndicate insisting on Suediah, while the Turks held out for Alexandretta or Yourmoutalik on the opposite side of the bay.

[14] Einstein to Knox, No. 1106, Aug. 27, 1909, DS 5012/25–26; Straus to Knox, No. 2, Sept. 23, 1909, DS 5012/29; A. Rustem Bey (Ottoman Chargé in Washington) to Knox, No. 50, Dec. 21, 1909, DS 5012/39.

[15] Lewis Einstein (Chargé at Constantinople) to the Secretary of State No. 1045, July 15, 1909, DS 20784/–; Einstein to Secretary of State, No. 1065, July 29, 1909, DS 5012/21.

understandable. Previously, the embassy had helped him pursue the more modest Aleppo-Mediterranean railroad scheme and an application for installing a telephone system in Constantinople. This time, however, he acted without prior consultation at the embassy before confronting Lewis Einstein, American Chargé, with the news that he had applied for many of the same lines the White Company was seeking. Even then, Chester did not formally file his new claims with the embassy, although Einstein agreed to introduce him to appropriate Turkish officials.[16]

For his part, Arthur Chester felt his plans for American enterprise in Turkey were being obstructed from all sides. Some of his sponsors at home appeared to question his application for the additional lines in Asia Minor. Chester complained also that Glasgow of the White Company was spreading information that he was a fraud, that Einstein and the embassy were plotting with Glasgow against him, and that articles in the Turkish press were attacking his proposals unfairly.[17]

The competition between two American groups for the same lines embarrassed the State Department, which feared the rivalry might jeopardize the favorable disposition of the Turks toward American capital.[18] Einstein informed his Washington superiors that he tried to support Glasgow, whose success, he believed, would mean a very great victory for American enterprise and prestige in the Near East. When the Chester interests spurned Einstein's urging that they come to an agreement with the White Company, the Chargé felt he must support both groups diplomatically without partiality, leaving Turkish officials to decide between them.[19]

The upshot of the Chester-Glasgow competition was the virtual elimination of the White Company by late summer. The Chesters offered superior terms — a broad-gauge instead of a narrow-gauge line, and a land grant of 10 kilometers instead of 20 on either side of the railway. But on August 20, the Turkish parliament's Committee on Public Works postponed action to allow additional bidding. The Turks knew how to drive a hard bargain and were maneuvering for the most advantageous terms. The granting of the

[16] *Ibid.*; Einstein to Knox, No. 1081, Aug. 5, 1909, DS 20784/1; Einstein to Knox, No. 1106, Aug. 27, 1909, DS 5012/25–26.

[17] To his father he wrote: "I hate to think what I will do if I am not backed at home. I have staked my honor on our desire to take this option. . . ." Chester would have to bury himself "on a lonely island away from mankind" if he was not backed. "I absolutely have to carry this through. There is no turning back." Arthur Chester to Admiral Colby M. Chester, Aug. 29, 1909, Chester Family Papers through the courtesy of Colby M. Chester, Jr.

[18] Straus to Knox, No. 2, Sept. 23, 1909, DS 5012/29.

[19] Einstein to Knox, No. 1045, July 15, 1909, DS 20784/–; Einstein to Knox, No. 1065, July 29, 1909; Einstein to Knox, No. 1106, Aug. 27, 1909, DS 5012/21 and /25–26.

railroad concessions had, moreover, become a factional issue in Turkish politics.[20]

This was the state of affairs in September, 1909, when Ambassador Oscar S. Straus arrived in Constantinople.[21] He summarized the scramble for concessions to Secretary Knox on September 23 indicating that many agents — some who were American and some who were not — were claiming to represent American interests in seeking various contracts for public utilities from the Turkish government.[22] Many an operator without capital was making a play for big financial returns in Turkey at this time.

Straus pressed the department repeatedly to improve the chaotic system by requiring that all American companies desiring to apply for concessions make their plans known initially in Washington where the department could ascertain whether they were bona fide American companies, investigate their financial standing, and decide what support they were entitled to from the department's agents in the field. Improved procedures, he felt, might mitigate the disadvantage of American merchants and manufacturers in competing with their western European counterparts. The latter sent to Turkey representatives who were usually connected with their firms as managers or part owners. By way of contrast, American concession-seekers and contractors were too often represented by "commercial soldiers-of-fortune," that is, men not directly connected with the firms they represented, and "who seek concessions or contracts, with some kind of arrangement or understanding with American concerns, which pay a fixed sum or commission to such agents and then endeavor to organize a company to finance the concession and, if successful, arrange to carry on the work required." [23]

Straus may well have made his recommendation on the basis of his early experience with the Chester syndicate. The Admiral and his elder son do not seem to have been men of capital and business connections in their own right; and, although the younger son, Colby M. Chester, Jr., was treasurer of a substantial and well-established firm, he does not appear to have had sizable personal funds for investment. In this case, then, the Admiral was the soldier-of-fortune who arranged an understanding with several important American

[20] *Ibid.*; Einstein to Knox, No. 1124, Sept. 16, 1909, DS 5012/28.

[21] Constantinople had been raised to an embassy in 1906. Prior to this Straus had twice been American Minister to Turkey.

[22] Straus to Knox, No. 2, Sept. 23, 1909, DS 5012/39.

[23] Straus to Knox, No. 46, Nov. 25, 1909, DS 5012/34. Knox evaded Straus' proposals for departmental screening by merely stating that the general policy of the department was to afford opportunities equally to reputable American concerns for submitting proposals to foreign governments. Knox to Straus, No. 24, Nov. 1, 1909, *Foreign Relations, 1909* (Washington, 1914), pp. 595–596.

concerns for financing the railroad and mining venture if a concession could be obtained from the Ottoman authorities. As for Arthur Chester, Straus complained that he had no conception of the proper limits of official assistance in such matters. Chester's feeling that his various adversaries had hatched a plot against him made it difficult for the embassy to deal with him.[24] Straus' efforts to convince Chester of the desirability of harmonizing his conflicting interest with the White group's were as little heeded as Einstein's had been.[25]

* * *

By the autumn of 1909, the Chester group, after virtually eliminating the White Company, was ready to organize formally and to press for the strongest possible official support from top officials in Washington.[26] In November the syndicate organized as the Ottoman-American Development Company with a New Jersey charter,[27] after which they began in earnest the first of three unsuccessful attempts between 1909 and 1911 to consummate a concession agreement with the Ottoman government.

As the new company sought active support from the Taft administration, it impressed the State Department with evidence of strong financial backing. Those principally involved financially were C. A. Moore, president of Manning, Maxwell, and Moore, Incorporated; E. G. Converse, a director of United States Steel; Admiral Chester; MacArthur Brothers, who were among the country's foremost railroad builders; the Foundation Company, general contractors; and the banking firm of Laidlaw and Company. The Ottoman-American Development Company had provided its field representatives with letters of commendation from leading New York financial institutions indicating their faith in the ability of this combination to carry out effectively any concession it might undertake for the Ottoman government. The company then made a direct bid for diplomatic

[24] Einstein to Knox, No. 1081, Aug. 5, 1909, DS 20784/1/; Einstein to Knox, No. 1106, Aug. 27, 1909, DS 5012/25-26; Straus to Knox, No. 2, Sept. 23, 1909, DS 5012/29.

[25] Straus to Knox, No. 2, Sept. 23, 1909; Straus to Knox, No. 4, Sept. 24, 1909, DS 5012/29 and /30. For further details on Straus' difficulties with concession-seekers, see Straus to Knox, No. 24, Oct. 27, 1909, DS 20784/5-6.

[26] The Chester interests had from the inception of their more modest proposals concentrated efforts on high officials in Washington. C. A. Moore to Elihu Root, Oct. 14, 1908; Root to V. H. Metcalf (Secretary of the Navy), Oct. 20, 1908; Metcalf to Root, Oct. 22, 1908, all DS 16251/– and/1. As late as the summer and fall of 1909 the embassy reported knowing little firsthand of the burgeoning Chester plans. Einstein to Knox, Aug. 27, 1909; Straus to Knox, Sept. 23, 1909, DS 5012/25–26 and /29.

[27] The company reported that its authorized capitalization was $100,000, fully subscribed, with 10 per cent paid in. James M. Laidlaw to Knox, enclosed in C. A. Moore to Knox, both Nov. 24, 1909, DS 5012/31–32; Reports for Mr. Carr of the State Department by R. G. Dun and Co. ("The Mercantile Agency"), Dec. 23 and Dec. 28, 1909, DS 5012/39.

support both in Constantinople and with the Turkish embassy in Washington.[28]

Company officials were delighted with Secretary Knox's assurances of the administration's desire to encourage American enterprise, especially in Turkey, in every way possible.[29] Their representatives would receive official aid in meeting appropriate Turkish officials, although diplomatic assistance would be held within limits.[30]

Pressure from the Turkish side was added to the importuning of the company for diplomatic support. The Turkish Chargé in Washington, Rustem Bey, tried to maneuver Secretary Knox into an official endorsement of the Ottoman-American Development Company, arguing that the company's position with the Turkish government would be strengthened if the State Department would state specifically that the composition of the company was "such as to command the thorough confidence of the Imperial Ottoman Government both as regards to the general business standing of this concern and its ability to carry out any contract to which it would put its signature." [31]

Knox parried adroitly, placing the company in a favorable light but without committing his department to underwriting its financial solidity.[32] Instead, he shifted the burden to "substantial bankers and business men in the United States" who had "amply assured" the department that the men making up the Ottoman-American Development Company were "of the highest standing and that any undertakings made by them should inspire your Government's complete confidence. . . ." [33] A contract with such a company, Knox

[28] Laidlaw (president of the Ottoman-American Development Company) to Knox, Nov. 24, 1909, DS 5012/31-32. In addition to Arthur Chester, James W. Colt, a railway construction engineer, was also to represent the company.

[29] Moore to Knox, Nov. 24, 1909, enclosed in Laidlaw to Knox, Nov. 24, 1909, DS 5012/31-32. Copies of these letters were sent to Ambassador Straus for his information and to allay his fears that Chester was inadequately backed. Knox to Straus, No. 43, Dec. 8, 1909, same file.

[30] Established policy "would not permit the Ambassador to request the granting of the concession to the company which must rely on its own efforts and merits to obtain this." Knox to Moore, Dec. 8, 1909; Knox to Straus, No. 43, Dec. 8, 1909, both DS 5012/31-32.

[31] A. Rustem Bey to Knox, No. 50, Dec. 20, 1909, DS 5012/39.

[32] Before replying to Rustem Bey, the department had made some effort to ascertain the financial soundness of the company. Asst. Secy. of State (Huntington Wilson) to C. A. Moore, telegram, Dec. 23, 1909; Moore to Wilson, telegram, Dec. 23, 1909; M. S. Clayton to Wilson, Dec. 23, 1909; Report for Mr. Carr of the State Dept. by R. G. Dun and Co. ("The Mercantile Agency"), Dec. 23, 1909, DS 5012/39-41.

[33] Those listed by Knox were W. E. Corey, president of the United States Steel Corporation; Messrs. J. P. Morgan & Co.; D. E. Pomeroy, vice president of the Bankers' Trust Company; Thomas Cochran, Jr., vice president of the Astor Trust Company; S. H. Miller, cashier of the Chase National Bank; Paul Morton, formerly Secretary of the Navy and now president of the Equitable Life Assurance Society of the United States; Alvin W. Krech, president of the Equitable Trust Company of New York; F. A. Vanderlip, president of the National City Bank, and formerly Assistant Secretary of the Treasury; Gilbert G. Thorne, vice president of the National City Bank; James J. Hill, president of the Great Northern Railway; and others.

emphasized, would have a beneficial effect on all phases of Ottoman-American relations.[34] The endorsement of the company's standing was strong even though it did not commit the department as fully as Rustem Bey might have hoped.

* * *

During the early months of 1910, the representatives of the Chester interests made slow but satisfactory progress in Constantinople and by early March had signed a detailed preliminary agreement with the Minister of Public Works.[35] As evidence of its good faith, the company deposited £T 20,000 in a Constantinople bank.[36] Then followed a delay of nearly three months during which the Grand Vizier, Hakki Pasha, refused to act on the agreement, thereby preventing it from continuing through the prescribed channels — approval by the Council of Ministers and submission to parliament for final confirmation.

During this delay the Department of State showed how far it had moved from the position taken by Secretary Knox the previous autumn when he told company officials that they must rely on their own efforts to obtain the concession, except for routine embassy help. Within a few months the department intervened directly to persuade the Turks that they should grant the concession to this particular American group. The department used several pet objectives of the Young Turk regime as bargaining points: increase in Turkish customs duties from 7 to 11 per cent; purchase of warships in the United States to offset additions to the Greek navy; [37] abandonment by the United States of some capitulatory privileges, most especially the right of forum in cases where Americans were accused of criminal acts; [38] and foreign loans to ease their urgent financial needs.[39]

The Turks were perfectly willing to play this bargaining game

[34] Knox to A. Rustem Bey, No. 27, Dec. 27, 1909, DS 5012/39.

[35] Admiral Chester to Huntington Wilson, Jan. 25, 1909, DS 5012/43; Laidlaw to Wilson, March 8, 1910, DS 867.602 Ot 81/1; Henry Janes (Chargé in Constantinople) to Knox, No. 24, telegram, March 26, 1910; Janes to Knox, April 1, 1910, DS 867.602 Ot 81/6 and /13.

[36] Straus to Knox, No. 20, telegram 12 noon, March 7, 1910; Admiral Chester to Wilson, March 15, 1910; Janes to Knox, April 1, 1910, DS 867.602 Ot 81/–, /7, and /13.

[37] Wilson to American Embassy, Constantinople, March 12, 1910, telegram, DS 867.602 Ot 81/–. Turkey had requested in Jan., 1910, that the United States sell her a warship to counteract an addition to the Greek navy. This could not have been done without special authorization from Congress, which the department was unwilling to seek. Straus to Knox, No. 14, telegram, strictly confidential, Jan. 19, 1910; Wilson to the Secretary of the Navy, confidential, Jan. 20, 1910; Secretary of the Navy to Wilson, confidential, Jan. 20, 1910; Knox to Straus, telegram, Feb. 1, 1910, all DS 20186/1 and /2.

[38] Gordon, *American Relations with Turkey*, pp. 190–199; A. Rustem Bey to Knox, Dec. 21, 1909, DS 5012/39.

[39] Earle, *The Bagdad Railway*, pp. 224–226; Straus to Knox, May 12, 1910, DS 867.602 Ot 81/15.

by making it appear that they would be more favorably inclined toward American investors if the United States government proved willing to make concessions on these issues, extraneous to the Chester proposition but important to Turkey. Straus did his best to make this instrument of Turkish diplomacy a two-edged sword, but complained that the State Department would not give him enough room for maneuver on the issues.[40] The limit to which the department would go was outlined by Assistant Secretary Huntington Wilson in a communication to the Turkish Chargé in Washington on March 15, 1910, when he told him that the United States would assent to the increase in Turkish customs duties as soon as the Chester concession had been granted.[41] But capitulations were another matter. The United States played this issue more cautiously by suggesting that it might consider further negotiation on the matter after the granting of the concession.[42] The department was not willing, however, to seek the special congressional authorization required before Turkey could obtain the warship she had requested in January, 1910.[43] Straus did dangle tempting bait before the Turks in the form of possible future loans in the United States.[44]

The optimism expressed by the Ottoman-American Development Company throughout March[45] evaporated abruptly in April with evidence that German interests with the help of their embassy were enlisting formidable opposition to the American project. Prior to this time the European powers with vested interests in Turkey had not reacted openly against what they regarded as upstart American interests. The Germans decided not to tolerate a newcomer to the ranks of those interested in the economic exploitation of the Ottoman Empire.[46] It was soon apparent that the influence of the German Embassy was behind the procrastinating behavior of Grand Vizier Hakki Pasha in his refusal to place the preliminary agreement before the Council of Ministers.

The Germans charged that Admiral Chester was merely a front

[40] Straus to Knox, No. 20, March 7, 1910, DS 867.602 Ot 81/–.

[41] Knox to Rustem Bey, No. 35, March 15, 1910, DS 867.602 Ot 81/4A. "Favorable action on this concession would be considered by this Government as showing a sincere desire on the part of your Government to further these [commercial] relations. As giving to the United States a reality of actual material interest in Ottoman dominions it would also justify a more advanced position on the part of this Government in furthering various measures by the speedy consummation of which the present enlightened Ottoman Government so naturally and properly sets great store."

[42] *Ibid.*; Wilson to American Embassy, Constantinople, March 20, 1910, telegram, DS 867.602 Ot 81/–.

[43] See footnote 37.

[44] Straus to Knox, No. 167, May 12, 1910, DS 867.602 Ot 81/15.

[45] Laidlaw to Wilson, March 8, 1910; Janes to Knox, March 26, 1910, DS 867.602 Ot 81/1 and /6.

[46] G. B. Ravndal (Consul-General, Beirut) to the Assistant Secretary of State, No. 316, Nov. 23, 1909, DS 5012/35.

for cunning plans of the Standard Oil Trust which was allegedly angling for control of the oil lands of the Turkish Empire. Whether or not the Germans believed their allegation, the introduction of Standard Oil as a whipping boy was a clever and effective tactic in view of the past and current American attacks on the Rockefeller organization and a suspicious attitude toward the company in some Turkish circles.

The German attack worried officials of the Ottoman-American Development Company who enlisted the assistance of the State Department in an effort to blunt its influence. After company officials hurried to Washington on April 8 with their fears concerning the German-inspired rumors in the Turkish press, an explanation went out to the embassy in Constantinople denying any connection between the Chester interests and Standard Oil with instructions: "You will discreetly cause this to be well known." [47]

This German maneuver complicated Ambassador Straus' efforts to induce the reluctant Grand Vizier to press the project. Arthur Chester and James Colt, the railway construction engineer working with him, told Straus of their belief that the German Embassy strongly opposed the Chester Project because it would compete with the Baghdad railway already under construction. Meanwhile, Hakki Pasha, whose Germanophilia was notorious, found convenient excuses for delay by pleading the priority of imperial problems connected with the Albanian insurrection and affairs in Crete. Straus then tried to force the issue on May 11 by confronting the Grand Vizier with the request for a frank answer as to whether there were political reasons — opposition from Germany or other powers, for instance — which would prevent the granting of the concession to an American company. The Grand Vizier answered in the negative and assured Straus that he would complete his studies in the next ten days; the matter could then be submitted to the Council of Ministers after which a report would be made to parliament.[48]

Straus told his superiors in Washington that he might be able to make better headway in unblocking the Chester Project and countering German opposition if the department authorized him to give ground on the important but extraneous issues. Even then, Straus

[47] John R. MacArthur to Wilson, April 6, 1910, telegram; MacArthur to Wilson, April 6, 1910; Wilson to MacArthur, April 7, 1910, telegram; Wilson to American Embassy, Constantinople, April 9, 1910, telegram, all DS 867.602 Ot 81/9, /8, /9, and /10A, respectively. Rustem's reaction to the rumors led MacArthur and Moore (the trouble shooters for the company on this occasion) to think that official circles in Constantinople might be attaching real importance to the German charges. See MacArthur to Chief of the Near Eastern Division (Evan Young), April 9, 1910; Laidlaw to Wilson, April 13, 1910; Wilson to Laidlaw, April 15, 1910, DS 867.602 Ot 81/67 and /12.

[48] Straus to Knox, May 12, 1910, DS 867.602 Ot 81/15.

had deep misgivings about the prospects for the American promoters. He perceived more clearly than his superiors that these gigantic projects collided with the interest of the Great Powers. In his thoughtful analysis of May 12, 1910, he told the department: [49]

> The negotiations appear to me hopeful for the American company; but one can never judge about the ultimate result of any matter of negotiations here, until it is a *fait accompli.* Turkey is so dependent upon the cultivation of good relations with the six great Powers, who practically have in their keeping the political existence of the Empire, that should one or more of these Powers, as for instance Germany or Russia, strongly oppose, this would prove a serious, if not a definite, obstacle to the granting of such a concession. Ordinarily in commercial matters a neutral nation has an advantage, but such is not the case here, where the power to harm counts for much more than good, neutral relations.

It took Washington officials several weeks to comprehend fully that German opposition had thrown obstacles in the path of the American concession-seekers. A naive notion of "Dollar Diplomacy" as a commercial concept had not taken into account the realities of international politics. After he had been alerted by the Ottoman-American Development Company and by Straus, Knox began diplomatic inquiries in the European capitals. Instructions to Berlin on June 3 told Ambassador David Hill "to make a very discreet but strong oral representations [*sic*] to the German Foreign Office on the subject of the German opposition toward our railway enterprises in Turkey." Hill was to refer to the cooperation between the United States and Germany in Liberia, China, and Persia. Knox apparently hoped Hill might appeal to the better nature of the *Wilhelmstrasse* by observing that traffic arrangements could be made which would conserve both German and American railway interests in Turkey. As if these suggestions were not sufficient indication of Knox's inadequate grasp of the power equation, he also empowered Hill to intimate pointedly that if German cooperation was not forthcoming the United States might find it necessary to work with other powers in Turkey.[50]

Very shortly Washington had to ask whether Germany might, in

[49] Straus to Knox, May 12, 1910, DS 867.602 Ot 81/15. The published British, German, and French documents reveal little bearing directly on the Chester Project, but they are instructive of the interests and rivalries of the European Powers in the Near East. See G. P. Gooch and Harold V. Temperley (eds.), *British Documents on the Origins of the War, 1898–1914* (11 Vols.; London, 1922–1927), Vols. V and IX; Johannes Lepsius, Albrecht Mendelssohn Bartholdy, and Friedrich Thimme (eds.), *Die grosse Politik der europäischen Kabinette, 1871–1914* (40 Vols.; Berlin, 1922–1927), Vols. XXVII, XXVIII, XXXI, XXXIII; Ministère des Affaires Etrangères, *Documents diplomatiques français, 1871–1914,* 2d series, 1901–1911 (Paris, 1930–1955), Vols. XII and XIII; 3d Series, 1911–1914 (Paris, 1929–1936), *passim.*

[50] Knox to Hill, telegram, June 3, 1910, DS 867.602 Ot 81/18.

fact, be getting the jump by enlisting the support of the powers against American enterprise in Turkey. The department asked American representatives in Berlin, Paris, Rome, London, and St. Petersburg to make discreet inquiries as to the validity of the rumors that the German ambassador in Constantinople, Baron Marschall von Bieberstein, was endeavoring to secure support from his colleagues for the defeat of the American application.[51] The American ambassadors found no tangible evidence for the conspiracy charge, but the British made it clear that they could not accept any threat to their primacy in the Persian Gulf area.[52]

That the German Foreign Office had little trouble in dealing with Hill is suggested by the latter's response to Knox's instructions. Hill cabled that the "German Government fully upholds our position regarding the open door in Turkey as elsewhere and assert in a memorandum there is not opposition on their part to an American railroad concession in Turkey." Yet Hill was told at the same time that since the American group had taken no steps to come to an understanding with German interests, the latter would naturally seek to protect themselves. But the Germans assured Hill that the government "so far" had "not taken part in the affairs." They felt that the two groups might confer "in which case the German Government would willingly exercise its influence on the German interests in favor of an understanding." [53] Obviously, the bland assurances given Hill in Berlin did not square with the rumored actions of Germany's ambassador in Constantinople.[54]

[51] Knox to American Embassy, Berlin, June 11, 1910, telegram; Knox to American Embassy, Paris, June 11, 1910, telegram, both DS 867.602 Ot 81/118; Laidlaw to Knox, June 14, 1910, DS 867.602 Ot 81/23. Straus considered Marschall von Bieberstein the ablest ambassador in Constantinople. Straus, "My Third Mission to Turkey, 1909–1910," p. 10, Oscar S. Straus Papers, Division of Manuscripts, Library of Congress, Box 11. See also the appraisal in Earle, *The Bagdad Railway*, p. 43.

[52] Hill to Knox, confidential, June 13, 1910, telegram; Bacon (in Paris) to Knox, June 15, 1910, telegram; Reid (in London) to Knox, June 16, 1910, telegram; Leishman (in Rome) to Knox, June 22, 1910, telegram; Leishman to Knox, June 26, 1910, telegram; Post-Wheeler (in St. Petersburg) to Knox, June 29, 1910, all DS 867.602 Ot 81/22, /25, /26, /39, /29, and /36, respectively.

[53] By the time Hill sent his dispatch he had already been visited unofficially by Arthur von Gwinner, head of the Deutsche Bank of Constantinople, who had indicated on maps where, in his view, the American project invaded rights already held by the Baghdad and Anatolian railway concessions. He too complained that the American plan was not one "for bona fide railroad development but a scheme for controlling certain undeveloped oil fields in order to keep their product out of the market." Hill to Knox, confidential, June 13, 1910, telegram, DS 867.602 Ot 81/22.

[54] A few days later Hill forwarded an article from the *Berliner Lokal-Anzieger* of June 21, 1910, which used in a sensational way the same arguments von Gwinner had used on Hill. The article, called "American Artful Dodgers," ran in part as follows: "The general public did not know and does not yet know today just what this Mr. Chester, a straw man of the Standard Oil Company and of the financial groups allied with it, was really after." The article then comments that the concession proposed would give the Americans 16 months in which to lay pre-emptive claims to all minerals in the area which would give them first chance at these resources. The parting sentence reads that "The Turks were on the point of becoming dupes of Rockerfeller's [*sic*] genius, and while they were unsuspecting

The evidence funnelling into Washington during June from Hill, Straus, and the Ottoman-American Development Company pointed clearly to the obstructionist role of the German ambassador. There was, for instance, a report that Baron Marschall had told the Turks at a recent dinner he gave for the Turkish cabinet that the advent of American capital into their country would be harmful and that the Americans were interested solely in securing the valuable Turkish petroleum fields for Standard Oil. Threats and cajolery were reputedly used. Germany might withhold consent to the customs increase if the concession was granted, and there was the attractive suggestion of German support for Turkey in her Cretan difficulties.[55]

For an interval early in June, it had looked as if the Chester Project would reach parliament before its summer adjournment. Ambassador Straus reported that the papers had successfully passed the Council of State; they had then been approved by the War Department and returned to the Council of State. Straus considered the "outlook hopeful" except for the opposition from the German Embassy.[56]

Excitement heightened during the latter part of June. Although time was running out because of the approaching adjournment of parliament, Straus could do little more to meet stern exhortations from Washington that he exert all his power to see the concession through parliament. He did prepare a careful legal argument to refute the latest German attack.[57] Straus reported on June 21 that the case was *in statu quo*; the Grand Vizier had not yet referred the concession to parliament. Straus went on to say that the memorandum from the German government, denying its opposition, was not correct: [58]

British Ambassador informed me again today that German Ambassador

enough yesterday, today they have something of the feeling of having had a very narrow escape." Translation enclosed in Hill to Knox, June 22, 1910, DS 867.602 Ot 81/34.

[55] Laidlaw to Knox, June 14, 1910; Straus to Knox, June 27, 1910, telegram; both DS 867.602 Ot 81/23 and /30; Gordon, *American Relations with Turkey*, pp. 260–261.

[56] Straus to Knox, telegram undated, received June 2, 1910; Straus to Knox, undated, received June 3, 1910, both DS 867.602 Ot 81/17 and /18. Von Bieberstein then attacked the project directly, protesting that it conflicted with the mining law of 1907 passed as one condition for German consent to an earlier increase in customs duties. As a result of the German attack, the project was sent to a board of Turkish legal advisers for review. Straus to Knox, telegram, undated, received June 18, 1910, 6 p.m., DS 867.602 Ot 81/27.

[57] Knox to Straus, June 18, 1910, telegram; Straus to Knox, telegram, undated (received June 18, 1910, 6 p.m.); Laidlaw to Wilson, June 23, 1910, DS 867.602 Ot 81/24, /27, and /43, respectively. Laidlaw quoted a dispatch from a company agent: "Grand Vizier openly in opposition to mining feature of our proposition. Will do all in our power and the necessary plans are now being made but result is in doubt."

[58] Straus to Knox, undated, received, June 21, 1910, 8:45 a.m., DS 867.602 Ot 81/28. Two men on the four-man legal board had turned in reports holding that the concession did not conflict with the 1907 mining law.

**told him he had opposed it before the Grand Vizier. Only yesterday Austrian Ambassador informed me that German Ambassador has opposed the concession, and stated that as Austrians are interested in the Bagdad railroad they also oppose it as conflicting with their rights.**

Despite the concerted efforts of the company, its Turkish supporters, and the mounting pressure from the State Department, parliament adjourned on June 28 without receiving the concession. After this defeat, gloom and disappointment pervaded company quarters making doubtful whether the project would be pursued. Although the Grand Vizier promised to take the matter up after adjournment, the company's representative felt this would be futile, because parliament would not meet for some time and the many amendments suggested would mean further delays.[59]

Straus appraised the failure in terms of German opposition and its effect upon the Grand Vizier and the Minister of War. The latter was particularly opposed to the mineral clauses which relieved the company from building the railroad if, after sixteen months of investigation, it turned out that the mineral and oil deposits within the forty kilometer area were not sufficiently promising. Straus explained that the Germans were in a superior position because they consistently pushed forward their commercial enterprises to advance the political interests of Germany. This was particularly true in the case of the Baghdad railroad project on which the German groups had paid out at least 150,000 pounds in bakshish, some of which was believed to have reached the Sultan himself. "It is a great mistake to believe that any of the government concessions or contracts are awarded under an open competition. The openness as well as the competition are fictions, especially when large contracts or important interests are under consideration.[60] Straus contrasted the German diplomatic support for its commercial enterprises with the inadequate instruments with which the department had provided him. [61]

* * *

The Department of State decided promptly that it would underwrite another attempt to win the Chester concession. Even during the conduct of the "post mortem," influential individuals in the Department of State, unwilling to let the project die, prodded the com-

[59] Straus to Knox, June 27, 1910, telegram; Laidlaw to Wilson, June 28, 1910, both DS 867.602 Ot 81/30 and /33. The exact scope of the amendments suggested is not clear. Among other changes the government apparently was proposing the elimination of the Samsun-Sivas line. Adee to Wilson, Nov. 4, 1910, telegram, DS 867.602 Ot 81/56.

[60] Straus to Knox, No. 208, June 29, 1910, DS 867.602 Ot 81/37.

[61] *Ibid.*; Straus to Knox, June 27, 1910, DS 867.602 Ot 81/30.

pany to continue its efforts. Evan Young, chief of the Near Eastern Division, informed Assistant Secretary Huntington Wilson that he had telephoned MacArthur (an investor in the company) to send someone to Washington soon "for the purpose of conferring and mapping out a line of action in order that we may exert every pressure as soon as Parliament convenes looking to the early granting of the concession." [62] The frustrating second trial consumed nearly a year before it ended in failure in June of 1911.[63]

The company's half-hearted and haphazard efforts toward gaining the concession during the autumn and winter months raised doubts among American officials in Constantinople. The earlier enthusiasm of the promoters had turned sour, as their belated surveys indicated the economic prospects for their ventures appeared less promising than anticipated. There was also more than a hint of dissension and lack of cohesion within the company.

From Washington came pressure coaxing the company into a more aggressive course. This tenacious support of the department for the concession effort was surprising in view of the analyses from its agents in the field. Straus, Hoffman Philip, Huntington Wilson (sent on a special mission to Turkey late in 1910), and William W. Rockhill successively sent back pessimistic reports about the possibilities for American commercial enterprise in so notorious an international trouble spot.

Straus drew on his long diplomatic experience in Turkey to observe, as he had in previous dispatches, that "In a country such as this, the political and commercial interests are very closely allied." He felt this was shown in the activities and attitudes not only of Germany, but also in those of Great Britain and France. He told the department categorically that American commercial interests of the magnitude of the Chester concession could not "be successfully advanced and sustained in this Empire without the strong sup-

[62] Yellow memorandum by EEY [Evan E. Young] to Wilson, attached to letter from Laidlaw (see footnote 59). Wilson pencilled "a good idea" on Young's memorandum.

[63] The department took the initiative in recommending that during the interim until the Ottoman parliament should meet again in November, 1910, the company should try to reach an understanding with the complaining German interests. Before this strategy could be implemented, the department abandoned the idea, although why is not clear. The sole clue is a memorandum by Evan Young stating that a departmental conference had decided it was not an opportune time to make overtures to the German groups concerned. David J. Hill to Knox, No. 728, June 22, 1910, DS 867.602 Ot 81/34. Evan Young attached a memorandum (undated, but probably after the Turkish parliament had adjourned) suggesting that "after a very careful consideration of this matter" he believed the department should recommend that the company send one of its Constantinople representatives to Berlin "for the purpose of conferring with the German group." Same file. MacArthur to Knox, July 28, 1910, DS 867.602 Ot 81/41. Evan Young, undated, probably Aug. 2, 1910, same file. During the summer, talks with Russian diplomatic officials showed that accommodation of American and Russian interests could probably be achieved. DS 867.602 Ot 81/38, /40, /42, /44, and /45.

port of our Government." If this were tried he saw no escape from involvement in [64]

> the political maze of the "Eastern Question," either on the side of Turkey or on the side of the Triple Alliance. . . . This may not be so apparent in the initial stage as afterwards, when such concession shall have been obtained and the work shall have been begun thereafter. It must be remembered, judging the future by the past and the subtle diplomatic play of the Powers, that a railway, such as the Ottoman American Company is seeking the right to build, will not only meet with obstruction on the part of such Powers as will regard their commercial interest or spheres of political influence affected, but such a Company will most probably meet with serious hindrances on the part of the Ottoman Government seeking to avoid to live up to its obligations under the express terms of any contract it may enter into. In other words, commercial interests of this magnitude will need the strong arm of the Government all the time, not only to advance them but to protect them from unjust encroachment and from the violation of obligations.

Some years later Straus wrote that he had accepted the assignment to Turkey for a third time in 1909 because of his long-standing interest in the philanthropic activities of Americans in the Ottoman Empire. He wished to make secure the legal status and rights of these American activities under definite laws in the new Turkish regime, but felt that the commercial policy of the Taft administration would hinder these objectives as well as involve the United States in Near Eastern affairs "for a few American exploiters." [65]

Reservations on narrower grounds as to the wisdom of supporting the Chester concession were also expressed by Hoffman Philip, in charge of the embassy after Straus' departure for the United States. Philip indicated on October 14, 1910, that Colt, the company's engineer, had recently completed a survey of the territory through which the proposed railway would pass. Arthur Chester, discouraged with the results of the survey, questioned whether the company could attempt the project if it embodied modifications insisted upon, the previous summer, by the Ottoman government. A prevalent opinion in Turkish circles, reported Philip, considered the concession impractical, incapable of becoming a financial success, and perhaps designed for speculative purposes. Even in the face of such attitudes, Philip had tried to promote the interests of the company. His private view, however, was that the company should make a much larger

[64] Straus to Knox, No. 223, Aug. 4, 1910, DS 867.602 Ot 81/46. See also Straus, "My Third Mission to Turkey, 1909–1910," pp. 74–75, 98–99, 133–141, Straus Papers, Boxes IV and XI.

[65] Oscar S. Straus, *Under Four Administrations* (New York and Boston, 1922), pp. 296–298. See also Straus to Taft, Aug. 27, 1910, Box IV, 1909–1919, and Straus, "My Third Mission to Turkey, 1909–1910," pp. 104–105, Box XI, Straus Papers.

deposit in a bank in Turkey to guarantee its good faith and to show that it seriously intended sinking the large amounts of capital required if it won the concession.[66] He expressed surprise that the company had committed itself so deeply on the basis of so little specific and practical information. In view of the Colt report, he suggested that the department inquire carefully into the exact plans and attitude of the company.[67]

The department showed Philip's observations to Colby M. Chester, Jr., to enable the company to state its position. Chester assured the department that the company would not undertake a project which it could not complete, and that "as businessmen we would not undertake anything that was destined to be a failure." Participants did take the position that the company might ask for some changes to compensate for elimination by the Turkish government of profitable features of the original proposal. If the Turks would agree to such changes he could "assure the Department that the road will be built and operated by Americans."[68]

Any reassurance felt by Washington officials must have been quickly dispelled when they received conflicting information from one of their own men, Assistant Secretary Huntington Wilson, who had been assigned a special mission to the Ottoman Empire. Ostensibly as a courtesy gesture in honor of the new regime, he had been designated on September 30, 1910, as ambassador extraordinary on special mission to Turkey. Wilson testified in his memoirs that he "was also expected to look into the pending Chester Concession" and the possibilities for American trade and expansion.[69] His on-the-spot survey must have been a revealing experience, for the tone of his observations was radically different from what it had been before he left Washington.

The information Wilson had received after his arrival increased his "fear that the syndicate may have proposed more than it wishes to perform."[70] There was danger of a fiasco, which would be highly prejudicial to general American prestige. He recommended that the department send for the responsible agents of the company and insist on a definite understanding concerning "their line of action and and efficient execution of their plans."

[66] The company had deposited 20,000 pounds Turkish in the British bank in Constantinople in 1909.

[67] Philip to Knox, No. 257, confidential, Oct. 14, 1910, DS 867.602 Ot 81/53.

[68] C. M. Chester, Jr., Secretary, Ottoman-American Development Company to the State Department, Nov. 1, 1910, DS 867.602 Ot 81/55.

[69] F. M. Huntington Wilson, *Memoirs of an Ex-Diplomat* (Boston, 1945), p. 223.

[70] Wilson was astonished to find that on the day he arrived in Constantinople, Arthur Chester had departed for Vienna. The company had assured the department that both the

Wilson now shared Straus' views on "the weighty questions of policy involved" in efforts to push American commercial enterprise in Turkey. He apparently was not convinced that France and England would welcome the United States as a check to Germany. He also questioned whether it was wise for the United States to have "admitted financial and industrial vested interest" in a country whose internal administration was so chaotic "and which is pressed by such complex outside influences."[71] Recalling his mission years later he wrote: "the very air was thick with German influence."[72] He had felt that Turkey was no natural sphere of interest for the United States in the political sense. To him our heavy interests in the Caribbean area and our newly acquired responsibilities in China gave us as much as we could handle; he could not see any useful purpose in courting rebuff in the Near East. He preferred to lay emphasis on the good that had come from American educational efforts in the Near East.[73]

The department followed Wilson's suggestion that it have an understanding with the company. When Colt visited the department on November 4, he again assured government officials of the group's complete readiness to carry out the revised concession, except that it might require compensation for the omission of the lucrative Samsun-Sivas line. The department cabled Wilson that it had "entire confidence in the good faith of these assurances."[74]

Wilson spent his several days in Constantinople in a series of whirlwind conferences with various top Ottoman officials — the Grand Vizier; and the Ministers of Interior, Public Works, Finance, and War — always stressing the importance his government attached to the granting of the concession. The Turkish officials repeatedly told him that three obstacles stood in the way of the concession: its conflict with the rights of the German Baghdad enterprise; its monopolistic mining provisions; and, finally, the American insistence on the right of forum under article 4 of the 1830 treaty. When the latter issue proved to be the one emphasized by the Grand Vizier before parliament in December, the department gave ground by permitting John R. Carter to inform Ottoman authori-

Admiral and Arthur Chester would be in Constantinople throughout Wilson's visit. Wilson to Knox, telegram, Nov. 2, 1910, DS 867.602 Ot 81/56.

[71] *Ibid.*

[72] Wilson, *Memoirs of an Ex-Diplomat*, p. 227.

[73] *Ibid.*, pp. 227–228. Straus had presented essentially these same ideas to Secretary Knox on Oct. 25, 1910, after the former's return to the United States. Straus, "My Third Mission to Turkey, 1909–1910," pp. 137–138, Straus Papers.

[74] Adee to Wilson, Nov. 4, 1910, telegram, DS 867.602 Ot 81/56. Adee told Wilson that the company was ordering Arthur Chester back to Constantinople, although Chester did not return for more than a month, that is, until a few days after Colt had arrived from the United States.

ties that "this obstacle could be overcome."[75] Knox told Carter, confidentially, that the department was drafting a proposed convention interpreting this right in a way that might satisfy Turkey.[76]

Laborious negotiations continued into 1911 with a Turkish cabinet crisis complicating their progress in February.[77] The Turks shifted the basis for their delay again claiming that it was not yet acceptable to the Germans. The Minister of War told Carter that "nothing would compensate [the] Ottoman Government for the loss of German friendship."[78]

The will of the company to continue its efforts showed signs of breaking before the end of March. The delays and deceits of oriental diplomacy were proving too much for the American promoters, who were preparing to instruct their Turkish representatives to deliver to the Ottoman government an ultimatum that, if the concession was not granted by May 1, the company would withdraw. The department urged that these instructions be withheld until a further report could be requested from the embassy.[79] A dispatch already on the way to Washington explained that with so little remaining to be done, the issue should be decided within a few days.[80]

More than a month passed before Carter sent encouraging news that all disputed points had been settled, that the application had gone to the Council of Ministers, and that it would probably reach

[75] At the time of Huntington Wilson's special mission to Constantinople, the department did not want the embassy in the hands of a Chargé. Carter was transferred from Bucharest to be temporary Minister. Adee for Knox to Carter, Oct. 20, 1910, DS 867.602 Ot 81/59A.

[76] Carter to Knox, Dec. 19, 1910, telegram; Carter to Knox, No. 294, Dec. 20, 1910, DS 867.602 Ot 81/61 and /62. "Although the controversy between the Governments of the United States and the Ottoman Empire over the interpretation of article 4 of the treaty of 1830 is of long standing, but few cases calling for the application of the provision of that article have actually occurred, and therefore under present conditions the question is perhaps academic rather than practical. It is clearly recognized, however, that the granting of the railway concession will bring about such a change in the existing conditions as to render very desirable a more definite and mutual understanding in regard to this matter, and when the necessity for such an understanding thus becomes evident this Government will be glad at once to enter into the negotiation of a convention which shall make appropriate concessions in the matter of the right of forum." Knox to Carter, Dec. 22, 1910, telegram, DS 867.602 Ot 81/61.

[77] Carter to Knox, confidential, Feb. 16, 1911, DS 867.602 Ot 81/75. During this stage the disagreement over the Mediterranean terminal was in the foreground. Carter to Knox, Feb. 1, 1911, telegram; Knox to Carter, Feb. 4, 1911, telegram; Carter to Knox, Feb. 5, 1911, telegram, all DS 867.602 Ot 81/70; Evan Young, Memorandum for Wilson, Feb. 1, 1911, DS 867.602 Ot 81/73.

[78] Carter to Knox, Feb. 1, 1911, telegram; Carter to Knox, Feb. 5, 1911, telegram, both DS 867.602 Ot 81/70. The Grand Vizier made the absurd claim that negotiations had been going on for only three months which prompted Carter to retort, more accurately, that they had been started more than two years earlier. Carter to Knox, confidential, No. 332, March 8, 1911, DS 867.602 Ot 81/77.

[79] EEY [Evan Young] to Wilson, Memorandum, March 21, 1911; Wilson to embassy, Constantinople, March 21, 1911, telegram, DS 867.602 Ot 81/77A.

[80] Carter's optimism was tempered by a closing observation that "in any other country I should say that the negotiations were practically finished, but my brief experience here has taught me that Turkey has very special methods of its own, so that I dare not be too sanguine." Carter to Knox, No. 333, confidential, March 15, 1911, DS 867.602 Ot 81/79.

the parliament in a few days.[81] Another of the periodic ministerial crises then intervened to cause further delay.[82] Carter wrote the department that "It is difficult to explain these dilatory proceedings; and all sorts of suggestions are made to us as to their origin . . . among them . . . 'bakshish.'"[83] On May 14 Carter finally cabled that the Grand Vizier had signed the project and it was now in the hands of parliament for the first time.

At the department, tension and expectation increased during the latter half of May in view of the impending adjournment of parliament. The session was prolonged a few days beyond its projected adjournment to consider the railway plan and the budget. The blow fell on June 1, 1911, when parliament voted 77 to 64 to postpone consideration until the next session on grounds that too little time remained to consider it intelligently. Carter was convinced that this was a "preconceived plan to defeat [the] project" on the part of the Grand Vizier.[84]

* * *

The news from Turkey that the concession had not been approved by parliament created consternation in the New York office of the Ottoman-American Development Company where some participants showed a "strong disposition to give up the whole proposition." This time encouragement to continue the fight came from Minister Carter in Constantinople, who now argued that the difficult work had been accomplished in getting the concession before parliament where there was enough favorable sentiment to augur well for affirmative action during the autumn session. With this in mind, he cabled: "Earnestly hope that the Department will persuade the Ottoman Development Company not to abandon the project but at least wait until the autumn session of Parliament. . . ." Fortified to reconsider by Carter's optimism, Admiral Chester wrote the department that the full board would meet soon to make the decision. He felt sure that company officials would be "ready

[81] Carter to Knox, April 22, 1911, telegram, DS 867.602 Ot 81/82; Wilson to MacArthur, confidential, April 25, 1911, DS 867.602 Ot 81/84; Carter to Knox, April 26, 1911, telegram, DS 867.602 Ot 81/86.

[82] Carter to Knox, May 6, 1911, telegram, DS 867.602 Ot 81/87; Hoffman Philip to William W. Rockhill, May 8, 1911, William W. Rockhill Papers, Houghton Library, Harvard University.

[83] Carter to Knox, No. 348, confidential, May 12, 1911, DS 867.602 Ot 81/100.

[84] Carter to Knox, May 14, 1911, telegram; Wilson to Carter, May 15, 1911, telegram; Carter to Knox, May 16, 1911, telegram; Knox to Carter, May 22, 1911, telegram; Carter to Knox, May 23, 1911, telegram; Carter to Knox, May 26, 1911, telegram; Carter to Knox, May 27, 1911, telegram; Carter to Knox, June 1, 1911, telegram; all DS 867.602 Ot 81/89, /89, /91, /91A, /93, /94, /96, and /99 respectively.

to come to Washington and arrange for the next campaign to be carried on under the American Flag in Turkey." [85]

After Secretary Knox and Assistant Secretary Wilson had seen the Admiral's letter, the Near Eastern Division wrote the Admiral that the department was "much gratified" to learn of the company's plans to continue its efforts, and assured the company of "all possible proper support." [86] The company then announced early in September that it intended to send its authorized representative to Constantinople before the opening of the approaching session of parliament.[87]

The extent of the administration's commitment to the Chester Project is revealed in the instructions to the new ambassador to Turkey, William W. Rockhill, veteran diplomat and orientalist, reassigned from St. Petersburg. In the name of President Taft, Secretary Knox instructed Rockhill in a private letter of June 17, 1911, to direct his energies constantly "to the real and commercial rather than the academic interests of the United States in the Near East." [88]

Rockhill soon mastered the previous history of the difficult negotiations for the railway concessions.[89] The chances for approval at the forthcoming session appeared reasonably good to him, but he thought the company should have an agent on the spot who should not even overlook "the judicious expenditure of money" as a method of dispelling "the adverse influences. . . ." All companies had found such methods needed in Turkey and other Oriental countries.[90]

The bold measures urged by Rockhill came to naught with the development of a crisis from which the company could not recover. At issue was a rift within the company, deepened by the outbreak of war between Turkey and Italy in September, 1911, which influenced the decision of important elements of the syndicate to withdraw their financial support. The department's first intimation that the company contemplated withdrawing the deposit of 20,000 pound Turkish (which had been on deposit at the British bank in Constantinople for two-and-a-half years) came from Colby M. Chester, Jr., on September 28. Chester revealed that some members of the syndicate felt that the Italo-Turkish War would occupy the

[85] Carter to Knox, June 1, 1911, telegram; Carter to Knox, June 4, 1911, telegram; Admiral Chester to Evan E. Young, June 22, 1911, all DS 867.602 Ot 81/99, /101, and /104, respectively.

[86] Young to Chester, June 27, 1911, DS 867.602 Ot 81/104.

[87] J. W. Colt to Wilson, Sept. 2, 1911, DS 867.602 Ot 81/109.

[88] Knox to Rockhill, June 17, 1911 (carbon in DS 867.602 Ot 81/102A); Rockhill "Diary," Vol. IV, May 2, May 4, Aug. 3, Aug. 6, Aug. 28, all 1911, Rockhill Papers.

[89] Rockhill to Knox, No. 16, Sept. 18, 1911, DS 867.602 Ot 81/111.

[90] *Ibid.*; also Rockhill to Knox, Oct. 10, 1911, telegram, DS 867.602 Ot 81/115.

full attention of parliament in November, and they would, therefore, be unwilling to continue their share of the cautionary deposit. In this case, the other members felt they would be obliged to withdraw the entire sum, although there was talk of redepositing the amount when conditions became more promising. An official of the department summarized the syndicate's argument, as follows: [91]

> That they have for almost three years tied up approximately $88,000 pending a result to negotiations which have involved their yielding to the wishes of the Turkish Government on every point, and have resulted in nothing more than the same assurances that were held out to them at the beginning. They do not fear that there is danger of the Turkish Government's giving the concession to other applicants while their claims remain in abeyance. They are convinced, on the other hand, that the withdrawal of the deposit will induce the Turkish Government to reach a definite decision whether or not it desires to grant the concession to the Development Company.

As the debate continued among members of the syndicate, the internal differences became more pronounced.[92] Finally, the Board of Directors informed the department on October 18, 1911, of its final decision to withdraw its application and the money deposit. The "controlling interests" argued "that conditions have so wholly changed since the concession was first sought that, if obtained, it would probably be burdensome and difficult or impossible to finance, and they are unwilling to proceed further in the matter." [93] While professing a desire to carry out the railroad project, the company pressed for changes in the terms of the concession, arguing that it had ceased to be a sound business proposition as then drafted. Unless modifications could be arranged, the company was determined to drop the project.[94]

[91] MacMurray to Wilson, "Memorandum of a Conversation with Mr. Chester in regard to the Concession Sought by the Ottoman American Development Company," Sept. 28, 1911; Adee to Rockhill, No. 24, Oct. 12, 1911; Knox to Rockhill, Oct. 18, 1911, telegram; Rockhill to Knox, Oct. 19, 1911, telegram; DS 867.602 Ot 81/110, /113, /117, and /118, respectively.

[92] MacArthur brothers felt "that this was a very inopportune time to show a lack of confidence in Turkey's good faith or a feeling of insecurity with regard to the deposit of some $90,000 which the syndicate has in Turkey," but they failed to convince their colleagues. C. W. Fowle to Adee, Oct. 4, 1911; John R. MacArthur (personally as a member of MacArthur Bros.) to Adee, Oct. 13, 1911, DS 867.602 Ot 81/114 and /116. For further evidence of the opinion among some elements of the syndicate that the Chesters had not been well suited for the negotiations and should have been withdrawn earlier, see J. G. A. Leishman (Ambassador to Italy) to Knox, Personal, Oct. 4, 1911, DS 867.602 Ot 81/119.

[93] J. W. Colt to Knox, Oct. 18, 1911, DS 867.602 Ot 81/117.

[94] The company expressed willingness to reopen negotiations on the basis it had originally suggested by which Turkey would grant either a kilometric guarantee with mining privileges, such as other railway concessions had included, or some other form of subsidy. If the Turks did not want to proceed on these terms, the company proposed as an alternative that the concession contain a twelve-month option for preliminary reconnaissance and study of traffic and resources along the projected routes. If further work seemed warranted the company would deposit 30,000 pounds Turkish and proceed with the work, but if they were not satisfied after the survey they would surrender to the Turkish government the studies already made. The mining provisions must, of course, remain in the bill. Colt

Concurrently with the efforts to force modifications in the terms of the concession, a frantic effort was being made to obtain sufficient financial backing to replace that withdrawn.[95] Failure in both efforts was the result. Pasdermadjian, the friendly deputy from Erzerum, notified Colt on November 7, 1911, that "No modification whatever" was possible in the bill.[96] The company did not at once give up its efforts to bring in other capital, but finally concluded it was "hopeless to seek to interest American capital unless the modifications which we set forth early in November are granted." It would only put both the company and the department in an awkward position if the concession were granted on the terms laid down in the bill now unacceptable to the company.[97]

Until the end, the department had refused to give official sanction to the withdrawal. The syndicate had proposed that the Department of State lend prestige to its withdrawal by allowing it to announce that the action was taken upon the advice, or at least with the concurrence, of the department. After Adee and Wilson counselled Secretary Knox against official endorsement of the withdrawal, the company was informed of the department's attitude, and Knox made it clear to Ambassador Rockhill that "this Department, while unable to acquiesce in this decision is not in a position to avert such action by the Company." [98]

Adee in Washington and Rockhill in Constantinople did not concur in the belief of the Ottoman-American Development Company that the Turco-Italian War posed an insuperable obstacle to the concession's chances in the autumn of 1911. On the contrary, with a favorable change in cabinet personnel and the diminution of German opposition the prospects had seemed quite bright. Although the uncertainty created by the war contributed to the internal troubles within the company, it is clear that the root of the company's troubles lay in the unwillingness of the majority interests to accept the concession without major modifications.[99]

to Knox, Oct. 31, 1911; Adee to Rockhill, Nov. 2, 1911, telegram, confidential, DS 867.602 Ot 81/126 and /121.

[95] CWF (Charles W. Fowle) to Adee, Oct. 27, 1911, concerning conversation with Admiral Chester; Adee to Rockhill, confidential, Nov. 2, 1911, telegram; Knox (by Adee) to Rockhill, Nov. 10, 1911, telegram, DS 867.602 Ot 81/120, /121, and /124.

[96] Rockhill to Knox (from Pasdermadjian for Colt), Nov. 7, 1911, telegram; DS 867.602 Ot 81/124.

[97] Rockhill to Knox, Nov. 18, 1911, telegram; MacArthur to Fowle, Dec. 4, 1911, DS 867.602 Ot 81/131 and /140.

[98] MacMurray to Wilson, "Memorandum," Sept. 28, 1911; Adee to Knox, Memorandum, Sept. 30, 1911; Adee to Knox, Memorandum, Oct. 18, 1911; Knox to Rockhill, Oct. 18, 1911, telegram; Adee, acting, to Rockhill, No. 30, Oct. 20, 1911, all DS 867.602 Ot 81/110, /112, and /117.

[99] Adee to Knox, Memorandum, Sept. 30, 1911; Adee, acting, to Rockhill, No. 24, Oct. 12, 1911; Adee to Knox, Memorandum, Oct. 18, 1911; Rockhill to Knox, Oct. 26, 1911, telegram; Charles W. Fowle to Adee, Memorandum, Oct. 27, 1911; Colt to Knox,

Embarrassment on all sides followed the company's withdrawal. The chagrin in the department was matched by the dismay among the Turkish supporters of the concession, for the bill was still scheduled to come up in parliament and its friends were in doubt as to what action the company would take if the bill passed. They believed that "withdrawal of [the] deposit was only a protest against dilatoriness of [the] former administration." [100]

Now that Washington officials had burned their fingers badly, the Taft administration hastened to disengage itself as completely as possible from its untenable position. By the end of the year, the department had reverted to the traditional policy of avoiding possible political involvement in the Eastern Question.[101] Rockhill was instructed "to take necessary steps to obviate further purposeless discussion of [the] present bill in Parliament, and to refrain from all further connection with [the] project" unless terms agreeable to both the Ottoman authorities and the company had been agreed upon.[102]

The department could not complain that Ambassador Rockhill had lacked zeal in trying to implement the policy of the department. He had played the role in spite of his personal misgivings that nothing would come of the efforts of the syndicate. These views he could pour out in a personal letter to a friend in the State Department. He was disgusted, "but in no way surprised, by the ending of the Ottoman American Development Company's schemes. . . ." This collapse, he believed, would make it difficult for the embassy to attempt additional efforts for "any further participation of American financial or industrial enterprise in this country." [103] In Washington, too, the department felt it had been let down awk-

Oct. 31, 1911; MacArthur to Fowle, Dec. 4, 1911, DS 867.602 Ot 81/112, /113, /117, /120, /126, and /140.

[100] Rockhill to Knox, Oct. 26, 1911, telegram, DS 867.602 Ot 81/120. Early in November the Erzerum deputy, Pasdermadjian, urged the company to redeposit the cautionary money, and guaranteed acceptance of the project if this was done. Rockhill to Knox (from Pasdermadjian for Colt), Nov. 1, 1911, telegram, DS 867.602 Ot 81/121.

[101] Contemporaneously, the department even discouraged suggestions that the United States offer its services as a mediator during the Italo-Turkish War of 1911–1912 on grounds that the Middle East was a European question; it was argued that the United States should not irritate the European Powers by injecting itself into the situation, and no excuse should be given for European interference in the Western Hemisphere. William C. Askew, *Europe and Italy's Acquisition of Libya* (Durham, 1942), pp. 163–164, 241–242; Askew and Rippy, *Journal of Politics*, Vol. IV, pp. 73–74.

[102] Knox to MacArthur, Dec. 7, 1911, telegram; Knox to Rockhill, Dec. 8, 1911, telegram, both DS 867.602 Ot 81/136; Rockhill, "Diary," Vol. IV, Dec. 12, 1911, Rockhill Papers.

[103] Rockhill to MacMurray, Nov. 6, 1911, Rockhill Papers. "The Department is very anxious, I know, to extend our relations here; but how the devil are you going to do it if nobody in America, I mean in the business world is willing to give to the extension of our interests in this country either time or trouble or even to pledge to keep good faith with the people here in case something is given them. I trust that you, in your wisdom, will give me full instructions as to how I am to act here because I really don't see what we are to do in the matter of carrying out the wishes of our country."

wardly and that American prestige had suffered as a result of the failure of a project pressed so strongly by American diplomats.[104]

* * *

Admiral Chester did not give up easily. Early in 1912 he approached the State Department again explaining that the syndicate had been reconstituted and was now stronger financially than before, although he did not give details.[105] This time chastened Washington officials outlined a more cautious policy. Rockhill received instructions that "the Department is disposed neither to assist nor to encourage any effort to revive the project" until the financial strength and seriousness of purpose of the backers were clear beyond a doubt. Assistant Secretary Adee described the new attitude as one of "benevolent neutrality" until the new syndicate made good on its own.[106]

The suspicions of the department were warranted; the Admiral's assurances that strong new financial backing had been found were apparently premature. Some months after the Admiral's visit, the Chester interests asked the banking firm of J. P. Morgan & Company to participate in the scheme. Before committing itself, this company sent John R. Carter, formerly of the State Department, to Turkey in June of 1912 to learn the status of the project and the condition on which the Ottoman government was willing to approve it. The results of the inquiry did not make Carter sanguine about the prospects for obtaining the concession, and the Morgan company did not become involved.[107]

Apparently the State Department heard no more from the Chester interests until after the Wilson administration had been installed, when they made another futile attempt to bring about a reversal of official policy in their favor. On July 1, 1913, Colt wrote Secretary of State William J. Bryan that a new company called the Ottoman-American Exploration Company had been formed and its agent sent to Constantinople where he was negotiating with the Ottoman authorities. The company stated that it was going after the same railroad and mining concession which the defunct company had sought.[108]

[104] MacMurray to Clark, Memorandum, Feb. 28, 1912; Wilson to Rockhill, No. 109, Feb. 29, 1912, DS 867.602 Ot 81/146.

[105] Memorandum by MacMurray, Feb. 29, 1912; Memorandum, MacMurray to Clark, Feb. 28, 1912; Wilson to Rockhill, No. 109, Feb. 29, 1912, DS 867.602 Ot 81/147, /146, and /146.

[106] *Ibid.*; MacMurray to Rockhill, March 12, 1912, Rockhill Papers.

[107] Colt to Knox, June 7, 1912; Rockhill to Knox, No. 227, June 22, 1912, DS 867.602 Ot 81/149 and /152.

[108] Colt to Bryan, July 1, 1913; Colt to MacMurray, July 1, 1913, DS 867.602 Ot

The new company sought from the department as strong an endorsement as possible, but the Wilson administration was not disposed to reverse the chary attitude which the Taft administration had finally adopted. An intradepartmental memorandum expressed the policy position to which the government had reverted after three years of active diplomatic intervention to secure extensive economic rights in the Ottoman Empire: [109]

> **the obtaining of this concession — which, though purporting and purposing to be purely commercial in character, could not be divested of political bearings — would result in no real and permanent national advantage to this country, but would, on the other hand, entail upon this Government the liability to very serious obligations which might involve us in the international politics of Europe and the Near East, which we have always been solicitous to avoid.**

Accordingly, the department instructed the Constantinople embassy that the new company must deal primarily with the Ottoman government expecting from the United States government only the usual support given American enterprises abroad both in its negotiations for the concession and in its use if obtained.[110]

The department's policy disappointed the company, which tried to convince the State Department that more positive assistance was imperative if the company was to compete on equal terms with government-backed European interests. The chances for success seemed fairly favorable, the company believed, if the State Department would use for bargaining purposes the desire of the Ottoman authorities to raise customs duties from 11 per cent to 15 per cent, to which the United States must assent according to treaty.[111]

The department replied in January, 1914, that in authorizing the Constantinople embassy to consent to the increase in Turkish customs, the ambassador was instructed to request a pledge from the Turkish government that it would "grant fair consideration to American merchants, manufacturers and contractors who may desire to participate in the commercial and industrial development of Turkey." The company considered the proposed line of attack far short of what was required and argued that a mere hint was not

---

81/154 and /153. The principals in the new company were MacArthur Brothers Company, C. M. Chester, Jr., H. C. Keith, and Colt. See also Moore to Colt, Nov. 21, 1913, and Colt to Moore, Dec. 9, 1913, DS 867.602 Ot 81/156 and /159.

[109] MacMurray to John Bassett Moore, Memorandum, July 12, 1913, DS 867.602 Ot 81/154. Moore was in general agreement with this point of view. Moore to MacMurray, Memorandum, July 12, 1913, same file.

[110] Moore to Hoffman Philip (Chargé d'Affaires), Constantinople, No. 261, July 24, 1913, DS 867.602 Ot 81/154.

[111] Moore to Colt, July 24, 1913; Colt to Moore, Nov. 15, 1913; Colt to Moore, Dec. 9, 1913, DS 867.602 Ot 81/154, /156, and /159.

sufficient for the Oriental mind unless accompanied by real pressure such as the embassies of other nations exerted in behalf of their citizens. Colt suggested that the instructions be strengthened with a statement that the United States government insisted upon a favorable consideration of the desired concession. "Unless something of this kind is done," Colt wrote, "I fear that we may as well consider our matter as dead." [112]

This gratuitous advice to the department on how to run its business exhausted the patience of State Department officials and elicited the following curt reply: [113]

> I have to advise you that the instructions heretofore given by the Department were sent out after full consideration of all the various aspects of the situation on which this Government was called upon to act, and that the language originally used by the Department in stating the conditions on which consent would be given to an increase of customs duties is thought to cover the ground sufficiently and to be fair to all the various interests concerned.

With this letter the Chester Project drops out of the State Department files until 1920 when the Admiral sought to revive it as a method of meeting the oil shortage scare.[114]

This first serious flirtation with the Eastern Question had exposed America's lack of sophistication for major league international politics in Asia Minor. Both the American businessmen and the State Department found themselves outmaneuvered. The evidence available casts doubts on the competence of the negotiators, who proposed a grandiose undertaking without adequate surveys and with little appreciation of the international complications certain to accompany their proposed entry into a country already heavily mortgaged to the Great Powers.

In Washington, President Taft and Secretary Knox became ardent supporters of the Chester Project, not because of congressional or public pressures, for there were none, but because the administration wished to employ the engines of diplomacy to promote American business activity abroad as part of its policy of "Dollar Diplomacy." Ambassador Straus and others in the field judged correctly when they insisted that American commercial penetration of the Ottoman Empire would require a political policy. But the time was not ripe. As yet the ambitious commercial interests comprised

[112] Moore to Colt, Jan. 15, 1914; Colt to Moore, Jan. 24, 1914, DS 867.602 Ot 81/160 and /161.

[113] Moore to Colt, Feb. 3, 1914, DS 867.602 Ot 81/161.

[114] For a detailed treatment of the postwar Chester Project, see John A. DeNovo, "Petroleum and American Diplomacy in the Near East, 1908–1928" (Ph.D. thesis, Yale University, 1948), Chap. 8.

only a negligible group, and there was no popular ground swell demanding intervention. The possible commercial advantages did not appear commensurate with the political risks which would accompany a permanent abandonment of the long-standing policy of abstention from the politics of the Eastern Question. The issue was raised, but not faced squarely, as to whether commercial prospects were more important than humanitarian stakes Americans had built up in the region, and whether the latter would be helped or hindered by American political involvement at that particular time. These issues would arise again in changed contexts and with different results. In the meantime, the United States had reverted to its traditional abstention from the international politics of the Eastern Question.

# [13]

# The United Fruit Company in Latin America

## *Business Strategies in a Changing Environment*

This chapter examines the evolution of the United Fruit Company's business strategies throughout the twentieth century. The company had to adapt to the changing political environment in Latin America; these changes were facilitated by technical improvements in the banana industry. Prior to World War II, the company built its production and distribution empire following vertical integration. This system ensured the coordinated flow of highly perishable bananas to their final markets. United Fruit had good relationships with most of the governments of the countries in which it operated, so its huge investments were safe from any threat. Additionally, United Fruit used its growing power to eliminate its competitors either by absorbing them or by forcing them out of the market through price wars. In this way, the company eventually managed to control more than half of the international banana market. Because of this, United Fruit was repeatedly accused of creating a monopoly.

After World War II, however, the situation changed. In the decades following the war, the company was faced with a different political-economic environment—one characterized by increased labor union activity, higher taxes on exports, growing nationalism, competition from independent producers in Ecuador, and a technological transformation that made vertical integration less important. In addition, United Fruit faced the growing hostility of the U.S. government itself, which accused the company of violating antimonopoly legislation. Well aware of these changes, the company slowly transformed its operations from being a direct producer of bananas into a marketer of tropical fruit. This change was made with the support of the company's shareholders and American institutional investors.

In this way, during the 1960s the United Fruit Company got rid of its fixed assets—its main source of risk. In the decades after 1970, United Fruit faced new political problems in Latin America that reinforced its decision to stay out of the direct production of bananas. Later, in the 1990s, United Fruit faced new kinds of problems in the policies followed by European banana importers, which created high costs for United Fruit and eventually made it file for bankruptcy in 2001.[1]

## *The Creation of the Banana Empire*

Marketing bananas in the United States existed before the United Fruit Company was created. Between 1860 and 1870, several companies attempted to create a banana market in the United States, but they failed to keep a constant flow of the fruit going to final markets. This was because some of them did not have boats fast enough or with adequate enough refrigeration systems to keep the fruit fresh until it reached U.S. ports. According to Robert Read, 114 banana import companies were created between 1870 and 1899, but only 22 had survived by 1899.[2] These companies did not have their own plantations, but bought their fruit from unreliable Central American and Caribbean producers. Therefore, before 1870, no large banana import company existed in the United States.

The challenges of the banana business were resolved in 1870 when Boston ship captain Lorenzo Dow Baker imported some of the fruit from Jamaica to Boston. Baker sold his fruit to Andrew Preston, a local businessman, who then sold the fruit to consumers at reasonable prices. After their initial success, Preston and Baker organized more shipments, which initially came in irregular intervals. However, by 1885, they accumulated enough capital to create a company specialized in banana imports—the Boston Fruit Company. Preston and Baker were aware that developing a reliable transportation system consisting of a large number of ships was crucial for business success. With this in mind, they made their first big investment and created what would be later known as the Great White Fleet—a fleet of ships conditioned solely for banana transportation, which later also operated as passenger ships.[3]

Around the same time, another Boston entrepreneur, Minor C. Keith was developing a railway network in Central America. Keith was the nephew of Henry Meiggs, a legendary entrepreneur who built several railways in South America. In 1871, Meiggs invited Keith to work with him to build a railroad in Costa Rica, contracted by the Costa Rican government. The railroad was to stretch from San José to the port of Limón on the Caribbean coast, and Meiggs had already successfully built the

Callao-Lima and the Oreja railroads in Peru some years before. Keith accepted the invitation and went to Costa Rica with his two brothers to work on the railroad project.

During the construction of the first twenty-five miles of the railroad, Meiggs and the Keith brothers faced incredible odds. Building in the jungle was much harder than they had calculated because disease and difficult working conditions cost them greatly; around five thousand men died during the construction, including Meiggs and Minor Keith's two brothers. In 1874, Keith was left in charge of the project and stubbornly continued with it despite the odds. The large number of deaths made it hard for him to recruit new workers in Central America, so one source of labor was prisoners from the jails of New Orleans. With the seven hundred convicts Keith began with, it is said only twenty-five survived the end of the construction. When Keith brought in two thousand Italian immigrants from Louisiana by boat, many of them rose in rebellion when they discovered the miserable working conditions. Many ran away, and sixty were lost in the jungle.

By 1882, Keith had carried the construction of the railroad seventy miles—from the coast to Río Sucio—but he was running out of money and had received no help from the Costa Rican government, which had defaulted on promised payments. The situation was so difficult that at one point, Keith encouraged banana trees to be planted along the railroad tracks to feed the workers. With time, Keith began using the train to export the bananas he planted, and, by 1883, he owned three banana export companies. Keith's financial situation, however, did not improve, and he was obliged to obtain a loan of 1.2 million pounds that permitted him to finish the railroad to San José in 1890.

Once the railroad was finished, however, Keith faced a new problem—there were not enough passengers to travel on it. Neither operating costs nor Keith's debts could be paid. But Keith quickly found that he could keep his business alive by exporting the bananas he had planted for the railroad workers. His experiment proved successful, and, by 1890, the train was used solely to transport bananas, and the new plantations surpassed the value of the train.

During a business trip to London, Keith organized the Tropical Trading and Transport Company to coordinate his banana business and to provide transportation for his increasing shipments to the United States. In addition, his new company managed a chain of stores he established along the Costa Rican coasts to trade local produce. He also expanded his banana business to the region of Magdalena, Colombia, through the

Colombian Land Company and made a deal to export fruit to the United States with the Snyder Banana Company of Panama (at that time Colombian territory). With these deals, by 1899, Keith dominated the banana business in Central America. But new problems for Keith were not slow to arrive. In 1899, Hoadley and Company, a New York brokerage firm against which Keith held $1.5 million in drawn bills, declared bankruptcy, and Keith lost all of his money. The Costa Rican government and several members of the local elite tried to help him, but Keith's financial situation did not improve.[4] He was forced to go to Boston and talk with Andrew Preston and Lorenzo Baker of the Boston Fruit Company, Keith's rivals. Keith hoped a merger of his Tropical Trading and Transport Company and the Boston Fruit Company would end his debt. They all agreed to the deal, and the United Fruit Company was born on March 30, 1899.

The United Fruit Company was led by Preston with Keith as vice-president. Their diverse interests and skills complemented each other. Keith had his railroad network and plantations in Central America and an established market in the southeastern United States, and Preston grew bananas in the West Indies, ran the Great White Fleet of steamships, and sold to the northeastern United States. As the company grew, Keith continued with his railroad projects in Central America.[5]

The United Fruit Company needed to ensure a steady output of bananas to its consumer market in the United States. This was a difficult task because of the nature of bananas—unlike other goods, bananas rot quickly and easily. Given that bananas could not be produced in U.S. consumer markets, it was necessary to develop a production and distribution network between the Caribbean and the United States. This required the United Fruit Company to closely coordinate the whole banana production process from beginning to end.

Before the integration of the independent banana companies into the single United Fruit Company, most of the difficulties and losses these companies faced resided in problems of coordination between the production centers, the transporters, and the final distribution in the United States.[6] When a shipment was lost it was usually for the same reason—the fruit perished quickly. The invention of the closely coordinated vertically integrated structure of the company included plantations (with health and housing infrastructure), railways, ports, telegraph lines, and steamships. Most of the lands the company owned were given as concessions by the producing countries' governments, which were eager to promote foreign investment as a way to modernize their economies.

Shortly after the merger, the new United Fruit Company continued its expansion to other sectors in order to have under its roof most of the stages of banana production. United Fruit established the Fruit Dispatch Company—a subsidiary in charge of distributing bananas in the United States. United Fruit became a major shareholder of the Hamburg Line, a German shipping company, and also bought 85% of the shares of the British banana import and shipping company, Elders and Fyffes, with which United Fruit was assured a privileged position in the British market. (By 1928, United Fruit had bought 99% of Elders and Fyffes's shares.) In 1913, United Fruit created the Tropical Radio and Telegraph Company to keep in constant communication with its ships and plantations.[7] Additionally, the company owned newly developed steamships that permitted faster trips between the plantations and the final markets than the older sailing vessels.[8] With these operations, United Fruit was successfully monopolizing the banana market.

In the second decade of the 1900s, United Fruit saw its monopoly challenged by a newcomer—maverick Samuel Zemurray. A Jewish Russian-born New Orleans entrepreneur, Zemurray established the Hubbard-Zemurray Fruit Company in 1910 with his plantations in Honduras. Zemurray financed and organized a military coup against Honduran president, Miguel Dávila, replacing him with Manuel Bonilla. Once in power, Bonilla granted the Hubbard-Zemurray Fruit Company generous tax concessions and grants. For a time, Zemurray's business continued to operate and expand up the Honduran coast and created a new banana export corporation—the Cuyamel Fruit Company.

However, as Cuyamel Fruit grew, the competition between Cuyamel and United Fruit grew as well. To improve the size and quality of his bananas, Zemurray built an expensive irrigation system, and, in 1922, he acquired the Bluefields Fruit and Steamship Company. By 1929, the Cuyamel Fruit Company had thirteen steamships running between ports in Honduras and Nicaragua and New Orleans. Cuyamel Fruit also had a sugar plantation and refinery, and, in 1929, Cuyamel's stock rose while United Fruit's fell. The two companies went into a fierce price war that included a short armed conflict between Honduras and Guatemala until United Fruit decided its best option was to acquire Cuyamel. In 1930, Zemurray sold Cuyamel to United Fruit for 300,000 shares of the latter's stock, making him United Fruit's largest shareholder. He was also given a seat on the board of directors. The acquisition of Cuyamel meant 250,000 more acres of land in Honduras, fifteen more steamships, port facilities, and the concession on the Honduran national railway for United Fruit. With Cuyamel out of the way, United Fruit continued as the biggest and most powerful banana producing and marketing corporation in the world, reinforcing the monopolistic nature of the banana market in the decades to come.[9]

United Fruit maintained its vertical integration in the years after the acquisition of Cuyamel. Early studies viewed United Fruit's move toward vertical integration as either a triumph of civilization over nature[10] or as an example of what Lenin called "the latest stage of imperialism."[11] More recent scholarship sees the company's shift as part of a broader trend toward vertical integration within corporate America during the late nineteenth and early twentieth centuries.[12] In this argument, the reasons behind vertical integration were purely technical—ships were not fast enough, agriculture was uncertain, and bananas are a perishable fruit that can not be grown in the principal places they are marketed. Companies that marketed bananas had to ensure a smooth flow of fruit from production sites in Latin American to consumers in Europe and the United States. The best way to reduce uncertainties was to control all stages of the production process from plantation to market. By so doing, United Fruit was able (during the first half of the twentieth century) to coordinate the entire process.

This vertical integration was done under particular political circumstances. Central American and Caribbean countries were gradually falling under the United States–dominated economic sphere. The United States paid some of the debt of these countries' to European powers, changing the debtors' creditors to private American banks or to the American government. This debt payment was at the same time as what Mira Wilkins calls the United States' "spill-over" into the Caribbean. According to Wilkins, in the late nineteenth century, American companies considered Mexico and the Caribbean natural extensions of U.S. territory, and they expanded in these regions to open new markets and ensure their control of raw materials. While this spill-over covered the mining and oil sectors of countries like Chile, Mexico, Peru, and Venezuela, the effect was concentrated in the agricultural sector in Central America. These Central American countries were relatively young because they all had belonged to the short-lived United Provinces of Central America in the nineteenth century and had gone through several civil wars when this federation collapsed. The republics were ruled by military *caudillos* who had little affection for democratic institutions. In the early twentieth century, the Central American republics were ruled by infamous, grotesque, and corrupt dictators such as the Somozas, Ubico, Estrada, and Trujillo, who ruled their countries like their personal fiefs.

The Central American military dictators were initially friendly toward foreign investors. Because they ruled by decree, it was easy for them to grant concessions to foreign corporations without opposition. Political scientist Paul Dosal has found that in pre–World War II Guatemala, it was much easier for United Fruit to get concessions from military dictators than from the few and short-lived elected presidents. Some of these dictators ruled in countries extremely dependent on banana exports, such as Panama, Guatemala, and Honduras, which each depended on bananas for more than half of their total exports.[13]

Additionally, there was strong American intervention in the region in the period before World War II. Using the guise of protecting American interests (or American lives), the United States invaded Honduras, the Dominican Republic, Cuba, Nicaragua, Panama, Haiti, Guatemala, and El Salvador during this time, and some were invaded more than once. These invasions helped to perpetuate the dictatorial systems in these countries.

In summary, in the period before World War II, the United Fruit Company followed a vertical integration process both because of a need for a closely coordinated system and because of a friendly political environment. The need for coordination in production and distribution made it more advantageous to vertically integrate. Furthermore, the political reality of Central America and the Caribbean before World War II created a situation in which foreign investors, especially American investors, could feel secure operating in the region. Not only did the investors know the Central American governments would not bother them, but they also knew that if they did try to intervene, the American government would back the foreign investor with force. This scenario, however, changed with time (especially during the 1950s), and United Fruit had to adapt.

## *The Octopus Loses Its Arms: United Fruit's Vertical Disintegration*

The vertical disintegration of the United Fruit Company has not been studied. Scholars have focused their attention either on United Fruit's vertical integration process in the first decades of the twentieth century or on the political conflicts the company faced in post–World War II. However,

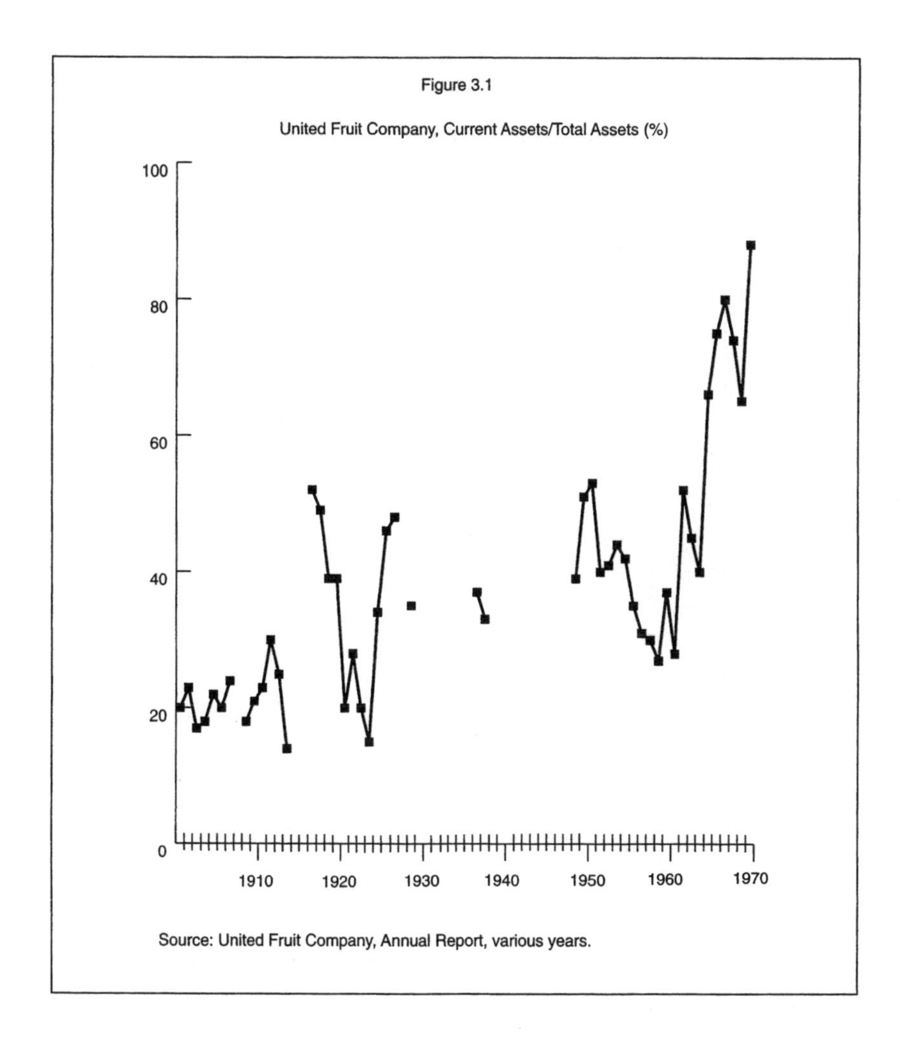


Figure 3.1

United Fruit Company, Current Assets/Total Assets (%)

Source: United Fruit Company, Annual Report, various years.

no one has tried to see any relationship between the disintegration of United Fruit and the political changes in Latin America. In this section I will show that the company faced increasing political uncertainties in the 1950s that led to its divestiture in the 1960s.

Three different sources indicate United Fruit's internal shift from a production company to a marketing company in the decades after World War II: the relation of current assets and total assets, land ownership, and steamship ownership. One way to see this shift is by tracing the evolution of the company's current assets in relation to its total assets. Total assets

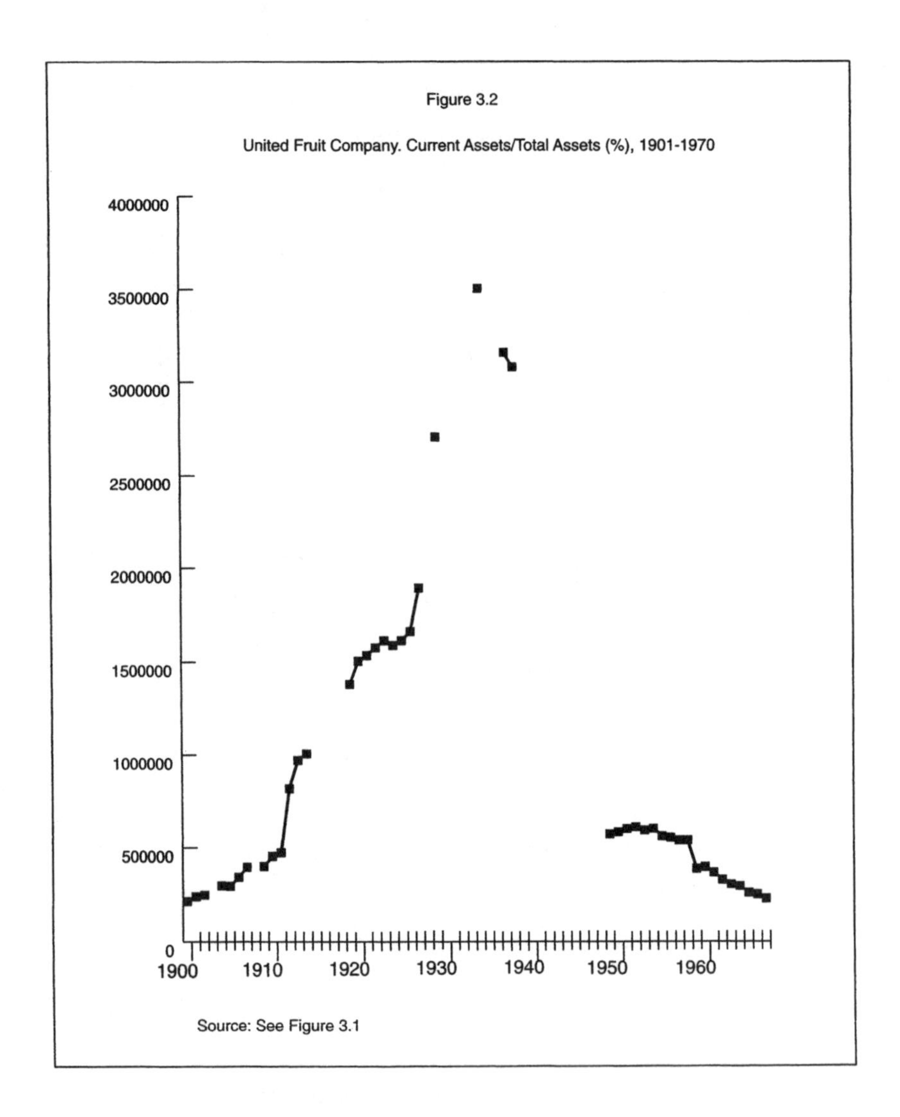


include current assets and fixed assets. United Fruit's current assets were the wealth the company had in financial securities, cash, and future sources of income, like accounts receivable. Its fixed assets included the company's physical wealth, such as buildings, ships, cars, trucks, lands, furniture, and other wealth. Service companies, such as banks, tend to have a larger percentage of their assets in current assets than in fixed assets. Production companies, on the other hand, tend to have a significant

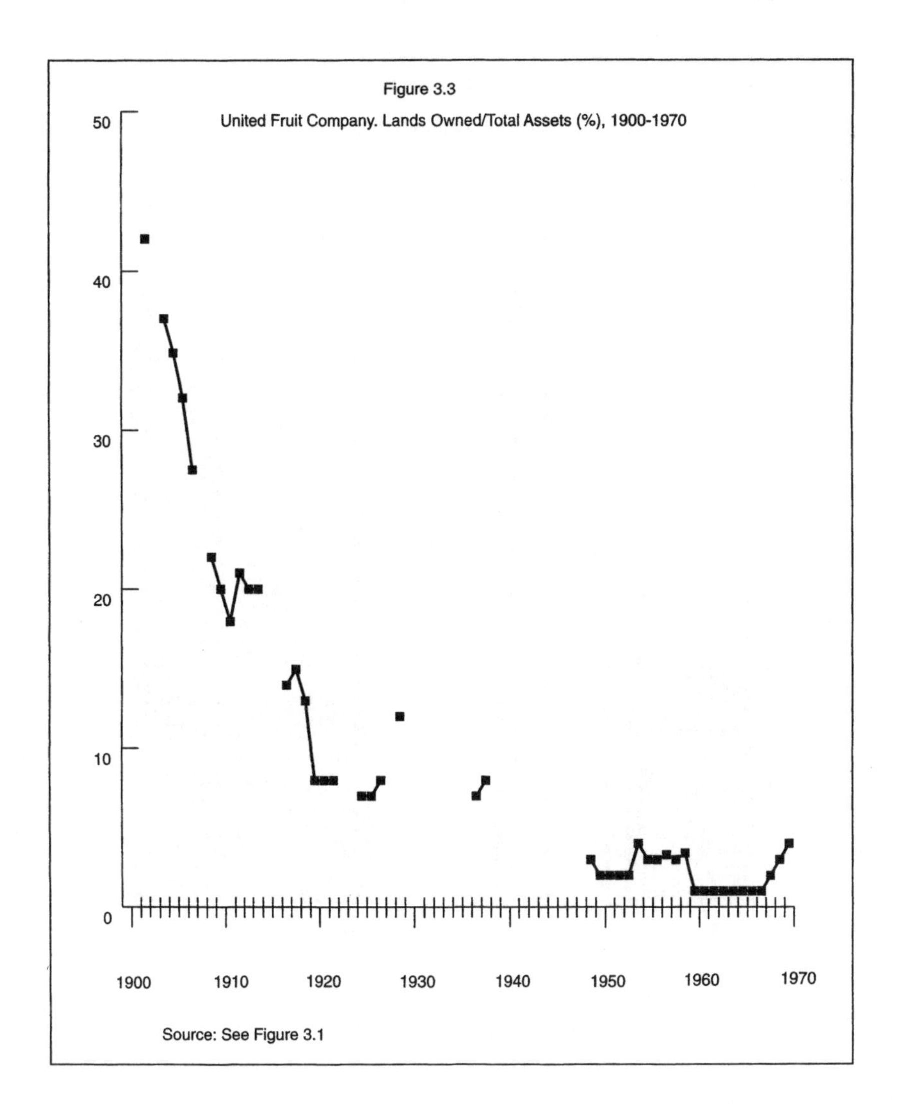


Figure 3.3

United Fruit Company. Lands Owned/Total Assets (%), 1900-1970

Source: See Figure 3.1

portion of their assets in fixed assets. If United Fruit's current assets are weighed in relation to its total assets, a clear tendency toward service is seen after 1961 (see figure 3.1). This tendency becomes clearer when we analyze the behavior of the most important asset United Fruit owned to produce its product—land. Figure 3.2 shows that after World War II, United Fruit decreased its landholdings dramatically, and it did so much more aggressively after 1960.[14] Figure 3.3 shows how land also decreased

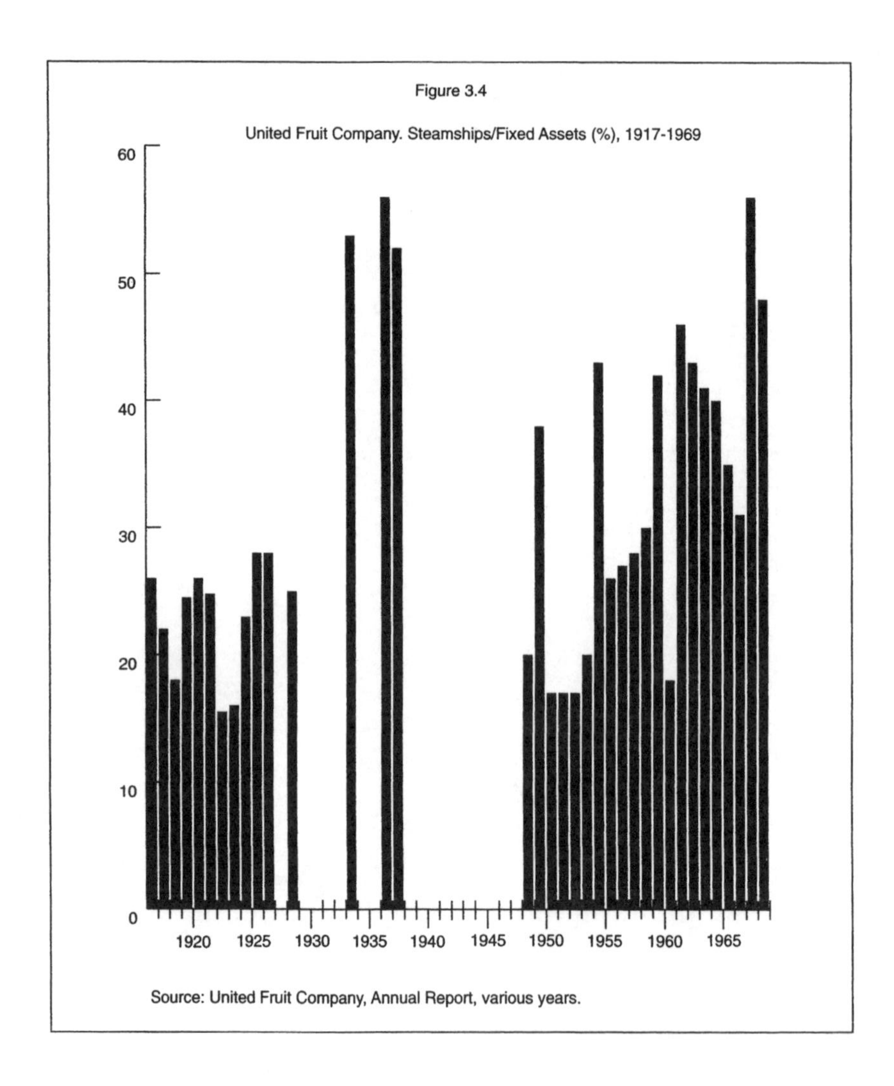


in importance as a proportion of United Fruit's total assets. Figure 3.3 also shows that after 1960, lands decreased in proportion to total assets even more. United Fruit did not get rid of all its fixed assets, however; ships remained an important fixed asset (figure 3.4), because the company still needed them to effectively focus on marketing.

The evolution of United Fruit's assets shows that in the late 1950s and 1960s there was a clear change in the company's strategy; its internal structure began to resemble more that of a marketing company than a production company. One way to understand why the company changed is to see the evolution of its profit rate in the long term.

## *Profitability of United Fruit's Operations*

Given the company's image throughout Latin America as *El Pulpo* (the Octopus), one would expect United Fruit to have exorbitantly high profit rates. Indeed, in some years, especially early in its history, the company did well. However, if we examine the company's return on equity and return on as-

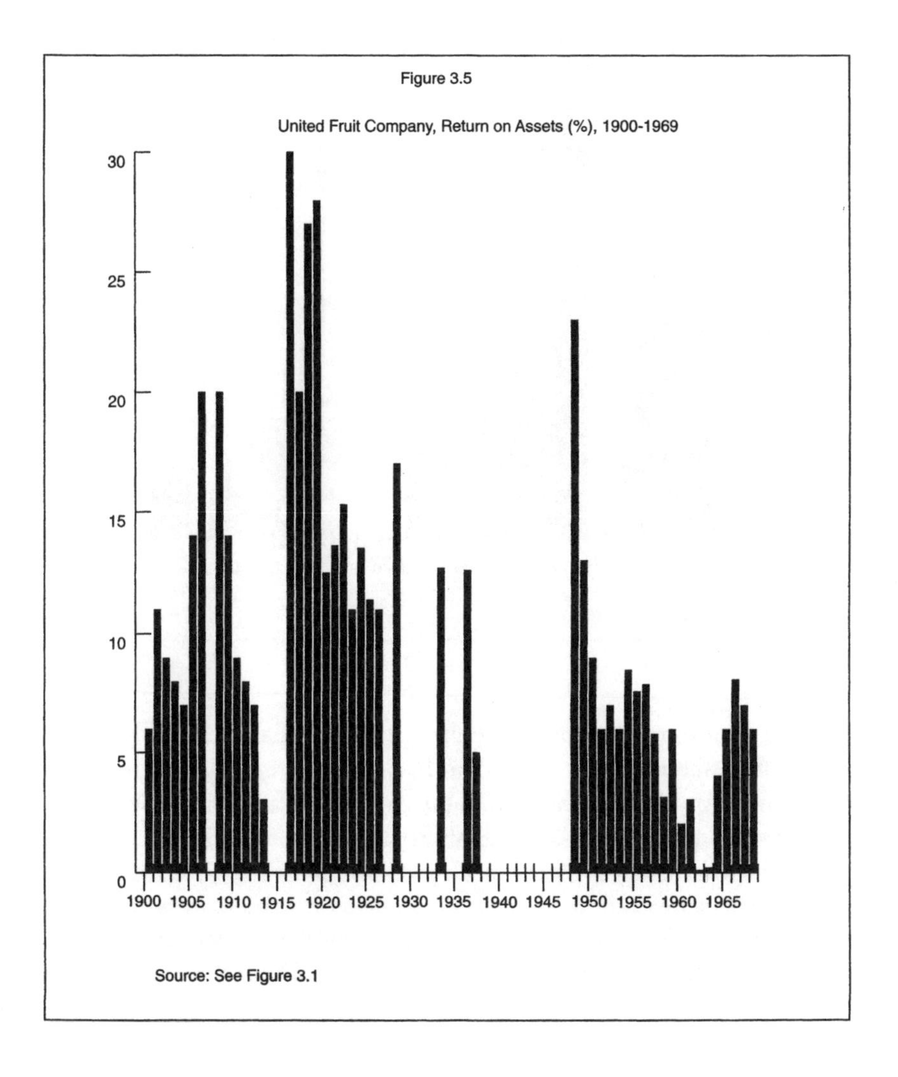


Figure 3.5

United Fruit Company, Return on Assets (%), 1900-1969

Source: See Figure 3.1

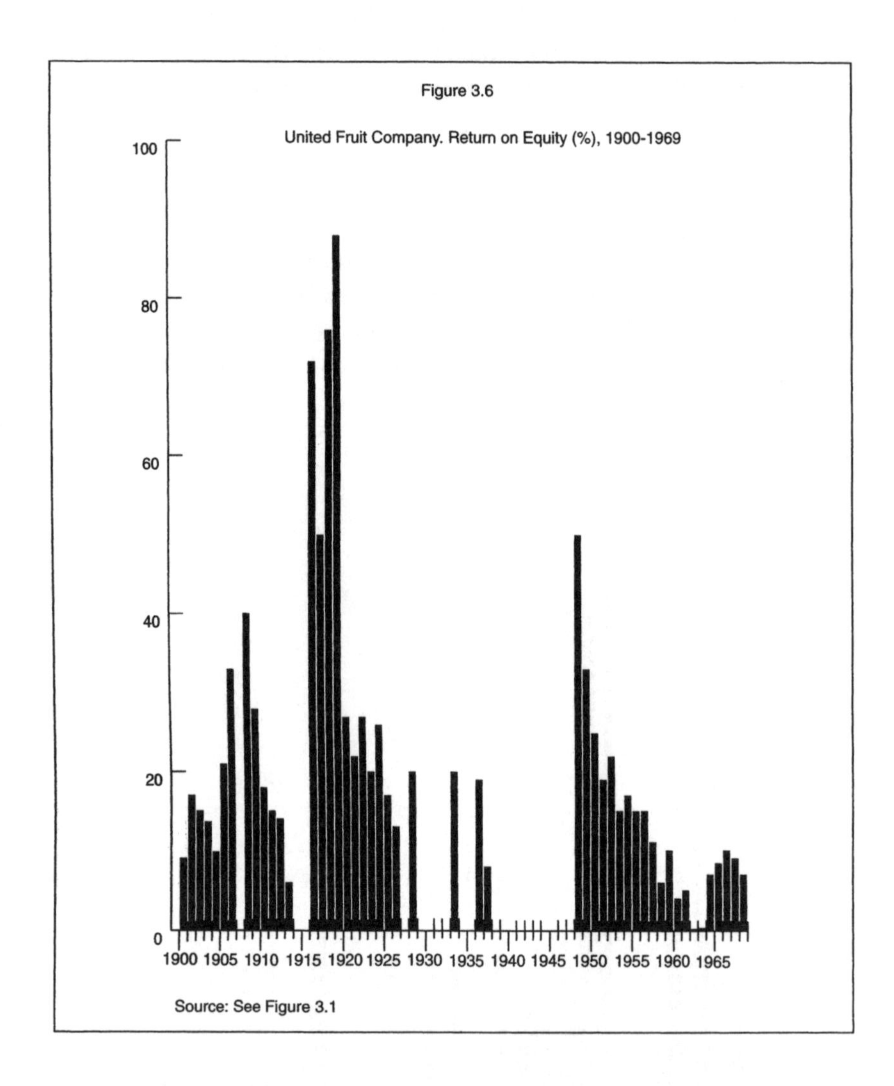


sets, we get a somewhat more complicated picture characterized by declining profits, especially after World War II. Return on equity is how much income the company brought in from the amount of capital it received from its investors. Return on assets establishes the relationship between net income and total assets; it is how much profit the company earns from its assets. The higher each of these ratios is, the better the company is doing.[15]

The return on assets shows a variable rate for the pre–World War II period, but a decreasing tendency in the post–World War II period. Late in the second decade of the 1900s, it reached levels of 30%, falling to around 5% just prior to World War II. After the war, the return on assets began at levels around 25% and then fell below 5% in the early 1960s. In short, United Fruit's return on assets peaked in the 1920s and declined dramatically in the postwar period (see figure 3.5).

The return on equity ratio shows a similar pattern. Figure 3.6 shows how this ratio reached levels over 20% in the early 1920s and then decreased. During the postwar period, it fell dramatically, actually having a negative value in 1970.[16]

One potential counter-argument to United Fruit's declining profits is that the fall in United Fruit's profit rate came from one of the other businesses in which the company was involved. Although United Fruit is recognized for its banana business, it was not their only line of operation. After World War II, the company's management showed an increasing interest in diversifying its operations. United Fruit began an aggressive diversification program in 1960, with businesses in sugar, transportation, processed foods, fast food products, communications, and others. However, despite a strong effort to decrease the company's dependence on bananas, this remained the most important of the company's businesses, and banana marketing always represented more than half of all of United Fruit's other businesses combined (see table 3.1).[17] Therefore, even in times of diversification, the business that counted was bananas.[18]

United Fruit's profitability ratios suggest the earlier period of the company's history—the one defined by vertical integration—was actually more profitable. Why, then, did the multinational choose switch to a sys-

TABLE 3.1

*United Fruit Company: Sales of Products and Services. Percentage of participation, bananas vs. other businesses*

| *Year* | *Bananas (%)* | *Sugar, transportation, communications, processed food, and others combined (%)* |
|---|---|---|
| 1962 | 63 | 37 |
| 1963 | 60.4 | 39.6 |
| 1964 | 60.8 | 39.2 |
| 1965 | 65 | 35 |
| 1966 | 65 | 35 |
| 1967 | 63.8 | 36 |
| 1968 | 63 | 37 |

Source: Author's calculations, made with information taken from United Fruit Company, *Annual Report to the Stockholders* (Boston: Various Years)

tem that appears to have been less profitable in the long run? Was this decision a strategic miscalculation or were there other factors that compelled the company to divest itself of landholdings and production?

## *United Fruit's Risks and Shareholders Fears*

Why did the company continue to divest (that is, pull out of direct production and switch its resources into marketing), despite the fact that the strategy resulted in decreased profit rates? Part of the explanation has to do with the expectations of United Fruit's investors. What was the perception the investors had of the company? What did financial analysts think? What was the risk perception related to the company's internal structure? Two ways to answer these questions are by analyzing the company's own views of what their problems were (such as, by looking at their annual reports) and by looking at the perception of independent financial analysts such as Moody's Investors Service. Moody's is one of the two most important analysts in the United States. Because negative evaluations from Moody's can prove fatal to a company's share prices, no publicly traded American corporation can afford to ignore Moody's recommendations. This was especially true during this time period, when the stock market was dominated by major institutional investors.

Before 1949, Moody's considered United Fruit a fairly good investment option. As late as 1946, the company was even included among Moody's "Recommended Investment Stocks." By 1949, however, doubt about the company's activities emerged. Although Moody's still considered United Fruit a good option, it attributed the company's decreasing profits to rising social and political problems in Central America. Moody's warned, "future political developments remain an uncertainty."[19] This warning coincided with a gloomy letter from United Fruit's president to its stockholders. Whereas at the beginning of 1949, the company had expectations of exceeding the prior year both in tonnage of bananas marketed and in sales volume, conditions arose that made this impossible. Labor trouble in Guatemala interrupted shipments from that country for six weeks; labor troubles in Colombia and Costa Rica of shorter duration also resulted in the loss of fruit from these countries.[20] The market reacted to the company's situation by raising its risk ratio, as shown in figure 3.9. Moody's overall concern emanated from labor unrest in United Fruit's Central American divisions. These concerns were highlighted in the opening statements of three analyses from 1950 and 1951: "The lower earnings last year were caused by abnormal weather conditions and labor troubles in several important Latin American areas."[21]

In 1950 and 1951, Moody's saw conflicts with the Guatemalan labor movement as an important issue affecting the company's stock:

> Outcome of the company's wage dispute with Guatemalan labor could have longer term effects than the mere reduction in earnings this year. If United Fruit were to abandon production there, other companies would probably move in and develop a competitive position. Or, if the company compromises the issue, labor in other countries would probably demand similar concessions.[22]

The 25% price decline of this stock from its 1951 all-time high can be attributed primarily to the impact upon earnings of a hurricane and a six month work stoppage at the company's Guatemala plantations.[23]

The company's report to its stockholders was not more optimistic:

> During recent years banana production in Guatemala has been declining due to frequent windstorms, inroads of disease, and the absence of conditions conducive to the planting of new cultivations. At the same time labor costs have been rising sharply. The company has always paid wages far greater than those paid by others in Guatemala for similar work, and up to the last few years its labor relations have been most satisfactory. During recent years, however, extremists who are not employees of the Company have kept the laborers in a constant state of unrest. . . . To date the Company's offer to negotiate participation contracts with Guatemala similar to those negotiated with other countries has not been accepted.[24]

Moody's suggested the problems in Central America were not limited to labor but to potential difficulties United Fruit could have with local governments. Moody's proved prophetic. United Fruit faced its most infamous problem in 1951 when Jacobo Arbenz was elected president of Guatemala. With United Fruit in mind, in 1953, Arbenz developed an agrarian reform law and expropriated some of the company's uncultivated lands.[25] The company saw its conflict with Arbenz as serious and gave a long explanation of the conflict in its annual report, but United

Fruit president Kenneth Redmond was nonetheless unable to assure shareholders the company would prevail:

> The Company has filed with the Department of State, for presentation to the Government of Guatemala, a claim for just compensation for the expropriation including the appraised present value of the lands and improvements expropriated, and the damage caused to the Company by depriving it of its reserve banana lands and greatly shortening the useful life of its expensive facilities on the west coast. Since the lands have actually been expropriated, the acreage has been dropped from the records. . . . Under the present conditions the Company is not planting additional acreage in Guatemala, and the acreage of banana cultivations in production will become less each year. As long as the political atmosphere remains inimical to American enterprise, the Company must of necessity follow a policy of retrenchment.[26]

But Moody's was worried about the broader implications: "This is not a question of immediate crucial importance to the company's earning power. More important is whether Guatemalan events are indicative of what may happen elsewhere in Latin America where United Fruit operates."[27]

Arbenz was eventually ousted by opposition from certain sectors of the Guatemalan army, the U.S. Department of State, the Organization of American States, and Guatemalan large land owners. Colonel Castillo Armas, who took power after the coup, overturned Arbenz's social reforms and returned the expropriated lands to United Fruit. The twenty-five-year-old Argentinian, Ernesto Guevara (later known as "El Ché"), who had previously applied for a position as a medical doctor with United Fruit, witnessed the coup. He was living in Guatemala at the time as a doctor and bookseller and organized resistance militias against Castillo's army. Facing an inevitable defeat, he escaped to Mexico where he met another political refugee who would become one of his closest friends—Cuban Fidel Castro.[28]

The United Fruit Company reported the change of government with great relief to its shareholders and emphasized the negotiations it was holding with other Central American governments regarding land, labor, taxes, and welfare: "The overthrow of the Communist-dominated government of Guatemala, while causing a cessation of shipments from that country for a period of about three weeks, was a decidedly favorable development which will have far-reaching effects in the future."[29]

United Fruit also reported its cooperation with the new Guatemalan government in land distribution and welfare policies. However, despite the company's optimism, Moody's was skeptical. In 1954, Moody's published an article—"United Fruit's Prospects under Political Pressures"—that suggested the problems in Guatemala reflected United Fruit's general inability to manipulate Latin American governments in the postwar period (which an unfavorable tax policy in Costa Rica quickly confirmed). Three years after the ouster of Arbenz, Moody's still warned, "Further political disturbances in the Caribbean area can never be ruled out."[30] Similarly, in 1956, Moody's reported, "United Fruit has finances that are proportionately among the strongest of any United States corporation. . . . Unfortunately, however, the company's operations are subject to natural and foreign political hazards beyond its control."[31]

United Fruit's political risks were not limited to Central America; it also had to face the hostility of the U.S. government. In 1954, the U.S. Department of Justice filed a lawsuit against United Fruit for violating antitrust legislation. As a result, in 1956, the company had to sell its holdings of the International Railways of Central America (IRCA), as well as the lands in its Guatemalan division (an obligation the company eventually met in 1972 when Del Monte acquired these lands). Three years later, in 1959, United Fruit reported bad news from the Caribbean. First, the Cuban revolutionary government was expropriating Cuban land.[32] Second, in Costa Rica (a country with a very different political regime), United Fruit clashed with the government on labor legislation. For United Fruit's efforts, it was rewarded with a massive strike by its workers.

In November 1959, the Costa Rican congress passed (over the president's veto) a law requiring all employers to pay laborers a year-end bonus. As some of the terms of the law were clearly discriminatory and in direct violation of United Fruit's operating contracts with the government, United Fruit refused to comply with the improper and discriminatory provisions. United Fruit's refusal was used as a means to provoke an illegal strike and, by threats and intimidation, prevented laborers from working.[33]

Following these events, Moody's began to advise investors to look elsewhere: "United Fruit has been hurt by political troubles in several Latin American countries and periodic weather damage to its banana crops. . . . Management is currently attempting to combat its problems . . . but any appreciable effect will be far in the future. . . . We therefore see no reason to hold the stock, and would switch into U.S. Rubber for better prospects."[34]

The changing situation in the 1950s for United Fruit was not limited to Central America; United Fruit also faced competition from the emergence of a fairly independent banana industry in Ecuador. Table 3.2 shows the rapid emergence of Ecuador as the world's largest banana producer by the mid-1950s.[35] Ecuador was unique in the sense that its government helped keep the industry in the hands of domestic planters. The dramatic increase in exports from Ecuador threatened United Fruit by leading to a general decrease in international banana prices.[36] Ecuador had a tremendous competitive advantage in terms of production costs, as summarized in table 3.3, and was seen as a problem by United Fruit's president:

> [In Ecuador] the local growers were not required to furnish housing, schools, hospitals, the necessary access roads, port facilities, as United Fruit had to as its own cost [in Central America]. . . . Wages of banana workers in these areas were also far less than United Fruit paid its workers in other producing countries. The small compensatory tax put on export bananas in Ecuador was insignificant compared with the costs to United Fruit elsewhere. . . . Large quantities of bananas became available at costs less than United Fruit's costs.[37]

In Ecuador, United Fruit was in a different situation than in Central America. United Fruit never had a significant share in banana production, producing just 2% of the national total banana crop.[38] Additionally, no associate producer program existed in Ecuador, so United Fruit had to compete with other marketing companies in the open market.[39] By the late 1950s, the company's lands in Ecuador suffered from the banana destroying disease Sigatoka and peasant activism, which encouraged the company to get rid of these minor plantations.[40]

United Fruit also faced difficulties when its main rival, Standard Fruit, dramatically increased its productivity and decreased the risks inherent to banana production by pursuing the biggest technological change in the banana industry since the 1900s. In 1956, Standard Fruit began conducting experiments to develop a new kind of banana resistant to the Panama Disease that had destroyed many of its (and United Fruit's) plantations in Central America.[41] Before the 1950s, all bananas traded worldwide were from the Gros Michel family, which had a thick skin that made them easy to export in bunches, but were not resistant to the Panama Disease. The fruit developed by Standard, known as Valery, was smaller, less tasty, and had a weaker skin, but it was resistant to the disease and pro-

TABLE 3.2
*Banana Exports by Country (thousand of tons), 1950-1970*

| *Year* | *Colombia* | *Costa Rica* | *Ecuador* | *Guatemala* | *Honduras* | *Panamá* |
|---|---|---|---|---|---|---|
| 1950 | 143.8 | 222.0 | 169.6 | 160.2 | 262.1 | 145.6 |
| 1951 | 154.5 | 216.0 | 246.5 | 124.1 | 241.7 | 142.2 |
| 1952 | 152.6 | 412.0 | 429.8 | 95.1 | 261.7 | 118.9 |
| 1953 | 196.2 | 355.0 | 406.4 | 170 | 248.4 | 184.6 |
| 1954 | 195.7 | 355.3 | 492.2 | 153 | 221.6 | 221.7 |
| 1955 | 209.6 | 329.4 | 612.6 | 134.5 | 133.8 | 275.1 |
| 1956 | 215.9 | 232.0 | 578.9 | 124.8 | 181.4 | 247.8 |
| 1957 | 191.2 | 315.4 | 677.6 | 129.8 | 261.5 | 289.6 |
| 1958 | 189.0 | 302.4 | 742.2 | 112.9 | 398.2 | 273.2 |
| 1959 | 203.3 | 213.4 | 885.6 | 146.2 | 359.6 | 291.5 |
| 1960 | 190.7 | 272.8 | 897.4 | 197.6 | 363.0 | 263.3 |
| 1961 | 205.6 | 230.9 | 842.3 | 153.5 | 430.4 | 271.5 |
| 1962 | 147.1 | 287.3 | 656.8 | 81.3 | 334.5 | 262.3 |
| 1963 | 202.6 | 323.6 | 632.3 | 118.5 | 290.7 | 308.7 |
| 1964 | 171.6 | 347.8 | 624.9 | 92.6 | 306.6 | 377.0 |
| 1965 | 253.5 | 402.2 | 531.2 | 32.7 | 489.8 | 483.6 |
| 1966 | 310.9 | 293.3 | 653.1 | 60.9 | 668.9 | 543.7 |
| 1967 | 325.6 | 453.0 | 505.9 | 42.7 | 723.8 | 595.8 |
| 1968 | 401.5 | 711.8 | 556.5 | 66.4 | 787.8 | 682.3 |
| 1969 | 334.5 | 944.8 | 518.5 | 20.1 | 715.1 | 833.5 |
| 1970 | 261.8 | 839.5 | 540.1 | 28.0 | 737.2 | 825.3 |

Source: Table made with information taken from Colombia, Departamento Administrativo Nacional de Estadística, *Anuario de Comercio Exterior* (Bogota: various years); Economic Commission for Latin America (ECLA), *Boletín Económico para América Latina* (Santiago: 1950-1959); International Monetary Fund, *International Financial Statistics* (Washington: September 1968, September 1970)

TABLE 3.3
*Comparative costs of banana production.*
*Ecuador vs. Central America*

| | *Ecuador* | *Central America* |
|---|---|---|
| Cost of opening a banana plantation ($/hectare) [1958] | 120 | 2000–3100 |
| Workers/hectare [1964] | 0.5 | 0.60–0.75 |
| Cost of harvested bananas [1958] | 1.16 cents | 1.98 cents |
| Share of total freight plus unloading of the CIF Price [1964] | 36% | 32% |

Source: Table made with information taken from Valles, Jean-Paul, *The World Market for Bananas, 1964–72: Outlook for Demand, Supply, and Prices* (London: Praeger, 1968) 115, 117, 119, 123, 136, 137.

duced more fruit per acre. This resistance was enough incentive for Standard to begin a gradual change from Gros Michel to Valery bananas. Despite the advantages of Valery bananas over Gros Michel bananas, United Fruit did not change its crop immediately but waited until 1962. As a result of the delay, Standard Fruit increased its participation in the international market dramatically, from 8.9% in 1950 to 31% in 1965.[42]

Shifting from Gros Michel to Valery required huge changes. Valery's fragility made it necessary to change the entire transportation process of the bananas from the time they were harvested at the plantation until they reached the last consumer. United Fruit developed a system of "air wires" inside its plantations to avoid damaging the bunches. The air wires consisted of poles connected to each other with a moving wire going from the banana trees to the packing plant where the fruit was selected and packed. When the workers cut the banana bunch off the tree, they hung the bunch on a hook on the moving wire; in this way, the bananas were transported to the packing plant with minimum damage because they were not hit by anything. The stems of the bananas were then cut from the bunch, and they were packed in cardboard boxes. But, although the fruit was resistant to the Panama Disease it was not resistant to insects, so the company also had to cover the bunches with plastic bags while they were growing. All of these new processes required extensive changes; the company installed the air wire system, cardboard and plastic manufacturing plants, and packing plants.

A study by the Harvard Business School also pointed to the rise of Ecuadoran production as one of the most worrisome issues faced by United Fruit in the early 1960s. According to the study, the company had just two options: to get rid of all of its Central American production and associate producers and buy only from Ecuadoran producers in the open market or drastically reduce its costs and increase its productivity in the areas in which it operated.[43] United Fruit could survive only if a radical change was made.

## *The Banana Empire Strikes Back: Changes and Adaptations in the 1960s*

It was under these circumstances that United Fruit appointed Thomas Sunderland as president of the company. In his 1960 letter to shareholders, Sunderland announced that the company was going through a long-range readjustment program. The main transformations included a switch from the Gros Michel to Valery banana variety, a growing reliance on contract producers, an increase in purchases from Ecuador, and a general diversification of operations.[44] Indeed, a number of factors reflected the company's withdrawal from direct production. Total income from the sale of tropical properties increased dramatically from $2,871,094 in 1960 to $16,483,492 in 1961.[45] Indeed, the Harvard Business School study noted that although United Fruit could produce bananas more cheaply on its own, it made sense to get out of direct production for a number of reasons that were not strictly economic in nature:

> By encouraging the nationals to enter the banana industry, Mr. Sunderland believed United Fruit could contribute to the development of stable conditions in the tropics (i.e., aid in the creation of a growing middle class), gain partners who would be valuable allies in the development of joint interests, and reduce the frequent attacks by "trouble makers" against United Fruit as a large land owner and employer. . . . as a straight matter of production United Fruit could probably produce bananas at less cost on its own.[46]

Despite United Fruit's positive outlook, Moody's remained only cautiously optimistic about the company's prospects:

> Symbolic of management's innovations is its policy of selling Latin American land holdings to local interests while contracting to take their produce. This defense against possible expropriations has had mixed success, but it has aided in a 37% cut in the number of 'tropical' employees in the last four years.[47]

A year later, in 1962, Moody's maintained a similar attitude:

> Fourth quarter earnings were hurt by windstorm damage last summer, and the continuing longshoremen's strike. This may cool near-by investor enthusiasm for the stock, but with the price still well below book value, and the longer range outlook brighter, we would hold it.[48]

However, in spite of these transformations, United Fruit had not solved its remaining political problem—its unfinished antitrust trial—and Moody's reminded investors of this looming issue.[49] In fact, the only year

United Fruit's yield was again above the average yield of the top 200 companies traded on Wall Street was in 1965, when it informed its shareholders that the following year's earnings would fall by 15% of the gross revenue when the antitrust legislation consent would be implemented.[50] After the company presented a plan in 1966 to be implemented in 1968, both the market perceptions calculated in the yield and Moody's analyses improved. After having mentioned little about the company in its stock survey for two years, in 1967, Moody's saw United Fruit with optimism and advised investors to hold the stock because of its future growth perspectives.

The replacement of the Gros Michel strain of banana with the Valery also proved successful, improving productivity (now mostly under the associate producers' control) and return on equity (after 1966). The increase in Central American productivity due to Valery was enough to counterweigh the low production costs in Ecuador in such a way that by the late 1960s, Ecuador had lost its comparative advantage.[51] Central American production increased after 1965, quickly reaching levels similar to those of Ecuador, as shown in table 3.4.

In the late 1960s, United Fruit's management made it clear to shareholders it was aware of the social and political changes in Latin America and the company had no other choice than to adapt. In a retrospective analysis of United Fruit's operations, company president Herbert Cornuelle wrote, "No matter how successful we are in this process, we still will be perceived, however, I am sure, as a threat to national independence and sovereignty. The fact that we are domiciled in a foreign country and that we are big assures that."[52]

In 1970, United Fruit merged with the AMK Corporation to create a new company, United Brands. This event marked the end of United Fruit's transformation process. The company became part of a giant food conglomerate that included processed foods and meat packing. In his initial letter to shareholders, Eli Black, the first president of the conglomerate, again emphasized the political issues the company had to deal with:

> While these operations are in stable countries with enlightened governments, the fact is that all Latin American countries are being swept by strong winds of nationalist aspiration. [The company] knows that it must adjust to change in Latin America. It is adjusting. . . . One of the most sensitive areas is that of land use policies. . . . Since 1952 the Company has divested itself of 65% of its holdings in the four countries. Many thousand acres have been given to the governments for distribu-

TABLE 3.4
*Productivity of the Central American Banana Industry.*
*Tons per hectare, 1947-1970*

| *Year* | *Costa Rica* | *Guatemala* | *Panama* | *Honduras* |
|---|---|---|---|---|
| 1947 | 622 | 870 | 940 | 870 |
| 1948 | 762 | 860 | 1163 | 860 |
| 1949 | 957 | 513 | 1196 | 513 |
| 1950 | 879 | 712 | 1051 | 712 |
| 1951 | 841 | 515 | 1030 | 515 |
| 1952 | 955 | 252 | 810 | 252 |
| 1953 | 849 | 796 | 825 | 796 |
| 1954 | 919 | 811 | 904 | 811 |
| 1955 | 878 | 647 | 1043 | 646 |
| 1956 | 663 | 664 | 909 | 663 |
| 1957 | 1045 | 627 | 1071 | 627 |
| 1958 | 1111 | 528 | 930 | 528 |
| 1959 | 756 | 595 | 985 | 595 |
| 1960 | 965 | 829 | 839 | 829 |
| 1961 | 757 | 830 | 917 | 830 |
| 1962 | 843 | 552 | 867 | 552 |
| 1963 | 764 | 948 | 852 | 948 |
| 1964 | 929 | 1734 | 984 | 1734 |
| 1965 | 1083 | 738 | 1082 | 739 |
| 1966 | 1253 | 1275 | 1262 | 1275 |
| 1967 | 1339 | 1763 | 1598 | 1763 |
| 1968 | 1547 | 2330 | 1652 | 2330 |
| 1969 | 1982 | 2351 | 1952 | 2351 |
| 1970 | 2203 | 2561 | 2386 | 2561 |

Source: Ellis, *Las transnacionales del banano*, 410.

tion; the remainder has been sold to individuals and firms. . . . In several countries land has been given to unions to build low-cost housing financed by the company.[53]

The change in risk perception by the company's shareholders and potential investors can be quantified by calculating the yield on common stock. This is a widely accepted measure of risk and can show how the market perceives a certain stock in relation to other alternatives. The higher the yield, the riskier the investment is considered.

I calculated the yield on common stock for United Fruit and compared it with the average yield calculated by Moody's Investors Service for the top 200 companies traded on Wall Street.[54] If the company's ratio is higher than those of the top 200 companies, its stock is riskier than the average stock of the top 200 companies traded in the stock market. If its risk ratio is lower than the top 200, investing in United Fruit faces a lower risk than investing in the average company. Figure 3.7 displays the results of this calculation and clearly shows that before 1949, the company was considered less risky by investors than after that year. Perceived risk increased from 1950 to 1959. From 1960 on, however, United Fruit was seen as a less risky investment because it announced it would pull out of direct production and depend more heavily on contract producers.[55]

These events and their relationship to investors' perceptions of the company are summarized in table 3.5. This table compares yields on the company's common stock with the average yield calculated by Moody's for the top 200 companies traded on Wall Street.[56] The yield on common stock measures how risky an investment is perceived by the market—the higher the yield, the higher the risk perception.[57] A calculation of the yield in itself does not say much, as investors need to know if a stock is more or less risky than other stocks. When United Fruit's yield is compared with that of the top 200 companies, it can be seen whether the company was considered more or less risky than other investments.[58] The data show the risk perception of United Fruit decreased when the company diminished its direct operations in Latin America and, therefore, reduced its labor and political problems in the region.

As labor unions grew more powerful, governments sought more revenue from exports and local elite became less reliable agents of foreign capital, the company witnessed an erosion of the political and economic control on which its vertical integration rested. Simultaneously, the company could no longer count on the unconditional support of the American government, at least where direct military intervention was concerned. All of these developments contributed to a perception among investors that because of the political and social environment in Latin America, it was an increasingly risky place to do business.

Examination of the data presented in this chapter shows how United Fruit adapted to these perceptions, eventually choosing to withdraw from direct production and become a marketing company. These changes were made possible, in part, by the technical improvements of the post–World

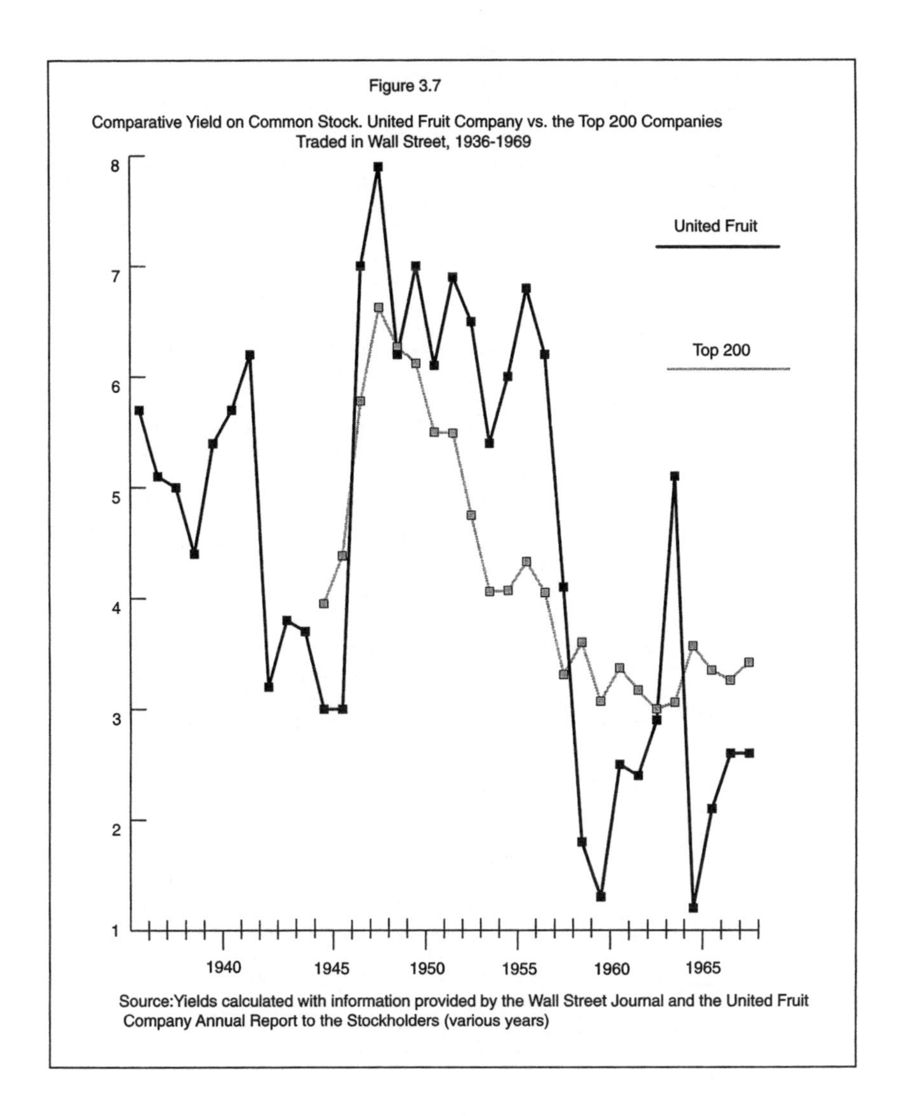


Figure 3.7

Comparative Yield on Common Stock. United Fruit Company vs. the Top 200 Companies Traded in Wall Street, 1936-1969

Source: Yields calculated with information provided by the Wall Street Journal and the United Fruit Company Annual Report to the Stockholders (various years)

War II period in the banana industry. Despite nationalist politicians and labor leaders creating the conditions leading to the company's divestiture from Latin America, these corporate policies were intended not as concessions to company adversaries but as strategies to please both financial analysts and investors. The "octopus" of the "Banana Empire" in the early twentieth century consciously dismantled itself in later years, largely to insure a continued place on top of the banana world.

TABLE 3.5

*Comparison of the Yield on Common Stock for United Fruit, Yield for the top 200 Companies, and Issues Affecting Earnings from United Fruit Annual Reports*

| *Year* | *Yield: United Fruit* | *Yield: Top 200 Companies* | *Issues having significant impact on earnings in the Annual Reports* |
|---|---|---|---|
| 1946 | 3 | 3.95 | |
| 1947 | 3 | 4.38 | |
| 1948 | 7 | 5.98 | |
| 1949 | 7.9 | 6.62 | Labor problems in Guatemala, Colombia, and Costa Rica decrease production and interrupt shipments |
| 1950 | 6.2 | 6.27 | |
| 1951 | 7 | 6.12 | Labor unrest in Guatemala plantations. United Fruit has problems at solving the conflict. |
| 1952 | 6.1 | 5.5 | Slow recovery of Guatemalan operations after strike. |
| 1953 | 6.9 | 5.49 | Expropriation of some company lands in Guatemala under Arbenz. The company reports problems in the negotiations. |
| 1954 | 6.5 | 4.75 | The U.S. Department of Justice files antitrust suit against United Fruit. |
| | | | The company faces ten-week strike in Honduras. |
| 1955 | 5.4 | 4.06 | Big losses from weather problems. |
| 1956 | 6 | 4.07 | Heavy windstorms provoke new losses. |
| 1957 | 6.8 | 4.33 | Company losses lawsuit from International Railways of Central America's (IRCA) shareholders. |
| 1958 | 6.2 | 4.05 | Company announces change of banana from Gros Michel to Valery to decrease potential losses from windstorms and Panama Disease. |
| 1959 | 4.1 | 3.31 | Conflict with Costa Rican government for "discriminatory" labor legislation followed by strike by workers. |
| | | | The Cuban Agrarian Reform Law makes almost all company's lands subject to expropriation. Little hope of succeeding in a conflict with revolutionary government. |
| 1960 | 1.8 | 3.6 | United Fruit announces long-term plan to restructure the company that includes larger role of the associate producers. |
| 1961 | 1.3 | 3.07 | The company reports no labor problems with larger participation of associate producers. |
| 1962 | 2.5 | 3.37 | Losses due to windstorms. |
| 1963 | 2.4 | 3.17 | |
| 1964 | 2.9 | 3 | |
| 1965 | 5.1 | 3.06 | The company announces it will lose about 15% of gross revenue when antitrust legislation consent is implemented. |
| 1966 | 1.2 | 3.57 | |
| 1967 | 2.1 | 3.35 | |
| 1968 | 2.3 | 3.25 | |
| 1969 | 2.6 | 3.42 | |

Source: Yields calculated with information taken from The *Wall Street Journal* and the United Fruit Company annual reports. Information on issues taken from United Fruit Company annual reports various years.

## *The Banana Republics Rebel: United Brands and the Creation of the Unión de Países Exportadores de Banano [UPEB]*

The structure of the international banana market witnessed radical changes in the 1970s. First, United Brands began to lose ground to rival, Standard Fruit, after Standard Fruit merged with Castle and Cook in 1972. Second, when Del Monte merged with the West Indies Fruit Company and purchased United Brands's banana plantations in Guatemala (as a result of the antitrust action against United Brands), it made Del Monte a stronger and more aggressive competitor in the banana market. Third, hurricane Fifi destroyed most of United Brands's production areas in Honduras in 1974. Last, United Brands had to confront the challenge of the creation of the Unión de Países Exportadores de Banano [UPEB] by the Central American governments in 1974 to control banana exports.

When Eli Black took over United Brands, he wanted to transform the company's image in Latin America and the United States. The company awarded several Central American students with scholarships and made significant improvements in the health and housing services of its employees. In his letter to the company's shareholders in 1973, Eli Black proudly presented the company's social programs in the opening letters of the 1972 and 1973 annual reports. In 1972, he said,

> [There] was a dramatic change in the image of our company. It is a reflection of many years of effort to improve the working and social conditions of our employees, especially in Latin America. Our changing image was exemplified in numerous articles in the *New York Times*, the *Chicago Daily News*, the *Boston Globe*, etc., in which it was said of the company, "It may well be the most socially conscious American company in the hemisphere."[59]

In another section of the same report, the company quoted the *New York Times*: "What emerges from talks with labor, management and government is a picture of a company that anticipated the changes that have swept Latin America and has quietly set about to adjusting them."[60] To show how things had changed, United Brands gave a detailed description of the economic and social aid it provided Nicaraguans after the devastating earthquake the country had in 1972.[61]

In spite of these changes, Black faced new political problems in Latin America in 1974.

In March 1974, the governments of Costa Rica, Guatemala, Honduras, Panama, and Colombia signed the Panama Agreement, forbear of the Unión de Países Exportadores de Banano. The agreement's main goals were to increase taxation on banana multinationals, control supply to manipulate prices, and modify the tax and land concessions granted to the multinationals decades earlier. This was a response to the steady decline of the international price of bananas and the hardships of these countries due to an international oil crisis and hurricane Fifi, which destroyed hundreds of Central American banana plantations.[62]

The founders of the UPEB claimed producing countries were getting an unfair share of banana export profits. According to the founders, Central American countries were getting 11% of the income generated in the banana market, while the multinationals received 37%, and the retailers in consuming countries earned 19%.[63] The export taxes the producing countries wanted to impose violated what had been originally agreed on in the concessions given to the multinationals. These concessions had been granted for long periods of time (between fifty-eight and ninety-nine years, and sometimes with an indefinite deadline) and established an average tax of 2 cents per bunch, which is equivalent to 80 cents per ton. In order to increase the tax to 55 dollars per ton, the governments of Costa Rica, Honduras, and Panama passed laws that nullified the previous contracts between their governments and the multinationals in 1974, 1975, and 1976, respectively. These laws not only increased taxes but also eliminated many of the generous concessions the foreign corporations had enjoyed.[64]

The multinational corporations did not remain passive and protested by interrupting shipments and threatening the countries with export strikes and layoffs. Standard Fruit interrupted its exports from Honduras, and United Brands reduced its Costa Rican exports by 30%.[65] In response, the Central American governments began to use harsher language against the multinationals, and strong mutual accusations began. The situation reached a tense point in June 1974 when two high-ranking officials of the Panamanian government accused Standard Fruit and United Brands of conspiracy to murder Panama's president, Omar Torrijos, and of supporting military coups in the region.[66] In the meantime, banana workers in Costa Rica went on several strikes supporting the creation of the UPEB. Torrijos, a charismatic president known for his strong nationalism, anti-imperialistic discourse, and close friendship with Fidel Castro, refused to give in to United Brands, saying he would "take the war to its last consequences," and showed the conflict as a war for national sovereignty. United Brands continued its boycott by destroying around $1 million worth of bananas and refusing to continue exporting. Torrijos promised United Brand's 15,000 banana workers he would pay their wages as long as the conflict continued, and Castro offered to buy the Panamanian bananas.[67]

The conflict was settled in September 1974, when UPEB was formally created with strong resistance from Torrijos and no help from the U.S. government, United Brands accepted the new policies of the Panamanian government, which also meant accepting the UPEB and the new political environment in Central America. Shortly afterward, the company restarted its operations.

The year of these conflicts was not a profitable one for United Brands. That year alone, the company reported a net loss of $43,607,000, for which they blamed weather problems and the conflict with the Central American republics.[68] Figure 3.8 shows United Brands's dip in net revenues in 1974. In that year's report, the company informed its shareholders the new agreements with the local governments were going to mean higher taxes and fees and less property in Central America, but added the company

> is proud of the long working relationships it has had with the nations of Latin America. We look forward to continued associations which are mutually beneficial both to our company and to the peoples of the nations in which we work. We further have pledged to those nations our support as a responsible corporate citizen.[69]

The conflict around the creation of the UPEB revealed the new political realities of the region. On one hand, local governments stubbornly insisted on pushing ahead with their new policies despite strong opposition from the largest two banana corporations. On the other hand, it was clear that the U.S. government distanced itself from what was going on in the banana producing regions despite pleas made by both United Brands and Standard Fruit.

Under the UPEB, the producing countries increased their participation in the banana market via tax income. Central American producers increased their earnings from banana export taxes from $25.4 million in 1974 to $44.5 million in 1975 to $51.4 million in 1976. This growth continued steadily to a peak of $102.1 million in 1981. The UPEB countries

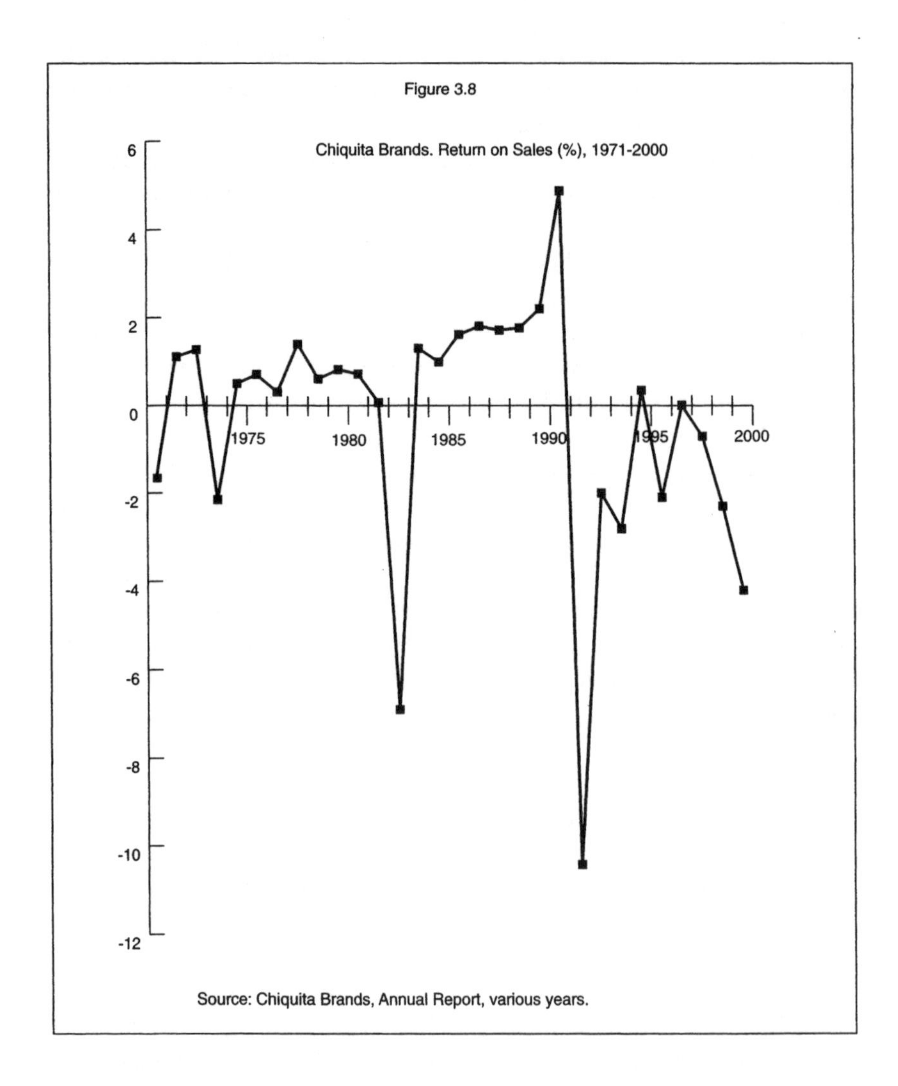


also attempted to participate in the international marketing of bananas by creating Comunbana, their own export corporation, in 1977. This enterprise was owned jointly by the governments (with 80% of the shares) and local entrepreneurs of each Central American country, and it exported to Eastern Europe and the United States in the early 1980s. Comunbana was a short-lived effort and was never a real competitor for the traditional multinationals, which actually increased their international market participation from 58% in 1973 to 70% in 1981.[70]

The multinational corporations adapted to the political changes in Central America by using the mechanisms created by the UPEB to expand their share in the banana industry. In the 1970s, the Central American governments channeled loans provided by multilateral agencies (such as the World Bank or the Inter-American Development Bank) to local producers in order to stimulate local production to gain more independence from the multinational corporations. According to José Roberto Lopez's calculations, from the twelve Costa Rican farms that received subsidized governmental loans in 1980, United Brands had a stake of more than 40% in five of them; similar results could be observed in Honduras.[71] At the same time, the multinational corporations gradually increased their participation in Ecuador.[72]

## *Eli Black's Suicide: United Brands at the Center of Scandal*

The creation of the UPEB not only cost United Brands financially, but it also damaged their reputation. In February 1975, president Eli Black committed suicide by jumping from the 44th floor of his office building. The investigations by the Securities Exchange Commission uncovered a corrupt scheme by the company to negotiate a reduction in the UPEB's export tax in Central America. Black was at the center of a bribery case involving several high-ranking officials of the Honduran government, including Honduran president, Oswaldo López Arellano. When the results of the investigation became public, United Brands admitted it had paid $1.25 million in bribes to Honduran officials through the company's subsidiaries, whose books were falsified to cover up these transactions. According to United Brands, the whole scheme had been authorized by Black. The deeper the investigations went, the worse the situation became for the company. The Securities Exchange Commission also discovered United Brands had paid $750,000 in bribes in Italy to get favorable business opportunities in Europe.[73]

In the 1974 annual report, Wallace W. Booth, Black's replacement as president of the company, claimed the bribes had been made without the knowledge of the board of directors.[74] The company's new management made a huge effort (with some success) to recover the company's reputation, but by 1974 analysts still described United Brands as a "case of corporate calamity."[75]

## *Chiquita versus Europe: A New Era of Political Conflict in the 1990s*

United Brands began the 1980s precariously. It was losing market share to Standard Fruit (renamed Dole) and Del Monte; a new Ecuadoran enterprise (Noboa) was on the rise; and the diversification process started by Black did not seem to help the company regain its prior domination of the banana market. The importance of banana sales in the company's operations had gradually decreased in the 1970s to a point where, in 1979, the company reported that meat represented 62% of its sales, while bananas and related products represented only 27%.[76] The diversification process had been successful, but United Brands lost a substantial share of the banana market to its competitors during the second half of the 1970s. It was during those years that a high school dropout (but successful businessman) named Carl Lindner began to acquire shares of United Brands and became its largest shareholder and CEO in 1984.[77] Lindner's strategy was to follow a divestiture process selling several subsidiaries (the sale of Elders and Fyffes being the most significant) and nonagriculture related business, refocusing the company's attention on bananas. In 1989, Lindner changed the name of the company to Chiquita Brands International, Inc., emphasizing the company's best-known brand.

During the first seven years of Lindner's management, it looked like his strategy was successful. Between 1984 and 1991, the company's profitability improved (see figure 3.8), its dividends per share increased from 2 cents to 55 cents, its earnings per share increased from 27 cents to $2.52, and its market value per share increased remarkably from $3.58 to $40.[78] Lindner's luck, however, radically changed in the 1990s—one the worst decades in the company's history.

Chiquita's problems in the 1990s stemmed from the way the European banana market evolved during that decade. One of Lindner's greatest ambitions was to take advantage of the promising European market due to the establishment of the European Union (EU) and the fall of Communism in Eastern Europe in the late 1980s. Particularly, Lindner had enormous hopes for the reunified Germany market. Germany was the largest importer of bananas in Europe with the highest level of per capita consumption, so Lindner's strategy anticipated a much larger market with Germany and the former Communist countries.[79]

To prepare for a larger market, Chiquita focused its efforts on banana production and shipping.[80] During the late 1980s and early 1990s the company again began to buy lands in Latin America and purchased and conditioned more ships, all at a cost of around $1 billion, most of it financed with debt.[81] However, Lindner's optimistic calculations proved wrong for two reasons. First, the Eastern European market did not grow as much as Chiquita anticipated, which hurt all the companies that invested in increasing their production capabilities. And second, in the early 1990s the European Union decided to establish a quota system on banana imports that favored the producers of Africa, the Caribbean, and the Pacific (the ACP countries) and left out Latin American producers—the main providers of bananas for Chiquita. Lindner challenged the European Union through his high-level political connections and started what became the most serious economic conflict between the European Union and the United States.

The predicted large consumer market in the former Communist countries was a disappointment for banana companies that anticipated a market in Eastern Europe. According to the Food and Agriculture Organization [FAO], the deep economic crisis Russia suffered in the late 1990s made bananas more expensive for Russian consumers and many of the distribution companies and supermarkets that distributed them went bankrupt. An FAO study reported that the sudden impoverishment of Russian consumers made them choose locally grown fruits instead of bananas. This created problems for Chiquita, which had heavily invested in increasing their production infrastructure.[82]

In addition to the miscalculation of the Eastern European market, the import system instituted by the European Union took Chiquita by surprise (although the roots of the import system can be traced back to the creation of the European Economic Community [EEC] in 1957).[83] From the beginning, the founding nations of the EEC had different views on how to deal with the banana market. While Germany wanted free market imports, France wanted a quota system that favored its former colonies. As long as a common external tariff existed, the two countries would never agree on how to include bananas in their common agricultural policy. In the end, bananas enjoyed a particular status among agricultural goods imported in Europe—the French imported only from its former colonies under a quota system and the Germans imported freely, mostly from Latin America.[84] The fruit coming into France was shipped from Africa and the Caribbean by French companies, while that imported into Germany was shipped from Latin America by United Brands and Standard Fruit.

The expansion of the EEC in the 1960s and early 1970s created more differences surrounding the policies on banana imports. Italy wanted a quota to protect Somalian producers; the United Kingdom wanted a quota for its former colonies in the Caribbean; Spain wanted to protect its production in the Canary Islands; Greece its production in Crete; and Portugal its production in Madeira. On the other hand, Denmark, Ireland, and the Benelux countries joined the Germans in advocating a free market. As a result, bananas continued to be imported into Europe under a different system for each country. The bananas imported into France and Britain were brought in by French and British corporations, while the American multinationals still were selling their Latin American fruit mostly in the German market.[85]

With the reunification of Germany in 1989 and its subsequent expansion of markets, the European Union considered it imperative to create a common policy toward banana imports. After the reunification, consumption in the former East Germany jumped from "3.1 kg in 1987–88 to 22.5 kg in 1991, more than 50% above the level in Western Germany,"[86] which reinforced the German preference for a free market system. In the early 1990s, the European Union began to look for a solution to the banana import disagreements that would not only be consistent with its commitments to some African and Caribbean producers under the treaties of the Lomé Convention, but also would be consistent with the negotiations with the General Agreement on Tariffs and Trade (GATT).[87] As a member of the GATT, the European Union could not simply raise the tariffs of Latin American bananas in order to protect their former colonies' production. Between 1992 and 1993, two crucial votes took place among European Union members in order to define a common policy toward bananas. With the opposition of Germany, the Netherlands, and Belgium, but the support of all the other members, the European Union approved a quota system that favored Caribbean and African producers.[88] The agreement became effective in July 1993.

The new European policy was a blow for Chiquita. The company already had suffered losses of $284 million in 1992, generated mostly by reduced production and decreased quality of bananas due to unusual weather patterns created by El Niño, so the new quota system was a disaster. Between 1992 and 1997, Chiquita's share in the world market fell from 32% to 26%, in the EU market it fell from 30% to 19%, and in

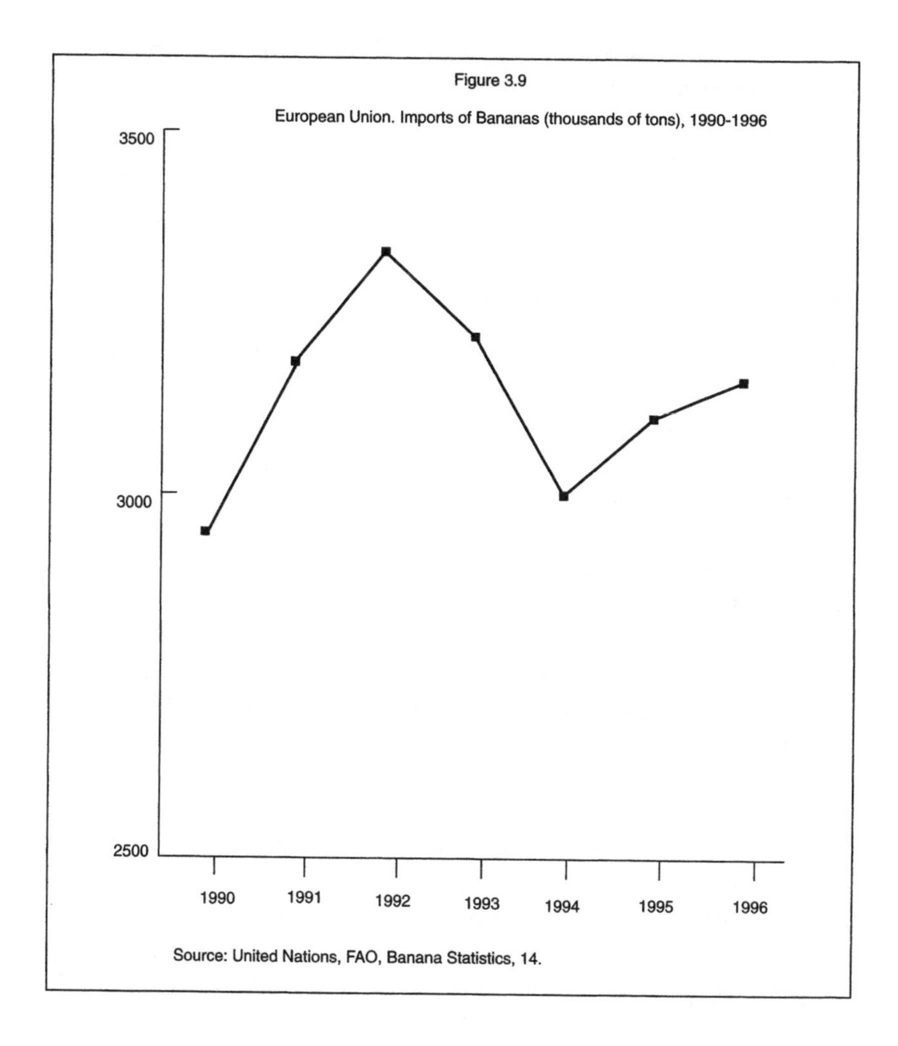


Figure 3.9

European Union. Imports of Bananas (thousands of tons), 1990-1996

Source: United Nations, FAO, Banana Statistics, 14.

Germany, its largest customer, its share fell from 40% to 20%.[89] During this period, and as a result of the new quota system, European consumption of bananas decreased as a whole, as shown in figure 3.9. While Chiquita was facing these difficulties, its rival, Dole, was doing better because it had prepared itself for the possibility of a regulated market in Europe by investing in African production, reducing its dependence on bananas, and focusing its marketing on Asian markets.[90] In a desperate attempt to survive, Chiquita belatedly tried to diversify its operations. This was not enough, and the company announced in January 2001 it was unable to meet its public debt obligations of $862 million.[91]

During the early stages of the European banana dispute in the 1990s, the U.S. government did not intervene because it felt the issue was not important to the American economy. However, this attitude changed when Lindner approached high-ranking politicians, especially Republican Senator Bob Dole.[92] Dole was beginning his presidential campaign and received a sizable donation of $1.5 million from Lindner plus an airplane owned by Chiquita for his campaign tour. Even though Lindner was closer to the Republicans than to the Democrats, he donated $5 million to both parties between 1993 and 1999 and became a frequent visitor at the White House, holding meetings with President Clinton and U.S. Trade Secretary Mickey Kantor.[93]

By August 1994, a group of twelve senators, including Dole, wrote a document urging President Clinton to intervene in what they considered an "illegal" measure by the European Union against American corporations. In January 1995, the U.S. government made its first official complaints to Europe, threatening with retaliation if the European Union did not drop the quota system. The Europeans rejected the U.S.'s complaints.[94] In response, the United States brought the case to the newly formed World Trade Organization [WTO] in September 1995.

Chiquita gained several new allies in its struggle against the European Union in the first months of the conflict with the EU quota system. It could count on the support of the Clinton administration and the Republican Party. Ecuador, the world's largest producer of bananas, brought the case to the WTO shortly afterward. Additionally, American beef producers requested help from the U.S. government to overturn the European ban on hormone beef, expanding the case against the European Union in the WTO to include both beef and bananas.

Senator Dole not only targeted the European Union but also the governments of Costa Rica and Colombia. In 1993, the two countries signed the Framework Agreement with the European Union, which gave them access to the European market under a quota system similar to the ACP countries' system. Although this meant Chiquita bananas produced in these two countries would reach the European Union, Chiquita complained to the U.S. government, accusing the two Latin American countries of unfair trade practices and cooperation with the restrictive European system. Even with some access to Europe for the Costa Rican and

Colombian bananas, Chiquita still could not export its bananas produced in the rest of its Latin American divisions.

In September 1994, Chiquita Brands and Senator Dole requested that the U.S. trade representative investigate the Colombian and Costa Rican banana exports to find out whether or not these countries were following discriminatory practices against U.S. corporations and to impose economic sanctions if they were.[95] In late 1995, the U.S. government threatened Colombia and Costa Rica with sanctions unless they abandoned the Framework Agreement. But the Clinton administration eventually dropped this threat, despite Senator Dole's strong opposition and let the two countries continue with the agreements they had previously signed with the European Union. In exchange, both Colombia and Costa Rica promised to fully cooperate with the WTO's final ruling in this matter.[96]

In May 1997, the WTO ruled in favor of the United States, but the policies followed by the European Union after January 1998 did not show that the Europeans were willing to comply with the decision. This marked the beginning of what the media called the "Banana War."[97]

The "Banana War" was the WTO's first serious issue, and it tested the organization's ability to settle differences. By January 1999, the United States established the first sanctions against some luxury European imports valued at $191 million as a retaliation for not complying with WTO regulations. The conflict continued throughout the year 2000—the last year of the Clinton administration. The administration rejected any EU proposal that would not benefit Chiquita by claiming the proposals were not compatible with WTO rules. Simultaneously, the Republican-dominated Congress continued pressuring the president to impose tougher sanctions on Europe.[98] Clinton finished his term without resolving the problem and passed it on to his successor, George W. Bush.

President Bush was also close to Lindner, who donated $1.03 million to his campaign (plus $677,000 to Democratic candidate Al Gore).[99] The Bush administration continued negotiations and reached a final agreement with the involved European countries (approved by the WTO) in April 2001. The new agreement established import licenses distributed based on past trade, which gave Chiquita the possibility of importing into Europe a volume of bananas similar to that it had in the early 1990s. The European Union and the United States agreed this system would last until 2006, when a new "tariff only" system would be established instead of per-country quotas.[100] Chiquita had won the "Banana War" but at a high cost.

## *The Fall of a Giant: Chiquita Files for Bankruptcy*

At the end of the "Banana War" with the European Union, Chiquita was in a terrible financial situation. According to the company, before the imposition of the quota system by the European Union, 70% of the bananas consumed in Europe came from Latin America, and Chiquita imported 40% of them, giving the company control of 22% of the European market. This market share was reduced by half during the quota system, costing Chiquita around $200 million.[101] During the period that Chiquita concentrated its efforts and resources in its conflict with the Eu-

Figure 3.10

United Brands/Chiquita Brands. Debt to Equity Ratio, 1985-2000

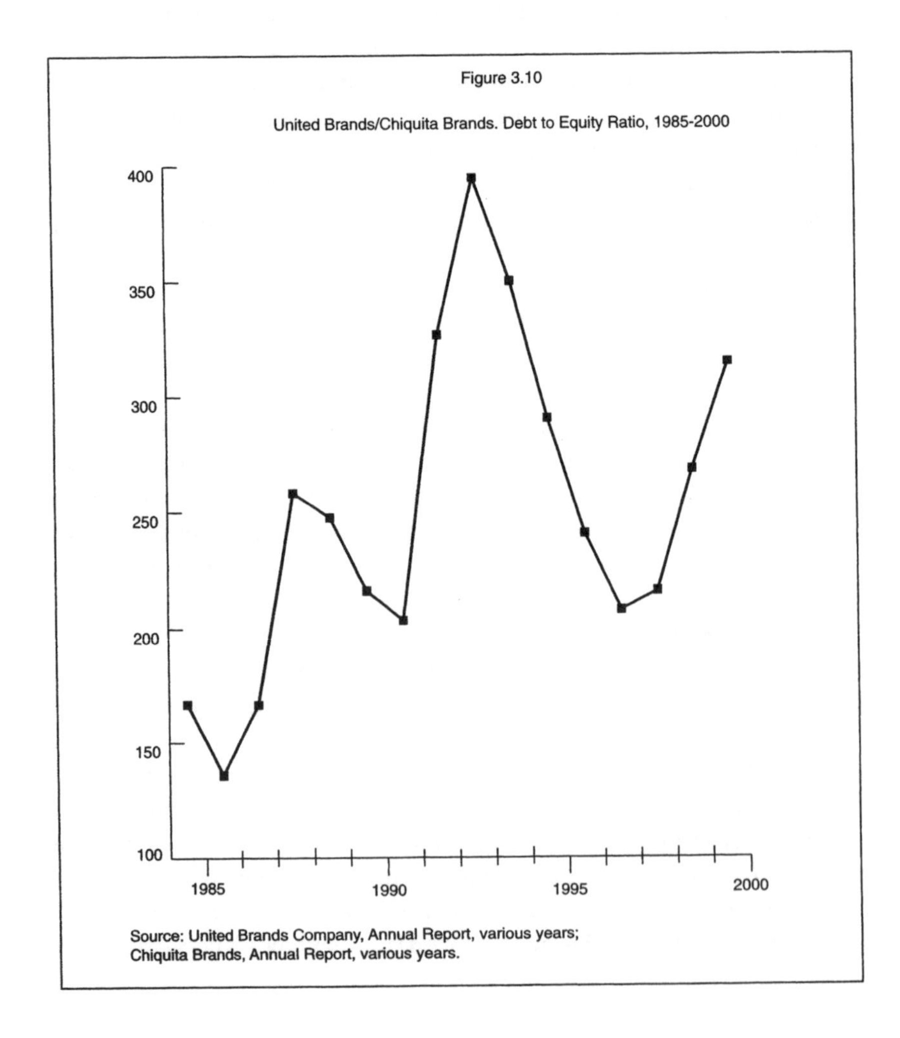


Source: United Brands Company, Annual Report, various years; Chiquita Brands, Annual Report, various years.

ropean Union, its closest rival, Dole, was adapting to Europe's regulations by investing in African production and diversifying its operations. Additionally, during this period Chiquita lost market share in the Japanese market when it withdrew from the Philippines as a result of agrarian reform.[102]

Chiquita finished the century with enormous debt and high losses. As figure 3.10 shows, the debt on equity ratio of the company increased from 167% in 1985 to a peak of 394% in 1993 and decreased to a still high 315% in 2000. The company made a huge effort to recover by restructuring itself—strengthening its nonbanana and vegetable businesses, diversifying into other products (the opposite process Lindner originally followed), and selling many of its subsidiaries to repay its debt. The company's management, however, could not save Chiquita, and, in 2001, the company filed for bankruptcy. Exactly one century after it started operations with Minor Keith and Andrew Preston as heads of United Fruit, the company began the twenty-first century in its worst financial condition ever, trying to recover from bankruptcy.

## *Conclusion*

The ever-expanding banana empire that Kepner and Soothill described in their 1930s classic has had its counterparts in the political and literary imaginations of Latin Americans throughout the twentieth century. From the leaf storm that swept through García Márquez's Macondo to the sinister interests that installed Asturias's Green Pope, United Fruit has been seen by scholars, activists, and writers alike as an implacable and overwhelming force throughout the hemisphere. Yet even as these images were being fixed in the minds of United Fruit's opponents, the conditions that had given rise to United Fruit's unrivaled control over land and national governments were rapidly changing.

By the mid-twentieth century, altered conditions in Latin America obliged the company to transform itself or lose significant terrain. In Central America, where national governments once had nearly surrendered sovereignty over the company's areas of operation, United Fruit found itself confronting increasingly assertive workers, less compliant national officials, and growing demands from would-be landowners. More ominous for the company, by mid-century, similar pressures were growing throughout the hemisphere, all of which threatened United Fruit's ability to marshal the quantities of land and labor necessary to maintain production on a large scale.

Until now studies have cared only about United Fruit's vertical integration process and the political conflicts the company faced in the countries in which it operated. United Fruit needed to vertically integrate in the first decades of the twentieth century because of technological constraints in banana production and marketing. Vertical integration was facilitated by the favorable political conditions in the area. In the 1950s, the company faced political uncertainties that made it change its internal structure once again, the changes this time facilitated by the technical innovations at the time.

The dynamics after 1970 must be seen under a different light because United Brands was more than just United Fruit with a different name. The new conglomerate had a more diversified structure and, therefore, did not depend on bananas as did the pre-1970 company. United Brands faced new political conflicts in Latin America with the creation of the UPEB and a lack of much U.S. government support, but the company adapted itself by reinforcing its marketing activities and its business in processed foods.

The conflict over European quotas in the 1990s did not begin as a political issue but became one when Chiquita decided to use its political connections to change the EU's policy. This strategy proved extremely costly for the company and was one of the main reasons for its bankruptcy in the year 2000. After a century of operations, Chiquita began the twenty-first century still with powerful market control but with weak finances and an uncertain future.

## *Appendix*

The risk ratio of United Fruit is measured by calculating the yield on common stock, a widely accepted ratio. The ratio is calculated by dividing the share's dividend earnings by its market price and tells how much of a return investors would have if they purchased a share of the company. The higher this ratio is, the riskier an investment is considered. The calculation was made in the following way: first, I took the information on the stock price and dividends from the *Wall Street Journal* as published on the last day of each month for the years 1936 to 1970. Though this information is published daily, this method is considered a good proxy. Second, I calculated the year's average stock price and dividend using the monthly information. Third, I calculated the company's annual yield using those averages. Fourth, I compared these yields with the annual yields calculated by Moody's Investors Service for the top 200 companies traded on Wall Street. Moody's did not publish an annual yield for the top 200 in 1947, 1949, and 1968, but published a monthly yield. For those three years, I calculated the yearly average with the monthly information.

NOTES TO CHAPTER 3

1. In order to understand how the company adapted to a changing political and social environment, I use a set of sources and methodology that have not been utilized by other scholars. The information on the general consolidated balance of the company is taken from the United Fruit, United Brands, and Chiquita Brands Annual Reports to the Stockholders for the years 1900 to 2000. Data on dividends and stock prices come from the *Wall Street Journal.* The yields of other industries in the American economy during this period and some analyses (when quoted) of the company are taken from the *Moody's Investors Service Stock Survey* for the years 1945 to 1970. Together, these sources take us inside United Fruit itself and help us understand the motives, perceptions, and forces that were driving changes in United Fruit's corporate strategy during the post–World War II period.

2. Taylor, "Evolution of the Banana Multinationals," 2.

3. McCann, *An American Company*, 26–27.

4. Brungardt, "The United Fruit Company," 234, 244.

5. May and Plaza, *United States Business Performance Abroad*, 6–8.

6. See Read, "The Growth and Structure of Multinationals." According to Read, the international banana business followed the same pattern Alfred Chan-

dler described for American big enterprises in the second half of the nineteenth century and the early twentieth century. See Chandler, *The Visible Hand*, "The Emergence of Managerial Capitalism," "The Growth of the Transnational Industrial Firm," and *Scale and Scope*.

7. White, "United Fruit Company," 29.

8. Taylor, "Evolution of the Banana Multinationals," 72.

9. Although the company had its own production and distribution network, it also increasingly relied on local growers who provided it with part of the fruit it marketed. See Kepner and Soothill, *The Banana Empire*, 265–75. However, in spite of relying significantly on local planters, the company did not change its internal structure by the time Kepner and Soothill published their book. This means it had the structure of a production company rather than of a marketing company. The actual internal change of the company began after World War II.

10. See Adams, *The Conquest of the Tropics*.

11. See Kepner and Soothill, *The Banana Empire*.

12. Read, "The Growth and Structure of Multinationals"; Wilkins, *The Emergence*, and *The Maturing of Multinational Enterprise*.

13. See Dosal, *Doing Business*.

14. Before World War II the company did not include depreciation on fixed assets in its annual report. I took the market value of those goods for these years.

15. Equity and assets are different measures of the company's capital. Total assets is the value of all assets held, regardless of how they were financed. For instance, the company could have bought its assets using debt. Equity is the capital provided by shareholders plus the profits reinvested. So, assets financed through debt are not included in the equity measure. Return on equity treats interest and debt payment as a cost. Return on assets does not.

16. This trend holds true despite the fact that the company tried to diversify its holdings during this period. Bananas remained the main source of income and profit for United Fruit prior to 1970.

17. For the years before 1962 and after 1968, the company did not record this information and only published an aggregate of sales of products and services.

18. During the diversification phase from 1959 to 1961, the company's management made it clear that its earnings would still depend on bananas. In his letters to the shareholders during these years, president Thomas Sunderland emphasized that bananas continued to be the most important good in the company's business: "Of course, bananas will be our principal source of income for some time in the future" (United Fruit Company, Annual Report 1959, 2); "The mainstay of our business is and will continue to be bananas" (Annual Report 1960, 2); "Bananas are and will continue to be the principal source of our income" (Annual Report 1961, 2).

In the years to follow, the studies of analyst firms also showed the company as highly dependent on bananas despite its diversification efforts. In 1963, a

Standard and Poor's report on the company's diversification program stated, "Bananas represent around 70% of the company's business" (Standard Corporation Description 1962, 7311). The Standard and Poor's reports continued giving the same percentage for the next three years. In its 1967 report, Standard and Poor's data showed the success of the diversification: "In 1967 bananas represented 63.8% of sales, sugar 11.9%, fruits and vegetables 3.5% fast food operations 3.5%, communications 1%. In 1966 it had been 65.2%, 13.2%, 8.2%, 6.1%, 3.6%, 1.6%, 1%, and 1.1% respectively" (Standard Corporation Description 1968, 9123). What the information of the company's annual reports and the analyses of Standard & Poor's suggest is that the company's business was heavily influenced by its banana operations. Therefore, it makes sense to analyze the trends on profitability as largely the result of the banana business behavior.

19. Moody's Investors Service, Moody's Stock Survey (April 1949), 528.

20. United Fruit Company, Annual Report 1949, 7.

21. Moody's Investors Service, Moody's Stock Survey (March 20, 1950), 561.

22. Moody's Investors Service, Moody's Stock Survey (November 26, 1951), 133.

23. Moody's Investors Service, Moody's Stock Survey (November 17, 1952).

24. United Fruit Company, Annual Report 1951, 9–10.

25. For a good analysis of the Arbenz affair, see Coatsworth, *Central America and the United States*; Gliejeses, *Shattered Hope*; and Schlesinger and Kinzer, *Bitter Fruit*. Thomas McCann's insider view is worth reading in *An American Company*.

26. United Fruit Company, Annual Report 1954, 4.

27. Moody's Investors Service, Moody's Stock Survey (March 30, 1953), 561.

28. The story of Guevara and Castro is in Castro's memoirs. See Castro, *Che*.

29. United Fruit Company, Annual Report 1954, 3.

30. Moody's Investors Service, Moody's Stock Survey (March 14, 1955), 589.

31. Moody's Investors Service, Moody's Stock Survey (December 24, 1956).

32. In 1959's annual report, the company's president wrote, "The estimated present value of these [expropriated] properties is two and one-half million dollars. Occupation of these lands has not been carried out in conformance with the terms of the law. The company is taking every legal recourse open to it under the laws of Cuba against these illegal occupations, but thus far without results" (8).

33. United Fruit Company, Annual Report 1959, 6.

34. Moody's Investors Service, Moody's Stock Survey (August 17, 1959).

35. Larrea, *El banano en el Ecuador*, 46.

36. See United Fruit Company, Annual Report 1960.

37. Thomas Sunderland, quoted by Arthur, Houck, and Beckford, *Tropical Agribusiness*, 147.

38. May and Plaza, *United States Business Performance Abroad*, 170.

39. Organization of American States, *Sectoral Study*, 20; Larrea, "Los cambios recientes," 165.

40. In his analysis on United Fruit in Ecuador, Steve Striffler shows how peasant activism in this country also encouraged the company to follow a process of divestiture. See Striffler, *In the Shadows of State and Capital*. Also, see Glover and Larrea, "Changing Comparative Advantage," 95.

41. Ellis, *Las transnacionales del banano*, 174.

42. Taylor, "Evolution of the Banana Multinationals," 78, 81.

43. Arthur, Houck, and Beckford, *Tropical Agribusiness*, 148.

44. United Fruit Company, Annual Report 1960, 2.

45. United Fruit Company, Annual Report 1961, 1.

46. Arthur, Houck, and Beckford, *Tropical Agribusiness*, 148.

47. Moody's Investors Service, Moody's Stock Survey (March 26, 1962).

48. Moody's Investors Service, Moody's Stock Survey (January 14, 1963), 772.

49. Moody's told investors that "United Fruit's antitrust difficulties were aggravated last month when it was indicted on a charge of trying to monopolize the banana market in seven western states. This could dampen the investment appeal of the stock, particularly in view of recent weak earnings. . . . Despite the company's capabilities for eventually solving its current problems, the new antitrust suit adds to the intermediate uncertainties. Hence we should feel holdings of this stock should be disposed of" (Moody's Investors Service, Moody's Stock Survey [August 12, 1963]), 455.

50. United Fruit Company, Annual Report 1965.

51. Glover and Larrea, "Changing Comparative Advantage," 95.

52. United Fruit Company, Annual Report 1968.

53. United Brands Company, Annual Report 1970.

54. For an explanation of how I calculated this yield, see appendix to chapter 3.

55. United Fruit Company, Annual Report 1960 and 1961.

56. The opinion about the company did not only change among investors or within the company itself. A recent study shows that the American media, represented in the *New York Times*, also changed its perception of United Fruit through the twentieth century. While before the 1940s the company was perceived as "civilizer" of the Caribbean and as an important ally in World War II, after the war, the media became more concerned on the way the company managed its labor conflicts. See Read, "Reinterpreting the United Fruit Company."

57. For a detailed explanation of how I calculated United Fruit's yield on common stock, see appendix.

58. The comparison between United Fruit's and the top 200 companies' yields is also shown in graph 8.

59. United Brands Company, Annual Report 1972, 5.
60. Ibid., 38.
61. Ibid., 38–39.
62. "La UPEB, el problema bananero, inversión extranjera y empresas multinacionales," *Augura*, vol. 2, no. 5; United Nations, FAO, *La economía mundial del banano*, 79–80; Vallejo, *Productos básicos*, 83–88.
63. López, *La Economía del banano*, 33–34.
64. United Nations, FAO, *La economia mundial del banano*, 79–80.
65. Vallejo, *Productos básicos*, 284; Presa Fernández, *Aportes*, 11, 54, 55; Clairmonte, "El imperio de la banana," 21, 22.
66. Vallejo, *Productos básicos*, 285.
67. Ibid., 286–87.
68. United Brands Company, Annual Report 1975, 1, 2, 4, 10.
69. Ibid., 3.
70. According to the FAO, Comunbana failed because it never managed to create a marketing infrastructure and organization similar to that of the multinational corporations. Additionally, this company could never reduce production costs enough to become competitive at the international level (United Nations, FAO, *La economía mundial del banano*, 80). Roche, *The International Banana Trade*, 50. The companies' individual shares in the market increased from 28% to 30% for United Brands between 1973 and 1981, 22% to 25% for Standard Fruit, and 8% to 15% for Del Monte. United Brands increased its participation even in Panama where the most heated debate took place. In 1973, the company controlled 100% of exports, by 1975 it had decreased to 97%, and to 90% in 1977. However, by 1983, it had recovered to 97%. In fact, the market participation of the independent producers never reached levels above 12% (López, *La economía del banano*, 94–98).
71. López, *La economía del banano*, 122, 123. López also shows that Standard Fruit and Del Monte chose a different strategy. These two companies decreased the participation of their associate producers and decided to refocus on producing the fruit themselves in a smaller number of plantations of higher productivity.
72. Ibid., 124, 125.
73. "Honduran Bribery," *Time Magazine* (April 21, 1975): 46. McCann, *An American Company*, 232–34.
74. United Brands Company, Annual Report 1974.
75. Taylor, "Evolution of the Banana Multinationals," 80.
76. United Brands Company, Annual Report 1979, 1.
77. Taylor, "Evolution of the Banana Multinationals," 80; Stein, "Yes, We Have No Profits," 190.
78. Chiquita Brands International, Annual Report 1991, 1.
79. In his letter to the stockholders of 1990, Lindner showed great optimism

on the possibilities of the new European market. That year, the company forecasted a potential increase of European customers from 180 million to 675 million (Chiquita Brands International, Annual Report 1990, 3, 10).

80. Chiquita Brands International, Annual Report 1991, 4.

81. Stein, "Yes, We Have No Profits," 192; Chiquita Brands International, Annual Report 1990, 9.

82. United Nations, FAO, *Intergovernmental Group on Bananas*, 2–10.

83. In his 1992 letter to shareholders, Lindner expressed his concern on this unexpected change in policy by the European Union and gave it partial blame for the company's poor performance in that year (Chiquita Brands International, Annual Report 1992, 2).

84. Tangermann, "European Interests," 21–24.

85. The bananas imported into Germany could not be re-exported to the other EU members that had established restrictive quotas. Although one of the main goals of the European Union is to eliminate tariffs between countries, this restriction was legally acceptable under EU legislation. For a detailed explanation, see ibid., 28–31.

86. By 1997, a kilo of bananas cost the Russians 40.7% of the price of a kilo of beef, and, by 1998, bananas were 25% more expensive than apples (ibid., 27–28).

87. The Lomé Convention guaranteed a market for bananas in favorable conditions to some former European colonies over the Latin American producers.

88. Tangermann, "European Interests," 33–36.

89. Taylor, "Evolution of the Banana Multinationals," 85.

90. Ibid., 86.

91. Chiquita Brands International, Annual Report 2000, and Form 10-K 2000, 0.

92. Senator Bob Dole has no relation with Dole Corporation, Chiquita's main rival.

93. Stein, "Yes, We Have No Profits," 194.

94. Stovall and Hathaway, "U.S. Interests," 154.

95. Harding, "U.S. Banana Exporters File 301 Petition," 36; "Banana Republican," 48.

96. "Senator Dole: Frequent Flier in Battle for Chiquita Bananas," *Associated Press*; Collymore, "Trade-Bananas"; Sanger, "Dole at the Forefront of the Trade Battle to Aid Donor's Banana Empire."

97. In 1998, Chiquita also made headlines for a different reason. The *Cincinnati Enquirer* published an eighteen-page article that accused Chiquita of hidden political, environmental, and human rights abuses in Central America. The article claimed the company had several dummy companies in the region and manipulated local politicians using bribery and threats. Reporter Mike Gallagher got this information by hacking the company's voicemails from general head-

quarters in Cincinnati. Chiquita sued the newspaper for $14 million for having hacked its voicemails illegally. The newspaper was forced to publish an apology to Chiquita and fired Gallagher. However, the actual charges made in Gallagher's articles were never dismissed. If ever proved true, they will make it imperative to do new studies of the company's operations in the 1980s and 1990s. Gallagher, "Chiquita Secrets Revealed," *Cincinnati Enquirer*, May 3, 1998.

98. Stovall and Hathaway, "U.S. Interests," 161.

99. Ibid., 164.

100. Stein, "Yes," 194.

101. Ibid., 192.

102. Van de Kasteele, "The Banana Chain," Appendix A, 2.

# Part IV
# The Impact of International Entrepreneurship on Host Economies

# [14]

# Cakes and Oil: Technology Transfer and Chinese Soybean Processing, 1860–1895

SHANNON R. BROWN
*University of Maryland, Baltimore County*

## I

Economists have increasingly recognized that one of the main sources of economic development is technological change.[1] Since it is much easier to borrow than to invent new technology, an important source of technological change has been the diffusion of new technology from its place of origin to subsequent users. When such diffusion involves movement between two countries, it is usually referred to as *technology transfer*.

Given the obvious importance that technology transfer has played in the economic development of all countries, including that of the first industrial nation, Great Britain, it is surprising how little has been written on the subject. One reason for this, perhaps, lies in the nature of neoclassical economics, especially in its preoccupation with static analysis and its relative lack of interest in institutions and institutional change. Another reason may be that economists and economic historians have concentrated on the historical experience of the successful developers—i.e., certain countries of Western Europe, Canada, the United States, and Japan.[2] Many of these countries have political and economic institutions which are similar or, at least, not sufficiently different to have been major impediments to the transfer of technology. The history of the rest of the world, however, has been quite different.

In neoclassical economics, the theory of technology transfer relies heavily on the study of comparative costs and is simply a special case of the general theory of the profit-maximizing firm. It assumes that at least some entrepreneurs will be well enough informed about foreign technology to consider its use and that they will do so, providing it is more profitable than the indigenous technology they are already using. Usually discussions of profitability

[1] For a survey of economists' knowledge of technological change see C. Kennedy and A. P. Thirlwall, "Surveys in Applied Economics: Technical Progress," *Economic Journal*, 82 (March 1972), 11–72; and Arnold Heertje, *Economics and Technical Change* (London, 1977).

[2] See, for example, W. O. Henderson, *Britain and Industrial Europe, 1750–1870* (Liverpool, 1954); Rondo Cameron, *France and the Economic Development of Europe, 1800–1914* (1961; reprint ed., New York, 1975); John P. McKay, *Pioneers for Profit: Foreign Entrepreneurship and Russian Industrialization, 1885–1913* (Chicago, 1970).

focus on the relative costs of capital and labor, but some authors have also pointed out that the nature and structure of the demand will influence the choice of technology. Utilizing this approach, a number of economists and historians have written valuable studies of technology transfer.[3]

Most of these existing studies, however, devote little attention to the values and institutions of the country importing the new technology.[4] This is because the data on supply and demand usually are sufficient to explain the outcome. Implicitly this means that the values and institutions of the exporting and importing countries are not functionally different, at least with respect to technology transfer. Although that may have been the case in the presently developed countries, much of the rest of the world, until quite recently, has obviously possessed values and institutions which have impeded such transfer. As a consequence, the study of the spread of technology to those countries must pay more attention than has been traditional in economic studies to the precise nature of those values and institutions, i.e. to the system of political economy and to how it interacts with attempts at technological borrowing.[5] Although neoclassical economic analysis is still necessary, it is not sufficient and a complete analysis must go further. In particular, it must examine the extent to which values and institutions will transform the supply and demand conditions after an effort to introduce new technology has begun. Such an analysis, attentive to the changes induced by attempted innovation, will provide a clearer understanding of success or failure than one relying solely on information concerning supply and demand before the event.

## II

Following the loss of the second Sino-British War in 1860, China's economy became, against the wishes of its leaders, more open to foreign influence. In 1860 there were fifteen Chinese ports where foreign businessmen were allowed to reside and do business, and by 1895 this number had grown to twenty-two. Tariffs on both imports and exports were quite low, averaging

[3] Good examples of such studies are Peter Temin, "A New Look at Hunter's Hypothesis about the Antebellum Iron Industry," *American Economic Review,* 54 (1964), 344–51; Edward Ames and Nathan Rosenberg, "The Enfield Arsenal in Theory and History," *Economic Journal,* 78 (1968), 827–42; Gary Saxonhouse, "A Tale of Japanese Technological Diffusion in the Meiji Period," *Journal of Economic History,* 34 (1974), 149–65. For a general survey of the literature, mostly on the American experience, see Paul Uselding, "Studies of Technology in Economic History" in *Recent Developments in the Study of Business and Economic History: Essays in Honor of Herman E. Krooss,* Robert E. Gallman, ed. (Greenwich, Conn., 1977), 159–219.

[4] In several as yet unpublished papers, Mancur Olson has explored the effect of institutions upon economic activity. See, for example, "The Political Economy of Comparative Growth Rates," unpublished, 1978.

[5] For a more complete treatment of this subject, see Shannon R. Brown, "Technology Transfer and Economic Systems: The Case of China in the Nineteenth Century," *ACES Bulletin,* forthcoming, 1981.

about 6 percent and 8 percent, respectively.[6] And because of extraterritoriality, foreign business firms were subject to the laws of their own countries rather than those of China. All this certainly suggests a more open economy, but it is important to remember that outside the foreign enclaves in a limited number of treaty ports, the Chinese government was still strong and the Chinese system of political economy was still dominant.[7]

One of the largest commercial activities in that system was the trade in soybeans and soybean by-products. A considerable quantity of soybeans, which were grown in north China, was pressed into cakes that found their market in south China, mostly as a fertilizer for sugar cane. The oil that was extracted in pressing had a number of culinary and other uses. This extensive trade, in both bean cake and oil, operating over considerable distances, quite naturally developed a number of interested parties. Among them were the growers of soybeans, the merchants who traded in them, the carters who carried them, the owners and employees of bean-crushing mills, the traders in bean cake and oil, and the junk owners and sailors who transported the products from north to south China. In addition, there was a large number of officials who were symbiotically connected with these interests. It is not surprising, then, that in the middle of the nineteenth century, when foreigners sought to enter this trade and, through their superior technology, to dominate it, they met with considerable opposition. But while such opposition was predictable, the forms that it took were not, and it is precisely those forms that help us to understand some of the problems facing the transfer of technology to China in the nineteenth century.

Initially, foreign interest in the soybean trade was confined to transporting bean cake. Because of the superiority of steamships in handling this commodity, their operation as common carriers, and the insurability of Western ships and cargo, the foreigners eventually were able to take over this sector of the soybean trade, though not without considerable opposition from the junk guild which had previously monopolized it. Western domination became complete in 1867 when the Chinese government finally intervened to break a two-year boycott, organized by the junk guild, of Chinese merchants who bought bean cake carried by foreign ships.[8]

At about the same time, in 1866, foreigners were also beginning to consider

[6] Chuan-ting Lu, "The Evolution of the Chinese Tariff Schedule 1840-1910," in *Modern Chinese Economic History*, Chi-ming Hou and Tzong-shian Yu, eds. (Taipei, Taiwan, 1979), 643.

[7] For a fuller discussion, see Shannon R. Brown, "The Partially Opened Door: Limitations on Economic Change in China in the 1860s," *Modern Asian Studies*, 12 (1978), 177-92.

[8] For a general survey of the soybean industry, see Imperial Maritime Customs (hereafter IMC), *The Soya Beans of Manchuria*, Special Series, no. 31 (Shanghai, 1911). On Chinese efforts to keep foreigners out of the trade, see Britten Dean, *China and Great Britain: The Diplomacy of Commercial Relations, 1860-1864* (Cambridge, Mass., 1974), ch. 4.

the introduction of Western technology in soybean processing. The traditional technology and process which the foreigners expected to replace was quite simple.[9] It involved only four steps: crushing, steaming, packing, and pressing. In the first step, the beans were crushed by means of a large millstone, usually turned by a pair of mules. Next the flattened beans were placed in large wooden baskets, holding about 55.5 catties each, a catty being equal to approximately one and a third pounds, and were steamed over open iron pots for about a quarter of an hour. Steaming, which rendered the beans soft and pliable, made them easier to pack and facilitated the extraction of oil. The water absorbed in this process also raised the weight of a basket of crushed beans to about 60.5 catties. In the third step, the steamed beans were packed, in layers separated by grass, into a cylinder formed by several metal hoops laid one on top of the other. This created a stack of five partially formed cakes which were then taken to the press. The press consisted of a large A-shaped wooden structure below which the cylinders of beans were placed and capped with a wooden lid that acted as the face of the press. The lid was then pressed downward by means of wooden wedges driven in between it and the top of the press, the increasing distance between the two being periodically bridged by inserting wooden blocks. The oil squeezed out of the beans then ran out the bottom of the cylinders into collecting tanks. This process took about two hours to complete and yielded (by weight) about 9 percent oil and 91 percent bean cake.

The economics of this activity were also quite simple, though subject to close tolerances. In the decade 1882–91, for example, the total value of the oil and bean cake produced from a given quantity of beans was less than 7 percent larger than the cost of the beans themselves.[10] Added to this difficulty was the fact that there were separate, though related, markets for soybeans, oil, and bean cake. Increased demand or supply for one of them was not instantly and proportionately carried over to the others and, as a consequence, the relative prices of the three commodities were not constant.[11] The result was that profitability in the industry was quite sensitive to these relative prices as well as to more obvious considerations such as the oil-yield rate and the cost of obtaining the oil.

[9] This description of the indigenous technology is based on Alexander Hosie, *Manchuria: Its People, Resources, and Recent History* (London, 1901), 218–33. Additional description, but for a later era, can be found in Rudolph P. Hommel, *China at Work* (Cambridge, Mass., 1969), 133–42.

[10] The actual values in Newchwang taels per 100 catties were: beans .97; oil 3.43; and bean cake .70 (assuming a weight of 53 catties each). Assuming the 9 percent yield rate for oil and the increase in weight due to steaming mentioned in the previous paragraph, this results in a value added by manufacturing of 6.3 percent. Hosie, *Manchuria*, 223.

[11] In the period 1 January 1869 to 22 March 1870, for example, a catty of oil cost from 3.4 to 3.9 times as much as a catty of beans, while a catty of bean cakes cost from 0.64 to 0.71 times as much as a catty of beans.

Trade in these commodities was strongly dominated by a variety of craft guilds and regional merchant guilds, or *landsmanschaften*. The purchase of soybeans from the peasants and their resale to bean mills or to exporters was controlled by the soybean guild, whose headquarters were in Shenyang and which was dominated by merchants from Shansi. The transporting of beans from Shenyang, their major market, to Newchwang was dominated by a cart guild that, like the soybean dealers, set a common price each day. The native mills in Newchwang were also organized in a guild, most of whose members and employees came from Chefoo. The Chinese firms that exported the soybean products were members of a guild dominated by merchants from Swatow, while the junk owners who carried the products were members of the Shanghai junk guild.[12] The presence of such a pervasive system of trade guilds and *landsmanschaften* meant that would-be entrants would have to come to terms with the existing organizations or face heavy opposition.

## III

It is against the technological and economic background outlined above that one must assess the first effort by foreigners, in 1866, to employ Western technology in the production of soybean cakes and oil. The location of this effort was the port of Newchwang, the center of the Manchurian soybean trade, and the initial promoter of the attempt was Thomas Platt, a British merchant who had established a trading company in Newchwang soon after it was opened to foreign trade in 1861. Observing the growing trade in bean cakes and their method of production, Platt was convinced that Western technology would provide a more profitable method of producing soybean cakes and oil than the indigenous methods. The British consul in Newchwang was less optimistic, perhaps because of the boycott of foreign ships then in effect. He predicted "the continuation of the old mischiefs and the arise of new ones." More specifically, he feared that local officials would "prevent the owners of the new steam factory from purchasing pulse [soybeans] at this port town, on the same terms as the owners of the existing native factories."[13]

In 1866, after deciding on a location for a factory and the type of equipment needed, Platt ordered the necessary machinery from England. Part of the financing for this equipment was advanced by Jardine, Matheson and Com-

[12] Jardine, Matheson Archive, Cambridge University Library, Unbound Correspondence, Newchwang (hereafter JMA), 9 January 1869; 6 February 1869; 3 March 1869. Unless noted, all letters are from Charles E. Hill to F. B. Johnson or to Jardine, Matheson and Company (JM). On Chinese guilds, see Hosea Ballou Morse, *The Guilds of China* (New York, 1909).

[13] Public Records Office, London, FO 228/418, T. T. Meadows to R. G. Alcock, 12 May 1866. It is interesting to note that this same form of opposition—increasing the price of a necessary input—though achieved by guild rather than official action, led to the demise of the first effort to introduce Western technology in silk-reeling. See Shannon R. Brown, "The Ewo Filature: A Study in the Transfer of Technology to China in the Nineteenth Century," *Technology and Culture*, 20 (1979), 550–68.

pany, the largest British trading firm in China. The machinery arrived in August of 1867, but soon thereafter Platt defaulted on the loan, and the machinery came into Jardine's possession along with Platt's land and buildings in Newchwang.[14] After a brief assessment of the equipment and survey of the prospects for such a mill in March of 1868, the new owners decided to go ahead with the project and construction was begun.[15] By October of that year the mill was basically completed and trial production had begun. But as cold weather reduced the amount of oil obtained from the beans, operations were soon suspended for the winter, as was the practice with the Chinese mills. In the spring of 1869, operations were recommenced, but the results for the season were unsatisfactory.[16] And in the summer of 1870, after a disappointing spring, the plant was closed.[17] The reasons for closure are both specifically applicable to the Newchwang soybean mill and also generally suggestive of the difficulties facing innovation in nineteenth-century China.

Jardine's reason for building the Newchwang mill was the expectation that it would be at least as profitable as the company's other investment opportunities. Undoubtedly it was expected that the cost advantages of Western technology would be the main source of these profits. A good estimate of the profits actually achieved can be made from the firm's ledgers and journals, which fortunately have survived. Since these books were not kept in accordance with modern cost accounting concepts, however, it was necessary to reorganize the data, as shown in Table 1, before an analysis could be made.

The figures in Table 1 show that operating expenses exceeded revenues in the first year by $52,238, but that in the following year there was a positive balance of $11,415, which increased in the final year to $31,146, although the figures for this last year are obviously inflated by the nonreplacement of inventories. Since there are no data on the use of inventories, however, it is impossible to determine exactly why the cash flow became positive. But what seems clear is that the fortunes of the mill were improving—so why was it closed?

First of all it must be recalled that the concept "net operating cash flow" is not the same as "profits," since it does not include charges for depreciation or interest. Depending on the rate assumed, the inclusion of depreciation would worsen the operating results since there was nearly $80,000 invested in fixed capital. But fixed capital is a sunk cost, as are the large operating losses of the first year, so they would not be taken into account when deciding whether to keep the plant open. The owners saw it this way, too, as can be seen in their decision, shown in the Jardine account books, to write off $25,000 in each of

[14] JMA, Account Books, A1/61, A2/42.
[15] JMA, 25 March 1868.
[16] JMA, 6 September 1869.
[17] JMA, 17 June 1870.

TABLE 1

*Cash Flow on Newchwang Mill Operation, 1868–1871 (in Mexican $)*[a]

| | *1 July 1868– 30 June 1869* | *1 July 1869– 30 April 1870* | *1 May 1870– 30 April 1871* |
|---|---|---|---|
| Net sales | | | |
| Bean cake | $47,618 | $49,386 | $33,887 |
| Oil | 8,534 | 27,904 | 18,988 |
| Total | $56,152 | $77,290 | $52,875 |
| Net input purchases | | | |
| Soybeans | $84,802 | $49,486 | $19,995 |
| Coal | 8,822 | 3,650 | 0 |
| Wages | 6,307 | 3,608 | 1,734 |
| Miscellaneous | 8,459 | 9,131 | 0 |
| Total | $108,390 | $65,875 | $21,729 |
| Net operating cash flow | ($52,238) | $11,415 | $31,146 |

*Note:* To avoid confusion with modern cost accounting concepts, the term *cash flow* is used instead of net operating income because the account books recorded inputs when purchased (not when used) and outputs when sold (not when produced).

[a] Mexican money was the currency commonly used in China trade during this period.

SOURCE: JMA, Account Books, A1/59–64; A2/39–44.

the first two years of operations.[18] What could not be ignored, however, was the large amount of operating capital—nearly $100,000—which was tied up in the enterprise and the likelihood that it would not earn what the company considered to be its normal return, i.e., between 6 and 9 percent. Consequently, Jardine's managers closed the mill because they felt that their capital had a better use than being tied up in a marginally profitable bean-crushing mill in Manchuria.

To say that Jardine closed the mill because it seemed unlikely to earn the normally expected rate of return still does not explain why the profits were so low. The answer to that question is more difficult, and it requires a careful consideration of the technology, economics, and social institutions which, collectively, determined the outcome.

The technology introduced by the foreigners was, of course, quite different from the indigenous technology described earlier. Essentially, it consisted of a coal-fired boiler, steam engine, three sets of horizontal rollers to crush the beans, equipment for steaming, and hydraulic presses which formed the bean

[18] JMA, Account Books, A1/62–63.

TABLE 2
*Noncapital Inputs and Outputs, Newchwang Mill, 1868–1871 (in Mexican $)*

| *Inputs* | | | *Outputs* | | |
|---|---|---|---|---|---|
| *Items* | *Value* | *Percent* | *Items* | *Value* | *Percent* |
| Soybeans | $154,283 | 79 | Bean cake | $130,891 | 70 |
| Coal | 12,472 | 06 | Soybean oil | 55,426 | 30 |
| Wages | 11,649 | 06 | | | |
| Miscellaneous | 17,590 | 09 | | | |
| Total | $195,994 | 100 | Total | $186,317 | 100 |

SOURCE: JMA, Account Books, A1/59–64; A2/39–44.

cakes and extracted the oil. Extracting the oil took about thirty minutes, though the presses could produce six cakes simultaneously. In addition to this equipment and the factory which housed it, there were two warehouses for storing beans, cakes, and oil, and a dormitory for the workers.[19]

The structure of costs produced by this technology can be seen in Table 2, which shows the total of noncapital input and output over the lifetime of the enterprise. What these figures show is that the value of the products produced—bean cakes and soybean oil—was nearly 21 percent higher than the value of the soybeans used to produce them, a result which compares favorably with a value added of less than 7 percent for native mills. This reflects the fact that the quality of the bean cakes and oil produced by the foreign mill was higher than that of the native mills and, consequently, commanded a higher price.[20] But the data also show that the direct costs of production exceeded the value of the products produced. There are several reasons for this, which will be examined in turn.

Contrary to the expectations of the British consul in Newchwang, there is no evidence that the foreign mill had greater difficulty in purchasing soybeans than did native mills or that it paid a higher price for what it bought. Perhaps this was because the foreign mill posed no threat to the traders in soybeans who obviously had interests different from the native mill owners. But it may also have been because the native mill owners, who were undoubtedly aware

[19] JMA, *passim*. The oil mill technology used in this mill was similar to that described in Alexander Samuelson, "On Oil Mill Machinery," *Proceedings of the Institution of Mechanical Engineers* (1858), 27–43.

[20] British Consular Report (hereafter BCR), *Newchwang 1868*. All British Consular Reports cited in this paper are reprinted in *Irish University Press Area Study Series, British Parliamentary Papers: China*, 42 vols. (Shannon, 1971).

of the Jardine mill's difficulties (to which they contributed, as discussed below) and lack of profits, had other ways of pressuring the foreign enterprise. However, when Charles E. Hill, the American manager of the mill, became interested in the direct purchase and storing of soybeans in an effort to reduce costs by bypassing the Chinese middlemen, he soon met with resistance. He wrote, "The whole Chinese community are working against it. If I can get one man of good reputation to begin with me I will make it a profitable business."[21] Not surprisingly, he found no such partner.

Nor is there any evidence that the foreign mill paid an excessive price for coal. Initially, the mill used English coal which cost nearly $14 a ton, but soon thereafter Hill discovered that Chinese coal, which came from the interior of Manchuria and cost about $7 a ton, would work quite well when mixed with English coal in the ratio of half and half or even three parts Chinese to one part English.[22]

The input that proved to be the greatest problem was labor, and here the difficulty arose, at least in the beginning, because the new technology required a pattern of labor discipline considerably different from what the Chinese workers were used to. Essentially, the problem was to get the Chinese workers to adapt to the needs of the foreign machinery.

The first difficulty, which was rather quickly overcome, was to get the Chinese to work at night as well as in the daytime. This schedule was devised in order to economize on the cost of steam, which was nearly as great for twelve hours of operation as for twenty-four, and in order to spread the fixed costs of the plant over a larger volume of production.[23] But hardly had the work begun, in March 1869, when the mill was closed by a strike of the men who packed the bean cakes for pressing. The strike occurred, according to Hill, because the locally recruited labor force, which was of Chefoo origin, "was all more or less under the influence of their old masters and all these masters, since they find [that] the mill cake sell [*sic*] readily, and that there is every indication of its working regularly, are doing all in their power to prevent our keeping men."[24] It was also true, however, that the packers had more work to do than in a Chinese mill because of the pace of the machinery, but Hill maintained that he had explained this to them before they undertook the work and that, moreover, they were paid more than workers in native mills. In any case, Hill's response to the strike was to send the mill's compradore to Chefoo ("All men here who make bean cake are Chefoo men") to obtain some new "Chefoo men who have never been here."[25] At the same time, Hill sought three Cantonese "engineers" to operate the steam engines.

[21] JMA, 8 October 1869.
[22] JMA, 6 February 1869; 3 June 1869.
[23] JMA, 9 January 1869.
[24] JMA, 3 March 1869.
[25] *Ibid.*

After the new men arrived work was resumed, but the equipment could not be worked to capacity. Hill observed in May that the "presses are large enough to hold six cakes at a time, but as yet I have not been able to get them to pack more than the usual 5 at a time. The compradore is doing his best to make these men pack 6 or get men who will."[26] If this could have been achieved, then the same equipment, the same wage expenditure, and nearly the same coal consumption would have produced 1,728 cakes per day instead of 1,440, as well as an equivalent increase in oil. Success in that effort would have reduced unit costs by about 7 percent.[27]

Before it could be achieved, however, Hill discovered that the standard Chefoo bean cake, on which he had modelled his own product, in fact weighed 60 catties and not the 50 he had originally assumed.[28] Consequently, in August of 1869 he began to produce 5 bean cakes of 60 catties each, an output that would have achieved the same results as the previously desired objective of 6 cakes of 50 catties each. But in response to his efforts, the packers again went on strike, and although the strike was nominally precipitated by the increased work attending the larger size cake, the real issue was one of work pattern.[29] One point of conflict was the regularity of work. In the summer of 1869, the high price of soybeans relative to that of bean cake and oil led the native mills to close down for several months. Such closures were common among the native mills and provision for them consequently was built into the labor contract. But this particular form of adaptation to fluctuating market conditions was less attractive to the foreign mill which, having a higher ratio of fixed to variable costs, stood to gain less by closing down than did the native mills. It was at this point that the packers struck, arguing, as Hill reported, that "the Chinese mills had not been at work for more than a month and the men received pay all the same and they should take the same privilege. I then tried to reason with them and explained that they were employed for foreigners and that all our rules and customs were made clear to them before they signed agreements to work."[30]

In an attempt to avoid collective action enhanced by craft or regional solidarity and in anticipation of the forthcoming season, Hill then sought to put together a polyglot mixture of workers from different places. His head

[26] JMA, 17 May 1869.

[27] A 20 percent increase in output, achieved by such means, would have required a 20 percent increase in the input of soybeans. As soybeans constituted about two-thirds of total (variable and fixed) costs, a 20 percent increase in output would require a 13 percent increase in inputs.

[28] JMA, 3 July 1869. Cakes were sold by weight and oil content.

[29] JMA, 3 August 1869; 7 August 1869.

[30] JMA, 7 August 1869. Having found the locally recruited labor intransigent, Hill had then brought in new men from Chefoo who had now gone on strike. Consequently, his bile is more understandable than his optimism when he wrote, "All this year's troubles can be avoided by getting Chinchew [South China, near Swatow] men who can be managed and work for the same wages. Men used to the work can be found and who will be entirely foreign to these dogs." *Ibid.*

practical engineer, a Mr. Kite, was an Englishman.[31] His compradore was from Swatow, while the three men who ran the steam engines were Cantonese, as was the oil mill shroff, the moneychanger. To pack the bean cakes, he contracted for one shift of twelve men from Swatow, who had once made bean cake in Chefoo, and for the other shift he sought twelve men from Chefoo. The dozen or so men who operated the presses, as opposed to those who packed the beans, were from Newchwang, as were most of the coolies employed in the warehouses.[32] How well this work force might have done under more favorable conditions is hard to say, since 1870 turned out to be a bad year for all soybean mills, both native and foreign. The cause of this circumstance was, in part, the strong Japanese demand for soybeans, which drove up the price of beans more than that of oil and bean cake, thereby putting the mills in a cost-price squeeze. This development, combined with an abnormally cold spring which lowered the oil-yield rate, finally convinced Jardine, Matheson and Company that the mill was unlikely ever to become a sufficiently profitable venture.[33]

It has been suggested that the mill closed because the oil-yield rate was below that of the Chinese mills,[34] but such an explanation is based on a misunderstanding of the economics of the new technology. Even though the foreign technology obtained a lower percentage of the high-priced oil from a given quantity of soybeans than did the Chinese method, this fact in itself would not prevent it from being more profitable than the traditional technology, provided the costs of producing a given quantity of output were less or the value of the output were higher. As mentioned above, the products produced by the foreign mill were higher in quality than their Chinese counterparts and thus commanded a higher price on the market. It was also shown that the value added by manufacture was greater for the foreign mill than for the Chinese ones. Still, the costs of the foreign mill exceeded its revenues. While it is true that a higher oil-yield rate would have increased profits, provided it was not offset by an increase in costs, so also would any other action which reduced costs. For example, Hill's efforts to reorganize traditional work patterns and his attempt to initiate large-scale direct purchase of soybeans would have reduced costs and increased profits, had they been successful. But both failed—the former because of opposition from native mill owners and the latter because of opposition from soybean dealers.

[31] Mr. Kite full satisfied his Victorian employer, who in recommendation for Kite's furthor employment with Jardine said of him: "Never drinks, never neglects his duty, always ready, and never impertinent. A combination hardly ever seen in one man of his profession." JMA, 1 October 1870.

[32] JMA, 8 January 1870.

[33] JMA, 6 March 1870; 22 April 1870; 17 June 1870.

[34] BCR, *Newchwang 1873*. This same source maintains, however, that the foreign mill experimented successfully with modifications but that "still the profit would not be large enough to tempt foreign speculators who have other outlets for their capital."

## IV

Given the difficulties experienced with this first venture, it is perhaps not surprising that the next attempt to establish a soybean mill using Western technology was in Swatow, in south China, where no native mills are known to have existed, and not in Manchuria or Chefoo where vested interests were well entrenched. It is also of interest that this mill seems to have been "entirely a Chinese venture... situated among the foreign hongs [firms] at Swatow."[35] One of the principals involved in this enterprise was also simultaneously employed as Jardine's compradore in Swatow.[36] Swatow, it should be recalled, was located in the center of the Chinese sugar-producing district which constituted the main market for soybean cake.[37]

The mill in Swatow, begun in 1880, was on a smaller scale than the one in Newchwang. In its first year of operation, the rate of production was only 200 bean cakes per day, but daily output rose steadily to 300 in 1881, 400 in 1882 and, after an expansion in 1883, to 600 cakes per day in 1884. In 1893, when construction of a second plant was said to be imminent, the rate of production was given as 800–900 cakes per day.[38] The Newchwang mill, by comparison, had a capacity of 1,728 cakes per day, although production never seems to have exceeded 1,440.

Although the Swatow mill was steam powered, and probably used equipment purchased from the Newchwang mill, it does not seem to have been as fully mechanized as the Newchwang mill.[39] This likelihood is suggested by descriptions of the mill as well as by its smaller scale and higher oil-yield rates. For instance, 1,000 catties of beans were said to produce 19 bean cakes of 47.5 catties each as well as 112 catties of oil, indicating an oil-yield rate of about 11 percent, which was slightly higher than that obtained in the native mills of Newchwang. The cakes were said to be "in the form of the Chefoo bean cakes, and their cost is about the same as those imported from that port and Newchwang."[40] Probably the crushing and steaming operations were similar to those at Newchwang, but the pressing operation may have been less mechanized. Such mixtures of old and new technologies became common in Manchuria later in the century.[41]

[35] BCR, *Swatow 1882*.

[36] JMA, B7/42, Robert Craig to JM, 8 October 1881; and C29/1, JM to Robert Craig, 10 October 1881.

[37] "Bean cake is used almost exclusively as a manure for sugar cane...." BCR, *Swatow, 1886*.

[38] BCR, *Swatow 1882; Swatow 1883; IMC, Decennial Reports, 1882–91*, 2 vols. (Shanghai, 1893), II, 537.

[39] See note 36.

[40] BCR, *Swatow 1882*.

[41] In the late nineteenth and early twentieth centuries, many Chinese mills in Manchuria employed a Japanese-made hand-powered iron capstan press for extracting the oil from beans which were crushed and steamed by steam-powered machinery. Despite its seemingly primitive

In addition to the lack of opposition from vested interests mentioned above, Swatow may have had other advantages as a site for a bean-crushing mill using Western technology. It was cheaper and easier to handle and ship the beans south than the finished oil. Perhaps more important, the beans were also subject to a lower tariff.[42] Furthermore, the warmer weather in Swatow may have helped since it allowed year-round operation, an important consideration given the relatively greater importance of fixed capital in the Western technology. The warmer weather may also have contributed to the higher oil-yield rates. Even so, the advantages of the Swatow location must have been limited since the firm grew slowly and failed to attract imitators.

Given the apparent financial success of the Swatow mill—an inference justified both by the statements of outsiders and, more important, by the continual expansion of the enterprise—it is rather surprising that similar mills were not established elsewhere in China. In the case of foreign enterprise, the explanation for this may be due, in part, to the controversy that arose in 1881 concerning the right of foreigners to establish factories in the treaty ports. Prior to that date, foreigners had established numerous industrial enterprises in the treaty ports without the Chinese questioning their right to do so.[43] But in 1881, a German businessman in Amoy sought to establish a foundry to manufacture iron cooking pans.[44] This was strongly opposed by two local Chinese producers of such items and the local officials refused to let the foreign firm ship its products from the port. As the main market for such items was among the overseas Chinese community in Southeast Asia, this was a severe blow. Consequently, the foreign consuls protested this action, and when the argument was eventually carried to Peking, it became enmeshed with a similar controversy involving Li Hung-chang, the governor-general of Chih-li.[45] In 1878, Li had become the main backer of a project to establish China's first cotton textile mill, in Shanghai, and he sought to ensure its profitability by having it declared an official monopoly.[46] When in 1881 an American merchant also sought to establish a cotton mill in Shanghai, the conflict began and

nature, such a press nevertheless required foreign technology since Chinese metallurgical techniques could not produce iron which could withstand such pressure. See IMC, *Soya Beans of Manchuria*, 13; and Hosie, *Manchuria*, 223.

[42] The tariff on oil was Tls .50 per picul and that on soybeans Tls .29. In 1870, for instance, oil cost Tls 3.80 per picul in Newchwang, which gave Swatow a Tls .31, or 8 percent, cost advantage, other things being equal. JMA, 10 March 1870.

[43] According to one listing there were sixty foreign "industrial enterprises" established in the treaty ports before 1881. Sun Yu-t'ang, *Chung-kuo chin-tai kung-yeh shih tzu-liao, ti-i-chi* [Materials on the history of modern industry in China, first collection] (Peking, 1957), 234–38. I have found no evidence of any official objection to the establishment of the Newchwang mill.

[44] BCR, *Amoy 1881*.

[45] For a general survey of this controversy, see G. E. Paulsen, "Machinery for the Mills of China: 1882–1896," *Monumenta Serica*, 27 (1968), 320–42.

[46] Albert Feuerwerker, *China's Early Industrialization* (Cambridge, Mass., 1958), 207–25. BCR, *Shanghai 1878*.

it remained unresolved until 1895. Which side had the better legal argument need not detain us here, since for our purposes it is enough to note that the controversy clearly deterred new foreign investment in the treaty ports. At least one of the investments which was discouraged, in 1893, was another bean mill.

In that year, Butterfield and Swire (B&S), second only to Jardine, Matheson and Company among the British firms in China, was seriously considering establishing a steam-powered bean mill in Newchwang.[47] But in the summer of that year the controversy over foreign rights to establish factories in the treaty ports was again revived by a Japanese effort to establish a cotton gin at Ningpo. As a result, B&S developed cold feet. Considering the reputation for arrogance which has been assigned to the foreign firms operating in China during that time, it is interesting to note the caution with which B&S considered the decision. The head of the firm, John Samuel Swire, wrote from London to his partners in China: "Unless Li's decision, that foreigners cannot own industrial works in China, be abrogated, we had better have nothing to do with the bean cake mill in Newchwang. To attempt an evasion of the law, by placing a native as nominal principal, would bring us into trouble, the property might be seized, and our right to realize any security contested, on the grounds that we had been law breakers."[48] But in September 1895, immediately after the Japanese-imposed Treaty of Shimonoseki explicitly gave foreigners the right to establish factories in the treaty ports, B&S finally decided to establish a bean-crushing mill in Newchwang. Swire then wrote to his partners: "Two years ago when we decided against being interested in this scheme, it was on grounds of possible trouble with the Chinese government if we attempted to evade the then existing laws. This difficulty is now removed."[49]

## V

The Treaty of Shimonoseki in 1895 gave foreigners a clear legal right to establish factories in the treaty ports. Before that time, and especially after 1881, a cloud of uncertainty had hung over foreign ventures and, while it did not completely prevent new enterprises from being established, it was definitely a factor in reducing their number. After 1895, foreign-run factories using Western technology rapidly increased in number as, revealingly, did privately owned Chinese factories using Western technology.[50]

[47] Butterfield and Swire Archives, School of Oriental and African Studies, London, *Letterbook*, vol. 1179, John Samuel Swire to J. H. Scott, 27 October 1893; 2 November 1893; 3 November 1893; 23 January 1894.

[48] *Ibid.*, 3 November 1893.

[49] *Ibid.*, 11 September 1895.

[50] Wang Ching-yu, *Chung-kuo chin-tai kung-yeh shih tzu-liao, ti-erh-chi* [Materials on the history of modern industry in China, second collection] (Peking, 1957), 234; IMC, *Soya Beans of Manchuria*, 19. By 1911, there were at least thirteen steam- or internal-combustion powered mills in Newchwang, of which seven were large mills owned by Chinese. *Ibid.*, 21.

In Newchwang, B&S finally opened their steam-powered bean mill in 1896. According to the local customs officer, it was "under foreign auspices, probably to avoid Chinese official supervision" but, as a visitor shortly thereafter observed, "The mill is worked by Chinese only, and is practically Chinese owned."[51] So successful was the mill that imitators quickly followed—one each in the summer of 1899, the fall of 1900, and the fall of 1901. By the latter year, the modern factories of Newchwang, using a technology quite similar to that of the original foreign mill, had a combined capacity of 15,600 bean cakes per day. This figure represented most of the port's total output of bean cakes. Furthermore, the costs per cake were about 20 percent less in the new mills and the yield of oil higher. This cost advantage enabled them "to make a profit at prices which caused a loss to the old-style mills."[52]

What this study seeks to demonstrate is that the failure to introduce Western technology more rapidly in nineteenth-century China, at least in the case of soybean processing, was not due to the incompatability of that technology with Chinese conditions. Rather it was due to the strength of China's system of political economy. That system—a symbiotic coalition of Chinese merchants, organized in guilds, and government officials—was quite effective at preventing innovation it did not desire. Also, it did not matter whether the innovators were foreigners or Chinese since both were seen as threats to the wealth and comfort of established interests. But in 1895 the Treaty of Shimonoseki dealt a heavy blow to this system, by giving foreigners the legal right to establish factories in the treaty ports. After that date it was much more difficult for traditional producers to prevent innovation and, as a consequence, both foreign and Chinese firms using Western and Chinese technology grew rapidly. The "gales of creative destruction" unleashed by these innovating entrepreneurs accelerated the transfer of technology to China, which stimulated the growth of industry and, not so incidentally, contributed to the downfall of the old regime.[53]

[51] IMC, *Decennial Reports, 1892-1901*, 2 vols. (Shanghai, 1904), I, 22; Lord Charles Beresford, *The Break Up of China* (London, 1899), 70.

[52] IMC, *Returns and Reports on Trade, Newchwang, 1899* (Shanghai, 1900), 4. Bean crushing by mechanical means does not appear to have changed greatly during these years, though incremental improvement undoubtedly took place. See Harold W. Brace, *History of Seed Crushing in Great Britain* (London, 1960), 57–79.

[53] Schumpeter's classic description of the innovating entrepreneur can be found in his *Theory of Economic Development* (Cambridge, Mass., 1934), ch. 2, especially pp. 66 67. For a more general discussion of foreign efforts to introduce new technology to China see Shannon R. Brown, "The Transfer of Technology to China in the Nineteenth Century: The Role of Direct Foreign Investment," *Journal of Economic History*, 39 (1979), 181–97.

# [15]

# Multinational Enterprises in Less Developed Countries: Cultural and Economic Interactions

## 6.1. INTRODUCTION

This chapter analyses the operations of MNEs in LDCs in terms of the interplay between two types of culture. The MNE, it is claimed, personifies the highly entrepreneurial culture of the source country, while the LDC personifies the less entrepreneurial culture of the typical social group in the host country. This view places MNE–LDC relations in an appropriate historical perspective. It is the entrepreneurial culture of the source country which explains why in the past that country had the economic dynamism to become a developed country (DC). Conversely, the limited entrepreneurial culture of the host country explains why it has been so economically static that it has remained an LDC. The current problems perceived by MNEs in operating in certain LDCs—and also the problems perceived by these LDCs with the operation of foreign MNEs—reflect the difficulties of attempting to bridge this cultural gap.

The concept of entrepreneurial culture is, of course, related to the concept of 'modernization' which appears in the sociology of development (Eisenstadt, 1973; Herskovits, 1961; Inkeles and Smith, 1974). There are important differences, however. The concept of entrepreneurial culture derives from economic theories of the entrepreneur (see Chapter 3) which identify specific functions, such as arbitrage, risk-bearing, and innovation, needed for economic develoment. It describes the cultural values which stimulate the emergence of individual personalities capable of performing these functions competently. Modernization, on the other hand, typically begins with a wide range of attitudes associated with Western industrial societies, and examines how far these attitudes have permeated LDCs. Entrepreneurial theory suggests that not only are some 'modern' attitudes irrelevant to economic development, but others are actually inimical to it. Emphasis on entrepreneurial culture does not therefore imply a trite endorsement of 'modern' values. Entrepreneurial theory has been applied to development issues by a number of previous writers—Hagen (1962), Hoselitz (1961), Kilby (1971), Leff (1978), and McClelland and Winter (1969), for example—but along rather different lines.

Countries classified as LDCs form an extremely heterogeneous group. Indeed, differences between the poorest and the wealthiest LDCs are in some respects greater than between the wealthiest LDCs and many DCs. This chapter is concerned principally with the poorest and most persistently underdeveloped LDCs—such as some countries of sub-Saharan Africa. Since these countries are, generally speaking, the ones with the lowest MNE involvement, it may be asked why a focus on these countries is appropriate. One reason is that this low involvement itself merits explanation, since the continuing confinement of these countries to the periphery of the world economy is of considerable policy interest (Wallerstein, 1979). By examining the difficulties encountered by the small number of MNEs that actually invest in these countries, the lack of interest of the majority can be explained in terms of a rational perception of the size of the problem. The second reason is that the starker contrast between wealthy DCs and the poorest LDCs reveals cultural influences in a sharper relief.

Levels of development can vary not only across LDCs but also across regions within any one of them. This point is fully recognized by the analysis in this chapter, which emphasizes that regional differences in development are endemic in DCs as well (Berger and Piore, 1980). The difference between urban (especially metropolitan) and rural areas is fundamental in this respect. Indeed the analysis below suggests that many international differences in levels of development can be ascribed to differences in the relative influence of urban as opposed to rural culture.

Multinationals differ too; in the present context, differences between source countries are likely to be most significant, because these affect the national culture upon which the headquarters of the firm draws. There can also be differences between firms from the same country, due, for example, to the religious affiliations of the founders, or the impact of the size of the firm on its organization and leadership style. Due to limited space, however, this chapter abstracts from such considerations by working with the concept of a representative MNE.

Section 6.2 delineates the main areas in which conventional economic theory appears to be deficient in explaining MNE behaviour in LDCs. The 'residual' phenomena which remain unexplained by economic factors, it is suggested, may be explicable by cultural factors instead. The analytical core of the chapter comprises Sections 6.3–6.7. These sections consider in detail the interaction between geographical and cultural factors in the process of development. Section 6.3 identifies three conditions for successful economic development; one is geographical—entrepôt potential—and two are cultural—a scientific outlook and a commitment to voluntary methods of social and economic co-ordination. Sections 6.4–6.6 elaborate on each of these factors in turn, generating a check-list of country characteristics relevant to economic development. Section 6.7 draws on the core analysis to expound an evolutionary model of world development, which focuses on the dynamics of the linkages between DCs and LDCs, as mediated by MNEs. Section 6.8 returns to the key issues identified in Section 6.2. It explains how difficulties faced by some LDCs in learning new technologies originate in specific cultural factors, and argues that these same cultural factors explain other phenomena too. Attention is drawn to the weaknesses as well as the strengths of contemporary entrepreneurial cultures, and it is suggested that some of the cultural values transmitted by MNEs to LDCs hinder rather than help the process of development. Section 6.9 concludes the chapter with suggestions for further research.

## 6.2. KEY ISSUES

Any analysis of multinational operations in LDCs must address a number of key stylized facts. Some of these facts are readily explained by conventional economic theory (see, for example, Casson and Pearce, 1987), but others are not. The facts that conventional theory can explain include

1. *The limited scale and disappointing economic performance of import-substituting manufacturing investments in LDCs*. This is partly attributable to inappropriate LDC trade policies. By protecting relatively small domestic markets for finished manufactures, LDC governments have encouraged the proliferation of

downstream assembly-type operations of less than efficient scale. It is only the ability to charge domestic monopoly prices well above world export prices that has encouraged MNEs to continue operating in these protected markets.

2. *The increase in foreign divestments since the oil price shocks of the mid-1970s* is partly explained by the reduction in real consumer incomes in oil-exporting LDCs, which has reduced local demand for relatively sophisticated MNE-produced goods. The threat of blocked profit repatriations from countries with balance of payments difficulties has also encouraged a pre-emptive liquidation of foreign investments by MNEs.

3. *The recent poor performance of resource-based investments in Africa and Latin America* is partly explained by another consequence of the oil price shocks—namely the recession in Western heavy industries—and by the continuing protection of domestic agriculture in industrial societies. It is also due partly to the development of new mineral deposits in the Asia-Pacific region. Finally, the emergence of synthetic substitutes has reduced the long-term demand for certain minerals (although the price advantage of oil-based substitutes has declined).

4. *The use of capital-intensive technologies by MNEs in labour-abundant LDCs* can be explained partly by the cost of adapting to local conditions a technology originally developed for use in Western locations. It can also be explained by the importance of mechanization in meeting quality standards in export markets—and in home markets dominated by wealthy consumers (in countries with a highly skewed distribution of income). The distortion of factor prices in LDC markets through minimum wage legislation, capital subsidies, etc., may also be significant.

Some of the salient points which existing theory cannot easily explain are

5. *The failure of technology transfer to generate sustained innovative capability in LDC industries*. The much slower rate at which foreign technologies are assimilated by the poorest LDCs compared to newly industrializing countries such as Korea, or successfully industrialized countries such as Japan, suggests that cultural factors may inhibit the acquisition of scientific ideas and Western working practices.

6. *The confinement of modern industry to 'enclaves', and in particular the failure of foreign investors to develop backward

*linkages with indigenous suppliers*. Where resource-based investments are concerned, there may be limited opportunities for backward linkages in any case. Even in developed countries, furthermore, large-scale investments often fail to develop a local supply base; the disciplined routine of work in large plants seems to inhibit the 'incubation' of entrepreneurial skills in the local workforce. Nevertheless, the frequent claim by MNE managers of medium-size manufacturing operations that the quality of local supplies is persistently deficient suggests that there may be a systematic failure in LDCs to appreciate the importance of component quality and of precision work in manufacturing industries.

7. *Poor internal relations, both between headquarters and subsidiary, and between management and labour within the foreign subsidiary*. Conflicts between different groups within the firm over the distribution of profit, the level of investment, and so on, are common in any business activity, and there may be special reasons—such as the high risks perceived by foreign investors and their consequently short-term perspective on cash flow—why these conflicts may be particularly acute in respect of LDC operations. Nevertheless, it is also possible that the failure to resolve these conflicts effectively is due to frequent misunderstanding caused by cross-cultural barriers to communication.

8. *The tendency for industrialization through foreign technology to precipitate the disintegration of traditional social groups within the host economy*. All innovation does, of course, involve 'creative destruction', but the social groups of developing countries seem to be much more vulnerable in this respect than do equivalent social groups in the developed world.

It is worth noting that even the 'successful' explanations in (1)–(4) involve only the most proximate causes of the effects involved. Thus in respect of (1), for example, it is possible to ask the more fundamental question of why so many LDC governments opted for protectionism in the first place. Were they susceptible to economic analysis supporting import-substitution because they were predisposed to break economic as well as social and political ties with their colonial powers in order to bolster independence? It seems that—in this case at least—the more fundamental the questions asked, and the further back the quest for explanation goes, the more likely cultural factors are to become significant.

A good theory often has the capacity to explain more than was originally asked of it, and it is claimed that this is also true of the analysis presented here. The theory can explain not only contemporary differences between DCs and LDCs, but also certain aspects of the historical process of industrialization in countries which have become DCs. Thus the vulnerability of traditional social groups, for example, noted above, applies also to the social groups which became extinct a century or more ago during the industrialization of DCs. There is insufficient space in the present book, however, to document all the relevant facts, let alone substantiate the claim of the theory to explain them.

## 6.3. THE PROCESS OF DEVELOPMENT

A necessary condition for development in any locality is that there are resources with potential for exploitation. Conventional economic theory tends to underestimate the obstacles that lie in the path of realizing this potential, however. Working with traditional concepts of resource endowment—land, labour, and capital—cross-section regressions using the total factor-productivity approach have only limited success in explaining international differences in material economic performance (as measured by per capita GNP) (Pack, 1987). Some countries clearly underperform by failing to realize their potential, and the question is why this should be so (Leibenstein, 1978).

Differences in education and training are commonly cited as a possible explanation, and the analysis presented here is generally consistent with this view. It goes beyond it, however, in recognizing that education takes place largely outside formal institutions. Early education, in particular, is effected through family influence, peer-group pressure within the local community, and so on. To benefit fully from formal education it may be necessary for people to 'unlearn' beliefs from their informal education. But if the conflict between the two sets of beliefs is acute then psychological obstacles to unlearning may arise. Measures of educational input based on gross expenditure fail to capture these important factors. The analysis in this chapter helps to identify those aspects of the formal curriculum which are crucial in supporting economic development. It also identifies those elements of general culture which prepare people to benefit from such education.

Two main obstacles to the efficient use of national resources can be identified. The first is geographical: the inability to effect a division of labour due to obstacles to transportation. In this context, it is argued below that the presence of a potential entrepôt centre is crucial in facilitating the development of a region. The second is the absence of an entrepreneurial culture. An entrepreneurial culture (see Chapter 4) provides an economy with flexibility—in particular, the structural flexibility to cope with changes in the division of labour. These changes may be progressive changes, stemming from essentially autonomous technological innovations, or defensive changes, made in response to resource depletion or various environmental disturbances. The role of geographical and cultural factors is summarized in Table 6.1.

TABLE 6.1. *Factors in the long-run economic success of a nation*

*GEOGRAPHICAL FACTORS THAT INFLUENCE ENTREPÔT POTENTIAL*

1. Location near to major long-distance freight transport routes
2. Natural harbour with inland river system
3. Extensive coastline
4. Land and climate suitable for an agriculture with potential for local downstream processing
5. Mineral deposits and energy resources

*ENTREPRENEURIAL CULTURE*

Technical aspects

1. Scientific attitude, including a systems view
2. Judgemental skills, including
   (a) ability to simplify
   (b) self-confidence
   (c) detached perception of risk
   (d) understanding of delegation

Moral aspects

3. Voluntarism and toleration
4. Association with trust, including
   (a) general commitment to principles of honesty, stewardship, etc.
   (b) sense of corporate mission
   (c) versatile personal bonding (friendship not confined to kin)
   (d) weak attachments to specific locations, roles, etc.
5. High norms in respect of effort, quality of work, accumulation of wealth, social distinction, etc.

Geographical and cultural factors are linked because the geography of a territory can influence the kind of culture that emerges within it. This is because geographical impediments to communication reduce personal mobility and partition a country into small isolated social groups. Internal co-ordination within these groups tends to rely on simple mechanisms of reciprocity, etc., which depend crucially on stability of membership. As explained below, the cultures of these groups are likely to emphasize conformity and coercion rather than individuality and choice, and so inhibit spontaneous entrepreneurial activity.

Good communications, on the other hand, provide opportunities for appropriating gains from interregional trade. Groups that inhabit areas with good communications will tend to prosper, provided their leaders adopt a tolerant attitude towards entrepreneurial middlemen who promote trade. Groups which develop an entrepreneurial culture will tend to expand the geographical scope of their operations (through commercially inspired voyages of discovery, and so on). Technological advances in transportation will be encouraged because their liberal policies permit the appropriation of material rewards by inventors and innovators. Geographical expansion eventually brings these groups into contact with isolated groups who occupy resource-rich locations. These locations would be inaccessible without the transportation technology and logistical skills of the entrepreneurial group. Equipped with superior technology, the entrepreneurial group can, if its leaders wish, subdue the isolated groups by military means. Different entrepreneurial groups may become rivals in pre-empting opportunities for the exploitation of overseas resources. This may lead to military conflict between the groups, or to a compromise solution where each group maintains its own economic empire and political sphere of influence.

The creation of a transport infrastructure within these hitherto isolated territories not only gives access to resources (and incidentally improves imperial defence); it also tends to undermine the viability of indigenous cultures. Ease of transportation promotes personal mobility and so destroys the stability of membership on which the local groups' methods of internal co-ordination depend. The confrontation between MNEs and LDCs can be understood as one aspect of this final phase, in which the technologies of the entrepreneurial societies are transferred to the regions occupied by the hitherto isolated social groups. To understand fully the nature of this confrontation, however, it is necessary to study in detail the various aspects of the process of development outlined above.

## 6.4. GEOGRAPHICAL DETERMINANTS OF ENTREPÔT POTENTIAL

A division of labour creates a system of functionally specialized elements (see Chapter 1). System operation over space depends on ease of transportation, and in this context the existence of low-cost facilities for the bulk movement of intermediate products is crucial.

Water transport has significant cost advantages for the bulk movement of freight, and this implies that a good river system and a long coastline (in relation to land area) is an advantage. These conditions are most likely to be satisfied by an island or peninsula with low-lying terrain. Water transport is, however, vulnerable through icing, flooding, etc., and so geological features that facilitate road and rail construction are also useful.

Good transportation expands the area of the market for the final output of each process. It permits a much finer division of labour, because economies of scale in individual plants can be exploited more effectively. In general, steady expansion of the market permits the evolution of system structure. The horizontal division of labour expands to proliferate varieties of final product, while the vertical division of labour extends to generate a larger number of increasingly simple (and hence more easily mechanized and automated) stages of production.

The development of a region depends not only on the progress of its internal division of labour, but also on its ability to participate in a wider division of labour beyond its boundaries. The external division of labour (as traditional trade theory emphasizes) allows the region to specialize in those activities which make the most intensive use of the resources with which it is best endowed.

The interface between the internal and external division of labour is typically an entrepôt centre. Whether or not a region includes a location with entrepôt potential will exert a significant influence on its development (Hodges, 1988). The general advantages of water transport, noted earlier, are reflected in the fact that the cost of long-distance bulk transportation is normally lowest by sea. This means that port facilities are normally necessary for successful entrepôt operation. Since ships afford significant economies of scale in their construction and operation, a successful port must be designed to handle large sea going (and ocean-going) vessels.

A port located close to major international and intercontinental shipping routes may become an important node on a global network of trade. Port activities will comprise both the transhipment of bulk consignments on connecting trunk routes and also 'break-bulk' and 'make-bulk' operations geared to local feeder services. In this context, the location of the port on the estuary of an extensive river system is advantageous. A centre of transhipment and consolidation is, moreover, a natural place at which to carry out processing activities. Handling costs are reduced, because goods can be unloaded directly into the processing facility from the feeder systems, and then later loaded directly from the processing facility onto the trunk system (or vice versa).

The need for processing exported goods depends upon the type of agricultural and mineral production undertaken in the hinterland of the port. In the pre-industrial phase of port development, agricultural processing is likely to be particularly significant. Crops such as corn and barley offer relatively limited opportunities for downstream processing before consumption—baking and brewing being respectively the main activities concerned—while rice feeds into even fewer activities. Animal production, by contrast, generates dairy product, meat, and hides, while hides, in turn, feed into the leather and clothing sequence. Sheep are particularly prolific in generating forward linkages, as their wool feeds into the textile sequence. The textile sequence is simple to mechanize and has the capacity to produce a wide range of differentiated fashion products. (Cotton feeds into a similar sequence, but unlike sheep does not generate meat and hides as well.) The potential for forward linkages varies dramatically, therefore, from rice growing at one extreme to sheep farming at the other.

The location of the processing at the port depends, of course, on it being cheaper to locate the processing in the exporting rather than the importing country., This requirement is generally satisfied by both agricultural and mineral products. The perishability of agricultural products means that processing is usually done as close to the source as possible. Mineral products, though durable, lose weight during processing, and so to minimize transport costs it is usually efficient to process close to the source as well.

Mineral processing is, however, energy-intensive, and energy sources, such as fossil fuels, are often even more expensive to transport than mineral ores themselves. The absence of local energy resources can therefore lead to the relocation of processing away from the exporting country. Mineral processing can also generate hazardous by-products. Access to a coastline near the port where such by-products can be dumped is important, therefore, if minerals are to be processed before export.

While the processing of imported products is likely to be of much less economic significance, for reasons implicit in the discussion above, there are a few exceptions. Imports from an LDC, for example, may well arrive in a raw state, because of the lack of suitable energy supplies or labour skills in the exporting country. Furthermore, the more sophisticated consumer tastes are in the importing country, the more extensive is the processing likely to be required. Thus the greater the gap in development between the exporting and importing country, the more likely it is that the amount of value added in import-processing will be significant.

The agglomeration of activities within a port provides an opportunity for exploiting economies of scale in the provision of defence, law and order, drainage and sewage systems, and so on. It also provides a large local market which promotes the development of highly specialized services—not only commercial services, but also consumer services—of the kind that could never be provided in country areas with dispersed populations. (Such economies of urbanization can, of course, be provided without a port, and many countries do, in fact, contain inland administrative capitals which support such services. The viability of such capitals often depends, however, on cross-subsidization from tax revenues generated at an entrepôt centre, and the social benefits derived from them may therefore be imputed to entrepôt activity.)

It is sometimes claimed that, contrary to the argument above, entrepôts devoted to the bulk export of agricultural products and raw materials are inherently enclavistic. The crucial question here is how fast the linkages between the entrepôt and the village communities of the hinterland develop. In the history of Western DCs provincial agricultural marketing and light manufacturing have grown up in medium-sized towns whose merchants intermediate between the village and the entrepôt. Even in LDCs with limited rural transport infrastructure, the tentacles of trade can extend to the village in respect of livestock farming, because livestock can be driven to market over distances that are prohibitive so far as the carriage of crops is concerned. It is, therefore, only if rural culture is strongly opposed to merchant activity that the entrepôt is likely to remain an enclave indefinitely.

The conditions most favourable to industrialization, it may be concluded, are the existence of a natural harbour close to major shipping routes, good internal communications between the port and its hinterland, livestock farming in the hinterland, abundant endowments of both minerals and primary energy sources, and a coastline suitable for the disposal of pollutants. These considerations alone go some way towards explaining both the early industrialization of temperate-climate, mineral-rich island countries with coastal deposits of fossil fuels and good inland river systems, such as the UK, and their relative decline once their minerals and fossil fuels have been depleted and their comparative advantage in livestock farming undermined by the development of overseas territories.

## 6.5. SCIENTIFIC OUTLOOK AND SYSTEMS THINKING

A territory with entrepôt potential can find its development inhibited by an unsuitable culture. Cultural constraints inhibit entrepreneurship both directly, by discouraging individual initiative, and indirectly, by encouraging political leaders to distort incentives and over-regulate the economy.

In some societies the absence of a scientific outlook may well be a problem. Western analysts studying LDCs tyically perceive this problem as resulting from the absence of any Renaissance or Enlightenment. The society has not gone through an intellectual revolution in which a mystical view of the world gives way to a more realistic one. The society still relies on anthropomorphic explanations of natural processes, interprets unusual but scientifically explicable events as omens, and perceives its real-world environment as the centre of a metaphysical cosmos. This emphasis on things as symbols of something beyond inhibits recognition of things as they really are. It discourages the understanding of nature in terms of mechanism and system interdependency.

A realistic systems view of nature does, however, raise philosophical problems of its own, which can be resolved in various ways. A major difficulty is that if man himself, as a part of nature, is pure mechanism, then choice and moral responsibility become simply an illusion caused by lack of self-knowledge. Western liberal thought resolves this problem through Cartesian dualism, in which the moral world of intentional action coexists alongside the physical world of mechanism.

The scientific outlook does not imply, as is sometimes suggested, a completely secular view of the world. Western Christian thought has also embraced dualism by redefining the role of God as the creator and architect of a self-contained universe rather than as a supernatural force intervening directly through everyday events. The view that man is fashioned in the image of God encourages the idea that man too has creative abilities. Rejection of the view that the earth is the centre of the universe diminishes man's stature and raises that of nature, encouraging the idea that nature is worthy of serious investigation. Man's contact with God can no longer reasonably be maintained through sacrifices offered in anticipation of favours, but it can be sustained in other ways, such as an appreciation of the elegance and simplicity of the physical laws which express this design. Man's creative abilities can be used to explore this design through observation and experiment.

The systems view of nature translates readily into a systems view of production. Production involves a system created by man and superimposed on the system of nature, with which it interacts. A systems view of production involves awareness of the principle of the division of labour—in particular, the importance of decomposing complex tasks into simple ones and allocating resources between these tasks according to comparative advantage. The systems view also emphasizes that the strong complementarities between different elements of the system make it vulnerable to the failure of any single element and so create a strong demand for quality control.

The close connection between religious beliefs and attitudes to nature means that in countries where mysticism or superstition prevail, a scientific outlook and systems thinking are unlikely to develop. The concept of harnessing nature to control the future is absolute folly to people who believe that the future is already pre-ordained, or is in the hands of powerful and arbitrary gods. As a consequence, their ability to assimilate technological know-how will be very low. Awareness of how local operations fit into a global division of labour will be minimal. For example, the idea that system complementarities necessitate continuity of operation, rigorous punctuality, etc., will be quite alien to local operatives. Appreciation of the importance of quality control in the manufacture of components and intermediate products will be missing too.

## 6.6. COMPETITIVE INDIVIDUALISM VERSUS VOLUNTARY ASSOCIATION

The development of a scientific attitude in the West was associated with the rise of individualism. The idea that people are intelligent and purposeful was applied democratically. Intelligence was not something confined to a traditional élite, but a feature of every mature adult. Emphasis on intelligence led to demands for reasoned argument rather than appeal to traditional authority or divine revelation for the legitimation of moral objectives.

Individualism asserts that each person is the best judge of how his own interests are served. He can deal with other individuals as equals, and use his intelligence to safeguard his own interests in his dealings with them. Interference in other people's affairs on paternalistic grounds is unacceptable. Individualism claims that everyone is capable of forming judgements on wider issues too. Since different people have different experiences, no one should assume that his own opinion is necessarily correct, and so toleration of other people's views is required. Differences of opinion over collective activity need to be resolved peacefully, and so in political life commitment to the democratic process is regarded as more important than approval of the outcome of the process.

Four aspects of individualism are worthy of special mention. The first is the alienability of property, which helps to promote markets in both products and labour. The demystification of the world through the emergence of a scientific outlook undermines the view that people impart something of themselves to the things they produce. It breaks the anthropomorphic link between production and use. As the product of labour becomes depersonalized and objectified, it becomes acceptable to alienate it for use by others. Conversely, it becomes acceptable to claim ownership of things one did not produce. So far as natural resources are concerned, they no longer need to be held in common by the territorial group. They can be privately appropriated, giving the owner an incentive to manage them properly and avoid excessive depletion.

The second aspect is freedom of entry (and of exit), which allows individuals to switch between trading partners and between markets without the permission of established authority. Such freedom also implies freedom from statutory regulation of entry too.

Thirdly, respect for contract and a right of recourse to an independent judiciary for the resolution of contractual dispute are aspects of individualism which are important in reducing transaction costs.

Finally, an individualist appreciates that multilateral trade is most easiy established through separately negotiated bilateral trades in which goods are bought and sold using a medium of exchange. He recognizes that currency is useful as a specialized medium of exchange, and that the most convenient currency is the debt of a reputable debtor such as the sovereign or the state. Individualism is therefore tolerant of debt and of the personality cult that surrounds notes and coin that carry the head of the sovereign. It imposes obligations on the debtor, however, to live up to his reputation through self-restraint: in particular he must not debase the currency through over-issue.

A major cultural weakness of LDCs seems to be a lack of individualistic thinking. In the extreme case of a primitive rural economy, the link between production and consumption remains unbroken: individuals consume what they themselves produce, and thereby forgo the gains from trade. In so far as there is a division of labour, it is confined within a social group. Different activities are co-ordinated both by relations of reciprocity between individual members and by members' common sense of obligation to the leader. These mechanisms are most effective within small, stable, and compact groups, such as the extended family or the village community. In such groups members regularly expect to encounter one another again, offenders quicky acquire a reputation for bad behaviour and can be easily punished by the leader and, indeed, by other members of the group.

A major defect of such co-ordination mechanisms is that they depend crucially on stability of membership. If it becomes easy for members to quit, then reputations become less valuable, and punishment is easier to evade. Moreover, conditions of geographical isolation, which tend to promote stability of membership, also mean that the threat of expulsion from the group can be very severe. This allows a leader to acquire enormous power over individual members, provided he can 'divide' the members against each other or otherwise prevent them joining forces to overthrow him. Thus, while isolation may help to promote close emotional ties between the followers, the leader may be feared rather than respected or loved.

Individualism has its own problems, however, in co-ordinating the activities of groups. Because individualism promotes inter-group mobility, it not only undermines the 'despotic' solution to intra-group co-ordination, but also the internal reputation mechanism too. A purely competitive form of individualism, which encourages individuals to join teams purely for the material benefits, offers no effective substitute for primitive reciprocity.

When followers' efforts can be easily monitored by the leader, there is little problem for competitive individualism, because the material rewards of each member can be linked to his individual performance. When effort becomes difficult to monitor, however, material incentives have to be related to team output, and when the team is large, a share of the team bonus may be insufficient to prevent team members slacking. Unless there is a shared sense of corporate mission, individuals are likely to put too little effort into team activity. The leader cannot trust his followers not to slack. If the leader cannot be trusted either then the followers may not respond to his incentives anyway, because they believe he will default on the agreement if he can get away with it.

Another problem of individualism is that the inalienability of the individual's right to quit may induce higher rates of inter-group mobility than are compatible with efficiency. Successful teamwork often requires members to accumulate on-the-job experience in learning to anticipate each other's actions; unrestricted freedom to enter and exit can allow transitory members, who lack this experience, to profit at the expense of their colleagues.

Widening the range of an individual's legitimate commitments from mere respect for property and contract to generate trust by instilling a sense of corporate mission significantly modifies the moral basis of individualism. The resulting philosophy is essentially one of voluntary association. This philosophy retains many of the attributes of competitive individualism, but emphasizes that the contract of group membership involves acceptance of discipline imposed by the leader. Freedom exists principally in choosing between alternative group commitments, rather than in maintaining full discretion within the chosen group. It also emphasizes that commitment to a group is a source of emotional satisfaction, and that more commitment rather than less may make people better off. It does not attempt to repudiate the 'minimal commitment' of competitive individualism, but rather to augment this commitment with others.

Widening the range of commitments creates the possibility of moral conflicts. To a heavily committed individual, indeed, it is the resolution of moral dilemmas that often appears to be the essence of choice. Experience in coping with moral dilemmas of this kind may well improve general decision-making skills.

The global organization of production implemented by sophisticated MNEs depends crucially upon such commitments to mitigate what would otherwise be insuperable agency problems. However intense the competition between MNEs, within each MNE cooperation between the parent and each subsidiary needs to be maintained at a high level. A clear group mission, articulated by a charismatic business leader who makes an effective role model, can be crucial in this respect.

It is therefore worth noting that the kind of individualism harnessed by the successful MNE is very different from the culture of unrestrained self-assertion—or even exhibitionism—which can be found in many societies, including LDCs. The extrovert 'individualism' of adolescent males, for example, has little connection with the mature individualism of the successful entrepreneur. People who exhibit no self-restraint cannot normally be trusted, and so make poor business risks for financiers, and bad employees. The observation, often heard, that there is 'too much individualism' rather than too little in LDCs confuses exhibitionism with the mature individualism described above. It is not too much individualism that is the problem, but too little individualism of the appropriate kind.

## 6.7. GEOGRAPHICAL AND CULTURAL ASPECTS OF A GLOBAL TRADING SYSTEM

The preceding analysis suggests that the differences between DCs and LDCs lie not only in resource endowments, but in the fact that the territories of the former embrace potential entrepôt centres and that cultural obstacles to the realization of this potential are relatively weak. An LDC is likely to be a country that has no entrepôt potential and poor internal communications, which make it unlikely to develop an indigenous entrepreneurial culture. A DC, on the other hand, is a country with both entrepôt potential and an entrepreneurial culture.

A country that has entrepôt potential but lacks an indigenous entrepreneurial culture is likely to find that, in the course of time, entrepôt operations emerge under the ownership and control of foreign entrepreneurs based in DCs. These entrepreneurs have the systems thinking needed to recognize the entrepôt potential, and so are likely to control the international transpsort and distribution systems into which the new operations can be integrated. The external commercial relations of these countries may become heavily dependent upon an international trading system governed by the requirements of DC markets, and controlled by DC interests, while profits generated by entrepôt operations may be repatriated too.

Within any given historical epoch, the process of development begins with the countries that later emerge as the DC investors in LDCs. These countries may subsequently go into decline, but this process of decline is not considered here—it is treated as a separate issue, involving the transition from one historical epoch to another (cf., Wiener, 1981).

In modelling the process of development in global terms, the advantages of water transport over land-based transport—emphasized earlier—play an important role. These advantages mean that maritime trade between entrepôt centres in different countries is likely to be of much greater significance for each country than inland trade between the entrepôt and its remoter hinterland. The fortunes of individual countries are therefore closely linked to their place in the world trading system. Another consequence of the dominance of maritime trade is that even DCs may experience a degree of dualism in their development, between the entrepôt centre on the one hand, and the remoter hinterland on the other. A somewhat ironic corollary of this is that the most unfortunate LDCs, which have no valuable resources and no entrepôt potential, may be the only countries not to experience dualism, purely because they have no development either.

A typical sequence of global development is shown in Figures 6.1 and 6.2. There are two phases. The first involves the rise of DCs prompted by the development of trade between them. The second involves the emergence of LDCs and their own subsequent development.

In the first phase (see Figure 6.1) it is assumed that there are two

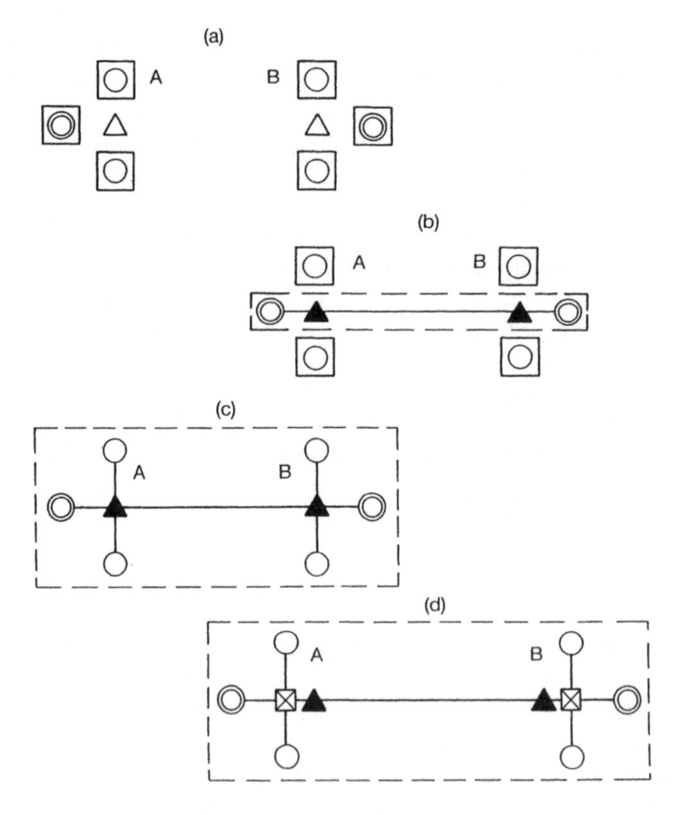


FIG. 6.1. Evolution of international linkages
*Note*: For explanation of symbols, see text.

potential DCs, A and B, each of which is initially segmented into isolated social groups which control particular resources (see sector (a) ). Resource endowments are denoted by circles, with large endowments that have foreign trade potential (because, for example, the output is non-perishable and has a high value per unit weight) being denoted by two concentric circles. Each square box encloses a group of people who share a common culture and reside close to a given resource endowment.

Both countries have a natural harbour which forms a potential entrepôt centre. The resources all lie in a hinterland which can be accessed given suitable investment in transport infrastructure. The harbour represents a potential entrepôt centre, and is denoted by a white triangle. It is assumed that in each country the indigenous culture around the major resource is reasonably progressive, so that this potential can be realized. A line of communication is established between the groups controlling the major resources of each country, and two-way trade develops through the entrepôt ports. Realization of the entrepôt potential is indicated by the switch from the white triangle to the black one in sector (b).

The trade flow intensifies communications between the two countries, leading to cultural homogenization. This is illustrated by the fact that the two countries now lie within the same box—at least so far as the entrepôt centres and the export-oriented hinterlands are concerned. This culture differs from the cultures of the isolated groups in the less promising hinterlands. The trading system strengthens the progressive element in the indigenous culture of the export-oriented hinterland by giving greater emphasis to the individual's right to hold property and his ability to fend for himself in the negotiation of trades. Competition between the port and the hinterland for employees also stimulates a friendlier and less autocratic style of leadership within social groups. This new commercial culture is distinguished from the culture of the isolated groups by the use of a dashed line in the figure.

As each entrepôt centre develops, the advantages of utilizing more fully its indivisible facilities—notably the port—encourage the generation of additional feeder traffic by investment in transport links with the less promising areas of hinterland (see section (c) ). The entrepôt now handles not only additional export traffic, but also interregional traffic between different parts of the hinterland. In other words, the entrepôt becomes a hub for domestic freight transport too. Each country becomes homogenized around the commercial culture as a result. This stage of evolution may well be protracted. Many so-called developed countries still contain isolated rural areas where the commercial culture has made only limited inroads.

Before this stage has been completed, the fourth stage may begin. This involves processing exports at the port, in order to reduce the bulk and increase the value of long-distance cargo. Downstream processing of this kind is illustrated in the figure by a cross within a square (see sector (d) ). Industrialization around the port will have further cultural consequences, but these are not considered here.

The second phase of the development sequence begins when one of the developed countries, say A, makes contact with an LDC, C. C is still in the situation that A was in at the beginning of the first phase, but with this difference—that C remains undeveloped partly because it has a less progressive culture. Its initial state is illustrated in sector (a) of Figure 6.2. The figure has

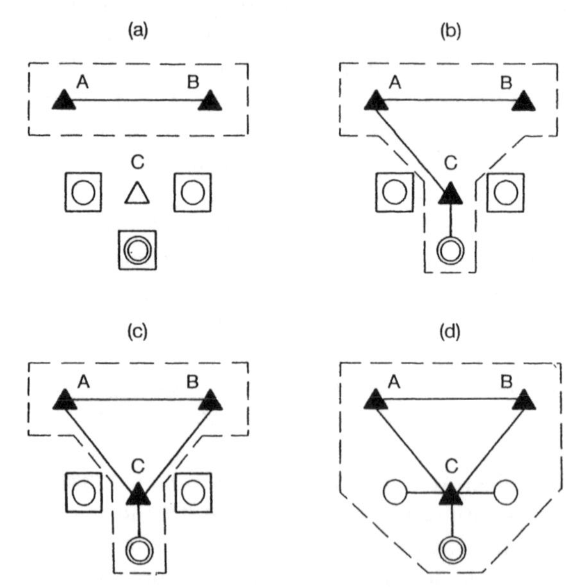


**Fig. 6.2.** Integration of an LDC into a global trading system
*Note*: For explanation of symbols, see text.

been simplified by omitting the domestic trade flows within countries A and B.

If A discovered C before B does, A may attempt to monopolize trade with C, so that all trade between B and C has to be routed via A. Colonial occupation or control of international shipping lanes may be used to enforce the exclusion of B. So far as C is concerned, it is faced with the impact via A of an established commercial culture which has evolved over a long time from roots which were, in any case, more progressive. This opens up a wide cultural gap within C, between the highly commercial imported culture of the entrepôt centre on the one hand, and the less promising areas of hinterland on the other. This is illustrated in sector (c). Cultural dualism impedes the final stage of development, shown in sector (d), where linkages are established with the remaining hinterland. Downstream processing around the entrepôt centre may also develop in this final stage, but this is not shown in the figure.

Two main social groups are available to bridge this cultural gap. One is the resident expatriates, who may have moved abroad originally as employees of the MNE or the DC government. The other is the group of indigenous individuals—merchants and other educated people drawn mainly from the middle and upper ranks of the host society—who are quick to take advantage of the profit opportunities from cultural brokerage. They are willing to learn the language and customs, and adopt the style of dress, of the DC—and perhaps send their children to be educated there as well—in order to consolidate their position. The size of these two groups, and their ability to combine forces where necessary, is crucial in determining the spread of entrepôt influence within the DC.

The analysis suggests that while the process of development in an LDC is similar in outline to that previously followed by an established DC, there are three important differences, which arise chiefly because the LDC is a latecomer to development.

First, the reason why it is a latecomer is partly that it has an unprogressive culture. There may be considerable resistance to the development of entrepôt activity, and indigenous entrepreneurs may be so slow off the mark that foreigners dominate the operations. There may even be political support for a policy of closing the harbour to foreign merchants.

Secondly, if the entrepôt centre is opened up under colonial rule, foreign merchants may enjoy significant market power. Thus few of the gains of trade that accrued to the DC in the early stages of its own development may accrue to the LDC as it passes through a similar stage itself.

Thirdly, the LDC is confronted with a very sophisticated trading system organized by DC trade, and with a matching culture very much at variance with its own. Thus, although superficially it might seem that an LDC should be able to catch up quickly with DCs, its vulnerability to the exercise of market power and the magnitude of the cultural gap may well cause discrepancies in the level of development to persist for a very long time.

## 6.8. CULTURAL ASPECTS OF MNE OPERATIONS

The MNE is the major institution through which both the technology and the entrepreneurial culture of the DC is transferred to the LDC economy. The largest and most sophisticated MNEs are based in DCs; they utilize advanced technologies to operate internationally rationalized production systems. Systems thinking is highly developed in the headquarters of these firms. Strategic attitudes to competition are also well developed because of continuing oligopolistic rivalry between MNEs in major DC markets.

The analysis in this chapter shows that there are substantial cultural barriers to disseminating attitudes of this kind to indigenous managers, and to their subordinates, in LDCs. One obvious way of educating local employees is to send out managers from headquarters on short-term overseas appointments. This may encounter difficulties if the location is sufficiently unattractive to Western eyes that managers resist reassignment to the extent that they prefer to resign instead. In any case, these managers may have difficulties communicating with their subordinates, so while headquarters–subsidiary relations may be good, internal relations within the subsidiary may be poor. In some cases resident expatriates may be employed instead, though there is a risk that they will be out of touch with the more sophisticated ideas developed at headquarters.

An alternative is to hire locally and send recruits to headquarters for extensive training before they return to the subsidiary. Training is, however, likely to be difficult—even at headquarters—unless the local recruits already have some Western-style education, which may well mean that indigenous recruitment is confined to a small social élite. This strategy is inappropriate, moreover, when establishing a new subsidiary; managers will normally have to be sent out from headquarters to organize recruitment, and they can only be replaced when the flow of trained recruits has come on stream.

Cross-cultural barriers also explain why spill-overs from MNE operations in LDCs are so limited. The capacity of indigenous competitors to imitate—let alone adapt or improve upon—imported technologies is limited by their lack of a scientific outlook. Similarly, the inability of local firms to emerge as sub-contractors competing against imported component supplies stems from their failure to appreciate the importance of precision and punctuality—an importance that is so transparent once a systems view of production is adopted.

This is not to deny that profit-oriented indigenous innovation will occur. It will proceed slowly, however—because, for example, the nature of the innovation may have to be explained with the aid of an expensive foreign-run 'demonstration' plant, if the basic scientific logic cannot be assimilated. Cautious indigenous businessmen may wait for an indigenous innovator to operate successfully before committing themselves. Unfortunately, if the indigenous innovator does not understand the logic of the situation, he may be unable to improvise solutions to unforeseen difficulties, and so the innovation may gain an undeserved reputation for being unworkable.

When significant spill-overs do occur, and agglomerations of local industries begin to develop, the effect on the cultural life of the indigenous communities can be devastating. The development of urban areas in which MNE activities are concentrated draws labour away from the rural areas. The migration of rural labour is a selective process. Younger and more entrepreneurial workers are attracted to the towns, leaving the least entrepreneurial workers, and the immigrants' aged dependants, behind. Although rural incomes may be partially sustained by intra-family remittances from the towns, the loss of the more productive and entrepreneurial individuals may well harden the conservative and inward-looking attitudes of those that are left behind. Faced with rising out-migration, the reputation mechanisms that co-ordinate the activities of rural communities are undermined. Rural economic performance declines, and the dualistic structure of the economy is reinforced.

Meanwhile, cut off from their traditional life-style, new urban workers tend to consume a higher proportion of the convenience products and sophisticated durables marketed by the MNEs. Some of these products are promoted using advertising strongly influenced by Western-style competitive individualism. Instead of creating an urban culture based upon voluntary association, which could lead in the long run to a lively entrepreneurial society, commercial media tend to promote attitudes of unrestrained self-assertion, which are inimical both to industrial discipline and to honest business practices.

The social disruption caused by MNE activities does not end here, however. The tradition of subservience to despotic authority, sustained in isolated communities, can sometimes be usefully exploited by MNEs searching for cheap unskilled labour that is easily disciplined by intimidation. Women and children accustomed to absolute paternal authority may become useful factory or plantation employees, for example. Once the women acquire a measure of economic independence, however, the economic basis for paternal authority is undermined, and attempts to sustain it through religious teaching may only be able to slow the trend rather than reverse it. As a result, the whole fabric of traditional family organization may be thrown into disarray.

Another form of disruption is to encourage mass immigration of refugees or landless peasants from other areas in order to depress wages in the locality of the subsidiary. Besides redistributing income away from labour, this strategy carries major problems of cultural integration within the local community, which may spill over into violence, particularly where the immigrants are readily recognized by their language, style of dress, or physical characteristics.

Finally, there is the political disruption which may result from the fragmentation of political alliances which occurs when some local leaders opt for co-operation with foreign interests while others oppose it. Both groups may be forced into extreme positions—one as lackeys of the foreign power and the other as intransigent fundamentalists favouring isolation. This fragmentation of the polity may enable the foreign power to 'divide and rule' the country.

This rather negative view of the social consequences of the MNE may be countered by many instances in which MNEs have attempted to become good corporate citizens of the host country. The difficulty here is that many LDCs—particularly former colonies—are in fact agglomerations of different tribes and castes, and that the concept of a good citizen with which the MNE conforms is merely the view held by the social group that is currently in power. Thus in a country with a long history of internal divisions, being officially recognized as a good citizen may require covert discrimination against rival indigenous groups.

Situations of this kind pose various dilemmas for the MNE. In a country, for example, where the religion of the dominant group stresses paternal authority, should contracts for the employment of married women be negotiated through their husbands, so that women in effect become wage-slaves? Is obstructing the economic liberation of women a satisfactory price to pay for being a good corporate citizen and maintaining the economic basis of traditional family life?

In many recently independent LDCs political power changes frequently, often in response to military initiatives. Should the MNE favour political stability and, if so, use its economic influence on the military to secure the kind of stable regime most acceptable to the liberal Western conscience? If the MNE remains aloof, and instability continues, it is likely to be confronted with a series of corrupt demands for payments to government officials, as the holders of influential offices attempt to make their fortunes before they are deposed in the next change of government. Should the MNE jeopardize the interests not only of its shareholders, but also of its indigenous employees by refusing to make payments, or should it respect 'local culture' and support the bribery endorsed by the 'unofficial constitution'?

The way managers resolve these moral issues will be determined by the MNE's own corporate culture, which will in turn reflect, at least in part, the national culture of the DC in which it is headquartered. In this respect the balance between the philosophies of competitive individualism and voluntary association in the source country culture will be a critical factor in determining how far broad moral concerns dominate the pursuit of shareholders' short-term interests.

## 6.9. CONCLUSION

Previous economic literature on MNEs in LDCs has tended to concentrate on issues of market power and the choice of contractual arrangements (for example, Lall and Streeten, 1977; Calvet and Naim, 1981). The integration of cultural issues into an economic analysis of the subject is necessary because economic factors such as these cannot entirely explain the relevant phenomena.

A great deal of further work needs to be done before the hypotheses advanced in this chapter can be properly tested. The full extent of the cultural differences among LDCs, and among the DC countries in which MNEs are based needs to be recognized. The performance of a given MNE in a given LDC is likely to be governed by (a) the degree of entrepreneurship in the culture of the firm, (b) the degree of entrepreneurship in the culture of the host country, and (c) an 'interaction' or 'coupling' term which captures the overall degree of similarity between the cultures, recognizing that culture is a multifaceted phenomenon.

To apply this method it is necessary to profile the cultures of both the entities involved. It may require in-depth interviews with many people to establish profiles which can make any claim to objectivity. Complete objectivity can never be achieved, of course, in any study of cultural phenomena, because of the distortion created by the culture-specific prejudices of the observer. Nevertheless, it is unnecessary to go to the other extreme and adopt an entirely relativistic view. Different observers may still be able to agree on some things, even if they cannot agree on everything.

Cultures contain a certain amount of inertia because of the way they are transmitted between generations through family upbringing. Nevertheless, the advent of public education and mass-media communications has the potential to accelerate cultural change. Much contemporary change is directed towards increasing the uniformity of beliefs and tastes in order to promote economic integration and develop large global markets. The trend towards greater rapidity of cultural change does, indeed, give a sense of urgency to understanding the mechanisms and the economic effects involved.

Economic changes can themselves precipitate cultural change, because they affect the shared experiences of members of a society. The increasing interdependence within the world economy is, in fact, another reason why the process of cultural change may have speeded up. This chapter has, unfortunately, treated culture as though it were an exogenous parameter rather than an endogenous variable. A full study of cultural factors would, however, involve a dynamic analysis containing feedback loops of a kind far too complex to be considered here.

Even in its present state, though, the theory provides some simple predictions about comparative economic development. It suggests, for example, that small island economies which enjoy a sophisticated cultural legacy may be better equipped to develop than mainly land-locked countries whose cultural traditions are derived almost exclusively from small isolated rural communities. The entrepôt potential and cultural legacy of Hong Kong, Singapore, and Taiwan, say, may therefore explain why they have been able to industrialize and develop indigenous business services so much faster than many sub-Saharan African economies. This is quite consistent with the view that outward-looking trade policies have also promoted their development. It underlines, however, the earlier suggestion that trade policy itself may, in the long run, be culturally specific. Imposing outward-looking trade policies on a less entrepreneurial country in Africa is unlikely to have the same dramatic result as has the voluntary adoption of such policies in South East Asian NICs.

Finally, it should be noted that recognition of cultural factors has significant welfare implications. The emotional benefits that individuals derive from group affiliation are commonly omitted from the preference structures assumed in conventional social cost–benefit analysis of foreign investment. The cultural specificity of the policy-maker's own attitudes are also ignored, although these attitudes are crucial in validating the highly materialistic individual preferences assumed in conventional policy analysis. On a more specific level, the failure of conventional analysis to recognize the important economic function of culture in reducing transaction costs means that conventional analysis has overlooked the significant material as well as emotional costs that cultural disintegration imposes on many sectors of the economy. A number of judgements about the net benefits of foreign investment derived from conventional analysis will have to be carefully reconsidered in the light of this cultural analysis.

## References

Berger, S., and Piore, M. J. (1980), *Dualism and Discontinuity in Industrial Societies* (Cambridge: Cambridge University Press).

Calvet, A. L., and Naim, M. (1981), 'The Multinational Firm in Less Developed Countries: A Markets and Hierarchies Approach', paper presented at Academy of International Business/European International Business Association Conference, Barcelona, Spain.

— and Pearce, R. D. (1987), 'Multinational Enterprises in LDCs', in N. Gemmell (ed.), *Surveys in Development Economics* (Oxford: Blackwell), 90–132.

Eisenstadt, S. N. (1973), *Tradition, Change, Modernity* (New York: Wiley).

Hagen, E. E. (1962), *On the Theory of Social Change: How Economic Growth Begins* (Homewood, Ill.: Dorsey Press).

Herskovits, J. J. (1961), 'Economic Change and Cultural Dynamics', in R. Braibanti and J. J. Spengler (eds.), *Tradition, Values, and Socio-Economic Development* (Durham, NC.: Duke University Press), 114–38.

Hodges, R. (1988), *Primitive and Peasant Markets* (Oxford: Blackwell).

Hoselitz, B. F. (1961), 'Tradition and Economic Growth', in R. Braibanti and J. J. Spengler (eds.), *Tradition, Values, and Socio-Economic Development* (Durham, NC: Duke University Press), 83–113.

Inkeles, A., and Smith, D. H. (1974), *Becoming Modern: Individual Change in Six Developing Countries* (London: Heinemann).

Kilby, P. (1971), 'Hunting the Heffalump', in P. Kilby (ed.), *Entrepreneurship and Economic Development* (New York: Free Press), 1–40.

Lall, S., and Streeten, P. (1977), *Foreign Investment, Transnationals and Developing Countries* (London: Macmillan).

Leff, N. H. (1978), 'Industrial Organization and Entrepreneurship in the Developing Countries: The Economic Groups', *Economic Development and Cultural Change*, 26: 661–75.

Leibenstein, H. (1978), *General X-Efficiency Theory and Economic Development* (New York: Oxford University Press).

McClelland, D. C., and Winter, D. G. (1969), *Motivating Economic Achievement* (New York: Free Press).

Pack, H. (1987), *Productivity, Technology and Economic Development* (New York: Oxford University Press).

Wallerstein, I. (1979), *The Capitalist World-Economy* (Cambridge: Cambridge University Press).

Wiener, M. J. (1981), *English Culture and the Decline of the Industrial Spirit* (Cambridge: Cambridge University Press).

# [16]

## *The Role of Private Business in the International Diffusion of Technology*

CLEARLY, private business is but one agent for the diffusion of technology. Yet it is an important one. In the normal pursuit of business, technological knowledge and skills pass over political boundaries and private enterprise takes part in the international diffusion of technology. In this paper I want to try to delineate the means by which private companies have shared in the international diffusion of technology in the nineteenth and twentieth centuries. I will note briefly the "imitation lag" and then what I want to call the "absorption gap." From generalizations, I will turn to some explicit examples and analysis. Finally, in conclusion, I want to return to my concept of the absorption gap and the role of private enterprise in bridging that gap.[1]

### I

In theory at least there appear to be eight distinct ways by which a private company can act to transfer technology across political borders. The eight methods are broad and each contains sub-categories. First, a private concern can export for sale or for exhibition a new or improved product. If the exports are capital goods, they transfer technology directly when used in modernizing production processes. But any export, whether of a producer or a consumer good, may be imitated in foreign lands and by this means move technology from one country to another. Thus, the first manner by which a company transfers technology involves simply the *export of products.* Second, a private enterprise can take out patents in a foreign country, patents that may be worked in that nation. In reg-

This paper has been revised since its delivery on September 14, 1973, in light of comments made at the Economic History Association meeting by Professors Kozo Yamamura, Ralph Hidy, Stuart Bruchey, David Felix, and others.

[1] Technology has been defined in narrow terms to comprise simply tools and machines. I prefer a more comprehensive definition, including in addition to tools and machines, product design, knowhow, and organizational ability, that is, concept along with technique. I am well aware that technological diffusion often takes place in "bits and pieces." Indeed, technology itself evolves in a complex fashion. While these points are not elaborated on herein, there is nothing in my paper to imply otherwise.

istering a patent, there is disclosure. There are opportunities for its sale or licensing, or for designing similar but not covered products. Thus, the second approach involves the *export of patents.* Third, a firm can make a range of different types of technical assistance agreements or provide technical aid to foreign companies or governments. Here there is the *export of technical knowledge and services.* And, fourth, a company can undertake direct foreign investments, that is, act as a multinational enterprise and transfer its technology abroad with its investment. This fourth approach involves an *export of, or rather an extension of, the firm itself abroad.* All these methods are those of enterprises that possess technology to transmit.[2] Note that a single company can participate in all four forms of transfer. The distinctions between these methods of transfer may be real or simply theoretical, depending on the particular circumstances.

The second four manners by which a company transfers technology are counterparts of the first group. These four are associated with the receipt of technology: One, a firm can *import* machines used in production processes new to its nation; an importer can sell or present any new product, which is then imitated within the recipient nation. Two, a company can commercialize the *patents* of a foreign enterprise in its domestic market. Three, it can make *technical assistance arrangements* from which it will benefit. Four, it can acquire technology from a *direct foreign investor.* All these last four approaches involve the utilization of foreign technology. Perhaps these four manners of receiving technology may be as much or more responsible for international technological diffusion as the four manners used by the holders of the technology.

Still, the second group of businessmen is often, although not always, reliant on the first group, since it is impossible to import if something is not exported; a patent must exist before any one can work or modify that particular patent; someone must have the technology before a technical assistance agreement can be made; for there to be technology derived from a direct foreign investor, there must be that investor. Note, however, that the holder of the technology—the exporter, the owner of the patent, the provider of tech-

[2] If the exporter of the product is independent of the producer of the product, it can be argued that the export firm does not have the technology of production; yet, it is still the holder of (owner of or agent for) the product that contains within it the technology.

nological assistance, or even the direct foreign investor—need not be a private company. In short, there need not be symmetry in the relationship between our two groups of private companies.[3] Note, too, the second group of businessmen may in certain instances be one and the same as the first group; exporter and importer may be part of one company; holder of the patent and exploiter of it abroad may be identical; and so forth.[4] Once again, the distinctions may be real or simply theoretical.

There are additional ways by which a technologically-advanced company participates in a passive manner in the transfer of technology.[5] The eight modes described above seem to be the *active* ways by which private companies take part in technological transfers.

## II

Before I elaborate on these eight modes of transfer, it is worth considering the difference between mere transfer and the absorption of technology within the host country. A company can export capital goods. In one country the machines installed might be allowed to break down and eventually fall into disrepair; in another country, the same machines might be used efficiently in modern industry, copied, adapted, and produced locally. A company can ex-

[3] The holder of the technology may be, for example, a national or international public agency, or an individual or individuals, a periodical, or a scholarly text. Technology obviously does not have to be received by private companies from other private companies, or alternatively, transmitted by private companies to other private companies.

[4] By identical I mean within the same corporate group—company and branch or foreign subsidiary of that company. I am in this case piercing the corporate arrangements to determine the actuality.

[5] An employee of the technologically-advanced firm may leave it and travel abroad, taking with him technological information or proficiency. Nathan Rosenberg, "Economic Development and the Transfer of Technology: Some Historical Perspectives," *Technology and Culture*, XI (July 1970), 553ff., points out that in the nineteenth century it was common for technological transfers to be made by the migration of trained personnel. See also William Woodruff, *The Impact of Western Man* (New York: St. Martin's Press, 1967), chap. 5. A technologically-advanced company may open its plants to visiting foreign technicians, who see processes they can imitate in their homelands. A firm may sell or exhibit its products domestically, which products may be seen by foreigners who may reproduce the innovations in their own countries. A man may conduct industrial espionage in a plant of a technologically-advanced company and then transmit the secrets across the border. In each of these cases, technological transfer occurs, but the technologically-advanced private firm is essentially passive. It does not send goods, patents, technology, capital, or men across borders; instead, the agency for the transfer is an individual, an ex-employee, or a visitor who may or may not be associated with a private business *abroad.*

port consumer goods to two countries. In one the product might continue as an import; while in the second, host-nation businesses might manufacture the product. A company may register patents in countries abroad. In one nation the patents may not be worked, or be worked by foreigners; in a second, the patents may be commercialized by nationals of that land. A firm may transfer its technology through a technical assistance arrangement and in one country no one may be able or willing to utilize the advanced methods, whereas by contrast the technical assistance in another country might effectively train nationals of the host country. Similarly, a direct foreign investment carries with it technology but the technologies transmitted may be confined to the foreign corporation, or alternatively, may be absorbed by enterprises within the host nation. In each of these paired cases there is a transfer of technology, but only in the second situation in the pair does absorption or true international diffusion occur.

These comments distinguishing transfer and absorption are obviously too black and white, since they do not take into account time lags.[6] The poles are lack of absorption and rapid absorption; between the poles, absorption may take years or even decades. There seems to be not only an "imitation lag," but an "absorption gap." The literature on technological transfers says a great deal about the international imitation lag, defined by others as the lapsed time between when a product is first produced in the innovator country and in each subsequent nation.[7] The imitation lag is relatively uncomplicated to determine, yet it seems to me inadequate, because it says nothing about absorption (or true international diffusion). It does not differentiate whether the product was produced by nationals of the "imitating" country on their own, or by such nationals with extensive foreign assistance or by subsidiaries of multinational enterprises.[8] It would seem that only when nationals on their own

[6] Everett Rogers, *Diffusion of Innovations* (New York: The Free Press, 1962), pp. 18-19, 79-120, and his second edition of the same book, *Communication of Innovations* (New York: The Free Press, 1971), pp. 128-132, are excellent on time lags between awareness of the innovation and adoption.

[7] To my knowledge, the term "international imitation lag" was first used by Michael Posner, "International Trade and Technical Change," *Oxford Economic Papers*, XIII (October 1961), 323-341. See also G. C. Hufbauer, *Synthetic Materials and the Theory of International Trade* (Cambridge, Mass.: Harvard University Press, 1966), chaps. 1 and 5, and Louis T. Wells, Jr., ed., *The Product Life Cycle and International Trade* (Boston, Mass.: Division of Research, Graduate School of Business Administration, Harvard University, 1972), pp. 23-25.

[8] John R. Tilton, *International Diffusion of Technology: The Case of Semi-Con-*

(or virtually on their own) are able to produce the product does true diffusion—in contrast with mere geographical transfer—of the technology occur. Tentatively, I will define the absorption gap as the lapsed time between the introduction of a new technology, process or product, into a nation and the point when that technology is used in processes of comparable or near comparable efficiency and the manufacture of products of comparable or near comparable quality under ownership and control (defined here as technological ability) of nationals of that country. "Near comparable" is probably a better formulation than "comparable," for with effective absorption there will be modification when appropriate and also improvement to fit national requirements. Note that I am referring here to the initial—original—absorption of the new technology within a recipient nation. In going beyond international diffusion and dealing with economic development, obviously one must consider two absorption gaps, one defined, as above, to indicate simple *international* diffusion of the new technology, and the second defined to indicate infusion (or successful *national* diffusion), that is when the new technology is not only adopted and adapted by nationals but also becomes the dominant technology of the host nation industry.[9] In

---

*ductors* (Washington, D.C.: Brookings Institution, 1971), p. 23, introduces four different "lags" (including the imitation lag) but none takes into account the question of national ownership and control, although Tilton's book has much of value to say on this matter.

[9] Thus, for example, absorption gap (1) would indicate the lapsed time between the first introduction of British-made cotton textiles into India and the efficient production of such machine-made cotton textiles in a plant owned by Indian capital, run by Indian management, and operated in the main by Indian technicians. Absorption gap (2) might indicate the lapsed time between the first introduction of British machine-made cotton textiles into India and the time when say 50 percent of the output of the Indian cotton textiles came from the modern Indian cotton textile industry. I find myself very much in agreement with Stuart Bruchey's statement that "it is not so much the first appearance of new techniques as their spread [within a nation] that matters in economic growth." *The Roots of American Economic Growth* (New York: Harper & Row, 1965), p. 139. Nonetheless, the entry of new techniques in a nation and their initial absorption are clearly a precondition for their spread. Professor Solomon Barkin of the Department of Economics at the University of Massachusetts, Amherst, has been helpful to me in stressing that in considering "absorption" of technological ability—as I have defined it—I should consider separately managerial and technical personnel. I find this idea both stimulating and troubling. For example, in the 1890's, The Royal Dutch Company in the Dutch East Indies used American drillers in its crude oil producing operations. Royal Dutch had complete ownership and management control. Was the foreign technology absorbed? It seems to me that it was under Dutch corporate control, and one can legitimately refer to true technological diffusion as having taken place. Perhaps the test should be: If the business would fail or be seriously disrupted were foreign technicians removed, the control of technology cannot be said to be in national

this paper, I am considering only the first absorption gap involving diffusion over international boundaries. In short, the international imitation lag (as defined by others) covers the transfer of technology to a foreign nation and does not take into account the nationality of the producer in the host country. The absorption gap stresses the absorption of the new technology by nationals of the recipient country. As I have defined these terms, international transfers are a necessary but not a sufficient condition for absorption or true international diffusion.[10]

With the concept of the absorption gap we are brought squarely to the need to analyze the conditions under which the international technology is received—that is, the institutional structure prepared to accept the technology, and for purposes of this paper, specifically private companies within the host country that can digest the technology. Our second group of four modes by which technology is transferred deals with this matter. Only if the companies in the second group (the receivers of technology) are nationals of the host country, I suggest, does effective international diffusion take place.

Since I am arguing that transfer does not necessarily mean diffusion, this brings me to the point that there are barriers to effective diffusion of new technology that directly relate to the receivers of technology. These often co-existent and sometimes overlapping barriers include: (1) demand barriers (there may not be sufficient de-

hands; if, by contrast, the business would remain viable and can find substitutes for the foreign technicians then it may be that despite the presence of foreign technicians in the operations, the technology has been effectively assimilated.

[10] In the literature on international technological transfer and diffusion, definitions vary. Sometimes the ideas of transfer, diffusion, and adoption are used interchangeably. (See for instance Tilton, *International Diffusion*, pp. 2, 163.) Sometimes "transfer" refers to the crossing of borders and "diffusion" to the spread within the borders. See John Joseph Murray's article in Daniel L. Spencer and Alexander Woronick, eds., *The Transfer of Technology to Developing Countries* (New York: Praeger, 1967), p. 9. Rogers, *Diffusion of Innovation*, p. 76, differentiates diffusion from adoption in that diffusion for him involves the spread from source to user or adopter, while adoption is an "individual matter"—"the mental process through which an individual passes from first hearing about an innovation to final adoption." In *Communication of Innovations*, pp. 12, 26, 99ff., Rogers defines diffusion as a special type of communication—"the process by which innovations spread to the members of a social system" and changes his definition of adoption to a "decision to make full use of a new idea." For purposes of this paper, as my reader is now aware, I am distinguishing between mere international transfers and true international diffusion (that is absorption)—the first implying the physical, geographical transfer of an innovation (specifically new technology) over borders, and the second designating the spread of that new technology to nationals of the host country to the extent that they can and do utilize the new technology in production.

mand to warrant national production); (2) capital barriers (local producers may not have or be able to obtain the capital to utilize the technology)[11]; (3) natural resource barriers (a nation's commercially-developed natural resources may be inappropriate for the effective utilization of the technology)[12]; (4) labor-cost barriers (low labor costs relative to other costs may discourage the application of a particular technology); (5) technological barriers (local producers may not have the skills or education to absorb the incremental technological knowhow)[13]; (6) scale barriers (foreign producers may have economies of scale that cheapen costs vis-à-vis host nation producers; without government protection, national producers may have no possibility of meeting foreign competition); (7) infrastructure barriers (there may not be sufficient supporting services or complementary techniques to warrant diffusion); (8) cultural barriers (there must be values and norms of behavior conducive to the absorption of technology); and (9) most easily overcome, language barriers, which may slow absorption. There may also be "priority barriers" within a particular economy.[14] Herein, I do not intend to elaborate on these barriers, which are obviously of vast importance. The barrier, however, that directly concerns me is one that should be (but is often not) included on the above list—that of "business organization." There must be effective business organization (private or governmental) to absorb the technology.[15]

11 As Joseph Bower points out in *Managing The Resource Allocation Process* (Boston: Division of Research, Graduate School of Business Administration, Harvard University, 1970), p. 39, "Studies of the research and development process indicate that expenditures rise exponentially as a product moves from the basic and applied research steps to development and production. It is factories, tools, and dies, trained labor, reoriented channels of distribution and promotion which are the truly expensive part of innovation."

12 See Nathan Rosenberg, ed., *The Economics of Technological Change* (London: Penguin Books, 1971), pp. 210, 274-281.

13 Professor Rosenberg has put it, in describing the United States in the nineteenth century, "it required considerable technical expertise to borrow and exploit a foreign industrial technology." *Technology and American Economic Growth* (New York: Harper & Row, 1972), p. 82.

14 See note 54 below for an example of priority barriers. Priority barriers may be erected by governments as well as faced by private companies. Thus, the Soviet government may decide not to manufacture certain consumer goods, not because of demand, capital, natural resource, labor-cost, technological, scale, infrastructure, cultural, or language barriers, or even business organization barriers, but because of priority barriers.

15 Effective business organization includes attitudes of management. G. F. Ray, "The Diffusion of New Technology—A Study of Ten Processes in Nine Industries," *National Institute Economic Review* (May 1969), 83, concludes that the attitude of management has the "greatest impact on the application of new techniques." I am

III

With these general comments, I am now ready to examine the actual process of technological transfer by private companies. Regrettably, my examples are unsystematic. The difficulty lies in the shortness of the paper. The examples should, however, demonstrate forms of transfer and their relation to diffusion, as well as provoke thought about methodology in dealing with international technological diffusion by private business. Whether the classification scheme proves useful in studying the success of the particular type of international diffusion has to be tested in subsequent research.

All the eight modes of transfer that I have outlined in the early part of this paper have existed in the nineteenth and twentieth centuries. First, exports: The British, fearing the diffusion of technology in the early nineteenth century, barred the sale abroad of certain textile machinery.[16] Britishers bypassed the law and established manufacturing enterprises on the continent and *exported* from there, directly transferring and diffusing British manufacturing methods.[17] In the late 1820's and 1830's, English builders sold

far from alone in talking about the absorptive capabilities of recipient firms. See Jack Baranson, "Technology Transfer Through the International Firm," *American Economic Review*, LX (May 1970), 435-436. Baranson in this article is concerned with factors affecting transfer logistics of the international firm; he barely touches on the problems of transfer as distinct from diffusion but he does recognize the importance of absorptive capabilities. In my general analysis in this paper, I find myself influenced by the body of work that deals specifically with transfers without diffusion, for example, the seminal article by Hans Singer, "Distribution of Gains between Investing and Borrowing Countries" (1950), reprinted in Hans Singer, *International Development* (New York: McGraw-Hill, 1964), pp. 161-172; the concept of "a dual economy" that now appears in most textbooks on less developed countries; and statements such as the one that appeared in a 1956 National Planning Association Study. After noting that U.S. firms had been transferring technology to Latin America for years, this study concluded, "Unfortunately, however, only a low proportion of the many small firms which are still using primitive practices throughout Latin America have as yet been reached by the methods and techniques which are being introduced by U.S. firms and their affiliates." National Planning Association Special Committee on Technical Cooperation, *Technical Cooperation in Latin America—Recommendations for the Future* (Washington, D.C.: National Planning Association, 1956), p. 77. This will henceforth be cited as NPA Technical Cooperation Study. I have a number of reservations about the legitimacy of such views, but find it essential to take their premises into account in a consideration of the history of the international diffusion of technology. These views touch on the basic question of the abilities of recipients of technology to absorb the technology.

16 Details on such British restraints appear in Great Britain, "First Report from Select Committee to Inquire into the Operation of the Existing Laws Affecting the Exportation of Machinery," *Parliamentary Papers*, Vol. 7 (1841).

17 For example the Cockerill firm, using British methods and manufacturing in Belgium and Germany, sold its machines as far east as Poland; new textile enterprises developed, incorporating the new technology. David S. Landes, *The Unbound*

their locomotives in the United States; these were copied and improved upon and "a locomotive-building industry sprang up in the United States almost at once."[18] In the 1840's, Stephen Moulton carried to (exported to) England samples of Charles Goodyear's vulcanized rubber, exhibiting the product to prospective manufacturers; these samples were seen by Englishman Thomas Hancock, who had worked on rubber manufacture for many years; not long after, Hancock took out his own patents that virtually duplicated Goodyear's process. He then proceeded to manufacture rubber goods.[19] The Singer records are full of data expressing concern about the imitation of Singer sewing machines in western Europe.[20] In the twentieth century, capital equipment exports were often a means of transferring technology abroad. Likewise, exported products of all sorts were imitated.

Second, registering of patents abroad served to transfer technology. In the nineteenth and twentieth centuries U.S. companies in Europe and European enterprises in the United States obtained patents. The patents were worked in the foreign country. Examples include manufacture of revolvers, aluminum, electrical equipment, and chemicals.[21]

---

*Prometheus* (Cambridge, Eng.: Cambridge University Press, 1969), pp. 150, 148. Bruchey notes that despite the ban on British machinery exports, a substantial number of British machines reached the United States to be copied and, more important, modified to meet U.S. requirements. Bruchey, *Roots of American Economic Growth*, p. 167.

18 Eugene S. Ferguson, "The Steam Engine Before 1830," in *Technology in Western Civilization*, eds. Melvin Kranzberg and Carroll W. Pursell, Jr. (New York: Oxford University Press, 1967), I, p. 299.

19 Moulton was British, emigrated to the United States, and established his business there. He took the rubber samples to England, hoping to sell "the inventor's secret." William Woodruff, "Origins of An Early English Rubber Manufactory," *Bulletin of the Business Historical Society*, XXV (March 1951), pp. 32-36. Hancock's lawyers denied that the latter had gained technological information directly from Goodyear's samples. Woodruff suggests, "Perhaps his [Hancock's] genius lay in appreciating what Goodyear had done. . . .There can be no doubt that Goodyear's discovery stimulated the English inventor to still further effort."

20 Singer Manufacturing Co. records, State Historical Society of Wisconsin, Madison, Wisconsin.

21 Thus Colt licensed companies on the European continent to make revolvers under Colt patents in the 1850's. See Mira Wilkins, *The Emergence of Multinational Enterprise: American Business Abroad from the Colonial Era to 1914* (Cambridge, Mass.: Harvard University Press, 1970), p. 30. The predecessor of Aluminum Company of America, The Pittsburgh Reduction Company, that acquired the Hall patents for making aluminum in 1888, granted in 1895 a license under these patents to a small French firm, rights that soon passed to d'Alais et Camargues, later Cie. Pechiney. See George W. Stocking and Myron W. Watkins, *Cartels in Action* (New York: Twentieth Century Fund, 1946), pp. 220, 227. Annual reports and company prospectuses in the Scudder Collection, Columbia University Library, reveal numerous licens-

Third, a range of technical assistance arrangements have been made by private firms to communicate technology. Often capital equipment exports were accompanied by a single mechanic or a group of technicians that installed the equipment and instructed the customer in its operation and maintenance.[22] When, for example, American elevators and electrical equipment were marketed abroad in the late nineteenth century, technicians frequently accompanied the export.[23] The German Von Kohorn Company sold machinery and technical aid for the establishment of the viscose rayon industry in Czechoslovakia (1919), Greece (1923), Turkey (1935), Rumania (1937) and then farther afield in Peru (1946) and Egypt (1948).[24] In more recent times, as well, this phenomenon of exporters sending technical knowhow with their exports has persisted.[25] Likewise, when patents were worked abroad, often the innovating firm would transfer technological information beyond what was in the patent registration. Thus, for instance, when in the 1850's, the Singer Company sold its French patent, it agreed to send to the purchaser an aide for his manufacturing department so that merchant could make "perfect machines."[26] Frequently, in the twentieth century, the licensing of patents and technical assistance accords went together.[27]

While associated with exports and patents, technical assistance arrangements may go far beyond the other two modes of transfer. There were patents included in the interchange of information between Standard Oil (N.J.) and I. G. Farben and between du Pont and the large European chemical companies before World War II, but the technological assistance transcended the mere licensing of

ing relationships. Sometimes patents were taken out abroad under the names of individuals on behalf of a company, sometimes by the company itself. U.S. Bureau of Census, *Historical Statistics of the United States* (Washington, D.C.: G.P.O., 1960), pp. 607-608, gives data on the number of patents issued in the United States to residents of foreign countries and foreign corporations. I know of no one who has attempted to use these data in considering problems of international technological transfer.

22 See, for example, Landes, *Unbound Prometheus*, p. 150, on Cockerill exports.

23 Data from company records of exporters of these products.

24 Hufbauer, *Synthetic Materials*, p. 93.

25 All through the twentieth century, American firms have sent technicians to install machinery in plants in Latin America and over time have trained local employees to operate and maintain the machinery. NPA Technical Cooperation Study, pp. 76-77.

26 Wilkins, *Emergence of Multinational Enterprise*, p. 38.

27 See Mira Wilkins, *The Maturing of Multinational Enterprise: American Business Abroad from 1914 to 1970* (Studies in Business History, Cambridge, Mass.: Harvard University Press, forthcoming).

patents.[28] In recent years, the many agreements between U.S. and Japanese enterprises for technological exchanges sometimes include patent exchanges yet they comprise far more than the licensing of such patents.[29] Some technical assistance accords may be entirely independent of patents. In 1908, Herbert Hoover organized an international mining consulting firm to sell U.S. technological services.[30] British Managing Agents in India transferred technological knowhow.[31] When management contracts are made between western companies and firms or governments in less developed countries there is a sale of organizational and technological skills.[32]

Private business enterprise has had experience with a particular technology that it has developed or used. It has trained individuals to work with the technology. It has knowledge of the problems and difficulties in commercializing the particular technology. It has organizational knowledge. It is in short in a unique position in the transfer of the specific technology. It seems clear that often the product, or the description in the patent, or mere drawings and instructions, are inadequate for transfers of technology; men are needed to carry, explain, and facilitate the introduction of the new processes or products. The private firm can provide the institutional framework whereby these men can transfer the technology.[33]

Four, technology also crosses boundaries through direct foreign investment. Closely associated with exporting, registering patents abroad, and technical assistance is direct foreign investment. Generally, the international business carries on all these functions and has done so since the nineteenth century, if not before.[34] As prac-

28 *Ibid.*

29 Data obtained in Japan from U.S. and Japanese companies and the Ministry of International Trade and Industry.

30 Herbert Hoover, *Memoirs* (New York: Macmillan, 1952), I, pp. 28ff.

31 P. S. Lokanathan, *Industrial Organization in India* (London: George Allen & Unwin, 1970), pp. 15-16.

32 See Peter Gabriel, *The International Transfer of Corporate Skills* (Boston: Division of Research, Graduate School of Business Administration, Harvard University, 1967).

33 These comments are especially true of the twentieth century as technology became more complex. But even in the nineteenth century, as others have noted, imitation of products and processes and development of patents often required foreign personnel familiar with the techniques. Such men in the nineteenth century were sometimes (and sometimes not) associated with private companies. In recent times, when a company has moved away from specific to "overall technology," it may fail completely. This was the case with Litton Industries' much discussed contract with Greece for the economic development of Crete and the Peloponnesus peninsula.

34 There are numerous instances in the nineteenth century wherein private companies carried technology over borders through direct investments. For the activities

tically every writer on the subject has pointed out, direct investors communicate management, technology, and skills across national boundaries. Recent studies have indicated that the firm that invests abroad generally has an advantage, an advantage in technology, product design, marketing, or managerial expertise.[35] It has this advantage to communicate. Corporations that own foreign factories, mines, oil properties, and plantations transmit technology in various ways: (1) There is clearly a physical (geographical) transfer. Beyond that, the products made and the processes used abroad are there to be imitated within the host nation.[36] Also, there can be a shift of the technology of the direct investor to host country nationals should expropriation occur or should a national firm purchase the properties of the direct investor.[37] (2) Host nation workers and managers gain knowledge of products and processes. The training may be on the job, in the corporation's home operations, at local educational institutions supported by the company, or at foreign universities (subsidized by scholarships granted by the multinational business).[38] The training can range from that in simple skills to that in highly-sophisticated modern technology and business administration. (3) If the activity of the international en-

of American companies in this respect see Wilkins, *Emergence of Multinational Enterprise.* How many cases of technological transfer through direct investment one can find in the eighteenth century is unknown to the present author, but clearly European companies before 1800 through direct investment appear to have played a role in technological transfer. Thus, in 1770, a French company operated a coal mine at Hagenbach in Baden and appears to have transferred the more advanced French methods to Germany. See Rondo E. Cameron, *France and the Economic Development of Europe 1800-1914* (Princeton, N.J.: Princeton University Press, 1961), p. 372. Alexander Gerschenkron, *Economic Backwardness in Historical Perspective* (New York: Praeger, 1965), pp. 38-39, suggests such activities by the Fuggers in the fifteenth and sixteenth centuries.

[35] See for example Raymond Vernon, *Sovereignty at Bay* (New York: Basic Books, 1971); Wilkins, *Emergence of Multinational Enterprise;* and Wilkins, *Maturing of Multinational Enterprise.*

[36] On imitation abroad see Robert B. Stobaugh, "The Product Life Cycle, U.S. Exports, and International Investment," DBA dissertation, Graduate School of Business Administration, Harvard University, 1968, and Tilton, *International Diffusion,* p. 164.

[37] These two types of diffusion are seldom discussed, yet they are of some significance.

[38] Today multinational corporations boast of their contributions in this sphere. It wasn't always so: William Woodruff tells of how in the 1850's American investors in a rubber plant in Scotland imported skilled labor from the United States; part of the reason was the company's fear that skilled British rubber workers "might only stay long enough to make off with the firm's secrets." William Woodruff, "The American Origins of a Scottish Industry," *Scottish Journal of Political Economy,* II (February 1955), 28.

terprise is a joint-venture, foreign technology is brought under partial host nation ownership.[39] (4) Suppliers of the direct foreign investor frequently obtain significant technological assistance.[40] (5) If technology is broadly defined to encompass marketing experience (including the servicing of complex products), technology is often transferred to dealers and distributors. (6) In addition, indirectly, but of great significance, the multinational corporation acts to transfer technology by paying taxes and offering employment in the host nation, which actions create capital resources and demands there. The resources and demands often in turn become magnets that will result in the emergence of agencies for the subsequent transfer of technology not specifically required by the multinational corporation.[41] Examples of all these types of transfers of technology abound.[42]

The fact of transfer by export, by patent, by technical assistance, or by direct investment says nothing about the appropriateness of the technology transferred for the host country. Some argue that technology suitable in one country may be less suitable in a second nation that has different relative costs of factors of production and a different demand structure. Indeed, in the main (although far from always) when a firm transfers technology, it does little to modify manufacturing methods; it transmits what it has developed at

[39] A number of governments in recent years have forced multinational enterprises to have local partners in part in order to diffuse technology.

[40] There is marvelous, detailed material to illustrate this point that I have uncovered in the files of Ford-Werke, Cologne. When in the early 1930's, Ford began to manufacture in Germany, it needed local suppliers. It made arrangements for German suppliers to learn about U.S. technology so that its German subsidiary could buy quality German-made parts. See Frederick C. Young to E. C. Heine, Dec. 19, 1934; Frederick C. Young, "Report on Cologne," Dec. 22, 1934; and T. F. Gehle to A. M. Wibel, Jan. 31, 1935 and Mar. 14, 1935, Ford-Werke Archives, Cologne. Moving to a totally different area, multinational corporations that are buyers of rubber, cotton, and bananas have given technical assistance to small growers. See NPA Technical Cooperation Study, p. 76.

[41] Thus, for example, the Kuwait Oil Company pays taxes to the Kuwaiti government. That government used part of its revenue to buy technology to build a water desalination plant for Kuwait City. Using tax revenues, the host government becomes the vehicle for technological transfers. Or, as a second example, employees of Kuwait Oil Company have demands. Technologically-advanced goods are imported into Kuwait to meet the new demands.

[42] The literature on the multinational corporation and its technological contributions is substantial. The National Planning Association published in the 1950's and early 1960's a series of Case Studies on United States Business Performance Abroad, many of which studies sought to reveal the technological contributions of multinational corporations. James Brian Quinn, "Technology Transfer by Multinational Companies," *Harvard Business Review,* XLVII (Nov.-Dec. 1969), 147-161, provides numerous examples of transfers of technology.

home. In many industries, the high engineering costs of designing plants "strongly militate against redesigning [them] to employ more labour and less capital" or to take advantage in other ways of different resource availability in the recipient nation.[43] Brazilian economist Celso Furtado insists that the introduction of new technology in manufacturing in less developed countries by giant technologically-advanced international business creates "structural imbalances."[44] On the other hand, many feel that not only in industrial nations, where there is more comparability in factor costs, but also in less developed countries, the advanced technology is appropriate.[45] More research needs to be done and better tests of appropriateness developed. Yet I would suggest—as I have earlier—that it is more the receiver than the communicator of the technology that is responsible for diffusion and the most stringent tests lie in that arena.

This brings me to the second group of transmitters of technology. First, the importer: Within the host country, private companies (the importer or other firms) may undertake to manufacture an import locally. Such import substitution is far from automatic. There must be a demand for the new product or processes and also an in-

43 Quotation is from Hufbauer, *Synthetic Materials*, p. 68, and applies to his work on the chemical industry; it is also applicable to other industries, although in some industries there is clear evidence that multinational corporations have adapted to foreign conditions—if not too frequently to differences of factor availability at least to diverse foreign demand. Recent research at the Harvard Business School by Professor Robert B. Stobaugh indicates that often adjustments of technology by multinational corporations occur in *material handling* and *packaging* rather than in the actual production activity.

44 Celso Furtado, *Obstacles to Economic Development* (Garden City, N.Y.: Doubleday & Co., 1970). On the many advocates of some technological adjustment, see Louis T. Wells, Jr., "Economic Man and Engineering Man: Choice of Technology in a Low-Wage Country," *Public Policy*, XXI (Summer 1973), 319, n. 1. This article has fascinating data on the selection of technology in plants in contemporary Indonesia.

45 Such is certainly the thrust of the N.P.A. studies, cited in note 42 above. It is the policy implicitly accepted by Brazilian *government* economists. Gerschenkron, *Economic Backwardness in Historical Perspective*, pp. 9, 26, argues that largely by the application of "modern and efficient techniques" can a backward country achieve success and that the advanced technology is the right one. From a different point of view, others agree that techniques to be appropriate should be modified and feel that some international firms are "more willing and able than others to adjust industrial transfers to the specialized needs of developing countries." Baranson, "Technology Transfer through the International Firm," p. 440. For an intelligent, although limited, consideration of the impact of the foreign investor's communication of technology on the Canadian economy, see Report of the Task Force on the Structure of Canadian Industry, *Foreign Ownership and the Structure of Canadian Industry* (Ottawa: Privy Council Office, 1968), pp. 56-60, 66-70.

stitutional structure to undertake the import substitution. While a great deal has been written about import substitution by less developed countries in recent times, there appears to be a paucity of analysis on the pace and character of import substitution in the nineteenth and early twentieth centuries and the extent to which import substitution has involved "mere transfer" or full absorption. For example, there are figures available on the number of power looms in France and Germany in the 1860's and 1870's,[46] but not the number actually manufactured within those countries; we have figures on the capacity of steam engines worldwide in the late nineteenth century,[47] but not the breakdown on the steam engines from abroad and those produced within a host nation. We have inadequate data on the extent to which power looms or steam engines that were made within a particular country were manufactured by nationals of that country and the extent to which they were produced by foreign companies operating within that country.

From available information, it is clear that one aspect of technological diffusion in the nineteenth century lay in the significant import substitution in the United States and western Europe. There is substantial evidence that in certain products, American firms, for example, rapidly substituted locally-produced goods for imports. Likewise, in the late nineteenth century, when British shoe manufacturers met American competition, *they* replicated U.S. methods to meet competition.[48] On the other hand, comparable import substitution did not occur when U.S. shoe manufacturers, for instance, sold in Latin America—at least in the nineteenth century. Americans and Britishers had companies capable of—and determined to—copy and adapt the methods of foreigners. In the twentieth century numerous cases exist of imitation of imports, resulting in the diffusion of technology.[49] On the other hand, not every nation has

[46] Landes, *Unbound Prometheus*, p. 214.

[47] *Ibid.*, p. 221.

[48] Rosenberg, *Technology and American Economic Growth*, p. 45n. The British started to import American shoe-making machinery to obtain the appropriate technological processes. See John H. Dunning, *American Investment in British Manufacturing Industry* (London: George Allen & Unwin, 1958), pp. 31-32, and International Management Association, *Case Studies in Foreign Operations* (New York: International Management Association, 1957), pp. 77-78, on United Shoe Machinery's activities in Britain providing American machinery for the "modernized industry."

[49] Product cycle theory argues that products are exported, imitated abroad, and that this becomes a basis for direct investment in foreign countries by the exporter. See Raymond Vernon, "International Investment and International Trade in the Product Cycle," *Quarterly Journal of Economics*, LXXX (May 1966), 190-207.

companies able or ready to imitate or adapt the technology. It may be foreign and not national business that provides for the import substitution, closing the imitation lag but not the absorption gap.[50]

Two: Firms operating on the basis of foreign patents sometimes merely transfer as distinct from diffuse technology. This may be the case when the manufacturer abroad is part of a multinational enterprise. It was the case when the revolvers produced by Europeans under Colt license never reached the high standards of the American product.[51] By contrast, often, the exchange of patents between private firms has proved highly effective in the diffusion of technology. Data available to business historians reveal substantial evidence of domestic-incorporated companies that have obtained licenses to work foreign patents at home.[52] The German General Electric Company (Allgemeine Elektrizitäts Gesellschaft) started its business on the basis of American patents and a minimum of technical aid. The assimilation of technology was highly successful, and A.E.G. was soon innovating.[53] Diffusion was not always so rapid; German chemical patents were registered in the United States in the nineteenth and early twentieth centuries. Some of these patents were worked by German subsidiaries in the United States. There was a transfer of the technology to this side of the Atlantic. Then, with World War I, these patents were confiscated and made available to American companies; only at this time was there absorption of the technology. In 1917-1918 there existed in the United States companies capable of working these patents and a domestic demand for the output under them.[54]

[50] The automobile industry is a fine example of this proposition. The mass produced American automobile made with interchangeable parts was exported to Europe. William Richard Morris (later Lord Nuffield) set out to compete with the Model T, producing his first car, the Morris-Oxford in April 1913. Morris borrowed American technology. Mira Wilkins and Frank Ernest Hill, *American Business Abroad: Ford on Six Continents* (Detroit: Wayne State University Press, 1964), p. 51. On the other hand, when in the late 1950's and 1960's Brazil and Argentina determined to substitute domestic car and truck production for imports, it was in the main foreign rather than domestic capital that undertook to manufacture. *Ibid.*, pp. 416-419.

[51] Wilkins, *Emergence of Multinational Enterprise,* p. 30.

[52] Such data are highly miscellaneous, ranging from annual reports, company records, government hearings and reports, antitrust case materials, to business histories.

[53] Wilkins, *Emergence of Multinational Enterprise,* p. 54.

[54] Why were Americans so slow to imitate in this case? The reason seems to lie not in business organization, not in capital, natural resource, labor-cost, technological, scale, infrastructure, cultural, or language barriers, or even completely in demand factors but rather in priorities. The demand was small; the profit potentials did not seem great; and more important up until World War I the Germans adequately filled the existing demand. With the war, the demand structure changed and the

We turn next to item three in this group: the receivers of technical assistance. Technical assistance may be communicated to firms incapable of absorbing this aid. It may be communicated to foreign subsidiaries of the holder of the technology and thus kept within the holders' own family group—a geographical transfer. On the other hand, technical assistance from abroad may be *requested* by —sought out by—host nation companies, be effectively utilized, and serve as a highly viable means of both technological transfer and diffusion. Technical assistance obtained from abroad may be particular or general, informal or formal, short-term or long-term. A few examples will suffice. In the late 1860's or early 1870's, Henry Phipps, financial director of Union Iron Mills Company (one of the firms that would become part of Carnegie Steel Company) visited a mill in Germany and noticed that the piles made ready for the heating furnace, to be used for rolling "I" beams, contained more than double the amount of scrap iron rails employed in Pittsburgh. He sketched the pile and once home ordered a change in Union Mills' practice. We are told that "the cost of this trip to Europe was saved almost daily thereafter to his firm."[55] Here was a case of specific technological assistance, informally obtained, on the basis of one journey. Similarly, on a European trip in 1872, Andrew Carnegie studied Bessemer steel works, recognized the significance of the new technology, and on his return made plans based on what he saw in England.[56] Here, too, we have technical information, informally obtained, on a single trip, but in this case general technological know-how transmitted by the chief executive of the recipient firm. Earlier in American history, when in 1801-1802, Irénée du Pont planned a powder mill in the United States, he drew on French technical aid. He sought out and arranged that French government draftsmen would draw the plans for his company's machinery, that the machines would be constructed in France, and that if needed, the French would send technical aid. Soon, however, Irénée du Pont's powder plant had absorbed the French technology and was

former sources of supply were gone. Working chemical patents became of high priority. Diffusion occurred.

[55] James Howard Bridge, *The Inside History of the Carnegie Steel Company* (New York: The Aldine Book Co., 1903), p. 35.

[56] *Ibid.*, pp. 75, 86. It is important that Carnegie grasped the potentialities of the new technology. See Robert A. Solo, "Technology Transfer," in Robert A. Solo and Everett M. Rogers, eds., *Inducing Technological Change for Economic Growth and Development* (East Lansing: Michigan State University Press, 1972), p. 18.

on its own.[57] Here we have general technical assistance on a formal but short-term basis.

Sometimes technical assistance came from the men hired. Thus, British mining companies in South Africa sought out and employed American technicians.[58] When the Belgian firm SIDAC began producing cellophane in 1925, it did so with the aid of the chief engineer from La Cellophane (a French company that was the first producer of cellophane in 1917). The engineer brought to the Belgian company blueprints and complete data on the French firm's secret processes for cellophane manufacture.[59]

J. S. Fforde in his volume, *An International Trade in Managerial Skills*, tells of how Britishers "of the technical managerial type" went to the Indian sub-continent and Latin America for "career service" in one business and would be recruited by one enterprise after another (in jute manufacture, cotton spinning and weaving, paper manufacture, flour milling, and light engineering) as "a type of efficiency expert."[60] Unfortunately Fforde does not tell when this practice started; presumably it relates to the late nineteenth and twentieth centuries. He also implies but does not state that these men were hired by local capitalists as well as foreign enterprise. How effective this was in diffusion of technology still needs closer study.

On a more formal basis we have the technological assistance arrangements that existed between Standard Oil of New Jersey and I. G. Farben and between du Pont and the major European chemical companies. In the chemical industry in the first part of the twentieth century, European, especially German, technology greatly impressed Americans. "I was plunged into a world of research and development on a gigantic scale such as I had never seen," wrote Frank A. Howard of Standard Oil Development Company (a subsidiary of Jersey Standard) after a tour of the Badische Anilin und Soda research laboratories at Ludwigshaften in early 1926. What Howard saw was a pilot plant for the hydrogenation of oil. Badische was then being merged into the newly-formed I. G. Farben and Jersey Standard entered into arrangements with the giant Ger-

[57] William S. Dutton, *Du Pont* (New York: Scribners, 1942), p. 31 and *passim*.
[58] Interviews in South Africa.
[59] Hufbauer, *Synthetic Materials*, pp. 88-89, 131.
[60] J. S. Fforde, *An International Trade in Managerial Skills* (Oxford: Basil Blackwell, 1957).

man firm to obtain technological knowledge. Jersey Standard's historians have recorded that "with the help of I. G. Farben 'know-how'" engineers of Jersey Standard's affiliates "mastered a new, difficult, and promising process." The company's historians conclude that from I. G. Farben, Jersey Standard gained "research concepts and techniques" as well as "the stimulus that [in time] contributed to the building up of a large research staff soundly trained in chemistry and chemical engineering."[61] In a similar vein, an internal memo from du Pont's files, dated December 9, 1936, shows the impact of the international exchange of technical aid on that receiving company. "It should be borne in mind that a number of the du Pont Company's most important activities have originated from technical information derived from European sources, examples being rayon, 'Cellophane,' ammonia, hydrogen peroxide, titanium dioxide, to mention only a few." The memo noted that as a result of its technical agreements with European groups "the du Pont Company has been able to offer numerous products developed in Europe in the American market."[62]

Perhaps the most impressive (and successful) technical assistance accords have been between Japanese and Western firms in the post-World War II years. Here, too, in the main, Japanese companies seem to have taken the initiative in seeking out the technology. Over the years 1950 to 1970, the Japanese government approved 8,324 contracts made by Japanese concerns involving the purchase of technology from western enterprises.[63]

These are only a scattering of technical assistance arrangements prompted by actions (desires) of *recipient* private enterprises. Clearly, one needs more than assorted instances and a systematic treatment by industry, as well as by country and region, of the effectiveness of the various types of technical assistance in technological diffusion. My point here is simply that often domestic—

[61] Henrietta M. Larson, Evelyn H. Knowlton, and Charles S. Popple, *New Horizons, 1927-1950* (New York: Harper & Row, 1971), pp. 153-159.

[62] J. K. Jenney, Foreign Relations Department to J. E. Crane, Dec. 9, 1936, Eleutherian Mills Historical Library, Greenville, Wilmington, Dela., Accession 1231, Box 2.

[63] See Terutomo Ozawa, "Should the United States Restrict the Technology Trade," *MSU Business Topics*, XX (Autumn 1972), 35. An excellent piece on technology transfers to Japan is George Hall and Robert Johnson, "Transfer of U.S. Aerospace Technology to Japan" in *Technology Factor in International Trade*, edited by Raymond Vernon (Special Conference Series No. 22; New York: National Bureau of Economic Research, 1970).

receiving—firms took the initiative in obtaining technological assistance from abroad and that this type of initiative should be tested as possibly one of the most effective forms of international technological diffusion. I might suggest that the reason for its effectiveness was that when this occurred there was an existing private business structure, an agency, that could absorb the technology. The defined demand was determined by the recipient rather than by the donor. The selection of the technology to be received was by the recipient, who hoped to profit from its receipt.

The last of our four modes by which private companies obtain technology involves the receipt by companies of technology from direct foreign investors. As we have earlier noted, when a company invests abroad, in a geographical sense it transfers technology; yet, as we have also noted, it may not diffuse technology for the latter may be contained within the corporation. Yet there do exist imitators (absorbers) of the processes and products introduced by multinational corporations. In developed countries, it is commonplace that when a direct foreign investor undertakes operations, competitors using similar processes and making similar products emerge. (Sometimes the direct investment is made because the imitation of the export has taken place and the holder of the technology can not maintain its market unless it manufactures nearby; often imitation seems likely and occurs *after* the direct investment has been made.)[64] This type of absorption by private companies in the host country is, however, more difficult in less developed countries, where private companies have neither the organization nor the capital to replicate the methods of the foreign investor.[65] Sometimes technology is diffused when a direct investor sells out to a private domestic firm. In England, for example, before World War I Westinghouse set up a foreign manufacturing subsidiary; this subsidiary was sold to the British, Metropolitan-Vickers, which obtained Westinghouse's technology in the transaction.[66] U.S. direct investors dominated the Cuban sugar industry in the 1920's, introducing new technology; gradually, over time, a number of the properties were

[64] The formulation often made is that direct foreign investment takes place after the market for exports is "threatened"—meaning by the existence of imitators or the *potential* for competition.

[65] Here the government, which is beyond the subject limits of this paper, may take over the technology.

[66] Wilkins, *Maturing of Multinational Enterprise.*

transferred to Cuban capital, and Cuban businessmen took the place of Americans.[67]

Employees and managers of foreign subsidiaries often have been hired by host nation enterprises and serve to transfer technology. In recent years, European companies have eagerly sought personnel who have worked for foreign subsidiaries of American firms.[68]

When the direct investor participates in a joint-venture with a host nation firm, that company obtains valuable technology. This has been the motive of a number of host-nation companies that have approached foreign firms, suggesting joint-venture relationships.[69]

Because a direct investor in a foreign country creates certain demands, there are linkage effects resulting from the direct investor's activities. Private companies in the host country often seek to fill the demands. Here the technological diffusion often will be *associative* rather than direct. For example, when a foreign company invests in an extractive industry in a less developed country, its employees probably need housing; local private companies often learned from the foreign company not the basic technology of the latter's industry but rather a new technology of home building.[70] So, too, when Sears, Roebuck opened a department store in Peru in 1955, it did not create other mass marketers in Peru. Rather, its technological diffusion was associative. Soon it was seeking local suppliers, and local suppliers started to seek out Sears. In 1959, the president of the Lima firm of Industrias Reunidas, S. A. asked Sears whether it would be interested in marketing a nationally-made refrigerator. Sears was interested; the Peruvian firm obtained with Sears' help a license from an American manufacturer. Two years

[67] *Ibid.* From 1934 to 1958 there had been a steady decline in U.S. influence in the Cuban sugar industry.

[68] J.-J. Servan-Schreiber, *The American Challenge* (New York: Atheneum, 1968), p. 4.

[69] For example, in 1904 Gordon M. McGregor, a Canadian wagon builder, visited Henry Ford and convinced him operations in Canada were desirable. Ford agreed that he and the American company would furnish the Canadian enterprise with patents, plans, drawings and specifications needed to build Ford cars, and Ford personally would give "such reasonable and sufficient oversight" as was required. In return for the technology, the stockholders in Ford Motor Company obtained a 51 percent interest in the Canadian firm and Ford was paid a fee for his services. (Wilkins and Hill, *American Business Abroad,* pp. 14-18). In the late 1920's and early 1930's, the Japanese wanted to build their own refining industry. One way was through a joint-venture with an American oil company. In this case the Japanese held control, while obtaining U.S. technology. Data from the Archives, Mitsubishi Oil Company, Tokyo, Japan.

[70] Based on my own visits to such enterprises in Latin America and the Middle East.

later, using American technology, the first refrigerator was made in Peru. The demand created by the direct investor had been the stimulant for such production; Sears had been the catalyst for the transfer and diffusion of technology; the Peruvian firm, however, had initiated the suggestion.[71]

Sometimes the linkage effects are more general; thus, in Canada, employment offered by multinational corporations has contributed to a higher standard of living and the raising of the level of demand. Canadian firms have sought to attract new technology to meet the demands.[72]

These are but a few of the many instances wherein private companies in receiving countries have tried to obtain technology and have been successful in obtaining that technology from, through, or based on the presence of the direct foreign investor.

## IV

In conclusion, then, this paper has been a modest attempt to define various aspects of the role of private business as a vehicle for the diffusion of technology. It has been difficult to write because there are so many facets of this fascinating subject that seem to cry out for exploration. Because of space limitations, I have had to be highly selective. Among the numerous relevant topics not discussed or barely considered are: (1) the relations between the *motive* behind technological diffusion by private enterprise and the effectiveness of that diffusion; (2) the process whereby private enterprise changes its strategies through time and takes on over the years an altered role in the diffusion of technology; (3) the attributes of successful diffusers of technology (do such attributes exist in the abstract?); (4) the variation between and among industries and technologies in technological diffusion by private firms (are certain industries and technologies more amenable to technological transfers by private enterprise than others?); (5) the success of technological diffusion by private firms as compared with other agencies for diffusion (has this varied through time?); (6) a systematic look at differences in receptivity to international diffusion of technology

[71] William R. Fritsch, *Progress and Profits: The Sears, Roebuck Story in Peru* (Washington, D.C.: Action Committee for International Development, 1962), pp. 22, 50-51.

[72] Often in Canada, it was other multinational corporations that met the new demands. Yet, there were cases wherein Canadian private companies took on that role.

by various nations; (7) a comparison of the demand structure and factor proportions within both the donor and recipient nations and the effects on international diffusion by private firms; (8), which is associated with point (7), the appropriateness of technology developed by private firms for international diffusion; (9) the distinctions between what is economically sound for the private enterprise and for the nations receiving the technology; and (10) an exploration of the types of measures that might be employed as indices of the effectiveness of private enterprise in technological diffusion (how much, for example, can productivity data be used as a measure of technological diffusion?). On each of these topics, and many others as well, there is a vast amount to be learned. Because of space constraints, I have, however, limited my content.

I have herein presented eight ways by which private enterprise in technologically advanced and in receiving countries acts to transfer technology. Clearly, private enterprise transfers technology in a variety of manners within these eight categories. I have tried to emphasize that for true international diffusion there must be more than simple geographical transfer of technology; there must be absorption of technology by national enterprises within the host country. While there are a number of factors affecting absorption by the host nation, ranking high among them is the existence or non-existence of agencies to receive the technology. One of the most significant of such agencies has, in the past, been private business. Thus, I have argued in this paper that one must not only study the holders of technology as vehicles of diffusion but also the receivers of technology. I have suggested that with the existence of international business, the concept of the "imitation lag" may cover more transfers and not diffusion per se. A more fruitful concept might be that of an "absorption gap," a notion that considers the time that true international diffusion takes, the time between the introduction of a new technology into a nation and that point when the innovation is utilized in processes of near comparable efficiency and in the production of products of near comparable quality under the ownership and control of nationals of that land. Using such a concept may offer a more meaningful guide to questions of international diffusion. I hope the distinctions made in this paper will provoke further research on the agencies for technological diffusion, particularly the role of private business.

MIRA WILKINS

# [17]

*By John P. McKay*
ASSOCIATE PROFESSOR OF HISTORY
UNIVERSITY OF ILLINOIS, URBANA

# Foreign Enterprise in Russian and Soviet Industry: A Long Term Perspective

*This examination of the role of foreign enterprise in Russian and Soviet industrial development from 1632 to the present indicates that it was a significant one. Tsarist and Soviet Russia used foreign enterprise to their own advantage very skillfully by periodically acquiring advanced industrial technology and thereby reducing their own "backwardness" relative to the West. In doing so, they succeeded in remaining firmly in control of their own economic affairs, an achievement that often eluded other countries.*

For more than three centuries, foreign enterprise has been a significant if highly variable factor in Russian industrial development. To be sure, this statement might have seemed highly debatable or patently false until quite recently. Both hagiographers and critics of central planning models and the "Soviet achievement" had consigned the foreign capitalist to a most distant historical limbo as far as the Soviet economy was concerned. But our perception of the Soviet economy as neither wanting nor needing foreign enterprise is being overtaken by both events and research. The main question today, for example, would seem to be whether the present wave of foreign enterprise has already topped out, or whether it will eventually swell to the mammoth proportions of the 1890s or an Occidental Petroleum Company press release.

Of course it is obvious that the forms of foreign business activity changed profoundly as the Russian economy and society moved from feudalism to capitalism to socialism, to adopt for a moment the grand divisions of Soviet historiography. But many of these changes have indeed been in form only, and certain commanding relationships in the whole process have remained remarkably constant. This view is valid for the conception of foreign industrial enterprise utilized in this article, namely as an undertaking involving significant foreign decision-making capability and technical, managerial skills, but not necessarily requiring foreign ownership. It is my hope that this brief, wide-ranging study, based upon much

*Business History Review*, Vol. XLVIII, No. 3 (Autumn, 1974). 

more detailed investigations, may provide insights into the general problem of active foreign entrepreneurship, which differs so profoundly from the passive, foreign portfolio investment with which it is sometimes confused.

### The Seventeenth Century Iron Industry

Although there were numerous instances of foreign entrepreneurial activity in sixteenth century Russia, where the English Muscovy Company held pride of place, our analysis may best begin with foreign effort in the iron industry in the seventeenth century. This was the first important case of foreign industrial enterprise in Russia, and it was of great significance.[1]

Two Dutch merchants resident in Moscow, Andrei Vinius and Peter Marselis, took the lead in developing large-scale, water-powered Russian ironworks – the first in the country's history. Thus in 1632 Vinius successfully petitioned Tsar Michael for a charter to manufacture iron and all manner of military supplies for state needs in works to be established near Tula, some 150 kilometers south of Moscow. With renewed war with Poland a certainty, with high prices being paid for much-needed cannon and projectiles, and with only small artisan producers as competitors within Russia, Vinius agreed to attractive prices spelled out in his charter, even though the state was not clearly obligated to make any purchases. Should that occur, however, Vinius and his partners could sell to other buyers at home or abroad, and they had a monopoly on all iron production by foreigners within Russia for ten years.[2]

Vinius, Marselis, and their partners, including Boris Morozov, an important boyar and merchant with close ties to the tsar, planned to build several interrelated workshops which would constitute an integrated and advanced ironworks. Four dams for four sets of workshops were built on the Sine-Tulitsa River to provide dependable water power needed to operate the large and relatively powerful bellows of the blast furnace, as well as the forging hammers used to refine the pig iron into blooms, bars, and merchant iron.

[1] See, in particular, Erik Amburger, *Die Familie Marselis: Studien zur russischen Wirtschaftsgeschichte* (Giessen, 1957); S. G. Strumilin, *Istoriia chernoi metallurgii v SSSR*, vol. 1 (Moscow, 1954); and N. N. Stoskova, *Pervye metallurgicheskie zavody Rossii* (Moscow, 1962). These and other relevant sources are used and discussed by Joseph T. Fuhrmann, *The Origins of Capitalism in Russia: Industry and Progress in the Sixteenth and Seventeenth Centuries* (Chicago, 1972). Despite certain flaws and a rather pretentious title, this work is a useful drawing together of existing knowledge on the foreign contribution to early Russian iron manufacturing, and I have used it extensively in conjunction with the above-mentioned monographs.

[2] Fuhrmann, *Origins of Capitalism*, 59–63.

This meant that in addition to castings, such as cannon and cannon balls, the works also produced rifles, armor, and sidearms from the finished iron. From all indications the technology of the works, and particularly of the blast furnaces, was developed to "an extraordinarily high degree." [3] Indeed, these Russian blast furnaces of the early 1640s produced 1,600 to 1,900 kilograms of pig iron in twenty-four hours, at a time when the best German and Swedish furnaces were smelting only 600 to 900 kilograms in a like period.[4]

While capital for the Tula works came from the Dutch entrepreneurs and their Russian partner in Moscow, both plant construction and management were largely in the hands of Dutch and Walloon furnace masters and skilled iron workers, who were recruited in the home country by agents of the Dutch owners. As might be expected, these foreign specialists received high salaries and wages. The good pay, however, did not prevent rapid turnover of the foreign portion of the work force. A good deal of hired Russian labor was used under foreign direction in skilled tasks, such as the preparation of charcoal, and Vinius's charter specifically stipulated that the foreigners were to train Russian metallurgical experts. The wages of these hired Russians were fairly high by domestic standards. The Tula works also relied extensively upon feudal rights over state peasants, who were assigned by the tsar to be unskilled laborers at the works in return for payment to the Russian ruler.[5]

By the early 1640s, the four "manufactories" making up the Vinius-Marselis ironworks near Tula were producing roughly 500 metric tons of pig iron per year.[6] A relatively modern Russian iron industry was launched, and in the next hundred years it sped forward: by the 1670s pig iron production reached about 2,300 metric tons; by 1700, roughly 4,200 metric tons; and by 1740, 25,000 metric tons.[7] This meant that Russia was the world's leading producer of pig iron from at least 1740 to about 1800, after which England became the largest producer on the basis of coke smelting technology perfected in the industrial revolution.[8]

The foreign contribution to this Russian growth was unquestionably substantial. In his analysis of iron manufactories, Joseph T.

[3] *Ibid.*, 70.
[4] *Ibid.*, 68–72, and the sources cited there, particularly Strumilin, *Istoriia*, I, 98–118.
[5] Fuhrmann, *Origins of Capitalism*, 72–79.
[6] Strumilin, *Istoriia*, I, 105.
[7] B. B. Kafengauz, *Istoriia khoziaistva Demidovykh v xviii–xix vv* (Moscow, 1949), 33; Strumilin, *Istoriia*, I, 204.
[8] In 1780 Russia produced 110,000 metric tons of pig iron while England produced 40,000; in 1800 they were about even at 162,000 tons for Russia and 156,000 tons for England. Strumilin, *Istoriia*, I, 204.

Fuhrmann concluded that between 1637 and 1662 the group of Dutch entrepreneurs just discussed built ten iron factories (the Tula works being counted as four), while Russian nobles built three and the state one.[9] Between 1668 and 1700 the share attributed to foreigners declined somewhat, however, as they built eight iron factories while Russian commoners built four and the state two. Nor was the iron industry, clearly the single most important industrial sector, the only area of extensive foreign penetration: fifteen of twenty-nine manufactories in all industries were constructed by foreigners, while the state was second, by a wide margin, with nine. In sum, almost three-fifths of all large industrial plants in Russia before 1700 were established by foreign enterprise.

In the eighteenth century the trend toward Russian entrepreneurship seen in the late seventeenth century continued and the foreign components declined. In accounting for this decline one should note that – in the iron industry at least – the Dutch entrepreneurs compromised their position through bitter conflicts and mutually damaging public recriminations. Some time after those conflicts were resolved, Peter Marselis was caught redhanded in league with treasury officials embezzling coins from the state mint.[10] Although Marselis later recovered most of his ironworks, a series of deaths in the Marselis family went far toward destroying the firm.

Another factor in the foreign decline was the great increase in state-owned enterprises under Peter the Great, enterprises which often called upon foreign specialists but retained a basically Russian orientation.[11] This was part of the general growth of Russian entrepreneurial capacity. Such capacity was exhibited by Russian merchants as well as by the state, the most famous example being that of the famous Urals iron magnate Nikita Demidov.[12] After the death of Peter the Great in 1725, merchant entrepreneurs were increasingly joined by nobles in industrial activities, especially in the latter part of the eighteenth century.[13] There is more work to be done here, but it seems that both Russian merchants and the Russian state were stimulated to copy and expand upon the more advanced industrial models which foreigners, like Marselis and his technical experts, had first installed in their midst.[14]

[9] *Origins of Capitalism*, 244–245.

[10] Amburger, *Die Familie Marselis*, 124–126.

[11] *Ibid.*, 186–189; P. I Liashchenko, *History of the National Economy of Russia to the 1917 Revolution* (New York, 1949), 292–294.

[12] *Ibid.*; Roger Portal, *L'Oural au XVIIIe siècle: Etude d'histoire économique et sociale* (Paris, 1950), 54–60.

[13] Liashchenko, *History*, 294–296; William L. Blackwell, *The Beginnings of Russian Industrialization, 1800–1860* (Princeton, 1968), 24–28.

[14] For evidence supporting this hypothesis, see Portal, *L'Oural*, 54–57, and Fuhrmann, *Origins of Capitalism*, 131–134.

## The Nineteenth Century

The growth and transformation of European industry, which began in England in the late eighteenth century, created new economic opportunities which led to a resurgence of foreign entrepreneurial activity in Russia. The overall scale of this activity was fairly modest but nonetheless of occasional strategic importance until 1861, when the serfs were emancipated. Even as late as 1880 foreigners accounted for only about 17 per cent of all capital invested in industrial corporations operating in Russia. Only in the last years of the century did foreign industrial investment reach higher and eventually startling proportions, accounting for an estimated 26 per cent of the Russian total in 1890, 45 per cent in 1900, and 47 per cent in 1914.[15] No other major European state even came close to having a comparably significant infusion of foreign investment.

Before looking at these two phases in the history of foreign enterprise in Russia, it is well to point out certain conceptual and definitional problems. In the first place, it seems clear that "the bulk of foreign enterprise in Russia before 1860 was commercial." [16] As with the Dutch entrepreneurs of the seventeenth century, the foreign trade activities of leading merchants might lead to involvement in industrial pursuits, but for most, commerce remained the primary focus. The same might be said for financial activities. Ludwig Stieglitz, born in Germany and attaining the height of financial influence in Russia as its semi-official court banker by the 1820s, also invested in numerous industrial ventures, including one of the largest cotton-spinning factories in St. Petersburg.[17] Yet for Stieglitz, as for other foreigners in finance and commerce, industrial operations were a secondary consideration, almost incidental to their main activity. To pin the label of "foreign industrialists" on such leading commercial figures would be to exaggerate the importance of foreign influence in manufacturing enterprise.

Another difficulty is the very broad definition of foreign entrepreneurs often used in Russian history. Specifically, was someone like Ludwig Knoop, who was born in Germany, clerked in England, and arrived in Russia before he was twenty, and who then proceeded to build a great textile empire, became a Russian citizen and even a baron, really a "foreign entrepreneur" – as he is gen-

[15] These figures are based upon P. V. Ol', *Inostrannye kapitaly v narodnom khoziaistve dovoennoii Rossi* (Leningrad, 1925), as processed by L. Ia. Eventov, *Inostrannye kapitaly v russkoi promyshlennosti* (Moscow, 1931), 20. These and other estimates of foreign investment in Russian industry are discussed in detail in John P. McKay, *Pioneers for Profit: Foreign Entrepreneurship and Russian Industrialization, 1885–1913* (Chicago, 1970), 24–37.
[16] Blackwell, *Beginnings*, 243.
[17] *Ibid.*, 255–261.

erally considered to have been ever since Gerhardt von Schulz-Gävernitz's eulogistic study?[18] As William L. Blackwell suggests, Knoop was perhaps no more a foreigner than many other permanent immigrants in other countries, persons such as Andrew Carnegie, who was also born and raised abroad, but who is not considered a foreign enterpreneur by American economic historians.[19]

All of this is connected to the problem of assimilation of businessmen of foreign origins, which the Russian state strongly encouraged in the early nineteenth century with measures designed to "russify" the foreign element. Yet such measures were only partially successful, particularly for businessmen of Germanic origins. True, they often became Russian citizens, but they still retained ties abroad and a sense of separateness, thereby compounding the problem of determining who was a foreign entrepreneur and to what extent.[20] In order to mitigate these uncertainties, which give rise to questions that cannot be investigated adequately here, this study concentrates on businessmen of foreign origin who long maintained a separate identity within Russia, or who were foreign in the sense that they ultimately left Russia and returned home.

A number of early English entrepreneurs fell into this class and were of considerable importance, particularly in the textile and machinery industry.[21] The career of Charles Baird, one of the most successful of these English-speaking entrepreneurs, illustrates the general process. Baird's career began in his native Scotland at the famous Carron ironworks, whence Baird and Carron's director went to Russia. There Baird and Carron were invited to reorganize iron and cannon foundries. Setting up on his own with another Englishman as partner, Baird proceeded to build some of Russia's first steam engines and steam-driven machines.[22] Baird also received a ten-year monopoly for a steamship line between St. Petersburg and its port area, Kronstadt, which led to the complete domination of the local transfer traffic. Extremely successful in 1860, when Baird's machine works was one of the largest in Russia with 1,200 to 1,500

[18] Gerhardt von Schulze-Gävernitz, *Volkswirtschaftliche Studien aus Russland* (Leipzig, 1899), 90–97.

[19] Blackwell, *Beginnings*, 241–242.

[20] *Ibid.*, 246–247; Erik Amburger, "Der fremde Unternehmer in Russland bis zur Oktoberrevolution im Jahre 1917," *Tradition*, II (1957), 337–355.

[21] There is no equivalent for Russia of W. Henderson's *Britain and Industrial Europe, 1750–1870* (Leicester, 1965), which deals only with Western Europe, although the transfer of skills and technology from the more to less advanced industrial area is similar. The following discussion of English entrepreneurs is based primarily on Blackwell, *Beginnings*, 249–253.

[22] *Ibid.*, 252; Richard Mowbray Haywood, *The Beginnings of Railway Development in Russia in the Reign of Nicholas I, 1835–42* (Durham, N.C., 1969), 20–21, 51–52.

workers, Baird's heirs combined with French firms in two ventures in rail production and ship building in 1877 and 1880, when the now Russianized foreigners were invigorated with a fresh infusion of foreign enterprise and technology.[23]

A similar example of trail-blazing enterprise in the machinery industry was that of the American firm of Harrison, Eastwick, and Winans in the construction of railway equipment.[24] Tsar Nicholas's decision in 1842 to build the St. Petersburg-Moscow railroad as a state enterprise was followed by the decision to produce all the locomotives and rolling stock within the Russian Empire. Such a course would no doubt be more costly in the short run, but it would lead to the establishment of a new domestic railway equipment industry, a much more favorable development in the long run. The problem of course was that Russian industry, technology, and labor were as yet quite unable to build and maintain the locomotives and rolling stock. Therefore, at the suggestion of George Washington Whistler, the American engineer called in to help supervise construction of the St. Petersburg-Moscow line, the Russian government turned to the American firm of Harrison, Eastwick, and Winans. And it was this firm which won the contract to supply the new road with equipment produced entirely within Russia.

The provisions of the contract, which was to make the American partners wealthy men, were significant. The Russian government provided a large portion of the fixed capital by leasing the buildings of the Aleksandrovsk iron foundry to the Americans. These buildings were in good condition and could be converted to car and locomotive production. Prices and quantities of equipment to be delivered were fixed in the contract. In addition, the Americans were authorized to import duty-free all the machinery necessary to equip the plant, and they were to be supplied with Russian workmen, some of whom they were expected to train for skilled tasks.[25] In short, the Russian party to the contract – the state – from the very beginning supplied the market, most of the labor force, and much of the capital for this indubitably foreign enterprise.

The Americans, on the other hand, were long on technical and managerial skills, but they were very short on capital. Here again local forces were crucial: while the government made some advances, those great Ural iron masters, the Demidovs, offered to sell to Harrison on long-term credit any of their products that he could

[23] Blackwell, *Beginnings*, 253; McKay, *Pioneers for Profit*, 41, 114–116.

[24] My discussion is based primarily upon Professor Blackwell's excellent presentation in *Beginnings*, 303–323. Further detail and clarification will undoubtedly come with the second volume of Professor Haywood's comprehensive history of Russian railroads.

[25] Blackwell, *Beginnings*, 303–304.

use. Harrison was able to repeat the process in England, where he convinced another legendary iron and metalworking firm, the Crawshays of Cyfarthfa, to supply much of the specialized machinery on credit. Thus Harrison's suppliers financed their sales, and Harrison was able to pay them off as he himself was paid by the Russian government for the equipment he delivered.

Subsequently, the production skills of Harrison and his partners allowed them to equip the plant and to stay ahead of schedule. By December 1845, two years after signing the first contract, 1,600 workmen were turning out ten cars a day and one locomotive a week. A year and a half later the plant was producing two locomotives a week and was a year ahead of schedule. Harrison could write that "this beats our old operation at home and it is about two engines a month ahead of any establishment in any country we have knowledge of." [26] The American firm subsequently entered into two maintenance contracts for the equipment it had built, the first in 1850 and the second in 1865. These contracts were very advantageously fulfilled, and they added considerably to the fortunes of the partners of the American firm.

Foreigners were also active in railroads *per se*, as state construction and ownership of the railroad from St. Petersburg to Moscow came between two periods of private enterprise. The first Russian railroad, a short "suburban" line of seventeen miles from St. Petersburg to Tsarskoe Selo and Pavlovsk, begun in 1836, was due largely to the initiative of an Austrian engineer and railway pioneer, Franz Anton von Gerstner. Von Gerstner conceived of this line as the first stage of a road from St. Petersburg to Moscow, which he was seeking to build. The capital was raised both in Russia and abroad, in roughly equal proportions. Many of the stockholders in Russia were of the nobility, although a few of the larger shareholders were merchants and naturalized Germans. The foreign component was also largely German and Austrian, with the banking houses of Dresden playing the leading role.[27] Subsequently, agreement was almost reached with the Leipzig bankers and merchants Albert Dufour-Feronce and Gustav Harkort for foreign capitalists to build the St. Petersburg-Moscow line, before the state finally did so.

The decision to turn to foreign entrepreneurs once again came swiftly after the disasters of the Crimean War, reversals which showed beyond all doubt that accelerated railway construction was a military and economic necessity. The audacious businessmen be-

[26] Quoted by Blackwell, *Beginnings*, 311.

[27] The origins of Russian railways have been most thoroughly studied by Haywood in his *Beginnings of Railway Development in Russia*, upon which the above is based.

hind the Crédit Mobilier, who figured so prominently in railway construction throughout Europe in the 1850s, won in competition with a German-Belgian group headed by A. Oppenheim an enormous concession to build four major lines in 1856. Three new lines, running from Moscow to the Black Sea, from Moscow to Nizhni-Novgorod, and from the central provinces (Orel) to the Baltic Sea, coupled with the completion of the previously authorized line from Warsaw to St. Petersburg, were to give Russia the first outlines of a unified system of railroads.[28] These concessions totaled about 4,250 kilometers, at a time when only 1,100 kilometers of railways had been constructed in Russia. Not only was capital for the new company, the Main Company of Russian Railways, raised largely in France, but also the engineering personnel and much of the equipment were of French origin. Although it succeeded in building 1,700 kilometers by 1862, the company was not a financial success and could not raise additional capital for the lines to Libau on the Baltic and to Theodosia on the Black Sea. Therefore, while the dividend of 5 per cent guaranteed by the state was regularly paid, the Russian government revoked the unfulfilled concessions in 1861 and sharply reduced French influence in the company.[29]

The setback of the Main Company coincided with an infusion of German capital and railroad builders, as well as the appearance of indigenous railroad tycoons, many of whom were Jewish. Yet most of the German investment was in railroad bonds guaranteed by the Russian state and was tied to a considerable extent to the financing of German exports of railway equipment.[30] This re-enforces the conclusion that, although foreign enterprise and investment were clearly present in Russia before 1880, "the foreign contribution was still decidedly of a minor nature, and in the general process of company organization the major share continued to come from Russian capital." [31]

## The Great Foreign Surge and After

The pattern of foreign enterprise in the last two decades of the nineteenth century differed sharply from that which had prevailed

[28] Rondo E. Cameron, *France and the Economic Development of Europe, 1800–1914* (Princeton, 1961), 275–283; Joachim Mai, *Das deutsche Kapital in Russland, 1850–1894* (Berlin, 1970), 44–45.

[29] Our knowledge of foreign enterprise in Russian railroad construction in this period is sketchy and often contradictory. Cameron states that Russian investors unloaded their shares of the Main Company in Paris as quickly as possible (*France*, 115), while Liashchenko (*History*, 491) states that normally it was the foreign constructors who dumped their shares on Russian capital markets.

[30] Mai, *Das deutsche Kapital*, 44–63.

[31] Liashchenko, *History*, 490.

throughout most of the century. In the first place, there was the enormous size of the new foreign infusions of managerial expertise and investment. Although the statistical data are far from perfect, the most comprehensive estimates of the Russian statistician, P. V. Ol', suggest that between 1880 and 1913 roughly 50 per cent of all new capital invested in industrial corporations doing business in Russia was of foreign origin.[32] The crucial surge clearly came between 1893 and 1900, when foreign investment in such corporations jumped more than fourfold (from 136,000,000 to 628,000,000 rubles) and the foreign share of the total increased from 27 per cent in 1893 to 45 per cent in 1900. This increase coincided with a rate of growth for industrial production of approximately 9 per cent, and about 8 per cent for the 1890s as a whole.[33] Neither the United States nor any of the major countries in Western Europe had attained a comparably high rate of change previously, or grew as rapidly in the 1890s.[34]

In terms of nationality groups, the French and the Belgians, who had previously played a secondary role behind the Germans and the English, now took a very active part. French and Belgian enterprise was particularly important in developing the new industrial region in southern Russia, which emerged as the leading steel-producing area in the nation in little more than a decade.[35] The English concentrated their new investment in extractive industries, mainly petroleum and precious metals, while the Germans rose to dominate the chemical and electrical industries. In short, all the leading industrial nations of Western Europe participated in what the Belgians later termed the "Russian adventure."[36]

Much more than previously, foreign enterprise operated primarily through independent, publicly-listed, joint-stock companies, incorporated either in Russia or abroad. (The few examples of the wholly owned subsidiary, associated with so much of recent direct investment, were confined primarily to German investment in the chemical and electrical industries.) Typically, the principal founder was a leading western corporation, which provided the Russian venture with technology, management, and some capital, and which worked with underwriting institutions for immediate public placement of a

[32] McKay, *Pioneers for Profit*, 28, and footnote 15 above.

[33] Alexander Gerschenkron, "The Rate of Growth of Industrial Production in Russia Since 1885," *Journal of Economic History*, 7, Supplement (1947), 147.

[34] Gerschenkron, *Economic Backwardness in Historical Perspective* (New York, Praeger edition, 1965), 129; *Vierteljahrshefte zur Konjunkturforschung* 31 (1933), 18.

[35] R. S. Livshits, *Razmeshchenie promyshlennosti v dorevoliutsionnoi Rossii* (Moscow, 1954), 278–285.

[36] Fernand Baudhuin, *Le capital de la Belgique et le redement de son industrie avant la guerre* (Louvain, 1924), 164–167.

large portion of the total capital requirements. Individual foreign speculative promoters, often living in Russia or having extensive contacts there, were another source of initiative and entrepreneurship, presenting preliminary projects to leading firms and financial institutions. Nor should one overlook the activities of "groups" of foreign enterprises, which directed several companies and often grew out of the opportunities uncovered by a single successful Russian venture.[37]

On the basis of archival materials, it seems clear that these different types of entrepreneurial initiatives shared a common strategy to a remarkable extent.[38] They did indeed seek high returns (which Russian Marxists have assumed they also secured) largely through the establishment of plants embodying Western technology. That technology often represented a remarkable improvement over Russian norms. Indeed, foreign entrepreneurs and their engineers usually acted as if they believed that their advanced industrial technology could be transplanted in its highly developed form to Russia without significant modification. They were willing to compromise with Russian private and governmental interests on many issues, but not on the question of the use of foreign technical expertise. As Théophile Lombard of the Paris International Bank told Adolphe Rothstein of the St. Petersburg International Bank in 1896, in connection with a discussion over whether Russian or French expertise should be used in any joint venture, "I can say that industry in Russia has not yet attained such a level of perfection that we could dream of asking any existing Russian industrial firm to get our venture on its feet. . . . Thus I am obliged to reject any [technical] aid which would not be exclusively French." [39] Foreign technical direction was clearly superior, and it was also an essential prerequisite for enlisting the support of passive foreign investors.

Perhaps the best detailed evidence concerning the degree to which foreign enterprise actually implemented its strategy of establishing advanced technology relates to the southern steel and coal industries. As Alexander Gerschenkron has correctly noted, the new south-Russian steel plants of the 1890s were as large as any in Europe and they utilized the latest, most capital-intensive tech-

[37] The best example of this was the Bonnardel Group, which grew from an investment of considerably less than 1,800,000 francs placed in the Huta-Bankova Steel Company of Tsarist Poland in 1877 to a number of firms with a stock-market capitalization of 168,-000,000 francs in 1900. See McKay, *Pioneers for Profit*, 39–71, 337–367.

[38] *Ibid.*, 72–111.

[39] Iu. B. Solov'ev, "Mezhdunarodnyi bank i frantsuzskii finansovyi kapital," in Akademiia Nauk SSSR, Trudy leningradskogo otdeleniia instituta istorii, *Monopolii i inostrannyi kapital* (Moscow, 1962), 395.

nology.[40] It should be stressed, however, that *all* these large integrated steel producers were planned, executed, and initially directed by Western technical experts. Indeed, one of the distinguishing marks of the Briansk Ironworks Company, which was the only example of Russian entrepreneurs successfully participating in the rapid growth of the south-Russian steel industry, was its skillful use of foreign technical personnel.[41] The results obtained by foreign enterprises and their engineers in coal mining were almost as impressive. There Western firms took the lead in washing, sorting, and coking of coal, as well as in the ventilation, electrification, and centralization of mines. There, as elsewhere, foreign enterprise applied advanced techniques almost universally, and thereby accelerated the diffusion of such techniques through these key industries.

In addition to the basic strategy of growth based on technical superiority, two other factors were particularly noteworthy in the influx of foreign enterprise. First, as opposed to the rather suspicious and russifying attitude of the first half of the nineteenth century (and probably the eighteenth century as well), the Russian state aggressively sought foreign entrepreneurial investment as an integral part of its strategy for economic development. This embracing of foreign enterprise is particularly associated with Sergei Witte, Minister of Finance from 1892 to 1903 and chief architect of Russian economic policy in these crucial years.[42] Witte summed up his position in 1899 in a secret memorandum for Tsar Nicholas II, a portion of which is worth quoting: [43]

> The inflow of foreign capital is, in the considered opinion of the Minister of Finance [i.e., Witte], the only way by which our industry will be able to supply our country quickly with abundant and cheap products. Each new wave of capital, rolling in from abroad, knocks down the excessively high level of profits to which our monopolistic businessmen are accustomed and forces them to seek equal profits through technical improvements which lead to price reductions.

Witte's establishment of the gold standard in a series of steps between 1894 and 1897, which guaranteed the repatriation of profits at a fixed rate of exchange, and his widely publicized balanced budgets were both indications of his policy of attracting foreign enter-

[40] Gerschenkron, *Economic Backwardness*, 10, 127–130.

[41] See McKay, "Elites in Conflict in Tsarist Russia: The Briansk Company," in Frederic C. Jaher, ed., *The Rich, the Well-Born, and the Powerful: Elites and Upper Classes in History* (Urbana, Ill., 1974), 179–202.

[42] See the valuable study of Theodore Von Laue, *Sergei Witte and the Industrialization of Russia* (New York, 1963).

[43] McKay, *Pioneers for Profit*, 11, for full citation. (This important document has been translated by Theodore Von Laue, *Journal of Modern History* 26 [1954], 60–75.)

prise. What is perhaps less widely known is that Witte was largely building on the policy of his predecessor, Ivan Vyshnegradskii, as far as financial stability and a more positive attitude toward foreign enterprise was concerned. This helps explain why Witte's policy paid off so spectacularly in the late 1890s.[44]

Second, there was the powerful example of a few exceptionally fortunate pioneering firms. The Belgian consul at Odessa summed up this pattern in 1894 when he wrote that "the prodigious success of some firms has bowled over the business world completely. Everyone moves toward Russia now."[45] In southern metallurgy the South Russian Dnieper Metallurgical Company, founded in 1886 by Société John Cockerill and paying 10 per cent on its capital in 1891 and 40 per cent in 1895, pulled Belgian and French followers to the new industrial area like a magnet.[46] Similarly, the remarkable results of an English firm with the Taguieff Oil Company elicited so many followers that by 1898 an unbiased contemporary could speak of a general English take-over. Indeed, examination of the chronology of foreign investment in various industries shows again and again a pioneer reaping high profits followed by a rush of competitors who soon pushed the rate of return downward toward the "normal" level of the "average" firm. Data on dividends support this proposition to some extent: whereas foreign capital in joint-stock companies was receiving 8.9 per cent at its high point in 1895, this had fallen to a low of 3.8 per cent a decade later with the 1900–1905 depression, and then recovered to 6.8 per cent in 1913 with prewar expansion.[47]

It has been a common enough mistake of both critics and admirers of foreign enterprise in Russia in this period to assume or imply that local Russian participation was either unwanted or unnecessary for the average foreign firm. Yet nothing could be farther from the truth: in general, foreign enterprise worked closely with local forces, and the degree of success for the individual firm was directly related to how skillfully this was done. Take, for example, the question of capital resources. Foreign firm after foreign firm raised a substantial proportion of its capital in Russia, supporting the view that in Russia, as in some developing countries today, there was less a lack of

[44] See Vyshnegradskii's general rationale, as well as his specific intervention in favor of foreign enterprise in the petroleum industry, in Akademiia Nauk SSSR, Institut istorii, Leningradskoe otdelenie, *Monopolisticheskii kapital v neftianoi promyshlennosti Rossii, 1883–1914* (Moscow, 1961), 114–116.

[45] McKay, *Pioneers for Profit*, 83.

[46] For details, see John P. McKay, "John Cockerill in Southern Russia, 1885–1905: A Study of Aggressive Foreign Entrepreneurship," *Business History Review*, XLI (Autumn, 1967), 243–256.

[47] Ol', *Inostrannye kapitaly v narodnom khoziaistve*, 12–13.

savings *per se* than a lack of investment opportunities or able financial intermediaries, which foreign enterprise helped provide.[48]

Foreign enterprises also needed Russian managers, particularly for knotty nontechnical problems, such as negotiations with the ubiquitous Tsarist officials, legal questions, means of marketing the product, and labor disputes. The most successful firms seem to have realized the need for both foreign and Russian top management from the beginning. Therefore they often used foreigners in the top technical positions and Russians in some top managerial and commercial positions. Those firms which lacked this managerial balance initially learned its value after a few expensive lessons. The fact that top foreign managers were more expensive than their Russian counterparts also encouraged extensive russification of personnel by 1913. Those enterprises which remained under effective foreign control did, however, always retain a core of foreign top managers in Russia, no matter how small it might become.[49]

To sum up an enormous topic all too briefly, foreign enterprise had a very positive impact on Russian economic development in this period. It provided advanced technology, called up underutilized resources, and infused a missing dynamism into the economy. Foreign enterprise also stimulated dormant Russian entrepreneurial potential, as may be seen in part by the fact that in the boom immediately preceding World War I, Russian businessmen tended to replace foreigners as the driving force in the economy. That trend was evident even in such closed preserves as the electrical industry.[50] That foreign enterprise stimulated Russian enterprise and thereby fostered its own relative decline is perhaps the strongest piece of evidence for its largely positive impact in this period.

This does not imply that foreign enterprise always and everywhere has such beneficial results; indeed, it may not. In any event, it seems certain that the fact that Russia was an independent, sovereign nation, willing and able to control unwanted foreign behavior, was of great significance in this outcome. There was never that imbalance of power in the foreigner's favor which David Landes has argued was the mainspring of imperialism and exploitation.[51] Rather, contrary to popular opinion, any imbalance within Russia was clearly in the state's favor. Thus the looting, exploitation, and

[48] See Albert Hirschman, *The Strategy of Economic Development* (New Haven, 1958), 35–39; McKay, *Pioneers for Profit*, 201–241.

[49] For details see the chapter on management in McKay, *Pioneers for Profit*, 158–200.

[50] See V. S. Diakin, *Germanskie kapitaly v Rossii: elektroindustriia i elektricheskii transport* (Leningrad, 1971), 135–161.

[51] David S. Landes, "Some Thoughts on the Nature of Economic Imperialism," *Journal of Economic History*, XXI (1961), 496–511.

draining, which might conceivably have occurred in a politically weak and defenseless Russia and which did occur on occasion in colonial areas where European governments and businessmen could use coercion, was simply impossible. Foreign economic gain depended upon foreign economic performance, and that in turn depended upon cooperation and partnership with the Russians themselves.

## The Soviet Era

In the last month of 1917 and the first half of 1918, when the new Bolshevik government was hurling down decree after decree on nationalization and expropriation, it would have seemed highly unlikely that within three years that same government would be avidly seeking foreign enterprise, or that foreign enterprise, confiscated without compensation, would respond to such an appeal. Yet both developments occurred. By 1921 the Soviet economy had collapsed, though most of the sizable prewar industrial plant was intact if not in operation. The result was Lenin's New Economic Policy (NEP), which included a partial restoration of foreign enterprise within Soviet Russia to help reverse the mounting economic crisis.[52] As Lenin told a group of party secretaries in April 1921, "We are energetically seeking to conclude agreements with [foreign] concessionaires but, to my deep regret, we have not yet concluded any." [53] A year later, however, foreign business, specifically German, began to arrive in force.[54]

Foreign enterprises had, of course, to operate within the Soviet system, where their freedom of action was greatly reduced relative to the capitalist framework of Tsarist Russia. Initially there were two types of foreign activity, one which involved direct investment and one which did not. Within the direct investment category there was, first of all, the "pure concession." This included a specific agreement between the Soviet government and a foreign enterprise, "whereby the foreign firm was enabled to develop and exploit an opportunity within the U.S.S.R., under the legal doctrine of *usufruct*,

[52] On NEP and its origins, see Alec Nove, *An Economic History of the U.S.S.R.* (London, 1969).

[53] Address of April 9, 1921, as quoted in Alexandre Krimmer, *Sociétés de capitaux en Russie impériale et en Russie soviétique* (Paris, 1934), 394.

[54] By the Treaty of Rapallo, signed April 16, 1922, the Soviet Union and the Weimar Republic "reciprocally renounced all war claims and war losses. Germany also agreed to renounce compensation for nationalized property in the U.S.S.R., 'provided that the Soviet Government does not satisfy similar claims of other States.' " Anthony C. Sutton, *Western Technology and Soviet Economic Development, 1917 to 1930* (Stanford, 1968), 316–317. This and the second volume of Dr. Sutton's projected three-volume study have provided invaluable data for this article.

i.e., without acquiring property rights. Royalty payments to the U.S.S.R. were an essential part of the agreement, and in all cases the foreign enterprise was required both to invest stipulated capital sums and to introduce the latest in Western technology and equipment." [55] The second type was the "mixed" joint-stock company, in which Soviet and foreign shares were approximately equal. Here the foreigners furnished the capital and technical-managerial skills, while the Soviets provided the opportunity and location. In both cases foreign firms were normally permitted to import tools and equipment duty free, while arbitration procedures in case of disagreement were spelled out.[56] Roughly 330 concessions of these two kinds were granted between 1921 and sometime in 1926, after which there was a sharp decline.[57] In 1930 the policy of both pure concessions and mixed companies to attract foreign enterprise was discontinued.

The pure concession was most extensively used to develop natural resources. In the petroleum industry, at least four such concessions were granted to Western firms, mainly for exploration in secondary or unproven fields. In the primary producing area of Baku, however, technical assistance concessions (discussed below) were normally the rule. This was in keeping with the general policy of using pure concessions mainly for the development of previously untapped resources requiring extensive new investment, while the Soviets themselves concentrated on the already existing facilities they had inherited from the tsars. In addition to concessions for bauxite, mica, manganese and other mineral resources, some pure concessions were granted in coal mining, but again only in connection with remote, largely untouched regions.

It seems clear that foreign enterprise involving some capital investment made a positive contribution to Soviet recovery in the 1920s. Yet it appears equally certain that Anthony Sutton overestimated this contribution in his enthusiasm for the foreign technical infusion.[58] In the West, Alexander Baykov calculated that total output from foreign concessions accounted for only 0.4 per cent of total gross output of large-scale industry in 1925–1926.[59] Russian economist E. Preobrazhenskii calculated that at the begin-

[55] Sutton, *Western Technology*, I, 8.

[56] Krimmer, *Sociétés de capitaux*, 400–415.

[57] Sutton, *Western Technology*, I, 9. Krimmer, *Sociétés de capitaux*, 417, using different Soviet sources, gives only 138 concessions of these two types through September 1926. No doubt there is a problem of definition, since the Soviet government considered any contract with foreign companies or individuals as being a concession, according to Krimmer.

[58] Part of the problem is that Sutton tends to lump all foreign activity together in his analysis, although he is aware of the different types and indeed spells them out.

[59] *The Development of the Soviet Economic System* (Cambridge, 1948), 125–126.

ning of 1925 only 4,400,000 rubles were invested by foreigners in pure concessions, and perhaps a similar amount in mixed companies. The high point was reached in 1926 when perhaps 50,000,000 rubles were invested by foreigners in pure concessions and mixed companies, or something like 2½ per cent of the amount of foreign investment in joint-stock companies in Russia in 1913.[60] Foreign industrial enterprise operating in the direct investment mode may have had some strategic importance in restarting the Russian economy, but it was always a small capitalist island in a vast socialist sea.

Sutton is on firmer ground when he stresses the contributions of foreign enterprises which did not involve direct investment but instead operated under technical-assistance contracts. Such contracts were and continue to be of greatest long-term significance, especially since some concessions and mixed companies were more nearly technical-assistance agreements than direct investments. Under this arrangement, the foreign firm made no permanent investment, but provided technical expertise and managerial skills for a fixed fee. Such firms were also joined by large numbers of "free-lance" engineers – largely Germans in the early 1920s and then increasingly Americans after 1927–1928 – who also sold their knowledge to Soviet industry.[61] To the extent that the technical-assistance contract might involve large equipment sales, the successful foreigner bidder was usually called upon to extend credit, but only in order to facilitate the commercial transaction and not to acquire any degree of ownership. In essence, this method permitted the Soviets to "rent" the foreign enterprise they needed without compromising the ideology of complete state control and ownership.

Foreign businesses operating under such technical-assistance contracts were active by 1922. An excellent example of the pattern and its importance is found in the Baku petroleum industry. This industry survived the Revolution and Civil War without major structural damage, but it was badly disorganized by 1922. In order to help restore output and modernize the Baku industry, the Soviet oil trust, Azneft, worked out an agreement with International Barnsdall Corporation, a New York-based oil company. Barnsdall was to import equipment necessary to deepen old wells and drill new ones with the new rotary method, and it was to substitute electrical deep-pumping for less advanced extractive techniques. Barnsdall was paid a scheduled fee for its drilling and a percentage of gross

[60] See Krimmer, *Sociétés de capitaux*, 416–425, for various estimates.
[61] Sutton, *Western Technology*, I, 320.

crude output for its pumping equipment.[62] With this and other foreign assistance, Caucasian oil production revived, contributing significantly to the exchange earnings so desperately needed to pay for imports of capital goods. In the petroleum industry, as in other industries, the Soviets developed the capacity to survey systematically the state of technology throughout the world, and thereby determine what the best processes were. Then they would seek out an American, European, or even Japanese firm to install such processes in the Soviet Union and train the necessary Soviet technical personnel.

Foreign firms continued to be of great importance in the construction and operation of new capacity associated with the Five-Year Plans. This was especially so until about 1932. In those years American firms planned and supervised construction of plants similar to the best in America. Such plants not only increased Soviet industrial capacity and efficiency, but provided models for further expansion.

The Soviet steel industry, one of the unquestioned showpieces of socialist construction, provided an excellent example of the process. Freyn Engineering Company of Chicago directed all aspects of construction of the Kuznetsk plant, while Arthur G. McKee and Company of Cleveland directed the famous Magnitogorsk plant, which was modelled very closely on that of U.S. Steel at Gary, Indiana. The specifications for these plants were then transformed into the standard Soviet designs, with American engineers also doing much of that work within the Soviet metallurgical trust.[63] Another case was that of Albert Kahn Company, "the foremost industrial architects in the United States." [64] First approached to design the Stalingrad Tractor Plant in 1928, this firm was quickly presented with "an outline of a program for an additional two billion dollars' worth of buildings. About a dozen of these factories were done in Detroit; the rest were handled in a special office with 1,500 draftsmen in Moscow." [65] In effect, Albert Kahn Company was the industrial architect for the First and Second Five-Year Plans.

To summarize the enormous quantity of material presented by Anthony Sutton for the period 1920–1939, several observations seem justified. Foreign enterprise did indeed play an important role in Soviet economic development, even if direct foreign investment was limited and circumscribed under NEP and almost nonexistent after

[62] *Ibid.*, 16–27.

[63] Anthony Sutton, *Western Technology and Soviet Economic Development, 1930–1945* (Stanford, 1971), 61–64.

[64] *Ibid.*, 249.

[65] G. Nelson, *Industrial Architecture of Albert Kahn Co., Inc.* (New York, 1939), 18–19, as quoted in Sutton, *Western Technology*, II, 249.

1928. This was because foreign corporations and individuals provided technical and operating expertise to help start up the disorganized prerevolutionary industrial sector, and then expand it. Such technical expertise, often furnished in connection with the export of equipment, has, however, always been under the control of the Soviet political-economic leadership.

This leads in turn to the conclusion that the Soviets have used foreign enterprise to their own advantage with great skill. Because the central government was the sole Soviet buyer of Western enterprise – the complete monopsonist – it could pick and choose among atomized competing Western sellers, who ended up accepting relatively low prices for the technology they furnished. The Soviets have also sought the best and most advanced methods, which they have skillfully identified, purchased, and then mastered.

It is also clear that this basic pattern is still being used with success, although any serious discussion of current developments should await the careful analysis of the third volume of Anthony Sutton's study. Nonetheless, a recent press notice provides a brief epilogue.

On November 23, 1973, it was announced that the Soviet Union would purchase a $100,000,000 petrochemical complex, which was to have an annual capacity of 150,000 metric tons of acetic acid, used in the production of acetates for tapes for computers and textile filaments, among other goods. All the equipment and technology, totalling about $45,000,000 will be American-made, with an American engineering firm, C. E. Lummus of Bloomfield, New Jersey, directing construction, and with Monsanto of St. Louis providing processes. American private capital and the American Export-Import Bank were apparently slated to provide $40,000,000 in financing, in roughly equal shares. With disarming candor, one Soviet official noted that "the process which Monsanto suggested is the best in the world." The process was one of Monsanto's most recent, and was currently in use only in its Texas City, Texas, plant.[66] The Soviets have done it again: with such opportunities, who needs the capacity for independent technological development, except of course for armaments?

## Conclusions

The first conclusion is that a primary and ever present factor in the activity of foreign enterprise in Russian and Soviet industry has

[66] *Chicago Tribune*, November 24, 1973, sec. 2, p. 7.

been the foreigners' possession of superior technology. Thus while the initiating force for foreign economic activity came from a number of sides – powerful Western firms, foreign speculators, Russian businessmen, the Russian state, etc. – the subsequent infusions of foreign enterprise rested to a large extent upon technological gaps between Russia and the West, which foreign activity was intended to close or reduce. Furthermore, foreign enterprise attained the goal set before it, establishing very successfully large numbers of industrial operations using vastly improved techniques. This is of course a tremendous achievement, and it is easy for someone who regards the foreign contribution of the 1890s with sympathy and enthusiasm to see the element of truth in such statements as Anthony Sutton's regarding socialist electrification and, by implication, Soviet industrialization. "This [electrification in the 1920s] was heralded," Sutton wrote, "as a triumph of socialist construction, but unless one defines the latter as Western enterprise operating in a socialist economy, it should be hailed as a triumph of Western private enterprise working under enormously difficult technical and political conditions." [67]

There is, however, another side to the coin. The fact that foreign enterprise has established more advanced industrial technology again and again also means that Tsarist and Soviet Russia could fairly readily master and operate that technology, and thereby reduce the nation's dependence on the foreign component. This too is a great achievement, an accomplishment occurring in the period from 1890 to 1913 as well as the one from 1920 to 1939. Surely this is also a major commentary on the whole problem of Russian "backwardness," a question which has fascinated most students of industrialization and modernization. Tsarist and Soviet Russia have indeed been relatively backward, but as S. G. Strumilin says in speaking of the period to 1861 (and which I would extend to at least the 1950s), Russia was "never proven to be in a condition of extreme backwardness compared to its western neighbors." [68] This was so in large part because time and again the Russians were able to reduce technological lags by assimilating the superior technology which Western enterprise has been willing to provide. At the same time, this catching-up with Western industrial technology is a Sisyphean task. No sooner is the rock rolled to the top of the mountain than it falls again, as the boundless dynamism of Western technology and private enterprise reopens tomorrow the gap that was

[67] Sutton, *Western Technology*, I, 340.
[68] Strumilin, *Istoria*, I, 85.

being closed yesterday, and recreates for itself new opportunities in the Eastern empire.

No doubt many factors have accounted for this impressive Russian-Soviet success. Yet in taking the long perspective, one is struck by the way in which foreign enterprise has almost invariably been integrated into an over-all Russian framework and subject to unquestionable Russian political control, a reflection of the independence of the Russian-Soviet state and the fact that its technical backwardness vis-à-vis the West was never very great, or at least never so pronounced as to prevent a ready assimilation of more advanced technologies. This is particularly clear in the Soviet period, when foreign enterprise has been "rented" to solve specific deficiencies, but it was also true of Tsarist Russia. Foreign enterprise with its impressive technology has always needed local capital, management, and skilled personnel. And it has worked to supply the Russian market in most cases and has operated within the state's general economic policy. In the Russian-Soviet context, foreign enterprise could not operate in an autonomous, fortified foreign enclave; rather it had to enter into a partnership with indigeneous forces and infuse them with its special talents.

# [18]

*The Journal of Modern African Studies*, 35, 1 (1997), pp. 101–128


# Contacts, Contracts, and Green Bean Schemes: Liberalisation and Agro-Entrepreneurship in Burkina Faso

by SUSANNE FREIDBERG*

SOON after midnight in early January 1994, an Air Afrique cargo jet took off from the airport of Bobo-Dioulasso in Burkina Faso. It roared north over the sleeping city carrying 15 tons of *première-qualité*, extra-fine green beans bound for Paris. Within several hours, the beans would be unloaded and trucked to the sprawling wholesale docks of Rungis, on the outskirts of the French capital, and put up for sale to restaurant and supermarket buyers from throughout Europe. The jet's blast marked the first time in over a decade that a cargo flight had carried the region's garden produce overseas. It represented, perhaps, the opening of an isolated and stagnant economy, the linking of local producers to the global market. It was exactly the kind of 'take-off' the World Bank hoped for from this poor but deadly earnest country when it began a structural adjustment loan programme in Burkina Faso in 1991.

The months of negotiations and labour preceding this landmark flight, however, had hardly gone as smoothly as the lift-off from the darkened savannah runway. Indeed, the whole enterprise was so fraught with mishap that simply the arrival of that first shipment in Europe mattered more, especially to those who initiated the 'green bean scheme', than the fact that it made no money.

Africa's states and foreign financiers are calling on entrepreneurs to pull the continent out of its economic doldrums. Until the current trickle of multinational investment picks up, 'least-developed countries' like Burkina Faso must depend on the domestic private sector to replace the state as the motor of economic growth and job creation. Given that structural adjustment conditions mandate increased primary commodity exports over industrialisation, the agricultural sector in particular – where 85 per cent of the population makes

* Visiting Lecturer, Department of Geography, University of California, Berkeley.

its living – awaits what the World Bank calls the 'entrepreneurial catalyst'. But given declining world markets for traditional tropical commodities such as cotton or palm oil, the sector needs not only increased output but also intensification, diversification, and the means to find and reach overseas 'niche' markets – in short, more green bean schemes.

At a time of great expectations and even greater uncertainty, it is worth asking at least two questions about contemporary agricultural 'entrepreneurship' in sub-Saharan Africa. First, how are changing economic and ideological conditions – namely liberalisation, austerity, and 'scientific' capitalism[1] – transforming both practice and meaning: that is, both the day-to-day production and exchange relations, as well as the professional norms, identity, and aspirations? Second, who is leading the charge into new crops, technologies, and markets, and how are they able to do so? What, in other words, is the source of entrepreneurial 'spirit' and capacity? Yield and earning statistics, the usual measures of agricultural development, are not much help here; like a glimpse inside the cargo jet, they reveal only the end product, not how it got there.

This article, by contrast, takes a biographical approach as the outcome of information collected in a series of interviews conducted in and around Bobo-Dioulasso between October 1993 and July 1994.[2] By recounting the career histories and current ventures of a number of 'agro-entrepreneurs' operating in southwestern Burkina Faso, it will show that while they are finding both new opportunities and perils in high-value export horticulture, they are also running up against obstacles to agricultural accumulation familiar to generations of entrepreneurs throughout West Africa and, arguably, much of the continent. As in earlier eras, the real challenge lies in mastering both the 'old' and 'new' ways of doing business, and knowing when and where each applies. Meeting this challenge, I will argue, requires a combination of skills, resources, and status that effectively limits who can even participate in the emerging horticultural export trade, much less hope to succeed.

[1] James Ferguson, 'From African Socialism to Scientific Capitalism: reflections on the legitimation crisis in IMF-ruled Africa', in David B. Moore and Gerald J. Schmit (eds.), *Debating Development Discourse: institutional and popular perspectives* (New York, 1995).

[2] See Susanne Freidberg, 'Making a Living: a social history of market-garden work in the regional economy of Bobo-Dioulasso, Burkina Faso', Ph.D. dissertation, University of California, Berkeley, 1996, and 'Tradeswomen and Businessmen: the social relations of contract gardening in southwestern Burkina Faso', in *African Urban and Rural Studies* (East Lansing, MI), forthcoming.

## ECONOMIC MAN IN AFRICA

The guiding principles of structural adjustment assume that beneath the mire of over-sized bureaucracies, over-regulated markets, and over-staffed parastatals waits the rational, self-interested actor of neo-classical economic theory. According to this model, clearing the mire – primarily through deregulation, privatisation, and public sector 'downsizing' – should leave *homo oeconomicus* 'free to accumulate capital', and thus invest in the productive activities necessary for sustainable economic growth.[3]

### *The World Bank Line: from swamp to seedbed*

While early structural adjustment programmes (SAPs) in Africa adhered relatively closely to this bare-bones formula, the plan signed by the Government of Burkina Faso in 1991 reflects the World Bank's revised appreciation for the rôle of the state and other institutions in preventing 'market failure', not to mention social anarchy. It views the state's proper function in free-market economic development as 'capacity-building', both in infrastructural and human terms. Accordingly, the Bank and its bilateral partners are financing not only a number of the state's road construction projects, but also a variety of 'entrepreneurial development' programmes, where would-be businessmen (and women) can find all manner of advice, training, and start-up loans. The US Agency for International Development in particular supports the new government bureau for small and medium-sized companies, *les petits et moyens entreprises*. These programmes assume that, once 'market mechanisms' are in place, the transfer of certain basic skills such as book-keeping and personnel management will suffice to sprout the 'seedbed of indigenous entrepreneurship'.[4]

The areas in which the Bank anticipates such developments include the so-called informal sector and non-traditional high-value export agriculture. The first is viewed as a 'training ground' for resourceful, flexible, competitive entrepreneurs held back only by the cost and nuisance of small-business regulations. Cutting red tape, it is argued, should encourage bootstrap business people in trade, services, and micro-manufacturing to 'formalize' and expand, thus generating

[3] World Bank, *Sub-Saharan Africa. From Crisis to Sustainable Growth: a long-term perspective study* (Washington, DC, 1989), p. 135.

[4] Ibid. p. 136.

linkages and employment.[5] Although I will not be discussing the informal sector in any detail, the Bank's supportive stance is worth noting here because it reflects a fundamental assumption about the future of African entrepreneurship: namely, that the emerging market economy will be an open playing-field, where skill and hard work will count for more than nepotistic connections. It also reflects the Bank's efforts to promote the economic activities of women, though as I shall suggest below, it is not clear that the recommended 'capacity-building' steps will propel many out of shoe-string trades and into modern 'formal' sector businesses.

The Bank's enthusiasm for high-value non-traditional agro-exports assumes that the 'successes' (in terms of export earnings) of Thai shrimps, Chilean fruits, and Kenyan horticulture can be repeated elsewhere. In the case of Kenya, many of the products (including French green beans) are grown by rural smallholders under contract with private export firms of varying size and origin. Contract farming appears especially suited for perishable horticultural commodities because it allows, in theory, for standardised production, efficient distribution, and sophisticated marketing while taking advantage of the 'careful crop husbandry' of small farm households. Contract horticulture also has the potential, according to its proponents, to promote both rural welfare and dynamism, by bringing higher returns than traditional agro-exports while preserving the autonomy of smallholders. In addition, it could prove particularly promising for indigenous entrepreneurs who lack the capital and expertise for, say, industrial ventures, but are more familiar with the region's lands, languages, and customs than foreign investors.[6]

Whether any of the boons of contract arrangements can be realised through horticultural development in a region known, like south-western Burkina Faso, for its abominable transport and communications infrastructures, as well as a historically 'uncooperative' indigenous rural population, remains to be seen. The exploits of the agro-entrepreneurs described in this article, at least, give cause for scepticism. None the less, these are arrangements that the World Bank typically promotes as a means to expand and diversify agro-exporting through private rather than state-run agricultural marketing. So when

[5] Ibid. p. 142.

[6] For case-studies as well as critiques, see Peter D. Little and Michael Watts (eds.), *Living Under Contract: contract farming and agrarian transformation in sub-Saharan Africa* (Madison, WI, 1994). Also, Nurad Islam, *Horticultural Exports of Developing Countries: past performances, future prospects, and policy issues* (Washington, DC, 1990).

Burkina Faso signed a structural adjustment programme in 1991, the sectoral plan for agriculture called for increased horticultural production, as well as the total privatisation of marketing fruit and vegetable exports.

*Rethinking Economic Rationality*

While neo-liberal models of economic activity and entrepreneurship lend themselves to neat policy measures, they do not hold up well in the face of detailed portrayals of the lives and circumstances of Africa's commercial farmers, traders, and industrialists. The following discussion draws together some of the major contributions of Africanist economic history and anthropology, including the francophone school of 'enterprise anthropology'.

In both bodies of literature, much of the analysis in the past two decades has focused, of course, less on *how* African economies work but why they have *not*. Especially as famine swept through much of the continent in the mid-1980s, scholars as well as policy-makers were pressed to explain why national and foreign agency-sponsored agricultural development programmes had largely failed, and why, then, many Africans were more vulnerable to hunger than they had been 20 years earlier. While the neo-classical analysis placed blame on the overbearing states and misguided policies borne of 1960s developmentalism, the history of most African countries reveals that conditions discouraging 'productive' investments in agriculture long preceded Independence – and, indeed, even colonial occupation. On a continent characterised for centuries by abundant land and relatively scarce labour, wealth came to be measured and invested in *people*, not landed property.[7] This did not preclude, especially in the West African savannah states, the development of extensive trade networks or artisanal commodity production, but neither did it provide fertile ground for a British-style agricultural revolution. Instead, the central importance of human relations to both social security and status gave rise to practices and norms of 'social investment' and wealth redistribution quite foreign to Britain and the other colonial powers.[8]

The efforts of bureaucratic colonial states to bring Africa into the economic and cultural empires of Europe, while straining many kinds

[7] Ferguson, loc. cit.

[8] Sara Berry, *No Condition is Permanent: the social dynamics of agrarian change in sub-Saharan Africa* (Madison, 1993), p. 160.

of customary social ties and hierarchies, did not undermine the logic of investing in social institutions more generally. To the contrary: as Sara Berry argues, the insecurity, uncertainty, and social conflict inherent in the project of colonial rule reinforced the logic of accumulating memberships and status within as many social groups and networks as possible.[9] In other words, regardless of the size of particular colonial régimes or their specific forms of intervention, the institutions and ideologies necessary to colonial administration and surplus extraction both introduced new definitions of rights and status and provoked disputes over 'customary' definitions. The resulting legal and normative ambiguity permitted some groups to pursue new freedoms and economic opportunities.[10] But it also made accumulating wealth (whether through farming, trade, or, most often, a combination of activities) heavily dependent on an individual's or family's influence within certain realms of decision-making and resource distribution. This influence was built through the ongoing cultivation of allies, clients, and benefactors, especially those connected to the colonial bureaucracy and court system.

The confusion and negotiation over access to resources at all levels, from the household to the state, did not end with decolonisation. If anything, expanding governments and newly arrived foreign development agencies only multiplied the institutions that Africans needed to understand, join, and seek to manipulate if they were to assure their livelihoods and career ambitions, especially as national economic and political prospects looked increasingly bleak. Under such conditions, 'rational' entrepreneurs continue to invest, on the one hand, in the 'means of negotiation' by building social status and networks and, on the other, in multiple sources of income – a civil service job, a 'weekend' farm, a part-time trade, a rent-collecting house.[11]

Those most successful at these diversified strategies now rank among what Jean-François Bayart calls the 'dominant elite' of bureaucrats,

[9] Ibid. ch. 7.

[10] In colonial Upper Volta (now Burkina Faso), for example, women used the marriage laws of the Catholic church to avoid undesired arranged marriages, and those of the colonial courts to seek divorce. Mission-educated young men became civil servants and later politicians, while some of their elders accumulated small fortunes as 'chiefs' appointed by colonial administrations. Joseph-Roger de Benoist, *Église et pouvoir colonial au Soudan français : les relations entre les administrateurs et les missionnaires catholiques dans la Boucle du Niger, de 1885 à 1945* (Paris, 1987).

[11] Case-studies of African entrepreneurship in the anglophone literature include Peter Kilby, *African Enterprise: the Nigerian bread industry* (Stanford, CA, 1965), and Janet MacGaffey, *Entrepreneurs and Parasites: the struggle for indigenous capitalism in Zaire* (Cambridge, 1987); and in Burkina Faso, Mahir Saul, 'The Organization of a West African Grain Market', in *American Anthropologist* (Washington, DC), 89, 1, 1987, pp. 74–95.

politicians, and business operators who, whatever their formal titles, have risen to and maintained an enviable status precisely because their individual careers and social networks 'straddle' the public and private sectors. The ways in which such élites 'fed from the trough' of colonial and post-colonial developmentalist states are by now well-documented,[12] but a recent crop of francophone work sheds light on how West African merchants and industry operators continue to capitalise off political connections in the 1980s and 1990s, despite the purported 'depoliticisation of the market' under structural adjustment.[13] In some cases they tap these connections for relatively conventional purposes – i.e. to obtain export licenses, project contracts, government-controlled goods, especially petrol – or to avoid persecution for underground trading or workplace violations.

But the transition to multi-party electoral politics in a number of West African nations has also opened new possibilities for influence-building. The same *hommes d'affaires* who have been cultivating clientelistic relations with non-elected state officials for decades (and who may have once been civil servants themselves), have now become major party financiers or are even running for political office. Given that few citizens in, for example, Mali, Niger, or Burkina Faso can afford to support campaigns financially, the economic clout of business communities in these emerging democracies goes largely uncontested. Arguably, they have simply found new and somewhat more legitimate ways to buy off the state.[14]

None of the agro-entrepreneurs profiled in this article have launched campaigns for elected office – at least not yet. But they circulate in the same social milieu as politicians and upper-level bureaucrats, and they employ very similar strategies of networking and constituency-building. Their accounts make two additional points about entrepreneurs in contemporary Africa. First, they show the extent to which both the milieu and the strategies of successful businessmen remain, indeed,

[12] Gavin Kitching, *Class and Economic Change in Kenya: the making of an African petite-bourgeoisie, 1905–1970* (New Haven, CT, and London, 1980); Paul M. Lubeck (ed.), *The African Bourgeoisie: capitalist development in Nigeria, Kenya and the Ivory Coast* (Boulder, CO, 1987); and Jean-François Bayart, *The State in Africa: the politics of the belly* (London and New York, 1993).

[13] See, for example, Emmanuel Grégoire and Pascal Labazée (eds.), *Grands commerçants d'Afrique de l'Ouest* (Paris, 1993); *Politique africaine* (Paris), 56, 1994, 'Entrepreneurs, ajustement et démocratie', which includes Yves A. Fauré, 'Les Politiciens dans les entreprises en Côte d'Ivoire: investisseurs ou courtiers?', pp. 26–40; and Stephen Ellis and Yves A. Fauré (eds.), *Entreprises et entrepreneurs africains* (Paris, 1995).

[14] Emmanuel Grégoire, 'Démocratie, état et milieux d'affaires au Niger', in *Politique africaine*, 56, 1994, pp. 94–107, and Pascal Labazée, 'Les Entrepreneurs africains entre ajustement et démocratie', in ibid. pp. 000–000.

open only to men. The stories of renowned 'market queens' and 'Mama Benzes' should not obscure the fact that women still comprise a tiny minority of Africa's medium and large business owners, that most made their fortunes in a limited number of historically 'female' trades – i.e. perishable foodstuffs and textiles – and that they often did so at great personal cost.[15] Entrepreneurial 'capacity' is gendered and stratified by norms and practices that deny women access not only to critical resources, but also to critical *places* for doing business.

Second, the way that the agro-entrepreneurs describe their careers and ambitions express what I believe is a widely felt sense of ambivalence about any kind of occupation that quite obviously enriches the 'patron' much more than his employees or, in this case, the contracted vegetable growers. Despite the ruling party's official approval of entrepreneurial ambition, the moral status of the practising capitalist has become, if anything, more dubious during recent years of SAP-imposed austerity. In the popular view becoming wealthy is fine and admirable, but assiduously using one's assets to become wealthier still, when almost everyone else seems to be getting poorer, is not. Ever careful of their image, the men profiled below describe their own work both in bold terms, as 'pioneering modern agro-enterprise', but also modestly, as a way to make ends meet, and a form of public service to the peasantry.

Current events in the horticultural sector around Bobo-Dioulasso suggest that both the social legitimacy and economic viability of export-contracting remain, like the broader socio-economic climate under structural adjustment, too unsettled to recommend the unfettered pursuit of profit – in other words, without regard to local norms of patronage or the etiquette of commercial relations. So once again, the instability and ambiguities borne of a new era make it unwise for would-be modern entrepreneurs to abandon entirely old ways of 'doing business'. Those who do, or those foreign business operators ignorant of the customary expectations of their rôle, may find their ambitions thwarted or at least complicated by misunderstandings, non-co-operation, or outright resistance. The biographical accounts include examples of such instances, as well as of the many conventional frustrations and risks facing any horticultural export venture under-

[15] Claire C. Robertson, *Sharing the Same Bowl: a socioeconomic history of women and class in Accra, Ghana* (Bloomington, IN, 1984), and Gracia Clark, *Onions are My Husband: survival and accumulation by West African market women* (Chicago and London, 1994), examine the lives of 'market queens'. Several chapters in Christine Oppong (ed.), *Female and Male in West Africa* (London, 1983), analyse the strategies of and stigmas against ambitious women.

taken in the less-than-ideal social and infrastructural conditions typical of much of rural Africa. By the end it should be clear that those entrepreneurs best suited to adapt to new challenges will continue to be those who have the means and status to gain access to many different places of work and sociability, and the wits to know how to conduct themselves most profitably in each.

## THE HISTORICAL CONTEXT OF MARKET-GARDENING

European-style intensive commercial vegetable production, or *maraîchage*, was introduced to the hinterlands of Bobo-Dioulasso during the early years of French colonial rule, as one of the many forms of compulsory service used to feed the town's military base and administrative population. After the abolition of forced labour in 1946, local villagers continued market-gardening as a means of earning dry-season income. The network of small but numerous waterways north of 'Bobo' offered some of the best gardening conditions in sudano-savannah West Africa, and rapidly growing urban populations created strong local and regional demand for fresh vegetables. For some 30 years after World War II market-gardening was considered a lucrative and desirable occupation, and many young men preferred it to migrant labour in Côte d'Ivoire, or even wage work in town.

But gradual ecological deterioration combined with political and economic instability in the 1980s put an end to what older gardeners now refer to as the 'honeymoon years' of their profession. By the mid-1970s, a falling water table and declining soil fertility in the longest-cultivated village gardens were requiring growers to spend more on fertilisers and motorised pumps. The *coup d'état* staged in 1983 by Thomas Sankara, a military officer and self-proclaimed revolutionary, while welcomed by many of the urban and rural poor, cost gardeners in and around Bobo-Dioulasso some of their most valued customers. High-paying Ivoirian and Togolese wholesalers stopped coming after Sankara banned fresh-produce imports, and many local expatriates and Burkinabé businessmen left the country, fearing retribution from the President who referred to merchants as 'greedy compradores'.

Such rhetoric generated enmity among groups far more powerful than the market-gardeners, so when an internal coup in 1987 ended Sankara's life and brought to power his former friend, Blaise Campaoré, the new President lost no time repairing relations with both the merchant community and western donors. His ruling party now refers to private sector enterprise as the 'motor' of economic development, and political élites openly display the wealth earned through sideline businesses. The market-gardeners, however, have found Campaoré's 'rectification' no better for *their* business than revolution. Trade, industry, and international development agencies have become increasingly concentrated in Ouagadougou, the capital, leaving in Bobo-Dioulasso a relatively small number of consumers wealthy enough to afford the pricier garden crops, such as green beans. The rest of the inhabitants, meanwhile, have been tightening their belts since Burkina Faso agreed to stabilisation and structural adjustment measures in 1991. Austerity has not only hurt demand for fresh vegetables but also led more and more unemployed school-leavers, laid-off workers, and cash-poor grain farmers to become gardeners themselves, even though these days they complain that 'there are more producers than consumers'.

They also say, in light of the depressed local economy, that more than anything else they need access to higher-paying exterior markets. The 50 per cent devaluation of the CFA in 1994 did at least initially increase demand for Burkina Faso vegetables abroad, especially in Abidjan and the other large coastal capitals which had previously imported much of their 'European' produce from Europe itself. But the cost and limited supply of public transportation, combined with the volume and quality specifications of the supermarket buyers in those cities, pose formidable entry barriers to most small-scale gardeners, even those organised in village co-operatives. Women wholesalers do take tomatoes and cabbages south by train and bus from Bobo-Dioulasso, but their commerce does not absorb enough of the region's high-season production to prevent colossal gluts on the city's market. Nor does it always offer very remunerative prices, since most of this produce is destined for sale to lower and middle class consumers, not supermarket shoppers.

It is in this context that a small number of men have recently either begun or expanded high-end export vegetable trades. Unlike the women wholesalers, all are by national standards well educated, and have built prior careers in government or industry. All describe their methods not as inherited customs but rather as the scientific, profit-minded techniques of modern agro-enterprise. All have undertaken horticultural export-contracting, sometimes in combination with other forms of commercial agriculture, hoping to profit from the improved domestic business climate, the promising international trade and monetary policy reforms (in particular the currency devaluation), and the dire need of local village gardeners for new markets.

The following biographical sketches of four such agro-entrepreneurs show how over the course of their careers they have accumulated not only monetary savings, but also skills, knowledge, contacts, and social standing, all of which are very useful in their latest ventures. On the other hand, at a time when both the economy and the norms governing economic relations are highly uncertain, the clashing expectations and ambitions of these self-proclaimed 'pioneers' in export horticulture and those of local producers can, at times, turn this 'seedbed' of indigenous entrepreneurship into a minefield of misunderstanding and misadventure.

## THE AGRO-ENTREPRENEURS

### 1. *The Bureaucrat*

'Moussa' was born near Orodara, a mid-sized orchard town about 40 miles west of Bobo-Dioulasso. He came from a family sufficiently well-off to send him to the University of Ouagadougou for a degree in agronomy. Like most of the college-educated of his generation, he went on immediately to work for the state, in his case as an agricultural extension agent. Now in his 40s, he is the chief agronomist at the provincial bureau of the agricultural ministry in Bobo-Dioulasso. On the job, he makes frequent forays into the countryside to observe and counsel farmers, and in particular commercial gardeners. On the side, he runs a large and diversified farm enterprise, as men of his standing often do. 'It's a profitable way for *fonctionnaires* to spend their free time', he says.

Moussa began devoting his weekends to gardening in 1982, when he acquired 25 hectares of riverside land in a village 45 kilometres north of Bobo-Dioulasso, just off the main road to the Mali border. Although it is still common in rural Burkina Faso for 'outsiders' to gain long-term usufruct rights to farm land through borrowing rather than purchase, in this case the village authorities wanted to sell – an arrangement which suited Moussa because, he said, formal title would be more secure over the long term. At one point he planted up to 12 hectares each season with tomatoes, cabbages, and green peppers, but has currently only about a quarter, due to lack of time and reliable workers. Labour supervision is a common problem for 'weekend farmers', and although Moussa drives out to inspect his farm every Saturday (it helps that the road is paved) this may not be often enough if the hired help is less than trustworthy. He built on-site housing for his workers, as well as an office and warehouse, with financing from one of the national banks, and like other state employees, enjoys relatively easy access to credit, because his regular salary serves as collateral.

After selling only his own product for several years, Moussa began looking into bigger and more lucrative markets. The Togolese traders offered the best tomato prices, but only for large deals. So he contacted some of the many gardeners he knew through his job and found several in each of four different villages willing to co-operate. They agreed in advance on a price and schedule, and at harvest time the women came in trucks to collect the produce. In 1993, the gardeners sold 30 tons of tomatoes altogether.

This informal co-operative arrangement is not without its problems. 'The peasants', Moussa says, 'are disorganised', and some jeopardise contracts by trying to raise their prices when the buyers arrive at season's end. In addition, at certain times of the year the Lomé market is glutted with Ghanaian and Togolese tomatoes; on other occasions, must less predictably, political unrest in Togo has closed borders and disrupted trade. But Moussa says his 'liaisons' in Lomé fax him immediately with news of important developments. He can also turn to other markets, if necessary; his wife sometimes sends truckloads of tomatoes to Abidjan, where she has her own buyers. Moussa originally found his contacts abroad by travelling during annual vacations – another benefit of a ministry job. By 'asking around', he eventually found interested produce buyers in Lomé's commercial district.

Considered one of the local horticultural experts, given his education and employment, Moussa has served as a 'consultant' to the *Union régionale des coopératives agricoles et maraîchères de Bolo-Dioulasso* (Urcabo) and other groups attempting to form gardener co-operatives. He blames their difficulties in finding export markets on 'bad presentation': they mix ugly vegetables with good ones, and box them carelessly in old and dirty cartons. Familiar with the stringent aesthetic standards of capital-city supermarkets, Moussa himself puts a high priority on attractive packaging, even though it adds considerably to his expenses.

Familiar as well with the risks of exporting highly perishable crops across volatile borders, Moussa has not limited his weekend farming endeavours to vegetable gardening. He recently began planting maize and rice on his original piece of land, as well as raising sheep and chicken on another site closer to town. He claims the chickens lay as many as 600 eggs a day, so far all for the local market. The maize feeds the sheep; their manure fertilises the crops. This, he laughs, is '*l'agriculture autosuffisante*'.

Moussa fully recognises the advantages he enjoys as a *fonctionnaire*-farmer. He has a monthly salary, easy access to credit, and plenty of opportunities to make rural contacts. His background in agronomy helps too. Unlike some 'gentlemen farmers', he says, 'I know the techniques, I know how to cultivate'. He also keeps abreast of new trends in vegetable production and marketing by reading seed catalogues and farm journals. Finally, unlike many local commercial gardeners, Moussa sees in the 1994 currency devaluation great opportunities, both for increasing horticultural sales to Lomé and other coastal capitals (where fruits and vegetables imported from France and North Africa have become prohibitively expensive even for expatriate consumers) and for expanding grain sales locally (where prices of imported wheat and rice have also risen significantly). As for other farmers' complaints about higher production costs, he shrugs, 'It's not so bad as all that. My sales went very well this year.'

2. *The Ex-Politician*

What we're doing is not just an intellectual and moral accomplishment. Not at all. Economically, Madame, it's profitable! Provided, of course, you've got the means. – Lionel, Ouagadougou, 1 April 1994

'Lionel' is a native of north-central Burkina Faso, and came to the Bobo-Dioulasso area in 1968 as a young military officer assigned to a regional army post. The late-1960s Sahelian drought was causing increasingly severe hardships for family members in his rural homeland, so shortly after settling in Bobo he borrowed a piece of land from local villagers, and recruited some brothers to grow rainy-season maize. But since the land was located near enough to a river to be arable the year-round, he decided to put them to work producing dry-season vegetables for the local market.

And thus, Lionel says, took root his 'passion'. At first market-gardening simply helped him fulfil the responsibilities of a young educated salary-man, expected to support the many family members back home. 'I saw in this modern agriculture not only a means of generating revenue from my investments', he says, 'but also of easing the burden of the *fonctionnaire*'. Eventually, however, his ambition became that of an '*alpiniste*', or mountain climber: 'the more difficulties I encountered, the more the challenge attracted me'.

Indeed, his career path became rocky from time to time. During the 1970s he was promoted first to Secretary of Rural Development, then to Minister of Finances. On the side, he built his commercial gardening venture into a full-scale *société familiale* called 'Pionnier' – appropriate for what he claims was the first 'modern agricultural enterprise' in the region. He bought farm machines, a large combination office-villa in Bobo-Dioulasso, a cold-storage room, a refrigerated truck. He read agronomy books, and asked experts for advice. He secured deals with supermarket buyers in Abidjan, and to meet their large-volume orders began contracting with local villagers to grow lettuces.

Then a *coup d'état* in 1980 landed him in prison, along with many other high-ranking officials. He was released briefly and later re-imprisoned by Sankara, on uncertain grounds, until 1985. When his name was finally cleared, government work remained an option. 'I'd spent 35 years in the army as a superior officer. I had seven years of ministerial experience, and plenty of connections. I could have got a post. But instead I decided to return to *la passion*'. All the property supporting his passion, however, had been seized by the state. Both the Sankara and Campaoré régimes ran Pionnier as a money-losing parastatal until it eventually failed in the early 1990s.

Lionel was still trying to reclaim his land and tractors in 1994, but meanwhile had started a new company, 'Promagri', with some friends. They began with three million FCFA (approximately $11,000), and this time, rather than investing in machines and acreage for his own production, Lionel concentrated on developing the productivity and loyalty of prospective contract growers. Since most gardeners in the Bobo-Dioulasso region were cultivating lands outside 'managed' irrigation zones, using labour-intensive methods and limited inputs, Lionel's first step was to find external financial and technical assistance... or rather, to make local growers *eligible* for assistance. So he returned to the village where several gardeners had grown lettuces for Pionnier years before, and proposed they organise a co-operative.

> When I arrived in 1987, some people were watering their little tomato plots with calabashes. They had nothing. Well, four or five had motorpumps. So we met, and located a site where we were sure to have water... They already had a co-op in name, but no statutes, no regulations. So it was necessary to put all that together, and to draw up a project. And then I submitted the dossier everywhere... the BCEAO [*Banque centrale des états de l'Afrique de l'Ouest*] refused; the French also refused; the Canadians, they were interested.

The Canadian Government agreed to pay for 20 hectares of mechanised irrigation, a warehouse, shipping crates – in short, everything the gardeners would need to produce export-quality vegetables for Promagri. By the early 1990s Lionel had organised and found aid for two other village co-operatives, and was again shipping a wide variety of vegetables to Abidjan, including cauliflowers, beets, and carrots. Meanwhile, gardeners in the first village patronised by the 'former minister' were selling their high-value produce to other wholesalers (who sought out speciality crops), as well as to retail outlets in downtown Bobo-Dioulasso.

Lionel had been looking for new buyers 'all over the place' when one of Europe's biggest green bean importers, whom he had met while at the agricultural ministry in the 1970s, proposed a new product for Promagri: fresh herbs. Lionel liked the idea and arranged for a village to grow basil, rosemary, and a number of other varieties for the European winter market. He participated little in the on-site activities (a French herb specialist was flown in to supervise training, production, and transport), but did spend a great deal of time negotiating finance with the Parisian importer. The latter's unwillingness to pay for necessary equipment made it difficult for Promagri to meet the specifications of the contract, not least since the lack of a refrigerated truck led to some spoilage, and Lionel vowed to find a new European partner. Still, the first season's basil arrived in good condition in Paris, accompanying the green beans of the aforementioned cargo jet in January 1993. 'We managed', Lionel later noted proudly, 'to inscribe the name of Burkina Faso among the exporters of *herbes aromatiques*'.

Lionel is particularly excited about his prospects in Abidjan, where even 'picky' French expatriates have become more receptive to competitively priced Burkinabé vegetables. If Promagri can simply meet half of Abidjan's demand for carrots – ten tons a week, he estimates – 'I won't need anything else to live on!'. This sounds like a tall order, but Lionel says he is optimistic, having resolved to devote his life to contract vegetable-exporting. He plans to limit his rôle in this business, however, to that of the intermediary between foreign financiers, gardeners, and buyers. Even if he does eventually win back his confiscated property from the state (the case was still in court in 1994), he claims he has no need or desire to resume production himself.

### 3. *The Scientist's Family*

'Jean' is a French plant biologist who has lived 30 years in Africa, most of them in a spacious villa on an agricultural research station just south of Bobo-Dioulasso. His knowledge of vegetable diseases and breeding led to the introduction and improvement of numerous crop varieties now grown in the region, ranging from premier-quality butter lettuces to, most recently, seedless Japanese egg-plants. His contacts throughout France and the academic community help both to win foundation support and attract students (both French and African) to the research station.

Hardly a 'foreigner' to these parts, despite French citizenship, Jean speaks Dioula and knows intimately those parts of the countryside which grow vegetables. Like many long-time expatriates of his generation, however, his views of and behaviour towards '*les Africains*' remain those of an old *colon*. Acting as though he assumes everyone around him is either corrupt or stupid, he is respected but not terribly well-liked.

In 1993, Jean recruited his wife and two adult sons, one of whom has an MBA, to help him launch a vegetable export business. He had contacts with a major Parisian wholesaler, and his businessman son negotiated with Air Afrique to fly cargo out of Bobo-Dioulasso. The airline's agreement to resume service to this airport (which it had cut a decade earlier, for lack of profits) was crucial, Jean believed, to the success of any regional horticultural export venture. In the past, vegetables trucked to the next nearest airport in Ouagadougou often deteriorated or were even spoiled by the time they arrived in Paris.

Jean and his family began the 1993–4 growing season quite methodically. They selected a number of sites with appropriate soil and water conditions, arranged tonnage, price, and harvest dates with village authorities, and distributed seeds, fertilisers, and pesticides. Then the entire family spent the next several weeks making daily excursions to oversee the work. Complications quickly arose, however. First, because Burkinabé law still made it very difficult for non-nationals to undertake single-handedly this kind of business, Jean had needed to find a Burkinabé partner. The Bobo-Dioulasso businessman who agreed to collaborate (whose biography follows), while experienced in commercial agriculture and well-known among regional gardeners, proved to be exceedingly unreliable. Like many local businessmen, he was involved in several different money-making activities simultaneously, and the joint venture with the Frenchman ranked low on his list of priorities. A few weeks into the season, Jean charged that his partner was not checking up on sites assigned to his supervision, and was in fact absconding with fertilisers he was supposed to distribute. As a result, several of the neglected growers ended up with poor or failed harvests.

In addition, the French family found that even the growers they monitored themselves did not respect the terms of their contract when it did not suit them. Jean complained that some did not water the green beans at the correct intervals, or did not properly tie up the vines. Worst of all, on one pre-arranged harvest day an entire village refused to work because the chief had died the previous night. Such a delay could prove disastrous not only because of flight schedules, but also because 'string' green beans quickly grow too thick to command top prices on the Parisian market. Jean did in fact have to cancel the next day's flight, for lack of adequate tonnage. Indeed, he had to cancel a number of weekly flights during the three-month season, and at the end his son announced that they had lost money. But several late-night shipments did reach Paris, and both men had faith that if they trained their growers better and found a new business partner, the next season would go more smoothly. They even talked of diversifying into snow peas and cherry tomatoes.

4. *The Ex-Accountant*

My father is not a farmer, nor is my mother. I was not born into agriculture; I do not know the rural world. But I love agriculture – I *came* to this world... As a practising Catholic I said to myself, I have the good fortune, the education to be discerning, to choose my investments. I am capable of drawing up a financial plan [for a commercial farm], and I have done nothing to deserve all this. My God has given it to me... so I must give it to others. – Joseph, Bobo-Dioulasso, 15 February 1994

If export horticulture represents a weekend vocation for the bureaucrat, a mountain-climber's passion for the politician, an entrepreneurial experiment for the botanist, then for 'Joseph' it is a divine calling. The pursuit of his 'God-given' talent for making money from commercial agriculture has earned him wide though mixed renown throughout the vegetable-producing region of southern Burkina Faso, where everyone, it seems, has done some kind of business with the large grey-haired man in the white pick-up truck.

Joseph is the son of a prominent local lawyer whose 'weekend farm' consisted of a few well-watered hectares of fruit trees and farmland on the outskirts of town. He received his education at the Catholic mission in Bobo-Dioulasso, and after completing secondary school took a job managing a Uniroyal tyre store while at the same time studying for his *baccalauréat*. Aged 25, he went to the Netherlands in 1973 to become an apprentice in a similar firm, but not long afterwards returned to Bobo, where the national tyre company hired him as chief accountant. In 1980 he quit, he says, to start his own auto-parts import–export firm, and to go back to school. Two years later, he finished a master's thesis in business management through a correspondence course with tutors in Mauritius. He taught briefly in Bobo, and ran a private accounting service. In 1983 he took a job at the national battery factory, but after only one month there decided that his future lay on the land, not in the corporate world.

Joseph claims to have been moving ('called') in this direction for several years, and during business trips abroad as a corporate accountant he often visited farm enterprises in Benin, Togo, Mali, and Côte d'Ivoire. 'I realised', he says, that 'agriculture is *un métier*, just like accounting'. By 1983 he had taken over the management of his father's land, and acquired additional acreage in a more distant village. Consulting fellow farmers, technicians, and textbooks along the way, he planted new mango and papaya varieties in the old orchard, and installed canal irrigation for vegetable production. He also bought pedigreed hens and hogs, which are more difficult to raise but produce bigger eggs and better meat than common varieties. Within a number of years Joseph had established himself among the region's farming élite, well-known for his exotic and premier-quality products:

> now I can say that I'm a professional. I'm not an 'agriculturalist' – that's vast, like general medicine... rather, I'm specialised – in horticulture, and fruit trees, and pork-raising, and poultry. And I want to know more and more... it's a conviction.

Quite early on, Joseph began selling his vegetable crops to buyers in Abidjan, and later Lomé. But like other local exporters, he found that his harvests alone could not always fill the high-volume orders of large wholesalers or supermarkets. So like the aforementioned 'Lionel', he proposed to a number of experienced and reputable gardeners that they form a co-operative, more exclusive and profitable than that run previously by the state. Joseph would be an active member of this venture – in fact, its president – and would use his own reputation as a 'dynamic' commercial farmer to secure start-up funds from an international non-governmental agency.

Enthusiasm for this new and improved co-operative faded as members realised that it was not helping them to find new markets or sell more goods. It was not doing much at all, it appeared, besides collecting membership fees. Six years later, Joseph resigned from the enterprise after fellow members alleged that he had embezzled several thousand dollars. He does not mention the accusation in his own version of events, but says that he was fed up with trying to 'manage the peasants', and would thenceforth only buy certain produce from them on contract, on a one-on-one basis. In the meantime, he continues to oversee affairs on his own farm, and has opened a high-end grocery in downtown Bobo-Dioulasso, featuring his own garden produce, eggs, meat, even fruit jams. Next door, he has also established a sort of business school for farmers, where local growers are invited to take courses in accounting and marketing. In addition, he continues to travel to neighbouring cities and countries, ever in search of new markets, while maintaining a visible presence in the local Catholic community.

Considering this range of commitments it would hardly be surprising if, in fact, Joseph was neglecting his responsibilities to the French scientist's export venture. The Burkinabé businessman may not actually care much about jeopardising a partnership where his autonomy and potential gains appear limited. But among commercial gardeners and traders his reputation also suffers from his tendency to 'disappear' – that is, to leave town suddenly, miss appointments, and especially to back out on contracts without warning or explanation. Although a potentially valuable acquaintance, given Joseph's wealth and connections – what locals call *les bras longs*, or 'long arms' – the only gardeners who continue to produce on contract for him are usually those who are themselves relatively affluent and well-connected to top-end vegetable buyers. Only they can risk devoting three months and all or much of their garden to a crop of export-quality green beans that he may never return to purchase.

For someone described by most who know him as over-ambitious, even unethical, Joseph depicts himself as a businessman of modest and honourable goals. Having already witnessed one troubled season of the French scientist's 'green bean scheme', he expresses concern about the difficulties of expanding into the trans-Atlantic trade in, ironically, moral terms:

> Everyone says we must export to Europe. But I am still not convinced of the potential of this market. You must excuse me, but I think that's where the biggest bandits in the world are. They have no faith, no religion, they think only of their pockets. If I have the possibility of forging south–south relations, I prefer that... After all, I'm not trying to become a millionaire. You earn your daily bread in this; you manage to feed the family. You provide for future needs.

## CONNECTIONS AND COCKTAILS

Together, the stories of the four agro-entrepreneurs raise a number of points worth further discussion. First, past or concurrent employment has clearly helped each man to undertake and expand export-oriented agricultural enterprises. In terms of building from line of work to the next, however, the salary or pension is only one among many benefits of salaried employment; at least as important are the skills, *savoir-faire*, contacts, and prestige acquired while on the job. Second, if such benefits are achieved advantages for these businessmen, what are their ascribed advantages? In other words, what aspects of their social status, what privileges have effectively enabled them to pursue entrepreneurial ambitions further, and with fewer constraints, than other men and especially women? Finally, these individuals are engaging in their commercial agricultural ventures during a time of post-socialist liberalisation and state austerity. We need to consider precisely how shifts in official ideology and policies of resource distribution have transformed the conditions of entrepreneurship – and how, perhaps, they have not.

The professional backgrounds of the agro-entrepreneurs have endowed them with various means of tapping the resources of the state, the foreign donor community, even the Air Afrique board of directors. In part, their advantages derive from their 'expert' status in, for example, agronomy or international marketing. Employed as experts, they exercise at least some clout over the decisions and practices of gardeners, funders, and policy-makers. Their salaries or pensions also, of course, have enabled them to spend far more on transport, labour, machines, and so forth than can most gardeners, or traders. But just as importantly, their careers have provided opportunities to acquire information, contacts, and experience, which in turn have bolstered their expertise, and expanded their influence.

The ex-politician, for example, began his career as a military officer, but learned in later ministerial positions the organisational tactics and bureaucratic procedures needed to form rural co-operatives, draw up project dossiers, and apply for aid. For all four men, regular vacations and business trips have provided time to investigate potential markets and find likely buyers. Their jobs have also introduced them to 'experts' in related fields, to useful media (trade journals, scientific texts, seed catalogues), as well as to various people passing through their offices for whatever reason, who might someday prove useful – as, for example, the French importer of green beans who became a helpful acquaintance to the ex-politician.

Contacts made within or through the state, as well as through kin and ethnic networks, are everywhere used in the world of African enterprise. Identifying these relations helps explain why enterprises take certain forms, and why and how people are involved in particular entrepreneurial activities, but does not by itself explain an individual or firm's success. Family ties and state patronage can stifle as well as support, and especially in an era of public-sector cutbacks and widespread economic hardships, many informal 'connections', not to mention institutionalised government resources, have become much less reliable. In Burkina Faso, for example, structural adjustments designed to shrink and limit the regulatory power of state ministries mean that having a relative or acquaintance in the régime is helpful but no longer necessarily sufficient to secure a public sector job, or even a minor favour. Bureaucrats find themselves besieged with requests they no longer have either the official authority or the personal financial means to fulfil.

In the interests of minimising such claims on their wealth, Burkinabé merchants often launch their trades with family capital and labour, but later distance themselves as much as possible from kin who are likely to prove more burden than boon to the enterprise.[16] Similarly, the Burkinabé agro-entrepreneurs described here all initially received some form of support from relatives, at the very least for the education which qualified them for salaried employment, but now run their businesses relatively independently. Ironically, only the French plant biologist – the man so condescending towards African backwardness – depends on the full-time help of his spouse and children.

What most accounts neglect – but which the entrepreneurs themselves cannot – is the time-consuming, tiring, but critical work of *finding* business. The interviewed exporters of vegetables all made initial contact with most of their buyers and contract-producers by simply walking down the streets of Abidjan and Lomé and inquiring in the supermarkets and wholesale yards, by driving through the countryside and introducing themselves to villagers. One gardener on the outskirts of Bobo-Dioulasso, for example, who periodically grows green beans for Joseph, remembers meeting him years ago when the businessman, whose own property lies nearby, simply wandered into his garden to look at the vegetables.

So at least initially, would-be agro-entrepreneurs must spend considerable time and energy *making* connections, and turning relative strangers into potential buyers, suppliers, and collaborators. In addition, as the conditions for receiving financial and technical assistance from the state and many foreign donor agencies become increasingly stringent, they must devote considerable effort to the procedures and politics of aid-seeking. Lionel and Joseph, for example,

[16] Pascal Labazée, *Entreprises et entrepreneurs du Burkina Faso* (Paris, 1988).

won financial and technical assistance for village co-operatives which ultimately improved their personal commercial opportunities at least as much as it did any of the villagers. To do so they had to know not only how to draw up an application for aid, but also where and how to pitch their appeals. The Canadian aid agency approved Lionel's proposal for an irrigated horticultural production site not to make him a rich man, but because it appeared that the project, as described, would benefit the local peasantry as well as the growing export of vegetables.

Hunting for aid is a logical entrepreneurial strategy in a country where foreign governments, banks, and private agencies have long underwritten much of agricultural and infrastructural development, and it remains so at a time when the uncertain prospects of the national economy, government reforms, and international trade policy make many agro-entrepreneurs hesitant to invest much of their own capital (assuming they have any) in a risky and unproven export trade. Unlike the cash-strapped national banks, foreign donors not only provide grants or low-interest loans for approved projects, but also bring in technology and expertise not available locally. In addition, the businessman becomes a local hero if the aid proves beneficial (as in Lionel's irrigation project), but incurs relatively few losses if it does not. The businessman is only the go-between, not the investor. So although winning aid takes considerable experience and perseverance, it offers entrepreneurs involved in contract-gardening a relatively low-risk, low-cost means of improving the productivity of their enterprises.

Clearly, the agro-entrepreneurs benefit from the capital, skills, experience, and connections they bring from their other occupations. But these advantages bear fruit only if used to cultivate further contacts, more skills, and bigger sources of financing. Much of this footwork takes place in markets and villages, in offices, libraries, and banks. But the activities conducted at 'after-hours' meeting places are also crucial, both for what they produce and whom they exclude. Food-and-drink establishments are abundant and often short-lived in Bobo-Dioulasso, as in many West African cities, but those frequented primarily by businessmen (both local and foreign), aid workers, politicians, and top level bureaucrats are relatively few, and easily identified. The bars and swimming-pool patios of luxury-class hotels are prime rendezvous spots, as is any place with a television set that can show closed-circuit international soccer. All are popular sites not only for business lunches and drinks with clients, but also as strategic locations for 'being seen', for establishing oneself among the city's respectable business class. The contacts made, deals forged, and ideas generated in this milieu can do at least as much for an aspiring entrepreneur's career as the most diligent research and record-keeping.

Such establishments are not, however, open to everybody. Although most are not private clubs, the price of the drinks combined with an oftentimes unmistakably élitist atmosphere effectively shuts out most of the local population, including the scruffy small-time 'informal' entrepreneurs. Many young men who spend their days in downtown Bobo-Dioulasso, for example, come from families in neighbouring villages who control local gardens and orchards. Some of them spend part of the year working on the land, and know enough about market-gardening to have plenty of ideas and opinions about how *they* would run a vegetable export firm (or other venture) if they had the 'means' and the contacts. Many have made it at least partway through secondary school, but under current economic conditions have little chance of finding steady jobs. So they spend a great deal of time piecing together '*bizness*' – an afternoon's work as a guide, messenger, or delivery boy; spotting transactions in cheap handicrafts, used clothes, or pirated music tapes; or simply sitting outside the hotels or bars where important people pass by, hoping someone might request their services. They dress in jeans and baseball caps, and are often broke and bored.

Even though a number of these young men possess skills, access to land, and fierce 'entrepreneurial spirit', they appear idle and unremarkable, and lack entirely the social standing (as well as the cash and the clothing) needed to be welcomed or taken seriously in the 'businessman bars'. In 1994, I met only one from this age group and background in Bobo-Dioulasso whose future in agro-enterprise looked at all promising. A 27-year old bartender at the most popular downtown luxury hotel, he was unusually well-positioned to eavesdrop and to learn about the people passing through town, and the business they were conducting. He had eventually managed to arrange, albeit tentatively, finance and buyers for a scheme to turn several hectares of family land into an export-oriented orchard and vegetable farm.

## THE MEN'S CLUB?

Besides most young men, the other people absent from the world of negotiations and casual meetings, from the circuits of information and contacts, are women. They may have controlled the regional and urban vegetable commerce for decades, and some have become by local standards quite wealthy. But not even the two or three women reputed to be the richest, most successful traders in the Bobo-Dioulasso wholesale market, have operations comparable to the enterprises described in the preceding biographies. They make smaller transactions, deal in fewer and usually lower-value commodities, and have no overseas markets or sources of financing.

In part, women are less likely to build agro-enterprises comparable to men's because even the tiny percentage who attend university and find salaried employment do not necessarily acquire the right skills and contacts. Although more and more fill clerical or extension-agent posts in the government bureaucracy, the few women appointed to higher positions are concentrated in the ministries of social welfare, culture and tourism, not agriculture or trade.[17] Moreover, they will probably have, like women in other sectors, more domestic obligations than their male colleagues, and so less time to pursue sideline businesses.

Women who do climb relatively high in the fresh produce trade, in other West African cities as well as Bobo-Dioulasso,[18] have historically done so with little or no education, and without prior remunerated employment, though they may receive monetary aid from a salaried spouse or relative. A woman who begins full-time trading in adolescence will eventually accumulate considerable experience, contacts, and perhaps wealth. But she will probably not gain access to the kinds of information useful to larger international vegetable export enterprises (faxed reports on market conditions in Lomé and green bean prices in Paris, trade journals on new lettuce varieties and farm chemicals, texts of government trade regulations), nor will she acquire the knowledge needed to find and apply for large-scale financial aid. Nor, ultimately, will a woman who builds a wholesaling career learning from and dressing like her female peers – most in Bobo typically speak little or no French, do business in a loud, aggressive 'marketplace Dioula', and wear 'traditional' cloth wraps – easily win the respect of male agro-entrepreneurs, or feel at ease in the clubby locales where they relax and do business.[19]

[17] Women in these positions may also run sideline businesses, but these are likely to be those which accommodate their professional background and social milieu, the day-to-day constraints on their time, and prevailing norms about appropriate enterprises for bourgeois women. In Burkina Faso, women commonly own textile firms, clothing, and jewellery boutiques, as well as residential real estate.

[18] See, for example, in addition to Robertson, op. cit. and Clark, op. cit., Niara Sudarkasa, *Where Women Work: a study of Yoruba women in the marketplace and in the home* (Ann Arbor, MI, 1973).

[19] For two ethnographies of market women that describe typical career paths, as well as how they differ and are kept separate from men's, see Ellie Bosch, *Les Femmes de marché de Bobo-Dioulasso* (Leiden, 1985), and Claudia Roth, *La Séparation des sexes chez les Zara au Burkina Faso* (Paris, 1996).

Even market women who could easily afford to patronise popular basrs will not do so unless accompanied by a man. Besides the fact they are usually too busy, many prefer not to be seen in places where, except for expatriates and well-known wives of prominent local men, most of the female 'customers' are assumed to be prostitutes. Bar and hotel owners tolerate (even welcome) the 'regulars' provided they are well-dressed and discreet, a condition which obviously makes it harder for other women present not to be suspected of the same profession. So most stay away, and consequently miss out on the casual but important after-hours socialisation, conversation, and networking of male entrepreneurs.

On the other hand, although most women do not have access to the realms of 'contacts and cocktails', or to the various resources necessary to building agro-enterprises like those described, they are by no means unaware of the changes wrought by structural adjustment. While for most women in the vegetable trade these have brought only greater hardships – in the form of higher living costs, slumping sales, and perhaps laid-off spouses – a few are managing to exploit the opportunities of the contemporary liberalising market.

Consider the case of 'Fatou', a 25-year old Bobo-Dioulasso woman who grew up helping her grandmother sell vegetables and spices at a neighbourhood retail market. She never went to school, but learned maths on the job by hawking fruits and vegetables on the busiest downtown streets after her grandmother had given her 500 CFA (less than two dollars). Fatou claims that by selling everything at a 100 per cent mark-up (not inconceivable in the centre of town) for 12 years she was able to turn her 500 into 100,000 CFA, and hence able to set up a produce stall outside the most popular Lebanese grocery. Here she greets the élite clientele in lilting, if limited, French – '*Bonjour Madame, il ya des belles tomates, et des fraises très douces*' – and earns, she says, 10,000 CFA on a good day.

But this is only a small part of Fatou's business. She also exports local produce (mainly carrots, since the devaluation) to Abidjan and Cotonou, and buys and sells according to current market conditions rather than placing large pre-season orders with suppliers. Unlike most other women (or men, for that matter) in the regional trade, she does not export by train or truck, but instead boards one of Air Burkina's regular passenger flights, which gets her to Abidjan in a mere two hours, Cotonou slightly longer. Fatou only takes one or two 50 kg sacks at a time – she does not mention paying excess baggage charges – but can earn 50,000 CFA for each (again, about a 100 per cent mark-up).

Since airfares cost at least twice that, how can such a venture make a profit? 'I don't do just one thing', she explains. Rather, she uses cash from the carrot sales to buy luxury imports for expatriate customers in Bobo: Granny Smith apples from South Africa, peaches and cherries from France, even fresh shrimps packed on ice if specially ordered. Sometimes she also buys several metres of expensive batik cloth to resell to African customers, or to add to her already sizeable personal collection. Finally, before catching the flight back to Bobo, she goes to the airport 'free shop' and buys as much champagne and whisky as she can legally (she says) take with her. These purchases, according to her calculations, make the price of the airline ticket worthwhile, especially since the whole trip can be done in less than two days, and under conditions much less gruelling than on the 20+ hours, one-way train ride.

During 1993–4 Fatou was perhaps the only woman produce trader in Bobo who came into the main downtown hotel not just to dispose of a headpan of strawberries or sweetpeas, but to buy a soda or even an occasional beer. She has been selling produce in the neighbourhood (and to the hotel kitchen itself) for so long that she now refers to the gruff Lebanese hotel owner by his first name, and he buys champagne from her for the hotel's New Year's Eve party. In these ways, Fatou is not remotely 'typical', even among the small number of local women who sell top-quality fruits and vegetables in front of the downtown groceries. She has worked her way into a set of privileged business relations through an unparalleled combination of market savvy, charisma, and sheer gall.

On the other hand, Fatou has paid a price: local opinion assumes that any woman who does so well in a cross-border trade must use sex to get through customs. Women of such repute are generally considered less desirable wives, and indeed, she is teased for not having found a husband yet. Not every woman would choose her line of work, given the sacrifices it entails, and she herself sometimes hints at wanting to settle down into respectable married motherhood. Fatou's career is the exception proving what has historically been the rule for ambitious women: success comes through different kinds of entrepreneurial strategies than those pursued by men, and brings them often rather more ambivalent rewards.

## CONCLUSION

By now it should be apparent that the ongoing economic reforms in Burkina Faso and elsewhere in Africa are, for better or worse, only that – reforms. While certain measures have had a huge and immediate impact on the conditions of most people's daily work and survival (mass lay-offs and the currency devaluation, in particular), it looks much less likely that the overall effects of adjustment programmes will in fact dramatically transform the historical–structural conditions of African entrepreneurship. As for the men and woman profiled above, nepotism and patronage alone clearly do not explain their career trajectories. Yet neither could one argue that they have been eager and able to exploit new and risky markets simply because liberalisation measures have freed them from dependency on, and obligations to, family and state – which, in fact, they have not. Nor, as Fatou and other women traders are well aware, has it created a market that is more free of handicapping prejudices and old-boyism than commerce under socialism or colonialism.

This is not a comment, one way or the other, on whether the coming years will bring the expansion and proliferation of export-oriented agro-enterprises in Burkina Faso and other liberalising African countries. Any such projection would have to take into account many more variables than I have discussed here, including domestic politics and international trade and aid policies. The point is rather that because the norms, practices, and sites of economic activity are constructed in all kinds of places under different social and material conditions, with different uses and understandings of wealth, entrepreneurship simply does not work in the same way everywhere. It may be structured by relations of gender, class, and so forth – but again, in historically specific ways. That these are hardly new observations makes it all the more remarkable that World Bank policies continue to assume that entrepreneurship is a generic, even innate human quality. Arguably, only the metaphors and some of the methods of developing this quality have changed over the past 50 years: modernisation theorists expected *homo oeconomicus* to evolve, but now, in the hurried era of structural adjustment, he must be 'unleashed'.

In southwestern Burkina Faso, the entrepreneurial dynamism so far unleashed by liberalisation reflects not so much a broad-based acceptance of the rules of the market economy as a scramble to readapt earlier strategies to new conditions. Best positioned to adapt are those individuals who have already accumulated during their working lives not just capital (though that, clearly, is not unimportant), but also the skills, knowledge, social relations, and status needed to win acceptance and 'do business' in all kinds of social contexts, from the village to the bank office or hotel bar. As the case-studies above illustrate, no amount of technical skill will compensate for the inability to communicate or understand the other parties in a contract, partnership, or exchange; nor will fierce ambition necessarily compensate entirely for long-standing social inequalities and prejudice. What precisely constitutes entrepreneurial capacity varies over time and place, but in all cases it is both ascribed and achieved, a product of particular life situations put to most profitable use.

# Name Index